1,001

LOW-FAT

vegetarian

RECIPES

THIRD EDITION

SUE SPITLER

with Linda R. Yoakam, R.D., M.S.

Surrey Books
CHICAGO

1,001 LOW-FAT VEGETARIAN RECIPES, 3rd Edition, is published by
Surrey Books, Inc., 230 E. Ohio St., Suite 120, Chicago, IL 60611.

Third edition: 1 2 3 4 5

This book is manufactured in the United States of America.

Library of Congress Cataloging-in-Publication data:

Spitler, Sue.
    1,001 low-fat vegetarian recipes / Sue Spitler with Linda R. Yoakam. —
3rd ed.
        p. cm.
    Includes index.
    ISBN 1-57284-057-9
    1. Vegetarian cookery. 2. Low-fat diet—Recipes. I. Title: One thousand
and one low-fat vegetarian recipes. II. Yoakam, Linda R. III. Title.
    TX837.S698 2003
    641.5'636—dc21   2003006436

Editorial and production: *Bookcrafters, Inc., Chicago*
Art direction and book design: *Joan Sommers Design, Chicago*
Nutritional analyses: *Linda R. Yoakam, R.D., M.S.*
Cover illustration: *Vicki Rabinowitz*

For prices on quantity purchases or for free book catalog,
contact Surrey Books at the above address.

This title is distributed to the trade by Publishers Group West.

CONTENTS

Introduction   v

Ingredient Information   ix

1 *Appetizers and Snacks*   1

2 *Soups*   57

3 *Stews and Casseroles*   141

4 *Vegetarian Entrées*   209

5 *Roasted and Grilled Dishes*   261

6 *Pasta*   307

7 *Loaves, Patties, and Sandwiches*   367

8 *Pizza, Calzones, and Dinner Pies*   417

9 *Egg and Cheese Dishes*   477

10 *Bean Dishes*   509

11 *Grain Dishes*   545

12 *Vegetable Side Dishes*   583

13 *Salads and Dressings*   625

14 *Breads*   653

15 *Sauces and Condiments*   699

16 *Desserts*   737

17 *Veg Express*   818

Index   839

ACKNOWLEDGMENTS

To friend and associate Pat Molden, heartfelt thanks for sharing your culinary expertise and for your support in making this cookbook a reality. Much gratitude to Jane Ellis and Kathie German for your willingness to help whenever and wherever needed—your friendship is boundless. Also thanks to Cheryl Flynn and Barbara Krueger for their cooking assistance. Thank you, Linda Yoakam for providing nutritional information so necessary for recipe development as well as final documentation. I'm also grateful to publisher Susan Schwartz for her encouragement, to editor Gene DeRoin for his tireless hours of editing, to Phyllis Stark for her computer wisdom and advice, and to Lauren Mistretta for her enthusiastic assistance with countless details!

To my family and many friends who contribute so much to the world—
this cookbook is a gift to pleasure and nourish you!

INTRODUCTION

E ATING VEGETARIAN is probably America's fastest growing food trend. According to a survey by *Vegetarian Times* magazine, 7 percent of the United States population is vegetarian—that translates to about 12.5 million people today! The North American Vegetarian Society offers statistics that indicate that at least 1 out every 5 meals ordered in restaurants today is vegetarian. Most restaurants offer vegetarian fare to meet the demand for meatless meals, and vegetarian restaurants are popping up in every city with the growth rate of alfalfa sprouts!

If you are already a vegetarian, this book will provide you with more than 1,000 new and delicious low-fat healthy recipes in 17 recipe categories, from appetizers to desserts. If you are interested in becoming vegetarian but are not quite sure how to approach the transition, this book will serve as a recipe encyclopedia to get you started! You'll also find the book helpful if you are a "sometimes vegetarian," interested in incorporating delicious meatless meals into current family meal patterns. No doubt about it, new vegetable recipes are welcome in any kitchen!

Busy lifestyles afford precious little cooking time, so recipes are designed to get you in and out of the kitchen as quickly as possible. In Veg Express (see pg. 818), streamlined recipes boast preparation times of 30 minutes or less! All recipes are easy to make, requiring no special ingredients or skills.

There are recipes for every occasion, with most being appropriate for casual entertaining as well as family dining. Spinach and Cheese Mini-Quiches or Curried Onion Croustades will start any party in tasteful style. Tuscan Bean Soup, Mexican "Meatball" Soup, Mediterranean Curried Stew, and Goulash Casserole entice with a travelogue of flavors. Tempeh Fajitas, Smoked Tofu "Burgers," Moo Shu Tempeh, Swedish "Meatball" and Dilled Potato Casserole, and Oriental Loaf are a few of the creative uses of the many soy products available today. Ever popular pasta dishes entice with Artichoke Ravioli, Rice Noodle Salad, Ziti with Gremolata, and Curried Tortellini with Beans and Squash. Pizzas with pizzaz include Chili Poblano Pizza, Feta Pizza with Pesto Sauce, and Tuscan Potato Pizza accented with a generous sprinkling of smoked mozzarella cheese. Sweet Potato Hash and Poached Eggs and Spring Vegetable Terrine are delicious brunch or lunch offerings. Adzuki Bean Pastitsio, Asian Fried Rice, Wheat Berry Waldorf, and Bean and Pasta Salad with White Bean Dressing are tempting dishes from the bean and grain chapters. Creative salads and side dishes include Caribbean Potato Salad, Vegetable Salad with Millet, Greens and Smashed Potatoes, and Gulfport Okra. English Muffin Bread, Focaccia, or Lima Bean Wheat Bread are perfect accompaniments to any meal. Healthful sweet endings such as low-fat Flourless Chocolate Cake, Mom's Rhubarb Streusel Cake, Rustic Fruit Tart, and Sugared Lemon Squares will have everyone scheming for second helpings!

Eating vegetarian is extremely healthy. Medical research increasingly supports the health benefits of including increased amounts of fruits, vegetables, grains, beans, breads, cereals, and pasta in our diets while limiting, if not totally eliminating, meat, poultry, fish, dairy foods, and fats. Recommendations from the U.S. Department of Agriculture suggest eating 6 to 11 servings of bread, cereal, rice, and pasta per day; 2 to 4 servings of fruits; and 3 to 5 servings of vegetables. Dr. Arlene Spark, professor of nutrition at the New York Medical College, concurs with this information in her Vegetable Pyramid for vegetarian eating. In addition to the suggested servings in the three food groups above, the Vegetable Pyramid includes 2 to 3 servings of milk products or milk substitutes and 2 to 3 servings of dry beans, nuts, seeds, peanut butter, soy products, or eggs daily. Special needs for vegans, who eat only plant-based foods, include 1 tablespoon each of blackstrap molasses and brewer's yeast and 3 to 5 teaspoons of vegetable oil, if extra calories are needed.

It's commonly thought that vegetarian cooking is high in fat, due to ingredients such as nuts, cheese, or oil that are included as meat substitutes and for flavor and nutrition. We've proven here that vegetarian cooking *can* be low in fat without losing a bit of delicious flavor. To achieve optimal nutrition and low-fat percentages, we emphasize the use of fresh versus processed ingredients and use the many excellent fat-free, reduced-fat, reduced-sodium, and no-salt-added products currently available. The use of olive oil and vegetable oil cooking sprays for sauteing greatly reduces or eliminates the amounts of oil or fat needed in recipes. Flavors are fresh, with an integrity further enhanced by herbs and seasonings.

In accordance with American Heart Association guidelines, very few recipes in this book exceed 30 percent calories from fat, and almost all adhere to the following nutritional criteria:

Type of Recipe	Maximum Amounts per Serving		
	Calories	*Cholesterol (mg)*	*Sodium (mg)*
Soups, First Courses	200	50	600
Main-Dish Soups, Entrées, Salads, Sandwiches	400	100	800
Main-Dish Meals (including pasta, rice, grains)	500	125	800
Main-Dish Eggs, Cheese	400	450	800
Side-Dish Salads, Pasta, Grains, Vegetables	200	50	600
Sauces, Condiments	200	25	600
Breads	200	50	600
Desserts	350	90	600

Specific nutritional information is provided for each recipe (not including variations) in this book, but remember that nutritional data are not always infallible. The nutritional analyses are derived by using computer software highly regarded by nutritionists and dietitians, but they are meant to be used only as guidelines. Figures are based on actual laboratory values of ingredients, so results may vary slightly, depending upon the brand or manufacturer of an ingredient used.

Ingredients noted as "optional" or "to taste" or "as garnish" are not included in the nutritional analyses nor are they considered in assigning the vegetarian classification. When alternate choices or amounts of ingredients are given, the ingredient and amount listed first are used for analysis. Similarly, data is based on the first number of servings shown, where a range is given. Nutritional analyses are also based on the reduced-fat cooking methods used; the addition of margarine, oil, or other ingredients to the recipes will invalidate data.

Other factors that can affect the accuracy of nutritional data include variability in sizes, weights, and measures of fruits, vegetables, and other foods. There is also a possible 20 percent error factor in the nutritional labeling of prepared foods.

If you have any health problems that require strict dietary requirements, it is important to consult a physician, dietitian, or nutritionist before using recipes in this or any other cookbook. Also, if you are a diabetic or require a diet that restricts calories, fat, or sodium, remember that the nutritional data may be accurate for the recipe as written, but not for the food you cooked due to the variables explained above.

Recipes are coded so you can quickly tell whether they are vegan, lacto-ovo vegetarian, lacto-vegetarian, or ovo-vegetarian.

 V (vegan)—Recipes contain only plant-based food, with no dairy products or eggs.

 LO (lacto-ovo vegetarian)—Recipes contain dairy products and eggs.

 L (lacto-vegetarian)—Recipes contain dairy products, but no eggs.

 O (ovo-vegetarian)—Recipes contain eggs, but no dairy products.

Variety abounds in this collection of more than 1,000 recipes. We hope you enjoy preparing and eating these dishes as much as we enjoyed creating them for you!

INGREDIENT INFORMATION

ALL THE INGREDIENTS in this book are readily available in super-markets and health food stores. Following is helpful information on some of the ingredients we've used, with explanations of those you may not be very familiar with.

Achiote, or *Annatto, Seeds*—These are small red seeds from the annatto tree, which grows in the Caribbean and Mexico. They are used to make achiote oil, which has a deep yellow color and a subtle flavor. In Mexican recipes from the Yucatan region, the seeds are sometimes ground to make a seasoning paste; the seeds are extremely hard and require long soaking in boiling water to soften before grinding. The seeds are available in Latin American sections of supermarkets, or in Latin American groceries. There is no substitute; but a pinch or two of ground turmeric can be added to vegetable oil to obtain a yellow color.

All-vegetable Protein Products—A number of interesting and flavorful all-vegetable protein products are available in the freezer section of the supermarket. Some are "beef" flavored and come in "crumbles" to be used as ground beef substitutes. Some are "sausage" flavored and come in patties or links. There are numerous brands and flavors of "burgers" available. We've used these convenience products in recipes such as Basic "Burgers" and Italian-Style "Meatballs." Usually soy-based, these products may also contain grains, vegetables, and cheese.

Bead Molasses—Used mostly in Asian recipes, bead molasses is very dark and thick with an intense flavor. Like other molasses products, it is refined from the concentrated juice of sun-ripened sugar cane. It is readily available in Asian sections of supermarkets; other molasses products can be substituted.

Chili Oil—As the name implies, this oil is *hot!* Use sparingly. The oil is found in the Asian section of supermarkets; store at room temperature.

Cream Cheese, Fat-Free—The block-type of fat-free cream cheese is usually specified in the recipes in this book; the tub-type is much softer in texture and does not always work the same in recipes. If substituting fat-free cream cheese in your favorite recipes for dips, use the block type and add any liquid ingredients gradually, as the cream cheese thins much more quickly than full-fat or reduced-fat cream cheese. Fat-free cream cheese can be used to make cake glaze but not frosting, as it thins with the addition of powdered sugar and can't be thickened.

Fillo Pastry—These paper-thin pastry sheets are found in the freezer section of supermarkets or in Mediterranean groceries; store in the freezer. Before using, thaw the entire package of fillo overnight in the refrigerator, or for several hours at room temperature. After removing fillo from the package, always cover the unused sheets with a damp cloth to keep them soft; they dry and become brittle very quickly. Unused fillo can be rolled or folded, sealed in plastic wrap, and refrozen.

Herbs and Spices—In most recipes, dried or ground forms are called for, but where no such designation is made, fresh or whole items are intended. Remember, fresh herbs and spices may be substituted in most cases, using about twice as much as indicated for the dried or ground version.

Margarine—In all cases, we call for the all-vegetable product. Use regular rather than diet varieties.

Olive Oil—As we have kept the use of oil to a minimum, we prefer using the dark-colored virgin olive oil to take advantage of the more intense flavor.

Pasta, Grains, and Beans—When dried forms are called for, the quantities indicated are *uncooked* to begin with: "8 ounces spaghetti, cooked." Conversely, some recipes call for *cooked* quantities: "12 ounces cooked spaghetti."

When dry pasta or rice noodles are called for, they are always forms that do not contain egg and can be used in vegan dishes. Fresh pasta or refrigerated pasta such as ravioli, tortellini, wontons, and some flat noodles do contain egg and can be lacto-ovo and ovo-vegetarian dishes.

Roasted Garlic—See Roasted Garlic and Three-Cheese Spread, Step 1 (p. 27) for directions on roasting garlic. Our tip—roast several heads at a time to keep extra on hand for your favorite recipes. Roasted garlic stores well, wrapped in plastic wrap, in the refrigerator for 2 to 3 weeks. Jars of chopped roasted garlic can be purchased in the supermarket and used for convenience, but the flavor is less robust.

Sesame Oil—We have specified dark sesame oil in recipes, as it has an intense sesame flavor; it can be purchased in Asian sections of supermarkets. There is also a light-colored sesame oil which is found in the vegetable oil section of the supermarket; it can be substituted, but the sesame flavor is extremely subtle. Store at room temperature.

Tahini Paste—This flavorful paste is made with ground toasted sesame seeds and is used in Greek hummus and other Mediterranean dishes. See our recipes for Black Bean Hummus and Sun-Dried Tomato Hummus (pp. 20, 18). Store tahini in the refrigerator.

Tamari Soy Sauce—This highly flavored soy sauce is naturally brewed and is made without sugar. It is available in regular or low-sodium brands in Asian sections of supermarkets. Other soy sauce products can be substituted. Store in the refrigerator.

Tempeh—A nutritious cultured product made from cooked soybeans, tempeh has its origins in Indonesia. The soybean mixture is pressed into cakes, sometimes being combined with grains and/or other ingredients, and has a texture that is firmer, or "meatier," than tofu. Like tofu, it readily absorbs flavors from soy sauce or marinades. Because of its firm texture, tempeh is great for grilling. Purchased in the produce section of supermarkets, tempeh can be stored in the refrigerator or freezer.

Textured Vegetable Protein (TVP)—This versatile product made from soy flour can be added as a meat substitute to recipes such as chili or Meatless Sloppy Joes (see p. 407) and used to make delicious "meat loaves," "meatballs," or "burgers" (see Oriental Loaf, Chunky Loaf with Vegetables, and Mexi "Meatballs," pp. 376, 377, 405). Textured vegetable protein is dry and comes in either granular or chunk-style form; it must be reconstituted with water, vegetable broth, or liquid before using in recipes like loaves and patties. Like tofu and tempeh, textured vegetable protein takes on the flavor of whatever it is cooked with. Purchase in supermarkets or health food stores and store in an airtight package at room temperature.

Tofu, or *Bean Curd*—Originating in China, tofu is made by coagulating soy milk, which is the liquid remaining from cooked ground soy beans. Pressed into cakes, tofu is made in a variety of textures—soft or silken, firm, and extra-firm. It is also available seasoned and in baked and smoked forms. Soft tofu has a very fine, delicate texture and is perfect for dips, sauces, soups, and dressings; the firmer textures are better for cooking, stir-frying, broiling, and baking. As tofu is extremely mild in flavor, it is generally marinated in soy sauce or other marinades before cooking.

Tofu is extremely nutritious, but it is not low in fat, ranging between 40 and 45 percent calories from fat. A light tofu is now available and is the tofu we call for in most recipes.

Purchase tofu in the produce section of supermarkets; it is most commonly packaged in liquid in plastic tubs. Once opened, tofu has a several-day limited storage time in the refrigerator; it should be stored covered in water, and the water should be changed daily. Tofu can also be frozen; it changes to an amber color in the freezer and when thawed is firmer in texture and somewhat crumbly.

A few recipes in this book call for "pressed tofu." To press tofu, place it in a shallow dish such as a pie plate; place a plate over the tofu, with one or two 16-ounce cans on top. Let stand until excess liquid has drained from the tofu, 15 to 30 minutes. Although the resulting tofu is firmer in texture, the process can be omitted if desired.

Vegetable Stocks—There are five homemade vegetable stock recipes and a recipe for a quick-and-easy stock made with canned vegetable broth at the beginning of the soup chapter (see pp. 58-63). A good-quality canned vegetable broth or reconstituted vegetarian vegetable bouillon cubes can be substituted for the homemade stocks, but we suggest diluting each can of broth or 2 cups of broth made from cubes with about ½ cup of water so that the flavor will be more subtle. Canned reduced-sodium vegetable broth is also available. A nicely flavored oriental broth is available, too, and can be diluted as above.

Check your local grocery periodically for new convenience food items. Literally hundreds of fresh, frozen, canned, and packaged new food products find their way to grocery shelves each year. An occasional visit to gourmet stores may garner specialty items to keep in your pantry or freezer for interesting menu additions.

ONE

Appetizers

AND

Snacks

GORP, BY GOLLY!

The right kind of snack mix for curing the munchies or for sharing with a gathering of friends.

16 servings   (about ½ cup each)

3	cups low-fat granola
2	cups pretzel goldfish
½	cup sesame sticks, broken into halves
3	cups coarsely chopped mixed dried fruit
	Butter-flavored cooking spray
1	teaspoon ground cinnamon
½	teaspoon ground nutmeg
¼	teaspoon ground allspice

Per Serving:
Calories: 172
% Calories from fat: 13
Fat (gm): 2.6
Saturated fat (gm): 0.2
Cholesterol (mg): 0
Sodium (mg): 82
Protein (gm): 2.7
Carbohydrate (gm): 37.8
Exchanges
Milk: 0.0
Vegetable: 0.0
Fruit: 2.0
Bread: 0.5
Meat: 0.0
Fat: 0.5

1. Mix granola, pretzel goldfish, sesame sticks, and dried fruit on large jelly roll pan. Spray mixture generously with cooking spray; sprinkle with combined spices and toss to coat.

2. Bake at 350 degrees 15 to 20 minutes, stirring after 10 minutes. Cool; store in covered container at room temperature.

HOT STUFF!

And if this snack mix is not hot enough for you, add a few sprinkles of red pepper sauce! Use 2 cups of purchased plain pita chips, or make your own.

16 servings (½ cup each)

2	cups oyster crackers
	Pita Chips (see p. 53)
½	cup dry-roasted smoked almonds
1	cup coarsely chopped mixed dried fruit
1	cup dried pineapple chunks
	Butter-flavored cooking spray
1	teaspoon dried oregano leaves
1	teaspoon garlic powder
1	teaspoon chili powder
1-1¼	teaspoons cayenne pepper
1-1¼	teaspoons black pepper

Per Serving:
Calories: 120
% Calories from fat: 22
Fat (gm): 3.2
Saturated fat (gm): 0.2
Cholesterol (mg): 0
Sodium (mg): 160
Protein (gm): 3.2
Carbohydrate (gm): 21.7
Exchanges
Milk: 0.0
Vegetable: 0.0
Fruit: 0.5
Bread: 1.0
Meat: 0.0
Fat: 0.5

1. Mix crackers, Pita Chips, almonds, and fruit on large jelly roll pan. Spray mixture generously with cooking spray; sprinkle with combined herbs and peppers and toss to coat.

2. Bake at 350 degrees 15 to 20 minutes, stirring after 10 minutes. Cool; store in covered container at room temperature.

CHILI BONZOS

 These highly spiced crisp snackers are great tasting and good for you too!

8 servings (¼ cup each)

2 cans (15 ounces each) garbanzo beans
Olive oil cooking spray
1 tablespoon reduced-sodium Worcestershire sauce
1-2 teaspoons chili powder
1-2 teaspoons garlic powder
1-2 teaspoons onion powder
1 teaspoon paprika
2-3 dashes red pepper sauce
Salt, to taste

Per Serving
Calories: 109
% Calories from fat: 16
Fat (gm): 2.0
Saturated fat (gm): 0.3
Cholesterol (mg): 0
Sodium (mg): 440
Protein (gm): 5.1
Carbohydrate (gm): 18.5
Exchanges
Milk: 0.0
Vegetable: 0.0
Fruit: 0.0
Bread: 1.5
Meat: 0.0
Fat: 0.0

1. Rinse beans, drain, and dry well on paper toweling. Arrange beans in large skillet; spray generously with cooking spray. Cook over medium heat, stirring frequently, until beans begin to brown, about 10 minutes. Remove from heat.

2. Combine Worcestershire sauce, spices, and red pepper sauce; add to beans and stir to coat evenly. Sprinkle lightly with salt.

3. Transfer beans to jelly roll pan; bake at 325 degrees until beans are very crisp on the outside, 20 to 25 minutes, stirring twice. Cool; store in airtight container.

VEGGIE CRISPS

 So delicious and colorful, with intense vegetable flavors! Cut veggies as thinly as you can to ensure even cooking for crispness. And be sure they are completely dried; if slightly moist inside, spoilage can develop.

4 servings (about 1 cup each)

2 pounds assorted vegetables, peeled (sweet potatoes, russet potatoes, large radishes, butternut squash, large carrots, turnips, parsnips, rutabaga, beets)
Salt, to taste
Vegetable cooking spray

Per Serving:
Calories: 174
% Calories from fat: 1
Fat (gm): 0.3
Saturated fat (gm): 0.1
Cholesterol (mg): 0
Sodium (mg): 44
Protein (gm): 3.7
Carbohydrate (gm): 40
Exchanges
Milk: 0.0
Vegetable: 1.0
Fruit: 0.0
Bread: 2.0
Meat: 0.0
Fat: 0.0

1. Peel vegetables and slice very thinly, about $\frac{1}{16}$ inch thick. Sprinkle vegetable slices lightly and evenly with salt. Let stand 20 to 30 minutes, allowing vegetables to release moisture. Rinse well in cold water and dry completely on paper toweling.

2. To dry vegetables in the microwave, arrange slices in single layer on large microwave-safe plate sprayed with cooking spray. Spray vegetables lightly with vegetable spray. Microwave on high power until vegetables are dried, 5 to 7 minutes, checking and re-arranging after 4 or 5 minutes and removing vegetables as they are dry. The vegetables will become more crisp as they cool.

3. To dry vegetables in the oven, arrange slices in single layer on jelly roll pan sprayed with cooking spray. Spray vegetables lightly with cooking spray. Bake at 275 degrees for 40 to 50 minutes, checking occasionally and removing vegetables as they are dry. The vegetables will become more crisp as they cool.

4. Store cooled chips in airtight container at room temperature.

Note: Different kinds of vegetables cook in different times, so it is important to check for doneness frequently. In microwave cooking it is better to cook one kind of vegetable at a time.

FRUIT NUGGETS

 Bite-size and perfect for high-energy snacking or for a sweet ending to a meal.

3 dozen

2 cups finely ground low-fat graham cracker crumbs

½ cup finely ground ginger snaps, *or* low-fat graham cracker crumbs

½ teaspoon ground cinnamon

½ teaspoon ground nutmeg

¼ teaspoon ground ginger

½ cup dried apples

½ cup dried apricots

½ cup dates

½ cup golden raisins

½ cup orange juice

2-3 tablespoons honey

3 tablespoons sugar

Per Nugget
Calories: 57
% Calories from fat: 8
Fat (gm): 0.5
Saturated fat (gm): 0.1
Cholesterol (mg): 0
Sodium (mg): 29
Protein (gm): 0.8
Carbohydrate (gm): 12.8
Exchanges
Milk: 0.0
Vegetable: 0.0
Fruit: 0.5
Bread: 0.5
Meat: 0.0
Fat: 0.0

1. Combine graham cracker and ginger snap crumbs and spices in medium bowl. Finely chop fruit in food processor, using pulse technique, or by hand; add to crumb mixture.

2. Add orange juice and honey to fruit mixture, stirring until mixture holds together. Roll into 36 balls, about 1 inch in diameter.

3. Measure 1 tablespoon sugar into large plastic bag; add 1 dozen nuggets and shake to coat with sugar. Repeat with remaining sugar and nuggets. Store in covered container at room temperature.

TOASTED ONION DIP

Remember the popular onion dip made with packaged soup mix? This dip will bring back memories! Toasting the dried onion flakes is the flavor secret.

12 servings (generous 2 tablespoons each)

3-4 tablespoons dried onion flakes

1 package (8 ounces) fat-free cream cheese

⅓ cup reduced-fat plain yogurt

⅓ cup fat-free mayonnaise

2 small green onions and tops, chopped

2 cloves garlic, minced

¼ teaspoon crushed vegetable bouillon cube

2-3 tablespoons fat-free milk

½-1 teaspoon lemon juice

2-3 drops red pepper sauce

Salt and white pepper, to taste

Assorted vegetable relishes and bread sticks, as dippers

Per Serving
Calories: 32
% Calories from fat: 4
Fat (gm): 0.1
Saturated fat (gm): 0.1
Cholesterol (mg): 0.4
Sodium (mg): 223
Protein (gm): 3.3
Carbohydrate (gm): 3.9
Exchanges
Milk: 0.0
Vegetable: 0.0
Fruit: 0.0
Bread: 0.0
Meat: 0.5
Fat: 0.0

1. Cook onion flakes in small skillet over medium to medium-low heat until toasted, 3 to 4 minutes, stirring frequently. Cool.

2. Mix cream cheese, yogurt, mayonnaise, green onions, garlic, and bouillon in medium bowl until smooth, adding enough milk to make desired dipping consistency. Season to taste with lemon juice, pepper sauce, salt, and white pepper.

3. Spoon dip into serving bowl; serve with vegetable relishes and bread sticks (not included in nutritional data).

BAKED ARTICHOKE DIP

Everyone's favorite, modified for healthful, low-fat goodness.

16 servings (about 3 tablespoons each)

1	can (15 ounces) artichoke hearts, rinsed, drained
½	package (8-ounce size) fat-free cream cheese, softened
½	cup grated fat-free Parmesan cheese
½	cup fat-free mayonnaise
½	cup fat-free sour cream
1-2	teaspoons lemon juice
1	green onion and top, thinly sliced
2	teaspoons minced garlic
2-3	drops red pepper sauce
	Salt and cayenne pepper, to taste
	Assorted vegetables, bread sticks, *or* crackers, as dippers

Per Serving
Calories: 39
% Calories from fat: 2
Fat (gm): 0.1
Saturated fat (gm): 0
Cholesterol (mg): 0
Sodium (mg): 190
Protein (gm): 3.5
Carbohydrate (gm): 6.8
Exchanges
Milk: 0.0
Vegetable: 1.5
Fruit: 0.0
Bread: 0.0
Meat: 0.0
Fat: 0.0

1. Process artichoke hearts, cream cheese, Parmesan cheese, mayonnaise, sour cream, and lemon juice in food processor until smooth. Stir in onion, garlic, and red pepper sauce. Season to taste with salt and cayenne pepper.

2. Spoon dip into small casserole or baking dish. Bake, uncovered, at 350 degrees until hot through and lightly browned on the top, 20 to 25 minutes. Serve warm with assorted vegetables, bread sticks, or crackers (not included in nutritional data).

CURRY DIP

Sweet potatoes and broccoli are particularly good with this dip.

12 servings (2 generous tablespoons each)

1½	cups fat-free mayonnaise
½	cup fat-free sour cream
¼	cup thinly sliced green onions and tops
1½-2	teaspoons prepared horseradish
1½-2	teaspoons curry powder
2-3	teaspoons sugar
2-4	teaspoons lemon juice
	Salt and white pepper, to taste
	Assorted vegetable relishes, as dippers
	Pita Chips (see p. 53)

Per Serving
Calories: 34
% Calories from fat: 1
Fat (gm): 0
Saturated fat (gm): 0
Cholesterol (mg): 0
Sodium (mg): 393
Protein (gm): 0.7
Carbohydrate (gm): 8
Exchanges
Milk: 0.0
Vegetable: 0.0
Fruit: 0.0
Bread: 0.5
Meat: 0.0
Fat: 0.0

1. Mix mayonnaise, sour cream, green onions, horseradish, curry powder, and sugar. Season to taste with lemon juice, salt, and white pepper. Refrigerate several hours for flavors to blend.

2. Spoon dip into bowl; serve with vegetables or Pita Chips for dipping (not included in nutritional data).

GREEN TOMATO SALSA

Mexican green tomatoes (tomatillos) contain natural pectin, so the salsa will thicken when refrigerated. You can thin it to desired consistency with reserved cooking liquid or water.

16 servings (about 2 tablespoons each)

1½	pounds Mexican green tomatoes (tomatillos)
½	medium onion, finely chopped
2	cloves garlic, minced
¼	small jalapeño chili, seeds and veins discarded, very finely chopped
2	tablespoons finely chopped cilantro
½	teaspoon ground cumin

Per Serving
Calories: 17
% Calories from fat: 22
Fat (gm): 0.5
Saturated fat (gm): 0
Cholesterol (mg): 0
Sodium (mg): 2
Protein (gm): 0.5
Carbohydrate (gm): 3.1
Exchanges
Milk: 0.0
Vegetable: 0.5
Fruit: 0.0
Bread: 0.0
Meat: 0.0
Fat: 0.0

¼ teaspoon dried oregano leaves
⅛-¼ teaspoon sugar
Salt, to taste
Baked Tortilla Chips (see p. 55)

1. Remove and discard husks from tomatoes; simmer tomatoes in water to cover in large saucepan until tender, 5 to 8 minutes. Cool; drain, reserving liquid.

2. Process tomatoes, onion, garlic, jalapeño chili, cilantro, cumin, and oregano in food processor or blender, using pulse technique, until almost smooth, adding enough reserved liquid to make medium dipping consistency. Add sugar. Season to taste with salt.

3. Spoon salsa into bowl; serve with Baked Tortilla Chips (not included in nutritional data).

RED TOMATO SALSA

Poblano chilies can be quite hot in flavor, so taste before using. A green bell (sweet) pepper can be substituted if desired.

16 servings (about 2 tablespoons each)

2 large tomatoes, cut into wedges
1 small onion, finely chopped
1 small poblano chili, veins and seeds discarded, chopped
¼ jalapeño chili, seeds and veins discarded, chopped
1 clove garlic, minced
¼ cup loosely packed cilantro, finely chopped
Salt, to taste
Baked Tortilla Chips (see p. 55)

Per Serving
Calories: 9
% Calories from fat: 10
Fat (gm): 0.1
Saturated fat (gm): 0
Cholesterol (mg): 0
Sodium (mg): 4
Protein (gm): 0.4
Carbohydrate (gm): 1.9
Exchanges
Milk: 0.0
Vegetable: 0.5
Fruit: 0.0
Bread: 0.0
Meat: 0.0
Fat: 0.0

1. Process tomatoes, onion, chilies, and garlic in food processor or blender until finely chopped. Mix in cilantro; season to taste with salt.

2. Spoon salsa into bowl; serve with Baked Tortilla Chips (not included in nutritional data).

MEXICAN BEAN DIP

If a chunkier dip is desired, coarsely mash ½ cup of the beans and reserve. Make dip as directed, then stir the mashed beans into the dip. Purchased baked tortilla chips can be substituted for the homemade chips in the recipe.

12 servings (about 2 tablespoons each)

Vegetable cooking spray
½ cup thinly sliced green onions and tops
1-2 cloves garlic, minced
1 can (15 ounces) black beans, rinsed, drained
¾ cup (3 ounces) shredded reduced-fat Cheddar cheese
¼ teaspoon salt
⅓ cup vegetable broth, *or* water
1-2 tablespoons finely chopped cilantro
Baked Tortilla Chips (see p. 55)

Per Serving
Calories: 48
% Calories from fat: 21
Fat (gm): 1.3
Saturated fat (gm): 0.5
Cholesterol (mg): 3.8
Sodium (mg): 254
Protein (gm): 4.5
Carbohydrate (gm): 7
Exchanges
Milk: 0.0
Vegetable: 0.0
Fruit: 0.0
Bread: 0.5
Meat: 0.0
Fat: 0.0

1. Spray small skillet with cooking spray; heat over medium heat until hot. Saute onions and garlic until tender, about 3 minutes.

2. Process black beans, cheese, and salt in food processor or blender until almost smooth, adding enough broth to make desired dipping consistency. Mix in onion mixture and cilantro.

3. Spoon dip into bowl; serve with Baked Tortilla Chips (not included in nutritional data).

PINTO BEAN AND AVOCADO DIP

Avocado and tomato brighten this well-flavored bean dip. Increase the amount of jalapeño chili if you dare—or use the seeds and veins for maximum hotness.

12 servings (about 2 tablespoons each)

1 can (15 ounces) pinto beans, rinsed, drained

¾ cup finely chopped onion

2 cloves garlic

½ jalapeño chili, seeds and veins discarded, minced

3 tablespoons finely chopped cilantro

1 large tomato, chopped

½ medium avocado, peeled, pitted, chopped

2-3 tablespoons medium, *or* hot, prepared salsa

Salt and pepper, to taste

Baked Tortilla Chips (see p. 55)

Per Serving
Calories: 54
% Calories from fat: 25
Fat (gm): 1.7
Saturated fat (gm): 0
Cholesterol (mg): 0
Sodium (mg): 153
Protein (gm): 3
Carbohydrate (gm): 8.3
Exchanges
Milk: 0.0
Vegetable: 0.5
Fruit: 0.0
Bread: 0.5
Meat: 0.0
Fat: 0.0

1. Process beans in food processor or blender until smooth; add onion, garlic, jalapeño chili, and cilantro. Process, using pulse technique, until blended. Mix in tomato, avocado, and salsa; season to taste with salt and pepper. Refrigerate 1 to 2 hours for flavors to blend.

2. Spoon dip into serving bowl; serve with Baked Tortilla Chips (not included in nutritional data).

CHILE CON QUESO

This popular dip is generally made with full-fat Mexican Chihuahua, Monterey Jack, Muenster, or Cheddar cheese. Our "skinny" version is made with reduced-fat pasteurized processed cheese product for creamy texture and fat-free Cheddar cheese for added flavor.

12 servings (about 2 tablespoons each)

Vegetable cooking spray
5 medium anaheim, *or* 2 medium poblano, chilies, seeds and veins discarded, cut into halves
1 small onion, chopped
1 small tomato, chopped
½ teaspoon dried oregano leaves
2 cups (8 ounces) shredded reduced-fat pasteurized processed cheese product
1 cup (4 ounces) shredded fat-free Cheddar cheese
2-4 tablespoons fat-free milk
Baked Tortilla Chips (see p. 55)

Per Serving
Calories: 70
% Calories from fat: 26
Fat (gm): 2.1
Saturated fat (gm): 1.4
Cholesterol (mg): 8.5
Sodium (mg): 355
Protein (gm): 7.8
Carbohydrate (gm): 5.9
Exchanges
Milk: 0.0
Vegetable: 1.0
Fruit: 0.0
Bread: 0.0
Meat: 1.0
Fat: 0.0

1. Line jelly roll pan with aluminum foil; spray with cooking spray. Place chilies, skin sides up, on pan. Bake at 425 degrees until chilies are browned and soft, 20 to 25 minutes. Cool slightly; cut into strips.

2. Spray small saucepan with cooking spray; heat over medium heat until hot. Saute onion, tomato, and oregano until onion is tender, about 5 minutes. Add cheeses and chilies; cook over low heat until melted, stirring in milk for desired consistency.

3. Serve warm in serving bowl with Baked Tortilla Chips (not included in nutritional data) for dipping.

QUESO FUNDIDO

This melted cheese mixture is spooned onto warm tortillas, topped with a sprinkling of "Chorizo," onion, and cilantro, and then rolled up for easy eating! The "Chorizo" used is about ⅙ of the recipe; freeze the remaining "Chorizo" for another meal.

8 servings

Vegetable cooking spray
¼ cup chopped red bell pepper
¾ cup (3 ounces) shredded fat-free Cheddar cheese
½ cup (2 ounces) cubed reduced-fat pasteurized processed cheese product
¼-⅓ cup fat-free milk
8 corn tortillas, warm
½ cup (⅙ recipe) cooked, crumbled "Chorizo" (see p. 404)
2 tablespoons finely chopped green onions and tops
2 tablespoons finely chopped cilantro

Per Serving
Calories: 112
% Calories from fat: 15
Fat (gm): 1.9
Saturated fat (gm): 0.7
Cholesterol (mg): 12.8
Sodium (mg): 274
Protein (gm): 8.7
Carbohydrate (gm): 15.2
Exchanges
Milk: 0.0
Vegetable: 0.0
Fruit: 0.0
Bread: 1.0
Meat: 1.0
Fat: 0.0

1. Spray small saucepan with cooking spray; heat over medium heat until hot. Saute red bell pepper until tender, 2 to 3 minutes. Add cheeses; cook over low heat until melted, stirring in milk for desired consistency.

2. Spoon about 2 tablespoons cheese mixture in the center of each tortilla. Sprinkle with "Chorizo," green onions, and cilantro and roll up.

SOMBRERO DIP

The ingredients in this appetizer dip are layered in smaller and smaller circles, resembling the top of a sombrero when finished! Use Florida avocados for making the Guacamole, as they are lower in fat than California avocados.

6 servings

Vegetable cooking spray
¼ cup chopped poblano chili, *or* green bell pepper
¼ cup chopped onion
4-5 leaves romaine lettuce
1½ cups (½ recipe) Refried Beans (see p. 525), *or* 1 can (15 ounces) vegetarian refried beans
½ cup (¼ recipe) Red Tomato Salsa (see p. 9), *or* prepared salsa
½ cup (⅓ recipe) cooked, crumbled "Chorizo" (see p. 404)
½ cup chopped romaine lettuce
½ cup chopped tomato
Guacamole (recipe follows)
¼ cup (1 ounce) shredded fat-free Cheddar cheese
½ cup fat-free sour cream
1 green onion and top, thinly sliced
Baked Tortilla Chips (see p. 55)

Per Serving
Calories: 175
% Calories from fat: 16
Fat (gm): 3.2
Saturated fat (gm): 0.7
Cholesterol (mg): 23.7
Sodium (mg): 214
Protein (gm): 13.3
Carbohydrate (gm): 25
Exchanges
Milk: 0.0
Vegetable: 2.0
Fruit: 0.0
Bread: 1.0
Meat: 1.0
Fat: 0.0

1. Spray small skillet with cooking spray; heat over medium heat until hot. Saute poblano chili and onion until tender, 3 to 5 minutes; reserve.

2. Line a dinner-size serving plate with lettuce; cover with Refried Beans to within 2 inches of edge of lettuce. Spoon Red Tomato Salsa over beans, leaving edge of bean layer showing.

3. Combine "Chorizo" and reserved sauteed chili and onion; sprinkle over salsa. Sprinkle chopped lettuce and tomato over "Chorizo" mixture, leaving edge of "Chorizo" layer showing.

4. Spoon Guacamole over lettuce and tomato, leaving edge of previous layer showing; sprinkle with Cheddar cheese. Spoon sour cream in large dollop on top; sprinkle with green onion. Serve with Baked Tortilla Chips (not included in nutritional data) for dipping.

Guacamole

(makes about ⅔ cup)

> 1 medium Florida avocado (about 5 ounces), peeled, pitted
> ½ small onion, finely chopped
> ½ small jalapeño chili, seeds and veins discarded, minced
> 1-2 teaspoons finely chopped cilantro
> Salt and white pepper, to taste

1. Coarsely mash avocado in small bowl (mixture should be chunky, rather than smooth). Mix in onion, jalapeño chili, and cilantro. Season to taste with salt and pepper.

PINE NUT SPINACH PÂTÉ

Toasted pine nuts provide the flavor accent in this unique dip.

12 servings (about 2 tablespoons each)

> 1 package (10 ounces) frozen chopped spinach, thawed
> ¼ cup coarsely chopped onion
> ¼ cup coarsely chopped celery
> 1 clove garlic
> 2-3 teaspoons lemon juice
> ½ teaspoon dried dill weed
> 1-2 tablespoons toasted pine nuts, *or* slivered almonds
> ½ package (8-ounce size) fat-free cream cheese, softened
> Salt and pepper, to taste
> Bruschetta (see p. 54)

Per Serving
Calories: 19
% Calories from fat: 21
Fat (gm): 0.5
Saturated fat (gm): 0.1
Cholesterol (mg): 0
Sodium (mg): 73
Protein (gm): 2.1
Carbohydrate (gm): 1.9
Exchanges
Milk: 0.0
Vegetable: 0.5
Fruit: 0.0
Bread: 0.0
Meat: 0.0
Fat: 0.0

1. Drain spinach well between layers of paper toweling. Process spinach, onion, celery, garlic, lemon juice, and dill weed in food processor until almost smooth; add pine nuts and process until coarsely chopped, using pulse technique. Stir in cream cheese; season to taste with salt and pepper. Refrigerate several hours for flavors to blend.

2. Spoon pâté into crock or bowl; serve with Bruschetta (not included in nutritional data).

WILD MUSHROOM PÂTÉ

 This pâté is most flavorful when made with wild mushrooms, although brown or white mushrooms can be used.

8 servings (about 2 tablespoons each)

Olive oil cooking spray
12 ounces coarsely chopped shiitake, *or* portobello, mushrooms
½ cup chopped onion
2-4 cloves garlic, minced
¼ cup dry sherry, *or* Basic Vegetable Stock (see p. 58)
2 tablespoons grated fat-free Parmesan cheese
2-3 teaspoons lemon juice
Salt and pepper, to taste
Bruschetta, *or* Whole Wheat Lavosh (see pp. 54, 673)

Per Serving
Calories: 42
% Calories from fat: 2
Fat (gm): 0.1
Saturated fat (gm): 0
Cholesterol (mg): 0
Sodium (mg): 14
Protein (gm): 1.4
Carbohydrate (gm): 8.4
Exchanges
Milk: 0.0
Vegetable: 1.5
Fruit: 0.0
Bread: 0.0
Meat: 0.0
Fat: 0.0

1. Spray skillet with cooking spray; heat over medium heat until hot. Add mushrooms, onion, garlic, and sherry; cook, covered, over medium heat until mushrooms are wilted, about 5 minutes. Cook, uncovered, over medium to medium-low heat until vegetables are very tender and all liquid absorbed, 8 to 10 minutes. Cool.

2. Process mushroom mixture and Parmesan cheese in food processor until smooth. Season to taste with lemon juice, salt, and pepper. Refrigerate 2 to 3 hours for flavors to blend.

3. Spoon pâté into a crock or mound it on a serving plate. Serve with Bruschetta or Whole Wheat Lavosh (not included in nutritional data).

SOYBEAN AND VEGETABLE SPREAD

 A delicious and nutritious spread for snacking, or to serve as party fare.

12 servings (about 3 tablespoons each)

Vegetable cooking spray
¾ cup chopped carrot
½ cup chopped onion
2 cloves garlic, minced
2 tablespoons vegetable broth, *or* water
1½ cups cooked dried, *or* canned, soybeans
1 cup fat-free, *or* reduced-fat, sour cream
2 tablespoons minced parsley
1-2 teaspoons lemon juice
Salt and pepper, to taste
Assorted vegetables, Easy Herb Lavosh (see p. 53), *or* melba toast, as dippers

Per Serving
Calories: 56
% Calories from fat: 29
Fat (gm): 2
Saturated fat (gm): 0.3
Cholesterol (mg): 0
Sodium (mg): 17
Protein (gm): 5
Carbohydrate (gm): 5.6
Exchanges
Milk: 0.0
Vegetable: 1.0
Fruit: 0.0
Bread: 0.0
Meat: 0.5
Fat: 0.0

1. Spray small skillet with cooking spray; heat over medium heat until hot. Add carrot, onion, garlic, and broth; cook, covered, over medium heat until vegetables are tender and dry, 5 to 8 minutes. Cool.

2. Process soybeans and sour cream in food processor, using pulse technique, until smooth. Stir in vegetable mixture and parsley; season to taste with lemon juice, salt, and pepper. Refrigerate several hours for flavors to blend.

3. Spoon spread into bowl; serve with vegetables, easy Herb Lavosh, or melba toast (not included in nutritional data).

ROASTED GARLIC AND HERB CANNELLINI DIP

Another good-for-you dip that tastes terrific! Italian cannellini beans are white kidney beans that are similar in flavor and appearance to navy or Great Northern beans.

6 servings (about ¼ cup each)

1 can (15 ounces) cannellini, *or* Great Northern, beans, rinsed and drained
1 teaspoon minced roasted garlic
1 tablespoon olive oil
1 tablespoon prepared horseradish
2 tablespoons minced chives
½ teaspoon dried oregano leaves
½ teaspoon dried basil leaves
2-3 drops red pepper sauce
2-3 teaspoons lemon juice
Salt and white pepper, to taste
Pita Chips (see p. 53)
Assorted vegetables, as dippers

Per Serving
Calories: 75
% Calories from fat: 25
Fat (gm): 2.8
Saturated fat (gm): 0.3
Cholesterol (mg): 0
Sodium (mg): 167
Protein (gm): 5.3
Carbohydrate (gm): 13.1
Exchanges
Milk: 0.0
Vegetable: 0.0
Fruit: 0.0
Bread: 1.0
Meat: 0.0
Fat: 0.5

1. Process beans, garlic, olive oil, and horseradish in food processor until smooth. Mix in chives, herbs, and red pepper sauce. Season to taste with lemon juice, salt, and white pepper. Refrigerate 1 to 2 hours for flavors to blend.

2. Spoon dip into bowl; serve with Pita Chips, or vegetables (not included in nutritional data).

SUN-DRIED TOMATO HUMMUS

Sun-dried tomatoes and herbs embellish this Mediterranean favorite.

8 servings (about ¼ cup each)

1 can (15 ounces) chick peas, rinsed, drained
⅓ cup fat-free yogurt
2-3 tablespoons tahini (sesame seed paste)
3 cloves garlic

Per Serving
Calories: 73
% Calories from fat: 21
Fat (gm): 1.7
Saturated fat (gm): 0.2
Cholesterol (mg): 0.2
Sodium (mg): 256
Protein (gm): 3.6
Carbohydrate (gm): 11.4

3 tablespoons sun-dried tomato bits, *or* 4
sun-dried tomato halves (not packed in
oil), finely chopped

1 teaspoon dried oregano leaves

1 teaspoon dried mint leaves

2-3 teaspoons lemon juice

Salt and white pepper, to taste

Pita Chips (see p. 53), *or* pita breads,
cut into wedges, as dippers

Exchanges
Milk: 0.0
Vegetable: 0.0
Fruit: 0.0
Bread: 1.0
Meat: 0.0
Fat: 0.0

1. Process chick peas, yogurt, tahini, and garlic in food processor until smooth. Stir in sun-dried tomato bits and herbs; season to taste with lemon juice, salt, and white pepper. Refrigerate 1 to 2 hours for flavors to blend.

2. Spoon hummus into serving bowl; serve with Pita Chips (not included in nutritional data).

SPICY ORANGE HUMMUS

 Another flavorful variation of the traditional hummus.

8 servings (about ¼ cup each)

1 can (15 ounces) chick peas, rinsed,
drained

3 cloves garlic, minced

¼ cup orange juice

2 teaspoons soy sauce

1 teaspoon Dijon-style mustard

½ teaspoon curry powder

¼-½ teaspoon ground ginger

2 teaspoons grated orange rind

Salt and white pepper, to taste

Pita Chips (see p. 53), *or* pita breads,
cut into wedges, as dippers

Per Serving
Calories: 60
% Calories from fat: 15
Fat (gm): 1
Saturated fat (gm): 0.1
Cholesterol (mg): 0
Sodium (mg): 306
Protein (gm): 2.7
Carbohydrate (gm): 10.3
Exchanges
Milk: 0.0
Vegetable: 0.0
Fruit: 0.0
Bread: 1.0
Meat: 0.0
Fat: 0.0

1. Process chick peas, garlic, orange juice, soy sauce, mustard, curry powder, and ginger in food processor until smooth; stir in orange rind. Season to taste with salt and white pepper. Refrigerate 1 to 2 hours for flavors to blend.

2. Spoon hummus into serving bowl; serve with Pita Chips or breads (not included in nutritional data).

BLACK BEAN HUMMUS

Tahini, a ground sesame paste, and soy sauce season this unusual bean dip.

6 servings (about ¼ cup each)

1	can (15 ounces) black beans, rinsed, drained
¼	cup Basic Vegetable Stock (see p. 58), *or* water
2-3	tablespoons tahini (sesame seed paste)
3	cloves garlic
2-2½	tablespoons lemon juice
1½	tablespoons soy sauce
	Salt and cayenne pepper, to taste
	Pita Chips (see p. 53), *or* pita breads, cut into wedges for dippers

Per Serving
Calories: 100
% Calories from fat: 30
Fat (gm): 4
Saturated fat (gm): 0
Cholesterol (mg): 0
Sodium (mg): 480
Protein (gm): 7.6
Carbohydrate (gm): 13.9
Exchanges
Milk: 0.0
Vegetable: 0.0
Fruit: 0.0
Bread: 1.0
Meat: 0.0
Fat: 0.5

1. Process beans, stock, tahini, garlic, lemon juice, and soy sauce in food processor until smooth; season to taste with salt and cayenne pepper. Refrigerate 1 to 2 hours for flavors to blend.

2. Spoon hummus into serving bowl; serve with Pita Chips or breads (not included in nutritional data).

EGGPLANT CAVIAR

Middle Eastern flavors will tempt you to second helpings!

6 servings (generous 2 tablespoons each)

1	large eggplant (1½ pounds)
½	cup chopped tomato
¼	cup finely chopped onion
3	cloves garlic, minced
¼	cup fat-free yogurt

Per Serving
Calories: 59
% Calories from fat: 28
Fat (gm): 2.1
Saturated fat (gm): 0.3
Cholesterol (mg): 0.2
Sodium (mg): 19.1
Protein (gm): 1.8
Carbohydrate (gm): 10.1

2 teaspoons extra-virgin olive oil
½ teaspoon dried oregano leaves
1-2 tablespoons lemon juice
   Salt and pepper, to taste
2 ripe olives, sliced
   Lavosh, *or* pita bread wedges, as dippers

Exchanges
Milk: 0.0
Vegetable: 1.5
Fruit: 0.0
Bread: 0.0
Meat: 0.0
Fat: 0.5

1. Pierce eggplant in several places with fork; place in baking pan. Bake at 350 degrees until eggplant is soft, 45 to 50 minutes. Cool.

2. Cut eggplant in half; scoop out pulp with spoon. Mix eggplant, tomato, onion, garlic, yogurt, olive oil, and oregano in bowl; season to taste with lemon juice, salt, and pepper. Refrigerate 3 to 4 hours for flavors to blend.

3. Spoon eggplant into bowl; garnish with olives. Serve with lavosh or pita wedges (not included in nutritional data).

ROASTED ZUCCHINI AND GARLIC SPREAD

A great recipe for summer when garden zucchini are abundant.

12 servings (about 2 tablespoons each)

   Olive oil cooking spray
1¼ pounds zucchini, cut into 1-inch pieces
1 small onion, cut into wedges
2 garlic cloves, peeled
⅓ cup fat-free plain yogurt
2 tablespoons finely chopped parsley
   Lemon juice, to taste
   Salt and cayenne pepper, to taste
   Sliced vegetables, Baked Tortilla Chips, *or* Pita Chips (see pp. 55, 53), as dippers

Per Serving
Calories: 14
% Calories from fat: 6
Fat (gm): 0.1
Saturated fat (gm): 0
Cholesterol (mg): 0.1
Sodium (mg): 7
Protein (gm): 1
Carbohydrate (gm): 2.6
Exchanges
Milk: 0.0
Vegetable: 0.5
Fruit: 0.0
Bread: 0.0
Meat: 0.0
Fat: 0.0

1. Line jelly roll pan with aluminum foil and spray with cooking spray. Arrange zucchini, onion, and garlic in single layer on pan. Bake at 425 degrees until vegetables are very tender, about 15 to 20 minutes for garlic, 25 to 30 minutes for zucchini and onion. Cool.

2. Process vegetables in food processor, using pulse technique, until coarsely chopped. Stir in yogurt and parsley; season to taste with lemon juice, salt, and cayenne pepper. Serve with sliced vegetables or Pita Chips (see p. 53; not included in nutritional data).

ARTICHOKE PÂTÉ

For elegant presentation, spoon pâté on ends of Belgain endive leaves and arrange on a serving plate with vegetable garnishes.

16 servings (about 2 tablespoons each)

1	can (15 ounces) artichoke hearts or bottoms, drained
½	package (8-ounce size) fat-free cream cheese, softened
⅓	cup grated fat-free Parmesan cheese
2-4	tablespoons fat-free mayonnaise
1-1½	teaspoons minced roasted garlic
2	tablespoons finely chopped parsley
1-2	teaspoons lemon juice
	Salt and cayenne pepper, to taste
2	tablespoons chopped black olives
2	tablespoons chopped roasted red bell peppers
	Assorted vegetables, lavosh, or melba toast, as dippers

Per Serving
Calories: 31
% Calories from fat: 13
Fat (gm): 0.5
Saturated fat (gm): 0.1
Cholesterol (mg): 0
Sodium (mg): 142
Protein (gm): 2.7
Carbohydrate (gm): 4.7
Exchanges
Milk: 0.0
Vegetable: 1.0
Fruit: 0.0
Bread: 0.0
Meat: 0.0
Fat: 0.0

1. Process artichokes, cream cheese, Parmesan cheese, mayonnaise, and garlic in food processor until smooth. Stir in parsley; season to taste with lemon juice, salt, and cayenne pepper. Refrigerate several hours for flavors to blend.

2. Spoon mixture into a crock, or mound it on a serving plate. Garnish with olives and red peppers. Serve with vegetables, lavosh, or melba toast (not included in nutritional data).

GARDEN MUSHROOM SPREAD

Substitute zucchini, yellow summer squash, or bell peppers for the carrots in this flavor-fresh spread.

12 servings (about 2 tablespoons each)

Vegetable cooking spray
¾ cup chopped onion
½ cup chopped carrot
1-2 teaspoons grated lemon rind
2-3 cloves garlic, minced
12 ounces brown, *or* white, mushrooms, chopped
2 tablespoons dry sherry, *or* water
½ teaspoon dried thyme leaves
½ teaspoon dried savory leaves
½ package (8-ounce size) fat-free cream cheese
2 tablespoons grated fat-free Parmesan cheese
1-2 tablespoons minced parsley
Salt, cayenne, and black pepper, to taste
Assorted vegetables, Whole Wheat Lavosh, *or* Bruschetta (see pp. 673, 54), as dippers

Per Serving
Calories: 28
% Calories from fat: 5
Fat (gm): 0.2
Saturated fat (gm): 0
Cholesterol (mg): 0
Sodium (mg): 67
Protein (gm): 2.5
Carbohydrate (gm): 3.8
Exchanges
Milk: 0.0
Vegetable: 1.5
Fruit: 0.0
Bread: 0.0
Meat: 0.0
Fat: 0.0

1. Spray medium skillet with cooking spray; heat over medium heat until hot. Saute onion, carrot, lemon rind, and garlic until tender, about 5 minutes. Remove from skillet.

2. Spray skillet again; add mushrooms, sherry, and herbs. Cook, covered, over medium heat until mushrooms are wilted, about 5 minutes. Cook, uncovered, until mushrooms are tender and liquid absorbed, about 5 minutes. Cool.

3. Process cream cheese, Parmesan cheese, and half the mushroom mixture in food processor until smooth. Stir in onion mixture, remaining mushroom mixture, and parsley. Season to taste with salt and peppers. Refrigerate 2 to 3 hours for flavors to blend.

4. Spoon spread into bowl; serve with vegetables, Whole Wheat Lavosh, or Bruschetta (not included in nutritional data).

FAUX CHOPPED "LIVER"

 This pâté boasts incredible texture and flavor.

12 servings (2 tablespoons each)

1¾ cups Basic Vegetable Stock (see p. 58)
½ cup dried lentils
   Vegetable cooking spray
1 cup finely chopped onion
1 clove garlic, minced
¼-½ teaspoon dried thyme leaves
¼-⅓ cup chopped walnuts
   Salt and pepper, to taste
1 hard-cooked egg, *or* 2 egg whites, chopped
   Minced parsley, as garnish
24 slices cocktail rye bread, *or* crackers

Per Serving
Calories: 152
% Calories from fat: 19
Fat (gm): 3.5
Saturated fat (gm): 0.4
Cholesterol (mg): 17.8
Sodium (mg): 194
Protein (gm): 7.8
Carbohydrate (gm): 25.5
Exchanges
Milk: 0.0
Vegetable: 0.0
Fruit: 0.0
Bread: 0.0
Meat: 0.0
Fat: 0.5

1. Heat stock to boiling in medium saucepan; stir in lentils. Reduce heat and simmer, covered, until lentils are tender, but not mushy, and liquid absorbed, about 45 minutes.

2. Spray small skillet with cooking spray; heat over medium heat until hot. Saute onion, garlic, and thyme until onions are tender, 5 to 8 minutes.

3. Process lentils, onion mixture, and walnuts in food processor, using pulse technique, until almost smooth. Season to taste with salt and pepper. Refrigerate 2 to 3 hours for flavors to blend.

4. Mix hard-cooked egg into mixture; spoon into serving dish and garnish with parsley. Serve with cocktail rye bread or crackers (not included in nutritional data).

EGGPLANT MARMALADE

Minced roasted garlic is very rich in flavor. It can be purchased in jars, or regular minced garlic can be substituted. A quick kitchen tip—gingerroot does not have to be peeled before using! The eggplant mixture can be refrigerated up to 2 weeks.

12 servings (about 3 tablespoons each)

Per Serving
Calories: 75
% Calories from fat: 21
Fat (gm): 1.9
Saturated fat (gm): 0.3
Cholesterol (mg): 0
Sodium (mg): 6
Protein (gm): 1.6
Carbohydrate (gm): 14.9
Exchanges
Milk: 0.0
Vegetable: 2.0
Fruit: 0.5
Bread: 0.0
Meat: 0.0
Fat: 0.0

2	medium eggplant (1¼ pounds each), unpeeled
⅓	cup coarsely chopped onion
2	tablespoons minced roasted garlic
2-3	tablespoons minced gingerroot
3	tablespoons light brown sugar
1½	teaspoons fennel seeds, crushed
2	tablespoons red wine vinegar
2	teaspoons dark sesame oil
⅓	cup golden raisins
⅓	cup Basic Vegetable Stock (see p. 58)
2-3	tablespoons toasted pine nuts, *or* slivered almonds
	Whole Wheat Lavosh (see pp. 673), broken into pieces, as dippers

1. Cut eggplant into ½-inch slices; cut slices into scant ½-inch cubes. Combine eggplant, onion, garlic, gingerroot, brown sugar, and fennel; arrange in single layer on foil-lined and greased large jelly roll pan. Drizzle with combined vinegar and oil.

2. Bake at 425 degrees until eggplant is browned and wrinkled, about 1½ hours, stirring every 30 minutes. Stir raisins into mixture; drizzle with stock and toss. Bake until broth is absorbed, 10 to 15 minutes longer. Stir in pine nuts and cool. Refrigerate overnight for flavors to blend.

3. Spoon eggplant marmalade into serving bowl; serve with lavosh (not included in nutritional data).

CHUTNEY CHEESE SPREAD

Enjoy these flavors inspired from India. Ginger contributes "heat" as well as flavor to the spread, so adjust according to your taste. Make Pita Chips with curry powder or ground cumin.

8 servings (2 generous tablespoons each)

1 package (8 ounces) fat-free cream cheese (block, not tub, type), softened

1 cup (4 ounces) shredded reduced-fat Cheddar cheese

½ cup chopped mango chutney, divided

¼ cup finely chopped onion

2 tablespoons raisins, chopped

1-2 teaspoons finely chopped gingerroot

1 clove garlic, minced

½-1 teaspoon curry powder

1-2 tablespoons chopped dry-roasted cashews

Thinly sliced green onion tops, as garnish

Pita Chips, *or* Whole Wheat Lavosh, as dippers (see pp. 53, 673)

Per Serving
Calories: 116
% Calories from fat: 21
Fat (gm): 2.6
Saturated fat (gm): 1.1
Cholesterol (mg): 7.6
Sodium (mg): 367
Protein (gm): 7.4
Carbohydrate (gm): 14.6
Exchanges
Milk: 0.0
Vegetable: 0.0
Fruit: 1.0
Bread: 0.0
Meat: 0.5
Fat: 0.5

1. Mix cheeses, 2 tablespoons chutney, onion, raisins, ginger-root, garlic, and curry powder until blended (do not beat or fat-free cream cheese will become thin in texture). Refrigerate 1 to 2 hours for flavors to blend.

2. Mound spread on plate; spoon remaining 6 tablespoons chutney over or around spread. Sprinkle with cashews and on-ion tops; serve with Pita Chips or Whole Wheat Lavosh (not in-cluded in nutritional data).

ROASTED GARLIC AND THREE-CHEESE SPREAD

 For best flavor, make this dip a day in advance.

12 servings (2 generous tablespoons each)

1 small garlic bulb
Olive oil cooking spray
1 package (8 ounces) fat-free cream cheese, softened
1½-2 ounces goat's cheese
¼ cup (2 ounces) grated fat-free Parmesan cheese
⅛ teaspoon white pepper
2-4 tablespoons fat-free milk
Minced parsley, *or* dried tomato bits, as garnish
Vegetable relishes and assorted crackers, as dippers

Per Serving
Calories: 43
% Calories from fat: 28
Fat (gm): 1.3
Saturated fat (gm): 0.9
Cholesterol (mg): 3.8
Sodium (mg): 142
Protein (gm): 4.7
Carbohydrate (gm): 2.5
Exchanges
Milk: 0.0
Vegetable: 0.0
Fruit: 0.0
Bread: 0.0
Meat: 0.5
Fat: 0.5

1. Cut off top of garlic bulb to expose cloves. Spray garlic lightly with cooking spray and wrap in aluminum foil; bake at 400 degrees until very tender, 35 to 40 minutes. Cool; gently press cloves to remove from skins. Mash cloves with fork.

2. Mix cheeses, garlic, and white pepper in medium bowl, adding enough milk to make desired spread consistency. Refrigerate 2 to 3 hours for flavors to blend.

3. Spoon mixture into serving bowl; sprinkle with parsley or dried tomato bits. Serve with vegetable relishes and crackers (not included in nutritional data).

GOAT'S CHEESE QUESADILLAS WITH TROPICAL FRUIT SALSA

 Goat's cheese and tropical fruits combine for a new flavor in quesadillas.

8 servings

4 ounces fat-free cream cheese, softened
2 ounces goat's cheese
½ small jalapeño chili, minced
½ teaspoon dried marjoram leaves
¼ teaspoon dried thyme leaves
⅛ teaspoon white pepper
8 whole wheat, *or* white, flour tortillas
Butter-flavored cooking spray
Tropical Fruit Salsa (see p. 726)

Per Serving
Calories: 186
% Calories from fat: 25
Fat (gm): 5.2
Saturated fat (gm): 2.2
Cholesterol (mg): 7.5
Sodium (mg): 285
Protein (gm): 8
Carbohydrate (gm): 26.3
Exchanges
Milk: 0.0
Vegetable: 1.0
Fruit: 0.5
Bread: 1.0
Meat: 0.5
Fat: 0.5

1. Combine cream cheese, goat's cheese, jalapeño chili, herbs, and white pepper; spread about 3 tablespoons mixture on each of 4 tortillas. Top with remaining tortillas.

2. Spray medium skillet with cooking spray; heat over medium heat until hot. Cook 1 quesadilla on medium to medium-low heat until browned on the bottom, 2 to 3 minutes. Spray top of quesadilla with cooking spray; turn and cook until browned on the bottom. Repeat with remaining quesadillas.

3. Cut quesadillas into wedges; serve warm with Tropical Fruit Salsa.

BLACK BEAN QUESADILLAS

Substitute pinto beans for the black beans if you like, and vary the amount of jalapeño chili to taste.

12 servings

1 cup cooked dried black beans, *or* canned black beans, rinsed, and drained
1 cup mild, *or* hot, chili salsa, divided
¼ cup thinly sliced green onion
3 tablespoons finely chopped cilantro
2-3 teaspoons minced jalapeño chili
12 whole wheat, *or* white, flour tortillas
¾ cup (3 ounces) reduced-fat Monterey Jack cheese
¾ cup (3 ounces) fat-free Cheddar cheese
Butter-flavored cooking spray

Per Serving
Calories: 169
% Calories from fat: 21
Fat (gm): 3.9
Saturated fat (gm): 1.2
Cholesterol (mg): 5.1
Sodium (mg): 427
Protein (gm): 9
Carbohydrate (gm): 24.2
Exchanges
Milk: 0.0
Vegetable: 0.0
Fruit: 0.0
Bread: 1.5
Meat: 0.5
Fat: 0.5

1. Mash beans slightly; combine with ¼ cup salsa, green onion, cilantro, and chili. Divide mixture on 6 tortillas, spreading almost to edges. Sprinkle with cheeses and top with remaining tortillas.

2. Spray medium skillet with cooking spray; heat over medium heat until hot. Cook 1 quesadilla on medium to medium-low heat until browned on the bottom, 2 to 3 minutes. Spray top of quesadilla with cooking spray; turn and cook until browned on the bottom. Repeat with remaining quesadillas.

3. Cut quesadillas into wedges; serve warm with remaining ¾ cup salsa.

QUESADILLAS

The simplest quesadillas are made only with cheese. Our version adds the Mexican poblano chili, onion, and cilantro; "Chorizo" (see p. 404) would be a flavorful addition.

6 servings

Vegetable cooking spray

1 poblano chili, *or* green bell pepper, sliced

1 medium onion, finely chopped

1 teaspoon ground cumin

2 tablespoons finely chopped cilantro

1 cup (4 ounces) shredded reduced-fat Cheddar cheese

6 flour tortillas

¾ cup Red, *or* Green, Tomato Salsa (see pp. 9, 8)

6 tablespoons fat-free sour cream

Per Serving
Calories: 165
% Calories from fat: 26
Fat (gm): 4.8
Saturated fat (gm): 1.7
Cholesterol (mg): 10.1
Sodium (mg): 393
Protein (gm): 8.3
Carbohydrate (gm): 22.9
Exchanges
Milk: 0.0
Vegetable: 1.5
Fruit: 0.0
Bread: 1.0
Meat: 0.5
Fat: 0.5

1. Spray large skillet with cooking spray; heat over medium heat until hot. Saute poblano chili, onion, and cumin until vegetables are tender, 3 to 5 minutes; stir in cilantro.

2. Sprinkle cheese on half of each tortilla; spoon vegetable mixture over. Fold tortillas in half.

3. Spray large skillet with cooking spray; heat over medium heat until hot. Cook quesadillas over medium to medium-high heat until browned on the bottoms, 2 to 3 minutes. Spray tops of quesadillas with cooking spray; turn and cook until browned on the other side. Cut into wedges and serve warm with Salsa and sour cream.

TORTILLA WEDGES

Fun to make and eat—our Mexican-style version of pizza!

12 servings (2 wedges each)

"Chorizo" (see p. 404)
Vegetable cooking spray
½ cup chopped green bell pepper
½ cup chopped onion
Salt and pepper, to taste
4 large flour tortillas (10-inch)
1 cup (4 ounces) shredded reduced-fat Monterey Jack cheese
1 cup (4 ounces) shredded fat-free Cheddar cheese
1 cup Red Tomato Salsa (see p. 9), *or* prepared salsa
¾ cup fat-free sour cream

Per Serving
Calories: 206
% Calories from fat: 16
Fat (gm): 3.6
Saturated fat (gm): 1.4
Cholesterol (mg): 42.3
Sodium (mg): 551
Protein (gm): 25.2
Carbohydrate (gm): 18.4
Exchanges
Milk: 0.0
Vegetable: 0.5
Fruit: 0.0
Bread: 0.5
Meat: 3.0
Fat: 0.0

1. Make "Chorizo" mixture, deleting salt; do not form into patties.

2. Spray medium skillet with cooking spray; heat over medium heat until hot. Add "Chorizo" and cook over medium heat until brown, crumbling with fork; add green pepper and onion and cook until tender, 2 to 3 minutes. Season to taste with salt and pepper.

3. Place tortillas on baking sheets; sprinkle evenly with Monterey Jack cheese. Sprinkle with "Chorizo" mixture, and top with Cheddar cheese. Bake at 450 degrees until edges of tortillas are browned and cheese is melted, 6 to 8 minutes. Top with Red Tomato Salsa and sour cream. Cut each tortilla into 6 wedges.

NACHOS

A favorite, but high-fat and high-calorie, restaurant appetizer that can be made in a healthy "skinny" version at home! Canned refried beans can be substituted for the pinto beans, and purchased baked tortilla chips and salsa can be substituted for the homemade. Cooked, crumbled "Chorizo" (see p. 404) can be added to make these nachos "grandes"!

6 servings

Baked Tortilla Chips, made with corn tortillas (see p. 55)

1 can (15½ ounces) pinto beans, rinsed, drained, coarsely mashed

1 cup Red Tomato Salsa, *or* Green Tomato Salsa (see pp. 9, 8), divided

½-1 teaspoon chili powder

¾ teaspoon dried oregano leaves

2-3 cloves garlic, minced

Salt, to taste

½ cup (2 ounces) shredded reduced-fat Cheddar, *or* Monterey Jack, cheese

1 medium tomato, chopped

½ small avocado, chopped

2 green onions and tops, sliced

6 pitted ripe olives, sliced (optional)

¼ cup fat-free sour cream

Per Serving
Calories: 200
% Calories from fat: 22
Fat (gm): 5.4
Saturated fat (gm): 1.2
Cholesterol (mg): 5.1
Sodium (mg): 455
Protein (gm): 10.5
Carbohydrate (gm): 32.5
Exchanges
Milk: 0.0
Vegetable: 1.0
Fruit: 0.0
Bread: 2.0
Meat: 0.0
Fat: 1.0

1. Spread Baked Tortilla Chips in a single layer in jelly roll pan. Mix beans, ¼ cup salsa, chili powder, oregano, and garlic; season to taste with salt. Spoon bean mixture over tortilla chips; sprinkle with cheese. Bake at 350 degrees until beans are hot and cheese melted, 5 to 10 minutes.

2. Sprinkle with tomato, avocado, onions, and olives; garnish with dollops of sour cream. Serve with remaining salsa.

JICAMA WITH LIME AND CILANTRO

Very simple, and incredibly tasty!

4 servings

  1 medium jicama, peeled, thinly sliced
     Salt, to taste
     Lime juice, to taste
1-2 tablespoons finely chopped cilantro

Per Serving
Calories: 17
% Calories from fat: 2
Fat (gm): 0
Saturated fat (gm): 0
Cholesterol (mg): 0
Sodium (mg): 0
Protein (gm): 0.5
Carbohydrate (gm): 3.8
Exchanges
Milk: 0.0
Vegetable: 1.0
Fruit: 0.0
Bread: 0.0
Meat: 0.0
Fat: 0.0

1. Arrange jicama slices on large serving plate; sprinkle very lightly with salt. Then sprinkle with lime juice and cilantro.

FRIED RIPE PLANTAINS

When ripe, the plantain skin is black and the fruit is soft. If purchasing plantains when green, they will ripen more quickly if kept in a closed paper bag in a dark place.

4 servings

     Canola, *or* peanut, oil
2 ripe plantains, peeled, diagonally cut into ¼-inch slices
     Salt, to taste

Per Serving
Calories: 119
% Calories from fat: 10
Fat (gm): 1.5
Saturated fat (gm): 0.3
Cholesterol (mg): 0
Sodium (mg): 4
Protein (gm): 1.2
Carbohydrate (gm): 28.6
Exchanges
Milk: 0.0
Vegetable: 0.0
Fruit: 2.0
Bread: 0.0
Meat: 0.0
Fat: 0.0

1. Heat 1½ to 2 inches of oil to 375 degrees in large saucepan. Fry plantains until golden on both sides; drain well on paper toweling.

2. Sprinkle plantains with salt and arrange in a bowl; serve hot.

Note: For a sweet variation, plantains can be sprinkled with sugar and cinnamon instead of salt.

FRUIT EMPANADAS

Sweet empanadas can be served as an appetizer or dessert. Other dried fruits, such as pears or apples, can be substituted for the apricots and raisins.

24 empanadas

½ cup chopped dried apricots
½ cup raisins
½ cup water
¼ cup sugar
½ teaspoon ground cinnamon
⅛ teaspoon ground nutmeg
  Empanada Pastry (recipe follows)
3 tablespoons fat-free milk, for glaze
1 tablespoon sugar, for glaze

Per Empanada
Calories: 64
% Calories from fat: 23
Fat (gm): 1.7
Saturated fat (gm): 0.4
Cholesterol (mg): 0
Sodium (mg): 16
Protein (gm): 1
Carbohydrate (gm): 11.8
Exchanges
Milk: 0.0
Vegetable: 0.0
Fruit: 1.0
Bread: 0.0
Meat: 0.0
Fat: 0.0

1. Heat apricots, raisins, and water to boiling in small saucepan. Reduce heat and simmer, covered, until fruit is very soft, about 5 minutes. Mash fruit with fork until almost smooth; stir in ¼ cup sugar and spices.

2. Roll half the Empanada Pastry on lightly floured surface until ⅛ inch thick; cut into circles with 3-inch cookie cutter. Place slightly rounded teaspoon of fruit mixture in center of each pastry circle; fold pastries in half and crimp edges with tines of fork. Make slit in top of each pastry with knife.

3. Bake pastries on greased jelly roll pans at 350 degrees until golden, 12 to 15 minutes.

4. To glaze, brush pastries lightly with fat-free milk and sprinkle with sugar; bake 1 to 2 minutes more, until glazed. Serve warm.

Empanada Pastry

1¼ cups all-purpose flour
1 tablespoon sugar
¼ teaspoon baking powder
⅛ teaspoon salt
3 tablespoons vegetable shortening
1 teaspoon lemon juice, *or* distilled white vinegar
3-4 tablespoons fat-free milk, *or* water

1. Combine flour, sugar, baking powder, and salt in small bowl; cut in shortening until mixture resembles coarse crumbs. Mix in lemon juice and milk, a tablespoon at a time, to form soft dough. Refrigerate until ready to use.

RICOTTA-STUFFED SHELLS WITH SPINACH PESTO

Pesto sauces are traditionally served at room temperature. Spinach Pesto can be made up to 1 week in advance and refrigerated. Before serving, let it stand until room temperature, or microwave it in a glass bowl at medium setting until softened, about 30 seconds.

4 servings (3 shells each)

Vegetable cooking spray
¼ cup finely chopped onions
2-3 cloves garlic, minced
½ teaspoon dried basil leaves
½ cup chopped fresh spinach
¾ cup low-fat ricotta cheese
¼ teaspoon ground nutmeg
¼ teaspoon salt
¼ teaspoon pepper
12 conchiglie (jumbo pasta shells), about 4 ounces, cooked
Spinach Pesto (recipe p. 727)
2 tablespoons chopped red, *or* green, bell peppers, roasted *or* raw
Basil sprigs, as garnish

Per Serving
Calories: 178
% Calories from fat: 24
Fat (gm): 4.7
Saturated fat (gm): 0.8
Cholesterol (mg): 7.2
Sodium (mg): 216
Protein (gm): 9.5
Carbohydrate (gm): 24.6
Exchanges
Milk: 0.0
Vegetable: 1.0
Fruit: 0.0
Bread: 1.5
Meat: 0.5
Fat: 0.5

1. Spray medium skillet with cooking spray; saute onions, garlic, and dried basil until onions are tender, 3 to 4 minutes. Add spinach; cook over medium heat until spinach is wilted, about 5 minutes.

2. Heat oven to 350 degrees. Stir spinach mixture into cheese; stir in nutmeg, salt, and pepper. Stuff mixture into shells; place in baking pan. Bake, covered, until hot through, about 20 minutes.

3. Arrange shells on small serving plates; spoon Spinach Pesto over shells or serve on the side. Sprinkle with bell peppers; garnish with basil sprigs.

STUFFED VEGETABLES

 Vegetables can also be stuffed with any of the spread recipes in this chapter.

12 servings (4 pieces each)

12 cherry tomatoes
12 cucumber slices, ¾ inch thick
12 yellow summer squash slices (¾ inch thick)
12 medium mushrooms
1 cup (½ recipe) Roasted Garlic with Three-Cheese Spread (see p. 27)
    Parsley sprigs, ripe olive slices, chopped sun-dried tomato bits, as garnish

Per Serving
Calories: 55
% Calories from fat: 24
Fat (gm): 1.5
Saturated fat (gm): 0.9
Cholesterol (mg): 3.8
Sodium (mg): 145
Protein (gm): 5.4
Carbohydrate (gm): 5.2
Exchanges
Milk: 0.0
Vegetable: 0.5
Fruit: 0.0
Bread: 0.0
Meat: 0.5
Fat: 0.5

1. Cut tops off tomatoes; cut thin slices off bottoms, if necessary for tomatoes to stand up securely. Remove seeds from tomatoes using tip of vegetable peeler or melon baller. Scoop out centers of cucumber and squash slices with melon baller. Remove stems from mushrooms.

2. Using pastry bag or small spoon, fill vegetables with spread. Garnish with parsley, olives, and sun-dried tomatoes.

MUSHROOMS STUFFED WITH ORZO

Enjoy flavor accents of tangy goat's cheese and a trio of fresh herbs. Serve with Cilantro Pesto or Spinach Pesto (see pp. 730, 727).

4 servings (3 mushrooms each)

12 large mushrooms
   Vegetable cooking spray
 1 tablespoon finely chopped medium shallots
 2 cloves garlic, minced
 1 tablespoon finely chopped fresh basil leaves, *or* 1 teaspoon dried
 2 teaspoons finely chopped fresh oregano leaves, *or* ½ teaspoon dried
 ½ teaspoon finely chopped fresh thyme leaves, *or* ⅛ teaspoon dried
 ¼ cup (2 ounces) orzo, cooked
 1 tablespoon goat's cheese, *or* reduced-fat cream cheese
   Basil, *or* oregano, sprigs, as garnish

Per Serving
Calories: 86
% Calories from fat: 24
Fat (gm): 2.6
Saturated fat (gm): 0.6
Cholesterol (mg): 3.4
Sodium (mg): 18
Protein (gm): 5.3
Carbohydrate (gm): 13
Exchanges
Milk: 0.0
Vegetable: 1.0
Fruit: 0.0
Bread: 0.5
Meat: 0.0
Fat: 0.5

1. Remove stems from mushrooms and chop coarsely. Reserve caps. Spray medium skillet with cooking spray; heat over medium heat until hot. Saute mushroom stems 2 to 3 minutes. Add shallots, garlic, and chopped herbs; saute until shallots are almost tender, about 3 minutes. Stir in orzo and goat's cheese; cook until orzo is warm, 1 to 2 minutes.

2. Heat oven to 350 degrees. Spoon orzo filling into mushroom caps and place in 13 x 9-inch baking pan. Bake, covered with aluminum foil, until mushroom caps are tender, about 15 minutes. Remove foil and bake 5 minutes longer.

3. Arrange mushrooms on serving plates; garnish with herb sprigs. Serve warm.

CURRIED ONION CROUSTADES

The Croustades can be filled with the onion mixture and refrigerated several hours before baking.

8 servings (2 each)

Vegetable cooking spray
2 cups chopped onions
2 cloves garlic, minced
1 teaspoon curry powder
½ teaspoon ground cumin
2 tablespoons flour
1 cup fat-free half-and-half, *or* fat-free milk
2 tablespoons dried fruit bits
1 tablespoon minced cilantro
Salt, cayenne, and black pepper, to taste
Croustades (see p. 55)
4 teaspoons chopped almonds

Per Serving
Calories: 125
% Calories from fat: 13
Fat (gm): 1.8
Saturated fat (gm): 0.3
Cholesterol (mg): 0
Sodium (mg): 167
Protein (gm): 4.2
Carbohydrate (gm): 22.3
Exchanges
Milk: 0.0
Vegetable: 1.0
Fruit: 0.0
Bread: 1.0
Meat: 0.0
Fat: 0.5

1. Spray large skillet with cooking spray; heat over medium heat until hot. Add onions, garlic, curry powder, and cumin; cook, covered, over low heat until onions are very soft, about 20 minutes. Stir in flour; cook 2 minutes longer, stirring frequently.

2. Stir half-and-half and fruit into onion mixture; heat to boiling. Reduce heat and simmer until thickened, stirring constantly. Stir in cilantro; season to taste with salt, cayenne, and black pepper.

3. Spoon slightly rounded tablespoon of onion mixture into each Croustade; sprinkle each with ¼ teaspoon almonds. Bake at 425 degrees 10 minutes.

ARTICHOKE-STUFFED APPETIZER BREAD

For easy entertaining, assemble this appetizer a day or two in advance. Bread pieces removed from the loaf can be used to make fresh bread-crumbs or croutons.

8 servings (2 pieces each)

Per Serving
Calories: 151
% Calories from fat: 29
Fat (gm): 5.1
Saturated fat (gm): 0.3
Cholesterol (mg): 0
Sodium (mg): 600
Protein (gm): 6.9
Carbohydrate (gm): 20.9
Exchanges
Milk: 0.0
Vegetable: 1.0
Fruit: 0.0
Bread: 1.0
Meat: 0.0
Fat: 1.0

- 1 package (8 ounces) fat-free cream cheese, softened
- 1 can (14 ounces) artichoke hearts, drained, chopped
- ½ cup red bell pepper
- ½ cup chopped celery
- ¼ cup chopped pitted green, *or* black, olives
- 2 teaspoons drained capers
- 1 clove garlic, minced
- ½ teaspoon dried basil leaves
- ½ teaspoon dried oregano leaves
- 1-2 teaspoons white wine vinegar, *or* lemon juice
  Salt and white pepper, to taste
- 1 loaf French bread (8 ounces, about 15 inches long)

1. Mix softened cream cheese with artichoke hearts, bell pepper, celery, olives, capers, garlic, and herbs; season to taste with vinegar, salt, and white pepper.

2. Slice bread lengthwise in half. Remove bread from centers of bread halves, using paring knife or serrated grapefruit spoon, leaving ¾-inch shell of bread.

3. Spoon filling into each bread half; press halves together firmly and wrap in plastic wrap. Refrigerate 2 hours or until serving time. Cut into 16 pieces.

CURRIED PINWHEELS

Make these easy appetizers up to 2 days in advance and refrigerate until ready to serve.

3 dozen

6	pieces luncheon-size lavosh (5-inch)
1½	packages (8 ounces each) fat-free cream cheese, softened
2	tablespoons fat-free mayonnaise
1-2	teaspoons spicy brown mustard
1	clove garlic, minced
1-1½	teaspoons curry powder
½	teaspoon ground cumin
¼	teaspoon cayenne pepper
½	cup finely chopped cored apple
¼	cup chopped celery
¼	cup finely chopped green onions and tops
¼	cup chopped dry-roasted peanuts
¾	cup chopped chutney

Per Pinwheel
Calories: 38
% Calories from fat: 14
Fat (gm): 0.6
Saturated fat (gm): 0.1
Cholesterol (mg): 0
Sodium (mg): 79
Protein (gm): 1.9
Carbohydrate (gm): 6.2
Exchanges
Milk: 0.0
Vegetable: 0.0
Fruit: 0.5
Bread: 0.0
Meat: 0.0
Fat: 0.0

1. Brush lavosh lightly with water and place between damp kitchen towels until softened enough to roll, 20 to 30 minutes.

2. Mix cream cheese, mayonnaise, mustard, garlic, curry, cumin, and cayenne pepper in small bowl; spread about 3 tablespoons mixture on each lavosh. Combine remaining ingredients, except chutney, and sprinkle over cheese mixture. Roll lavosh tightly; wrap each roll in plastic wrap and refrigerate at least 4 hours.

3. Cut each roll into 6 pieces and arrange on plate. Serve with chutney.

MUSHROOM BRUSCHETTA

Use any desired wild mushrooms for richest flavor, and make this filling up to 2 days in advance. Heat briefly before assembling and broiling the bruschetta.

6 servings (2 bruschetta each)

Vegetable cooking spray
¼ cup chopped red bell pepper
¼ cup chopped yellow bell pepper
2 green onions and tops, thinly sliced
2 cloves garlic, minced
2 cups chopped portobello, shiitake, *or* white mushrooms
1 teaspoon dried basil leaves
¼ teaspoon dried thyme leaves
2-3 tablespoons grated fat-free Parmesan cheese
Few drops balsamic vinegar
Salt and pepper, to taste
Bruschetta (see p. 54)
¼ cup (2 ounces) shredded reduced-fat mozzarella cheese

Per Serving
Calories: 184
% Calories from fat: 17
Fat (gm): 3.4
Saturated fat (gm): 1.3
Cholesterol (mg): 5.1
Sodium (mg): 388
Protein (gm): 8.8
Carbohydrate (gm): 29.5
Exchanges
Milk: 0.0
Vegetable: 0.5
Fruit: 0.0
Bread: 2.0
Meat: 0.5
Fat: 0.0

1. Spray medium skillet with cooking spray; heat over medium heat until hot. Saute bell peppers, onions, and garlic 2 to 3 minutes. Add mushrooms; cook, covered, over medium heat until wilted, about 5 minutes. Stir in herbs and cook until mushrooms are tender and all liquid is gone, 8 to 10 minutes. Stir in Parmesan cheese; season to taste with balsamic vinegar, salt, and pepper.

2. Spoon mushroom mixture on Bruschetta and sprinkle with mozzarella cheese; broil until cheese is melted, 1 to 2 minutes. Serve warm.

SPINACH AND CHEESE MINI-QUICHES

The tiny fillo shells, delicious and wonderfully crisp, are available in the frozen food section of supermarkets. Pie pastry for a double-crust pie (see p. 763) can be substituted; roll pastry to a scant ¼ inch thickness and cut into 2½-inch rounds. Fit pastries into muffin cups and crimp the top edges with tines of a fork.

1½ dozen

1¼ cups fat-free cottage cheese
¼ cup grated fat-free Parmesan cheese
2 tablespoons fat-free milk
2 tablespoons flour
½ cup finely chopped fresh spinach
½ teaspoon dried oregano leaves
¼ teaspoon dried thyme leaves
Salt and white pepper, to taste
2 eggs
1½ dozen frozen mini-fillo shells, thawed

Per Mini-Quiche
Calories: 48
% Calories from fat: 30
Fat (gm): 1.6
Saturated fat (gm): 0.2
Cholesterol (mg): 23.7
Sodium (mg): 61
Protein (gm): 3.9
Carbohydrate (gm): 4.3
Exchanges
Milk: 0.0
Vegetable: 0.0
Fruit: 0.0
Bread: 0.5
Meat: 0.0
Fat: 0.5

1. Mix cottage cheese, Parmesan cheese, fat-free milk, flour, spinach, oregano, and thyme; season to taste with salt and pepper. Stir in eggs.

2. Arrange fillo shells on cookie sheet or in mini-muffin tins; fill with cheese mixture. Bake at 325 degrees until puffed and beginning to brown on the tops, about 20 minutes.

CHEESE AND SPINACH SQUARES

Lots of cheese and spinach are a team in these terrific appetizer squares. Substitute fat-free Swiss or mozzarella cheese for the Cheddar, if you want.

12 servings (2 squares each)

Vegetable cooking spray
1-2 tablespoons dry unseasoned bread-crumbs
2 cups fat-free cottage cheese
1½ cups (6 ounces) shredded fat-free Cheddar cheese

Per Serving
Calories: 81
% Calories from fat: 11
Fat (gm): 1
Saturated fat (gm): 0.3
Cholesterol (mg): 35.5
Sodium (mg): 231
Protein (gm): 11.8
Carbohydrate (gm): 6.7

2 eggs

6 tablespoons whole wheat flour

1 package (10 ounces) frozen, chopped spinach, thawed, well drained

¼ cup thinly sliced green onions and tops

¼ cup chopped roasted red bell pepper, *or* pimiento

¼ cup finely chopped parsley

¼ teaspoon cayenne pepper

½ teaspoon black pepper

⅛ teaspoon ground nutmeg

Exchanges
Milk: 0.0
Vegetable: 1.0
Fruit: 0.0
Bread: 0.0
Meat: 1.0
Fat: 0.0

1. Spray 13 x 9-inch pan with cooking spray; coat bottom and sides of pan with breadcrumbs.

2. Combine cheeses and eggs in bowl; stir in remaining ingredients until blended. Pour into prepared pan and bake at 350 degrees until set and lightly browned, 35 to 40 minutes. Cool 10 minutes before cutting into squares.

BAKED SPINACH BALLS

Often laden with butter, these savory treats have been made "skinny" with no loss in flavor.

12 servings (2 balls each)

2 cups herb-seasoned bread stuffing cubes

¼ cup grated fat-free Parmesan cheese

¼ cup chopped green onions and tops

2 cloves garlic, minced

⅛ teaspoon ground nutmeg

1 package (10 ounces) frozen chopped spinach, thawed, well drained

¼-⅓ cup Canned Vegetable Stock (see p. 63)

2 tablespoons margarine, *or* butter melted

Salt and pepper, to taste

2 egg whites, beaten

Mustard Sauce (see p.734)

Per Serving
Calories: 86
% Calories from fat: 24
Fat (gm): 2.4
Saturated fat (gm): 0.4
Cholesterol (mg): 0
Sodium (mg): 271
Protein (gm): 4.2
Carbohydrate (gm): 13
Exchanges
Milk: 0.0
Vegetable: 1.0
Fruit: 0.0
Bread: 0.5
Meat: 0.0
Fat: 0.5

1. Combine stuffing cubes, Parmesan cheese, onions, garlic, and nutmeg in medium bowl. Mix in spinach, stock, and margarine; season to taste with salt and pepper. Mix in egg whites.

2. Shape mixture into 24 balls. Bake at 350 degrees until spinach balls are browned, about 15 minutes. Serve with Mustard Sauce for dipping.

FIVE-SPICE POTSTICKERS

Purchased wonton wrappers make this recipe simple to prepare. Wonton wrappers can be cut into circles with a 2½-inch cutter, if you like. Won tons can be assembled up to 1 day in advance; dust lightly with flour and refrigerate in a single layer on a plate, covered tightly with plastic wrap.

12 servings (4 potstickers each)

Vegetable cooking spray

- 2 cups sliced Chinese cabbage
- ½ cup shredded carrot
- ¼ cup thinly sliced green onions and tops
- ¼ cup thinly sliced celery
- 1-2 teaspoons minced gingerroot
- 1 clove garlic, minced
- 1 tablespoon wheat germ
- 1 tablespoon reduced-sodium tamari soy sauce
- ¼-½ teaspoon hot chili paste
- ¼-½ teaspoon five-spice powder
- 2 ounces light tofu, cut into small cubes *or* coarsely crumbled
- 48 wonton, *or* gyoza, wrappers
- 1 egg white, beaten
  Plum Sauce, *or* Tamari Dipping Sauce
  (see pp. 734, 735)

Per Serving
Calories: 130
% Calories from fat: 4
Fat (gm): 0.6
Saturated fat (gm): 0.1
Cholesterol (mg): 4
Sodium (mg): 431
Protein (gm): 5.2
Carbohydrate (gm): 25.9
Exchanges
Milk: 0.0
Vegetable: 2.0
Fruit: 0.0
Bread: 1.0
Meat: 0.0
Fat: 0.0

1. Spray wok or large skillet with cooking spray; heat over medium heat until hot. Stir-fry cabbage, carrot, green onions, celery, gingerroot, and garlic over medium to medium-high heat until cabbage is wilted, 2 to 3 minutes. Remove from heat; stir in wheat germ, tamari soy sauce, chili paste, and five-spice powder. Add tofu, toss lightly, and cool.

2. Spoon ½ tablespoon filling on wonton wrapper; brush edges of wrapper with egg white. Fold wrapper in half and press edges to seal. Repeat with remaining filling, wrappers, and egg white.

3. Heat large saucepan of water to boiling. Add won tons 6 or 8 at a time and simmer, uncovered, until won tons rise to the surface, 2 to 3 minutes. Remove from water with slotted spoon and drain. Repeat with remaining won tons.

4. Spray wok or large skillet with cooking spray; heat over medium heat until hot. Add single layer of won tons and cook until browned on the bottom, 2 to 3 minutes. Spray tops of won tons lightly with cooking spray; turn and cook until browned. Repeat with remaining wontons. Serve hot with Plum Sauce.

CRANBERRY-CHEESE WONTONS

Dried cranberries and gingerroot add a lively accent to these unusual cheese wontons. When fried at the correct temperature, deep-fried foods absorb almost no fat.

6 servings (4 wontons each)

¾ package (8-ounce size) fat-free cream cheese

3 tablespoons chopped dried cranberries

2 tablespoons finely chopped chives

½-¾ teaspoon minced gingerroot

1 tablespoon minced parsley

Salt and white pepper, to taste

24 wonton wrappers

1 egg white, beaten

Canola, *or* peanut, oil, for frying

⅓ cup jalapeño jelly, heated, *or* Tamari Dipping Sauce (see p. 735)

Per Serving
Calories: 182
% Calories from fat: 10
Fat (gm): 1.9
Saturated fat (gm): 0.3
Cholesterol (mg): 4
Sodium (mg): 368
Protein (gm): 7.9
Carbohydrate (gm): 31.6
Exchanges
Milk: 0.0
Vegetable: 0.0
Fruit: 1.0
Bread: 1.0
Meat: 1.0
Fat: 0.0

1. Mix cream cheese, cranberries, chives, gingerroot, and parsley in small bowl; season to taste with salt and white pepper.

2. Spoon ½ tablespoon filling on wonton wrapper; brush edges of wrapper with egg white. Fold wrapper in half and press edges to seal. Repeat with remaining filling, wrappers, and egg white.

3. Heat 2 inches of oil to 375 degrees in large saucepan. Fry wontons, 6 to 8 at a time, until golden, 1 to 2 minutes. Drain very well on paper toweling. Serve hot with jalapeño jelly or Tamari Dipping Sauce.

MIXED VEGETABLE EGG ROLLS

The dark oriental sesame oil in this recipe has a more distinctive sesame flavor than the light domestic brands. Spinach, alfalfa sprouts, and black beans add a new dimension to these egg rolls.

1 dozen

1	tablespoon sesame seeds
2-3	teaspoons dark sesame oil
2	green onions and tops, sliced
1	tablespoon minced gingerroot
2	cloves garlic, minced
2	cups shredded spinach
½	cup chopped water chestnuts
½	cup shredded carrot
½	cup sliced small mushrooms
1	can (15½ ounces) black beans, rinsed, drained
1-1½	teaspoons reduced-sodium tamari, *or* reduced-sodium soy, sauce
	Salt and pepper, to taste
2	egg whites
1	cup alfalfa sprouts
12	egg roll wrappers
	Peanut, *or* vegetable, oil
	Plum Sauce, *or* Tamari Dipping Sauce (see pp. 734, 735)

Per Egg Roll
Calories: 101
% Calories from fat: 12
Fat (gm): 1.6
Saturated fat (gm): 0.2
Cholesterol (mg): 0
Sodium (mg): 342
Protein (gm): 5.8
Carbohydrate (gm): 19
Exchanges
Milk: 0.0
Vegetable: 1.5
Fruit: 0.0
Bread: 1.0
Meat: 0.0
Fat: 0.0

1. Saute sesame seeds in sesame oil in large skillet until beginning to brown, 1 to 2 minutes. Add green onions, gingerroot, and garlic; saute until onions are tender, 1 to 2 minutes. Add spinach, water chestnuts, carrot, and mushrooms; cook, covered, over medium heat until spinach and mushrooms are wilted. Stir in beans and tamari sauce; season to taste with salt and pepper. Cool 5 to 10 minutes; stir in egg whites and alfalfa sprouts.

2. Spoon about ⅓ cup vegetable mixture near corner of 1 egg roll wrapper. Brush edges of wrapper with water. Fold bottom corner of egg roll wrapper up over filling; fold sides in and roll up. Repeat with remaining filling and wrappers.

3. Heat about 2 inches of oil to 375 degrees in deep skillet or large saucepan. Fry egg rolls until golden, 4 to 5 minutes. Drain on paper toweling. Serve hot with Plum Sauce or Tamari Dipping Sauce.

AFRICAN FAVA PATTIES WITH YOGURT-CUCUMBER SAUCE

Make the pattie mixture up to 2 days in advance; shape and cook at serving time.

6 servings (4 patties each)

Per Serving
Calories: 171
% Calories from fat: 16
Fat (gm): 3.1
Saturated fat (gm): 0.5
Cholesterol (mg): 0.7
Sodium (mg): 109
Protein (gm): 10.4
Carbohydrate (gm): 26.3
Exchanges
Milk: 0.0
Vegetable: 0.0
Fruit: 0.0
Bread: 2.0
Meat: 0.0
Fat: 0.5

    2 cups cooked dried fava beans, *or* canned
      fava beans, rinsed, drained
    1 small potato, peeled, cooked, mashed
    ½ cup finely chopped onion
    ¼ cup minced parsley
    ¾ teaspoon ground coriander
    ½ teaspoon ground cumin
    5 drops red pepper sauce
      Salt and pepper, to taste
    2 egg whites
    ⅓ cup dry unseasoned breadcrumbs
  1-2 tablespoons extra-virgin olive oil
      Yogurt-Cucumber Sauce (see p. 733)

1. Mash fava beans with fork; combine with potato, onion, parsley, coriander, cumin, and red pepper sauce. Season to taste with salt and pepper; mix in egg whites and breadcrumbs. Shape mixture into 24 patties.

2. Cook patties in oil in large skillet over medium to medium-low heat until browned and crisp on both sides; drain well. Serve hot with Yogurt-Cucumber Sauce.

INDONESIAN-STYLE TOFU SATAY

Light extra-firm tofu is very low in fat, with only 26% calories from fat, compared to regular extra-firm tofu, which is about 39% calories from fat.

6 servings

1	package (10½ ounces) light extra-firm tofu
2-3	tablespoons reduced-sodium soy sauce, divided
2	tablespoons reduced-fat peanut butter
2	tablespoons honey
1	tablespoon bead, *or* unsulphured, molasses
1	tablespoon lemon juice
1	tablespoon chopped gingerroot
1	tablespoon finely chopped serrano, *or* jalapeño, chili
3	cloves garlic, minced
1	teaspoon chili powder
½	teaspoon dark oriental sesame oil
2	tablespoons thinly sliced green onions and tops

Per Serving
Calories: 94
% Calories from fat: 28
Fat (gm): 3.1
Saturated fat (gm): 0.5
Cholesterol (mg): 0
Sodium (mg): 235
Protein (gm): 5.8
Carbohydrate (gm): 11.9
Exchanges
Milk: 0.0
Vegetable: 0.0
Fruit: 0.0
Bread: 0.5
Meat: 0.5
Fat: 0.5

1. Weight the tofu (see p. xiii) to remove excess moisture. Cut tofu into ¾-inch cubes and arrange on 6 skewers. Place in single layer in baking dish; brush with 1 to 2 tablespoons soy sauce. Refrigerate, covered, 1 hour or longer.

2. Process 1 tablespoon soy sauce and remaining ingredients, except green onions, in food processor or blender until smooth. Stir in green onions.

3. Bake tofu kabobs at 400 degrees for 20 minutes. Arrange kabobs on serving plate; spoon sauce over.

TORTELLINI KABOBS WITH MANY-CLOVES GARLIC SAUCE

 A fun party food, but also a great idea for a casual meal. Serve 3 to 4 skewers each for an entrée, and accompany with broiled tomato halves, a crisp green salad, and Garlic Bread (see p. 676).

8 servings (2 kabobs each)

1½ packages (9-ounces size) mushroom tortellini, cooked
5 cups assorted whole, cubed, and sliced vegetables (mushroom caps, cherry tomatoes, bell peppers, zucchini, broccoli florets, artichoke hearts, etc.)
Olive oil cooking spray
Many-Cloves Garlic Sauce (see p. 710)

Per Serving
Calories: 146
% Calories from fat: 26
Fat (gm): 5
Saturated fat (gm): 1.8
Cholesterol (mg): 25.3
Sodium (mg): 171
Protein (gm): 7.4
Carbohydrate (gm): 23.3
Exchanges
Milk: 0.0
Vegetable: 2.0
Fruit: 0.0
Bread: 1.0
Meat: 0.0
Fat: 0.5

1. Alternate tortellini and vegetables on 16 long skewers and arrange on broiler pan. Spray generously with cooking spray and broil 6 inches from heat source 4 minutes; turn kabobs, spray with cooking spray, and broil 3 to 4 minutes longer.

2. Make Many-Cloves Garlic Sauce using only 1 tablespoon olive oil. Arrange tortellini kabobs on serving platter; serve with garlic sauce.

Note: Cook firm vegetables such as broccoli, carrots, and zucchini until crisp-tender before using.

APPLE-CABBAGE STRUDELS

Serve hot or at room temperature. The strudels can be assembled several hours in advance; refrigerate, tightly covered. Spray tops of strudels generously with cooking spray before baking.

12 servings (2 pieces each)

Vegetable cooking spray
½ cup thinly sliced onion
2 cloves garlic, minced
3 cups thinly sliced cabbage
⅓ cup apple cider, *or* apple juice
1½ cups peeled, chopped, tart, *or* sweet, apples
¼ cup dark raisins
1-1½ teaspoons curry powder
Salt and pepper, to taste
8 sheets frozen fillo pastry, thawed
Butter-flavored cooking spray

Per Serving
Calories: 34
% Calories from fat: 5
Fat (gm): 0.2
Saturated fat (gm): 0
Cholesterol (mg): 0
Sodium (mg): 8
Protein (gm): 0.6
Carbohydrate (gm): 8.5
Exchanges
Milk: 0.0
Vegetable: 0.0
Fruit: 0.5
Bread: 0.0
Meat: 0.0
Fat: 0.0

1. Spray large skillet with cooking spray; heat over medium heat until hot. Saute onion and garlic until tender, about 5 minutes. Add cabbage and apple cider; cook, covered, over medium heat until cabbage is wilted, about 5 minutes. Stir in apples, raisins, and curry powder; cook, uncovered, until apples are crisp-tender and mixture is almost dry, 5 to 8 minutes. Season to taste with salt and pepper. Cool.

2. Place 1 sheet fillo on clean kitchen towel; spray with butter-flavored cooking spray; top with second sheet of fillo and spray. Repeat with 2 more sheets of fillo. Spoon half the cabbage mixture evenly along short edge of fillo, leaving a 1-inch space from the edge. Roll up from short edge, tucking ends under. Place seam side down on greased cookie sheet. Repeat with remaining fillo, cooking spray, and cabbage mixture. Spray tops of strudels generously with cooking spray.

3. Bake strudels at 400 degrees until golden, about 15 minutes. Cool slightly; cut diagonally into 1-inch pieces with serrated knife.

ONION AND BLUE CHEESE FOCACCIA

Expect rave reviews when serving this delicious appetizer. Serve larger portions as a bread with entrée salads, too.

8 servings

Olive oil cooking spray
2 cups thinly sliced onions
4 cloves garlic, minced
½ teaspoon dried rosemary leaves
Salt and pepper, to taste
1 focaccia (Italian flat bread, 10 ounces)
¼ cup chopped sun-dried tomatoes (not in oil)
2-3 ounces crumbled blue cheese
2 tablespoons grated fat-free Parmesan cheese

Per Serving
Calories: 146
% Calories from fat: 21
Fat (gm): 3.5
Saturated fat (gm): 1.6
Cholesterol (mg): 5.2
Sodium (mg): 354
Protein (gm): 5.9
Carbohydrate (gm): 23.3
Exchanges
Milk: 0.0
Vegetable: 2.0
Fruit: 0.0
Bread: 1.0
Meat: 0.0
Fat: 0.5

1. Spray large skillet with cooking spray; heat over medium heat until hot. Cook onions and garlic, covered, over medium heat until wilted. Cook, uncovered, over low heat until tender and lightly browned; stir in rosemary and season with salt and pepper.

2. Arrange onions on bread; sprinkle with sun-dried tomatoes and cheeses. Bake at 350 degrees until bread is hot and cheese melted, about 15 minutes. Cut into 8 wedges.

CALZONES

These Italian-style pies, filled with cheese and vegetables, can also be served for a lunch or supper. A package mix makes a quick and easy dough.

16 servings

Olive oil cooking spray
1 cup chopped zucchini
1 cup sliced mushrooms
½ cup chopped onions
¼ cup chopped green bell pepper

Per Serving
Calories: 185
% Calories from fat: 28
Fat (gm): 5.8
Saturated fat (gm): 1.6
Cholesterol (mg): 7.6
Sodium (mg): 379
Protein (gm): 9.4
Carbohydrate (gm): 23.6

1 can (14½ ounces) diced tomatoes with roasted garlic, undrained

2 teaspoons Italian seasoning

1 cup fat-free ricotta cheese

2 cups (8 ounces) shredded reduced-fat mozzarella cheese

Salt and pepper, to taste

1 package (16 ounces) hot roll mix

1¼ cups hot water

1 tablespoon olive oil

Fat-free milk

Exchanges
Milk: 0.0
Vegetable: 1.5
Fruit: 0.0
Bread: 1.0
Meat: 1.0
Fat: 0.5

1. Spray large skillet with cooking spray; heat over medium heat until hot. Saute zucchini, mushrooms, onions, and bell pepper 5 minutes.

2. Add tomatoes with liquid and Italian seasoning to skillet; simmer until vegetables are tender and excess liquid is gone, about 10 minutes. Cool slightly; stir in cheeses and season to taste with salt and pepper.

3. Make hot roll mix according to package directions, using hot water and oil. Divide dough into 8 parts; roll each into a 7-inch circle. Place about ½ cup vegetable mixture on each; fold in half and seal edges with tines of fork. Brush tops of pastries with fat-free milk.

4. Bake at 350 degrees until browned, about 15 minutes. Cut each calzone in half and arrange on serving platter. Serve warm.

EASY HERB LAVOSH

Quick, easy, delicious—and versatile!

6 servings

1 Whole Wheat Lavosh (see p. 673), *or* plain lavosh
Vegetable, *or* olive oil, cooking spray
½-¾ teaspoon caraway seeds, *or* other desired herb (see Note below)

Per Serving
Calories: 132
% Calories from fat: 3
Fat (gm): 0.6
Saturated fat (gm): 0.1
Cholesterol (mg): 0
Sodium (mg): 1
Protein (gm): 5
Carbohydrate (gm): 29.9
Exchanges
Milk: 0.0
Vegetable: 0.0
Fruit: 0.0
Bread: 2.0
Meat: 0.0
Fat: 0.0

1. Spray top of lavosh generously with cooking spray and sprinkle with herbs. Bake on a cookie sheet or piece of aluminum foil at 350 degrees until browned, 4 to 6 minutes (watch carefully as lavosh can burn easily).

Note: Use any herb you want, such as Italian seasoning, bouquet garni, creole seasoning, or a mix of herbs. Fat-free grated Parmesan cheese can be sprinkled over the lavosh, too.

PITA CHIPS

Perfect to serve with any dip, or to eat as a snack.

6 to 8 servings (6 to 8 chips each)

3 whole wheat, *or* plain, pita breads
Butter-flavored, *or* olive oil, cooking spray
3-4 teaspoons Italian seasoning, *or* desired herbs

Per Serving
Calories: 86
% Calories from fat: 8
Fat (gm): 0.9
Saturated fat (gm): 0.1
Cholesterol (mg): 0
Sodium (mg): 171
Protein (gm): 3.2
Carbohydrate (gm): 17.7
Exchanges
Milk: 0.0
Vegetable: 0.0
Fruit: 0.0
Bread: 1.0
Meat: 0.0
Fat: 0.0

1. Open pita breads and separate each into 2 halves. Stack pita halves and cut into 8 wedges. Arrange pita wedges, soft sides up, in single layer on jelly roll pan. Spray generously with cooking spray and sprinkle with Italian herbs.

2. Bake at 425 degrees until pita wedges are browned and crisp, 5 to 10 minutes.

Variation: 1 to 2 teaspoons chili powder, ground cumin, or garlic powder; or 1 to 2 tablespoons grated fat-free Parmesan cheese can be substituted for the Italian seasoning.

BRUSCHETTA

These simple-to-make Italian garlic toasts are perfect for serving with any kind of savory appetizer spread.

12 servings (2 slices each)

1 loaf French bread (8 ounces, about 15 inches long)
Olive oil cooking spray
2 cloves garlic, cut into halves

Per Serving
Calories: 53
% Calories from fat: 10
Fat (gm): 0.6
Saturated fat (gm): 0.1
Cholesterol (mg): 0
Sodium (mg): 115
Protein (gm): 1.7
Carbohydrate (gm): 10
Exchanges
Milk: 0.0
Vegetable: 0.0
Fruit: 0.0
Bread: 1.0
Meat: 0.0
Fat: 0.0

1. Cut bread into 24 slices; spray both sides of bread lightly with cooking spray. Broil on cookie sheet 4 inches from heat source until browned, 2 to 3 minutes on each side.

2. Rub top sides of bread slices with cut sides of garlic.

Note: If desired, bread slices can be sprinkled with herbs, such as basil, oregano, or Italian seasoning, before broiling. Bread can also be sprinkled lightly with grated fat-free Parmesan cheese before broiling; watch carefully so cheese does not burn.

CROUSTADES

These crisp, buttery toast cups can be filled with just about any hot or cold, sweet or savory filling. Bake the Croustades up to a week in advance and store in an airtight container.

8 servings (2 croustades each)

16 slices soft bread
   Butter-flavored cooking spray

Per Serving
Calories: 67
% Calories from fat: 12
Fat (gm): 0.9
Saturated fat (gm): 0.2
Cholesterol (mg): 0
Sodium (mg): 135
Protein (gm): 2.1
Carbohydrate (gm): 12.4
Exchanges
Milk: 0.0
Vegetable: 0.0
Fruit: 0.0
Bread: 1.0
Meat: 0.0
Fat: 0.0

1. Cut 2½-inch rounds out of bread slices with cookie cutter (remaining bread can be used for croutons or soft or dry breadcrumbs).

2. Spray 16 mini-muffin tins with cooking spray; press 1 bread round firmly into each. Spray bread generously with cooking spray.

3. Bake at 350 degrees until browned and crisp, 10 to 12 minutes.

BAKED TORTILLA CHIPS

Make these chips with either flour or corn tortillas, using any combination of the suggested spices. Store at room temperature in an airtight container.

6 servings (8 chips each)

6 flour, or corn, tortillas (see separate nutritional data)
   Vegetable cooking spray

**Per Serving, flour tortillas
(corn tortillas in parens.)**
Calories: 84 (58)
% Calories from fat: 21 (11)
Fat (gm): 1.9 (0.7)
Saturated fat (gm): 0.3 (0.1)
Cholesterol (mg): 0 (0)
Sodium (mg): 122 (43)
Protein (gm): 2.2 (1.5)
Carbohydrate (gm): 14.3 (12)

½ teaspoon total of desired herbs: ground
cumin, chili powder, paprika, dried
oregano leaves

Salt, to taste

Cayenne pepper, to taste

Exchanges
Milk: 0.0 (0.0)
Vegetable: 0.0 (0.0)
Fruit: 0.0 (0.0)
Bread: 1.0 (0.5)
Meat: 0.0 (0.0)
Fat: 0.0 (0.0)

1. Cut each tortilla into 8 wedges; arrange in single layer on jelly
roll pan. Spray tortillas with cooking spray. Sprinkle lightly with
herbs, salt, and cayenne pepper.

2. Bake at 350 degrees until lightly browned, 5 to 7 minutes.

TWO

Soups

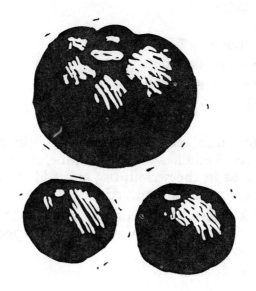

BASIC VEGETABLE STOCK

 As vegetables used in stocks are later discarded, they should be scrubbed but do not need to be peeled. This basic stock can be used in any of the soup recipes.

makes about 2 quarts

1 large onion, coarsely chopped
1 large leek, cleaned, cut into 1-inch pieces
1 large carrot, cut into 1-inch pieces
1 rib celery, cut into 1-inch pieces
½ teaspoon canola oil
8 cups water
1 cup dry white wine (optional)
4 cups mixed chopped vegetables (broccoli, green beans, cabbage, potatoes, tomatoes, corn, summer or winter squash, bell peppers, mushrooms, etc.)
6-8 parsley sprigs
1 bay leaf
4 whole allspice
1 tablespoon peppercorns
2 teaspoons bouquet garni
Salt and pepper, to taste

Per Cup
Calories: 12
% Calories from fat: 29
Fat (gm): 0.4
Saturated fat (gm): 0
Cholesterol (mg): 0
Sodium (mg): 12
Protein (gm): 0.4
Carbohydrate (gm): 1.8
Exchanges
Milk: 0.0
Vegetable: 0.0
Fruit: 0.0
Bread: 0.0
Meat: 0.0
Fat: 0.0

1. Saute onion, leek, carrot, and celery in oil in stock pot or large Dutch oven 5 minutes. Add water, wine, and chopped vegetables. Tie herbs in cheesecloth bag and add to pot. Heat to boiling; reduce heat and simmer, covered, 1½ to 2 hours.

2. Strain stock, pressing lightly on vegetables to extract all juices; discard solids. Season to taste with salt and pepper. Cool; refrigerate, or freeze.

ROASTED VEGETABLE STOCK

Roasting vegetables intensifies their flavors and makes this stock very rich in flavor. The beet adds a subtle sweetness to the stock, but use only if you don't object to the pink color it creates!

makes about 2 quarts

Vegetable cooking spray
1 large onion, quartered
1 medium bulb garlic, cut crosswise in half
1 large leek, cleaned, cut into 1-inch pieces
1 large carrot, cut into 4 pieces
1 rib celery, cut into 4 pieces
1 medium tomato, quartered
½ small butternut, *or* acorn, squash, cut into 2-inch pieces
1 small zucchini, cut into 4 pieces
1 small turnip, quartered
1 small beet, quartered (optional)
8 cups water
1 cup dry white wine, *or* water
3 cups coarsely chopped kale, *or* Swiss chard
6 sprigs parsley
1 bay leaf
1-2 teaspoons bouquet garni
1 teaspoon black peppercorns
4 whole allspice
Salt and pepper, to taste

Per Cup
Calories: 25
% Calories from fat: 1
Fat (gm): 0
Saturated fat (gm): 0
Cholesterol (mg): 0
Sodium (mg): 12
Protein (gm): 0.2
Carbohydrate (gm): 1.5
Exchanges
Milk: 0.0
Vegetable: 0.0
Fruit: 0.0
Bread: 0.0
Meat: 0.0
Fat: 0.0

1. Line large jelly roll pan with aluminum foil and spray with cooking spray. Arrange onion, garlic, leek, carrot, celery, tomato, squash, zucchini, turnip, and beet on pan; spray with cooking spray. Bake at 425 degrees until tender and browned, 35 to 40 minutes.

2. Combine vegetables and all remaining ingredients, except salt and pepper, in stock pot or large Dutch oven; heat to boiling. Reduce heat and simmer, covered, 1½ to 2 hours.

3. Strain, pressing lightly on vegetables to extract all juices; discard solids. Season to taste with salt and pepper. Cool; refrigerate or freeze.

MEDITERRANEAN STOCK

 A lovely stock, scented with orange, fennel, and saffron.

makes about 2 quarts

1	large onion, quartered
1	large leek, cleaned, cut into 1-inch pieces
1	large carrot, cut into 4 pieces
1	rib celery, cut into 4 pieces
1	medium sweet potato, cubed
1	small zucchini, cut into 4 pieces
½	small fennel bulb, sliced
½	red bell pepper, coarsely chopped
2	teaspoons olive oil
8	cups water
	Juice of 1 orange
1	cup dry white wine, *or* water
2	medium tomatoes, quartered
1	medium bulb garlic, cut crosswise in half
3	cups coarsely chopped spinach, *or* romaine lettuce
6	sprigs parsley
1	strip orange rind (3 x 1 inch)
1	bay leaf
1-2	teaspoons bouquet garni
1	teaspoon black peppercorns
4	whole allspice
	Pinch saffron
	Salt and pepper, to taste

Per Cup
Calories: 43
% Calories from fat: 24
Fat (gm): 1.2
Saturated fat (gm): 0.2
Cholesterol (mg): 0
Sodium (mg): 15
Protein (gm): 0.5
Carbohydrate (gm): 3.3
Exchanges
Milk: 0.0
Vegetable: 0.5
Fruit: 0.0
Bread: 0.0
Meat: 0.0
Fat: 0.5

1. Saute onion, leek, carrot, celery, sweet potato, zucchini, fennel, and bell pepper in oil in stock pot or large Dutch oven 8 to 10 minutes. Add remaining ingredients, except salt and pepper, and heat to boiling. Reduce heat and simmer, covered, 1½ to 2 hours.

2. Strain, pressing lightly on vegetables to extract all juices; discard solids. Season to taste with salt and pepper. Cool; refrigerate or freeze.

RICH MUSHROOM STOCK

 The dried shiitake mushrooms, also known as Chinese black mushrooms, add richness and depth of flavor to this stock.

makes about 2 quarts

Per Cup
Calories: 27
% Calories from fat: 22
Fat (gm): 0.7
Saturated fat (gm): 0.1
Cholesterol (mg): 0
Sodium (mg): 9
Protein (gm): 0.4
Carbohydrate (gm): 1.6
Exchanges
Milk: 0.0
Vegetable: 0.0
Fruit: 0.0
Bread: 0.0
Meat: 0.0
Fat: 0.0

1	large onion, sliced
1	large leek, sliced
2	ribs celery, sliced
3	teaspoons minced garlic
1	teaspoon olive oil
12	ounces cremini, *or* white, mushrooms, quartered
7	cups water
¾	cup dry white wine, *or* water
1½-2	ounces dried shiitake mushrooms
6	sprigs parsley
¾	teaspoon dried sage leaves
¾	teaspoon dried thyme leaves
1½	teaspoons black peppercorns
	Salt and pepper, to taste

1. Saute onion, leek, celery, and garlic in oil in small stock pot or large Dutch oven 5 minutes. Add cremini mushrooms and cook 2 to 3 minutes longer. Add remaining ingredients, except salt and pepper, and heat to boiling; reduce heat and simmer, covered, 1½ hours.

2. Strain, pressing lightly on vegetables to extract all juices; discard solids. Season to taste with salt and pepper. Cool; refrigerate or drain.

ORIENTAL STOCK

 A light, fragrant stock that can be used in many oriental soups and entrées.

makes about 2 quarts

8	cups water
6	cups shredded bok choy, *or* Chinese cabbage
1¼	cups loosely packed cilantro, coarsely chopped
1	large onion, sliced
1	large carrot, sliced
½	large red bell pepper, sliced
⅓	cup sliced gingerroot
3	teaspoons minced garlic
3-4	dried shiitake mushrooms
4-5	teaspoons reduced-sodium tamari soy sauce
2-3	star anise
1¾-2	teaspoons five-spice powder
1½	teaspoons toasted Szechuan pepper
	Salt and pepper, to taste

Per Cup
Calories: 8
% Calories from fat: 11
Fat (gm): 0.1
Saturated fat (gm): 0
Cholesterol (mg): 0
Sodium (mg): 110
Protein (gm): 0.6
Carbohydrate (gm): 1.1
Exchanges
Milk: 0.0
Vegetable: 0.0
Fruit: 0.0
Bread: 0.0
Meat: 0.0
Fat: 0.0

1. Combine all ingredients, except salt and pepper, in small stock pot or large Dutch oven; heat to boiling. Reduce heat and simmer, covered, 2 hours.

2. Strain, pressing lightly on vegetables to extract all juices; discard solids. Season to taste with salt and pepper. Cool; refrigerate or freeze.

CANNED VEGETABLE STOCK

A quick and easy solution for stock when you haven't the time or inclination to start from scratch.

makes about 1½ quarts

2 medium onions, coarsely chopped

2 medium leeks, cleaned, coarsely chopped

2 large carrots, cut into 1-inch pieces

2 large ribs celery, cut into 1-inch pieces

4 teaspoons minced garlic

1 teaspoon olive oil

2 cans (14½ ounces each) reduced-sodium vegetable broth

2 cups water

1 cup dry white wine, *or* water

2 medium tomatoes, quartered

4 sprigs parsley

2 bay leaves

Pepper, to taste

Per Cup
Calories: 62
% Calories from fat: 11
Fat (gm): 0.8
Saturated fat (gm): 0.1
Cholesterol (mg): 0
Sodium (mg): 55
Protein (gm): 0.8
Carbohydrate (gm): 6.7
Exchanges
Milk: 0.0
Vegetable: 1.0
Fruit: 0.0
Bread: 0.0
Meat: 0.0
Fat: 0.0

1. Saute onions, leeks, carrots, celery, and garlic in oil in Dutch oven 5 minutes. Add broth and remaining ingredients, except pepper, and heat to boiling. Reduce heat and simmer, covered, 30 minutes.

2. Strain, pressing lightly on vegetables to extract all juices; discard solids. Season with pepper. Cool; refrigerate or freeze.

VERY BERRY SOUP

A garden of berries in a bowl! When fresh berries are out of season, frozen unsweetened berries can be substituted.

4 first-course servings (about 1 cup each)

1½	cups raspberries
1½	cups quartered strawberries
1½	cups water
¾	cup dry red wine, *or* cranberry juice
3-4	tablespoons sugar
½	cup fat-free half-and-half, *or* fat-free milk
	Mint leaves, finely chopped, as garnish
4	tablespoons fat-free sour cream
¼	cup blueberries

Per Serving
Calories: 141
% Calories from fat: 3
Fat (gm): 0.5
Saturated fat (gm): 0
Cholesterol (mg): 0
Sodium (mg): 69
Protein (gm): 2.9
Carbohydrate (gm): 25.1
Exchanges
Milk: 0.0
Vegetable: 0.0
Fruit: 2.0
Bread: 0.0
Meat: 0.0
Fat: 0.0

1. Heat raspberries, strawberries, water, wine, and sugar to boiling in large saucepan. Reduce heat and simmer, covered, until berries are tender, 5 to 8 minutes. Remove from heat and cool.

2. Process soup in food processor or blender until smooth. Strain mixture, discarding seeds. Refrigerate until chilled, 3 to 4 hours.

3. Mix half-and-half into soup; pour into bowls. Sprinkle with mint and top each bowl with a tablespoon of sour cream and blueberries.

SWEET CHERRY SOUP

Serve as a first course--or a dessert! For year-round enjoyment, frozen unsweetened dark sweet cherries can be substituted for the fresh.

4 first-course servings (about 1 cup each)

1½	pounds dark sweet cherries, pitted
3-4	tablespoons sugar
3	cups plus 3 tablespoons water, divided
12	whole cloves
6	whole cardamom pods
1	large cinnamon stick, broken into pieces

Per Serving
Calories: 179
% Calories from fat: 8
Fat (gm): 1.6
Saturated fat (gm): 0.4
Cholesterol (mg): 0
Sodium (mg): 10
Protein (gm): 3
Carbohydrate (gm): 41.9

1½ tablespoons cornstarch
    Nutmeg, freshly ground, as garnish
4 tablespoons fat-free sour cream

Exchanges
Milk: 0.0
Vegetable: 0.0
Fruit: 3.0
Bread: 0.0
Meat: 0.0
Fat: 0.0

1. Combine cherries, sugar, and 3 cups water in medium saucepan. Tie spices in cheesecloth bag and add to saucepan. Heat to boiling; reduce heat and simmer, covered, until cherries are tender, 15 to 20 minutes. Remove from heat and cool to room temperature. Discard spices.

2. Process soup mixture in food processor or blender until smooth. Strain, discarding cherry skins. Return soup to saucepan and heat to boiling. Mix cornstarch and remaining 3 tablespoons water; whisk into boiling soup. Boil, whisking constantly, until thickened, 1 to 2 minutes. Cool; refrigerate until chilled.

3. Pour soup into bowls; sprinkle lightly with nutmeg and top each with a tablespoon of sour cream.

FRAGRANT MELON SOUP

 The flavor of the soup is dependent on the ripeness and flavor of the melon.

4 first-course servings (about 1 cup each)

1 quart peeled, seeded, cubed, ripe cantaloupe
½ cup orange juice
3-4 tablespoons lemon, *or* lime, juice
2 tablespoons honey
¼-½ cup fat-free half-and-half, *or* fat-free milk
4 thin lemon, *or* lime, slices
    Mint, *or* lemon, balm sprigs, as garnish

Per Serving
Calories: 116
% Calories from fat: 4
Fat (gm): 0.5
Saturated fat (gm): 0
Cholesterol (mg): 0
Sodium (mg): 30
Protein (gm): 2.2
Carbohydrate (gm): 28
Exchanges
Milk: 0.0
Vegetable: 0.0
Fruit: 2.0
Bread: 0.0
Meat: 0.0
Fat: 0.0

1. Process cantaloupe, orange and lemon juice, and honey in food processor or blender until smooth; stir in half-and-half. Refrigerate until chilled, 3 to 4 hours.

2. Pour soup into bowls; float lemon slice in each and garnish with herb sprigs.

DILLED BEET SOUP

Scrub beets well since the cooking liquid is reserved for use in the soup. It's not necessary to peel beets before cooking, as the skins slip off easily after cooking. Canned beets can be substituted for the fresh.

8 first-course servings (about 1¼ cups each)

12	medium beets, tops trimmed, scrubbed (about 3 pounds)
3	cups water
2-3	vegetable bouillon cubes
	Water
¾-1	cup dry red wine, *or* vegetable broth
1½-2	teaspoons dried dill weed
2-3	tablespoons red wine vinegar
	Salt and pepper, to taste
8	thin lemon slices, as garnish
	Chives, finely chopped, as garnish

Per Serving
Calories: 63
% Calories from fat: 3
Fat (gm): 0.3
Saturated fat (gm): 0
Cholesterol (mg): 0
Sodium (mg): 318
Protein (gm): 1.8
Carbohydrate (gm): 10.6
Exchanges
Milk: 0.0
Vegetable: 2.0
Fruit: 0.0
Bread: 0.0
Meat: 0.0
Fat: 0.0

1. Heat beets, 3 cups water, and bouillon cubes to boiling in large saucepan; reduce heat and simmer, covered, until beets are tender, 30 to 40 minutes. Let stand until cool; drain, reserving cooking liquid. Slip skins off beets and cut into scant 1-inch pieces.

2. Add enough water to reserved cooking liquid to make 6 cups. Process beets, wine, reserved cooking liquid, and dill weed in food processor or blender container until smooth. Season to taste with vinegar, salt, and pepper.

3. Heat soup and serve warm, or refrigerate until chilled and serve cold. Pour soup into bowls; garnish each with a lemon slice and sprinkle with chives.

HERBED CUCUMBER SOUP

This soup is very delicate in flavor. Use a serrated grapefruit spoon to seed cucumbers quickly and easily.

6 first-course servings (about 1⅓ cups each)

Vegetable cooking spray
½ cup chopped onion
6 medium cucumbers (about 3 pounds), peeled, seeded, chopped
3 tablespoons flour
4 cups Basic Vegetable Stock (see p. 58)
1 teaspoon dried mint, *or* dill weed
½ cup fat-free half-and-half, *or* fat-free milk
Salt and white pepper, to taste
Paprika, as garnish
6 thin slices cucumber

Per Serving
Calories: 70
% Calories from fat: 8
Fat (gm): 0.6
Saturated fat (gm): 0.1
Cholesterol (mg): 0
Sodium (mg): 33
Protein (gm): 3.1
Carbohydrate (gm): 13.7
Exchanges
Milk: 0.0
Vegetable: 1.0
Fruit: 0.0
Bread: 0.5
Meat: 0.0
Fat: 0.0

1. Spray large saucepan with cooking spray; heat over medium heat until hot. Saute onion until tender, 3 to 5 minutes. Add cucumbers and cook over medium heat 5 minutes; stir in flour and cook 1 to 2 minutes longer.

2. Add stock and mint to saucepan; heat to boiling. Reduce heat and simmer, covered, 10 minutes. Process soup in food processor or blender until smooth; stir in half-and-half; season to taste with salt and pepper. Cool; refrigerate until chilled, 3 to 4 hours.

3. Pour soup into bowls; sprinkle lightly with paprika and top each with a cucumber slice.

CUCUMBER AND SORREL SOUP

If cucumbers are mild in flavor, they do not need to be peeled. Spinach can be substituted for the sorrel.

6 first-course servings (about 1¼ cups each)

Vegetable cooking spray
¼ cup plus 2 tablespoons sliced green onions and tops, divided
1 clove garlic, minced
3 cups (about 1½ pounds) peeled, seeded, chopped cucumbers
1 cup coarsely chopped sorrel, *or* spinach
2 cups fat-free milk
2 cups Basic Vegetable Stock (see p. 58)
1 tablespoon cornstarch
2 tablespoons water
Salt and white pepper, to taste
1½ cups Herb Croutons (½ recipe, see p. 677)

Per Serving
Calories: 70
% Calories from fat: 10
Fat (gm): 0.8
Saturated fat (gm): 0.2
Cholesterol (mg): 1.3
Sodium (mg): 94
Protein (gm): 4.5
Carbohydrate (gm): 11.7
Exchanges
Milk: 0.0
Vegetable: 2.5
Fruit: 0.0
Bread: 0.0
Meat: 0.0
Fat: 0.0

1. Spray large saucepan with cooking spray; heat over medium heat until hot. Saute ¼ cup green onions and garlic until tender, 3 to 4 minutes. Add cucumbers and sorrel, and cook over medium heat 5 minutes.

2. Add milk and stock to saucepan; heat to boiling. Reduce heat and simmer, covered, until cucumbers are tender, 5 to 10 minutes. Process soup in food processor or blender until smooth; return to saucepan.

3. Heat soup to boiling. Mix cornstarch and water; whisk into boiling soup. Boil, whisking constantly, until thickened, about 1 minute. Season to taste with salt and white pepper. Cool; refrigerate until chilled, 3 to 4 hours.

4. Pour soup into bowls; top with Herb Croutons and remaining 2 tablespoons green onions.

EGGPLANT SOUP WITH ROASTED RED PEPPER SAUCE

Grilling gives eggplant a distinctive smoky flavor. For indoor cooking, eggplant can be oven roasted. Pierce the eggplant in several places with a fork and place them in a baking pan. Bake at 350 degrees until the eggplant is soft, 45 to 50 minutes.

4 main-dish servings (about 1 cup each)

2	medium eggplant (about 2½ pounds)
¾	cup chopped onion
¼	cup chopped green bell pepper
2	cloves garlic, minced
1	tablespoon extra-virgin olive oil
4-5	cups Mediterranean, *or* Roasted Vegetable, Stock (see pp. 60, 59)
	Salt and white pepper, to taste
	Roasted Red Pepper Sauce (see p. 709)

Per Serving
Calories: 250
% Calories from fat: 19
Fat (gm): 6
Saturated fat (gm): 0.7
Cholesterol (mg): 0
Sodium (mg): 25
Protein (gm): 6.8
Carbohydrate (gm): 44.8
Exchanges
Milk: 0.0
Vegetable: 2.0
Fruit: 0.0
Bread: 2.0
Meat: 0.0
Fat: 1.0

1. Pierce eggplant in several places with fork. Grill over medium hot coals, turning frequently, until eggplants are very soft, about 30 minutes. Cool until warm enough to handle; cut eggplants in half, scoop out pulp, and chop coarsely.

2. Saute onion, pepper, and garlic in oil in large saucepan until tender, 5 to 8 minutes. Add stock and eggplant to saucepan; heat to boiling. Reduce heat and simmer, covered, 10 minutes.

3. Process soup in food processor or blender until smooth. Season to taste with salt and white pepper. Refrigerate until chilled, 4 to 6 hours.

4. Pour soup into bowls; swirl about ¼ cup Roasted Red Pepper Sauce into each.

POBLANO CHILI SOUP

Poblano chilies give this soup its extraordinary flavor. Readily available in most large supermarkets, they can vary in flavor from mild to very picante. Taste the peppers before making this soup; if they are too hot for your taste, substitute some green bell peppers and decrease the amount of jalapeño.

6 first-course servings (about 1 cup each)

Vegetable cooking spray

2 medium onions, chopped

4 medium poblano chilies, seeds and veins discarded, chopped

½-1 small jalapeño chili, seeds and veins discarded, finely chopped

3½ cups Basic Vegetable Stock (see p. 58)

3 cups tomato juice

½ teaspoon ground cumin

½-1 cup water, divided

Salt and pepper, to taste

Cilantro, minced, as garnish

Per Serving
Calories: 63
% Calories from fat: 6
Fat (gm): 0.4
Saturated fat (gm): 0
Cholesterol (mg): 0
Sodium (mg): 374
Protein (gm): 1.8
Carbohydrate (gm): 13.1
Exchanges
Milk: 0.0
Vegetable: 2.5
Fruit: 0.0
Bread: 0.0
Meat: 0.0
Fat: 0.0

1. Spray large saucepan with cooking spray; heat over medium heat until hot. Saute onions and chilies until onions are tender, about 5 minutes. Add stock; heat to boiling. Reduce heat and simmer, covered, until chilies are very tender, about 5 minutes.

2. Process broth mixture in food processor or blender until smooth; return to saucepan. Add tomato juice, cumin, and enough water for desired consistency; heat to boiling. Reduce heat and simmer, uncovered, 10 minutes. Season to taste with salt and pepper. Serve soup in bowls; sprinkle with cilantro.

GAZPACHO

Gazpacho is Spanish in origin but popularly served throughout Mexico and South America. Easy to make and served cold, this is a wonderful soup to keep on hand in summer months.

6 first-course servings (about 1¼ cups each)

5 large tomatoes, divided
2 cups reduced-sodium tomato juice
2 cloves garlic
2 tablespoons lime juice
1 teaspoon dried oregano leaves
1 small seedless cucumber, coarsely chopped
1 cup chopped yellow bell pepper
1 cup chopped celery
6 green onions and tops, thinly sliced, divided
2 tablespoons finely chopped cilantro
Salt and pepper, to taste
Avocado Sour Cream (recipe follows)
Hot pepper sauce (optional)

Per Serving
Calories: 76
% Calories from fat: 17
Fat (gm): 1.6
Saturated fat (gm): 0.3
Cholesterol (mg): 0.1
Sodium (mg): 46
Protein (gm): 3.3
Carbohydrate (gm): 15.1
Exchanges
Milk: 0.0
Vegetable: 2.0
Fruit: 0.0
Bread: 0.0
Meat: 0.0
Fat: 0.5

1. Cut tomatoes into halves; remove and discard seeds. Chop tomatoes, reserving 1 cup. Process remaining tomatoes, tomato juice, garlic, lime juice, and oregano in food processor or blender until smooth.

2. Mix tomato mixture, reserved tomatoes, cucumber, yellow bell pepper, celery, 5 green onions, and cilantro in a large bowl; season to taste with salt and pepper. Refrigerate until chilled, 3 to 4 hours.

3. Serve soup in chilled bowls; top each with a dollop of Avocado Sour Cream and sprinkle with remaining green onion. Serve with hot pepper sauce if desired.

Avocado Sour Cream

½ medium avocado, peeled, pitted, chopped
¼ cup fat-free sour cream
2 tablespoons fat-free milk
Salt and white pepper, to taste

1. Process all ingredients in food processor until smooth; season to taste with salt and white pepper. Makes about ⅔ cup.

WHITE GAZPACHO

Something different that is sure to please!

4 first-course servings (about 1 cup each)

Vegetable cooking spray
1 large onion, sliced
4 cloves garlic, minced
1-2 cups fat-free milk
½-1 vegetable bouillon cube
1 cup fat-free plain yogurt
2 teaspoons lemon juice
2 dashes red pepper sauce
Salt and white pepper, to taste
⅓ cup chopped, seeded cucumber
⅓ cup chopped, seeded yellow tomato
⅓ cup cubed avocado
Cilantro, *or* parsley, finely chopped, as garnish

Per Serving
Calories: 109
% Calories from fat: 27
Fat (gm): 3.4
Saturated fat (gm): 0.6
Cholesterol (mg): 2
Sodium (mg): 196
Protein (gm): 6.7
Carbohydrate (gm): 14.3
Exchanges
Milk: 0.5
Vegetable: 2.0
Fruit: 0.0
Bread: 0.0
Meat: 0.0
Fat: 0.5

1. Spray large saucepan with cooking spray; heat over medium heat until hot. Cook onion and garlic over medium-low heat until very tender, about 15 minutes. Add milk and bouillon cube; cook over medium-high heat, stirring frequently, until mixture is hot and bouillon cube is dissolved.

2. Process soup, yogurt, lemon juice, and red pepper sauce in food processor or blender until smooth. Season to taste with salt and white pepper. Cool; refrigerate until chilled, 3 to 4 hours.

3. Stir cucumber, tomato, and avocado into soup; pour into bowls and sprinkle with cilantro.

BEAN GAZPACHO

Pureed beans contribute a creamy texture and subtle flavor to this unusual gazpacho. Canned pinto beans, rinsed and drained, can be substituted for the dried.

6 main-dish servings (about 1¾ cups each)

4	cups cooked dried pinto beans, divided
1	quart reduced-sodium tomato juice
3-4	tablespoons lime juice
2	teaspoons reduced-sodium Worcestershire sauce
1	jar (16 ounces) thick and chunky mild, *or* medium, salsa
1	cup peeled, seeded, chopped cucumber
1	cup thinly sliced celery
½	cup chopped onion
½	cup chopped green bell pepper
2	teaspoons minced roasted garlic
½	small avocado, peeled, chopped
1½	cups Herb Croutons (½ recipe, see p. 677)

Per Serving
Calories: 260
% Calories from fat: 13
Fat (gm): 3.8
Saturated fat (gm): 0.2
Cholesterol (mg): 0
Sodium (mg): 642
Protein (gm): 12.9
Carbohydrate (gm): 47.1
Exchanges
Milk: 0.0
Vegetable: 2.0
Fruit: 0.0
Bread: 2.5
Meat: 0.5
Fat: 0.0

1. Process 2 cups beans, tomato juice, lime juice, and Worcestershire sauce in food processor or blender; pour into large bowl. Mix in remaining beans and ingredients, except avocado and Herb Croutons. Refrigerate until chilled, 3 to 4 hours.

2. Mix avocado into soup and pour into bowls; sprinkle with Herb Croutons.

CHILLED PEA SOUP

 A refreshing soup for hot sultry days; serve with a ripe tomato salad and crusty bread or rolls.

4 main-dish servings (about 1½ cups each)

½ cup chopped onion
½ teaspoon dried marjoram leaves
¼ teaspoon dried thyme leaves
2 cups Basic Vegetable Stock (see p. 58)
2 packages (20 ounces each) frozen peas
2 cups sliced romaine lettuce
Salt and white pepper, to taste
½ cup fat-free sour cream, *or* fat-free half-and-half
Paprika, as garnish

Per Serving
Calories: 257
% Calories from fat: 4
Fat (gm): 1.1
Saturated fat (gm): 0.2
Cholesterol (mg): 0
Sodium (mg): 274
Protein (gm): 17.4
Carbohydrate (gm): 46.6
Exchanges
Milk: 0.0
Vegetable: 0.0
Fruit: 0.0
Bread: 3.0
Meat: 0.5
Fat: 0.0

1. Saute onion, marjoram, and thyme in large saucepan until onion is tender, about 5 minutes. Stir in stock, peas, and lettuce; heat to boiling. Reduce heat and simmer, covered, until peas are tender, 5 to 8 minutes.

2. Process soup in food processor or blender until smooth; season to taste with salt and pepper. Cool; refrigerate until chilled, 3 to 4 hours.

3. Stir sour cream or half-and-half into soup; pour into bowls and sprinkle with paprika.

SWEET RED PEPPER SOUP

Use jarred roasted peppers for this soup, or roast 2 medium red bell (sweet) peppers yourself. To roast the peppers, cut them in half and discard seeds. Place peppers, skin sides up, on an aluminum-foil-lined jelly roll pan. Broil 4 inches from heat source until skins are blackened. Place the peppers in a plastic bag for 5 minutes to loosen their skins, which may be discarded.

4 first-course servings (about 1 cup each)

Vegetable cooking spray
1 medium onion, chopped
½ small jalapeño chili, seeds and veins discarded, minced
1 clove garlic, minced
1 jar (15 ounces) roasted red bell peppers, drained
1 cup reduced-sodium tomato juice
1¾ cups Canned Vegetable Stock (see p. 63)
¼ teaspoon dried marjoram leaves
Salt and pepper, to taste
¼ cup fat-free sour cream
1 small green onion and top, thinly sliced

Per Serving
Calories: 77
% Calories from fat: 5
Fat (gm): 0.4
Saturated fat (gm): 0.1
Cholesterol (mg): 0
Sodium (mg): 264
Protein (gm): 2.9
Carbohydrate (gm): 13.4
Exchanges
Milk: 0.0
Vegetable: 3.0
Fruit: 0.0
Bread: 0.0
Meat: 0.0
Fat: 0.0

1. Spray medium saucepan with cooking spray; heat over medium heat until hot. Saute onion, jalapeño chili, and garlic until tender.

2. Process onion mixture, red bell peppers, and tomato juice in food processor or blender until smooth. Return mixture to saucepan and add stock and marjoram; heat to boiling. Reduce heat and simmer, covered, 15 minutes. Season to taste with salt and pepper.

3. Serve soup warm, or refrigerate and serve cold. Top each serving with a dollop of sour cream and sprinkle with green onion.

SNOW PEA SOUP

Make this soup a day in advance so that flavors can blend.

6 first-course servings (about 1¼ cups each)

½ cup sliced green onions and tops
½ cup chopped onion
1 tablespoon margarine, *or* butter
1 pound snow peas, trimmed
4 cups coarsely chopped romaine lettuce
4 cups Basic Vegetable Stock (see p. 58)
½ teaspoon dried tarragon leaves
½ teaspoon dried mint leaves
Salt and white pepper, to taste
6 tablespoons plain fat-free yogurt
Fresh mint, *or* tarragon, sprigs

Per Serving
Calories: 76
% Calories from fat: 28
Fat (gm): 2.5
Saturated fat (gm): 0.5
Cholesterol (mg): 0.3
Sodium (mg): 47
Protein (gm): 4.3
Carbohydrate (gm): 9.8
Exchanges
Milk: 0.0
Vegetable: 2.0
Fruit: 0.0
Bread: 0.0
Meat: 0.0
Fat: 0.5

1. Saute onions in margarine in large saucepan until tender, about 5 minutes. Add snow peas and lettuce; saute 3 to 4 minutes longer. Add stock, tarragon, and mint; heat to boiling. Reduce heat and simmer, covered, 15 minutes or until snow peas are very tender.

2. Process soup in food processor or blender until smooth; strain. Season to taste with salt and white pepper. Serve warm, or refrigerate and serve cold.

3. Pour soup into bowls; garnish each with a tablespoon of yogurt and fresh herb sprigs.

CHAYOTE SQUASH SOUP WITH CILANTRO SOUR CREAM

Chayote squash, often called a "vegetable pear," is native to Mexico. Readily available in supermarkets, the squash is light green in color and delicate in flavor.

6 first-course servings (about 1 cup each)

Vegetable cooking spray
1 large onion, chopped
2 cloves garlic, minced
3 tablespoons flour
3 large chayote squash, peeled, pitted, sliced
6 cups Basic Vegetable Stock (see p. 58), divided
½ cup water
Salt and white pepper, to taste
Cilantro Sour Cream (recipe follows)
Cilantro, finely chopped, as garnish

Per Serving
Calories: 68
% Calories from fat: 11
Fat (gm): 0.9
Saturated fat (gm): 0.1
Cholesterol (mg): 0.2
Sodium (mg): 27
Protein (gm): 2.9
Carbohydrate (gm): 13.3
Exchanges
Milk: 0.0
Vegetable: 2.5
Fruit: 0.0
Bread: 0.0
Meat: 0.0
Fat: 0.0

1. Spray large saucepan with cooking spray; heat over medium heat until hot. Saute onion and garlic until tender, about 5 minutes. Stir in flour; cook over medium heat 2 minutes, stirring constantly.

2. Add squash and 2 cups stock to saucepan; heat to boiling. Reduce heat and simmer, covered, until squash is tender, 15 to 20 minutes. Process mixture in food processor or blender until smooth; return to saucepan. Add remaining stock and water; season to taste with salt and white pepper. Heat over medium heat and serve warm, or refrigerate and serve chilled.

3. Serve soup in bowls; drizzle with Cilantro Sour Cream and sprinkle with cilantro.

Cilantro Sour Cream

⅓ cup fat-free sour cream
1 tablespoon finely chopped cilantro
¼-⅓ cup fat-free milk

1. Mix sour cream and cilantro in small bowl, adding enough milk for desired consistency. Makes about ½ cup.

SUMMER SQUASH SOUP

Use zucchini or yellow summer squash, such as pattypan or crookneck, in this soup.

6 first-course servings (about 1¼ cups each)

Vegetable cooking spray
½ cup chopped shallots
¼ cup sliced green onions and tops
2 cloves garlic, minced
4 medium zucchini (about 2 pounds), chopped
1 cup Idaho potato, peeled, cubed
4 cups Basic, *or* Roasted, Vegetable Stock (see pp. 58, 59)
1 cup chopped kale, *or* spinach leaves
1-½ teaspoons dried tarragon leaves
¼-½ cup fat-free half-and-half, *or* fat-free milk
Salt and white pepper, to taste
6 thin slices zucchini
6 thin slices yellow summer squash
Cayenne pepper, as garnish
1½ cups Sourdough Croutons (½ recipe, see p. 677)

Per Serving
Calories: 100
% Calories from fat: 7
Fat (gm): 0.8
Saturated fat (gm): 0.1
Cholesterol (mg): 0
Sodium (mg): 65
Protein (gm): 3.8
Carbohydrate (gm): 20.6
Exchanges
Milk: 0.0
Vegetable: 1.0
Fruit: 0.0
Bread: 1.0
Meat: 0.0
Fat: 0.0

1. Spray large saucepan with cooking spray; heat over medium heat until hot. Saute shallots, green onions, and garlic until tender, about 5 minutes. Add chopped zucchini and potato; saute 5 to 8 minutes longer.

2. Add stock, kale, and tarragon to saucepan; heat to boiling. Reduce heat and simmer, covered, until vegetables are tender, 10 to 15 minutes.

3. Process soup in food processor or blender until smooth; return to saucepan. Stir in half-and-half; season to taste with salt and white pepper. Heat and serve warm, or refrigerate and serve chilled.

4. Pour soup into bowls. Top each with a slice of zucchini and summer squash; sprinkle lightly with cayenne pepper and Sourdough Croutons.

ORANGE-SCENTED SQUASH SOUP

 Subtly seasoned with orange and spices, this delicious soup can be served warm or cold.

6 first-course servings (about 1⅓ cups each)

Vegetable cooking spray
¾ cup chopped onion
1 teaspoon ground cinnamon
¼ teaspoon ground nutmeg
¼ teaspoon ground cloves
1½ cups water
3 pounds winter yellow squash (Hubbard, butternut, or acorn), peeled, cubed
1 large, tart cooking apple, peeled, cored, cubed
1 strip orange rind (3 x ½ inch)
¼-½ cup orange juice
1½-2 cups fat-free half-and-half, *or* fat-free milk
Salt and white pepper, to taste
6 thin orange slices
Chives, finely chopped, as garnish

Per Serving
Calories: 144
% Calories from fat: 8
Fat (gm): 1.4
Saturated fat (gm): 0.3
Cholesterol (mg): 0
Sodium (mg): 64
Protein (gm): 4.1
Carbohydrate (gm): 30.2
Exchanges
Milk: 0.0
Vegetable: 0.0
Fruit: 0.0
Bread: 2.0
Meat: 0.0
Fat: 0.0

1.   Spray large saucepan with cooking spray; heat over medium heat until hot. Saute onion until tender, about 5 minutes. Stir in spices; cook 1 to 2 minutes longer.

2.   Add water, squash, apple, and orange rind to saucepan; heat to boiling. Reduce heat and simmer, covered, until squash is tender, 10 to 15 minutes.

3.   Process soup in food processor or blender until smooth; add orange juice and half-and-half. Season to taste with salt and white pepper. Serve soup warm, or refrigerate and serve chilled.

4.   Pour soup into bowls; top each with an orange slice and sprinkle with chives.

WINTER SQUASH SOUP

 An autumn or winter favorite, with apple cider, cinnamon, and spices for sweetness.

6 first-course servings (about 1 cup each)

½	cup chopped onion
1	tablespoon margarine
1	pound butternut, *or* other yellow winter, squash, peeled, seeded, cubed
1	cup peeled, cubed Idaho potato
1	cup cored, peeled, cubed tart cooking apple
1½	cups water
½	teaspoon ground cinnamon
¼	teaspoon ground ginger
⅛	teaspoon ground nutmeg
⅛-¼	teaspoon ground cumin
1	cup apple cider, *or* apple juice
½-1	cup fat-free half-and-half, *or* fat-free milk
	Salt or white pepper, to taste
	Nutmeg, ground, as garnish

Per Serving
Calories: 139
% Calories from fat: 13
Fat (gm): 2.2
Saturated fat (gm): 0.4
Cholesterol (mg): 0
Sodium (mg): 49
Protein (gm): 2.5
Carbohydrate (gm): 29.5
Exchanges
Milk: 0.0
Vegetable: 0.0
Fruit: 0.5
Bread: 1.5
Meat: 0.0
Fat: 0.0

1. Saute onion in margarine until tender, 3 to 4 minutes. Add squash, potato, and apple; cook over medium heat 5 minutes. Add water and spices and heat to boiling; reduce heat and simmer, covered, until squash and potato are tender, 10 to 15 minutes.

2. Process mixture in food processor or blender until smooth; return to saucepan. Stir in apple cider and half-and-half; cook over medium heat until hot through. Season to taste with salt and white pepper.

3. Pour soup into bowls; sprinkle lightly with nutmeg.

TOMATILLO SOUP WITH CILANTRO

Tomatillos look like tiny tomatoes, but they are not. The papery husks must be removed before using.

6 first-course servings (about 1¼ cups each)

Vegetable cooking spray
⅔ cup chopped onion
1-2 small jalapeño chilies, finely chopped
2 cloves garlic, minced
2 pounds tomatillos, husks removed, rinsed, quartered
4 cups Basic Vegetable Stock (see p. 58)
¼-⅓ cup fat-free half-and-half, *or* fat-free milk
3 tablespoons finely chopped cilantro
Salt and white pepper, to taste
Baked Tortilla Strips (recipe follows)

Per Serving
Calories: 92
% Calories from fat: 21
Fat (gm): 2.3
Saturated fat (gm): 0.1
Cholesterol (mg): 0
Sodium (mg): 58
Protein (gm): 2.9
Carbohydrate (gm): 16.2
Exchanges
Milk: 0.0
Vegetable: 2.0
Fruit: 0.0
Bread: 0.5
Meat: 0.0
Fat: 0.0

1. Spray large saucepan with cooking spray; heat over medium heat until hot. Saute onion, chilies, and garlic until tender, about 5 minutes. Add tomatillos and stock and heat to boiling; reduce heat and simmer, covered, until tomatillos are very tender, 10 to 15 minutes.

2. Process soup in food processor or blender until smooth; stir in half-and-half and cilantro. Season to taste with salt and white pepper. Refrigerate until chilled, 3 to 4 hours.

3. Pour soup into bowls; sprinkle with Baked Tortilla Strips.

Baked Tortilla Strips

1 flour, *or* corn, tortilla, cut into 2-inch-long, ¼-inch wide strips
Vegetable cooking spray
Salt, to taste

1. Arrange tortilla strips on cookie sheet; spray lightly with cooking spray and toss.

2. Bake at 375 degrees until browned, about 10 minutes, stirring occasionally.

RIPE TOMATO AND LEEK SOUP

Use the summer's ripest tomatoes for this soup, cooking only briefly to maintain their sweetness. Peel the tomatoes or not, as you prefer.

6 first-course servings (about 1¼ cups each)

2	cups (about 8 ounces) sliced leeks
3	cloves garlic, minced
1	tablespoon olive oil
6	large tomatoes (about 2½ pounds)
4	cups Basic Vegetable, *or* Mediterranean, Stock (see pp. 58, 60)
½-1	teaspoon dried basil leaves
	Salt and white pepper, to taste
6	tablespoons fat-free sour cream, *or* plain yogurt
	Basil sprigs, as garnish

Per Serving
Calories: 99
% Calories from fat: 24
Fat (gm): 2.9
Saturated fat (gm): 0.5
Cholesterol (mg): 0
Sodium (mg): 64
Protein (gm): 3.5
Carbohydrate (gm): 17.3
Exchanges
Milk: 0.0
Vegetable: 3.0
Fruit: 0.0
Bread: 0.0
Meat: 0.0
Fat: 0.5

1. Saute leeks and garlic in oil in large saucepan until tender, about 8 minutes. Add tomatoes, stock, and basil to saucepan; heat to boiling. Reduce heat and simmer, covered, 10 minutes.

2. Process soup in food processor or blender until smooth; season to taste with salt and white pepper. Heat and serve soup warm, or refrigerate and serve chilled.

3. Pour soup into bowls; top each with a tablespoon of sour cream and garnish with basil sprigs.

CREAM OF ARTICHOKE AND MUSHROOM SOUP

Shiitake or cremini mushrooms can be substituted for the portobello mushrooms. Serve with Sourdough Croutons (see p. 677), if desired.

4 first-course servings (about 1 cup each)

¾ cup chopped portobello mushrooms
2 tablespoons finely chopped onion
1 tablespoon margarine, *or* butter
1 tablespoon flour
3 cups fat-free milk
1 vegetable bouillon cube
1 package (9 ounces) frozen artichoke hearts, cooked, finely chopped
Salt and white pepper, to taste
Paprika, as garnish

Per Serving
Calories: 135
% Calories from fat: 22
Fat (gm): 3.6
Saturated fat (gm): 0.8
Cholesterol (mg): 3
Sodium (mg): 422
Protein (gm): 9.2
Carbohydrate (gm): 18.9
Exchanges
Milk: 1.0
Vegetable: 1.0
Fruit: 0.0
Bread: 0.0
Meat: 0.0
Fat: 0.5

1. Saute mushrooms and onion in medium saucepan in margarine until tender, about 5 minutes. Stir in flour; cook 1 minute longer. Stir in milk and bouillon cube; heat to boiling. Boil, stirring constantly, until thickened, about 1 minute.

2. Stir artichoke hearts into soup; simmer, uncovered, 5 minutes. Season to taste with salt and white pepper. Pour soup into bowls; sprinkle with paprika.

FRESH BASIL SOUP

For flavor variation, try another favorite garden herb such as rosemary, oregano, lemon thyme, marjoram, or sorrel.

6 first-course servings (about 1 cup each)

4 cups Roasted Vegetable Stock (see p. 59)
1 cup firmly packed basil leaves
1 cup firmly packed parsley sprigs
½ cup chopped onion
1 teaspoon sugar
2 cups potatoes, peeled, cubed

Per Serving
Calories: 147
% Calories from fat: 13
Fat (gm): 2.3
Saturated fat (gm): 0.5
Cholesterol (mg): 0.7
Sodium (mg): 61
Protein (gm): 4.1
Carbohydrate (gm): 25.3

1 cup fat-free milk
¼ cup all-purpose flour
1 tablespoon margarine, *or* butter
Salt and white pepper, to taste
Parsley, finely chopped, as garnish

Exchanges
Milk: 0.0
Vegetable: 1.0
Fruit: 0.0
Bread: 1.5
Meat: 0.0
Fat: 0.5

1. Heat stock, basil, parsley, onion, and sugar to boiling in medium saucepan. Simmer, covered, 30 minutes. Strain; return broth to saucepan.

2. Add potatoes to saucepan; heat to boiling. Reduce heat and simmer, covered, until potatoes are tender, about 15 minutes. Mix milk and flour; stir into saucepan and heat to boiling. Boil until thickened, 1 to 2 minutes, stirring constantly. Stir in margarine; season to taste with salt and white pepper.

3. Pour soup into bowls; sprinkle with parsley.

BEET BORSCHT

Several brands of soy-based vegetarian sausages are available, replacing the traditional Polish sausage often used in borscht.

8 first-course servings (about 1¼ cups each)

4 medium beets, peeled, cut into julienne strips
½-1 tablespoon margarine, *or* butter
6 cups Basic Vegetable Stock (see p. 58)
1 small head red cabbage, thinly sliced, *or* shredded
2 carrots, cut into julienne strips
1 clove garlic, minced
1 bay leaf
2-3 teaspoons sugar
2 tablespoons cider vinegar
Vegetable cooking spray
8 ounces all vegetable-protein sausage-style links
Salt and pepper, to taste
Dill weed, *or* parsley, finely chopped, as garnish

Per Serving
Calories: 104
% Calories from fat: 30
Fat (gm): 3.7
Saturated fat (gm): 0.6
Cholesterol (mg): 0
Sodium (mg): 230
Protein (gm): 6.2
Carbohydrate (gm): 12.9
Exchanges
Milk: 0.0
Vegetable: 2.0
Fruit: 0.0
Bread: 0.0
Meat: 1.0
Fat: 0.0

1. Saute beets in margarine in Dutch oven 3 to 4 minutes. Add stock, cabbage, carrots, garlic, bay leaf, sugar, and vinegar; heat to boiling. Reduce heat and simmer, covered, until vegetables are tender, 20 to 30 minutes.

2. Spray small skillet with cooking spray; heat over medium heat until hot. Cook sausage-style links over medium heat until browned on all sides, about 5 minutes. Cut links into 1-inch pieces and stir into soup; cook 5 minutes. Season to taste with salt and pepper.

3. Pour soup into bowls; sprinkle with dill weed.

CREAM OF BROCCOLI SOUP

 Fat-free half-and-half lends a wonderful richness to this soup.

6 first-course servings (about 1 cup each)

2	pounds broccoli
	Vegetable cooking spray
1	cup chopped onions
3	cloves garlic, minced
½	teaspoon dried thyme leaves
⅛	teaspoon ground nutmeg
3½	cups Basic Vegetable Stock (see p. 58)
½	cup fat-free half-and-half, *or* fat-free milk
	Salt and white pepper, to taste
6	tablespoons fat-free sour cream
2-3	teaspoons fat-free milk
1½	cups Croutons (½ recipe, see p. 677)

Per Serving
Calories: 99
% Calories from fat: 9
Fat (gm): 1.1
Saturated fat (gm): 0.2
Cholesterol (mg): 0
Sodium (mg): 110
Protein (gm): 6.8
Carbohydrate (gm): 17.6
Exchanges
Milk: 0.0
Vegetable: 2.0
Fruit: 0.0
Bread: 0.5
Meat: 0.0
Fat: 0.0

1. Peel broccoli stalks; cut broccoli into 1-inch pieces. Spray large saucepan with cooking spray; heat over medium heat until hot. Saute onions and garlic until tender, 3 to 5 minutes. Stir in broccoli, thyme, and nutmeg; cook 2 minutes longer.

2. Add stock to saucepan; heat to boiling. Reduce heat and simmer, covered, until broccoli is very tender, about 10 minutes.

3. Process soup in food processor or blender until smooth. Return soup to saucepan; add half-and-half and heat over medium heat until hot. Season to taste with salt and white pepper.

4. Pour soup into bowls. Mix sour cream and fat-free milk; swirl about 1 tablespoon mixture into soup in each bowl. Sprinkle with Croutons.

HERBED BROCCOLI AND PASTA SOUP

 A wonderfully versatile soup, as any vegetable in season and any choice of herb can be substituted for the broccoli and thyme.

4 main-dish servings (about 1½ cups each)

5½ cups Canned Vegetable Stock, *or* Basic Vegetable Stock (see pp. 63, 58)
4 cloves garlic, minced
2-3 teaspoons dried thyme leaves
3 cups small broccoli florets
2¼ cups (6 ounces) fusilli (spirals), uncooked
2-3 tablespoons lemon juice
¼ teaspoon salt
⅛ teaspoon pepper

Per Serving
Calories: 275
% Calories from fat: 7
Fat (gm): 2.2
Saturated fat (gm): 0.3
Cholesterol (mg): 0
Sodium (mg): 229
Protein (gm): 8.9
Carbohydrate (gm): 47.7
Exchanges
Milk: 0.0
Vegetable: 2.0
Fruit: 0.0
Bread: 3.0
Meat: 0.0
Fat: 0.5

1. Heat stock, garlic, and thyme to boiling in medium saucepan. Stir in broccoli and fusilli. Reduce heat and simmer, uncovered, until broccoli is tender and pasta is *al dente*, about 10 minutes.

2. Season soup with lemon juice, salt, and pepper. Serve immediately.

RUSSIAN CABBAGE SOUP

Use red or green cabbage, fresh or canned beets in this savory soup.

8 first-course servings (about 1½ cups each)

2 medium onions, sliced
1 tablespoon margarine, *or* butter
7 cups Basic Vegetable Stock (see p. 58)
1 can (16 ounces) reduced-sodium whole tomatoes, undrained, coarsely chopped
6 cups thinly sliced red cabbage
4 large beets, peeled, cubed
1 tablespoon cider vinegar
2 large carrots, sliced
1 turnip, cubed
1 large Idaho potato, peeled, cubed
Salt and pepper, to taste
8 tablespoons fat-free sour cream
Parsley, finely chopped, as garnish

Per Serving
Calories: 109
% Calories from fat: 17
Fat (gm): 2.2
Saturated fat (gm): 0.4
Cholesterol (mg): 0
Sodium (mg): 91
Protein (gm): 4
Carbohydrate (gm): 20.7
Exchanges
Milk: 0.0
Vegetable: 3.0
Fruit: 0.0
Bread: 0.5
Meat: 0.0
Fat: 0.0

1. Saute onions in margarine in Dutch oven until tender, about 5 minutes. Add stock, tomatoes, cabbage, beets, and vinegar; heat to boiling. Reduce heat and simmer, uncovered, 30 minutes; add carrots, turnip, and potato and cook 15 minutes longer. Season to taste with salt and pepper.

2. Pour soup into bowls; spoon 1 tablespoon sour cream into each and sprinkle with parsley.

DILLED CARROT SOUP

Carrots team with dill for a fresh, clean flavor.

6 first-course servings (about 1½ cups each)

Vegetable cooking spray
1½ cups chopped onions
2 cloves garlic, minced
6 cups Basic Vegetable Stock (see p. 58)
1 can (16 ounces) reduced-sodium diced tomatoes, undrained
2 pounds carrots, cut into ½-inch slices
1 medium Idaho potato, peeled, cubed
2-3 tablespoons lemon juice
1-1½ teaspoons dried dill weed
Salt and white pepper, to taste
6 tablespoons fat-free plain yogurt
2 tablespoons shredded carrot
Dill, *or* parsley sprigs, as garnish

Per Serving
Calories: 139
% Calories from fat: 6
Fat (gm): 1
Saturated fat (gm): 0.1
Cholesterol (mg): 0.3
Sodium (mg): 88
Protein (gm): 4.4
Carbohydrate (gm): 30.5
Exchanges
Milk: 0.0
Vegetable: 6.0
Fruit: 0.0
Bread: 0.0
Meat: 0.0
Fat: 0.0

1. Spray large saucepan with cooking spray; heat over medium heat until hot. Saute onions and garlic until tender, about 5 minutes. Add stock, tomatoes and liquid, sliced carrots, and potato; heat to boiling. Reduce heat and simmer, covered, until vegetables are tender, about 15 minutes.

2. Process soup in food processor or blender until smooth. Stir in lemon juice and dill weed; season to taste with salt and white pepper.

3. Serve soup warm, or refrigerate and serve chilled. Pour soup into bowls; top each with a tablespoon of yogurt and a teaspoon of shredded carrots. Garnish with dill sprigs.

CREAM OF CAULIFLOWER SOUP WITH CHEESE

Fat-free half-and-half adds a wonderful rich creaminess to the soup. Substitute broccoli for the cauliflower another time.

6 first-course servings (about 1 cup each)

Vegetable cooking spray
½ cup chopped onion
2 cloves garlic, minced
2 tablespoons flour
3½ cups Basic Vegetable Stock (see p. 58)
12 ounces cauliflower, cut into florets
1 large Idaho potato, peeled, cubed
¼-½ cup fat-free half-and-half, *or* fat-free milk
¾ cup (3 ounces) reduced-fat Cheddar cheese
Salt and white pepper, to taste
Mace, *or* nutmeg, ground, as garnish

Per Serving
Calories: 98
% Calories from fat: 22
Fat (gm): 2.4
Saturated fat (gm): 1.1
Cholesterol (mg): 7.6
Sodium (mg): 214
Protein (gm): 5.5
Carbohydrate (gm): 13.6
Exchanges
Milk: 0.0
Vegetable: 1.0
Fruit: 0.0
Bread: 0.5
Meat: 0.5
Fat: 0.0

1. Spray large saucepan with cooking spray; heat over medium heat until hot. Saute onion and garlic until tender, about 10 minutes. Stir in flour; cook 1 to 2 minutes longer. Add stock, cauliflower, and potato; heat to boiling. Reduce heat and simmer, covered, until vegetables are tender, 10 to 15 minutes.

2. Remove about half the cauliflower from the soup with a slotted spoon and reserve. Puree remaining soup in food processor or blender until smooth. Return soup to saucepan; stir in reserved cauliflower, half-and-half, and cheese. Cook over low heat until cheese is melted, 3 to 4 minutes, stirring frequently. Season to taste with salt and white pepper.

3. Pour soup into bowls; sprinkle lightly with mace or nutmeg.

LIME-SCENTED VEGETABLE SOUP

A soup with a fresh flavor, accented with lime and cilantro. Cubed light tofu can be added, if you want.

6 first-course servings (about 1¼ cups each)

Vegetable cooking spray
2 cups sliced carrots
1 cup chopped red bell pepper
¾ cup sliced celery
⅓ cup sliced green onions and tops
6 cloves garlic, minced
1 small jalapeño chili, finely chopped
6 cups Basic Vegetable Stock (see p. 58)
½-¾ cup lime juice
½ teaspoon ground cumin
1 cup chopped tomato
½ cup seeded, chopped cucumber
½ small avocado, peeled, chopped
3-4 tablespoons finely chopped cilantro
1½ cups Herb Croutons (½ recipe, see p. 677)

Per Serving
Calories: 106
% Calories from fat: 29
Fat (gm): 3.9
Saturated fat (gm): 0.1
Cholesterol (mg): 0
Sodium (mg): 100
Protein (gm): 3.3
Carbohydrate (gm): 17.6
Exchanges
Milk: 0.0
Vegetable: 2.0
Fruit: 0.0
Bread: 0.5
Meat: 0.0
Fat: 0.5

1. Spray large skillet with cooking spray; heat over medium heat until hot. Saute carrots, pepper, celery, green onions, garlic, and jalapeño chili 5 minutes.

2. Add stock, lime juice, and cumin to saucepan; heat to boiling. Reduce heat and simmer, covered, until vegetables are tender, 10 to 15 minutes.

3. Pour soup into bowls; add tomato, cucumber, and avocado to each bowl. Sprinkle with cilantro and Herb Croutons.

GARDEN HARVEST SOUP

 Vary the vegetables according to your garden's or greengrocer's bounty.

4 main-dish servings (about 2 cups each)

2 small onions, sliced
2 cloves garlic, minced
1 tablespoon olive oil
2 carrots, sliced
1 small red bell pepper, sliced
1 small yellow bell pepper, sliced
2 cups whole-kernel corn
5 cups Mediterranean, *or* Roasted Vegetable, Stock (see pp. 60, 59)
1 cup 1-inch pieces green beans
1 medium zucchini, sliced
1 yellow summer squash, sliced
½-¾ teaspoon dried basil leaves
½ teaspoon dried oregano leaves
Salt and pepper, to taste
⅓ cup fat-free half-and-half, *or* fat-free milk (optional)
Parsley, finely chopped, as garnish

Per Serving
Calories: 241
% Calories from fat: 19
Fat (gm): 5.7
Saturated fat (gm): 0.7
Cholesterol (mg): 0
Sodium (mg): 40
Protein (gm): 6.8
Carbohydrate (gm): 41.5
Exchanges
Milk: 0.0
Vegetable: 3.0
Fruit: 0.0
Bread: 1.5
Meat: 0.0
Fat: 1.0

1. Saute onions and garlic in oil in large saucepan until tender, about 5 minutes. Add carrots, bell peppers, and corn and saute 5 minutes. Add stock, green beans, zucchini, squash, and herbs; heat to boiling. Reduce heat and simmer, covered, until vegetables are tender, about 15 minutes. Season to taste with salt and pepper.

2. Stir half-and-half into soup just before serving. Pour soup into bowls; sprinkle with parsley.

HEARTY CORN AND POTATO CHOWDER

 Cut corn fresh from the cob for this soup, or for convenience use frozen, thawed whole-kernel corn.

4 main-dish servings (about 2 cups each)

2 cups fresh, *or* frozen, thawed, whole-kernel corn

1 medium onion, chopped

1 tablespoon canola oil

2 cups Basic Vegetable Stock (see p. 58)

2 cups unpeeled, cubed Idaho potatoes

½ cup sliced celery

½ teaspoon dried thyme leaves

1¾ cups fat-free half-and-half, *or* fat-free milk

Salt and pepper, to taste

Parsley and chives, finely chopped, as garnish

Per Serving
Calories: 298
% Calories from fat: 12
Fat (gm): 3.9
Saturated fat (gm): 0.5
Cholesterol (mg): 0
Sodium (mg): 134
Protein (gm): 9
Carbohydrate (gm): 57.0
Exchanges
Milk: 1.0
Vegetable: 1.0
Fruit: 0.0
Bread: 2.5
Meat: 0.0
Fat: 0.5

1. Saute corn and onion in oil in large saucepan until onion is tender, 5 to 8 minutes. Process ½ of vegetable mixture and all the stock in food processor or blender until finely chopped, using pulse technique. Return mixture to saucepan.

2. Add potatoes, celery, and thyme leaves to saucepan; heat to boiling. Reduce heat and simmer, covered, until vegetables are tender, 10 to 15 minutes. Stir in half-and-half; cook until hot through, 2 to 3 minutes. Season to taste with salt and pepper.

3. Pour soup into bowls; sprinkle with parsley and chives.

Note: If thicker soup is desired, mix 2 to 3 tablespoons flour with ⅓ cup water. Heat soup to boiling; stir in flour mixture and boil, stirring constantly, until thickened, about 1 minute.

CREAMED CORN SOUP

 Garnish this colorful soup with a sprinkling of finely chopped cilantro or parsley.

4 main-dish servings (about 1 cup each)

Vegetable cooking spray
½ cup chopped onion
1 medium Idaho potato, peeled, cubed
2 cloves garlic, minced
1 can (15½ ounces) whole-kernel corn, drained
3 tablespoons all-purpose flour
½ teaspoon ground coriander
⅛ teaspoon cayenne pepper
3½ cups Canned Vegetable Stock (see p. 63)
1 cup fat-free milk
2 medium tomatoes, chopped
Salt and pepper, to taste
Paprika, as garnish

Per Serving
Calories: 238
% Calories from fat: 8
Fat (gm): 2.3
Saturated fat (gm): 0.4
Cholesterol (mg): 1
Sodium (mg): 443
Protein (gm): 7.7
Carbohydrate (gm): 45.7
Exchanges
Milk: 0.0
Vegetable: 3.0
Fruit: 0.0
Bread: 2.0
Meat: 0.0
Fat: 0.5

1. Spray a large saucepan with cooking spray; heat over medium heat until hot. Saute onion, potato, and garlic until onion is tender, about 5 minutes. Stir in corn, flour, coriander, and cayenne pepper; cook 1 to 2 minutes, stirring frequently. Stir in stock and heat to boiling; reduce heat and simmer, covered, until potato is tender, about 10 minutes.

2. Process mixture in food processor or blender until almost smooth; return to saucepan. Stir in milk and tomatoes; heat just to boiling. Reduce heat and simmer, uncovered, 5 minutes. Season to taste with salt and pepper. Serve soup in bowls; sprinkle with paprika.

CORN SOUP WITH EPAZOTE

Epazote is a popular Mexican herb, which can be purchased in Mexican groceries. It's easy to grow but must be planted annually in northern climates. One-half to one teaspoon of dried epazote or dried thyme can be substituted.

4 main-dish servings (about 1½ cups each)

¾ cup chopped onion
1 medium jalapeño chili, finely chopped
1 clove garlic, minced
1 tablespoon olive oil
3½ cups Roasted, *or* Basic, Vegetable Stock (see pp. 59, 58)
5 cups fresh, *or* frozen, whole-kernel corn
2 tablespoons finely chopped fresh epazote, *or* ½ to 1 teaspoon dried epazote, *or* thyme leaves
Salt, cayenne, and white pepper, to taste
¾ cup Roasted Red Pepper Sauce (½ recipe, see p. 709)

Per Serving
Calories: 275
% Calories from fat: 12
Fat (gm): 4
Saturated fat (gm): 0.5
Cholesterol (mg): 0
Sodium (mg): 38
Protein (gm): 8.6
Carbohydrate (gm): 55.9
Exchanges
Milk: 0.0
Vegetable: 2.5
Fruit: 0.0
Bread: 2.5
Meat: 0.0
Fat: 0.5

1. Saute onion, jalapeño chili, and garlic in oil in large saucepan until tender, about 5 minutes. Add stock and corn; heat to boiling. Reduce heat and simmer, covered, 10 minutes.

2. Process soup in food processor or blender until almost smooth; stir in epazote and season to taste with salt and cayenne and white pepper.

3. Heat soup and serve warm, or refrigerate until chilled and serve cold. Pour soup into bowls; swirl about 3 tablespoons Roasted Red Pepper Sauce into each bowl.

GARLIC SOUP WITH TOAST

 Traditionally, a whole beaten egg is slowly stirred into the simmering soup before serving, similar to Chinese egg drop soup. Try this if you don't mind adding cholesterol.

4 first-course servings (about 1 cup each)

4 slices firm bread (French or sourdough)
Vegetable cooking spray
1 tablespoon olive oil
6-8 cloves garlic, finely chopped
½ teaspoon ground cumin
¼ teaspoon dried oregano leaves
¼ teaspoon cayenne pepper
3½ cups Canned Vegetable Stock (see p. 63)
Salt, to taste
Cilantro, finely chopped, as garnish

Per Serving
Calories: 162
% Calories from fat: 28
Fat (gm): 5
Saturated fat (gm): 0.7
Cholesterol (mg): 0
Sodium (mg): 202
Protein (gm): 3.2
Carbohydrate (gm): 20.6
Exchanges
Milk: 0.0
Vegetable: 1.0
Fruit: 0.0
Bread: 1.5
Meat: 0.0
Fat: 0.5

1. Spray both sides of bread slices generously with cooking spray; cook in large skillet, over medium heat, until golden on both sides. Keep warm.

2. Heat oil in medium saucepan until hot; add garlic and cook over low heat until garlic is very soft and very lightly browned, 5 to 8 minutes. Stir in cumin, oregano, and cayenne pepper; cook 1 to 2 minutes. Add stock to saucepan; heat to boiling. Reduce heat and simmer, covered, 5 minutes. Season to taste with salt.

3. Place slices of bread in bottoms of 4 shallow bowls; ladle soup over. Sprinkle with cilantro.

TORTELLINI SOUP WITH KALE

Fast and easy to make when there's no time to cook!

8 first-course servings (about 1½ cups each)

1 cup sliced leek, *or* green onions and tops

3 cloves garlic, minced

1 tablespoon olive oil

3 quarts Roasted Vegetable, *or* Rich Mushroom, Stock (see pp. 59, 61)

2 cups (12 ounces) kale, coarsely chopped

1 cup sliced mushrooms

½ package (9 ounce-size) mushroom, *or* herb, tortellini

Salt and white pepper, to taste

Per Serving
Calories: 105
% Calories from fat: 24
Fat (gm): 3.1
Saturated fat (gm): 0.8
Cholesterol (mg): 8.4
Sodium (mg): 69
Protein (gm): 3
Carbohydrate (gm): 11.6
Exchanges
Milk: 0.0
Vegetable: 2.0
Fruit: 0.0
Bread: 0.0
Meat: 0.0
Fat: 1.0

1. Saute leek and garlic in oil in Dutch oven until leek is tender, 5 to 8 minutes. Add stock and heat to boiling; stir in kale and mushrooms. Reduce heat and simmer, covered, 5 minutes.

2. Add tortellini to pan; simmer, uncovered, until tortellini are *al dente*, about 7 minutes. Season to taste with salt and white pepper.

BLACK MUSHROOM SOUP

Chinese black mushrooms, also called shiitake mushrooms, add the fragrant, woodsy flavor to this soup.

6 first-course servings (about 1¼ cups each)

1½ ounces dried Chinese black mushrooms (shiitake)

1 ounce dried cloud ear mushrooms

2 cups boiling water

Vegetable cooking spray

¼ cup chopped onion

¼ cup thinly sliced green onions and tops

5 cups Rich Mushroom, *or* Oriental, Stock (see pp. 61, 62)

Per Serving
Calories: 72
% Calories from fat: 16
Fat (gm): 1.4
Saturated fat (gm): 0.1
Cholesterol (mg): 0
Sodium (mg): 10
Protein (gm): 2.9
Carbohydrate (gm): 11.1
Exchanges
Milk: 0.0
Vegetable: 3.0
Fruit: 0.0
Bread: 0.0
Meat: 0.0
Fat: 0.0

3 cups sliced cremini mushrooms
Salt and white pepper, to taste
Parsley, finely chopped, as garnish

1. Place dried mushrooms in bowl; pour boiling water over. Let stand until mushrooms are softened, about 15 minutes. Drain, reserving liquid. Slice mushrooms, discarding tough stems from black mushrooms.

2. Spray large saucepan with cooking spray; heat over medium heat until hot. Saute onions until tender, about 5 minutes. Add sliced dried mushrooms, reserved 2 cups liquid, and stock; heat to boiling. Reduce heat and simmer, covered, 20 minutes, adding cremini mushrooms during last 10 minutes. Season to taste with salt and white pepper.

3. Pour soup into bowls; sprinkle with parsley.

CREAM OF MUSHROOM SOUP

Creamy and rich, this soup bears resemblance to the favorite-brand canned soup we remember. For a richer soup, use fat-free half-and-half instead of fat-free milk.

4 first-course servings (about 1¼ cups each)

1 pound mushrooms
2 tablespoons margarine, divided
1 cup chopped onion
2½ cups Canned Vegetable Stock, *or* Basic Vegetable Stock (see pp. 63, 58)
2½ cups fat-free milk, divided
2 tablespoons plus 2 teaspoons cornstarch
Salt and pepper, to taste
Parsley leaves, minced, as garnish

Per Serving
Calories: 207
% Calories from fat: 29
Fat (gm): 7
Saturated fat (gm): 1.4
Cholesterol (mg): 2.5
Sodium (mg): 185
Protein (gm): 8.6
Carbohydrate (gm): 25.3
Exchanges
Milk: 0.5
Vegetable: 2.5
Fruit: 0.0
Bread: 0.5
Meat: 0.0
Fat: 1.5

1. Slice enough mushroom caps to make 2 cups; finely chop stems and remaining mushrooms. Saute sliced mushrooms in 1 tablespoon margarine in large saucepan until browned, about 5 minutes; remove and reserve. Saute onion and chopped mushrooms in remaining 1 tablespoon margarine until onion is tender, about 5 minutes.

2. Add stock and 2 cups milk to saucepan; heat to boiling. Mix remaining ½ cup milk and cornstarch; whisk into boiling mixture. Boil, whisking constantly, until thickened, about 1 minute. Stir in reserved sliced mushrooms. Season to taste with salt and pepper. Serve in bowls; sprinkle with parsley.

TORTELLINI AND MUSHROOM SOUP

Porcini mushrooms, an Italian delicacy found fresh in Tuscany in fall, are available in dried form year round. Porcini impart a wonderful earthy flavor to recipes. Dried mushrooms, such as shiitake or Chinese black mushrooms, can be substituted for a similar flavor.

6 first-course servings (about 1 cup each)

2 ounces dried porcini mushrooms
Hot water
Vegetable cooking spray
8 ounces fresh white mushrooms, sliced
2 tablespoons finely chopped shallots, *or* green onions
2 cloves garlic, minced
½ teaspoon dried tarragon, *or* thyme, leaves
4 cups Rich Mushroom Stock, *or* Canned Vegetable Stock (see pp. 61, 63)
¼ cup dry sherry (optional)
1 package (9 ounces) fresh low-fat tomato-and-cheese tortellini
¼ teaspoon salt
¼ teaspoon pepper

Per Serving
Calories: 110
% Calories from fat: 16
Fat (gm): 2
Saturated fat (gm): 0.4
Cholesterol (mg): 4.2
Sodium (mg): 184
Protein (gm): 5
Carbohydrate (gm): 17.1
Exchanges
Milk: 0.0
Vegetable: 1.0
Fruit: 0.0
Bread: 1.0
Meat: 0.0
Fat: 0.5

1. Place dried mushrooms in bowl; pour hot water over to cover. Let stand until mushrooms are soft, about 15 minutes; drain. Slice mushrooms, discarding any tough parts.

2. Spray large saucepan with cooking spray; heat over medium heat until hot. Saute dried and white mushrooms, shallots, garlic, and tarragon until mushrooms are tender, about 5 minutes.

3. Add stock and sherry to vegetables; heat to boiling. Add tomato-and-cheese tortellini, salt, and pepper. Reduce heat and simmer, uncovered, until tortellini are *al dente*, about 5 minutes.

SAVORY MUSHROOM AND BARLEY SOUP

Fast and easy to make with quick-cooking barley. Other grains, such as wild rice or oat groats, can be substituted for the barley; cook before adding to the soup.

4 first-course servings (about 1½ cups each)

Vegetable cooking spray
1 cup chopped onion
1 cup sliced celery
⅔ cup sliced carrots
1 teaspoon dried savory leaves
¾ teaspoon fennel seeds, crushed
1 quart water
1 can (16 ounces) reduced-sodium whole tomatoes, undrained, coarsely chopped
½ cup quick-cooking barley
2 cups sliced cremini, *or* white, mushrooms
Salt and pepper, to taste
Parsley, finely chopped, as garnish

Per Serving
Calories: 151
% Calories from fat: 8
Fat (gm): 1.4
Saturated fat (gm): 0.1
Cholesterol (mg): 0
Sodium (mg): 53
Protein (gm): 5.6
Carbohydrate (gm): 32.1
Exchanges
Milk: 0.0
Vegetable: 2.0
Fruit: 0.0
Bread: 1.5
Meat: 0.0
Fat: 0.0

1. Spray large saucepan with cooking spray; heat over medium heat until hot. Saute onion, celery, and carrots until onion is tender, about 5 minutes. Stir in herbs; cook 1 to 2 minutes longer.

2. Add water, tomatoes with liquid, barley, and mushrooms to saucepan; heat to boiling. Cook, covered, until barley is tender, 10 to 15 minutes. Season to taste with salt and pepper.

3. Pour soup into bowls; sprinkle with parsley.

TEMPEH NOODLE SOUP

A light but nourishing soup that's also quick and easy to make.

4 first-course servings (about 1¼ cups each)

Vegetable cooking spray
2 cups sliced celery, including some leaves
1 cup sliced carrot
1 cup sliced onion
3½ cups Basic Vegetable Stock (see p. 58)
1 package (8 ounces) tempeh, *or* light firm tofu, coarsely shredded
1 teaspoon dried marjoram leaves
1 bay leaf
1 cup uncooked broad noodles
1 tablespoon minced parsley
Salt and pepper, to taste

Per Serving
Calories: 195
% Calories from fat: 22
Fat (gm): 5
Saturated fat (gm): 0.7
Cholesterol (mg): 0
Sodium (mg): 77
Protein (gm): 13.3
Carbohydrate (gm): 27.2
Exchanges
Milk: 0.0
Vegetable: 2.0
Fruit: 0.0
Bread: 1.0
Meat: 1.0
Fat: 0.5

1. Spray large saucepan with cooking spray; heat over medium heat until hot. Saute celery, carrot, and onion until crisp-tender, 5 to 8 minutes.

2. Add stock, tempeh, and herbs to saucepan; heat to boiling. Reduce heat and simmer, covered, until vegetables are tender, about 10 minutes.

3. Heat soup to boiling; add noodles. Reduce heat and simmer, uncovered, until noodles are tender, 7 to 10 minutes. Discard bay leaf. Stir in parsley and season to taste with salt and pepper. Serve in bowls.

VIDALIA ONION SOUP

The mild sweetness of Vidalia onions makes this soup special, but try it with other flavorful onion varieties too. Half of the soup is pureed, resulting in a wonderful contrast of textures.

8 first-course servings (about 1¼ cups each)

Vegetable cooking spray

6 cups (1½ pounds) thinly sliced Vidalia onions

2 cloves garlic, minced

1 teaspoon sugar

⅓ cup all-purpose flour

6 cups Roasted, *or* Basic, Vegetable Stock (see pp. 59, 58)

1½ teaspoons dried sage leaves

2 bay leaves

Salt, cayenne, and white pepper, to taste

Chives, snipped, as garnish

Per Serving
Calories: 88
% Calories from fat: 3
Fat (gm): 0.3
Saturated fat (gm): 0.1
Cholesterol (mg): 0
Sodium (mg): 13
Protein (gm): 2.2
Carbohydrate (gm): 16.4
Exchanges
Milk: 0.0
Vegetable: 2.0
Fruit: 0.0
Bread: 0.5
Meat: 0.0
Fat: 0.0

1. Spray Dutch oven with cooking spray; heat over medium heat until hot. Add onions and garlic and cook, covered, over medium-low heat until wilted, 8 to 10 minutes. Stir in sugar and cook, uncovered, over medium-low to low heat until onions are lightly browned. Stir in flour; cook 1 to 2 minutes longer.

2. Stir in stock, sage, and bay leaves; heat to boiling. Reduce heat and simmer, covered, 30 minutes. Discard bay leaves.

3. Process half the soup in food processor or blender until smooth; return to pan. Season to taste with salt, cayenne, and white pepper. Serve warm, or refrigerate and serve chilled.

4. Pour soup into bowls; sprinkle with chives.

FRENCH ONION SOUP

 This classic soup is topped with Crostini and fat-free cheese for healthful low-fat dining.

8 first-course servings (about 1¼ cups each)

Vegetable cooking spray
6 cups (1½ pounds) thinly sliced Spanish onions
2 cloves garlic, minced
1 teaspoon sugar
6 cups Roasted, *or* Basic, Vegetable Stock (see pp. 59, 58)
2 bay leaves
Salt and white pepper, to taste
8 Bruschetta (⅓ recipe, see p. 54)
8 tablespoons (2 ounces) shredded fat-free Swiss, *or* mozzarella, cheese

Per Serving
Calories: 131
% Calories from fat: 6
Fat (gm): 0.8
Saturated fat (gm): 0.2
Cholesterol (mg): 0
Sodium (mg): 221
Protein (gm): 5
Carbohydrate (gm): 22.9
Exchanges
Milk: 0.0
Vegetable: 2.0
Fruit: 0.0
Bread: 1.0
Meat: 0.0
Fat: 0.0

1. Spray Dutch oven with cooking spray; heat over medium heat until hot. Add onions and garlic and cook, covered, over medium-low heat until wilted, 8 to 10 minutes. Stir in sugar and cook, uncovered, over medium-low to low heat until onions are lightly browned.

2. Stir in stock and bay leaves; heat to boiling. Reduce heat and simmer, covered, 30 minutes. Discard bay leaves; season to taste with salt and white pepper.

3. Top each Crostini with 1 tablespoon cheese; broil 6 inches from heat source until cheese is melted. Pour soup into bowls; top each with a cheesy Crostini.

THREE-ONION SOUP WITH MUSHROOMS

Mushrooms add flavor and texture interest to this soup.

6 first-course servings (about 1½ cups each)

3	cups thinly sliced onions
1½	cups thinly sliced leeks
½	cup chopped shallots, *or* green onions and tops
1	tablespoon margarine, *or* butter
1	teaspoon sugar
4	ounces mushrooms, sliced
6½	cups Rich Mushroom Stock (see p. 61)
	Salt and pepper, to taste

Per Serving
Calories: 119
% Calories from fat: 21
Fat (gm): 3
Saturated fat (gm): 0.5
Cholesterol (mg): 0
Sodium (mg): 45
Protein (gm): 2.7
Carbohydrate (gm): 18.5
Exchanges
Milk: 0.0
Vegetable: 3.0
Fruit: 0.0
Bread: 0.0
Meat: 0.0
Fat: 0.5

1. Cook onions, leeks, and shallots in margarine in large saucepan, covered, over medium-low heat 15 minutes. Stir in sugar; continue cooking, uncovered, until onion mixture is golden, about 10 minutes longer.

2. Stir mushrooms into onion mixture; cook over medium heat until tender, about 5 minutes. Add stock and heat to boiling; reduce heat and simmer, uncovered, 15 minutes. Season to taste with salt and pepper. Serve in bowls.

ONION AND LEEK SOUP WITH PASTA

An Italian-style soup, this recipe combines onions, leeks, and pasta. Soup pasta, small shells, or bow ties can be alternate pasta choices.

4 main-dish servings (about 1¾ cups each)

	Vegetable cooking spray
4	cups sliced onions
2	cups sliced leeks
6	cloves garlic, minced
1	teaspoon sugar
7	cups Basic Vegetable Stock (see p. 58)
5	ounces small pasta rings, uncooked
	Salt and white pepper, to taste
6	teaspoons fat-free grated Parmesan cheese

Per Serving
Calories: 288
% Calories from fat: 6
Fat (gm): 1.9
Saturated fat (gm): 0.2
Cholesterol (mg): 0
Sodium (mg): 66
Protein (gm): 9.7
Carbohydrate (gm): 59.9
Exchanges
Milk: 0.0
Vegetable: 5.0
Fruit: 0.0
Bread: 2.0
Meat: 0.0
Fat: 0.0

1. Spray large saucepan with cooking spray; heat over medium heat until hot. Add onions, leeks, and garlic and cook, covered, over medium heat until wilted, 5 to 8 minutes. Stir in sugar; cook, uncovered, over medium-low heat until onion mixture is very soft and browned, 15 to 20 minutes.

2. Add stock to saucepan and heat to boiling. Add pasta, reduce heat, and simmer, uncovered, until pasta is *al dente*, 6 to 8 minutes. Season to taste with salt and white pepper.

3. Pour soup into bowls; sprinkle 1 teaspoon Parmesan cheese over each.

CREAMY PEANUT BUTTER SOUP

 This soup will tempt peanut butter lovers! In our low-fat version pureed beans contribute rich texture without detracting from the peanut flavor.

4 main-dish servings (about 1½ cups each)

Vegetable cooking spray
½   cup chopped onion
½   cup chopped carrot
½   cup sliced celery
1   leek, cleaned, sliced
2   cloves garlic, minced
3   cups Basic Vegetable Stock (see p. 58)
1   can (15 ounces) Great Northern beans, rinsed, drained
½   cup reduced-fat peanut butter
½   cup fat-free half-and-half, *or* fat-free milk
½   teaspoon curry powder
2-3   teaspoons lemon juice
1-2   dashes red pepper sauce
    Salt, cayenne, and black pepper, to taste
    Green onions, thinly sliced, as garnish

Per Serving
Calories: 379
% Calories from fat: 30
Fat (gm): 12.9
Saturated fat (gm): 2.7
Cholesterol (mg): 0
Sodium (mg): 88
Protein (gm): 19.2
Carbohydrate (gm): 48.6
Exchanges
Milk: 0.0
Vegetable: 2.0
Fruit: 0.0
Bread: 2.5
Meat: 1.5
Fat: 1.5

1. Spray large saucepan with cooking spray; heat over medium heat until hot. Saute onion, carrot, celery, leek, and garlic 5 minutes. Add stock and beans and heat to boiling; reduce heat and simmer, covered, until vegetables are tender, 10 to 15 minutes.

2. Process soup and peanut butter in food processor or blender until smooth. Return soup to saucepan; stir in half-and-half and curry powder. Heat over medium heat until hot. Season to taste with lemon juice, red pepper sauce, salt, cayenne, and black pepper.

3. Pour soup into bowls; sprinkle with green onions.

VICHYSSOISE

This classic French potato soup is traditionally served chilled, although it's good warm too!

4 main-dish servings (about 1½ cups each)

¾	cup sliced leeks, *or* green onions and tops
¾	cup sliced celery
2	tablespoons margarine, *or* butter
6	cups Basic Vegetable Stock (see p. 58)
2	pounds Idaho potatoes, peeled, cubed
¼	teaspoon dried thyme leaves
	Salt and white pepper, to taste
6	tablespoons fat-free sour cream
	Chives, finely chopped, as garnish

Per Serving
Calories: 282
% Calories from fat: 20
Fat (gm): 6.6
Saturated fat (gm): 1.2
Cholesterol (mg): 0
Sodium (mg): 134
Protein (gm): 6.2
Carbohydrate (gm): 51.5
Exchanges
Milk: 0.0
Vegetable: 1.0
Fruit: 0.0
Bread: 3.0
Meat: 0.0
Fat: 1.0

1. Saute leeks and celery in margarine in large saucepan until tender, about 8 minutes. Stir in stock, potatoes, and thyme and heat to boiling. Reduce heat and simmer, covered, until potatoes are tender, about 15 minutes.

2. Process soup in food processor or blender until smooth; season to taste with salt and white pepper. Refrigerate until chilled.

3. Pour soup into bowls; top each with 1 tablespoon sour cream and sprinkle with chives.

POTATO CHOWDER

A basic soup that is versatile: substitute any desired vegetables, such as carrots, zucchini, green beans, or corn, for part of the potatoes for a delectable vegetable chowder.

4 main-dish servings (about 1½ cups each)

1 cup chopped onion
¼ cup thinly sliced celery
2 tablespoons margarine, *or* butter
3 tablespoons flour
2 cups Canned Vegetable Stock, *or* Basic Vegetable Stock (see pp. 63, 58)
3½ cups peeled, cubed Idaho potatoes
¼-½ teaspoon celery seeds
2 cups fat-free milk
Salt and pepper, to taste

Per Serving
Calories: 338
% Calories from fat: 17
Fat (gm): 6.6
Saturated fat (gm): 1.4
Cholesterol (mg): 2
Sodium (mg): 175
Protein (gm): 9.3
Carbohydrate (gm): 58.4
Exchanges
Milk: 0.5
Vegetable: 1.0
Fruit: 0.0
Bread: 3.0
Meat: 0.0
Fat: 1.0

1. Saute onion and celery in margarine in large saucepan until tender, 5 to 8 minutes. Stir in flour; cook over medium-low heat, stirring constantly, 1 minute.

2. Add stock, potatoes, and celery seeds to saucepan; heat to boiling. Reduce heat and simmer, covered, until potatoes are tender, 10 to 15 minutes. Stir in milk; cook over medium heat until hot, 2 to 3 minutes. Season to taste with salt and pepper.

SPINACH AND TORTELLINI SOUP

Pasta soups can be made 2 to 3 days in advance, enhancing flavors. Add pasta to the soup when reheating for serving so that the pasta is fresh and perfectly cooked.

4 main-dish servings (about 1½ cups each)

Vegetable cooking spray
2 cups sliced carrots
¼ cup sliced green onions and tops
2 cloves garlic, minced
1 teaspoon dried basil leaves

Per Serving
Calories: 290
% Calories from fat: 9
Fat (gm): 2.8
Saturated fat (gm): 1
Cholesterol (mg): 3.8
Sodium (mg): 395
Protein (gm): 12.1
Carbohydrate (gm): 48

5 cups Canned Vegetable Stock, *or* Basic
   Vegetable Stock (see pp. 63, 58)
1 package (9 ounces) fresh low-fat
   tomato-and-cheese tortellini
3 cups torn spinach leaves
2-3 teaspoons lemon juice
⅛-¼ teaspoon ground nutmeg
   ⅛ teaspoon pepper

Exchanges
Milk: 0.0
Vegetable: 2.0
Fruit: 0.0
Bread: 2.5
Meat: 1.0
Fat: 0.0

1. Spray bottom of large saucepan with cooking spray; heat over medium heat until hot. Saute carrots, onions, garlic, and basil until onions are tender, about 5 minutes.

2. Add stock to saucepan; heat to boiling. Reduce heat and simmer, covered, 10 minutes.

3. Heat stock mixture to boiling; stir in tomato-and-cheese tortellini and spinach. Reduce heat and simmer, uncovered, until tortellini are *al dente*, about 5 minutes. Season with lemon juice, nutmeg, and pepper.

CINNAMON-SPICED PUMPKIN SOUP

 For convenience, 2 cans of pumpkin can be substituted for the fresh pumpkin. Any yellow winter squash such as butternut, Hubbard, or acorn can also be used.

4 first-course servings (about 1¼ cups each)

4 cups (about 2 pounds) pumpkin,
   peeled, seeded, cubed
2 cups fat-free half-and-half, *or* fat-free
   milk
1-2 tablespoons light brown sugar
   ½ teaspoon ground cinnamon
¼-½ teaspoon ground nutmeg
   Chives, snipped, as garnish

Per Serving
Calories: 125
% Calories from fat: 1
Fat (gm): 0.2
Saturated fat (gm): 0.1
Cholesterol (mg): 0
Sodium (mg): 122
Protein (gm): 5.2
Carbohydrate (gm): 23.2
Exchanges
Milk: 1.0
Vegetable: 0.0
Fruit: 0.0
Bread: 0.5
Meat: 0.0
Fat: 0.0

1. Cook pumpkin in medium saucepan, covered, in 1 inch of simmering water until tender, about 15 minutes. Drain well. Process pumpkin and half-and-half in food processor or blender; return to saucepan. Stir in brown sugar and spices and heat just to boiling; reduce heat and simmer, uncovered, 5 minutes.

2. Pour soup into bowls; sprinkle with chives.

SPINACH SOUP WITH ONION FLOWERS

An attractive appetizer offering! Roasted Vegetable, Mediterranean, Basic Vegetable, or Oriental stocks (see pp. 59, 60, 58, 62) can also be used to make this soup.

8 first-course servings (about 1 cup each)

8 small onions, peeled

9 cups Canned Vegetable Stock (1½ recipes, see p. 63), divided

1 package (10 ounces) frozen spinach
Salt and white pepper, to taste
Green onions and tops, thinly sliced, as garnish

Per Serving
Calories: 107
% Calories from fat: 9
Fat (gm): 1.1
Saturated fat (gm): 0.1
Cholesterol (mg): 0
Sodium (mg): 85
Protein (gm): 2.6
Carbohydrate (gm): 15.7
Exchanges
Milk: 0.0
Vegetable: 2.0
Fruit: 0.0
Bread: 0.5
Meat: 0.0
Fat: 0.0

1. Cut onions into ¼-inch slices, cutting to, but not through, the bottoms. Give onions a quarter turn; cut into ¼-inch slices, intersecting previous slices and cutting to, but not through, the bottoms.

2. Heat 6 cups stock to boiling in large saucepan; add onions. Reduce heat and simmer, covered, until onions are tender, about 20 minutes. Remove onions from stock with slotted spoon. Reserve stock.

3. Heat spinach and remaining 3 cups stock to boiling in medium saucepan; reduce heat and simmer, covered, 10 minutes. Strain, pressing lightly on spinach to extract all juice. Discard spinach, or reserve for other use.

4. Combine stock from onions and spinach; heat until hot. Season to taste with salt and white pepper. Arrange onions in serving bowls; pour soup around onions and sprinkle with green onions. Serve with knives, forks, and spoons.

SUN-DRIED TOMATO AND LINGUINE SOUP

For this skinny pasta soup, be sure to use plain sun-dried tomatoes rather than the ones packed in oil. One-half cup of uncooked orzo can be substituted for the linguine, if preferred.

4 first-course servings (about 1 cup each)

2 sun-dried tomatoes
Hot water
Vegetable cooking spray
½ cup thinly sliced celery
2 tablespoons thinly sliced green onions and tops
2 cloves garlic, minced
3½ cups Canned Vegetable Stock, *or* Basic Vegetable Stock (see pp. 63, 58)
2 ounces linguine, uncooked, broken into 2- to 3-inch pieces
1-2 teaspoons lemon juice
Salt and pepper, to taste

Per Serving
Calories: 111
% Calories from fat: 10
Fat (gm): 1.3
Saturated fat (gm): 0.1
Cholesterol (mg): 0
Sodium (mg): 155
Protein (gm): 3.3
Carbohydrate (gm): 16.8
Exchanges
Milk: 0.0
Vegetable: 1.0
Fruit: 0.0
Bread: 1.0
Meat: 0.0
Fat: 0.0

1. Place tomatoes in small bowl; pour hot water over to cover. Let tomatoes stand until softened, about 15 minutes; drain. Coarsely chop tomatoes.

2. Spray medium saucepan with cooking spray; heat over medium heat until hot. Saute celery, onions, and garlic until tender, 5 to 7 minutes. Stir in stock; heat to boiling.

3. Add linguine to boiling stock. Reduce heat and simmer, uncovered, until pasta is *al dente*, about 10 minutes. Season with lemon juice. Season to taste with salt and pepper.

WHITE BEAN AND SWEET POTATO SOUP WITH CRANBERRY COULIS

 An unusual but most pleasing combination of colors and flavors!

6 main-dish servings (about 1¼ cups each)

Vegetable cooking spray
1 cup chopped onion
1 pound sweet potatoes, peeled, cubed
1 large tart cooking apple, peeled, cored, chopped
1½ teaspoons minced gingerroot
2 cans (15 ounces each) navy or Great Northern beans, rinsed, drained
3 cups Basic Vegetable Stock (see p. 58)
½ teaspoon dried marjoram leaves
Salt, cayenne, and white pepper, to taste
Cranberry Coulis (see p. 732)

Per Serving
Calories: 310
% Calories from fat: 3
Fat (gm): 1.2
Saturated fat (gm): 0.3
Cholesterol (mg): 0
Sodium (mg): 650
Protein (gm): 12.6
Carbohydrate (gm): 64.6
Exchanges
Milk: 0.0
Vegetable: 1.0
Fruit: 1.0
Bread: 3.0
Meat: 0.0
Fat: 0.0

1. Spray large saucepan with cooking spray; heat over medium heat until hot. Saute onion, sweet potatoes, apple, and gingerroot 5 minutes. Add beans, stock, and marjoram and heat to boiling. Reduce heat and simmer, covered, until vegetables are tender, 10 to 15 minutes.

2. Process soup in food processor or blender until smooth; season to taste with salt, cayenne, and white pepper.

3. Pour soup into bowls; swirl 2 tablespoons Cranberry Coulis into each bowl.

LIGHTLY CREAMED VEGETABLE SOUP

 Fat-free milk, whipped with an immersion blender, lends a wonderful rich texture to this fragrant creamed soup. If you do not have an immersion blender, just stir ½ cup fat-free milk or fat-free half-and-half into the soup near the end of the cooking time.

6 first-course servings (about 1⅓ cups each)

1 medium onion, sliced
2 medium carrots, sliced
1 medium yellow summer squash, sliced
1 medium green bell pepper, coarsely chopped
1 medium red bell pepper, coarsely chopped
2 ribs celery, sliced
1 clove garlic, minced
1½ tablespoons margarine, *or* butter
4 peppercorns
3 whole cloves
1 bay leaf
4 cups Basic Vegetable Stock (see p. 58)
⅓ cup all-purpose flour
⅔ cup water
Salt and pepper, to taste
½ cup fat-free milk
Nutmeg, freshly ground, as garnish

Per Serving
Calories: 112
% Calories from fat: 27
Fat (gm): 3.6
Saturated fat (gm): 0.7
Cholesterol (mg): 0.3
Sodium (mg): 73
Protein (gm): 3.4
Carbohydrate (gm): 18
Exchanges
Milk: 0.0
Vegetable: 2.0
Fruit: 0.0
Bread: 0.5
Meat: 0.0
Fat: 0.5

1. Saute vegetables in margarine in large saucepan until onion is tender, 8 to 10 minutes. Tie herbs in cheesecloth bag; add to saucepan with stock and heat to boiling. Simmer, covered, until vegetables are tender, 10 to 15 minutes. Discard herb bag.

2. Heat soup to boiling. Mix flour and water; stir into soup. Boil, stirring constantly, until thickened, 1 to 2 minutes. Season to taste with salt and pepper.

3. Whip fat-free milk with an immersion blender; stir into soup just before serving. Pour soup into bowls; sprinkle lightly with nutmeg.

CREAM OF TOMATO SOUP

This tastes similar to the favorite-brand canned tomato soup we all remember! Canned tomatoes are necessary for the flavor, so don't substitute fresh.

4 first-course servings (about 1¼ cups each)

2	cans (14½ ounces each) no-salt whole tomatoes, undrained
1-3	teaspoons vegetable bouillon crystals
2	cups fat-free milk
3	tablespoons cornstarch
⅛	teaspoon baking soda
2	teaspoons sugar
1-2	tablespoons margarine, *or* butter
	Salt and pepper, to taste

Per Serving
Calories: 142
% Calories from fat: 22
Fat (gm): 3.7
Saturated fat (gm): 0.8
Cholesterol (mg): 2
Sodium (mg): 395
Protein (gm): 6.3
Carbohydrate (gm): 22.6
Exchanges
Milk: 0.5
Vegetable: 2.0
Fruit: 0.0
Bread: 0.5
Meat: 0.0
Fat: 0.5

1. Process tomatoes with liquid in food processor or blender until smooth; heat tomatoes and bouillon crystals in large saucepan to boiling. Mix milk and cornstarch; whisk into boiling mixture. Boil, whisking constantly, until thickened, about 1 minute.

2. Add baking soda, sugar, and margarine to soup, stirring until margarine is melted. Season to taste with salt and pepper. Ladle into bowls.

TWO-TOMATO SOUP

The concentrated flavor of sun-dried tomatoes enhances the taste of garden-ripe tomato soup.

6 first-course servings (about 1¼ cups each)

	Olive oil cooking spray
1	cup chopped onion
½	cup sliced celery
½	cup chopped carrot
2	teaspoons minced roasted garlic
4	cups Roasted Vegetable Stock (see p. 59)

Per Serving
Calories: 117
% Calories from fat: 5
Fat (gm): 0.8
Saturated fat (gm): 0.1
Cholesterol (mg): 0
Sodium (mg): 150
Protein (gm): 3.7
Carbohydrate (gm): 22.6

4 cups chopped ripe tomatoes, *or* 2 cans (16 ounces each) reduced-sodium whole tomatoes, undrained, coarsely chopped

1 large Idaho potato, peeled, cubed

½ cup sun-dried tomatoes (not in oil)

½ teaspoons dried basil leaves

½ cup fat-free half-and-half, *or* fat-free milk

2-3 teaspoons sugar

Salt and pepper, to taste

Basil, *or* parsley, finely chopped, as garnish

Exchanges
Milk: 0.0
Vegetable: 2.0
Fruit: 0.0
Bread: 1.0
Meat: 0.0
Fat: 0.0

1. Spray large saucepan with cooking spray; heat over medium heat until hot. Saute onion, celery, carrot, and garlic until tender, 5 to 8 minutes. Add stock, tomatoes, potato, sun-dried tomatoes, and basil; heat to boiling. Reduce heat and simmer, covered, until vegetables are tender, 10 to 15 minutes.

2. Process soup in food processor or blender until smooth; return to saucepan. Stir in half-and-half and cook over medium heat until hot through, 3 to 5 minutes. Season to taste with sugar, salt, and pepper.

3. Pour soup into bowls; sprinkle with basil or parsley.

TORTILLA SOUP

 Cubed tempeh can be added to the soup, if desired, to make this a more substantial dish.

8 first-course servings (about 1 cup each)

Vegetable cooking spray

3 corn, *or* flour, tortillas, cut into 2 x ¼-inch strips

1 small onion, chopped

1 cup chopped celery

1 medium tomato, coarsely chopped

½ teaspoon dried basil leaves

½ teaspoon ground cumin

Per Serving
Calories: 93
% Calories from fat: 9
Fat (gm): 1
Saturated fat (gm): 0.1
Cholesterol (mg): 0
Sodium (mg): 237
Protein (gm): 5.1
Carbohydrate (gm): 18.1
Exchanges
Milk: 0.0
Vegetable: 1.0
Fruit: 0.0
Bread: 1.0
Meat: 0.0
Fat: 0.0

5 cups Basic Vegetable Stock (see p. 58)
1 can (15½ ounces) pinto beans, rinsed, drained
2 teaspoons finely chopped cilantro
1–2 teaspoons lime juice
   Salt, to taste
   Cayenne pepper, to taste

1. Spray medium skillet with cooking spray; heat over medium heat until hot. Add tortillas; spray tortillas with cooking spray and cook over medium heat, tossing occasionally, until browned and crisp, about 5 minutes. Reserve.

2. Spray large saucepan with cooking spray; heat over medium heat until hot. Saute onions, celery, tomatoes, basil, and cumin until onions are tender, 3 to 5 minutes. Add stock and beans; heat to boiling. Reduce heat and simmer, uncovered, 3 to 5 minutes. Stir in cilantro; season with lime juice, and add salt and cayenne pepper to taste.

3. Add tortilla strips to soup bowls and ladle on soup.

POZOLE

 Pozole always contains hominy; our vegetarian version is served with a variety of crisp vegetable garnishes.

4 first-course servings (about 1⅓ cups each)

2 ancho chilies, stems, seeds, and veins discarded
1 cup boiling water
   Vegetable cooking spray
1 cup chopped onion
1 clove garlic, minced
2 cans (14½ ounces each) reduced-sodium vegetable broth
1 can (15½ ounces) hominy, rinsed, drained
1 can (14½ ounces) reduced-sodium tomatoes, drained, coarsely chopped
1 cup fresh, *or* frozen, whole-kernel corn

Per Serving
Calories: 186
% Calories from fat: 6
Fat (gm): 1.4
Saturated fat (gm): 0.2
Cholesterol (mg): 0
Sodium (mg): 323
Protein (gm): 5.3
Carbohydrate (gm): 40.8
Exchanges
Milk: 0.0
Vegetable: 2.0
Fruit: 0.0
Bread: 2.0
Meat: 0.0
Fat: 0.0

½ teaspoon dried oregano leaves
¼ teaspoon dried thyme leaves
   Salt and pepper, to taste
4 lime wedges
⅓ cup each, thinly sliced: lettuce, cabbage,
   green onion, radish, and shredded
   carrot

1. Cover chilies with boiling water in small bowl; let stand until softened, about 10 minutes. Process chilies and water in food processor or blender until smooth.

2. Spray large saucepan with vegetable cooking spray; heat over medium heat until hot. Saute onion and garlic until tender; add broth and heat to boiling. Reduce heat and simmer, covered, 10 to 15 minutes.

3. Add hominy, tomatoes, corn, oregano, and thyme to saucepan; cook, covered, over low heat 10 to 15 minutes. Season to taste with salt and pepper.

4. Serve soup in bowls; squeeze juice from one lime wedge into each bowl. Pass fresh vegetables (not included in nutritional data) for each person to add to soup.

MEXI "MEATBALL" SOUP

A great favorite in Mexico, this soup is traditionally seasoned with mint; we've offered oregano as an addition (or alternative), if you like.

4 main-dish servings (about 2 cups each)

   Vegetable cooking spray
¼ cup chopped onion
2 cloves garlic, minced
1 small jalapeño chili, seeds and veins
   discarded, minced
1 tablespoon flour
2 cups reduced-sodium tomato juice
2 cups water
3½ cups Basic Vegetable Stock (see p. 58)
3 medium carrots, sliced
2 medium zucchini, sliced

Per Serving
Calories: 245
% Calories from fat: 19
Fat (gm): 5.3
Saturated fat (gm): 2.1
Cholesterol (mg): 63.4
Sodium (mg): 630
Protein (gm): 16.3
Carbohydrate (gm): 34.7
Exchanges
Milk: 0.0
Vegetable: 3.0
Fruit: 0.0
Bread: 1.0
Meat: 2.0
Fat: 0.0

1½-2 teaspoons dried oregano leaves
   ½ teaspoon dried mint leaves
      Mexi "Meatballs" (see p. 405)
      Salt and pepper, to taste

1. Spray large saucepan with cooking spray; heat over medium heat until hot. Saute onion, garlic, and jalapeño chili until tender, about 5 minutes. Stir in flour; cook over medium heat 1 to 2 minutes.

2. Add tomato juice, water, stock, carrots, zucchini, oregano, and mint to saucepan; heat to boiling. Simmer until vegetables are tender, about 10 minutes. Add Mexi "Meatballs"; reduce heat and simmer, uncovered, until hot through, about 5 minutes. Season to taste with salt and pepper. Serve warm in bowls.

Note: Mexi "Meatballs" can be added to the soup after shaping; they do not need to be baked first.

ORIENTAL WATERCRESS SOUP

 Spinach can be substituted for the watercress in this fragrant Cantonese offering.

6 first-course servings (about 1 cup each)

   6 cups Oriental Stock (see p. 62)
   3 slices (scant ¼ inch thick) gingerroot
   2 large bunches (about 2 cups) watercress
      Salt and white pepper, to taste
   2 sliced green onions
   2 tablespoons shredded carrot

Per Serving
Calories: 11
% Calories from fat: 9
Fat (gm): 0.1
Saturated fat (gm): 0
Cholesterol (mg): 0
Sodium (mg): 116
Protein (gm): 0.9
Carbohydrate (gm): 1.8
Exchanges
Milk: 0.0
Vegetable: 0.0
Fruit: 0.0
Bread: 0.0
Meat: 0.0
Fat: 0.0

1. Heat stock and gingerroot to boiling in large saucepan; reduce heat and simmer, covered, 5 minutes. Remove gingerroot with slotted spoon and discard.

2. Trim stems from watercress and cut into 2-inch lengths. Add to soup and simmer, uncovered, 10 to 15 minutes. Season to taste with salt and white pepper.

3. Pour soup into bowls; sprinkle with green onions and carrot.

WONTON SOUP

 Your menu need not be oriental to begin with this soup; it goes well with any simple entrée.

6 first-course servings (about 1 cup each)

24 Five-Spice Potstickers (½ recipe, see p. 44)
6 cups Oriental Stock (see p. 62)
1 cup sliced spinach
Reduced-sodium tamari soy sauce
Pepper, to taste
1 medium green onion, sliced

Per Serving
Calories: 109
% Calories from fat: 7
Fat (gm): 0.9
Saturated fat (gm): 0.1
Cholesterol (mg): 3.3
Sodium (mg): 363
Protein (gm): 6.4
Carbohydrate (gm): 18.7
Exchanges
Milk: 0.0
Vegetable: 1.0
Fruit: 0.0
Bread: 1.0
Meat: 0.0
Fat: 0.0

1. Make Five-Spice Potstickers.

2. Heat stock to boiling in large saucepan. Add potstickers and simmer, uncovered, until potstickers rise to the surface, 2 to 3 minutes. Stir in spinach; simmer 2 to 3 minutes longer. Season to taste with soy sauce and pepper.

3. Pour soup into bowls; sprinkle with green onions.

HOT SOUR SOUP

The contrast in hot and sour flavors makes this Mandarin soup a unique offering. The hot chili sesame oil and Sour Sauce are intensely flavored, so use sparingly.

6 first-course servings (about 1 cup each)

½ ounce dried Chinese black mushrooms (shiitake)

¾ cup boiling water

4 cups Oriental Stock (see p. 62)

½ cup bamboo shoots

¼ cup white distilled vinegar

2 tablespoons reduced-sodium tamari soy sauce

1 tablespoon finely chopped gingerroot

1 teaspoon sugar

1 tablespoon cornstarch

3 tablespoons water

1½ cups cubed light extra-firm tofu

Salt, cayenne, and black pepper, to taste

1 egg, lightly beaten

1-2 teaspoons dark sesame oil

Green onions, sliced, as garnish

12-18 drops hot chili sesame oil, *or* Szechuan chili sauce

Sour Sauce (recipe follows)

Per Serving
Calories: 87
% Calories from fat: 24
Fat (gm): 2.4
Saturated fat (gm): 0.4
Cholesterol (mg): 35.5
Sodium (mg): 429
Protein (gm): 5.7
Carbohydrate (gm): 11.2
Exchanges
Milk: 0.0
Vegetable: 1.0
Fruit: 0.0
Bread: 0.5
Meat: 0.0
Fat: 0.5

1. Combine mushrooms and boiling water in small bowl; let stand until mushrooms are softened, 15 to 20 minutes. Drain; reserving liquid. Slice mushrooms, discarding tough stems.

2. Combine stock, mushrooms and reserved liquid, bamboo shoots, vinegar, tamari, gingerroot, and sugar in large saucepan. Heat to boiling; reduce heat and simmer, uncovered, 10 minutes. Heat soup to boiling; mix cornstarch and water and stir into soup. Boil until thickened, about 1 minute, stirring constantly.

3. Stir tofu into soup; simmer, covered, 5 minutes. Season to taste with salt, cayenne, and black pepper. Just before serving, stir egg slowly into soup; stir in sesame oil.

4. Pour soup into bowls; sprinkle with green onions. Serve with hot chili sesame oil, so each person can take 2 to 3 drops, and Sour Sauce.

Sour Sauce

(makes about ⅓ cup)

> 3 tablespoons white distilled vinegar
> 1 tablespoon reduced-sodium tamari soy sauce
> 2 tablespoons sugar

1. Mix all ingredients; refrigerate until serving time.

VIETNAMESE CURRIED COCONUT SOUP

Rice stick noodles, made with rice flour, can be round or flat. They must be softened in water before cooking. Angel hair pasta can be substituted.

6 first-course servings (about 1 cup each)

> Vegetable cooking spray
> 1 tablespoon minced garlic
> 3-4 tablespoons curry powder
> 3½ cups Basic Vegetable Stock (see p. 58)
> 3 cups reduced-fat coconut milk
> 2 tablespoons minced gingerroot
> ⅔ cup sliced green onions and tops
> ⅓ cup sliced onion
> 1 tablespoon minced parsley
> 1 tablespoon grated lime rind
> ½-1 teaspoon oriental chili paste
> ¼ cup lime juice
> ⅓ cup minced cilantro
> Salt and white pepper, to taste
> ½ package (8-ounce size) rice stick noodles
> Cold water
> 4 quarts boiling water

Per Serving
Calories: 138
% Calories from fat: 27
Fat (gm): 4.3
Saturated fat (gm): 0
Cholesterol (mg): 0
Sodium (mg): 112
Protein (gm): 3.4
Carbohydrate (gm): 22.9
Exchanges
Milk: 0.0
Vegetable: 1.0
Fruit: 0.0
Bread: 1.0
Meat: 0.0
Fat: 1.0

1. Spray large saucepan with cooking spray; heat over medium heat until hot. Saute garlic 1 minute; stir in curry powder and cook, stirring constantly, 30 seconds. Add stock, coconut milk, gingerroot, onions, parsley, lime rind, and chili paste; heat to boiling. Reduce heat and simmer, covered, 15 minutes.

2. Stir in lime juice and cilantro; season to taste with salt and white pepper. Simmer about 5 minutes longer.

3. Place noodles in large bowl; pour cold water over to cover. Let stand until noodles are separate and soft, about 5 minutes; drain. Stir noodles into 4 quarts boiling water. Reduce heat and simmer, uncovered, until tender, about 5 minutes; drain.

4. Spoon noodles into soup bowls; ladle soup over noodles.

GREEK LEMON-RICE SOUP

 Nicely tart; use fresh lemon juice for the best flavor. If making this soup in advance, do not add egg until reheating for serving.

4 first-course servings (about 1 cup each)

3½ cups Mediterranean, *or* Basic Vegetable, Stock (see p. 60, 58)
¼ cup converted long-grain rice
2 large cloves garlic, minced
¼-⅓ cup fresh, *or* frozen, thawed lemon juice
1 egg, lightly beaten
2 tablespoons finely chopped parsley
Salt and white pepper, to taste

Per Serving
Calories: 106
% Calories from fat: 20
Fat (gm): 2.4
Saturated fat (gm): 0.5
Cholesterol (mg): 53.3
Sodium (mg): 31
Protein (gm): 3
Carbohydrate (gm): 14.4
Exchanges
Milk: 0.0
Vegetable: 0.0
Fruit: 0.0
Bread: 1.0
Meat: 0.0
Fat: 0.5

1. Heat stock to boiling in medium saucepan; stir in rice and garlic. Reduce heat and simmer, covered, until rice is tender, about 25 minutes. Reduce heat to low.

2. Mix lemon juice and egg; slowly stir mixture into soup. Stir in parsley; season to taste with salt and white pepper. Pour soup into bowls.

MEDITERRANEAN-STYLE VEGETABLE SOUP

 A fragrant vegetable soup with a citrus accent.

6 first-course servings (about 1½ cups each)

Olive oil cooking spray
2 cups sliced mushrooms
1 medium onion, chopped
½ medium green bell pepper, chopped
3 cloves garlic, minced
3½ cups Mediterranean Stock (see p. 60)
1 can (16 ounces) reduced-sodium whole tomatoes, undrained, coarsely chopped
1 can (8 ounces) reduced-sodium tomato sauce
16 ounces light firm tofu, drained, cut into ¾-inch pieces
½ cup dry white wine (optional)
2 strips orange rind (3 x ½ inches)
2 bay leaves
1 teaspoon dried marjoram leaves
½-¾ teaspoon dried savory leaves
¼ teaspoon crushed fennel seeds
Salt and pepper, to taste

Per Serving
Calories: 109
% Calories from fat: 15
Fat (gm): 2
Saturated fat (gm): 0.1
Cholesterol (mg): 0
Sodium (mg): 104
Protein (gm): 8.1
Carbohydrate (gm): 13.8
Exchanges
Milk: 0.0
Vegetable: 2.5
Fruit: 0.0
Bread: 0.0
Meat: 0.5
Fat: 0.0

1. Spray large saucepan with cooking spray; heat over medium heat until hot. Add mushrooms, onion, bell pepper, and garlic; saute, covered, until vegetables are tender, 8 to 10 minutes.

2. Add remaining ingredients, except salt and pepper; heat to boiling. Reduce heat and simmer, covered, 10 to 15 minutes. Season to taste with salt and pepper. Remove bay leaves and serve in bowls.

LIGHT MINESTRONE

Minestrone does not always contain pasta, nor is it always a heavy, hearty soup. Enjoy this light version of an old favorite, selecting vegetables that are freshest and most plentiful. Without the Croutons, it is a vegan dish.

4 main-dish servings (about 2½ cups each)

Per Serving	
Calories: 293	
% Calories from fat: 20	
Fat (gm): 6.8	
Saturated fat (gm): 0.9	
Cholesterol (mg): 0	
Sodium (mg): 707	
Protein (gm): 11.2	
Carbohydrate (gm): 45.2	
Exchanges	
Milk: 0.0	
Vegetable: 4.0	
Fruit: 0.0	
Bread: 2.0	
Meat: 0.0	
Fat: 1.0	

    1 cup sliced carrots
    ½ cup chopped onion
    ½ cup chopped celery
    ½ cup sliced fennel bulb
    2 cloves garlic, minced
    1 tablespoon olive oil
    5 cups Roasted Vegetable Stock (see p. 59)
    1 can (19 ounces) garbanzo beans, rinsed, drained
    1 cup snap peas
    1 small zucchini, sliced
    1 cup broccoli florets
  ¾-1 teaspoon dried basil leaves
  ¾-1 teaspoon dried oregano leaves
    1 cup halved cherry tomatoes
    ¼ cup finely chopped parsley
       Salt and pepper, to taste
   1½ cups Parmesan Croutons (see p. 677)

1. Saute carrots, onion, celery, fennel, and garlic in oil in Dutch oven until onion is tender, 5 to 8 minutes. Add Roasted Vegetable Stock, beans, peas, zucchini, broccoli, and herbs; heat to boiling. Reduce heat and simmer, covered, until vegetables are tender, 10 to 15 minutes, adding tomatoes and parsley during last 10 minutes cooking time. Season to taste with salt and pepper.

2. Pour soup into bowls; sprinkle with Parmesan croutons.

SUMMER MINESTRONE

 Thick and savory, this traditional Italian soup is always a favorite.

6 main-dish servings (about 1⅓ cups each)

Vegetable cooking spray
2 medium potatoes, cubed
2 medium carrots, thinly sliced
1 small zucchini, cubed
1 cup halved green beans
1 cup thinly sliced, *or* shredded, cabbage
½ cup thinly sliced celery
1 medium onion, coarsely chopped
3-4 cloves garlic, minced
2 teaspoons Italian seasoning
1-2 teaspoons dried oregano leaves
4 cups Mediterranean Stock, *or* Basic Vegetable Stock (see pp. 60, 58)
1 can (15 ounces) no-salt-added stewed tomatoes
1 can (15 ounces) kidney beans, rinsed, drained
2 cups water
1½ cups (4 ounces) mostaccioli (penne), uncooked
½ teaspoon pepper
2 tablespoons grated Parmesan, *or* Romano, cheese

Per Serving
Calories: 264
% Calories from fat: 9
Fat (gm): 2.7
Saturated fat (gm): 0.6
Cholesterol (mg): 1.6
Sodium (mg): 216
Protein (gm): 12.3
Carbohydrate (gm): 50.5
Exchanges
Milk: 0.0
Vegetable: 3.0
Fruit: 0.0
Bread: 2.0
Meat: 1.0
Fat: 0.0

1. Spray bottom of large saucepan with cooking spray; heat over medium heat until hot. Saute fresh vegetables (next 8 ingredients) until crisp-tender, 10 to 12 minutes. Stir in Italian seasoning and oregano; cook 1 to 2 minutes more.

2. Add stock, tomatoes, beans, and water; heat to boiling. Reduce heat and simmer, covered, 10 minutes.

3. Heat soup to boiling; add pasta to saucepan. Reduce heat and simmer, uncovered, until pasta is *al dente*, 10 to 12 minutes. Stir in pepper.

4. Spoon soup into bowls; sprinkle with cheese. Serve immediately.

TWO-BEAN AND PASTA SOUP

 This substantial soup thickens upon standing; thin with additional stock or water, if necessary.

6 main-dish servings (about 2 cups each)

Vegetable cooking spray
1½ cups cubed carrots
1 medium green bell pepper, chopped
½ cup sliced green onions and tops
3 cloves garlic, minced
2 teaspoons dried basil leaves
2 teaspoons dried oregano leaves
4 cups Basic Vegetable Stock (see p. 58)
1 cup water
1 can (15 ounces) no-salt-added stewed tomatoes
1 can (15 ounces) cannellini, *or* Great Northern, beans, rinsed, drained
1 can (15 ounces) fava, *or* pinto, beans, rinsed, drained
1½ cups (4 ounces) rigatoni, uncooked
2-3 teaspoons lemon juice
¼ teaspoon salt
½ teaspoon pepper

Per Serving
Calories: 225
% Calories from fat: 7
Fat (gm): 2
Saturated fat (gm): 0
Cholesterol (mg): 0
Sodium (mg): 522
Protein (gm): 13.6
Carbohydrate (gm): 45.7
Exchanges
Milk: 0.0
Vegetable: 2.0
Fruit: 0.0
Bread: 2.5
Meat: 0.0
Fat: 0.0

1. Spray large saucepan with cooking spray; saute carrots, bell pepper, onions, and garlic until vegetables are tender, about 7 minutes. Stir in basil and oregano; cook 1 to 2 minutes.

2. Add stock, water, tomatoes, and both beans to saucepan; heat to boiling. Reduce heat and simmer, covered, 10 minutes.

3. Heat soup to boiling; add pasta to saucepan. Reduce heat and simmer, uncovered, until pasta is *al dente*, 12 to 15 minutes. Season with lemon juice, salt, and pepper. Serve immediately.

"MEATBALL" AND VEGETABLE SOUP

Made with one of the new-flavored prebrowned all-vegetable burger crumbles, or soy for recipes products, the "meatballs" are seasoned with Italian herbs and fennel.

8 main-dish servings (about 2½ cups each)

8 ounces winter squash, seeded, cut into scant ¾-inch cubes (Hubbard, acorn, butternut)

¾ cup chopped onion

2 cloves garlic, minced

1 tablespoon extra-virgin olive oil

5 cups Basic Vegetable Stock (see p. 58)

1 can (15 ounces) garbanzo beans, rinsed, drained

1 can (16 ounces) reduced-sodium diced tomatoes, undrained

1 cup frozen peas

1 teaspoon Italian seasoning
Italian-Style "Meatballs" (see p. 399)

4 ounces ditalini, *or* fusilli
Salt and pepper, to taste
Basil, *or* parsley, finely chopped, as garnish

Per Serving
Calories: 269
% Calories from fat: 16
Fat (gm): 5
Saturated fat (gm): 0.9
Cholesterol (mg): 53.3
Sodium (mg): 527
Protein (gm): 18.8
Carbohydrate (gm): 38.3
Exchanges
Milk: 0.0
Vegetable: 1.0
Fruit: 0.0
Bread: 2.0
Meat: 2.0
Fat: 0.0

1. Saute squash, onion, and garlic in oil in Dutch oven until onion is tender, about 5 minutes. Add stock, beans, tomatoes with liquid, peas, and Italian seasoning; heat to boiling. Reduce heat and simmer, covered, 10 minutes.

2. Heat soup to boiling; add meatballs and pasta. Reduce heat and simmer, uncovered, until pasta is tender, 7 to 10 minutes. Season to taste with salt and pepper.

3. Pour soup into bowls; sprinkle with basil.

CHILI *SIN* CARNE

For a Southwest version of this chili, substitute black or pinto beans for the kidney beans and add 1 minced jalapeño chili. Garnish each serving with a sprinkling of finely chopped cilantro leaves.

6 main-dish servings (about 1⅓ cups each)

Vegetable cooking spray
⅔ package (12-ounce size) frozen pre-browned all-vegetable protein crumbles
1½ cups chopped onions
1 cup chopped green bell pepper
2 cloves garlic, minced
1-2 tablespoons chili powder
2 teaspoons ground cumin
1 teaspoon dried oregano leaves
¼ teaspoon ground cloves
2 cans (14½ ounces each) no-salt-added whole tomatoes, undrained, coarsely chopped
1 can (6 ounces) reduced-sodium tomato paste
¾ cup beer, *or* water
1 tablespoon packed light brown sugar
2-3 teaspoons unsweetened cocoa
1 can (15 ounces) red kidney beans, rinsed, drained
Salt and pepper, to taste
½ cup (2 ounces) shredded fat-free, *or* reduced-fat, Cheddar cheese
½ cup thinly sliced green onions and tops
½ cup fat-free, *or* reduced-fat, sour cream

Per Serving
Calories: 255
% Calories from fat: 5
Fat (gm): 1.7
Saturated fat (gm): 0.1
Cholesterol (mg): 0
Sodium (mg): 436
Protein (gm): 22.5
Carbohydrate (gm): 43.5
Exchanges
Milk: 0.0
Vegetable: 4.0
Fruit: 0.0
Bread: 1.0
Meat: 1.5
Fat: 0.0

1. Spray large saucepan with cooking spray; heat over medium heat until hot. Add vegetable protein crumbles, onions, bell pepper, and garlic; cook over medium heat until vegetables are tender, 5 to 8 minutes. Add chili powder, cumin, oregano, and cloves; cook 1 to 2 minutes longer.

2. Add tomatoes, tomato paste, beer, brown sugar, and cocoa to soup mixture. Heat to boiling; reduce heat and simmer, covered, 1 hour. Stir in beans and simmer, uncovered, to thicken, if desired. Season to taste with salt and pepper.

3. Spoon chili into bowls; sprinkle each with 1 tablespoon cheese, green onions, and sour cream.

Variation: **Chili Mac:** In step 2, add 1 cup uncooked elbow macaroni, *or* chili mac pasta, and ½ cup water to chili after 45 minutes cooking time; heat to boiling. Reduce heat and simmer, covered, until macaroni is tender, about 15 minutes; stir in beans and simmer 5 minutes longer.

CLASSIC BLACK BEAN SOUP

Dried beans can also be "quick cooked" rather than soaked over-night before cooking. Place beans in a large saucepan and cover with 2 inches of water; heat to boiling and boil 2 minutes. Remove from heat and let stand 1 hour; drain and continue with step 2 in the recipe below. Or, substitute three cans (15 ounces each) of rinsed and drained black beans for the dried.

4 main-dish servings (about 1¼ cups each)

1½	cups dried black beans
	Vegetable cooking spray
1	large onion, chopped
4	cloves garlic, minced
1	tomato, chopped
1	teaspoon dried oregano leaves
½	teaspoon dried thyme leaves
	Salt and pepper, to taste
4-6	tablespoons fat-free sour cream
	Oregano or parsley, finely chopped, as garnish

Per Serving
Calories: 289
% Calories from fat: 4
Fat (gm): 1.3
Saturated fat (gm): 0.3
Cholesterol (mg): 0
Sodium (mg): 23
Protein (gm): 18.1
Carbohydrate (gm): 53.7
Exchanges
Milk: 0.0
Vegetable: 1.0
Fruit: 0.0
Bread: 3.0
Meat: 1.0
Fat: 0.0

1. Wash and sort beans, discarding any stones. Cover beans with 4 inches of water in a large saucepan; soak overnight and drain.

2. Spray large saucepan with cooking spray; heat over medium heat until hot. Saute onion and garlic 2 to 3 minutes; add tomato and herbs and cook 2 to 3 minutes longer. Add beans to saucepan; cover with 2 inches of water and heat to boiling. Reduce heat and simmer, covered, until beans are very tender, 1½ to 2 hours, adding water to cover beans if necessary. Drain mixture, reserving liquid.

3. Process bean mixture in food processor or blender until smooth, adding enough reserved cooking liquid to make desired consistency. Return soup to saucepan; heat over medium heat until hot through, 3 to 4 minutes. Season to taste with salt and pepper.

4. Serve soup in bowls; top each with a dollop of sour cream and sprinkle with oregano or parsley.

VEGETABLE SOUP WITH ORZO

 Escarole, which lends a unique taste to this hearty soup, is also a flavorful addition to green salads. Spinach leaves can be substituted for the escarole in this recipe, if desired.

4 main-dish servings (about 2 cups each)

Olive oil cooking spray
1 medium onion, coarsely chopped
2 medium carrots, sliced
2 medium ribs celery, sliced
3 cloves garlic, minced
2 medium zucchini, *or* summer yellow squash, sliced
1 cup sliced mushrooms
½ teaspoon dried thyme leaves
½ teaspoon dried oregano leaves
5 cups Canned Vegetable Stock (see p. 63)
½ cup (4 ounces) orzo, uncooked
½ cup frozen peas
6 medium leaves escarole, sliced or coarsely chopped
¼ teaspoon salt
½ teaspoon pepper
2 tablespoons grated Romano cheese

Per Serving
Calories: 265
% Calories from fat: 10
Fat (gm): 2.9
Saturated fat (gm): 0.9
Cholesterol (mg): 3.6
Sodium (mg): 298
Protein (gm): 9.1
Carbohydrate (gm): 44.3
Exchanges
Milk: 0.0
Vegetable: 3.0
Fruit: 0.0
Bread: 2.0
Meat: 0.0
Fat: 1.0

1. Spray large saucepan with cooking spray; heat over medium heat until hot. Saute onion, carrots, celery, and garlic in saucepan until onion is tender, about 5 minutes. Add zucchini, mushrooms, and herbs; cook, covered, 2 to 3 minutes.

2. Add stock to saucepan; heat to boiling. Stir in orzo, peas, and escarole. Reduce heat and simmer, uncovered, until orzo is *al dente*, about 7 minutes. Season with salt and pepper. Spoon soup into bowls; sprinkle with cheese.

ALSATIAN PEASANT SOUP

Root vegetables, cabbage, and beans combine for a robust soup that is almost a stew. Serve with a crusty rye bread and a good beer.

6 main-dish servings (about 1½ cups each)

½ cup chopped onion
½ cup sliced celery
1 tablespoon olive oil
1 large potato, unpeeled, cubed
1 cup peeled, cubed parsnip, *or* turnip
¾ cup sliced carrots
1 teaspoon dried thyme leaves
½ teaspoon crushed caraway seeds
1 bay leaf
3 cups Mediterranean, *or* Basic Vegetable, Stock (see pp. 60, 58)
2 cups thinly sliced cabbage
2 cans (15 ounces each) Great Northern beans, rinsed, drained
Salt and pepper, to taste
¾ cup (3 ounces) shredded reduced-fat Swiss cheese
1½ cups Rye Croutons (½ recipe, see p. 677)

Per Serving
Calories: 331
% Calories from fat: 17
Fat (gm): 6.5
Saturated fat (gm): 2.2
Cholesterol (mg): 10.1
Sodium (mg): 119
Protein (gm): 18
Carbohydrate (gm): 50.1
Exchanges
Milk: 0.0
Vegetable: 2.0
Fruit: 0.0
Bread: 2.5
Meat: 1.0
Fat: 1.0

1. Saute onion and celery in oil in large saucepan until tender, about 5 minutes. Add potatoes, parsnip, carrots, thyme, caraway, and bay leaf; cook over medium heat 5 minutes.

2. Add stock, cabbage, and beans to saucepan; heat to boiling. Reduce heat and simmer, covered, until vegetables are tender, 10 to 15 minutes. Discard bay leaf; season to taste with salt and pepper.

3. Pour soup into bowls; sprinkle each with 2 tablespoons shredded cheese and Rye Croutons.

FOUR-BEAN AND VEGETABLE SOUP

Any kind of dried beans can be used in the soup, or use prepackaged mixed dried beans.

12 main-dish servings (about 1½ cups each)

8 ounces dried black beans
8 ounces dried navy beans
8 ounces dried pinto beans
8 ounces dried garbanzo beans
Water
2 cups chopped green bell pepper
1 cup chopped onion
6-8 cloves garlic, minced
2 tablespoons olive oil
6 cups Roasted Vegetable Stock (see p. 59)
2-3 teaspoons dried thyme leaves
3 bay leaves
2 cans (16 ounces each) reduced-sodium diced tomatoes, undrained
2 cups sliced carrots
2 cups green beans, cut into 2-inch pieces
Salt, cayenne, and black pepper, to taste

Per Serving
Calories: 342
% Calories from fat: 11
Fat (gm): 4.3
Saturated fat (gm): 0.5
Cholesterol (mg): 0
Sodium (mg): 35
Protein (gm): 18.1
Carbohydrate (gm): 58.5
Exchanges
Milk: 0.0
Vegetable: 3.0
Fruit: 0.0
Bread: 3.0
Meat: 1.0
Fat: 0.0

1. Cover beans with water in large saucepan; heat to boiling. Remove pan from heat; let stand 1 hour. Drain.

2. Saute bell pepper, onion, and garlic in oil in Dutch oven until tender, 4 to 5 minutes. Add beans, stock, and herbs to pan; heat to boiling. Reduce heat and simmer, covered, until beans are tender (add water if necessary), 1 to 1½ hours, adding tomatoes with liquid, carrots, and green beans during last 15 to 20 minutes of cooking time. Discard bay leaves; season to taste with salt and cayenne and black pepper.

TUSCAN BEAN SOUP

 A hearty bean soup, savory with sage, rosemary, and thyme.

8 main-dish servings (about 1½ cups each)

1 cup chopped onion
½ cup sliced celery
½ cup chopped green bell pepper
2 teaspoons minced roasted garlic
2 tablespoons olive oil
1 tablespoon flour
¾-1 teaspoon dried rosemary leaves
½ teaspoon dried sage leaves
¼ teaspoon dried thyme leaves
2 bay leaves
7 cups Mediterranean, *or* Roasted Vegetable, Stock (see pp. 60, 59)
2 cans (15 ounces each) cannellini, *or* Great Northern, beans, rinsed, drained
2 tablespoons reduced-sodium tomato paste
½ cup quick-cooking barley
1 large Idaho potato, unpeeled, cut into ½-inch pieces
1 cup sliced carrots
1 cup packed sliced spinach leaves
Salt and pepper, to taste

Per Serving
Calories: 233
% Calories from fat: 18
Fat (gm): 5.6
Saturated fat (gm): 0.7
Cholesterol (mg): 0
Sodium (mg): 245
Protein (gm): 10.7
Carbohydrate (gm): 40.8
Exchanges
Milk: 0.0
Vegetable: 2.0
Fruit: 0.0
Bread: 2.0
Meat: 0.0
Fat: 1.0

1. Saute onion, celery, bell pepper, and garlic in oil in Dutch oven until tender, about 5 minutes. Add flour and herbs; cook 1 to 2 minutes longer.

2. Add stock, beans, and tomato paste to Dutch oven; heat to boiling. Reduce heat and simmer, uncovered, 20 to 25 minutes, adding barley, potatoes, carrots, and spinach during last 10 minutes of cooking time. Discard bay leaves. Season to taste with salt and pepper.

NAVY BEAN SOUP

A quick-soak method is used for the beans. If you prefer soaking the beans overnight, delete step 1 and proceed with step 2 in the recipe.

6 main-dish servings (about 1¾ cups each)

8 ounces dried navy, *or* Great Northern, beans, washed and sorted
Water
⅔ cup chopped onion
⅔ cup chopped carrot
1 rib celery, thinly sliced
2 cloves garlic, minced
1 tablespoon canola oil
1 tablespoon flour
4 cups Canned Vegetable Stock, *or* Basic Vegetable Stock (see pp. 63, 58)
1 cup water
¼ teaspoon dried thyme leaves
1 bay leaf
Salt and pepper, to taste

Per Serving
Calories: 312
% Calories from fat: 14
Fat (gm): 5.1
Saturated fat (gm): 0.8
Cholesterol (mg): 0
Sodium (mg): 79
Protein (gm): 14.3
Carbohydrate (gm): 47.8
Exchanges
Milk: 0.0
Vegetable: 1.0
Fruit: 0.0
Bread: 3.0
Meat: 1.0
Fat: 0.5

1. Cover beans with 2 inches of water in large saucepan; heat to boiling and boil, uncovered, 2 minutes. Remove from heat and let stand, covered, 1 hour; drain.

2. Saute onion, carrot, celery, and garlic in oil in large saucepan until vegetables are tender, 5 to 8 minutes. Stir in flour; cook over medium heat 1 minute.

3. Add beans, stock, water, and herbs to saucepan; heat to boiling. Reduce heat and simmer, covered, until beans are tender, 1¼ to 1½ hours. Discard bay leaf; season to taste with salt and pepper.

BEAN-THICKENED SOUP

 This soup is very quick and easy to make. The pureed beans contribute a hearty but not too thick texture and subtle flavor.

4 first-course servings (about 1⅓ cups each)

Vegetable cooking spray
2 carrots, sliced
1 small onion, chopped
2 large cloves garlic, minced
1¾ cups Basic Vegetable Stock (see p. 58)
1 can (16 ounces) whole tomatoes, undrained, coarsely chopped
1 can (15 ounces) Great Northern beans, rinsed, drained, pureed
¼-½ teaspoon dried thyme leaves
½-¾ teaspoon dried sage leaves
Salt and pepper, to taste
Parsley, minced, as garnish

Per Serving
Calories: 176
% Calories from fat: 5
Fat (gm): 1
Saturated fat (gm): 0.2
Cholesterol (mg): 0
Sodium (mg): 208
Protein (gm): 9.8
Carbohydrate (gm): 34
Exchanges
Milk: 0.0
Vegetable: 2.0
Fruit: 0.0
Bread: 1.5
Meat: 0.5
Fat: 0.0

1. Spray large saucepan with cooking spray; heat over medium heat until hot. Saute carrots, onion, and garlic until onion is tender, about 5 minutes. Stir in stock, tomatoes with liquid, pureed beans, and herbs. Heat to boiling; reduce heat and simmer, covered, until carrots are tender, about 10 minutes. Season to taste with salt and pepper.

2. Pour soup into bowls; sprinkle with parsley.

BLACK BEAN SOUP WITH SUN-DRIED TOMATOES AND CILANTRO CREAM

 Cilantro Cream adds a fresh accent to this South-of-the-Border favorite.

4 main-dish servings (about 1½ cups each)

¾ cup sun-dried tomatoes (not in oil)
1¼ cups boiling water
    Vegetable cooking spray
1 cup chopped onion
2 cloves garlic, minced
1 jalapeño chili, minced
3 cups Basic Vegetable Stock (see p. 58)
3 cups cooked dried black beans, *or* 2 cans (15 ounces each) black beans, rinsed, drained
¾ teaspoon ground cumin
½ teaspoon dried oregano leaves
¼-½ teaspoon hot pepper sauce
    Salt and pepper, to taste
¼ cup finely chopped cilantro
    Cilantro Cream (recipe follows)

Per Serving
Calories: 239
% Calories from fat: 5
Fat (gm): 1.5
Saturated fat (gm): 0.3
Cholesterol (mg): 0
Sodium (mg): 256
Protein (gm): 15.2
Carbohydrate (gm): 44.0
Exchanges
Milk: 0.0
Vegetable: 1.0
Fruit: 0.0
Bread: 3.0
Meat: 0.0
Fat: 0.0

1. Combine sun-dried tomatoes and boiling water in bowl; let stand until softened, about 10 minutes.

2. Spray large saucepan with cooking spray; heat over medium heat until hot. Saute onion, garlic, and jalapeño chili until tender, 5 to 8 minutes. Add stock, beans, cumin, oregano, and sun-dried tomatoes with liquid to saucepan; heat to boiling. Reduce heat and simmer, covered, 10 minutes. Season to taste with hot pepper sauce, salt, and pepper; stir in cilantro.

3. Process soup in food processor or blender until smooth. Pour into bowls; garnish with dollops of Cilantro Cream.

Cilantro Cream

(makes about ⅓ cup)

⅓ cup fat-free sour cream
2 tablespoons minced cilantro
1 teaspoon lemon, *or* lime, juice
¾ teaspoon ground coriander
2-3 dashes white pepper

1. Mix all ingredients; refrigerate until serving time.

CANNELLINI AND CABBAGE SOUP

Tuscany is known for its dishes with white cannellini beans. Cannellini beans are available in specialty sections of supermarkets or in Italian markets; canned Great Northern beans may be substituted.

4 main-dish servings (about 2 cups each)

Vegetable cooking spray
3 cups thinly sliced, *or* chopped, cabbage
1 small onion, coarsely chopped
3 cloves garlic, minced
1 teaspoon caraway seeds, crushed
5 cups Basic Vegetable Stock (see p. 58)
1 can (15 ounces) cannellini, *or* Great Northern, beans, rinsed, drained
½ cup (4 ounces) mostaccioli (penne), uncooked
¼ teaspoon salt (optional)
¼ teaspoon pepper

Per Serving
Calories: 226
% Calories from fat: 7
Fat (gm): 2
Saturated fat (gm): 0.1
Cholesterol (mg): 0
Sodium (mg): 234
Protein (gm): 12.9
Carbohydrate (gm): 47.8
Exchanges
Milk: 0.0
Vegetable: 2.0
Fruit: 0.0
Bread: 2.5
Meat: 0.0
Fat: 0.0

1. Spray large saucepan with cooking spray; heat over medium heat until hot. Saute cabbage, onions, garlic, and caraway seeds until cabbage begins to wilt, 8 to 10 minutes.

2. Add stock and beans to saucepan; heat to boiling. Stir in pasta; reduce heat and simmer, uncovered, until pasta is *al dente*, about 15 minutes. Stir in salt and pepper.

GARBANZO BEAN SOUP

 Cumin adds a Mexican flavor to this soup; curry powder can be substituted for a Mediterranean flavor.

4 main-dish servings (about 1⅓ cups each)

Vegetable cooking spray
2 medium onions, chopped
2 cloves garlic, minced
2 cans (15¼ ounces each) garbanzo beans, rinsed, drained
4 cups Basic Vegetable Stock, *or* Mediterranean Stock (see pp. 58, 60)
1 teaspoon ground cumin
½-¾ teaspoon dried thyme leaves
Salt and pepper, to taste
¼ cup fat-free sour cream
Paprika, *or* chili powder, as garnish

Per Serving
Calories: 267
% Calories from fat: 15
Fat (gm): 4.6
Saturated fat (gm): 0.6
Cholesterol (mg): 0
Sodium (mg): 627
Protein (gm): 12.4
Carbohydrate (gm): 46.4
Exchanges
Milk: 0.0
Vegetable: 1.0
Fruit: 0.0
Bread: 3.0
Meat: 0.0
Fat: 0.0

1. Spray large saucepan with cooking spray; heat over medium heat until hot. Saute onions and garlic until tender, about 5 minutes. Process onion mixture, garbanzo beans, and 2 cups stock in food processor or blender until smooth.

2. Return mixture to saucepan; add remaining stock, cumin, and thyme and heat to boiling. Reduce heat and simmer, covered, 5 minutes. Season to taste with salt and pepper.

3. Serve soup in bowls; top with dollops of sour cream and sprinkle with paprika.

CHICK PEA AND PASTA SOUP

Many fresh garden vegetables can be substituted for the zucchini and celery in this soup: carrots, cauliflower, broccoli florets, mushrooms, peas, and green beans are possible choices.

4 main-dish servings (about 1¾ cups each)

Olive oil cooking spray
1 small zucchini, cubed
2 ribs celery, thinly sliced
1 medium onion, chopped
3-4 cloves garlic, minced
1 teaspoon dried rosemary leaves
1 teaspoon dried thyme leaves
⅛ teaspoon dried crushed red pepper
4 cups Canned Vegetable Stock, *or* Basic Vegetable Stock (see p. 63, 58)
1 can (15 ounces) no-salt-added stewed tomatoes
1 can (15 ounces) chick peas, rinsed, drained
1 cup (4 ounces) farfalle (bow ties), uncooked
2 tablespoons finely chopped parsley
2-3 teaspoons lemon juice

Per Serving
Calories: 322
% Calories from fat: 10
Fat (gm): 3.7
Saturated fat (gm): 0.5
Cholesterol (mg): 0
Sodium (mg): 514
Protein (gm): 11.5
Carbohydrate (gm): 56.4
Exchanges
Milk: 0.0
Vegetable: 3.0
Fruit: 0.0
Bread: 3.0
Meat: 0.0
Fat: 0.5

1. Spray bottom of large saucepan with cooking spray. Saute zucchini, celery, onions, and garlic until zucchini is crisp-tender, about 8 minutes. Stir in herbs and red pepper; cook 1 to 2 minutes.

2. Add stock, tomatoes, and chick peas; heat to boiling. Reduce heat and simmer, covered, 10 minutes.

3. Heat soup to boiling; add pasta to saucepan. Reduce heat and simmer, uncovered, until pasta is *al dente*, about 8 minutes. Stir in parsley; season with lemon juice.

COUNTRY LENTIL SOUP

 A light soup, yet wholesome in flavor and texture. This soup freezes well, so make extra.

4 main-dish servings (about 1¾ cups each)

1½ cups chopped onions
1 cup sliced celery
1 cup sliced carrots
2 teaspoons minced garlic
1 tablespoon olive oil
3 cups Roasted Vegetable Stock (see p. 59)
2 cups water
1 cup dried lentils, washed, sorted
1 can (14½ ounces) reduced-sodium whole tomatoes, undrained, crushed
2 tablespoons finely chopped parsley
1 teaspoon dried marjoram leaves
½ teaspoon dried oregano leaves
¼ teaspoon dried thyme leaves
   Salt and pepper, to taste
4 tablespoons grated fat-free Parmesan cheese

Per Serving
Calories: 275
% Calories from fat: 14
Fat (gm): 4.4
Saturated fat (gm): 0.6
Cholesterol (mg): 0
Sodium (mg): 109
Protein (gm): 15.8
Carbohydrate (gm): 42.8
Exchanges
Milk: 0.0
Vegetable: 3.0
Fruit: 0.0
Bread: 2.0
Meat: 0.5
Fat: 0.5

1. Saute onions, celery, carrots, and garlic in oil in Dutch oven 5 to 8 minutes. Add Roasted Vegetable Stock, water, lentils, tomatoes, and herbs; heat to boiling. Reduce heat and simmer, covered, until lentils are tender, about 30 minutes. Season to taste with salt and pepper.

2. Pour soup into bowls; sprinkle each with 1 tablespoon Parmesan cheese.

INDIAN LENTIL SOUP

This soup (Dal Shorba) from India is flavored with curry powder and sweet coriander. Red, green, or brown lentils can be used.

6 main-dish servings (about 1⅓ cups each)

½ cup chopped onion

1 clove garlic

2 teaspoons curry powder

1 teaspoon crushed coriander seeds

1 teaspoon crushed cumin seeds

½ teaspoon ground turmeric

¼ teaspoon crushed red pepper flakes

1 tablespoon olive oil

5 cups Basic Vegetable Stock (see p. 58)

4 cups water

2 cups dried red, *or* brown, lentils, sorted, rinsed

Salt and pepper, to taste

6 tablespoons fat-free plain yogurt

Per Serving
Calories: 280
% Calories from fat: 11
Fat (gm): 3.6
Saturated fat (gm): 0.5
Cholesterol (mg): 0.3
Sodium (mg): 26
Protein (gm): 19.4
Carbohydrate (gm): 44.7
Exchanges
Milk: 0.0
Vegetable: 1.0
Fruit: 0.0
Bread: 2.5
Meat: 1.5
Fat: 0.0

1. Saute onion, garlic, herbs, and red pepper in oil in large saucepan until onion is tender, about 5 minutes, stirring frequently. Add stock, water, and lentils; heat to boiling. Reduce heat and simmer, covered, until lentils are tender, about 30 minutes. Season to taste with salt and pepper.

2. Pour soup into bowls; garnish each with a tablespoon of yogurt.

SPLIT PEA SOUP

A perfect main-dish soup for hearty appetites on a crisp autumn or winter day. Serve with thick slices of Garlic Bread (see p. 676).

6 main-dish servings (about 1⅓ cups each)

1½ cups chopped onions
1 cup chopped carrots
½ cup sliced celery
1 tablespoon canola oil
6 cups water
1¾ cups Canned Vegetable Stock, *or* Basic Vegetable Stock (see pp. 63, 58)
1 pound dried split peas, washed and sorted
1-2 teaspoons vegetable bouillon crystals (optional)
1 teaspoon dried marjoram leaves
Salt and pepper, to taste

Per Serving
Calories: 321
% Calories from fat: 10
Fat (gm): 3.5
Saturated fat (gm): 0.5
Cholesterol (mg): 0
Sodium (mg): 44
Protein (gm): 19.6
Carbohydrate (gm): 53.4
Exchanges
Milk: 0.0
Vegetable: 1.0
Fruit: 0.0
Bread: 3.0
Meat: 1.5
Fat: 0.0

1. Saute onions, carrots, and celery in oil in large saucepan until tender, 8 to 10 minutes. Add water, stock, split peas, bouillon crystals if used, and marjoram; heat to boiling. Reduce heat and simmer, covered, until peas are tender, 1 to 1¼ hours. Season to taste with salt and pepper.

THREE

Stews

AND

Casseroles

BEAN-THICKENED VEGETABLE STEW

Pureed beans provide the perfect thickening for the stew.

6 servings (about 1¼ cups each)

Vegetable cooking spray
3 carrots, sliced
1 medium onion, chopped
3 cloves garlic, minced
1¾ cups Basic Vegetable Stock (see p. 58)
2 cups chopped tomatoes
1½ cups sliced mushrooms
1 yellow summer squash, sliced
1 can (15 ounces) black beans, rinsed, drained
1 can (15 ounces) navy beans, rinsed, drained, pureed
1 cup frozen peas
¾ teaspoon dried thyme leaves
½ teaspoon dried oregano leaves
2 bay leaves
Salt and pepper, to taste
4 cups cooked noodles, warm
Green onions and tops, chopped, as garnish

Per Serving
Calories: 348
% Calories from fat: 5
Fat (gm): 1.9
Saturated fat (gm): 0.2
Cholesterol (mg): 0
Sodium (mg): 589
Protein (gm): 18.3
Carbohydrate (gm): 71.8
Exchanges
Milk: 0.0
Vegetable: 2.0
Fruit: 0.0
Bread: 4.0
Meat: 0.0
Fat: 0.0

1. Spray large saucepan with cooking spray; heat over medium heat until hot. Saute carrots, onion, and garlic until tender, about 5 minutes.

2. Stir in stock, tomatoes, mushrooms, squash, black beans, navy bean puree, peas, and herbs; heat to boiling. Reduce heat and simmer, uncovered, until vegetables are tender, 10 to 15 minutes. Discard bay leaves; season to taste with salt and pepper.

3. Spoon stew over noodles in shallow bowls; sprinkle with green onions.

HASTY STEW

Many vegetable stews are long-simmered to attain their goodness. This stew is easily made in less than 30 minutes and boasts fresh flavors and textures.

4 servings (about 1 cup each)

Vegetable cooking spray
2 medium onions, cut into wedges
8 ounces mushrooms, sliced
2 cloves garlic, minced
¼ cup finely chopped parsley leaves
1 teaspoon dried savory leaves
1 bay leaf
2 medium zucchini, sliced
¾ pound potatoes, unpeeled, cubed
8 ounces cauliflower florets
2 cans (14½ ounces each) vegetable broth
1 large tomato, cut into wedges
Salt and pepper, to taste
3 cups cooked millet, *or* couscous, warm

Per Serving
Calories: 404
% Calories from fat: 6
Fat (gm): 2.6
Saturated fat (gm): 0.4
Cholesterol (mg): 0
Sodium (mg): 116
Protein (gm): 13.4
Carbohydrate (gm): 84.6
Exchanges
Milk: 0.0
Vegetable: 3.0
Fruit: 0.0
Bread: 4.5
Meat: 0.0
Fat: 0.0

1. Spray large saucepan with vegetable cooking spray; place over medium heat until hot. Saute onions, mushrooms, garlic, and herbs until onions are tender, about 5 minutes.

2. Add vegetables (except tomatoes) and broth to saucepan; heat to boiling. Reduce heat and simmer, covered, until cauliflower is tender, about 10 minutes. Add tomato during last 5 minutes of cooking time. Season to taste with salt and pepper; discard bay leaf. Serve with millet.

CREAMY VEGETABLE AND "BURGER" STROGANOFF

 Fat-free half-and-half and sour cream contribute a wonderful rich flavor and creamy texture.

8 servings (about 1 cup each)

Vegetable cooking spray
2 medium onions, thinly sliced
12 ounces mixed wild mushrooms (shiitake, oyster, enoki, or cremini), sliced
2 cloves garlic, minced
¼ cup dry red wine, *or* Canned Vegetable Stock (see p. 63)
12 ounces broccoli florets and sliced stalks
1 package (9 ounces) frozen vegetable protein "burgers," thawed, crumbled
1 cup fat-free half-and-half, *or* fat-free milk
2 tablespoons flour
1½ teaspoons Dijon-style mustard
1 cup fat-free sour cream
½ teaspoon dried dill weed
Salt and white pepper, to taste
16 ounces noodles, cooked, warm

Per Serving
Calories: 352
% Calories from fat: 8
Fat (gm): 3.3
Saturated fat (gm): 0.5
Cholesterol (mg): 0
Sodium (mg): 283
Protein (gm): 15.2
Carbohydrate (gm): 66
Exchanges
Milk: 0.0
Vegetable: 2.0
Fruit: 0.0
Bread: 3.5
Meat: 1.0
Fat: 0.0

1. Spray large skillet with cooking spray; heat over medium heat until hot. Saute onions, mushrooms, and garlic until softened, about 5 minutes. Add wine, broccoli, and vegetable protein patties; heat to boiling. Reduce heat and simmer, covered, until broccoli is tender, 8 to 10 minutes.

2. Mix half-and-half, flour, and mustard; stir into vegetables. Heat to boiling; boil, stirring constantly, until thickened. Reduce heat to low; stir in sour cream and dill weed and cook 1 to 2 minutes longer. Season to taste with salt and white pepper. Serve over noodles.

VEGGIE STEW WITH DUMPLINGS

 Dumplings, soft, fluffy, and seasoned with herbs, top this colorful stew.

6 servings (about 1½ cups each)

1	cup coarsely chopped onion
1	large red bell pepper, sliced
1	rib celery, sliced
1	tablespoon canola oil
3⅔	cups Basic Vegetable Stock (see p. 58), divided
⅓	cup all-purpose flour
3	medium potatoes, unpeeled, cut into 1-inch pieces
2	cups cubed yellow winter squash (butternut or acorn)
1	medium zucchini, sliced
4	ounces halved cremini, *or* white, mushrooms
¾	cup frozen peas
1	teaspoon dried basil leaves
½	teaspoon dried oregano leaves
¼	teaspoon dried thyme leaves
	Salt and pepper, to taste
	Herb Dumplings (recipe follows)

Per Serving
Calories: 328
% Calories from fat: 13
Fat (gm): 5
Saturated fat (gm): 0.4
Cholesterol (mg): 0.4
Sodium (mg): 697
Protein (gm): 9.8
Carbohydrate (gm): 63.6
Exchanges
Milk: 0.0
Vegetable: 3.0
Fruit: 0.0
Bread: 3.0
Meat: 0.0
Fat: 1.0

1. Saute onion, bell pepper, and celery in oil in large saucepan until onion is tender, about 5 minutes. Stir in 3 cups stock; heat to boiling. Mix remaining ⅔ cup stock and flour; stir into boiling mixture. Boil, stirring constantly, until thickened, about 1 minute.

2. Stir potatoes, squash, zucchini, mushrooms, peas, and herbs into stew. Simmer, covered, until vegetables are tender, 10 to 15 minutes. Season to taste with salt and pepper.

3. Spoon dumpling mixture on top of stew in 6 large spoonfuls; cook over low heat, uncovered, 10 minutes. Cook, covered, 10 minutes longer or until dumplings are tender and toothpick inserted in center comes out clean. Serve in bowls.

Herb Dumplings

(makes 6)

>   2 cups reduced-fat baking mix
>   ½ teaspoon dried basil leaves
>   ¼ teaspoon dried oregano leaves
>   ⅛ teaspoon dried thyme leaves
>   ⅔ cup fat-free milk

1.   Combine biscuit mix and herbs in small bowl; stir in milk to form soft dough. Cook as directed in recipe.

VEGGIE MÉLANGE WITH BULGUR

Bulgur is a nutritious addition, and it also thickens this stew. Serve with warm, crusty Italian bread.

4 servings (about 1⅔ cups each)

>   ¾ cup boiling water
>   ½ cup uncooked bulgur
>   Vegetable cooking spray
>   2 medium onions, coarsely chopped
>   2 cups carrots, cut into 1-inch pieces
>   1 cup Idaho potatoes, unpeeled, cut into
>   1-inch pieces
>   1 red bell pepper, cut into 1-inch pieces
>   1 green bell pepper, cut into 1-inch pieces
>   2-3 cloves garlic, minced
>   1 can (14½ ounces) reduced-sodium
>   tomato wedges, undrained
>   2-3 cups spicy tomato juice
>   2 medium zucchini, cubed
>   1 medium yellow summer squash, cubed
>   2 cups halved cremini, *or* white, mush-
>   rooms
>   1½ teaspoons dried thyme leaves
>   1 teaspoon dried oregano leaves
>   Salt and pepper, to taste

Per Serving
Calories: 259
% Calories from fat: 5
Fat (gm): 1.4
Saturated fat (gm): 0.2
Cholesterol (mg): 0
Sodium (mg): 694
Protein (gm): 9.9
Carbohydrate (gm): 57.4
Exchanges
Milk: 0.0
Vegetable: 5.0
Fruit: 0.0
Bread: 2.0
Meat: 0.0
Fat: 0.0

1. Stir boiling water into bulgur in bowl; let stand until bulgur is softened, about 20 minutes.

2. Spray Dutch oven or large saucepan with cooking spray; heat over medium heat until hot. Saute onions, carrots, potatoes, bell peppers, and garlic until onions are tender, 8 to 10 minutes.

3. Add bulgur and remaining ingredients, except salt and pepper, to Dutch oven; heat to boiling. Reduce heat and simmer, uncovered, until vegetables are tender and stew is thickened, 10 to 15 minutes. Season to taste with salt and pepper. Serve in bowls.

CABBAGE RAGOUT WITH REAL MASHED POTATOES

Fresh fennel, gingerroot, and apple lend aromatic flavor highlights to this cabbage stew. If fresh fennel is not available, substitute celery and increase the amount of fennel seeds to 1½ teaspoons.

6 servings (about 1⅓ cups each)

Vegetable cooking spray

1 medium eggplant (about 1¼ pounds), unpeeled, cut into scant 1-inch slices

1 cup chopped onion

½ cup thinly sliced fennel

3 cloves garlic, minced

4 teaspoons minced gingerroot

1 teaspoon fennel seeds, crushed

8 cups thinly sliced cabbage

2 cups Basic Vegetable Stock (see p. 58)

2 medium apples, cored, cubed

1 cup fat-free sour cream

Salt and pepper, to taste

Fennel tops, chopped, as garnish

Real Mashed Potatoes (see p. 610), *or* 4 cups cooked no-yolk noodles

Per Serving
Calories: 283
% Calories from fat: 14
Fat (gm): 4.7
Saturated fat (gm): 0.9
Cholesterol (mg): 0.2
Sodium (mg): 124
Protein (gm): 9.3
Carbohydrate (gm): 55.6
Exchanges
Milk: 0.0
Vegetable: 3.0
Fruit: 0.5
Bread: 2.0
Meat: 0.0
Fat: 0.5

1. Spray large skillet with cooking spray; heat over medium heat until hot. Cook 5 or 6 eggplant slices over medium to medium-high heat until browned on the bottom, 3 to 5 minutes.

Spray tops of slices with cooking spray and turn; cook until browned on the bottom, 3 to 5 minutes. Repeat with remaining eggplant. Cut eggplant into 1-inch cubes and reserve.

2. Spray large saucepan with cooking spray; heat over medium heat until hot. Add onion, fennel, garlic, gingerroot, and fennel seeds to skillet; saute until onion is tender, 3 to 5 minutes. Add cabbage and stock; heat to boiling. Reduce heat and simmer, covered, until cabbage is wilted and crisp-tender, about 5 minutes.

3. Stir apples into cabbage mixture; cook, covered, until apples are tender, about 5 minutes. Stir in reserved eggplant and sour cream; cook over medium heat until hot through, 3 to 4 minutes. Season to taste with salt and pepper.

4. Spoon ragout into serving bowl; sprinkle with chopped fennel tops. Serve over Real Mashed Potatoes.

BEAN AND SQUASH STEW

Stews don't have to be long-cooked to be good—this delicious stew is simmered to savory goodness in less than 30 minutes. Serve with Garlic Bread (see p. 676).

6 servings (about 1¼ cups each)

Vegetable cooking spray

1½ cups chopped onions

1½ cups coarsely chopped green bell peppers

2 teaspoons minced roasted garlic

1 tablespoon flour

2 cups peeled, cubed, butternut, *or* acorn, squash (½-inch cubes)

2 cans (16 ounces each) reduced-sodium diced tomatoes, undrained   ⟍ 1 can

1 can (15 ounces) red kidney beans, rinsed, drained

1 can (13¼ ounces) baby lima beans,   — *other beans* rinsed, drained

½-¾ teaspoon Italian seasoning — *oregano, thyme*
Salt and pepper, to taste

Every one loves this 7/05

Per Serving
Calories: 239
% Calories from fat: 5
Fat (gm): 1.4
Saturated fat (gm): 0.2
Cholesterol (mg): 0
Sodium (mg): 160
Protein (gm): 14
Carbohydrate (gm): 50.5
Exchanges
Milk: 0.0
Vegetable: 3.0
Fruit: 0.0
Bread: 2.0
Meat: 0.5
Fat: 0.0

1. Spray large saucepan with cooking spray; heat over medium heat until hot. Saute onions, bell peppers, and garlic until tender, about 8 minutes. Stir in flour; cook 1 minute longer.

2. Add remaining ingredients, except salt and pepper, to saucepan; heat to boiling. Reduce heat and simmer 10 to 15 minutes. Season to taste with salt and pepper.

SOUTHERN STEWED PEAS AND BEANS

A hearty stew that can be made in less than 30 minutes with pantry-ready ingredients. Serve with Green Chili Corn Bread (see p. 678).

6 servings (about 1¼ cups each)

2 medium onions, chopped

2 cloves garlic, minced

1 tablespoon olive oil

1 can (28 ounces) reduced-sodium whole tomatoes, undrained, coarsely chopped

1 can (19 ounces) chick peas, rinsed, drained

1 can (15½ ounces) black-eyed peas, rinsed, drained

1 package (10 ounces) frozen spinach, partially thawed

2 cups fresh, *or* frozen, okra, cut into 1-inch pieces

1 teaspoon dried marjoram leaves

¾ teaspoon dried thyme leaves

¼ teaspoon hot pepper sauce

Salt and pepper, to taste

Per Serving
Calories: 258
% Calories from fat: 26
Fat (gm): 7.7
Saturated fat (gm): 1.1
Cholesterol (mg): 0
Sodium (mg): 627
Protein (gm): 10.9
Carbohydrate (gm): 39
Exchanges
Milk: 0.0
Vegetable: 3.0
Fruit: 0.0
Bread: 2.0
Meat: 0.0
Fat: 1.0

1. Saute onions and garlic in oil in large saucepan until tender, 5 to 8 minutes. Stir in remaining ingredients, except salt and pepper; heat to boiling. Reduce heat and simmer, covered, until okra is tender, 10 to 15 minutes. Season to taste with salt and pepper.

BLACK BEAN AND OKRA GUMBO

Lightly spiked with chili powder, the gumbo can also be served over soft polenta or another cooked grain. Substitute 2 cans (15 ounces each) of rinsed and drained black beans for the dried, if you prefer.

8 servings (about 1⅓ cups each)

Vegetable cooking spray
3 cups halved, small mushrooms
2 cups coarsely chopped onions
2 cups sliced carrots
1 cup chopped green bell pepper
1 cup chopped red bell pepper
4 teaspoons chili powder
1 teaspoon gumbo file powder
3 cups Basic Vegetable Stock (see p. 58)
3 cups cooked dried black beans
2 cups fresh, *or* frozen, cut okra
Salt and pepper, to taste
8 pieces Green Chili Corn Bread (see p. 678)

Per Serving
Calories: 454
% Calories from fat: 15
Fat (gm): 8
Saturated fat (gm): 1.7
Cholesterol (mg): 28
Sodium (mg): 754
Protein (gm): 14.8
Carbohydrate (gm): 85.5
Exchanges
Milk: 0.0
Vegetable: 3.0
Fruit: 0.0
Bread: 4.5
Meat: 0.0
Fat: 1.5

1. Spray large skillet with cooking spray; heat over medium heat until hot. Add mushrooms, onions, carrots, and bell peppers and cook, covered, over medium heat until mushrooms are wilted, 5 to 8 minutes. Stir in chili powder and file powder; cook 2 to 3 minutes.

2. Add stock, beans, and okra; heat to boiling. Reduce heat and simmer, uncovered, until vegetables are tender and broth thickened, 8 to 10 minutes. Season to taste with salt and pepper.

3. Serve stew over corn bread in shallow bowls.

EASY CREOLE SKILLET STEW

Easy to make, and fast too—dinner can be on the table in less than 30 minutes! Serve over rice, if desired.

4 servings

Vegetable cooking spray
1 package (8 ounces) all-vegetable protein sausage links
1 cup chopped onion
2 cloves garlic, minced
2 cups fresh, *or* frozen, whole-kernel corn
1 medium zucchini, sliced
2 cans (14½ ounces each) reduced-sodium stewed tomatoes
2 tablespoons flour
¼ cup water
Salt and pepper, to taste
2 green onions and tops, sliced

Per Serving
Calories: 245
% Calories from fat: 19
Fat (gm): 5.7
Saturated fat (gm): 0.9
Cholesterol (mg): 0
Sodium (mg): 392
Protein (gm): 14.9
Carbohydrate (gm): 38.7
Exchanges
Milk: 0.0
Vegetable: 2.5
Fruit: 0.0
Bread: 1.0
Meat: 2.0
Fat: 0.0

1. Spray large skillet with cooking spray; heat over medium heat until hot. Cook protein links over medium heat until browned, about 8 minutes, turning occasionally. Remove from skillet and reserve.

2. Add onion and garlic to skillet; saute until tender, about 5 minutes. Stir in corn, zucchini, and tomatoes; heat to boiling. Reduce heat and simmer, uncovered, 15 minutes. Heat mixture to boiling. Mix flour and water; stir into boiling mixture. Boil, stirring constantly, until thickened, about 1 minute.

3. Return sausages to skillet mixture; cook over medium heat 2 to 3 minutes longer. Season to taste with salt and pepper. Spoon into bowls to serve; sprinkle with green onions.

SOUTHERN VEGETABLE STEW

 Team this Southern favorite with Garlic Bread (p. 676).

4 servings (about 1¾ cups each)

Vegetable cooking spray
¼ cup sliced green onions and tops
1 medium green bell pepper, coarsely chopped
1 medium red bell pepper, coarsely chopped
4 cloves garlic, minced
2 cups Canned Vegetable Stock (see p. 63)
1 can (14½ ounces) reduced-sodium diced tomatoes, undrained
8 ounces pearl onions, peeled
2 teaspoons paprika
1 small eggplant, peeled, cut into 1-inch pieces
2 cups coarsely shredded carrots
1 medium zucchini, cut into ¾-inch pieces
4 ounces fresh, *or* frozen, thawed okra, sliced ½ inch thick
1½ teaspoons coarse-grain mustard
Red pepper sauce, to taste
Salt and pepper, to taste
Parsley, minced, as garnish

Per Serving
Calories: 170
% Calories from fat: 8
Fat (gm): 1.6
Saturated fat (gm): 0.2
Cholesterol (mg): 0
Sodium (mg): 94
Protein (gm): 5.7
Carbohydrate (gm): 34.4
Exchanges
Milk: 0.0
Vegetable: 6.0
Fruit: 0.0
Bread: 0.0
Meat: 0.0
Fat: 0.0

1. Spray large saucepan with cooking spray; heat over medium heat until hot. Saute green onions, bell peppers, and garlic until softened, about 4 minutes. Add stock, tomatoes, pearl onions, and paprika; heat to boiling. Reduce heat and simmer 10 minutes or until onions are tender.

2. Spray large skillet with cooking spray; heat over medium heat until hot. Saute eggplant, carrots, zucchini, and okra until slightly softened, about 5 minutes; add to saucepan. Stir in mustard and simmer until vegetables are tender, about 5 minutes. Season to taste with red pepper sauce, salt, and pepper.

3. Spoon stew into serving bowls; sprinkle with parsley.

BLACK AND WHITE BEAN CHILI

Made with black and white beans, this chili is uniquely accented in flavor and color with sun-dried tomatoes.

4 servings (about 1¼ cups each)

¼ cup sun-dried tomatoes (not in oil)

½ cup boiling water

    Vegetable cooking spray

⅔ package (12-ounce size) frozen pre-browned all-vegetable protein crumbles, thawed

1 cup chopped onion

½ cup chopped green bell pepper

1 medium jalapeño chili, finely chopped

2 teaspoons minced garlic

2-3 tablespoons chili powder

1-1½ teaspoons ground cumin

1 teaspoon dried oregano leaves

1 bay leaf

2 cans (16 ounces each) reduced-sodium whole tomatoes, undrained, coarsely chopped

1 can (15½ ounces) Great Northern beans, rinsed, drained

1 can (15 ounces) black beans, rinsed, drained

    Salt and pepper, to taste

4 tablespoons finely chopped cilantro

Per Serving
Calories: 396
% Calories from fat: 6
Fat (gm): 3
Saturated fat (gm): 0.3
Cholesterol (mg): 0
Sodium (mg): 748
Protein (gm): 34
Carbohydrate (gm): 69.8
Exchanges
Milk: 0.0
Vegetable: 3.0
Fruit: 0.0
Bread: 3.0
Meat: 2.0
Fat: 0.0

1. Cover sun-dried tomatoes with boiling water in small bowl; let stand until softened, about 10 minutes. Drain; reserve liquid. Chop tomatoes.

2. Spray large saucepan with cooking spray; heat over medium heat until hot. Saute vegetable protein crumbles, onion, bell pepper, jalapeño chili, and garlic until vegetables are tender, 8 to 10 minutes. Stir in herbs; cook 1 to 2 minutes longer.

3. Stir in sun-dried tomatoes with reserved liquid, tomatoes, and beans. Heat to boiling; reduce heat and simmer, covered, 30 minutes. Discard bay leaf; season to taste with salt and pepper. Stir in cilantro.

CHILI STEW

A squeeze of lime adds a cooling touch to this spicy favorite.

6 servings (about 1⅓ cups each)

Vegetable cooking spray
2 cups butternut squash, peeled, cut into 1-inch cubes
2 medium onions, cut into 1-inch pieces
2 cups chopped celery
1 red bell pepper, cut into 1-inch pieces
½ jalapeño chili, finely chopped
2 cloves garlic, minced
1 can (15 ounces) reduced-sodium chunky tomato sauce
1 can (15 ounces) red kidney beans, rinsed, drained
3 cups reduced-sodium tomato juice
½ package (12-ounce size) frozen pre-browned all-vegetable protein crumbles
1 medium zucchini, cubed
1 cup sliced mushrooms
1½ teaspoons chili powder
1½ teaspoons ground cumin
Salt and pepper, to taste
6 lime wedges

Per Serving
Calories: 236
% Calories from fat: 4
Fat (gm): 1.1
Saturated fat (gm): 0.1
Cholesterol (mg): 0
Sodium (mg): 691
Protein (gm): 16.9
Carbohydrate (gm): 46
Exchanges
Milk: 0.0
Vegetable: 3.0
Fruit: 0.0
Bread: 1.5
Meat: 1.0
Fat: 0.0

1. Spray Dutch oven or large saucepan with cooking spray; heat over medium heat until hot. Saute squash 5 minutes; add onions, celery, bell pepper, jalapeño chili, and garlic. Saute until tender, 8 to 10 minutes.

2. Add remaining ingredients, except salt, pepper, and lime wedges, to Dutch oven; heat to boiling. Reduce heat and simmer, uncovered, until vegetables are tender and stew is thickened, 10 to 15 minutes. Season to taste with salt and pepper.

3. Serve stew in bowls; squeeze lime wedge into each.

HOT 'N SPICY BEAN AND VEGETABLE STEW

 Make this stew as fiery as you like with serrano or other hot chilies!

6 servings (about 1½ cups each)

Olive oil cooking spray
1½ cups chopped onions
2-4 teaspoons minced serrano chilies
2-3 teaspoons minced garlic
1 tablespoon flour
1½ teaspoons dried oregano leaves
¾ teaspoon ground cinnamon
½ teaspoon ground cloves
1 bay leaf
2 cans (16 ounces each) reduced-sodium diced tomatoes, undrained
1½ cups Basic Vegetable Stock (see p. 58), *or* water
1 tablespoon red wine vinegar
4 medium carrots, sliced
4 medium red potatoes, unpeeled, cubed
1 can (15 ounces) black beans, rinsed, drained
1 can (15 ounces) pinto beans, rinsed, drained
Salt and pepper, to taste

Per Serving
Calories: 284
% Calories from fat: 5
Fat (gm): 2
Saturated fat (gm): 0.1
Cholesterol (mg): 0
Sodium (mg): 527
Protein (gm): 15.4
Carbohydrate (gm): 60.8
Exchanges
Milk: 0.0
Vegetable: 3.0
Fruit: 0.0
Bread: 3.0
Meat: 0.0
Fat: 0.0

1. Spray Dutch oven or large saucepan with cooking spray; heat over medium heat until hot. Saute onions, chilies, and garlic 5 minutes; stir in flour and seasonings and cook 1 to 2 minutes longer.

2. Add remaining ingredients, except salt and pepper; heat to boiling. Reduce heat and simmer, covered, until vegetables are tender and stew thickened, 15 to 20 minutes. Discard bay leaf; season to taste with salt and pepper.

TEX-MEX VEGETABLE STEW

Poblano chilies range from mild to very hot in flavor, so taste a tiny bit before using. If the chili is very hot, you may want to substitute some sweet green bell pepper.

6 servings (about 1½ cups each)

Vegetable cooking spray
1 medium red onion, chopped
1 poblano chili, seeded, chopped
3 cloves garlic, minced
3 cans (10 ounces each) tomatoes with chilies, undrained
12 small new potatoes, cut in halves
4 medium carrots, cut into 1-inch pieces
3 ears corn, cut into 2-inch pieces
1 cup Canned Vegetable Stock (see p. 63)
2 tablespoons balsamic vinegar
1 tablespoon chili powder
2 teaspoons ground cumin
½ teaspoon dried oregano leaves
¾ teaspoon ground pepper
1 can (15 ounces) black beans, rinsed, drained
2 cups frozen peas, thawed
Salt, to taste
½ cup finely chopped cilantro

Per Serving
Calories: 423
% Calories from fat: 5
Fat (gm): 2.4
Saturated fat (gm): 0.2
Cholesterol (mg): 0
Sodium (mg): 793
Protein (gm): 16.7
Carbohydrate (gm): 92.5
Exchanges
Milk: 0.0
Vegetable: 3.0
Fruit: 0.0
Bread: 5.0
Meat: 0.0
Fat: 0.0

1. Spray large saucepan with cooking spray; heat over medium heat until hot. Saute onion, chili, and garlic until softened, about 4 minutes.

2. Add tomatoes, potatoes, carrots, corn, stock, vinegar, chili powder, cumin, oregano, and pepper; heat to boiling. Reduce heat and simmer, uncovered, 30 minutes or until vegetables are tender.

3. Stir in beans and peas; cook until peas are cooked, about 5 minutes. Season to taste with salt. Serve stew in bowls; sprinkle with cilantro.

MEXICAN ANCHO CHILI STEW

This stew has lots of delicious sauce, so serve with crusty warm rolls or warm tortillas, or serve over Black Beans and Rice (see p. 526). Vary the amount of ancho chilies to taste.

4 servings (about 1⅓ cups each)

4-6 ancho chilies, stems, seeds, and veins discarded
2 cups boiling water
4 medium tomatoes, cut into wedges
   Vegetable cooking spray
6-8 Mexican-style all-vegetable "burgers," crumbled (18-24 ounces)
1 large onion, chopped
2 cloves garlic, minced
1 teaspoon minced serrano, *or* jalapeño, chili
1 teaspoon dried oregano leaves
1 teaspoon cumin seeds, crushed
2 tablespoons flour
   Salt and pepper, to taste

Per Serving
Calories: 275
% Calories from fat: 13
Fat (gm): 4.3
Saturated fat (gm): 0.1
Cholesterol (mg): 0
Sodium (mg): 735
Protein (gm): 11.9
Carbohydrate (gm): 50.9
Exchanges
Milk: 0.0
Vegetable: 2.0
Fruit: 0.0
Bread: 2.5
Meat: 0.5
Fat: 0.5

1. Place ancho chilies in bowl; pour boiling water over. Let stand until chilies are softened, about 10 minutes. Process chilies, with water, and tomatoes in food processor or blender until smooth.

2. Spray large saucepan with cooking spray; heat over medium heat until hot. Cook crumbled "burgers," onion, garlic, serrano chili, and herbs until onion is tender, about 5 minutes. Stir in flour; cook over medium heat 1 to 2 minutes more.

3. Add chili and tomato mixture to saucepan; heat to boiling. Reduce heat and simmer, covered, 15 to 20 minutes. Season to taste with salt and pepper. Serve in shallow bowls.

"MEATBALLS" IN TOMATO CHILI SAUCE

The "meatballs" can be made in advance and refrigerated or frozen; thaw before using. The pasilla chilies are picante—use 2 only if you enjoy a truly hot sauce!

4 servings (4 "meatballs" each)

Vegetable cooking spray
1-2 pasilla chilies
   1 can (28 ounces) reduced-sodium diced tomatoes, undrained
      Mexi"Meatballs" (see p. 405)
      Salt and pepper, to taste
   3 cups cooked brown, *or* white, rice, warm

Per Serving
Calories: 368
% Calories from fat: 15
Fat (gm): 6.4
Saturated fat (gm): 2.4
Cholesterol (mg): 63.4
Sodium (mg): 602
Protein (gm): 19
Carbohydrate (gm): 59.7
Exchanges
Milk: 0.0
Vegetable: 2.0
Fruit: 0.0
Bread: 3.0
Meat: 1.5
Fat: 0.5

1. Spray large saucepan with cooking spray; heat over medium heat until hot. Cook pasilla chilies over medium heat until softened; discard stems, seeds, and veins. Process chilies and tomatoes with liquid in blender until smooth.

2. Heat tomato mixture to boiling in large saucepan; add "meatballs". Reduce heat and simmer, covered, 10 minutes. Season to taste with salt and pepper. Serve "meatballs" and sauce over rice.

MEXICAN-STYLE VEGETABLE STEW

A winter vegetable offering with a Mexican flair, spooned over strands of spaghetti squash. Serve with warm squares of Green Chili Corn Bread (see p. 678).

4 servings (about 1⅓ cups each)

   1 medium spaghetti squash, halved, seeded
      Vegetable cooking spray
   2 medium russet potatoes, cut into 1-inch pieces
   1 medium onion, chopped

Per Serving
Calories: 166
% Calories from fat: 6
Fat (gm): 1.1
Saturated fat (gm): 0.2
Cholesterol (mg): 0
Sodium (mg): 437
Protein (gm): 5.3
Carbohydrate (gm): 37.3

1 large carrot, cut into ½-inch slices
1 cup cubed rutabaga (1-inch cubes)
½ cup chopped green bell pepper
2 cloves garlic, minced
1 tablespoon flour
1½ cups Basic Vegetable Stock (see p. 58)
1 can (14½ ounces) diced tomatoes and
    chilies, undrained
    Salt and pepper, to taste
    Cilantro, finely chopped, as garnish

Exchanges
Milk: 0.0
Vegetable: 2.5
Fruit: 0.0
Bread: 1.5
Meat: 0.0
Fat: 0.0

1. Place squash halves, cut sides down, in baking pan; add ½ inch water. Bake, covered, at 350 degrees until tender, 30 to 40 minutes. Using fork, scrape squash to separate into strands.

2. Spray large skillet with cooking spray; heat over medium heat until hot. Add vegetables, including garlic, and spray with cooking spray; saute until lightly browned, 8 to 10 minutes. Stir in flour; cook 1 minute longer.

3. Add stock and tomatoes with liquid; heat to boiling. Reduce heat and simmer, covered, until vegetables are tender, about 15 minutes. Season to taste with salt and pepper.

4. Spoon spaghetti squash onto serving plates; spoon vegetables over. Sprinkle with cilantro.

ORANGE AND GINGER SQUASH STEW

Any winter squash, such as acorn, butternut, or Hubbard, is appropriate for this orange-and-ginger accented stew; sweet potatoes can be substituted too.

6 servings (about 1½ cups each)

2 medium onions, chopped
2 medium green bell peppers, coarsely
    chopped
2 cloves garlic, minced
1 tablespoon basil-flavored olive oil, *or*
    regular olive oil
3 cups (about 2 pounds), winter yellow
    squash peeled, cut into ½-inch cubes

Per Serving
Calories: 327
% Calories from fat: 13
Fat (gm): 4.8
Saturated fat (gm): 0.8
Cholesterol (mg): 35.3
Sodium (mg): 55
Protein (gm): 11.3
Carbohydrate (gm): 60.8
Exchanges
Milk: 0.0
Vegetable: 2.5
Fruit: 0.0
Bread: 3.0
Meat: 0.0
Fat: 1.0

3 medium Idaho potatoes, peeled, cut
into ½-inch cubes

1 can (14½ ounces) reduced-sodium
diced tomatoes, undrained

2 cups Mediterranean Stock, *or* Basic
Vegetable Stock (see pp. 60, 58)

½ cup orange juice

¼ teaspoon ground ginger

1 cup fat-free sour cream

2 tablespoons minced parsley

1 tablespoon grated orange rind
Salt and pepper, to taste

4 cups cooked noodles, *or* brown basmati
rice, hot

1. Saute onions, peppers, and garlic in oil in large saucepan until tender, about 4 minutes. Add squash, potatoes, tomatoes, stock, orange juice, and ginger; heat to boiling. Reduce heat and simmer, uncovered, 30 minutes.

2. Reduce heat to low; stir in sour cream, parsley, and orange rind; season to taste with salt and pepper. Serve hot over noodles.

CARIBBEAN SWEET-AND-SOUR STEW

Sweet-and-sour flavors team with tofu, pineapple, and beans for this island-inspired dish.

6 servings (about 1¼ cups each)

Vegetable cooking spray

2 packages (10½ ounces each) light tofu,
cut into 1-inch cubes

2 medium onions, cut into 1-inch pieces

1 large red bell pepper, cut into strips

1 large green bell pepper, cut into strips

4 cloves garlic, minced

2 teaspoons minced gingerroot

1-2 jalapeño chilies, finely chopped

Per Serving
Calories: 388
% Calories from fat: 6
Fat (gm): 2.9
Saturated fat (gm): 0.2
Cholesterol (mg): 0
Sodium (mg): 361
Protein (gm): 17.8
Carbohydrate (gm): 76.8
Exchanges
Milk: 0.0
Vegetable: 2.0
Fruit: 1.0
Bread: 3.0
Meat: 1.0
Fat: 0.0

3 cups Canned Vegetable Stock (see p. 63)
1 can (20 ounces) pineapple chunks in juice, undrained
2 tablespoons light brown sugar
2-3 teaspoons curry powder
2-3 tablespoons apple cider vinegar
2 tablespoons cornstarch
¼ cup cold water
1 can (15 ounces) black beans, rinsed, drained
4 cups cooked rice, warm
3 small green onions and tops, sliced

1. Spray large skillet with cooking spray; heat over medium heat until hot. Add tofu and cook over medium heat until browned on all sides, 8 to 10 minutes. Remove from skillet and reserve.

2. Add onions, bell peppers, garlic, gingerroot, and jalapeño chilies to skillet; saute until onions are tender, about 5 minutes. Stir in stock, pineapple with juice, sugar, curry powder, vinegar, and reserved tofu; heat to boiling. Reduce heat and simmer, uncovered, 5 minutes.

3. Heat mixture to boiling. Mix cornstarch and water; stir into boiling mixture. Boil, stirring frequently, until mixture is thickened, about 1 minute. Stir in beans; cook over medium heat 2 to 3 minutes longer.

4. Serve mixture over rice; sprinkle each serving with green onions.

CARIBBEAN GINGER BEAN STEW

 Fresh gingerroot accents the taste contrasts in this flavorful stew.

6 servings (scant 1 cup each)

1 cup chopped onion
1 cup chopped red bell pepper
1 jalapeño chili, minced
2 teaspoons minced garlic
1 tablespoon olive oil
1 tablespoon minced gingerroot
½ teaspoon dried thyme leaves
½ teaspoon ground allspice
1 can (15 ounces) black beans, rinsed, drained
1 can (15 ounces) black-eyed peas, rinsed, drained
¾ cup fresh, or frozen, cut okra
⅓ cup orange juice
⅓ cup jalapeño chili jelly, or orange marmalade
1 can (11 ounces) Mandarin orange segments, drained
3 cups cooked brown, or white, rice

Per Serving
Calories: 369
% Calories from fat: 17
Fat (gm): 7.3
Saturated fat (gm): 1
Cholesterol (mg): 0
Sodium (mg): 461
Protein (gm): 13.2
Carbohydrate (gm): 69.2
Exchanges
Milk: 0.0
Vegetable: 2.0
Fruit: 0.5
Bread: 3.5
Meat: 0.0
Fat: 1.0

1. Saute onion, bell pepper, chili, and garlic in oil in large skillet until tender, about 5 minutes. Stir in gingerroot, thyme, and allspice; cook 1 to 2 minutes longer, stirring frequently.

2. Add black beans, black-eyed peas, okra, orange juice, and jelly to mixture; heat to boiling. Reduce heat and simmer, covered, until okra is tender, 5 to 10 minutes. Stir in orange segments; cook 1 to 2 minutes longer. Serve over rice.

SWEET-SOUR SQUASH AND POTATO STEW

 The vegetables are simmered in cider and seasoned with honey and vinegar for a refreshing sweet-sour flavor.

6 servings (about 1½ cups each)

Vegetable cooking spray
½ cup chopped shallots
1 medium red bell pepper, chopped
2 cloves garlic, minced
1 can (14½ ounces) reduced-sodium diced tomatoes, undrained
1 cup apple cider, *or* apple juice
1½ tablespoons honey
1½ tablespoons cider vinegar
1 bay leaf
¼ teaspoon ground nutmeg
3½ cups peeled, cubed, yellow winter squash (butternut or acorn)
4 medium Idaho potatoes, peeled, cut into ¾-inch cubes
2 medium sweet potatoes, peeled, cut into ¾-inch cubes
2 medium tart green apples, unpeeled, cored, cut into ¾-inch pieces
1½ cups fresh, *or* frozen whole-kernel corn
Salt and pepper, to taste
4 cups cooked basmati, *or* other aromatic, rice, warm

Per Serving
Calories: 411
% Calories from fat: 4
Fat (gm): 1.8
Saturated fat (gm): 0.2
Cholesterol (mg): 0
Sodium (mg): 52
Protein (gm): 9.7
Carbohydrate (gm): 95.9
Exchanges
Milk: 0.0
Vegetable: 3.0
Fruit: 1.0
Bread: 3.5
Meat: 0.0
Fat: 0.0

1. Spray large saucepan with cooking spray; heat over medium heat until hot. Saute shallots, bell pepper, and garlic until softened, about 4 minutes.

2. Add tomatoes, cider, honey, vinegar, bay leaf, nutmeg, squash, Idaho and sweet potatoes to saucepan. Heat to boiling; reduce heat and simmer, covered, 15 minutes or until potatoes are tender. Add apples and corn and simmer until apples are tender, about 5 minutes.

3. Discard bay leaf; season stew to taste with salt and pepper. Serve over rice.

TOFU AND VEGETABLE STEW

As with most stews, vegetables in this dish can vary according to season and availability; tempeh can be substituted for the tofu.

4 servings (about 1¾ cups each)

Vegetable cooking spray
1 medium onion, sliced
½ cup sliced celery
3 cloves garlic, minced
4 cups Rich Mushroom Stock, *or* Basic Vegetable Stock (see pp. 61, 58)
2 cups peeled, sliced red potatoes
6 medium carrots, sliced
1 bay leaf
1 teaspoon ground cumin
¼-½ teaspoon dried thyme leaves
⅛ teaspoon ground cloves
1 package (10 ounces) frozen chopped spinach
1 package (10½ ounces) firm light tofu, *or* tempeh, cut into ½-inch cubes
¼ cup minced parsley
Salt and pepper, to taste

Per Serving
Calories: 239
% Calories from fat: 8
Fat (gm): 2.3
Saturated fat (gm): 0.2
Cholesterol (mg): 0
Sodium (mg): 182
Protein (gm): 11.1
Carbohydrate (gm): 43.8
Exchanges
Milk: 0.0
Vegetable: 4.0
Fruit: 0.0
Bread: 1.5
Meat: 0.5
Fat: 0.0

1. Spray large saucepan with cooking spray; heat over medium heat until hot. Saute onion, celery, and garlic until softened, about 4 minutes.

2. Add stock, potatoes, carrots, bay leaf, cumin, thyme, and cloves to saucepan; heat to boiling. Reduce heat and simmer, covered, until vegetables are tender, about 20 minutes. Add spinach and simmer 2 to 3 minutes. Add tofu and parsley and cook until heated through, about 4 minutes. Season to taste with salt and pepper.

VIETNAMESE CURRIED VEGETABLE AND COCONUT STEW

Rice stick noodles, made with rice flour, can be round or flat. They must be softened in water before cooking. Angel hair pasta can be substituted.

6 servings (about 1½ cups each)

Vegetable cooking spray
1 cup chopped green onions and tops
½ cup chopped red bell pepper
½ cup chopped green bell pepper
2 tablespoons minced gingerroot
1 tablespoon minced garlic
3-4 tablespoons curry powder
3½ cups Oriental Stock, *or* Basic Vegetable Stock (see pp. 62, 58)
3 cups reduced-fat coconut milk
1 tablespoon grated lime rind
1 teaspoon oriental chili paste
1 cup broccoli florets
1 cup cubed yellow winter squash (acorn or butternut)
1 cup sliced zucchini
¼ cup all-purpose flour
¼ cup cold water
¼ cup lime juice
⅓ cup finely chopped cilantro
Salt and pepper, to taste
½ package (8-ounce size) rice stick noodles

Per Serving
Calories: 220
% Calories from fat: 27
Fat (gm): 6.9
Saturated fat (gm): 0.1
Cholesterol (mg): 0
Sodium (mg): 192
Protein (gm): 5.8
Carbohydrate (gm): 36.9
Exchanges
Milk: 0.0
Vegetable: 1.0
Fruit: 0.0
Bread: 2.0
Meat: 0.0
Fat: 1.0

1. Spray large saucepan with cooking spray; heat over medium heat until hot. Saute green onions, bell pepper, gingerroot, and garlic until tender, about 5 minutes. Stir in curry powder and cook 1 minute longer.

2. Add stock, coconut milk, lime rind, and chili paste to saucepan; heat to boiling. Add vegetables; reduce heat and simmer, covered, until vegetables are tender, about 15 minutes.

3. Heat stew to boiling. Mix flour, water, and lime juice; stir into boiling stew. Boil, stirring constantly, until thickened, about 1 minute. Stir in cilantro; season to taste with salt and pepper.

4. Place noodles in large bowl; pour cold water over to cover. Let stand until noodles are separate and soft, about 5 minutes. Stir noodles into 4 quarts boiling water in large saucepan. Reduce heat and simmer, uncovered, until tender, about 5 minutes; drain.

5. Serve stew over noodles in shallow bowls.

THREE-BEAN STEW WITH POLENTA

 Use any kind of canned or cooked dried beans you wish; one 15-ounce can of drained beans yields 1½ cups of beans.

4-6 servings (about 1-1½ cups each)

Olive oil cooking spray
1 cup chopped onion
½ cup chopped red bell pepper
1 teaspoon minced, roasted garlic
1 tablespoon flour
1 can (15 ounces) black-eyed peas, rinsed, drained
1 can (15 ounces) black beans, rinsed, drained
1 can (15 ounces) red beans, rinsed, drained
1 can (16 ounces) reduced-sodium diced tomatoes, undrained
¾ teaspoon dried sage leaves
½ teaspoon dried rosemary leaves
½ teaspoon dried thyme leaves
¾ cup Basic Vegetable Stock (see p. 58), *or* water
Salt and pepper, to taste
Polenta (see p. 579)

Per Serving
Calories: 299
% Calories from fat: 14
Fat (gm): 5.3
Saturated fat (gm): 0.6
Cholesterol (mg): 0
Sodium (mg): 587
Protein (gm): 17.5
Carbohydrate (gm): 56
Exchanges
Milk: 0.0
Vegetable: 2.0
Fruit: 0.0
Bread: 3.0
Meat: 0.5
Fat: 0.0

1. Spray large saucepan with cooking spray; heat over medium heat until hot. Saute onion, bell pepper, and garlic until tender, about 5 minutes. Stir in flour; cook 1 minute longer.

2. Add beans, tomatoes with liquid, herbs, and stock to saucepan; heat to boiling. Reduce heat and simmer, covered, 10 minutes. Season to taste with salt and pepper.

3. Spoon Polenta into shallow bowls; spoon stew over.

SPICED BEAN STEW WITH FUSILLI

 Use any favorite beans and any shaped pasta in this versatile stew.

8 servings (about 1¼ cups each)

Vegetable cooking spray
2 cups chopped onions
½ cup sliced celery
1 cup sliced cremini, *or* white, mushrooms
2 cans (14½ ounces each) diced tomatoes with roasted garlic
1 can (15½ ounces) garbanzo beans, rinsed, drained
1 can (15 ounces) dark red kidney beans, rinsed, drained
½ cup dry white wine, *or* water
1-2 tablespoons chili powder
1-2 teaspoons ground cumin
¾ teaspoon dried oregano leaves
½ teaspoon dried thyme leaves
8 ounces fusilli, cooked
Salt and pepper, to taste
3-4 tablespoons sliced green, *or* ripe, olives

Per Serving
Calories: 269
% Calories from fat: 9
Fat (gm): 2.9
Saturated fat (gm): 0.3
Cholesterol (mg): 0
Sodium (mg): 761
Protein (gm): 12.3
Carbohydrate (gm): 50.4
Exchanges
Milk: 0.0
Vegetable: 2.0
Fruit: 0.0
Bread: 2.5
Meat: 0.5
Fat: 0.0

1. Spray large saucepan with cooking spray; heat over medium heat until hot. Saute onions, celery, and mushrooms until onions are tender, 8 to 10 minutes.

2. Add tomatoes, beans, wine, and herbs to saucepan; heat to boiling. Reduce heat and simmer, covered, until vegetables are tender, about 10 minutes. Add pasta and cook 2 to 3 minutes longer. Season to taste with salt and pepper.

3. Serve stew in bowls; sprinkle with olives.

VEGETABLE STEW FROM ITALY

Make the "meatballs" in advance to save time; they can be frozen, too, for up to 3 months.

8 servings (about 1½ cups each)

Vegetable cooking spray
1 medium onion, chopped
1 large red, *or* green, bell pepper, sliced
2 cans (14½ ounces each) tomatoes with roasted garlic, undrained
4 medium potatoes, unpeeled, cubed
8 ounces broccoli rabe, coarsely chopped
2 medium carrots, sliced
2 ears corn, cut into 2-inch pieces
1 cup Mediterranean Stock, *or* Basic Vegetable Stock (see pp. 60, 58)
2 tablespoons balsamic vinegar
1 teaspoon dried oregano leaves
1 teaspoon dried basil leaves
½ teaspoon dried marjoram leaves
1 can (15 ounces) cannellini, *or* Great Northern, beans, rinsed, drained
1 cup frozen peas
½ cup finely chopped Italian parsley
    Salt and pepper, to taste
    Italian-Style "Meatballs" (see p. 399), warm
6 teaspoons grated, fat-free Parmesan cheese

Per Serving
Calories: 357
% Calories from fat: 7
Fat (gm): 2.9
Saturated fat (gm): 0.6
Cholesterol (mg): 53.3
Sodium (mg): 611
Protein (gm): 23.7
Carbohydrate (gm): 66.5
Exchanges
Milk: 0.0
Vegetable: 2.0
Fruit: 0.0
Bread: 3.0
Meat: 1.5
Fat: 0.0

1. Spray large saucepan with cooking spray; heat over medium heat until hot. Saute onion and bell pepper until tender, about 5 minutes. Add tomatoes with liquid, potatoes, broccoli, carrots, corn, stock, vinegar, and herbs; heat to boiling. Reduce heat and simmer, covered, until vegetables are tender, about 20 minutes.

2. Stir in beans and peas; cook 5 minutes longer. Stir in parsley; season to taste with salt and pepper. Serve stew in bowls; top each with "meatballs" and sprinkle with Parmesan cheese.

VEGETABLES MARENGO

A colorful dish that picks up flavors of the Mediterranean.

4 servings (about 1¼ cups each)

Vegetable cooking spray

1 package (10½ ounces) light tofu, cut into scant 1-inch cubes

2 medium onions, cut into wedges

2 medium zucchini, cubed

1 cup halved small mushrooms

2 cloves minced garlic

1 tablespoon flour

1 can (14½ ounces) reduced-sodium whole tomatoes, undrained, coarsely chopped

¾ cup Mediterranean Stock, *or* Basic Vegetable Stock (see pp. 60, 58)

1 strip orange rind (3 x 1 inch)

½ teaspoon dried thyme leaves

½ teaspoon dried oregano leaves

1 bay leaf

Salt and pepper, to taste

3 cups cooked couscous or rice, warm

Parsley, finely chopped, as garnish

Per Serving
Calories: 257
% Calories from fat: 6
Fat (gm): 1.9
Saturated fat (gm): 0.2
Cholesterol (mg): 0
Sodium (mg): 98.6
Protein (gm): 13.6
Carbohydrate (gm): 47.5
Exchanges
Milk: 0.0
Vegetable: 3.0
Fruit: 0.0
Bread: 2.0
Meat: 0.5
Fat: 0.0

1. Spray large saucepan with cooking spray; heat over medium heat until hot. Add tofu and cook over medium heat until browned on all sides, 8 to 10 minutes. Remove from skillet and reserve.

2. Add onions, zucchini, mushrooms, and garlic to saucepan; saute 5 minutes. Stir in flour and cook 1 to 2 minutes longer. Add tomatoes, stock, orange rind, herbs, and reserved tofu; heat to boiling. Reduce heat and simmer, covered, until vegetables are tender, 10 to 15 minutes. Discard bay leaf; season to taste with salt and pepper.

3. Serve mixture over couscous in shallow bowls; sprinkle with parsley.

GARDEN STEW WITH COUSCOUS

Take advantage of your garden's bounty with this quick and easy stew, substituting vegetables you have in abundance.

6 servings (about 1½ cups each)

Vegetable cooking spray

2 medium onions, cut into 1-inch pieces

8 ounces sliced shiitake, *or* cremini, mushrooms

1 small jalapeño chili, finely chopped

1 tablespoon flour

2 cups Rich Mushroom Stock, *or* Basic Vegetable Stock (see pp. 61, 58)

1 medium turnip, cut into ¼-inch cubes

8 ounces baby carrots

1 bay leaf

4 medium tomatoes, coarsely chopped

2 medium zucchini, cut into julienne strips

½ cup loosely packed cilantro leaves

Salt and pepper, to taste

4 cups cooked couscous, warm

Per Serving
Calories: 228
% Calories from fat: 4
Fat (gm): 1.2
Saturated fat (gm): 0.2
Cholesterol (mg): 0
Sodium (mg): 57
Protein (gm): 7.6
Carbohydrate (gm): 47.7
Exchanges
Milk: 0.0
Vegetable: 3.0
Fruit: 0.0
Bread: 2.0
Meat: 0.0
Fat: 0.0

1. Spray large saucepan with cooking spray; heat over medium heat until hot. Saute onions, mushrooms, and jalapeño chili until tender, 5 to 8 minutes. Stir in flour; cook 1 minute longer.

2. Add stock, turnip, carrots, and bay leaf to saucepan; heat to boiling. Reduce heat and simmer, covered, until vegetables are tender, 10 to 15 minutes. Add tomatoes, zucchini, and cilantro; simmer 5 minutes longer or until thickened to desired consistency. Season to taste with salt and pepper. Serve with couscous.

MEDITERRANEAN CURRIED STEW

Taste buds will be tantalized by the melding of cinnamon-spice and curry flavors this stew offers. Brightly colored Turmeric Rice completes the dish perfectly.

6 servings (about 1¼ cups each)

1 small eggplant (about 12 ounces), unpeeled, cut into 1-inch pieces
3 small onions, quartered
½ cup chopped green bell pepper
½ cup sliced celery
2 cloves garlic, minced
2 tablespoons extra-virgin olive oil
1 tablespoon flour
½ teaspoon ground cinnamon
½ teaspoon ground nutmeg
½ teaspoon ground cumin
¼ teaspoon curry powder
⅛ teaspoon cayenne pepper
2 cans (14½ ounces, each) reduced-sodium whole tomatoes, undrained, coarsely chopped
1 medium zucchini, cubed
1 cup peeled, cubed, seeded, butternut squash
1 can (15 ounces) garbanzo beans, rinsed, drained
½ cup Basic Vegetable Stock (see p. 58)
   Salt and pepper, to taste
   Turmeric Rice (see p. 578)
3 tablespoons raisins
3 tablespoons slivered almonds, toasted

Per Serving
Calories: 354
% Calories from fat: 22
Fat (gm): 8.8
Saturated fat (gm): 1.2
Cholesterol (mg): 0
Sodium (mg): 323
Protein (gm): 9.7
Carbohydrate (gm): 62.5
Exchanges
Milk: 0.0
Vegetable: 3.0
Fruit: 0.0
Bread: 3.0
Meat: 0.0
Fat: 1.5

1. Saute eggplant, onions, bell pepper, celery, and garlic in oil in large saucepan 10 minutes or until eggplant is beginning to brown. Stir in flour and spices; cook 1 to 2 minutes longer.

2. Add tomatoes, zucchini, squash, beans, and stock to saucepan; heat to boiling. Reduce heat and simmer, covered, until vegetables are tender, 10 to 15 minutes. Season to taste with salt and pepper.

3. Spoon Turmeric Rice into shallow bowls; spoon stew over. Sprinkle with raisins and almonds.

GREEK LENTIL STEW

The lentils are combined with fresh vegetables for flavor contrast.

6 servings (about 1¼ cups each)

Vegetable cooking spray
1 cup chopped onion
1 cup chopped green bell pepper
2 teaspoons minced garlic
2 cups peeled, diced potatoes
1 cup lentils, washed and sorted
1 can (14½ ounces) reduced-sodium diced tomatoes, undrained
3 cups Mediterranean Stock, *or* Basic Vegetable Stock (see p. 60, 58)
1 teaspoon dried oregano leaves
1 teaspoon dried mint leaves
½ teaspoon ground turmeric
½ teaspoon ground coriander
1 medium zucchini, sliced
½ pound green beans, trimmed
Salt and pepper, to atste

Per Serving
Calories: 159
% Calories from fat: 6
Fat (gm): 1.2
Saturated fat (gm): 0.2
Cholesterol (mg): 0
Sodium (mg): 26
Protein (gm): 5.2
Carbohydrate (gm): 32.7
Exchanges
Milk: 0.0
Vegetable: 3.0
Fruit: 0.0
Bread: 1.0
Meat: 0.0
Fat: 0.0

1. Spray large saucepan with cooking spray; heat over medium heat until hot. Saute onion, bell pepper, and garlic until tender, about 5 minutes. Add potatoes, lentils, tomatoes, stock, and seasonings; heat to boiling. Reduce heat and simmer, covered, until lentils are tender, about 25 minutes.

2. Add zucchini and green beans; simmer, uncovered, until vegetables are tender and stew is thickened, about 10 minutes. Season to taste with salt and pepper.

VEGETABLE TAJINE

From the Moroccan cuisine, tajines are traditionally cooked in earthenware pots. Serve with couscous and Pita Bread (see p. 672)

6 servings (about 1¼ cups each)

Vegetable cooking spray
1 medium onion, chopped
1 rib celery, sliced
1-2 teaspoons minced gingerroot
1 teaspoon minced garlic
1 cinnamon stick
2 teaspoons paprika
2 teaspoons ground cumin
2 teaspoons ground coriander
1½ teaspoons black pepper
2 cans (14½ ounces each) reduced-sodium diced tomatoes, undrained
1 can (16 ounces) garbanzo beans, rinsed, drained
1 cup chopped yellow winter squash (butternut or acorn)
1 cup chopped turnip, *or* rutabaga
1 large carrot, sliced
1½ cups whole green beans, ends trimmed
1 cup pitted prunes
¼ cup pitted small black olives
½ cup Basic Vegetable Stock (see p. 58)
Salt and pepper, to taste
4½ cups cooked couscous, warm
Parsley, minced, as garnish

Per Serving
Calories: 386
% Calories from fat: 10
Fat (gm): 4.6
Saturated fat (gm): 0.6
Cholesterol (mg): 0
Sodium (mg): 540
Protein (gm): 12.5
Carbohydrate (gm): 78.7
Exchanges
Milk: 0.0
Vegetable: 3.0
Fruit: 1.0
Bread: 3.0
Meat: 0.0
Fat: 1.0

1. Spray Dutch oven with cooking spray; heat over medium heat until hot. Saute onion, celery, gingerroot, and garlic until onion is tender. Stir in spices; cook 1 minute longer.

2. Add remaining ingredients, except salt and pepper, couscous, and parsley to Dutch oven. Bake, covered, at 350 degrees, until vegetables are tender, 20 to 30 minutes. Season to taste with salt and pepper. Serve over couscous in bowls; sprinkle with parsley.

MACARONI AND CHEESE

For kids of all ages—always a favorite.

4 servings (about 1 cup each)

¼ cup finely chopped onion

2 tablespoons margarine, *or* butter

¼ cup all-purpose flour

2½ cups fat-free milk

1 bay leaf

2 ounces light pasteurized processed cheese product, cubed

½ cup (2 ounces) shredded reduced-fat sharp, *or* mild, Cheddar cheese

1 teaspoon Dijon-style mustard

2 cups (10 ounces) elbow macaroni, cooked per package directions

Salt and cayenne, to taste

¼ teaspoon white pepper

2 tablespoons dry unseasoned bread-crumbs

Paprika, as garnish

Per Serving
Calories: 495
% Calories from fat: 21
Fat (gm): 11.6
Saturated fat (gm): 3.6
Cholesterol (mg): 17.7
Sodium (mg): 577
Protein (gm): 22
Carbohydrate (gm): 73.9
Exchanges
Milk: 0.5
Vegetable: 0.0
Fruit: 0.0
Bread: 5.0
Meat: 1.0
Fat: 1.0

1. Saute onion in margarine in medium saucepan until tender, 3 to 4 minutes. Stir in flour; cook over medium-low heat 1 minute, stirring constantly. Whisk in milk and bay leaf; heat to boiling. Boil, whisking constantly, until thickened, 1 minute.

2. Stir in cheeses and mustard; cook over low heat, stirring constantly, until melted. Discard bay leaf.

3. Combine sauce and macaroni in 2-quart casserole. Season to taste with salt, cayenne, and white pepper; sprinkle with bread-crumbs and paprika. Bake, uncovered, at 350 degrees, until bubbly, 30 to 40 minutes.

Note: Any shaped pasta, such as rotini, fusilli, or orrechiette, can be substituted for the macaroni.

Variations: **Macaroni and Cheese Primavera**—Stir 1 cup cooked broccoli florets, 1 cup sauteed sliced mushrooms, and ¼ cup sauteed chopped red bell pepper into the macaroni and sauce mixture in step 3; bake as above.

WILD RICE, CHEESE, AND VEGETABLE CASSEROLE

Delicious, with a generous amount of melty cheese. The vegetables can vary according to season and availability.

4 servings (about 1¼ cups each)

1	package (6¼ ounces) wild and white rice mix, cooked without spice packet
1½	cups cut asparagus spears, blanched
1½	cups halved small Brussels sprouts, blanched
3	ounces fat-free cream cheese, cubed
¾	cup (3 ounces) shredded fat-free mozzarella cheese
3-4	ounces goat's cheese, crumbled
	Salt and pepper, to taste

Per Serving
Calories: 307
% Calories from fat: 21
Fat (gm): 7.2
Saturated fat (gm): 4.3
Cholesterol (mg): 9.7
Sodium (mg): 200
Protein (gm): 21.7
Carbohydrate (gm): 39
Exchanges
Milk: 0.0
Vegetable: 2.0
Fruit: 0.0
Bread: 2.0
Meat: 1.5
Fat: 0.5

1. Mix rice, vegetables, and cheeses; season to taste with salt and pepper. Spoon into 1½-quart casserole.

2. Bake, covered, at 350 degrees until casserole is hot and cheese is melted, about 30 minutes.

MIXED GRAIN AND VEGGIE CASSEROLE

Vegetables baked in a creamy casserole with mixed grains will satisfy the heartiest appetites.

6 servings (about 1¼ cups each)

Vegetable cooking spray
2 medium zucchini, cubed
2 cups coarsely chopped portobello, *or* shiitake, mushrooms
1 medium onion, chopped
3 cloves garlic, minced
1 can (11 ounces) whole-kernel corn with red and green peppers
1 teaspoon dried marjoram leaves
Salt and pepper, to taste
2 cups cooked rice
2 cups cooked oat groats
1 cup fat-free sour cream
¾ cup shredded reduced-fat Colby, *or* Monterey Jack, cheese
2 green onions and tops, sliced

Per Serving
Calories: 254
% Calories from fat: 13
Fat (gm): 3.9
Saturated fat (gm): 1.7
Cholesterol (mg): 10.1
Sodium (mg): 323
Protein (gm): 13.6
Carbohydrate (gm): 45.5
Exchanges
Milk: 0.0
Vegetable: 1.0
Fruit: 0.0
Bread: 2.5
Meat: 0.5
Fat: 0.5

1. Spray large skillet with cooking spray; heat over medium heat until hot. Saute zucchini, mushrooms, onion, and garlic until tender, 8 to 10 minutes. Stir in corn and marjoram; season to taste with salt and pepper.

2. Combine rice and groats; season to taste with salt and pepper. Spoon 2 cups grain mixture into 2-quart casserole; top with vegetable mixture and sour cream. Spoon remaining grain mixture on top.

3. Bake casserole, loosely covered, at 300 degrees until hot through, 30 to 40 minutes. Uncover, sprinkle with cheese, and bake until cheese is melted, about 5 minutes longer. Sprinkle with green onions.

SPINACH PASTA BAKE

Jalapeño chili is an unexpected ingredient--add more if you enjoy really hot flavor.

6 servings (about 1⅓ cups each)

Vegetable cooking spray
2 cups sliced mushrooms
1 medium onion, chopped
1 jalapeño chili, minced
1 cup reduced-fat ricotta cheese
⅓ cup (1⅓ ounces) fat-free Parmesan cheese
¼-½ cup fat-free milk
2 packages (10 ounces each) frozen chopped spinach, thawed, well drained
¾ teaspoon ground nutmeg
Salt and pepper, to taste
1 egg
2 cups elbow macaroni, *or* other shaped pasta, cooked
½ cup (2 ounces) reduced-fat Monterey Jack cheese

Per Serving
Calories: 251
% Calories from fat: 16
Fat (gm): 4.5
Saturated fat (gm): 1.5
Cholesterol (mg): 47.7
Sodium (mg): 230
Protein (gm): 16.9
Carbohydrate (gm): 37
Exchanges
Milk: 0.0
Vegetable: 1.0
Fruit: 0.0
Bread: 2.0
Meat: 1.5
Fat: 0.0

1. Spray large skillet with cooking spray; heat over medium heat until hot. Saute mushrooms, onions, and jalapeño chili until mushrooms are lightly browned, 3 to 5 minutes.

2. Combine ricotta and Parmesan cheese, milk, spinach, sauteed vegetables, and nutmeg in bowl; season to taste with salt and pepper. Stir in egg. Spoon half the macaroni into lightly greased 2-quart casserole; top with half the spinach mixture. Repeat layers; sprinkle with Monterey Jack cheese.

3. Bake, uncovered, at 350 degrees until hot through, 20 to 30 minutes.

VEGETABLE AND MIXED RICE CASSEROLE

Vary the vegetables according to season or personal preference.

6 servings (about 1⅓ cups each)

Vegetable cooking spray
1½ cups sliced shiitake, *or* cremini, mushrooms
1 cup sliced zucchini
½ cup chopped onion
½ cup chopped green bell pepper
½ cup chopped red bell pepper
1 teaspoon dried thyme leaves
1 package (6 ounces) brown and wild rice
mix, cooked with spice packet
1 can (15 ounces) pinto beans, rinsed,
drained
1 cup fresh, *or* frozen, whole-kernel corn
1 cup fat-free sour cream
1 cup (4 ounces) shredded reduced-fat
Cheddar cheese, divided
Salt and pepper, to taste

Per Serving
Calories: 307
% Calories from fat: 12
Fat (gm): 4.2
Saturated fat (gm): 1.4
Cholesterol (mg): 10.1
Sodium (mg): 708
Protein (gm): 16.9
Carbohydrate (gm): 54.7
Exchanges
Milk: 0.0
Vegetable: 2.0
Fruit: 0.0
Bread: 3.0
Meat: 0.5
Fat: 0.5

1. Spray medium skillet with cooking spray; heat over medium heat until hot. Add mushrooms, zucchini, onion, bell peppers, and thyme; cook, covered, over medium heat until vegetables are tender, 8 to 10 minutes.

2. Combine rice, cooked vegetable mixture, beans, corn, sour cream, and ½ cup cheese; season to taste with salt and pepper. Spoon mixture into 2-quart casserole; sprinkle with remaining ½ cup cheese.

3. Bake, uncovered, at 350 degrees until hot through, 30 to 40 minutes.

MEXICAN-STYLE LASAGNE

A lasagne with a difference! Add "Chorizo" (see p. 404), if you want.

8 servings

2 cups fat-free ricotta cheese

2 cups (8 ounces) shredded reduced-fat Monterey Jack cheese

1 can (15 ounces) pinto beans, drained

1 can (15 ounces) black beans, drained
Chili-Tomato Sauce (recipe follows)

12 lasagne noodles (10 ounces), cooked, room temperature

¼ cup finely chopped cilantro, or parsley

Per Serving
Calories: 360
% Calories from fat: 18
Fat (gm): 8
Saturated fat (gm): 3.1
Cholesterol (mg): 26.3
Sodium (mg): 748
Protein (gm): 30.7
Carbohydrate (gm): 51
Exchanges
Milk: 0.0
Vegetable: 3.0
Fruit: 0.0
Bread: 2.0
Meat: 2.5
Fat: 0.5

1. Heat oven to 350 degrees. Combine ricotta and Monterey Jack cheeses. Combine pinto and black beans. Spread 1½ cups Chili-Tomato Sauce on bottom of 13 x 9-inch baking pan; top with 4 lasagne noodles, overlapping slightly. Spoon ⅓ of cheese mixture over noodles, spreading lightly with rubber spatula; top with ⅓ of beans and 1 cup Chili-Tomato Sauce. Repeat layers twice, ending with remaining 1½ cups sauce.

2. Bake lasagne, loosely covered with aluminum foil, until sauce is bubbly, about 1 hour. Sprinkle with cilantro before serving.

Chili-Tomato Sauce

(makes about 5 cups)

Olive oil cooking spray

2 cups chopped onions

3 cloves garlic, minced

2-3 teaspoons minced jalapeño peppers

2 cans (14½ ounces each) low-sodium stewed tomatoes

2 cans (8 ounces each) low-sodium tomato sauce

2 tablespoons chili powder

2 teaspoons ground cumin

1 teaspoon dried oregano leaves

¼-½ teaspoon salt

1. Spray large saucepan with cooking spray; heat over medium heat until hot. Saute onions, garlic, and jalapeño peppers until onions are tender, 5 to 8 minutes.

2. Stir in remaining ingredients, except salt; heat to boiling. Reduce heat and simmer, uncovered, until sauce is reduced to 5 cups, about 20 minutes. Stir in salt.

MEXICAN "MEATBALL" CASSEROLE

 Enjoy this colorful casserole with spunky flavors and moist "meatballs."

6 servings (about 1¼ cups each)

Vegetable cooking spray
1 medium onion, chopped
1 medium zucchini, cubed
1 cup sliced mushrooms
2 cloves garlic, minced
1 jalapeño chili, minced
1 can (15 ounces) reduced-sodium chunky tomato sauce
2 teaspoons chili powder
2 cups cooked rice
1 cup water
2 tablespoons sliced ripe olives
1 cup (4 ounces) shredded reduced-fat Cheddar cheese, divided
Salt and pepper, to taste
Mexi "Meatballs," baked (see p. 405)

Per Serving
Calories: 280
% Calories from fat: 23
Fat (gm): 7.1
Saturated fat (gm): 2.9
Cholesterol (mg): 52.4
Sodium (mg): 767
Protein (gm): 16.5
Carbohydrate (gm): 37.1
Exchanges
Milk: 0.0
Vegetable: 2.0
Fruit: 0.0
Bread: 2.0
Meat: 2.0
Fat: 0.0

1. Spray large skillet with cooking spray; heat over medium heat until hot. Saute onion, zucchini, mushrooms, garlic, and jalapeño chili until tender, 5 to 8 minutes. Stir in tomato sauce, chili powder, rice, water, and olives; heat to boiling. Reduce heat and simmer, uncovered, 5 minutes. Stir in ½ cup cheese; season to taste with salt and pepper.

2. Spoon half the rice mixture into ungreased 2-quart casserole; top with Mexi "Meatballs," remaining rice mixture, and remaining cheese. Bake, uncovered, at 350 degrees until cheese is melted and browned, 15 to 20 minutes.

ENCHILADA STACK

 A quick and easy casserole. Corn tortillas are layered and baked until hot—a Mexican fiesta of flavors, perfect for brunch!

4 servings

Vegetable cooking spray
1 medium onion, chopped
⅓-½ package (12-ounce size) frozen pre-browned all-vegetable protein crumbles, thawed
1 can (15 ounces) pinto beans, rinsed, drained
3 small tomatoes, chopped
1 jalapeño chili, minced
1½ teaspoons ground cumin
¼ teaspoon pepper
5 corn tortillas
Enchilada Sauce (see p. 720)
½ cup (2 ounces) shredded reduced-fat Cheddar cheese
¼ cup fat-free sour cream

Per Serving
Calories: 325
% Calories from fat: 11
Fat (gm): 4.4
Saturated fat (gm): 1.2
Cholesterol (mg): 7.6
Sodium (mg): 799
Protein (gm): 22.2
Carbohydrate (gm): 54.7
Exchanges
Milk: 0.0
Vegetable: 3.0
Fruit: 0.0
Bread: 2.5
Meat: 1.5
Fat: 0.0

1. Spray medium skillet with cooking spray; heat over medium heat until hot. Saute onion until tender, 3 to 4 minutes. Add protein crumbles, beans, tomatoes, jalapeño chili, cumin, and pepper; cook over medium heat until hot, 3 to 4 minutes.

2. Place 1 tortilla in bottom of 1-quart soufflé dish or casserole; spoon ¼ of the bean mixture over tortilla. Spoon ⅓ cup Enchilada Sauce over. Repeat layers three times, ending with a tortilla and remaining ⅔ cup of Enchilada Sauce. Sprinkle with cheese.

3. Bake, covered, at 350 degrees until hot through, 25 to 30 minutes. Let stand 5 minutes; cut into 4 wedges. Serve with sour cream.

CHILIQUILES

Chiliquiles is a family-style casserole dish usually made with day-old tortillas and leftover cooked foods. Vary this casserole with ingredients you have on hand!

8 servings

8 corn, *or* flour, tortillas
Vegetable cooking spray
1 medium green bell pepper, thinly sliced
½ teaspoon minced jalapeño chili pepper
¼ teaspoon cayenne pepper
Enchilada Sauce (see p. 720)
1½ cups cooked black beans, *or* 1 can (15 ounces) black beans, rinsed, drained
1 cup frozen whole-kernel corn, thawed, *or* fresh corn
⅔ package (12-ounce size) frozen pre-browned all-vegetable protein crumbles, thawed
1 large tomato, thinly sliced
Jalapeño con Queso Sauce (see p. 725)
Medium, *or* hot, salsa, to taste

Per Serving
Calories: 272
% Calories from fat: 13
Fat (gm): 4.1
Saturated fat (gm): 2.2
Cholesterol (mg): 10.3
Sodium (mg): 737
Protein (gm): 24.3
Carbohydrate (gm): 36.8
Exchanges
Milk: 0.0
Vegetable: 0.8
Fruit: 0.0
Bread: 2.5
Meat: 2.0
Fat: 0.0

1. Spray both sides of tortillas lightly with cooking spray; cook in small skillet over medium-high heat to brown lightly, 30 to 60 seconds per side. Cool slightly; cut into ½-inch strips.

2. Spray small skillet with cooking spray; heat over medium heat until hot. Saute peppers until tender, 2 to 3 minutes; sprinkle with cayenne pepper. Stir in Enchilada Sauce; heat until hot.

3. Arrange ⅓ of the tortilla strips in bottom of 2-quart casserole. Top with ⅓ of peppers mixture. Layer on ½ cup black beans, ⅓ cup corn, ⅓ of the vegetable protein crumbles, ⅓ of the tomato slices, and ⅔ cup Jalapeño con Queso Sauce. Repeat layers 2 times.

4. Bake casserole, uncovered, at 350 degrees until hot through, 25 to 30 minutes. Serve hot with salsa.

VEGETARIAN TETRAZZINI

A versatile dish—use any vegetable or pasta you care to substitute.

8 servings

8   ounces mushrooms, sliced
1   medium zucchini, sliced
1   cup sliced red bell pepper
½   cup chopped onion
1-2 tablespoons margarine, *or* butter
1   cup broccoli florets, cooked until crisp-tender
2   tablespoons flour
1¾ cups Canned Vegetable Stock (see p. 63)
1   cup fat-free milk
½   cup dry white wine, *or* fat-free milk
16 ounces thin, *or* regular, spaghetti, cooked, warm
¼   cup grated Parmesan cheese
¼   teaspoon ground nutmeg
¼   teaspoon salt
¼   teaspoon pepper

Per Serving
Calories: 344
% Calories from fat: 11
Fat (gm): 4.1
Saturated fat (gm): 1.2
Cholesterol (mg): 3
Sodium (mg): 176
Protein (gm): 12.9
Carbohydrate (gm): 60.3
Exchanges
Milk: 0.0
Vegetable: 2.0
Fruit: 0.0
Bread: 3.5
Meat: 0.0
Fat: 1.0

1. Saute mushrooms, zucchini, bell pepper, and onion in margarine in large saucepan until tender, about 5 minutes; stir in broccoli.

2. Mix flour and stock; stir into saucepan with milk and wine. Heat to boiling; boil, stirring constantly, until thickened, 1 to 2 minutes (sauce will still be very thin). Stir in pasta, Parmesan cheese, nutmeg, salt, and pepper.

3. Spoon pasta mixture into 2-quart casserole or baking dish. Bake, uncovered, at 350 degrees until lightly browned and bubbly, about 45 minutes.

FUSILLI AND CHEESE PRIMAVERA

Asparagus spears, broccoli florets, and sliced zucchini and carrots are other vegetable choices that can be used in this cheesy casserole.

6 servings (about 1½ cups each)

1	cup sliced cremini, *or* white, mush-rooms
¾	cup chopped onion
½	cup chopped red bell pepper
2	cloves garlic, minced
2	tablespoons margarine, *or* butter
3	cups fat-free milk
⅓	cup all-purpose flour
3	ounces light pasteurized processed cheese product, cubed
½	cup (2 ounces) shredded reduced-fat sharp, *or* mild, Cheddar cheese
1	teaspoon Dijon-style mustard
10	ounces fusilli, *or* rotini, cooked
1½	cups snow peas, *or* asparagus spears, cooked until crisp-tender
	Salt and pepper, to taste
2	tablespoons unseasoned dry bread-crumbs
	Paprika, as garnish

Per Serving
Calories: 386
% Calories from fat: 20
Fat (gm): 8.7
Saturated fat (gm): 2.8
Cholesterol (mg): 14.7
Sodium (mg): 462
Protein (gm): 18.3
Carbohydrate (gm): 58
Exchanges
Milk: 0.5
Vegetable: 1.0
Fruit: 0.0
Bread: 3.0
Meat: 1.0
Fat: 1.0

1. Saute mushrooms, onion, bell pepper, and garlic in margarine in large saucepan until tender, 8 to 10 minutes. Mix milk and flour until blended; stir into saucepan and heat to boiling, stirring constantly. Boil, stirring constantly, until thickened, about 1 minute.

2. Reduce heat to low; stir in cheeses and mustard, stirring until cheeses are melted. Combine sauce mixture, fusilli, and snow peas in 2-quart casserole; season to taste with salt and pepper. Sprinkle with breadcrumbs and paprika.

3. Bake, uncovered, at 350 degrees until bubbly, 30 to 40 minutes.

VEGGIE LASAGNE WITH EGGPLANT SAUCE

The hearty Eggplant Sauce is also wonderful served over shaped or tube pastas, such as corkscrews or ziti, or over cheese or herb tortellini.

8 servings

Olive oil cooking spray
1 medium onion, sliced
1 medium zucchini, sliced
1 medium red bell pepper, sliced
1 cup sliced mushrooms
3 cloves garlic, minced
2 cups fat-free ricotta cheese
¼ cup grated Parmesan cheese
Eggplant Sauce (see p. 708)
12 lasagne noodles (10 ounces), cooked, room temperature
2 medium-size sweet potatoes, sliced, cooked until crisp-tender
2 cups (8 ounces) shredded reduced-fat mozzarella cheese

Per Serving
Calories: 375
% Calories from fat: 24
Fat (gm): 10.4
Saturated fat (gm): 4.2
Cholesterol (mg): 2.3
Sodium (mg): 685
Protein (gm): 2.4
Carbohydrate (gm): 47
Exchanges
Milk: 0.0
Vegetable: 3.0
Fruit: 0.0
Bread: 2.0
Meat: 2.5
Fat: 0.5

1. Spray large skillet with cooking spray; heat over medium heat until hot. Saute onions, zucchini, bell pepper, mushrooms, and garlic until tender, about 10 minutes. In bowl, mix ricotta and Parmesan cheese.

2. Spread about ½ cup Eggplant Sauce in bottom of 13 x 9-inch baking pan; top with 4 lasagne noodles, overlapping slightly. Spoon ⅓ of ricotta cheese mixture over noodles, spreading lightly with rubber spatula. Add next layer, using ⅓ of sweet potatoes and ⅓ of sauteed vegetables. Spoon ⅓ of the sauce over vegetables; sprinkle with ⅓ of mozzarella cheese. Repeat layers 2 times.

3. Bake lasagne, loosely covered with aluminum foil, at 350 degrees until sauce is bubbly, about 1 hour. Let stand 10 minutes before cutting.

"SAUSAGE" LASAGNE

The traditional lasagne we all love, with a skinny rendering.

8 servings

Tomato and "Meat" Sauce (see p. 701)
1 package (8 ounces) sausage-style all-vegetable protein patties, *or* links, crumbled
1 can (6 ounces) reduced-sodium tomato sauce
2 cups fat-free ricotta cheese
¼ cup grated Parmesan cheese
3 cups (12 ounces) shredded reduced-fat mozzarella cheese
12 lasagne noodles (10 ounces), cooked, room temperature

Per Serving
Calories: 339
% Calories from fat: 29
Fat (gm): 11.1
Saturated fat (gm): 5.6
Cholesterol (mg): 25.3
Sodium (mg): 600
Protein (gm): 30.3
Carbohydrate (gm): 30
Exchanges
Milk: 0.0
Vegetable: 2.0
Fruit: 0.0
Bread: 1.5
Meat: 3.0
Fat: 0.0

1. Make Tomato and "Meat" Sauce, substituting the crumbled vegetable protein patties for the vegetable protein crumbles and adding tomato sauce.

2. Combine cheeses in bowl. Spread 1 cup sauce on bottom of 13 x 9-inch baking pan; top with 4 lasagne noodles, overlapping slightly. Spoon ⅓ of cheese mixture over noodles, spreading lightly with rubber spatula. Top with 1 cup sauce. Repeat layers 2 times, ending with layer of noodles, cheese, and remaining sauce.

3. Bake lasagne, loosely covered with aluminum foil, at 350 degrees until sauce is bubbly, about 1 hour. Let stand 10 minutes before cutting.

EGGPLANT LASAGNE

Generous slices of eggplant replace noodles in this flavorful version of lasagne.

6 servings

  1 large eggplant (about 1½ pounds),
    unpeeled, cut into ½-inch slices
  3 egg whites, lightly beaten
  ½ cup unseasoned dry breadcrumbs
  ¼ cup grated, fat-free Parmesan cheese
2-4 tablespoons extra-virgin olive oil
    Olive oil cooking spray
    Tomato and "Meat" Sauce (see p. 701)
  1 cup fat-free cottage cheese
¼-½ cup fat-free sour cream
¾-1 cup (3-4 ounces) shredded fat-free
    mozzarella cheese

Per Serving
Calories: 256
% Calories from fat: 19
Fat (gm): 5.7
Saturated fat (gm): 0.8
Cholesterol (mg): 0
Sodium (mg): 491
Protein (gm): 24
Carbohydrate (gm): 29.8
Exchanges
Milk: 0.0
Vegetable: 3.0
Fruit: 0.0
Bread: 1.0
Meat: 2.0
Fat: 0.0

1. Dip eggplant slices in egg whites; coat lightly with combined breadcrumbs and Parmesan cheese. Saute eggplant in oil in large skillet until browned, about 5 minutes on each side (if additional oil is needed, spray eggplant with cooking spray).

2. Spoon ⅓ of Tomato and "Meat" Sauce into 12 x 7-inch baking dish; arrange half the eggplant slices over the sauce. Mix cottage cheese and sour cream; spread half the mixture over eggplant. Repeat layers, ending with remaining sauce.

3. Bake, uncovered, at 350 degrees until bubbly, about 45 minutes, sprinkling with mozzarella cheese during last 10 minutes.

BROCCOLI AND CHEESE ROTOLI WITH MANY-CLOVES GARLIC SAUCE

Some people prefer cutting lasagne noodles into halves before filling, as they are easier to handle in eating. If cut, spread each rotolo with 1½ to 2 tablespoons of the cheese mixture.

6 servings

Olive oil cooking spray
1½ cups chopped broccoli
¾ cup chopped red bell pepper
3 cloves garlic, minced
¾ teaspoon dried marjoram leaves
½ teaspoon dried thyme leaves
1¼ cups reduced-fat ricotta cheese
Salt and pepper, to taste
12 lasagne noodles (10 ounces), cooked, room temperature
Many-Cloves Garlic Sauce (see p. 710)

Per Serving
Calories: 210
% Calories from fat: 20
Fat (gm): 4.9
Saturated fat (gm): 0.2
Cholesterol (mg): 6.6
Sodium (mg): 104
Protein (gm): 10.1
Carbohydrate (gm): 31.7
Exchanges
Milk: 0.0
Vegetable: 2.0
Fruit: 0.0
Bread: 1.5
Meat: 0.0
Fat: 1.0

1. Spray medium skillet with cooking spray; heat over medium heat until hot. Saute broccoli, bell pepper, and garlic until tender, about 8 minutes. Stir in herbs; cook 1 to 2 minutes longer and remove from heat.

2. Mix cheese and vegetable mixture; season to taste with salt and pepper. Spread 3 to 4 tablespoons of mixture evenly on each noodle; roll up and place, seam side down, in baking dish.

3. Spoon Many-Cloves Garlic Sauce over each rotolo. Bake, loosely covered with aluminum foil, at 350 degrees until rotoli are hot through and sauce is bubbly, 20 to 30 minutes.

SPINACH-MUSHROOM ROTOLI WITH MARINARA SAUCE

 Portobello or shiitake mushrooms would add a wonderful flavor and aroma to the pasta filling.

6 servings

Olive oil cooking spray
2 cups sliced mushrooms
1 package (10 ounces) fresh spinach, cleaned, chopped
2 cloves garlic, minced
1 teaspoon dried basil leaves
1 teaspoon dried tarragon leaves
½ package (8-ounce size) reduced-fat cream cheese, room temperature
½ cup fat-free ricotta cheese
¼ teaspoon salt
¼ teaspoon pepper
12 lasagne noodles, cooked, room temperature
Marinara Sauce (see p. 700)

Per Serving
Calories: 286
% Calories from fat: 30
Fat (gm): 10.3
Saturated fat (gm): 2.7
Cholesterol (mg): 8.7
Sodium (mg): 686
Protein (gm): 12.5
Carbohydrate (gm): 38
Exchanges
Milk: 0.0
Vegetable: 3.0
Fruit: 0.0
Bread: 1.5
Meat: 0.0
Fat: 2.0

1. Spray large skillet with cooking spray; heat over medium heat until hot. Cook mushrooms, covered, until they release juices, 3 to 5 minutes. Add spinach, garlic, and herbs to skillet; cook, covered, until spinach is wilted, 2 to 3 minutes. Cook, uncovered, over medium to medium-high heat until liquid is gone, about 10 minutes; cool.

2. Combine cheeses, salt, and pepper in bowl; stir in mushroom mixture. Spread 3 to 4 tablespoons of mixture on each noodle; roll up and place in baking dish.

3. Spoon Marinara Sauce over each rotolo. Bake, loosely covered with aluminum foil, at 350 degrees until rotoli are hot through and sauce is bubbly, 20 to 30 minutes.

SPAGHETTI AND EGGPLANT PARMESAN

Baked in a springform pan, the presentation of this dish is unusual and quite attractive.

6 servings

Olive oil cooking spray

1 large eggplant (about 3 pounds), unpeeled, cut into ¼-inch-thick slices

1 small onion, very finely chopped

3 cloves garlic, minced

1 tablespoon olive oil

2 cans (8 ounces each) low-sodium tomato sauce

8 medium plum tomatoes, chopped

⅛ teaspoon crushed red pepper

3 tablespoons finely chopped fresh basil leaves, *or* 2 teaspoons dried

12 ounces spaghetti, cooked, room temperature

¼ cup grated Parmesan cheese

2-3 tablespoons dry unseasoned breadcrumbs

Per Serving
Calories: 372
% Calories from fat: 13
Fat (gm): 5.4
Saturated fat (gm): 1.4
Cholesterol (mg): 3.3
Sodium (mg): 139
Protein (gm): 13.5
Carbohydrate (gm): 70
Exchanges
Milk: 0.0
Vegetable: 3.0
Fruit: 0.0
Bread: 3.5
Meat: 0.0
Fat: 1.0

1. Spray large skillet with cooking spray; heat over medium heat until hot. Cook eggplant slices until browned, about 4 minutes on each side. Set aside.

2. Saute onions and garlic in oil in large skillet until tender, 3 to 5 minutes. Add tomato sauce, tomatoes, and red pepper to skillet; heat to boiling. Reduce heat and simmer, uncovered, until mixture is medium sauce consistency, about 15 minutes. Remove from heat; stir in basil. Pour sauce over spaghetti and toss; stir in Parmesan cheese.

3. Spray 9-inch springform pan with cooking spray; coat with breadcrumbs. Line bottom and side of pan with ¾ of eggplant slices, overlapping slices and allowing those on side to extend 1 to 1½ inches above top of pan. Spoon spaghetti mixture into pan; press into pan firmly. Fold eggplant slices at top of pan over spaghetti mixture. Overlap remaining eggplant slices on top, pressing firmly into place.

4. Bake, uncovered, at 350 degrees until hot through, about 30 minutes. Let stand 15 minutes; remove side of pan. Cut into wedges to serve.

CANNELLONI CASSEROLE

Lasagne noodles are filled and rolled, then sauced and baked. Add other finely chopped vegetables, such as carrots or zucchini, to the cheese mixture if you like.

6 servings

2 packages (10 ounces each) frozen, chopped spinach, thawed, very well drained
2 cups fat-free small-curd cottage cheese
⅓ cup grated fat-free Parmesan cheese
1½ teaspoons dried basil leaves
¼ teaspoon ground nutmeg
   Salt and black pepper, to taste
3 eggs
12 lasagne noodles, cooked
¼ cup all-purpose flour
2 cups fat-free milk
2-3 tablespoons margarine, *or* butter
   Cayenne and white pepper, to taste
⅓ cup coarsely crushed garlic croutons
   Parsley, finely chopped, as garnish

Per Serving
Calories: 325
% Calories from fat: 26
Fat (gm): 9.5
Saturated fat (gm): 1.9
Cholesterol (mg): 107.8
Sodium (mg): 483
Protein (gm): 24.4
Carbohydrate (gm): 37.5
Exchanges
Milk: 0.0
Vegetable: 2.0
Fruit: 0.0
Bread: 2.0
Meat: 2.0
Fat: 0.5

1. Mix spinach, cheeses, basil, and nutmeg in bowl; season to taste with salt and black pepper. Stir in eggs.

2. Cut lasagne noodles crosswise into halves. Spread about 2 tablespoons cheese mixture on each noodle and roll up. Place rolls, seam sides down, in lightly greased baking pan, 11 x 12 x 7 inches.

3. Whisk flour into milk in small saucepan; heat to boiling, whisking frequently. Boil, whisking constantly, until thickened, about 1 minute. Remove from heat; stir in margarine until melted; season to taste with salt, cayenne, and white pepper. Pour sauce over pasta rolls; sprinkle with croutons.

4. Bake, uncovered, at 350 degrees until hot through, about 30 minutes. Sprinkle with parsley before serving.

EGGPLANT AND TOMATO SAUCE PARMESAN

 Eggplant layered with a Tomato and "Meat" Sauce and melty cheese, then baked to rich goodness.

6-8 servings

2 large eggplants, unpeeled (about 3 pounds), cut into scant ½-inch slices
Salt
Olive oil cooking spray
Tomato and "Meat" Sauce (see p. 701)
6 ounces (¾ cup) shredded fat-free mozzarella cheese
6 ounces (¾ cup) shredded reduced-fat mozzarella cheese
½ cup grated fat-free Parmesan cheese

Per Serving
Calories: 215
% Calories from fat: 15
Fat (gm): 3.7
Saturated fat (gm): 2.4
Cholesterol (mg): 11.4
Sodium (mg): 462
Protein (gm): 23.1
Carbohydrate (gm): 23.3
Exchanges
Milk: 0.0
Vegetable: 3.0
Fruit: 0.0
Bread: 0.0
Meat: 2.5
Fat: 0.0

1. Sprinkle eggplant slices lightly with salt; let stand 30 minutes. Rinse thoroughly and drain on paper toweling.

2. Line large jelly roll pan with aluminum foil; spray with cooking spray. Arrange eggplant on pan; spray generously with cooking spray. Bake at 425 degrees until tender, 20 to 30 minutes.

3. Layer ⅓ of eggplant slices, ⅓ of Tomato and "Meat" Sauce, and ⅓ of combined mozzarella cheeses in greased 13 x 9-inch baking pan. Repeat layers 2 times; sprinkle with Parmesan cheese. Bake, uncovered, at 350 degrees until bubbly, 30 to 40 minutes. Cool 10 minutes before cutting.

VEGETABLE-BARLEY MOUSSAKA

This meatless version of traditional moussaka is filled with sumptuous vegetables and hearty barley, topped with a creamy custard.

12 servings

1 large eggplant, unpeeled, sliced
Olive oil cooking spray
1 pound potatoes, unpeeled, sliced
3 cups chopped onions
8 ounces carrots, sliced
3 cloves garlic, minced
1 teaspoon ground cinnamon
1 teaspoon dried oregano leaves
½ teaspoon dried thyme leaves
¾ cup Canned Vegetable Stock (see p. 63)
2 cups chopped tomatoes
2 cups sliced mushrooms
2 cups cooked barley
1 small zucchini, sliced
Salt and pepper, to taste
Custard Topping (recipe follows)
Ground nutmeg to taste

Per Serving
Calories: 327
% Calories from fat: 25
Fat (gm): 9.3
Saturated fat (gm): 1.9
Cholesterol (mg): 28
Sodium (mg): 188
Protein (gm): 10.6
Carbohydrate (gm): 52.5
Exchanges
Milk: 0.0
Vegetable: 3.0
Fruit: 0.0
Bread: 2.5
Meat: 0.0
Fat: 1.5

1. Spray eggplant slices on both sides with cooking spray. Bake in sprayed aluminum-foil-lined jelly roll pan at 350 degrees until tender but still firm to touch, about 20 minutes. Arrange eggplant on bottom of 13 x 9 x 2-in. baking pan.

2. Heat potatoes, onions, carrots, garlic, cinnamon, oregano, thyme, and vegetable stock to boiling in large skillet; reduce heat and simmer, uncovered, 3 to 5 minutes. Add tomatoes and mushrooms; simmer, uncovered, until tomatoes are soft. Add barley and zucchini; cook, uncovered, until mixture is thick. Season to taste with salt and pepper.

3. Spoon vegetable mixture over eggplant. Pour Custard Topping over and sprinkle with nutmeg. Bake at 350 degrees until lightly browned on the top, about 45 minutes. Cool 5 to 10 minutes before cutting.

Custard Topping

⅓ cup margarine, *or* butter
½ cup all-purpose flour
3 cups fat-free milk
1 egg
2 egg whites
Salt and pepper, to taste

1. Melt margarine in medium saucepan; stir in flour. Cook over medium heat until bubbly, about 2 minutes, stirring constantly. Stir in milk; heat to boiling. Boil, stirring constantly, until thickened, about 1 minute.

2. Beat egg and egg whites in small bowl. Stir about 1 cup milk mixture into eggs; stir egg mixture back into saucepan. Cook over low heat until thickened, 2 to 3 minutes; season to taste with salt and pepper.

EGGPLANT PROVENÇAL

Serve this casserole as an entrée or half-portions as a side dish. It can be assembled several hours in advance; sprinkle with the breadcrumb mixture just before baking.

4 servings (1½ cups each)

Olive oil cooking spray
1 cup chopped onion
1 clove garlic, minced
2 small eggplant (about 1 pound each), peeled, cut into ¾-inch cubes
2 medium green bell peppers, cut into ¼-inch strips
2 cups chopped tomatoes
¼ cup finely chopped parsley
¼ cup sliced, pitted ripe, *or* pimiento-stuffed, olives
1 tablespoon drained capers
½-¾ teaspoon dried basil leaves
½-¾ teaspoon dried oregano leaves

Per Serving
Calories: 226
% Calories from fat: 28
Fat (gm): 7.6
Saturated fat (gm): 1.2
Cholesterol (mg): 0
Sodium (mg): 549
Protein (gm): 6.6
Carbohydrate (gm): 37.3
Exchanges
Milk: 0.0
Vegetable: 4.0
Fruit: 0.0
Bread: 1.0
Meat: 0.0
Fat: 1.0

Salt and pepper, to taste

½ cup dry unseasoned breadcrumbs

2 tablespoons grated, fat-free Parmesan cheese

1 tablespoon margarine, melted

1. Spray large skillet with cooking spray; heat over medium heat until hot. Saute onion and garlic 3 to 4 minutes; add eggplant, bell pepper, and tomatoes. Cook, covered, over medium heat until vegetables are tender, 8 to 10 minutes, stirring occasionally.

2. Stir parsley, olives, capers, and herbs into mixture; season to taste with salt and pepper. Spoon mixture into 11 x 7-inch baking dish. Combine breadcrumbs, Parmesan cheese, and margarine; sprinkle over casserole. Bake at 350 degrees, uncovered, until mixture is bubbly and top browned, about 30 minutes.

RATATOUILLE

We've baked this French vegetable stew in layers, the traditional way.

4 side-dish servings

Olive oil cooking spray

2 medium onions, sliced

½ large green bell pepper, sliced

4 cloves garlic, minced

3 medium tomatoes, coarsely chopped

Salt and pepper, to taste

1 medium eggplant (about 1¼ pounds), unpeeled

3 medium zucchini, sliced

3 tablespoons minced parsley

1-1½ teaspoons dried oregano leaves

1 teaspoon dried marjoram leaves

½ teaspoon dried thyme leaves

½ teaspoon dried savory leaves

Per Serving
Calories: 103
% Calories from fat: 7
Fat (gm): 1
Saturated fat (gm): 0.2
Cholesterol (mg): 0
Sodium (mg): 20
Protein (gm): 4.2
Carbohydrate (gm): 23.5
Exchanges
Milk: 0.0
Vegetable: 4.0
Fruit: 0.0
Bread: 0.0
Meat: 0.0
Fat: 0.0

1. Spray large skillet with cooking spray; heat over medium heat until hot. Saute onions, bell pepper, and garlic until tender, about 5 minutes. Add tomatoes and cook, covered, 5 minutes; cook uncovered until excess liquid is gone, about 5 minutes. Season to taste with salt and pepper. Transfer mixture to bowl and reserve.

2. Cut eggplant into strips measuring about 3 x ½ x ½ inches. Add eggplant and zucchini to skillet; spray generously with cooking spray. Cook over medium heat, stirring occasionally, until lightly browned; season to taste with salt and pepper.

3. Layer half the eggplant mixture in ungreased 1½-quart casserole; sprinkle with ¼ of combined herbs. Layer half the onion mixture over eggplant mixture; sprinkle with ¼ of herbs. Repeat layers, using remaining eggplant mixture, onion mixture, and herbs.

4. Bake, uncovered, at 400 degrees until hot through, 15 to 20 minutes.

EGGPLANT CASSEROLE SOUFFLÉ

Something different that's bound to please. Try Fresh Tomato and Herb Sauce or Fresh Tomato-Basil Sauce (see p. 702) as delicious alternatives to the sour cream sauce.

8 side-dish servings

Vegetable cooking spray
2 medium eggplants (1¼ pounds each), peeled, cut into ¾-inch slices
Vegetable cooking spray
¼ cup finely chopped onion
1 clove garlic, minced
¼ cup grated fat-free Parmesan cheese
2 tablespoons lemon juice
½-¾ teaspoon salt
¼ teaspoon pepper
4 eggs, separated
1 egg white
Minted Sour Cream (recipe follows)

Per Serving
Calories: 105
% Calories from fat: 23
Fat (gm): 2.8
Saturated fat (gm): 0.8
Cholesterol (mg): 106.5
Sodium (mg): 218
Protein (gm): 7.7
Carbohydrate (gm): 14
Exchanges
Milk: 0.0
Vegetable: 2.5
Fruit: 0.0
Bread: 0.0
Meat: 0.5
Fat: 0.5

1. Spray large skillet with cooking spray; heat over medium heat until hot. Cook eggplant slices over medium heat until browned on the bottom, 3 to 5 minutes. Spray tops of slices with cooking spray and turn; cook until brown on the bottom. Cut eggplant into coarse pieces; mix with onion, garlic, cheese, lemon juice, salt, and pepper.

2. Beat egg yolks in small bowl until thick and lemon colored, about 5 minutes. With clean beaters in large bowl, beat egg whites until stiff, but not dry, peaks form. Stir yolks into eggplant mixture; fold eggplant mixture into beaten egg whites.

3. Pour mixture into ungreased 2-quart soufflé dish. Bake at 350 degrees until puffed and brown, about 30 minutes. Serve with Minted Sour Cream.

Minted Sour Cream

(makes about 1 cup)

>   1 cup fat-free sour cream
>   3-4 tablespoons fresh or 1 teaspoon dried,
>   mint leaves
>   Salt and white pepper, to taste

1. Mix sour cream and mint; season to taste with salt and white pepper. Refrigerate until serving time.

EGGPLANT AND ZUCCHINI CASSEROLE

Herb-seasoned and baked with tomato-cheese and breadcrumb toppings, this casserole is both flavorful and healthful.

4 servings

>   Olive oil cooking spray
>   1 large eggplant, unpeeled, cut into ½-
>   inch thick slices
>   4 medium zucchini, cut in half length-
>   wise
>   1 medium red bell pepper, sliced
>   ½ teaspoon dried marjoram leaves

Per Serving
Calories: 206
% Calories from fat: 18
Fat (gm): 4.3
Saturated fat (gm): 0.5
Cholesterol (mg): 0.3
Sodium (mg): 660
Protein (gm): 13.8
Carbohydrate (gm): 31.2

½ teaspoon dried oregano leaves

¼ teaspoon garlic powder

Pinch crushed red pepper (or to taste)

Salt and pepper, to taste

¼ cup sliced ripe olives, rinsed, drained

4 medium tomatoes, seeded, coarsely chopped

1 package (8 ounces) fat-free cream cheese, cut into cubes

¼ cup fat-free milk

2 tablespoons reduced-sodium tomato paste

2 teaspoons sugar

Salt and pepper, to taste

3 tablespoons whole wheat breadcrumbs

Exchanges
Milk: 0.0
Vegetable: 5.0
Fruit: 0.0
Bread: 0.5
Meat: 0.5
Fat: 0.5

1. Spray aluminum-foil-lined large jelly roll pan with cooking spray. Arrange eggplant, zucchini, and bell pepper in pan; spray vegetables with cooking spray and sprinkle with marjoram, oregano, garlic powder, and crushed red pepper.

2. Roast vegetables at 475 degrees until beginning to brown, 15 to 20 minutes. Sprinkle lightly with salt and pepper. Arrange vegetables in greased 11 x 7-inch baking dish. Sprinkle olives and tomatoes over top.

3. Combine cream cheese, milk, tomato paste, and sugar in small saucepan; heat over low heat until cheese is melted, stirring constantly. Season to taste with salt and pepper; pour over vegetables and sprinkle with breadcrumbs. Lower oven temperature to 375 degrees and bake, uncovered, 15 minutes or until vegetables are tender.

ZUCCHINI AND MUSHROOMS PARMESAN

Yellow summer squash can be substituted for all or part of the zucchini in this dish.

4 side-dish servings

1¾ pounds zucchini, cut lengthwise into ⅛-inch slices

2 large portobello, *or* shiitake, mushrooms, sliced

1 pound plum tomatoes, thinly sliced
    Salt and pepper, to taste

½ cup finely chopped onion

3 cloves garlic, minced

1 teaspoon dried basil leaves

½ teaspoon dried marjoram leaves

¼-½ teaspoon crushed red pepper

¼ cup dry unseasoned breadcrumbs

1 cup (4 ounces) shredded reduced-fat mozzarella cheese

3 tablespoons grated fat-free Parmesan cheese

Per Serving
Calories: 184
% Calories from fat: 24
Fat (gm): 5.1
Saturated fat (gm): 3.2
Cholesterol (mg): 15.2
Sodium (mg): 311
Protein (gm): 13.1
Carbohydrate (gm): 22.3
Exchanges
Milk: 0.0
Vegetable: 3.0
Fruit: 0.0
Bread: 0.5
Meat: 1.0
Fat: 0.5

1. Layer zucchini, mushrooms, and tomatoes in lightly greased 11 x 7-inch baking dish; sprinkle lightly with salt and pepper. Sprinkle onion, garlic, basil, marjoram, and crushed red pepper over vegetables.

2. Combine breadcrumbs and cheeses; sprinkle over vegetable mixture. Bake, uncovered, at 350 degrees 30 minutes or until vegetables are tender.

PASTITSIO

Sweet cinnamon and nutmeg season this Greek favorite. Prebrowned all-vegetable protein crumbles substitute for the lamb or beef the dish would usually have.

6 servings

Olive oil cooking spray

1 package (12 ounces) frozen pre-browned all vegetable protein crumbles

1 cup chopped onion

1 can (8 ounces) reduced-sodium tomato paste

⅓ cup water

Salt and pepper, to taste

2 cups elbow macaroni, cooked

⅓ cup grated fat-free Parmesan cheese

¼-½ teaspoon ground cinnamon

¼ teaspoon ground nutmeg

2⅓ cups fat-free milk

2 tablespoons margarine

4 eggs, lightly beaten

Parsley, minced, as garnish

Per Serving
Calories: 322
% Calories from fat: 22
Fat (gm): 8
Saturated fat (gm): 2
Cholesterol (mg): 143.6
Sodium (mg): 452
Protein (gm): 26.2
Carbohydrate (gm): 37.1
Exchanges
Milk: 0.5
Vegetable: 2.0
Fruit: 0.0
Bread: 1.0
Meat: 3.0
Fat: 0.0

1. Spray large skillet with cooking spray; heat over medium heat until hot. Saute protein crumbles and onion until onion is tender, 5 to 8 minutes. Stir in tomato paste and water; cook 2 to 3 minutes longer. Season to taste with salt and pepper.

2. Spoon half the macaroni into 13 x 9-inch baking pan; spoon protein crumbles mixture over macaroni. Combine cheese and spices; sprinkle over casserole. Spoon remaining macaroni over the top.

3. Heat milk and margarine in medium saucepan, stirring until margarine is melted. Whisk about half the mixture into eggs; whisk egg mixture back into milk. Pour over macaroni.

4. Bake, uncovered, until casserole is bubbly, 50 to 60 minutes. Sprinkle with parsley.

BAKED EGGPLANT RAGOUT

 Sweet spices impart flavors of the Mediterranean.

6 servings

Olive oil cooking spray
2 medium eggplant (about 1¼ pounds each), peeled, cut into ½-inch slices
1 medium onion, sliced
4 cloves garlic, minced
1 package (12 ounces) frozen pre-browned all-vegetable protein crumbles, thawed
½ teaspoon dried marjoram leaves
¼ teaspoon dried thyme leaves
½ teaspoon ground cinnamon
⅛ teaspoon ground nutmeg
Salt and pepper, to taste
½ cup raisins
¼ cup sliced almonds, toasted
¾ cup uncooked converted rice
1¼ cups Canned Vegetable or Basic Vegetable, Stock (see pp. 63, 58)
2 green onions and tops, thinly sliced

Per Serving
Calories: 308
% Calories from fat: 9
Fat (gm): 3.3
Saturated fat (gm): 0.4
Cholesterol (mg): 0
Sodium (mg): 272
Protein (gm): 18
Carbohydrate (gm): 52.8
Exchanges
Milk: 0.0
Vegetable: 3.0
Fruit: 0.5
Bread: 1.5
Meat: 2.0
Fat: 0.0

1. Spray large skillet with cooking spray; heat over medium heat until hot. Cook eggplant over medium heat until browned on the bottom, about 5 minutes. Spray tops of eggplant slices with cooking spray and turn; cook until browned on the bottom. Remove from skillet and reserve.

2. Add onion and garlic to skillet; saute until tender, 3 to 5 minutes. Stir in protein crumbles, herbs, and spices; cook over medium heat 2 to 3 minutes. Season to taste with salt and pepper. Mix in raisins and almonds.

3. Spoon rice into bottom of 13 x 9-inch baking pan; top with half the eggplant slices and half the protein crumbles mixture. Repeat layers; pour stock over.

4. Bake, covered with aluminum foil, at 350 degrees until rice is tender, 35 to 45 minutes. Sprinkle with green onions. Cut into squares.

EGGPLANT BAKED IN EGGPLANT

A vegetable casserole baked in its own shell!

4 servings

4 medium eggplant (1¼ pounds each)
¾ cup finely chopped onion
2 cloves garlic, minced
2 tablespoons extra-virgin olive oil
½ package (12-ounce size) frozen pre-browned all-vegetable protein crumbles, thawed
1½ teaspoons dried basil leaves
½ teaspoon dried rosemary leaves
1 cup cooked bulgur, *or* brown rice
⅓ cup grated fat-free Parmesan cheese
Salt and pepper, to taste
1 cup (4 ounces) shredded reduced-fat, *or* fat-free, mozzarella cheese
Herbed Tomato Halves, ½ recipe (see p. 623)

Per Serving
Calories: 447
% Calories from fat: 24
Fat (gm): 12.5
Saturated fat (gm): 4.2
Cholesterol (mg): 15.2
Sodium (mg): 501
Protein (gm): 28.3
Carbohydrate (gm): 60.9
Exchanges
Milk: 0.0
Vegetable: 10.0
Fruit: 0.0
Bread: 0.5
Meat: 1.5
Fat: 2.0

1. Cut eggplant lengthwise into halves. Using grapefruit spoon or serrated knife, remove pulp from eggplant, leaving ¼-inch shells. Cut pulp into ½-inch cubes.

2. Saute eggplant, onion, and garlic in oil in large skillet until eggplant is barely tender, 7 to 10 minutes. Stir in protein crumbles and herbs; cook over medium heat 2 to 3 minutes. Stir in bulgur and Parmesan cheese; season to taste with salt and pepper.

3. Spoon mixture into eggplant shells and place in baking pan; pour 1 inch hot water in baking pan. Bake, covered with aluminum foil, at 350 degrees until eggplant mixture is tender, about 35 minutes.

4. Uncover eggplant; sprinkle with mozzarella cheese and bake at 350 degrees until cheese is melted, about 5 minutes. Serve with Herbed Tomato Halves.

GOULASH CASSEROLE

This sauerkraut dish, creamy with sour cream and seasoned with caraway, is excellent served with Real Mashed Potatoes and Lima Rye Bread (see pp. 610, 658).

6 servings (about 1⅓ cups each)

Vegetable cooking spray
2 medium onions, chopped
1 green bell pepper, chopped
1 red bell pepper, chopped
2 cloves garlic, minced
1 tablespoon flour
2 teaspoons paprika
1 teaspoon caraway seeds, crushed
½-¾ cup water
1 package (12 ounces) frozen pre-browned all-vegetable protein crumbles
1 can (14 ounces) sauerkraut, rinsed, drained
1 large tomato, coarsely chopped
1 cup fat-free sour cream
Salt and pepper, to taste
Parsley, minced, as garnish

Per Serving
Calories: 164
% Calories from fat: 3
Fat (gm): 0.5
Saturated fat (gm): 0.1
Cholesterol (mg): 0
Sodium (mg): 717
Protein (gm): 17.9
Carbohydrate (gm): 24.1
Exchanges
Milk: 0.0
Vegetable: 2.0
Fruit: 0.0
Bread: 1.0
Meat: 1.5
Fat: 0.0

1. Spray large skillet with cooking spray; heat over medium heat until hot. Saute onions, bell peppers, and garlic until tender, 8 to 10 minutes. Stir in flour, paprika, and caraway seeds; cook 1 to 2 minutes longer. Stir in water, protein crumbles, sauerkraut, tomato, and sour cream; season to taste with salt and pepper.

2. Spoon mixture into 11 x 7-inch baking dish or 2-quart casserole. Bake, covered, at 350 degrees until hot through, 20 to 30 minutes. Sprinkle with parsley before serving.

CABBAGE AND SAUERKRAUT CASSEROLE

Cabbage leaves are stuffed, then layered and baked with sauerkraut and tomatoes.

6 servings

1 small head cabbage (about 1¼ pounds)
⅔ package (12-ounce size) frozen pre-browned all-vegetable protein crumbles
1 cup cooked brown rice
2 cloves garlic, minced
2 tablespoons finely chopped parsley
1½-2 teaspoons paprika
Salt and pepper, to taste
1-2 eggs
1 can (16 ounces) sauerkraut, drained
1 can (16 ounces) reduced-sodium whole tomatoes, undrained, coarsely chopped
1 cup thinly sliced onion
1½ teaspoons caraway seeds, crushed
½ cup fat-free sour cream

Per Serving
Calories: 179
% Calories from fat: 9
Fat (gm): 1.8
Saturated fat (gm): 0.4
Cholesterol (mg): 35.5
Sodium (mg): 720
Protein (gm): 15.3
Carbohydrate (gm): 28
Exchanges
Milk: 0.0
Vegetable: 3.0
Fruit: 0.0
Bread: 0.5
Meat: 1.5
Fat: 0.0

1. Remove core from cabbage; remove 12 outside leaves. Thinly slice or shred remaining cabbage and reserve. Place cabbage leaves in large saucepan with water to cover; heat to boiling. Reduce heat and simmer, covered, until cabbage leaves are pliable but not too soft, 2 to 3 minutes. Drain and cool.

2. Mix vegetable protein crumbles, rice, garlic, parsley, and paprika; season to taste with salt and pepper. Mix in egg, using 2 if necessary for mixture to hold together. Place about ¼ cup of mixture in center of each cabbage leaf; fold in sides and roll up.

3. Mix sauerkraut, tomatoes, reserved cabbage, onion, and caraway seeds; sprinkle lightly with salt and pepper and toss. Spoon half the sauerkraut mixture into a large Dutch oven. Place cabbage rolls on sauerkraut mixture; spoon remaining sauerkraut mixture on top. Heat to boiling; transfer to oven and bake, covered, until cabbage is tender, 1 to 1½ hours.

4. Arrange sauerkraut mixture and cabbage rolls on serving platter; serve with sour cream.

SWEET-SPICED CABBAGE WITH QUINOA

Cabbage is baked with a tomato sauce uniquely flavored with apricots, ginger, and sweet spices. Served over quinoa, barley or an aromatic rice would also be excellent choices.

6 servings (about 1½ cups each)

Vegetable cooking spray
¼ cup sliced green onions and tops
2 cans (10 ounces each) diced tomatoes with chilies, undrained
3 tablespoons lemon juice
3 tablespoons cider vinegar
¼ cup packed light brown sugar
½ teaspoon ground cinnamon
¼-½ teaspoon ground ginger
¾ cup Basic Vegetable Stock (see p. 58), *or* water
¼ cup apricot nectar
½ cup chopped dried apricots
Salt and pepper, to taste
1 small cabbage (about 1 pound), sliced
½ cup gingersnap, *or* vanilla wafer, cookie crumbs
4 cups cooked quinoa, warm

Per Serving
Calories: 282
% Calories from fat: 11
Fat (gm): 3.5
Saturated fat (gm): 0.4
Cholesterol (mg): 0
Sodium (mg): 396
Protein (gm): 7.5
Carbohydrate (gm): 58.9
Exchanges
Milk: 0.0
Vegetable: 1.0
Fruit: 0.5
Bread: 3.0
Meat: 0.0
Fat: 0.5

1. Spray a medium saucepan with cooking spray; heat over medium heat until hot. Saute green onions until tender, about 4 minutes.

2. Stir in tomatoes, lemon juice, vinegar, brown sugar, cinnamon, ginger, stock, apricot nectar, and apricots. Heat to boiling; reduce heat and simmer 10 minutes. Season to taste with salt and pepper.

3. Arrange cabbage in lightly greased large baking dish. Pour tomato sauce over cabbage. Bake, covered, at 350 degrees 25 minutes. Sprinkle cookie crumbs over cabbage and bake, uncovered, 15 minutes or until cabbage is tender and crumbs are browned. Serve over quinoa.

SWEDISH "MEATBALL" AND DILLED POTATO CASSEROLE

 Serve this dill-flavored casserole with fried eggs and Herbed Tomato Halves (see p. 623) for brunch or a light supper.

6 servings

Swedish "Meatballs" (recipe follows)
Vegetable cooking spray
1 package (20 ounces) refrigerated, *or* frozen, thawed, shredded hash brown potatoes
1 medium onion, chopped
1 teaspoon dried dill weed, divided
1 cup chopped red bell pepper
1 cup (4 ounces) shredded reduced-fat Cheddar cheese
¾ cup fat-free milk
1 cup fat-free sour cream
Salt and pepper, to taste
Parsley, finely chopped, *or* green onions, as garnish

Per Serving
Calories: 262
% Calories from fat: 14
Fat (gm): 4.2
Saturated fat (gm): 1.7
Cholesterol (mg): 46.1
Sodium (mg): 682
Protein (gm): 16.5
Carbohydrate (gm): 41.8
Exchanges
Milk: 0.0
Vegetable: 1.0
Fruit: 0.0
Bread: 2.0
Meat: 1.5
Fat: 0.0

1. Make Swedish "Meatballs." Spray large skillet with cooking spray; heat over medium heat until hot. Cook "meatballs" until browned on all sides, 8 to 10 minutes.

2. Spray large skillet with cooking spray; heat over medium heat until hot. Add potatoes, onion, ½ teaspoon dill, and bell pepper; cook over medium heat until potatoes are lightly browned, about 10 minutes.

3. Heat cheese and milk in small saucepan over medium-low heat until melted. Stir in sour cream and remaining ½ teaspoon dill weed; stir into potato mixture. Season to taste with salt and pepper.

4. Spoon potato mixture into ungreased 1-quart casserole; top with "meatballs." Bake, uncovered, at 350 degrees until hot through, 15 to 20 minutes. Sprinkle with parsley or green onions.

Swedish "Meatballs"

(makes 1½ dozen)

>   1 cup textured vegetable protein
>   1 cup Basic Vegetable Stock (see p. 58)
>   1 egg, lightly beaten
>   ⅓ cup unseasoned dry breadcrumbs
>   ¼ all-purpose flour
>   ¼ cup chopped onion
>   1 clove garlic, minced
>   1½ teaspoon dried dill weed
>   ½ teaspoon salt
>   ¼ teaspoon cayenne pepper

1. Combine vegetable protein and stock in medium bowl; let stand until stock is absorbed, about 20 minutes. Mix in egg and remaining ingredients. Form mixture into 18 "meatballs."

FOUR

Vegetarian Entrées

SPAGHETTI SQUASH AND SPAGHETTI

Spaghetti squash is tossed first with spaghetti and then with a medley of flavorful vegetables.

4 servings

1	spaghetti squash, halved, seeded
	Olive oil cooking spray
2	small eggplant, unpeeled, cut into ½-inch cubes
2	medium onions, chopped
2	cups sliced mushrooms
4	cloves garlic, minced
4	medium tomatoes, chopped
1½	cups spicy tomato juice
½	cup loosely packed fresh, *or* 1½ teaspoons dried, basil leaves
	Salt and pepper, to taste
8	ounces thin spaghetti, cooked, warm
¼	cup grated fat-free Parmesan cheese

Per Serving
Calories: 442
% Calories from fat: 6
Fat (gm): 3
Saturated fat (gm): 0.5
Cholesterol (mg): 0
Sodium (mg): 557
Protein (gm): 17.7
Carbohydrate (gm): 91.6
Exchanges
Milk: 0.0
Vegetable: 3.0
Fruit: 0.0
Bread: 5.0
Meat: 0.0
Fat: 0.0

1. Place squash halves, cut sides down, in baking pan; add ½ inch water. Bake, covered, at 350 degrees until tender, 30 to 40 minutes. Using fork, scrape squash to separate into strands.

2. Spray Dutch oven or large saucepan with cooking spray; heat over medium heat until hot. Saute eggplant, onions, mushrooms, and garlic 10 minutes. Add tomatoes, tomato juice, and basil; heat to boiling. Reduce heat and simmer, covered, until vegetables are tender, 10 to 15 minutes. Season to taste with salt and pepper.

3. Toss spaghetti and spaghetti squash in large serving bowl; add vegetable mixture and toss. Sprinkle with cheese.

EGGPLANT AND VEGETABLE SAUTE

Another quick and easy recipe, guaranteed to get dinner on the table in record time!

4 servings (about 1 cup each)

Vegetable cooking spray
1 large eggplant (about 1¼ pounds), unpeeled, cubed
2 medium onions, chopped
1 yellow bell pepper, chopped
1 red bell pepper, chopped
4 teaspoons minced roasted garlic
¾ teaspoon dried rosemary leaves
½ teaspoon dried savory leaves
¼-½ teaspoon dried thyme leaves
1 can (15 ounces) cannellini beans, *or* Great Northern beans, rinsed, drained
Salt and pepper, to taste
8 ounces whole wheat spaghetti, *or* other pasta, cooked

Per Serving
Calories: 356
% Calories from fat: 5
Fat (gm): 2.3
Saturated fat (gm): 0.2
Cholesterol (mg): 0
Sodium (mg): 221
Protein (gm): 18.8
Carbohydrate (gm): 79.8
Exchanges
Milk: 0.0
Vegetable: 3.0
Fruit: 0.0
Bread: 4.0
Meat: 0.0
Fat: 0.0

1. Spray large saucepan with cooking spray; heat over medium heat until hot. Cook eggplant, onions, bell peppers, and garlic over medium heat, covered, 5 minutes; cook, uncovered, until vegetables are tender, 5 to 8 minutes. Stir in herbs and beans; cook until hot through, 3 to 5 minutes. Season to taste with salt and pepper.

2. Serve eggplant mixture over spaghetti.

SPICED CORN MÉLANGE

Quick and easy to make when kitchen time is at a premium! Serve with Smashed Potatoes and Greens (see p. 604), oat groats, or brown rice.

4 servings (about 1½ cups each)

Vegetable cooking spray

2 cups (8 ounces) green beans, cut into 1-inch pieces

1½ cups (8 ounces) cubed zucchini

1 medium onion, chopped

1 clove garlic, minced

1 package (16 ounces) frozen whole-kernel corn

1 can (14½ ounces) reduced-sodium diced tomatoes, undrained

¾ teaspoon dried marjoram leaves

¾ teaspoon dried thyme leaves

Salt and pepper, to taste

Per Serving
Calories: 155
% Calories from fat: 3
Fat (gm): 0.7
Saturated fat (gm): 0.1
Cholesterol (mg): 0
Sodium (mg): 23
Protein (gm): 6.5
Carbohydrate (gm): 37
Exchanges
Milk: 0.0
Vegetable: 2.0
Fruit: 0.0
Bread: 1.5
Meat: 0.0
Fat: 0.0

1. Spray large skillet with cooking spray; heat over medium heat until hot. Saute green beans, zucchini, onion, and garlic until onion is tender, 3 to 5 minutes.

2. Add corn, tomatoes, marjoram, and thyme to saucepan; heat to boiling. Reduce heat and simmer, covered, 8 to 10 minutes. Season to taste with salt and pepper.

SWEET POTATO CAKES

Saucer-sized and topped generously with sour cream! The recipe is simple to double or triple, and the cakes can be kept warm in the oven while more are cooking.

2 servings

2 cups shredded sweet potatoes

½ cup shredded carrot

½ cup shredded zucchini

½ cup shredded Jerusalem artichoke, *or* potato

Per Serving
Calories: 303
% Calories from fat: 9
Fat (gm): 3.2
Saturated fat (gm): 0.9
Cholesterol (mg): 106.5
Sodium (mg): 116
Protein (gm): 12.1
Carbohydrate (gm): 56.8

¼ cup finely chopped onion

¼ teaspoon dried sage leaves

Salt and pepper, to taste

1 egg

2 egg whites

¼ cup all-purpose flour

Butter-flavored cooking spray

4 tablespoons fat-free sour cream (optional)

Exchanges
Milk: 0.0
Vegetable: 2.0
Fruit: 0.0
Bread: 2.5
Meat: 1.0
Fat: 0.0

1. Combine vegetables and sage in medium bowl; season to taste with salt and pepper. Mix in egg, egg whites, and flour.

2. Spray medium skillet with cooking spray; heat over medium heat until hot. Add half the vegetable mixture to skillet, pressing down firmly to make a 7- to 8-inch cake. Cook over medium heat until browned on the bottom, 8 to 10 minutes. Loosen cake with spatula and invert onto plate.

3. Spray skillet generously with cooking spray and slide cake back into skillet. Cook until browned on the bottom, 8 to 10 minutes. Repeat with remaining potato mixture. Cut each cake in half and top with 1 tablespoon sour cream if desired.

STUFFED PORTOBELLO MUSHROOMS

These entrée-size mushrooms can also be served as appetizers: select a smaller size, or cut large mushrooms into halves or quarters.

4 servings (2 mushrooms each)

8 large portobello mushrooms (5 or more inches in diameter)

Vegetable cooking spray

1 cup chopped red bell pepper

1 cup chopped yellow bell pepper

½ cup chopped shallot, *or* onion

¼ cup thinly sliced green onions and tops

6 cloves garlic, minced

½ teaspoon dried basil leaves

½ teaspoon dried marjoram leaves

Per Serving
Calories: 168
% Calories from fat: 19
Fat (gm): 3.9
Saturated fat (gm): 2.1
Cholesterol (mg): 6.5
Sodium (mg): 357
Protein (gm): 20.8
Carbohydrate (gm): 15.1
Exchanges
Milk: 0.0
Vegetable: 2.0
Fruit: 0.0
Bread: 0.0
Meat: 2.0
Fat: 0.0

¼-½ teaspoon dried thyme leaves
     Salt and pepper, to taste
   6 ounces shredded fat-free mozzarella, *or*
     Cheddar, cheese
   2 ounces goat's cheese, crumbled
     Basil, *or* parsley, leaves finely chopped
     as garnish

1. Remove mushroom stems, chop, and reserve. Bake mushrooms, smooth sides down, in large greased jelly roll pan at 425 degrees for 15 minutes.

2. Spray large skillet with cooking spray; heat over medium heat until hot. Saute mushroom stems, bell pepper, shallot, green onions, and garlic until tender, 8 to 10 minutes. Stir in herbs and cook 1 to 2 minutes longer; season to taste with salt and pepper.

3. Spoon vegetable mixture onto mushrooms; sprinkle with cheeses. Bake at 425 degrees until mushrooms are tender and cheeses melted, about 10 minutes. Garnish with basil or parsley.

ORANGE-SCENTED VEGETABLES WITH TEMPEH

Both orange juice and rind are used to accent this family-style dish. Substitute light firm tofu for the tempeh, if you like.

6 servings

   2 packages (8 ounces each) tempeh, cut into strips, *or* cubes
1½ cups orange juice
   2 teaspoons grated orange rind
   2 cloves garlic, minced
   ¾ teaspoon dried marjoram leaves
   ½ teaspoon dried thyme leaves
   1 cinnamon stick (1-inch piece)
     Vegetable cooking spray
   1 large onion, sliced
   3 medium tomatoes, chopped
   1 tablespoon flour
   3 large carrots, cut into 1-inch pieces

Per Serving
Calories: 282
% Calories from fat: 20
Fat (gm): 6.5
Saturated fat (gm): 1.1
Cholesterol (mg): 0
Sodium (mg): 22
Protein (gm): 19.1
Carbohydrate (gm): 40.6
Exchanges
Milk: 0.0
Vegetable: 1.5
Fruit: 0.5
Bread: 1.5
Meat: 2.0
Fat: 0.0

3 medium potatoes, unpeeled, cubed
Salt and pepper, to taste

1. Arrange tempeh in shallow baking dish; combine orange juice and rind, garlic, marjoram, thyme, and cinnamon and pour over tempeh. Refrigerate 1 to 2 hours. Drain, reserving marinade.

2. Spray large skillet with cooking spray; heat over medium heat until hot. Saute tempeh until browned, 2 to 3 minutes. Add onion and saute until tender, 5 to 8 minutes. Stir in tomatoes; cook over medium heat 2 to 3 minutes. Add flour and cook 1 to 2 minutes longer.

3. Add reserved marinade, carrots, and potatoes to skillet; heat to boiling. Reduce heat and simmer, covered, until vegetables are tender, 10 to 15 minutes. Season to taste with salt and pepper.

BARBECUED TEMPEH AND PEPPERS

 Serve in toasted multigrain buns for fabulous sandwiches, too!

4 servings (generous 1 cup each)

1 package (8 ounces) tempeh
Tamari Marinade (see p. 735)
Vegetable cooking spray
1 cup sliced onion
2 medium red, *or* green, bell peppers, sliced
1 teaspoon minced garlic
1 cup water
¼ cup reduced-sodium tomato paste
1-2 tablespoons unsulphured molasses
1-2 tablespoons brown sugar
2 teaspoons prepared mustard
2 teaspoons cider vinegar
1 teaspoon chili powder
Salt and pepper, to taste
3 cups cooked brown basmati rice, warm

Per Serving
Calories: 371
% Calories from fat: 15
Fat (gm): 6.4
Saturated fat (gm): 0.8
Cholesterol (mg): 0
Sodium (mg): 394
Protein (gm): 20.1
Carbohydrate (gm): 64.1
Exchanges
Milk: 0.5
Vegetable: 3.0
Fruit: 0.0
Bread: 3.0
Meat: 1.0
Fat: 0.5

1. Place tempeh in shallow glass bowl; pour Tamari Marinade over. Refrigerate, covered, several hours or overnight, turning occasionally. Drain; reserve marinade. Cut tempeh into ½-inch cubes.

2. Spray large skillet with cooking spray; heat over medium heat until hot. Saute onion, bell peppers, and garlic until tender, 5 to 8 minutes.

3. Add reserved marinade and remaining ingredients, except salt and pepper and rice, to skillet; heat to boiling. Reduce heat and simmer, uncovered, until mixture is thickened, mashing cubes of tempeh slightly with a fork. Season to taste with salt and pepper; serve over rice.

GARDEN VEGETABLES AND TEMPEH SAUTE

 Vary the vegetables according to season and availability. Serve over rice, fresh Chinese-style noodles, or pasta, if desired.

4 servings (about 1¼ cups each)

Tamari Marinade (see p. 736)
1 package (8 ounces) tempeh
Olive oil cooking spray
1 cup sliced onion
2 medium red bell peppers, sliced
1 teaspoon minced garlic
1 cup reduced-sodium tomato juice
1 medium zucchini, sliced
2 cups (4 ounces) sliced mushrooms
1 teaspoon dried basil leaves
1 teaspoon dried oregano leaves
¼ teaspoon cayenne pepper
2 medium tomatoes, cut into wedges
Salt and pepper, to taste
Parsley, minced, as garnish

Per Serving
Calories: 218
% Calories from fat: 21
Fat (gm): 5.5
Saturated fat (gm): 0.8
Cholesterol (mg): 0
Sodium (mg): 323
Protein (gm): 17.4
Carbohydrate (gm): 30.3
Exchanges
Milk: 0.0
Vegetable: 3.0
Fruit: 0.0
Bread: 1.0
Meat: 1.0
Fat: 0.5

1. Make marinade, substituting red wine vinegar for the cider vinegar and Italian seasoning for the chili powder. Pour over tempeh in shallow glass bowl. Refrigerate, covered, 4 hours or overnight. Drain; reserve marinade. Cut tempeh into ½-inch cubes.

2. Spray large skillet with cooking spray. Saute onion, bell peppers, and garlic 5 minutes. Add tempeh and cook until vegetables are tender and tempeh is browned, about 5 minutes.

3. Stir in reserved marinade and remaining ingredients, except tomatoes, salt and pepper, and parsley; heat to boiling. Reduce heat and simmer, covered, until vegetables are tender, 5 to 8 minutes. Add tomato wedges; cook, covered, until softened, about 5 minutes. Season with salt and pepper. Sprinkle with parsley.

"SAUSAGE"-STUFFED ACORN SQUASH

Easy to make, delicious to eat!

4 servings

2	acorn squash (about 1 pound each)
	Vegetable cooking spray
1	small onion, chopped
1	clove garlic, minced
½	package (4-ounce size) sausage-style all-vegetable protein patties, *or* links, crumbled
½	cup chopped tomato
¼	cup water
½	cup cooked rice
½	teaspoon dried sage leaves
½	teaspoon dried thyme leaves
	Salt and pepper, to taste
	Parsley, minced, as garnish

Per Serving
Calories: 140
% Calories from fat: 16
Fat (gm): 2.7
Saturated fat (gm): 0.5
Cholesterol (mg): 0
Sodium (mg): 96
Protein (gm): 5.1
Carbohydrate (gm): 27.1
Exchanges
Milk: 0.0
Vegetable: 1.0
Fruit: 0.0
Bread: 1.5
Meat: 0.0
Fat: 0.0

1. Cut squash in half and scoop out seeds. Place squash, cut sides down, in baking pan; add ½ inch water. Bake, covered, at 400 degrees until flesh is fork-tender, about 30 minutes. Drain.

2. Spray large skillet with cooking spray; heat over medium heat until hot. Saute onion, garlic, and crumbled vegetable protein patties 2 to 3 minutes. Add tomato, water, rice, sage, and thyme. Cook over medium to medium-high heat until mixture is almost dry, about 5 minutes, stirring occasionally. Season to taste with salt and pepper.

3. Fill squash halves, sprinkle with parsley, and serve. Spoon squash from shell to eat with filling.

STUFFED TOMATO HALVES, RED AND YELLOW

Mushrooms, spinach, rice, and cheese are combined for the filling in this colorful dish.

4 servings

4	ounces mushrooms, chopped
¼	cup sliced green onions and tops
1	tablespoon margarine, *or* butter
½	package (10-ounce size) frozen chopped spinach, thawed, drained
3	tablespoons flour
1	cup fat-free milk
¼	teaspoon dried tarragon leaves
1-2	pinches ground nutmeg
1	cup cooked brown, *or* white, rice
½	cup shredded fat-free Cheddar, *or* Swiss, cheese
	Salt and pepper, to taste
2	large red tomatoes
2	large yellow tomatoes
	Parsley, minced, as garnish

Per Serving
Calories: 186
% Calories from fat: 19
Fat (gm): 4
Saturated fat (gm): 0.8
Cholesterol (mg): 1
Sodium (mg): 200
Protein (gm): 11.0
Carbohydrate (gm): 28.3
Exchanges
Milk: 0.0
Vegetable: 2.0
Fruit: 0.0
Bread: 1.0
Meat: 1.0
Fat: 0.0

1. Saute mushrooms and green onions in margarine in large skillet until tender, 5 to 8 minutes. Stir in spinach; cook until hot, 3 to 4 minutes. Stir in flour; cook 1 to 2 minutes longer.

2. Stir milk, tarragon, and nutmeg into vegetable mixture and heat to boiling; reduce heat and simmer 2 to 3 minutes. Remove from heat and stir in rice and cheese; season to taste with salt and pepper.

3. Cut tomatoes crosswise into halves; remove seeds and hollow out slightly. Chop removed portions of tomato and stir into filling. Spoon filling into tomatoes and place in lightly greased baking pan.

4. Bake tomatoes at 375 degrees until hot through, 15 to 20 minutes. Arrange 1 yellow and 1 red tomato half on each plate; sprinkle with parsley.

SPAGHETTI SQUASH STUFFED WITH VEGETABLE SAUTE

 Jerusalem artichokes, or sun chokes, add extra crunch to sauteed veggies.

4 servings

2 medium spaghetti squash (about 2 pounds each), cut lengthwise into halves, seeded

Olive oil cooking spray

2 medium Jerusalem artichokes (about 8 ounces), peeled, cubed

1 medium onion, cubed

2 medium carrots, diagonally sliced

1½ cups quartered mushrooms

½ cup sliced celery

2 cloves garlic, minced

2 teaspoons flour

2 medium tomatoes, coarsely chopped

½ cup Canned Vegetable Stock (see p. 63)

¾-1 teaspoon dried marjoram leaves

Salt and pepper, to taste

2 green onions and tops, thinly sliced

Per Serving
Calories: 186
% Calories from fat: 8
Fat (gm): 1.8
Saturated fat (gm): 0.3
Cholesterol (mg): 0
Sodium (mg): 48
Protein (gm): 6.9
Carbohydrate (gm): 39.9
Exchanges
Milk: 0.0
Vegetable: 2.0
Fruit: 0.0
Bread: 2.0
Meat: 0.0
Fat: 0.0

1. Place squash halves, cut sides down, in large baking pan; add ½ inch water. Bake, covered, at 350 degrees until squash is tender, 30 to 40 minutes. Scrape pulp into large bowl, separating strands with fork; reserve shells.

2. Spray large skillet with cooking spray; heat over medium heat until hot. Saute Jerusalem artichokes, onion, carrots, mushrooms, celery, and garlic until onion is transparent, about 5 minutes. Stir in flour and cook 1 minute longer.

3. Add tomatoes, stock, and marjoram to skillet; heat to boiling. Cook, covered, until vegetables are tender, about 10 minutes. Season to taste with salt and pepper.

4. Toss half the vegetable mixture with spaghetti squash; spoon mixture into reserved squash shells. Spoon remaining vegetable mixture on top; sprinkle with green onions.

CREAMED EGGPLANT IN EGGPLANT SHELLS

The eggplant shells are used as a container for baking and serving.

4 servings

2	large eggplant (1¼-1½ pounds each), unpeeled	
	Vegetable cooking spray	
1	cup chopped onion	
12	ounces mushrooms, sliced	
1	medium red bell pepper, chopped	
2	cloves garlic, minced	
2-3	teaspoons lemon juice	
2	tablespoons flour	
1	cup fat-free milk	
½	teaspoon Worcestershire sauce	
½	teaspoon dried marjoram leaves	
¼	teaspoon dried thyme leaves	
¼	cup finely chopped parsley	
	Salt and pepper, to taste	
¼	cup fat-free Parmesan cheese	
	Paprika, as garnish	

Per Serving
Calories: 185
% Calories from fat: 6
Fat (gm): 1.4
Saturated fat (gm): 0.3
Cholesterol (mg): 1
Sodium (mg): 98
Protein (gm): 10.1
Carbohydrate (gm): 38.6
Exchanges
Milk: 0.0
Vegetable: 6.0
Fruit: 0.0
Bread: 0.0
Meat: 0.5
Fat: 0.0

1. Cut one-third lengthwise off each eggplant; cut off stems. Scoop pulp from eggplant with serrated spoon, leaving ¼-inch thick shells. Coarsely chop pulp.

2. Place eggplant shells, cut sides up, in ungreased baking dish; spray with cooking spray. Place eggplant pulp in greased baking dish; spray with cooking spray. Bake both pans, uncovered, at 400 degrees until shells are slightly softened and eggplant pulp is tender, 10 to 15 minutes.

3. Spray large skillet with cooking spray; heat over medium heat until hot. Saute onion, mushrooms, bell pepper, and garlic until tender, 8 to 10 minutes. Add lemon juice. Mix in flour and cook 1 to 2 minutes longer.

4. Stir milk, Worcestershire sauce, and herbs into saucepan; heat to boiling. Boil, stirring constantly, until thickened, about 1 minute. Stir in eggplant pulp; season with salt and pepper.

5. Spoon eggplant mixture into eggplant shells. Sprinkle with Parmesan cheese and paprika. Reduce oven to 375 degrees and bake, uncovered, until lightly browned, about 20 minutes.

SPINACH CHEESE CREPES

For variation, saute ½ cup chopped portobello mushrooms and add them to the cottage cheese mixture.

4 servings (2 crepes each)

Vegetable cooking spray
- ¼ cup chopped onion
- 1 package (10 ounces) frozen chopped spinach, thawed, well drained
- 1 cup fat-free cottage cheese
- ¼ teaspoon dried thyme leaves
- 2-3 pinches ground nutmeg
- Salt and pepper, to taste
- 8 slices (½-¾ ounce each) fat-free mozzarella, *or* Swiss, cheese
- 8 Crepes (see p. 692), warm
- 1½ cups (½ recipe), Fresh Tomato and Herb Sauce (see p. 702)

Per Serving
Calories: 277
% Calories from fat: 25
Fat (gm): 7.9
Saturated fat (gm): 1.7
Cholesterol (mg): 107
Sodium (mg): 684
Protein (gm): 26.3
Carbohydrate (gm): 27.3
Exchanges
Milk: 0.0
Vegetable: 2.5
Fruit: 0.0
Bread: 1.0
Meat: 2.5
Fat: 0.0

1. Spray medium skillet with cooking spray; heat over medium heat until hot. Saute onion until tender, 3 to 4 minutes. Add spinach to skillet; cook until spinach is very dry, about 5 minutes. Remove from heat and mix in cottage cheese, thyme, and nutmeg; season to taste with salt and pepper.

2. Place 1 cheese slice on each crepe; spoon spinach-cheese mixture along centers of crepes. Roll up crepes and place, seam sides down, in lightly greased baking dish. Bake, loosely covered, at 325 degrees until filling is hot and cheese melted, about 10 minutes.

3. Transfer crepes to serving plates; spoon Fresh Tomato and Herb Sauce over.

VEGETABLE CREPES

Any vegetables you like can be used in these versatile crepes.

4 servings (2 crepes each)

Vegetable cooking spray
2 cups thinly sliced cabbage
1 cup thinly sliced celery
½ medium green bell pepper, thinly sliced
½ cup sliced mushrooms
⅓ cup chopped green onions and tops
2-3 teaspoons sugar
2 tablespoons water
2-3 teaspoons lemon juice
Salt and pepper, to taste
8 Crepes (see p. 692), warm
Mock Hollandaise Sauce (see p. 715)

Per Serving
Calories: 215
% Calories from fat: 25
Fat (gm): 5.8
Saturated fat (gm): 1.4
Cholesterol (mg): 107.2
Sodium (mg): 530
Protein (gm): 14.7
Carbohydrate (gm): 25.1
Exchanges
Milk: 0.5
Vegetable: 1.0
Fruit: 0.0
Bread: 1.0
Meat: 1.0
Fat: 0.5

1. Spray large skillet with cooking spray; heat over medium heat until hot. Add cabbage, celery, bell pepper, mushrooms, green onions, sugar, and water. Cook, covered, over medium heat until cabbage and mushrooms are wilted, about 5 minutes. Cook, uncovered, until vegetables are tender, about 5 minutes longer. Season to taste with lemon juice, salt, and pepper.

2. Spoon vegetable mixture along centers of crepes; roll up and arrange, seam sides down, on serving plates. Serve with Mock Hollandaise Sauce.

NIÇOISE PLATTER

A garden of vegetables on a plate, drizzled with vinaigrette and served with smooth-textured, garlic-spiked Tofu Aioli.

4 servings

12 small red potatoes (about 1¼ pounds), unpeeled, cooked

2 large beets, cooked

12 ounces green beans, ends trimmed, cooked

4 Braised Whole Artichokes (see p. 584)

2-4 hard-cooked eggs, halved

2 medium tomatoes, cut into wedges

3 cups mixed salad greens, torn into bite-size pieces

¼ cup halved ripe olives

4 teaspoons drained capers

½ cup salt-free, fat-free Italian dressing with herbs

1 small shallot, minced

1 clove garlic, minced

Salt and pepper, to taste

Tofu Aioli (recipe follows)

Per Serving
Calories: 424
% Calories from fat: 26
Fat (gm): 12.5
Saturated fat (gm): 2
Cholesterol (mg): 106
Sodium (mg): 652
Protein (gm): 16.7
Carbohydrate (gm): 65.2
Exchanges
Milk: 0.0
Vegetable: 4.0
Fruit: 0.0
Bread: 3.0
Meat: 1.0
Fat: 1.0

1. Cut potatoes into fourths; peel and slice or cube beets. Cool cooked vegetables to room temperature. Arrange with Braised Whole Artichokes, eggs, and tomatoes on plates lined with salad greens. Sprinkle with olives and capers.

2. Combine Italian dressing, shallot, and garlic; drizzle over vegetables, and sprinkle lightly with salt and pepper. Serve with Tofu Aioli.

Tofu Aioli

(makes about ¾ cup)

½ package (10½-ounce size) light firm tofu
1 tablespoon olive oil
¾ teaspoon tarragon vinegar
¾ teaspoon lemon juice
½ teaspoon Dijon-style mustard
3 cloves garlic, minced
Salt and white pepper, to taste

1. Process all ingredients, except salt and pepper, in food processor or blender; season to taste with salt and white pepper.

2. Refrigerate, covered, until ready to use.

VEGETABLE STRUDEL WITH WILD MUSHROOM SAUCE

A special dish for festive occasions.

4 servings

Vegetable cooking spray
½ cup chopped red bell pepper
½ cup chopped yellow bell pepper
¼ cup chopped shallot
2 cloves garlic, minced
1½ cups cubed butternut, *or* acorn, squash, cooked
1½ cups broccoli florets, cooked
Wild Mushroom Sauce (see p. 717), divided
¾ cup (3 ounces) shredded reduced-fat brick, *or* Swiss, cheese
Salt and pepper, to taste
5 sheets frozen fillo pastry, thawed
Tarragon, *or* parsley, sprigs, as garnish

Per Serving
Calories: 207
% Calories from fat: 19
Fat (gm): 4.6
Saturated fat (gm): 2.4
Cholesterol (mg): 15.2
Sodium (mg): 85
Protein (gm): 11.8
Carbohydrate (gm): 27.9
Exchanges
Milk: 0.0
Vegetable: 3.0
Fruit: 0.0
Bread: 1.0
Meat: 1.0
Fat: 0.0

1. Spray large skillet with cooking spray; heat over medium heat until hot. Saute bell peppers, shallot, and garlic until tender, 5 to 8 minutes. Stir in squash, broccoli, and half of the Wild Mushroom Sauce; cook until hot through, 2 to 3 minutes. Remove from heat and stir in cheese; season to taste with salt and pepper.

2. Lay 1 sheet of fillo on clean towel on table; spray generously with cooking spray. Cover with second sheet of fillo and spray generously with cooking spray; repeat with remaining fillo.

3. Spoon vegetable mixture along long edge of fillo, 3 to 4 inches from the edge. Fold edge of fillo over filling and roll up, using towel to help lift and roll; place seam side down on greased cookie sheet. Spray top of fillo generously with cooking spray.

4. Bake at 375 degrees until golden, about 30 minutes. Let stand 5 minutes before cutting.

5. Cut strudel into 4 pieces and arrange on plates. Spoon remaining Wild Mushroom Sauce over or alongside each serving. Garnish with tarragon sprigs.

LEEK AND MUSHROOM STRUDEL

The strudel is scented with 3 herb seeds: anise, fennel, and caraway.

4 servings

Vegetable cooking spray
½ cup chopped onion
2 cloves garlic, minced
2 pounds cleaned leeks (white part only), sliced
1 pound sliced shiitake, *or* portobello, mushrooms
½ cup Canned Vegetable Stock (see p. 63)
¼-½ teaspoon caraway seeds, crushed
¼-½ teaspoon fennel seeds, crushed
¼-½ teaspoon anise seeds, crushed
Salt and white pepper, to taste
5 sheets frozen fillo pastry, thawed

Per Serving
Calories: 225
% Calories from fat: 4
Fat (gm): 1.2
Saturated fat (gm): 0.2
Cholesterol (mg): 0
Sodium (mg): 66
Protein (gm): 5.8
Carbohydrate (gm): 52.5
Exchanges
Milk: 0.0
Vegetable: 6.0
Fruit: 0.0
Bread: 1.0
Meat: 0.0
Fat: 0.0

1. Spray large skillet with cooking spray; heat over medium heat until hot. Saute onion and garlic 2 to 3 minutes. Add leeks, mushrooms, stock, and herbs to skillet; heat to boiling. Reduce heat and simmer, covered, until vegetables are tender, 10 to 15 minutes. Cook, uncovered, until excess liquid is gone, about 5 minutes. Season to taste with salt and white pepper; cool.

2. Lay 1 sheet of fillo on clean towel on table; spray generously with cooking spray. Cover with second sheet of fillo and spray generously with cooking spray; repeat with remaining fillo.

3. Spoon vegetable mixture along edge of fillo, 3 to 4 inches from the edge. Fold edge of fillo over filling and roll up, using towel to help lift and roll; place seam side down on greased cookie sheet. Spray top of fillo generously with cooking spray.

4. Bake at 375 degrees until golden, about 30 minutes. Let stand 5 minutes before cutting. Cut strudel into 4 pieces and arrange on plates.

CABBAGE-FENNEL STRUDEL

If fresh fennel is not available, substitute sliced celery and add ½ teaspoon crushed fennel seeds to the recipe with the teaspoon of anise seeds.

4 servings

Vegetable cooking spray
1 cup chopped onion
½ cup leek, white parts only, *or* green onions, green and white parts, sliced
3 cloves garlic, minced
4 cups thinly sliced cabbage
1 cup sliced mushrooms
½ cup thinly sliced fennel bulb
1 cup Canned Vegetable Stock (see p. 63)
½ cup dry white wine, *or* Canned Vegetable Stock
1 teaspoon anise seeds, crushed
½ teaspoon caraway seeds, crushed
¾ cup cooked brown rice
¼ cup dark raisins

Per Serving
Calories: 266
% Calories from fat: 17
Fat (gm): 5.6
Saturated fat (gm): 0.8
Cholesterol (mg): 0
Sodium (mg): 212
Protein (gm): 6.8
Carbohydrate (gm): 46.7
Exchanges
Milk: 0.0
Vegetable: 4.5
Fruit: 0.5
Bread: 1.0
Meat: 0.0
Fat: 1.0

Salt and pepper, to taste

6 sheets frozen fillo pastry, thawed

Anise or caraway seeds, to taste

Herb-Tomato Sauce (see p. 702)

1. Spray large saucepan with cooking spray; heat over medium heat until hot. Add onions, leeks, and garlic; saute 3 to 5 minutes. Add cabbage, mushrooms, fennel, stock, wine, and anise and caraway seeds; cook, covered, until cabbage wilts, 5 to 10 minutes. Cook, uncovered, over medium heat until cabbage begins to brown, about 10 minutes. Stir in rice and raisins; season to taste with salt and pepper. Cool.

2. Lay 1 sheet of fillo on clean surface; cover remaining fillo with damp towel to keep from drying. Spray fillo with cooking spray; top with 2 more sheets fillo, spraying each with cooking spray. Spoon ½ cabbage mixture across dough, 2 inches from short edge; roll up and place, seam-side down, on greased cookie sheet. Flatten roll slightly; spray with cooking spray and sprinkle with anise seeds. Repeat with remaining fillo and cabbage mixture.

3. Bake at 375 degrees until strudel is golden, 35 to 45 minutes. Cool 5 to 10 minutes before cutting. Trim ends of strudels, cutting diagonally. Cut strudels diagonally into halves. Arrange on plates. Serve with Herb-Tomato Sauce.

SERBIAN LEEK CAKES

 Cooked leeks are made into pancakes, then baked with a creamy topping.

6 servings

1½ cups cleaned, chopped leeks

1 cup Canned Vegetable Stock (see p. 63)

1 cup all-purpose flour

1 egg, beaten

¼-½ teaspoon salt

Vegetable cooking spray

8 ounces all-vegetable protein "sausage" links, *or* patties, crumbled

½ cup chopped onion

Per Serving
Calories: 220
% Calories from fat: 19
Fat (gm): 4.7
Saturated fat (gm): 0.9
Cholesterol (mg): 35.5
Sodium (mg): 434
Protein (gm): 12.9
Carbohydrate (gm): 31.2
Exchanges
Milk: 0.0
Vegetable: 2.0
Fruit: 0.0
Bread: 1.0
Meat: 1.5
Fat: 0.0

¼ cup chopped green bell pepper
2 cloves garlic, minced
½ teaspoon paprika
⅛ teaspoon crushed red pepper
Salt and pepper, to taste
½ cup fat-free sour cream
1-2 tablespoons fat-free milk
¼ cup (1 ounce) shredded reduced-fat
Swiss cheese

1. Heat leeks and stock to boiling in medium saucepan; reduce heat and simmer, uncovered, 5 minutes. Strain, reserving stock. Add enough water to stock to make 1 cup.

2. Mix flour, reserved stock, egg, and salt. Stir in leeks. Spray medium skillet with cooking spray; heat over medium heat until hot. Pour ¾ cup batter into skillet; spread into 8-inch circle. Cook over medium heat until brown on the bottom, 3 to 5 minutes. Turn and cook until brown on other side. Repeat, making 2 more pancakes.

3. Spray medium saucepan with cooking spray; heat over medium heat until hot. Cook vegetable protein, onion, bell pepper, and garlic until onion is tender, about 5 minutes, stirring frequently. Stir in paprika and crushed red pepper; season to taste with salt and pepper.

4. Place a leek pancake in greased 9-inch pie plate; spread with ⅓ of the vegetable protein mixture. Repeat layers 2 more times. Mix sour cream and milk; pour over top. Sprinkle with cheese. Bake at 375 degrees, uncovered, until lightly browned, about 20 minutes. Cut into wedges to serve.

STUFFED CABBAGE WITH CHILI TOMATO SAUCE

 This dish can also be served in smaller portions as a side dish.

6 servings

1 large head green cabbage
1 large onion, chopped
1 clove garlic, minced
¼-½ jalapeño chili, seeds and veins discarded, minced
1 tablespoon canola oil
¾ teaspoon dried oregano leaves
½ teaspoon dried thyme leaves
1 can (15 ounces) black beans, rinsed, drained
2 medium tomatoes, chopped
½ cup cooked rice
½ cup raisins
1 tablespoon finely chopped cilantro
Salt and pepper, to taste
Chili Tomato Sauce (see p. 179)

Per Serving
Calories: 228
% Calories from fat: 14
Fat (gm): 4
Saturated fat (gm): 0.4
Cholesterol (mg): 0
Sodium (mg): 313
Protein (gm): 11.9
Carbohydrate (gm): 45.5
Exchanges
Milk: 0.0
Vegetable: 4.0
Fruit: 0.5
Bread: 1.0
Meat: 0.0
Fat: 0.5

1. Trim cabbage, discarding any wilted outside leaves. Place cabbage in large saucepan with water to cover; heat to boiling. Reduce heat and simmer, covered, 10 minutes. Drain cabbage; cool until warm enough to handle.

2. In a large skillet, saute onion, garlic, and jalapeño chili in oil until tender, about 5 minutes. Add oregano and thyme; cook 1 minute longer.

3. Add beans and tomatoes to skillet; cook over medium heat, lightly mashing beans with a fork, until tomatoes release liquid, about 10 minutes. Stir in rice, raisins, and cilantro; season to taste with salt and pepper.

4. Place cabbage on large square of double-thickness cheesecloth. Spread outer cabbage leaves as flat as possible without breaking them off. Cut out inner leaves of cabbage, chop them finely, and add to rice mixture; remove and discard core of cabbage.

5. Pack rice mixture into center of the cabbage; fold outer leaves up over mixture, reshaping cabbage. Gather up cheesecloth around cabbage and tie with string. Place cabbage in large saucepan and add water to cover; heat to boiling. Reduce heat and simmer, covered, 1 hour. Lift cabbage from saucepan and remove cheesecloth.

6. Place cabbage on serving plate; cut into wedges. Serve with Chili Tomato Sauce.

CABBAGE AND POTATO HASH

Serve with large dollops of fat-free sour cream and thick slices of a warm multigrain bread.

4 servings (about 1½ cups each)

Vegetable cooking spray
1 large onion, chopped
1 small head cabbage, cut into large pieces (about 4 cups)
6 medium red potatoes, unpeeled, cubed
3 carrots, sliced
3 cloves garlic, minced
4-5 teaspoons gingerroot, minced
½ cup Basic Vegetable Stock (see p. 58)
1½ teaspoons reduced-sodium tamari soy sauce
Salt and pepper, to taste
4 tablespoons fat-free sour cream

Per Serving
Calories: 254
% Calories from fat: 3
Fat (gm): 0.8
Saturated fat (gm): 0.1
Cholesterol (mg): 0
Sodium (mg): 153
Protein (gm): 7.9
Carbohydrate (gm): 57.6
Exchanges
Milk: 0.0
Vegetable: 4.0
Fruit: 0.0
Bread: 2.0
Meat: 0.0
Fat: 0.0

1. Spray large skillet with cooking spray; heat over medium heat until hot. Add onion, cabbage, potatoes, carrots, garlic, and gingerroot; spray with cooking spray and saute until lightly browned, about 8 minutes.

2. Add stock and soy sauce and cook, covered, over medium heat until vegetables are just tender, about 5 minutes. Season to taste with salt and pepper.

3. Spoon hash onto plates; top each serving with a tablespoon of sour cream.

VEGETABLES PAPRIKASH

Your preference of hot or sweet paprika can be used in this recipe. Serve over any pasta (flat shape preferred) or rice.

4 servings

2 cups thinly sliced cabbage
2 medium onions, sliced
1 medium zucchini, sliced
2 medium carrots, sliced
2 medium green bell peppers, sliced
1 tablespoon olive oil, *or* canola oil
1½ cups sliced mushrooms
1 medium tomato, chopped
3 tablespoons flour
1 tablespoon paprika
¾ cup Canned Vegetable Stock (see p. 63)
½ cup fat-free sour cream
Salt and pepper, to taste
12 ounces noodles, cooked, warm

Per Serving
Calories: 264
% Calories from fat: 17
Fat (gm): 5.2
Saturated fat (gm): 0.7
Cholesterol (mg): 0
Sodium (mg): 119
Protein (gm): 9.6
Carbohydrate (gm): 47.5
Exchanges
Milk: 0.0
Vegetable: 3.0
Fruit: 0.0
Bread: 2.0
Meat: 0.0
Fat: 0.7

1. Saute cabbage, onions, zucchini, carrots, and green peppers in oil in large skillet until tender, 5 to 8 minutes. Add mushrooms and tomatoes. Cook over medium heat, covered, until mushrooms and tomatoes are wilted.

2. Stir in flour and paprika; cook 1 to 2 minutes, stirring constantly. Stir in stock; heat to boiling. Boil, stirring constantly, until sauce thickens, about 1 minute. Stir in sour cream; season to taste with salt and pepper. Serve over noodles.

STUFFED GRAPEVINE LEAVES

This Mediterranean favorite, called "dolmades" in Greek cuisine, can be served hot or at room temperature, whichever you prefer.

8 servings (about 5 each)

1 jar (16 ounces) grapevine leaves, preserved in brine, drained
Olive oil cooking spray
2-4 ounces pine nuts
⅔ cup uncooked converted rice
3 cups Basic Vegetable Stock (see p. 58), *or* water, divided
½ cup currants, *or* chopped raisins
¼ cup finely chopped parsley
1½ teaspoons dried dill weed
1½ teaspoons dried mint leaves
1½ teaspoons ground allspice
2 teaspoons lemon juice
Salt and pepper, to taste
1 tablespoon olive oil (optional)
Mediterranean Roasted Eggplant and Tomatoes (see p. 287)
1 cup fat-free plain yogurt

Per Serving
Calories: 147
% Calories from fat: 25
Fat (gm): 4.3
Saturated fat (gm): 0.7
Cholesterol (mg): 0.5
Sodium (mg): 40
Protein (gm): 5.8
Carbohydrate (gm): 23.8
Exchanges
Milk: 0.0
Vegetable: 1.0
Fruit: 0.0
Bread: 1.0
Meat: 0.0
Fat: 1.0

1. Boil grapevine leaves in 2 quarts boiling water in large saucepan 2 minutes; drain well on paper toweling. Trim and discard any tough stems or veins. Arrange leaves, vein sides up, on clean surface.

2. Spray medium saucepan with cooking spray; heat over medium heat until hot. Add pine nuts and cook over medium to medium-low heat until browned; remove and reserve. Add rice to saucepan; cook until lightly browned, 2 to 3 minutes. Add 1½ cups stock; heat to boiling. Reduce heat and simmer, covered, until rice is tender and stock absorbed, about 25 minutes.

3. Mix rice, reserved pine nuts, currants, parsley, dill weed, mint, allspice, and lemon juice; season to taste with salt and pepper. Spoon about 1 tablespoon mixture on a grape leaf; fold stem end over filling, fold in sides, and roll up. Repeat with leaves and filling.

4. Line large skillet with torn and unused grape leaves; arrange filled grape leaves, seam sides down, in skillet. Pour remaining 1½ cups stock into skillet; drizzle filled leaves with olive oil, if using. Heat to boiling; reduce heat and simmer, covered, about 45 minutes.

5. Arrange stuffed grape leaves on serving platter with Mediterranean Roasted Eggplant and Tomatoes; serve with yogurt.

VEGETABLE CURRY

A variety of spices and herbs are combined to make the fragrant curry that seasons this dish.

4 servings

Vegetable cooking spray
½ cup chopped onion
2 cloves garlic, minced
1 large head cauliflower, cut into florets
2 medium potatoes, peeled, cut into ½-inch cubes
2 large carrots, cut into ½-inch slices
1½ cups Canned Vegetable Stock (see p. 65)
¾ teaspoon ground turmeric
¼ teaspoon dry mustard
¼ teaspoon ground cumin
¼ teaspoon ground coriander
1 tablespoon flour
2 tablespoons cold water
1 large tomato, chopped
2 tablespoons finely chopped parsley
1-2 tablespoons lemon juice
Salt, cayenne, and black pepper, to taste

Per Serving
Calories: 81
% Calories from fat: 6
Fat (gm): 0.6
Saturated fat (gm): 0
Cholesterol (mg): 0
Sodium (mg): 57.2
Protein (gm): 3.7
Carbohydrate (gm): 15.8
Exchanges
Milk: 0.0
Vegetable: 2.0
Fruit: 0.0
Bread: 0.5
Meat: 0.0
Fat: 0.0

1. Spray large saucepan with cooking spray; heat over medium heat until hot. Saute onion and garlic 3 to 4 minutes. Add cauliflower, potatoes, carrots, stock, and herbs to saucepan; heat to boiling. Reduce heat and simmer, covered, until vegetables are tender, 10 to 15 minutes.

2. Heat vegetable mixture to boiling. Mix flour and water; stir into boiling mixture. Cook, stirring constantly, until thickened. Stir in tomato, parsley, and lemon juice; simmer 2 to 3 minutes longer. Season to taste with salt, cayenne, and black pepper.

MARINATED TORTELLINI AND VEGETABLE KABOBS

The vegetables are served uncooked on these kabobs. Cook other vegetables, such as eggplant, broccoli, cauliflower, etc., until crisp-tender before marinating.

4 servings

1	large red bell pepper, cut into 1-inch pieces
1	small yellow summer squash, cut into ½-inch slices
1	small zucchini, cut into ½-inch slices
1	small cucumber, cut into ½-inch slices
24	cherry tomatoes
24	medium mushroom caps
16	pitted Greek, *or* ripe, olives
4	ounces fat-free mozzarella cheese, cut into cubes
4	ounces fat-free Cheddar cheese, cut into cubes
½	package (9-ounce size) mushroom, *or* cheese, tortellini, cooked
1¼-1½	cups fat-free, sodium-free Italian salad dressing
3	cloves garlic, minced
2	tablespoons grated fat-free Parmesan cheese
4	cups torn salad greens

Per Serving
Calories: 362
% Calories from fat: 16
Fat (gm): 6.2
Saturated fat (gm): 1.6
Cholesterol (mg): 13.3
Sodium (mg): 606
Protein (gm): 30.6
Carbohydrate (gm): 44.3
Exchanges
Milk: 0.0
Vegetable: 5.0
Fruit: 0.0
Bread: 1.5
Meat: 2.5
Fat: 0.0

1. Arrange vegetables, olives, cubed cheese, and tortellini on wooden skewers and place in large baking dish or plastic bag.

2. Mix salad dressing, garlic, and Parmesan cheese; pour over kabobs. Refrigerate 4 to 6 hours, turning kabobs occasionally.

3. Drain kabobs; reserving ¾ cup marinade. Arrange kabobs on lettuce on plates; drizzle each with 2 to 3 tablespoons of marinade.

LENTIL RAVIOLI WITH GINGERED TOMATO RELISH

 Delicate ravioli, bursting with myriad flavors! For luncheon portions, this recipe will serve 6 to 8 people.

4 servings (6 ravioli each)

Olive oil cooking spray

¼ cup finely chopped fennel bulb, *or* celery

2 teaspoons grated gingerroot

1 teaspoon curry powder

½ teaspoon ground cumin

¼ teaspoon ground turmeric

¼ teaspoon ground cinnamon

¼ teaspoon cayenne pepper

2⅔ cups water

⅔ cup dried lentils, cleaned, rinsed

2 tablespoons finely chopped cilantro

Salt, to taste

48 wonton wrappers

Gingered Tomato Relish (see p. 732)

Cilantro, *or* parsley, sprigs, as garnish

Per Serving
Calories: 324
% Calories from fat: 5
Fat (gm): 1.8
Saturated fat (gm): 0.3
Cholesterol (mg): 12
Sodium (mg): 569
Protein (gm): 12.1
Carbohydrate (gm): 65.4
Exchanges
Milk: 0.0
Vegetable: 2.0
Fruit: 0.0
Bread: 4.0
Meat: 0.0
Fat: 0.0

1. Spray large skillet and heat over medium heat until hot. Saute fennel and gingerroot 2 to 3 minutes; add spices and cook 1 minute longer.

2. Add water and lentils to skillet; heat to boiling. Reduce heat and simmer, covered, until lentils are just tender, about 15 minutes. Simmer uncovered, until excess liquid is gone, about 5 minutes. Stir in chopped cilantro; season to taste with salt.

3. Place 1 tablespoon lentil mixture in center of 1 wonton wrapper; brush edges of wrapper with water. Place second wonton wrapper on top and press edges to seal. Repeat with remaining wonton wrappers and filling.

4. Heat about 3 quarts water to boiling in large saucepan; add 4 to 6 ravioli. Reduce heat and simmer, uncovered, until ravioli float to surface and are cooked *al dente*, 3 to 4 minutes. Remove ravioli with slotted spoon; repeat cooking procedure with remaining ravioli.

5. Arrange ravioli on plates and top with Gingered Tomato Relish; garnish with cilantro.

GREEN ON GREEN STIR-FRY WITH TOFU

 The variety of green vegetables creates a beautiful presentation.

6 servings (about 1 cup each)

Vegetable cooking spray
3 cups sliced leeks, white parts only
1 cup sliced celery
1 teaspoon minced garlic
1 teaspoon minced gingerroot
½ teaspoon crushed red pepper
4 cups sliced bok choy
4 cups snow peas, strings removed
1 cup chopped green bell pepper
2 cups Oriental Stock, *or* Basic Vegetable Stock (see pp. 62, 58)
2 tablespoons cornstarch
2 teaspoons reduced-sodium tamari soy sauce
Salt and pepper, to taste
1 package (10 ounces) light firm tofu, cubed
4 cups cooked rice, warm

Per Serving
Calories: 275
% Calories from fat: 5
Fat (gm): 1.5
Saturated fat (gm): 0.2
Cholesterol (mg): 0
Sodium (mg): 194
Protein (gm): 11.9
Carbohydrate (gm): 54
Exchanges
Milk: 0.0
Vegetable: 3.0
Fruit: 0.0
Bread: 2.0
Meat: 1.0
Fat: 0.0

1. Spray wok or large skillet with cooking spray; heat over medium heat until hot. Stir-fry leeks, celery, garlic, gingerroot, and crushed red pepper 2 to 3 minutes. Add bok choy and stir-fry 1 minute; add snow peas and bell pepper and stir-fry 2 to 3 minutes longer.

2. Combine stock, cornstarch, and soy sauce; stir into wok and heat to boiling. Boil, stirring constantly until thickened, about 1 minute. Season to taste with salt and pepper. Gently stir in tofu; cook 1 to 2 minutes longer. Serve over rice.

CHEESE-STUFFED PASTA SHELLS WITH SIMPLE TOMATO SAUCE

 This dish can be made a day or two in advance of serving. Simply stuff the shells and refrigerate, covered. Spoon sauce over shells when ready to bake.

6 servings

1 package (15 ounces) fat-free ricotta cheese

1 cup grated Parmesan cheese, divided

2 eggs

½ cup finely chopped parsley leaves, divided

2 cloves garlic, minced

½ teaspoon salt

¼ teaspoon pepper

24 jumbo pasta shells, cooked
    Simple Tomato Sauce (recipe follows)

Per Serving
Calories: 356
% Calories from fat: 25
Fat (gm): 10.1
Saturated fat (gm): 4
Cholesterol (mg): 84.2
Sodium (mg): 747
Protein (gm): 25.8
Carbohydrate (gm): 43.6
Exchanges
Milk: 0.0
Vegetable: 2.0
Fruit: 0.0
Bread: 2.0
Meat: 2.0
Fat: 1.0

1. Mix ricotta, ¾ cup Parmesan cheese, eggs, ¼ cup parsley, garlic, salt, and pepper. Stuff shells with mixture and arrange in baking pan. Spoon Simple Tomato Sauce over shells.

2. Bake, covered, until hot through, 20 to 30 minutes. Sprinkle with combined remaining ¼ cup Parmesan cheese and ¼ cup parsley before serving.

Simple Tomato Sauce

 (makes about 3 cups)

1 small onion, finely chopped

1 clove garlic, minced

1 tablespoon canola, *or* olive, oil

2 cans (14½ ounces each) low-sodium tomatoes, undrained, coarsely chopped

½ teaspoon sugar

½ teaspoon dried basil leaves

¼ teaspoon dried oregano leaves

1 bay leaf

½ teaspoon salt

¼ teaspoon pepper

1. Saute onion and garlic in oil in large skillet 2 to 3 minutes. Add tomatoes and remaining ingredients; heat to boiling. Reduce heat and simmer, covered, 20 minutes. Discard bay leaf.

2. Process tomato mixture in food processor or blender until coarsely pureed.

SPRING VEGETABLE STIR-FRY

 The best of spring's bounty, seasoned with fresh ginger, sesame oil, and tamari soy sauce.

4 servings

Vegetable cooking spray
1 medium onion, sliced
8 small red potatoes, unpeeled, cut into ¼-inch slices
1 cup sliced mushrooms
1 pound asparagus, cut into 1½-inch pieces
½ cup chopped red bell pepper
2 cloves garlic, minced
2-4 teaspoons minced gingerroot
1½ cups Oriental Vegetable Stock (see p. 62)
4 teaspoons cornstarch
¼ cup cold water
1-2 teaspoons reduced-sodium tamari soy sauce
1 teaspoon sesame oil
Salt and pepper, to taste
2 cups cooked brown rice
1 cup cooked wild rice
1 teaspoon toasted sesame seeds

Per Serving
Calories: 443
% Calories from fat: 7
Fat (gm): 3.4
Saturated fat (gm): 0.6
Cholesterol (mg): 0
Sodium (mg): 125
Protein (gm): 13.5
Carbohydrate (gm): 94
Exchanges
Milk: 0.0
Vegetable: 2.0
Fruit: 0.0
Bread: 5.0
Meat: 0.0
Fat: 0.5

1. Spray wok or large skillet with cooking spray; heat over medium heat until hot. Stir-fry onion, potatoes, and mushrooms 3 to 5 minutes. Remove from wok and reserve. Add asparagus, bell pepper, garlic, and gingerroot to wok; stir-fry 5 minutes.

2. Add stock and reserved vegetables to wok and heat to boiling; reduce heat and simmer, covered, until vegetables are crisp-tender, 3 to 5 minutes. Heat mixture to boiling; stir combined cornstarch and water into mixture. Boil, stirring constantly, until thickened, about 1 minute. Stir in soy sauce and sesame oil; season to taste with salt and pepper.

3. Combine brown and wild rice and spoon onto serving platter; spoon vegetable mixture over. Sprinkle with sesame seeds.

FIVE-SPICE STIR-FRY

 Five-spice powder is a blend of spices and herbs that may vary according to the manufacturer. Fennel and anise seeds, ginger and anise root, cinnamon and cloves are usual ingredients.

4 servings (about 1 cup each)

2-3 teaspoons sesame oil

2 pounds broccoli florets and sliced stems

3 cups sliced bok choy, *or* Chinese cabbage

1 medium yellow bell pepper, sliced

1 medium onion, sliced

1 can (8 ounces) sliced water chestnuts, rinsed, drained

1⅓ cups Oriental Stock (see p. 62), *or* water

4 teaspoons cornstarch

1 teaspoon five-spice powder

1 teaspoon ground ginger

2-3 teaspoons reduced-sodium tamari soy sauce

Salt and pepper, to taste

4 cups cooked brown rice, *or* thin spaghetti, warm

¼ cup finely chopped cilantro, *or* parsley

Per Serving
Calories: 378
% Calories from fat: 12
Fat (gm): 5.2
Saturated fat (gm): 0.8
Cholesterol (mg): 0
Sodium (mg): 325
Protein (gm): 14.7
Carbohydrate (gm): 73.5
Exchanges
Milk: 0.0
Vegetable: 4.0
Fruit: 0.0
Bread: 3.0
Meat: 0.0
Fat: 1.0

1. Heat sesame oil in wok or large skillet until hot; stir-fry broccoli, bok choy, bell pepper, and onion until crisp-tender, 8 to 10 minutes. Stir in water chestnuts.

2. Mix stock, cornstarch, five-spice powder, ginger, and soy sauce; stir into wok and heat to boiling. Boil, stirring constantly, until thickened, about 1 minutes. Season to taste with salt and pepper.

3. Spoon vegetable mixture over rice on serving plates; sprinkle with cilantro.

SZECHUAN VEGETABLE STIR-FRY

The hot chili oil and crushed red pepper are hot, so begin with less, adding more to taste. Sesame oil can be substituted for the hot chili oil.

4 servings (about 1¼ cups each)

1	cup Oriental Stock, *or* Canned Vegetable Stock (see pp. 62, 63), divided
⅓	cup orange juice
¼	cup reduced-sodium tamari soy sauce
1-2	teaspoons hot chili oil
⅛-¼	teaspoon crushed red pepper
1	package (8 ounces) tempeh, *or* light firm tofu, cut into ¾-inch cubes
	Vegetable cooking spray
8	ounces asparagus, cut into 1½-inch pieces
4	ounces snow peas, strings removed
1	cup sliced carrots
1	cup sliced green onions and tops
1	medium red bell pepper, sliced
2-3	teaspoons minced gingerroot
4	cloves garlic, minced
½	cup sliced shiitake, *or* cremini, mushrooms
2	tablespoons cornstarch
	Salt and pepper, to taste
4	cups cooked brown rice, warm
¼	cup peanuts (optional)

Per Serving
Calories: 455
% Calories from fat: 15
Fat (gm): 8.0
Saturated fat (gm): 1.3
Cholesterol (mg): 0
Sodium (mg): 663
Protein (gm): 23.3
Carbohydrate (gm): 75.8
Exchanges
Milk: 0.0
Vegetable: 3.0
Fruit: 0.0
Bread: 4.0
Meat: 1.0
Fat: 1.0

1. Combine ½ cup stock, orange juice, soy sauce, hot chili oil, and red pepper; pour over tempeh in shallow glass dish and let stand 30 minutes. Drain, reserving marinade.

2. Spray wok or large skillet with cooking spray; heat over medium heat until hot. Add tempeh; stir-fry 2 to 3 minutes. Add asparagus, snow peas, carrots, green onions, bell pepper, gingerroot, and garlic; spray with cooking spray. Stir-fry until vegetables are crisp-tender, 8 to 10 minutes. Add mushrooms; stir-fry 3 to 4 minutes longer.

3. Add reserved marinade to wok; heat to boiling. Mix cornstarch and remaining ½ cup stock; stir into boiling mixture. Boil, stirring constantly, until thickened, about 1 minute. Season to taste with salt and pepper.

4. Spoon vegetable mixture over rice on serving plates; sprinkle with peanuts, if using.

CHOP SUEY

Bead molasses, a very dark molasses, adds the traditional flavor accent to this dish.

6 servings

1½ packages (8 ounces each) tempeh, cut into strips, *or* pieces

1-2 tablespoons reduced-sodium tamari soy sauce

Vegetable cooking spray

1 cup chopped onion

1 cup chopped red, *or* green, bell pepper

2 cloves garlic, minced

2 cups thinly sliced Chinese cabbage, *or* 1 cup sliced celery

1 cup sliced mushrooms

1 ½ cups Oriental Stock, *or* Basic Vegetable Stock (see p. 62, 58)

2 tablespoons cornstarch

½-1 tablespoon bead molasses

Per Serving
Calories: 402
% Calories from fat: 15
Fat (gm): 6.7
Saturated fat (gm): 1.2
Cholesterol (mg): 0
Sodium (mg): 149
Protein (gm): 20.6
Carbohydrate (gm): 67.9
Exchanges
Milk: 0.0
Vegetable: 2.0
Fruit: 0.0
Bread: 4.0
Meat: 1.0
Fat: 0.0

2 cups fresh, *or* canned, rinsed, bean
sprouts

½-1 can (8-ounce size) bamboo shoots,
rinsed, drained

½-1 can (8-ounce size) water chestnuts,
rinsed, drained
Reduced-sodium soy sauce, to taste
Salt and pepper, to taste

6 cups cooked brown, *or* white, rice,
warm

1. Brush tempeh with soy sauce; let stand 30 minutes.

2. Spray wok or large skillet with cooking spray; heat over medium heat until hot. Add tempeh and cook until browned, 3 to 4 minutes; remove.

3. Add onion, bell pepper, and garlic to wok; saute 2 to 3 minutes. Add cabbage and mushrooms; stir-fry until vegetables are crisp-tender, 3 to 5 minutes longer.

4. Mix stock, cornstarch, and molasses; stir into wok and heat to boiling. Boil, stirring constantly, until thickened, 1 to 2 minutes. Stir in tempeh, bean sprouts, bamboo shoots, and water chestnuts; cook until hot through, about 2 minutes. Season to taste with soy sauce, salt, and pepper. Serve over rice.

DIM SUM PLATTER WITH STIR-FRIED VEGETABLES

 The potstickers can be assembled a day in advance; the filling for the egg rolls also can be made a day in advance. Double the recipe for the stir-fried vegetables if serving them alone as an entrée.

6 servings

Vegetable cooking spray

12 ounces eggplant, cut into ¾-inch cubes
(about 3 cups)

6 ounces broccoli rabe, cut into 2-inch
pieces (about 3 cups)

1 medium onion, cut into thin wedges

2 cups sliced mushrooms

Per Serving
Calories: 354
% Calories from fat: 11
Fat (gm): 4.5
Saturated fat (gm): 0.7
Cholesterol (mg): 20.8
Sodium (mg): 632
Protein (gm): 15
Carbohydrate (gm): 67.8
Exchanges
Milk: 0.0
Vegetable: 4.0
Fruit: 0.0
Bread: 3.0
Meat: 0.0
Fat: 1.0

3 cloves garlic, minced

3 teaspoons minced gingerroot

1½ tablespoons cornstarch

1½ cups Oriental Stock, *or* Basic Vegetable
Stock (see pp. 62, 58)

2-3 teaspoons chili sesame oil

3 teaspoons reduced-sodium tamari soy
sauce

1½ cups sliced radicchio

3 cups oriental egg noodles, cooked,
warm

6 (½ recipe) Mixed Vegetable Egg Rolls
(see p. 46)

6 (½ recipe) Five-Spice Potstickers (see
p. 44)

1. Spray wok or large skillet with cooking spray; heat over medium heat until hot. Stir-fry eggplant until lightly browned, about 5 minutes. Add broccoli rabe, onion, mushrooms, garlic, and gingerroot. Spray vegetables with cooking spray; stir-fry until crisp-tender, about 8 minutes.

2. Mix cornstarch, stock, sesame oil, and soy sauce; add to wok and heat to boiling. Boil, stirring constantly, until thickened, about 1 minute. Stir in radicchio; cook 1 minute.

3. Spoon noodles onto plates; spoon vegetable mixture over. Arrange egg rolls and potstickers on plates.

TEEM SEEM LOAF

The loaf mixture is shaped and baked into one large round, then topped with sweet-sour stir-fried vegetables. The mixture can also be shaped into small "meatballs" or "burgers."

4 servings

Oriental Loaf (see p. 376)

Vegetable cooking spray

8 ounces snow peas, strings removed

¾ cup diagonally sliced carrots

1 can (8 ounces) water chestnuts, rinsed,
drained, sliced

Per Serving
Calories: 364
% Calories from fat: 11
Fat (gm): 4.6
Saturated fat (gm): 0.9
Cholesterol (mg): 53.3
Sodium (mg): 790
Protein (gm): 13.8
Carbohydrate (gm): 69

1 can (13¼ ounces) pineapple chunks in its own juice, drained, reserve ½ cup juice
1 tablespoon cornstarch
3-4 tablespoons sugar
¼ cup cider vinegar
3 tablespoons reduced-sodium tamari soy sauce
Salt and pepper, to taste

Exchanges
Milk: 0.0
Vegetable: 2.0
Fruit: 2.5
Bread: 1.5
Meat: 1.0
Fat: 0.0

1. Make Oriental Loaf, shaping mixture in pie pan into round loaf about 5 inches in diameter. Bake at 350 degrees until hot in the center, about 1 hour.

2. Spray wok or large skillet with cooking spray; heat over medium heat until hot. Stir-fry snow peas and carrots until crisp-tender, about 5 minutes. Add water chestnuts and pineapple chunks; cook 1 minute longer.

3. Mix cornstarch, reserved ½ cup pineapple juice, sugar, vinegar, and soy sauce; add to wok and heat to boiling. Cook, stirring constantly, until thickened, about 1 minute. Season to taste with salt and pepper.

4. Spoon vegetable mixture over loaf on serving platter. Cut into wedges to serve.

MOO-SHU TEMPEH

 Tempeh replaces pork in this traditional Mandarin favorite. The Mandarin Pancakes are fabulous and can be made in advance. If short on time, however, flour tortillas can be substituted.

6 servings (2 each)

1½ ounces dry Chinese mushrooms (shiitake)
Boiling water
2-3 tablespoons reduced-sodium tamari soy sauce
2 teaspoons sesame oil
1 tablespoon minced gingerroot
1 teaspoon sugar

Per Serving
Calories: 253
% Calories from fat: 23
Fat (gm): 6.5
Saturated fat (gm): 1.3
Cholesterol (mg): 71
Sodium (mg): 230
Protein (gm): 13.9
Carbohydrate (gm): 36.1
Exchanges
Milk: 0.0
Vegetable: 1.0
Fruit: 0.0
Bread: 2.0
Meat: 1.0
Fat: 0.5

  1 package (8 ounces) tempeh, cut into
     julienne strips
     Vegetable cooking spray
  2 eggs, lightly beaten
  ½ cup water
  2 teaspoons cornstarch
  ½ cup julienned bamboo shoots
  2 green onions and tops, sliced
     Mandarin Pancakes (recipe follows)
½-¾ cup oriental plum sauce
 12 medium green onions

1. Place mushrooms in bowl; pour boiling water over to cover. Let stand until mushrooms are softened, about 15 minutes. Drain. Slice mushrooms, discarding tough centers, and reserve.

2. Combine soy sauce, sesame oil, gingerroot, and sugar; pour over tempeh in bowl. Let stand 30 minutes, stirring occasionally.

3. Spray large skillet with cooking spray; heat over medium heat until hot. Add eggs and cook over low heat until scrambled, breaking into small pieces with a fork; set aside.

4. Add tempeh mixture to skillet; cook over medium heat 2 to 3 minutes, stirring occasionally. Mix water and cornstarch; add to skillet with reserved mushrooms, bamboo shoots, and sliced green onions. Heat to boiling; boil, stirring constantly, until thickened, about 1 minute. Stir in reserved egg; cook 1 minute longer.

5. To eat, spread 1 Mandarin Pancake with 2 to 3 teaspoons plum sauce; spoon about ⅓ cup tempeh mixture onto pancake. Top with a green onion and roll up. Repeat to make remaining pancakes.

Mandarin Pancakes

(makes 12 pancakes)

> ⅓ cup boiling water
> 1 cup all-purpose flour
>   Vegetable cooking spray

1. Stir water into flour in small bowl until crumbly; shape into a ball. Knead on lightly floured surface until smooth and satiny, about 10 minutes. Let stand, covered, 30 minutes.

2. Divide dough into 12 equal pieces; shape into balls. Roll 2 balls into 3-inch circles; spray 1 circle lightly with cooking spray and cover with remaining circle. Roll both circles together into a 6-inch circle being careful not to wrinkle dough when rolling.

3. Spray medium skillet with cooking spray; heat over medium heat until hot. Cook dough circle over medium to medium-high heat until pancake blisters and is the color of parchment paper, turning frequently with chopsticks or tongs. Remove from skillet; separate 2 pancakes with pointed knife.

4. Repeat rolling and cooking with remaining dough, making only 1 or 2 dough circles at a time. As pancakes are cooked and separated, they can be covered and kept warm in a 200-degree oven.

Note: Pancakes can be cooled, stacked with plastic wrap between each, and frozen in a freezer bag or aluminum foil for up to 2 months.

TEMPEH STEAK WITH RED AND GREEN STIR-FRY

If available, use red Swiss chard for its beautiful red and green color.

6 servings (about 1 cup each)

Vegetable cooking spray
2 cups sliced red onions
1 cup sliced celery
2 teaspoons minced garlic
1 teaspoon minced gingerroot
6 cups shredded red, *or* green, Swiss chard, *or* spinach
2 cups sliced red bell peppers
2 cups Oriental Vegetable Stock (see p. 62)
2 tablespoons cornstarch
4 teaspoons reduced-sodium tamari soy sauce, divided
½-¾ teaspoon hot chili paste
Salt and pepper, to taste
3 packages (8 ounces each) tempeh, cut into halves

Per Serving
Calories: 302
% Calories from fat: 26
Fat (gm): 9.4
Saturated fat (gm): 1.5
Cholesterol (mg): 0
Sodium (mg): 272
Protein (gm): 27.3
Carbohydrate (gm): 32
Exchanges
Milk: 0.0
Vegetable: 3.0
Fruit: 0.0
Bread: 1.0
Meat: 2.0
Fat: 1.0

1. Spray wok or large skillet with cooking spray; heat over medium heat until hot. Stir-fry onions, celery, garlic, and gingerroot 1 to 2 minutes. Add Swiss chard and stir-fry 1 to 2 minutes. Add bell peppers to wok; stir-fry until vegetables are crisp-tender, 2 to 3 minutes.

2. Combine stock, cornstarch, 2 teaspoons tamari, and chili paste; stir into wok. Heat to boiling; boil, stirring constantly, until thickened, about 1 minute. Season to taste with salt and pepper.

3. Spray large skillet with cooking spray; heat over medium heat until hot. Brush tempeh with remaining 2 teaspoons tamari. Cook in tempeh over medium heat until browned, 2 to 3 minutes on each side.

4. Arrange tempeh on serving platter; spoon vegetable mixture over.

TACOS PICADILLO

Picadillo is a Mexican beef or pork mixture that is uniquely seasoned with raisins, almonds, sweet spices, and jalapeño chili. We've substituted vegetable protein crumbles in this flavorful filling. Serve with Red or Green Tomato Salsa (see pp. 9, 8).

6 servings (2 tacos each)

Vegetable cooking spray
½ cup chopped onion
4 cloves garlic, minced
1 small jalapeño chili, seeds and veins discarded, minced
1 package (12 ounces) frozen pre-browned all-vegetable protein crumbles, thawed
2 medium tomatoes, chopped
½ cup dark raisins
2-4 tablespoons slivered almonds, toasted
2-3 teaspoons cider vinegar
1 teaspoon dried oregano leaves
2 teaspoons ground cinnamon
½ teaspoon ground cloves
½ teaspoon ground allspice
Salt and pepper, to taste
12 flour, *or* corn, tortillas

Per Serving
Calories: 365
% Calories from fat: 12
Fat (gm): 4.8
Saturated fat (gm): 0.8
Cholesterol (mg): 0
Sodium (mg): 278
Protein (gm): 20.8
Carbohydrate (gm): 61.2
Exchanges
Milk: 0.0
Vegetable: 0.5
Fruit: 0.5
Bread: 3.0
Meat: 2.0
Fat: 0.0

1. Spray medium skillet with cooking spray; heat over medium heat until hot. Saute onion, garlic, and jalapeño chili until tender, about 5 minutes. Add vegetable protein crumbles, tomatoes, raisins, almonds, vinegar, oregano, cinnamon, cloves, and allspice. Cook over medium heat, stirring occasionally, until mixture is hot through, about 5 minutes. Season to taste with salt and pepper.

2. Spoon about ⅓ cup of mixture on each tortilla and fold in half to make tacos. Spray large skillet with cooking spray; heat over medium heat until hot. Saute tacos until lightly browned, 1 to 2 minutes on each side.

TACOS WITH "CHORIZO" AND POTATOES

In many parts of Mexico, fried tacos are made by pan-sauteing folded, filled tortillas—a delectable alternative to the crisp taco shells we are accustomed to! Our low-fat version uses vegetable cooking spray in place of traditional lard for sauteing.

4 servings (2 tacos each)

1½ cups (½ recipe) "Chorizo" (see p. 404)
   Vegetable cooking spray
1 cup chopped onion
1 cup peeled, cubed, cooked potato
1 cup (4 ounces) shredded fat-free Cheddar cheese
2 tablespoons finely chopped cilantro
   Salt and pepper, to taste
8 corn, *or* flour, tortillas
½ cup Tomatillo Sauce, *or* Jalapeño con Queso Sauce (see pp. 724, 725)
¼ cup fat-free sour cream

Per Serving
Calories: 400
% Calories from fat: 10
Fat (gm): 4.7
Saturated fat (gm): 0.6
Cholesterol (mg): 53.3
Sodium (mg): 646
Protein (gm): 28.2
Carbohydrate (gm): 64.7
Exchanges
Milk: 0.0
Vegetable: 3.0
Fruit: 0.0
Bread: 3.0
Meat: 2.0
Fat: 0.0

1. Make "Chorizo" mixture but do not form into patties.

2. Spray large skillet with cooking spray; heat over medium heat until hot. Cook onion and potato until onion is tender and potatoes browned, about 5 minutes. Stir in "Chorizo" and cook 1 to 2 minutes longer. Remove from heat; stir in cheese and cilantro. Season to taste with salt and pepper.

3. Heat tortillas in skillet or microwave oven until softened. Spoon about ½ cup vegetable mixture on each tortilla and fold in half to make tacos. Spray large skillet with cooking spray; heat over medium heat until hot. Saute tacos until lightly browned, 1 to 2 minutes on each side. Serve with Tomatillo Sauce and sour cream.

VEGETARIAN BURRITOS WITH POBLANO CHILI SAUCE

Brushed with sauce and cooked twice for extra flavor, these burritos are a beautiful adobe red color.

4 servings

3 arbol chilies, stems, seeds, and veins discarded
Hot water
Olive oil cooking spray
¾ cup chopped zucchini
¾ cup chopped yellow summer squash
1 small onion, finely chopped
3 cloves garlic, minced
2 tablespoons finely chopped cilantro
1 teaspoon dried marjoram leaves
1 teaspoon dried oregano leaves
1 can (15 ounces) pinto beans, rinsed, drained
¼ cup water
1 cup chopped tomato
Salt and cayenne pepper, to taste
4 large (10-inch) flour tortillas
Poblano Chili Sauce (see p. 722)
½ cup fat-free sour cream
Medium, *or* hot, prepared salsa, to taste

Per Serving
Calories: 319
% Calories from fat: 10
Fat (gm): 3.7
Saturated fat (gm): 0.5
Cholesterol (mg): 0
Sodium (mg): 620
Protein (gm): 18.3
Carbohydrate (gm): 58.9
Exchanges
Milk: 0.5
Vegetable: 2.0
Fruit: 0.0
Bread: 3.0
Meat: 0.5
Fat: 0.5

1. Cover arbol chilies with hot water in small bowl; let stand until softened, 10 to 15 minutes. Drain; chop finely.

2. Spray medium skillet with cooking spray; heat over medium heat until hot. Saute zucchini, squash, onion, garlic, and herbs until onion is tender, 8 to 10 minutes. Add beans, water, and arbol chilies to skillet; mash coarsely with fork. Stir in tomato; cook over medium heat until hot. Season to taste with salt and cayenne pepper.

3. Spoon vegetable mixture along centers of tortillas; top each with ¼ cup Poblano Chili Sauce. Fold sides of tortillas in, overlapping filling; fold ends in, overlapping to make a square "package"; secure with toothpicks.

4. Spray large skillet with cooking spray; heat over medium heat until hot. Cook burritos until browned on all sides, brushing with remaining Poblano Chili Sauce. Serve hot with sour cream and salsa.

ENCHILADAS MOLE

For variation, the enchiladas can also be baked with Tomatillo Sauce or Jalapeño con Queso Sauce (see pp. 724 and 725). Serve with Jicama Salad (see p. 640) for fresh flavor contrast.

4 servings (2 enchiladas each)

8-12 ounces tempeh, cut into strips 2 x ½ x ½ inches

1 cup Enchilada Sauce (see p. 720), *or* prepared salsa

Garlic-flavored vegetable cooking spray

8 corn, *or* flour, tortillas

½ cup (2 ounces) shredded fat-free Cheddar cheese

½ cup sliced green onions and tops

4-8 tablespoons fat-free sour cream

¼ cup finely chopped cilantro

Mole Sauce (see p. 721)

Per Serving
Calories: 388
% Calories from fat: 22
Fat (gm): 10.2
Saturated fat (gm): 1.5
Cholesterol (mg): 0
Sodium (mg): 235
Protein (gm): 26.2
Carbohydrate (gm): 53.8
Exchanges
Milk: 0.0
Vegetable: 3.0
Fruit: 0.0
Bread: 2.5
Meat: 2.0
Fat: 1.0

1. Place tempeh in shallow glass baking dish; pour Enchilada Sauce over. Refrigerate 1 to 2 hours; drain, reserving Enchilada Sauce.

2. Spray medium skillet with cooking spray; heat over medium heat until hot. Add tempeh and spray lightly with cooking spray. Cook over medium heat until tempeh is browned, 3 to 5 minutes.

3. Dip tortillas in reserved Enchilada Sauce to coat lightly. Spoon tempeh along centers of tortillas; top with cheese, green onions, sour cream, and cilantro. Roll up and place, seam sides down, in large baking pan. Spoon Mole Sauce over enchiladas.

4. Bake, loosely covered, at 350 degrees until enchiladas are hot through, 20 to 30 minutes.

VEGETABLE ENCHILADAS

Vary these healthful enchiladas by substituting vegetables in season or best buys at the supermarket. Substitute 8 to 12 ounces of tempeh or light firm tofu for the vegetable protein if you wish.

6 servings (2 enchiladas each)

Vegetable cooking spray
2 cups chopped zucchini
1½ cups chopped tomatoes
¾ cup chopped carrots
¼ cup chopped poblano chili, *or* green bell pepper
¼ cup thinly sliced green onions and tops
4 cloves garlic, minced
1 teaspoon minced serrano, *or* jalapeño, chili
1 teaspoon dried oregano leaves
1-2 teaspoons ground cumin
1 package (12 ounces) frozen pre-browned all-vegetable protein crumbles
Salt and pepper, to taste
12 corn, *or* flour, tortillas
Enchilada Sauce (see p. 720)
¾ cup (3 ounces) shredded fat-free Cheddar cheese
3 tablespoons finely chopped cilantro

Per Serving
Calories: 269
% Calories from fat: 6
Fat (gm): 1.8
Saturated fat (gm): 0.3
Cholesterol (mg): 0
Sodium (mg): 449
Protein (gm): 22.5
Carbohydrate (gm): 42.7
Exchanges
Milk: 0.0
Vegetable: 2.0
Fruit: 0.0
Bread: 2.0
Meat: 1.5
Fat: 0.0

1. Spray large skillet with cooking spray; heat over medium heat until hot. Saute vegetables and herbs until vegetables are tender, about 10 minutes. Add vegetable protein crumbles; cook over medium heat until no excess juices remain, 5 to 8 minutes. Season to taste with salt and pepper.

2. Dip tortillas in Enchilada Sauce to coat lightly, and fill each with about ⅓ cup of vegetable mixture. Roll up and place, seam sides down, in large baking pan. Spoon remaining Enchilada Sauce over enchiladas; sprinkle with cheese.

3. Bake enchiladas, uncovered, at 350 degrees, 15 to 20 minutes. Sprinkle with cilantro.

FLAUTAS WITH TOMATILLO SAUCE

 Flautas are usually deep-fried; these are sauteed to achieve the same crispness.

4 servings (2 flautas each)

Vegetable cooking spray
1 cup chopped zucchini
1 cup chopped tomato
1 cup sliced mushrooms
½ cup chopped onion
½ cup finely chopped poblano chili
½ teaspoon ground cumin
¼ teaspoon dried thyme leaves
2 tablespoons finely chopped cilantro
Salt and pepper, to taste
8 flour, *or* corn, tortillas
1 cup Tomatillo Sauce (see p. 724)
4 tablespoons crumbled Mexican white cheese, *or* farmer's cheese
¼ cup fat-free sour cream
Cilantro sprigs, as garnish

Per Serving
Calories: 330
% Calories from fat: 22
Fat (gm): 8.1
Saturated fat (gm): 1.8
Cholesterol (mg): 5.1
Sodium (mg): 456
Protein (gm): 11
Carbohydrate (gm): 55.3
Exchanges
Milk: 0.0
Vegetable: 2.0
Fruit: 0.0
Bread: 3.0
Meat: 0.0
Fat: 1.5

1. Spray large skillet with cooking spray; heat over medium heat until hot. Saute vegetables until tender, about 5 minutes. Stir in cumin, thyme, and cilantro; cook 1 to 2 minutes longer. Season to taste with salt and pepper.

2. Spoon about ⅓ cup vegetable mixture on each tortilla; roll up and fasten with toothpicks. Spray large skillet generously with cooking spray; heat over medium heat until hot. Cook flautas over medium to medium-high heat until browned on all sides, spraying with cooking spray if needed.

3. Arrange flautas on plates; spoon Tomatillo Sauce over. Sprinkle with cheese; top with dollops of sour cream. Garnish with cilantro.

VEGETABLE TOSTADAS

A perfect brunch or lunch entrée, South-of-the-Border style! Serve with Yellow Salsa Rice or Refried Beans (see pp. 575, 525).

6 servings (1 tostada ecah)

Vegetable cooking spray
6 whole wheat tortillas
2 medium zucchini, chopped
1 small onion, chopped
½ serrano chili, seeds and veins discarded, finely chopped
3 cloves garlic, minced
1 package (12 ounces) frozen pre-browned all-vegetable protein crumbles, thawed
1½-2 teaspoons dried oregano leaves
Salt and pepper, to taste
2 cups chopped romaine lettuce
1 medium tomato, chopped
Chili Tomato Sauce (see p. 179), warm
¼ cup crumbled Mexican white cheese, *or* farmer's cheese
⅓ cup (½ recipe) Guacamole (see p. 15)

Per Serving
Calories: 291
% Calories from fat: 17
Fat (gm): 5.4
Saturated fat (gm): 1.3
Cholesterol (mg): 3.4
Sodium (mg): 543
Protein (gm): 20.1
Carbohydrate (gm): 41.3
Exchanges
Milk: 0.0
Vegetable: 2.0
Fruit: 0.0
Bread: 2.0
Meat: 2.0
Fat: 0.0

1. Spray medium skillet with cooking spray; heat over medium heat until hot. Cook tortillas until crisp and browned, about 1 minute on each side. Place tortillas on serving plates.

2. Spray large skillet with cooking spray; heat over medium heat until hot. Saute zucchini, onion, serrano chili, and garlic 2 to 3 minutes; stir in vegetable protein crumbles and oregano. Cook until hot through 3 to 4 minutes; season to taste with salt and pepper.

3. Top tortillas with chopped lettuce and tomato; spoon cooked mixture and Chili Tomato Sauce over. Sprinkle with crumbled cheese; top each with a large dollop of Guacamole.

TEMPEH FAJITAS

Fajitas are an American interpretation of soft tacos. They can include any combination of vegetables you want.

4 servings (2 fajitas each)

8-12 ounces tempeh, cut into strips 2 x ½ x ½ inches
Fajita Marinade (recipe follows)
Vegetable cooking spray
1 medium red bell pepper, sliced
1 medium onion, sliced
1 can (15 ounces) black beans, rinsed, drained
1 teaspoon ground cumin
½ teaspoon dried marjoram leaves
Salt and pepper, to taste
8 flour, *or* corn, tortillas, warm
2 tablespoons finely chopped cilantro
1 cup Red Tomato Salsa (see p. 9)
½ cup fat-free sour cream

Per Serving
Calories: 441
% Calories from fat: 18
Fat (gm): 9.7
Saturated fat (gm): 1.4
Cholesterol (mg): 0
Sodium (mg): 601
Protein (gm): 29.1
Carbohydrate (gm): 70.8
Exchanges
Milk: 0.0
Vegetable: 2.0
Fruit: 0.0
Bread: 4.0
Meat: 2.0
Fat: 0.0

1. Place tempeh in shallow glass baking dish; pour Fajita Marinade over. Refrigerate, covered, 1 to 2 hours; drain.

2. Spray large skillet with cooking spray; heat over medium heat until hot. Cook tempeh over medium heat until browned, 5 to 8 minutes; move tempeh to side of pan. Add bell pepper and onion; cook over medium heat until tender, about 5 minutes. Add beans, cumin, and marjoram; cook until hot, 2 to 3 minutes. Season to taste with salt and pepper.

3. Spoon mixture onto tortillas; sprinkle with cilantro, top with Red Tomato Salsa and sour cream, and roll up.

Fajita Marinade

(makes about ⅓ cup.)

- ⅓ cup lime juice
- 4 cloves garlic, minced
- 1½ teaspoons dried oregano leaves
- ½ teaspoon ground allspice
- ¼ teaspoon black pepper

1. Mix all ingredients.

CHIMICHANGAS

A quick and easy Mexican-style favorite that can vary according to the ingredients you have on hand. Garnish with cilantro or a spoonful of Guacamole (see p. 15), if you wish.

4 servings (2 chimichangas each)

Vegetable cooking spray
- ¾ cup chopped onion
- 1½ teaspoons minced garlic
- 1½ cups frozen prebrowned all-vegetable protein crumbles, thawed
- 2 tablespoons water
- 1-2 teaspoons taco seasoning
- 8 flour, *or* corn, tortillas, warm
- 1½ cups (6 ounces) shredded fat-free Cheddar, *or* Monterey Jack, cheese
- ½ cup hot, *or* mild, prepared salsa
- ½ cup fat-free, *or* reduced-fat, sour cream

Per Serving
Calories: 364
% Calories from fat: 8
Fat (gm): 3.3
Saturated fat (gm): 0.6
Cholesterol (mg): 0
Sodium (mg): 726
Protein (gm): 29.7
Carbohydrate (gm): 53.7
Exchanges
Milk: 0.0
Vegetable: 1.0
Fruit: 0.0
Bread: 3.0
Meat: 2.5
Fat: 0.0

1. Spray medium skillet with cooking spray; heat over medium heat until hot. Saute onion and garlic 2 to 3 minutes; stir in protein crumbles, water, and taco seasoning. Cook over medium heat until hot through, 2 to 3 minutes.

2. Spoon mixture onto tortillas; top with cheese, salsa, and sour cream. Roll up and fold one end for eating.

THREE-CHILI TAMALES

Ancho chilies are fresh poblano chilies that have been dried. Corn husks and masa harina (corn flour) can be purchased in large supermarkets or Mexican groceries.

4 servings (3 tamales each)

12 corn husks
   Hot water
2 ancho chilies, stems, seeds, and veins discarded
⅓ cup boiling water
1 large poblano chili, seeds and veins discarded, chopped
1 can (4 ounces) chopped green chilies, drained
¾ teaspoon dried oregano leaves
½ teaspoon dried thyme leaves
   Salt and pepper, to taste
   Tamale Dough (recipe follows)

Per Serving
Calories: 187
% Calories from fat: 26
Fat (gm): 5.6
Saturated fat (gm): 1
Cholesterol (mg): 0
Sodium (mg): 396
Protein (gm): 3.7
Carbohydrate (gm): 29.9
Exchanges
Milk: 0.0
Vegetable: 1.0
Fruit: 0.0
Bread: 1.5
Meat: 0.0
Fat: 1.0

1. Soak corn husks in hot water until softened, about 1 hour; drain well on paper toweling.

2. Crumble ancho chilies into bowl; pour ⅓ cup boiling water over and let stand until softened, 15 to 20 minutes. Cook ancho chilies and liquid, poblano chili, green chilies, and herbs over medium heat in medium skillet until chilies are tender, 5 to 8 minutes, stirring frequently. Season to taste with salt and pepper. Mix in Tamale Dough.

3. Spoon about ¼ cup of tamale mixture onto center of each corn husk; fold sides of husks over filling. Tie ends of tamales, making "bundles."

4. Place tamales on steamer rack in saucepan with 2 inches of water. Steam, covered, 2 hours, adding more water to saucepan if necessary. Serve warm.

Tamale Dough

    1   cup masa harina
    ¾   teaspoon baking powder
    1½ tablespoons margarine, softened
    ¼-½ teaspoon salt
    1   cup Canned Vegetable Stock (see p. 63)

1.   Combine masa harina, baking powder, margarine, and salt; gradually stir in stock (mixture will be soft).

VEGGIE TAMALES WITH BEANS

Tamales can be tied in "bundles," as in the preceding recipe, or in "envelopes," as in this recipe.

4 servings (3 tamales each)

    12 corn husks
        Hot water
        Vegetable cooking spray
    1   medium onion, chopped
    ¾   cup coarsely chopped zucchini
    ½   cup chopped poblano chili, *or* green
        bell pepper
    ¾   cup fresh, *or* frozen, thawed, whole-
        kernel corn
    3   cloves garlic, minced
    ¾   teaspoon dried marjoram leaves
    ¼   teaspoon ground allspice
    ½   can (15-ounce size) pinto beans, rinsed,
        drained, coarsely mashed
        Salt and cayenne pepper, to taste
        Tamale Dough (see above)

Per Serving
Calories: 257
% Calories from fat: 20
Fat (gm): 6
Saturated fat (gm): 1
Cholesterol (mg): 0
Sodium (mg): 457
Protein (gm): 8.5
Carbohydrate (gm): 44.7
Exchanges
Milk: 0.0
Vegetable: 2.0
Fruit: 0.0
Bread: 2.5
Meat: 0.0
Fat: 0.5

1.   Soak corn husks in hot water until softened, about 1 hour; drain well on paper toweling.

2.   Spray medium skillet with cooking spray; heat over medium heat until hot. Saute onion, zucchini, poblano chili, corn, and garlic until vegetables are tender, about 5 minutes. Stir in herbs and beans and cook 2 to 3 minutes; season to taste with salt and cayenne pepper. Mix in Tamale Dough.

3. Spoon about ¼ cup of tamale mixture onto center of each corn husk. Fold sides of husks over filling; fold tops and bottoms of husks toward center and tie in the center with string.

4. Place tamales on steamer rack in saucepan with 2 inches of water. Steam, covered, 2 hours, adding more water to saucepan if necessary. Serve warm.

TOFU RANCHERO

The Achiote Oil gives a deep golden color to the tofu, making it appear amazingly like scrambled eggs! See information on achiote seeds and pressing tofu (pp. ix, xii).

6 servings

1-2 teaspoons Achiote Oil (recipe follows)
  2 packages (10½ ounces each) light firm tofu, pressed, crumbled
  ¼ cup chopped onion
     Salt and pepper, to taste
     Serrano Tomato Sauce (see p. 723), warm
  ¼ cup finely chopped cilantro

Per Serving
Calories: 67
% Calories from fat: 27
Fat (gm): 2.2
Saturated fat (gm): 0.1
Cholesterol (mg): 0
Sodium (mg): 100
Protein (gm): 7.8
Carbohydrate (gm): 5.2
Exchanges
Milk: 0.0
Vegetable: 1.0
Fruit: 0.0
Bread: 0.0
Meat: 1.0
Fat: 0.0

1. Heat Achiote Oil over medium heat in medium skillet; add tofu and onion and cook, stirring frequently, until onion is tender and tofu hot through, 3 to 5 minutes. Season to taste with salt and pepper.

2. Spoon tofu mixture on plates; top with Serrano Tomato Sauce and sprinkle with cilantro.

Achiote Oil

(makes 2 teaspoons)

  2 teaspoons canola oil
  ½ teaspoon achiote (annatto) seeds

1. Heat oil and achiote seeds in small skillet or saucepan over medium heat until oil is a deep yellow color, about 5 minutes. Remove from heat and cool.

2. Remove achiote seeds with slotted spoon and discard.

FIVE

Roasted

AND

Grilled Dishes

ROASTED CORN AND POTATO CHOWDER

Perfect for summer's end, when evenings become cool.

8 main-dish servings (about 1½ cups each)

6 ears corn, in the husks
   Olive oil cooking spray
2 pounds new red potatoes, unpeeled, cut into halves
1 medium red bell pepper, cut into ¾-inch pieces
1 medium onion, cut into ¾-inch pieces
3 cloves garlic, peeled
2 teaspoons dried thyme leaves
2 teaspoons dried parsley leaves
6 cups Canned Vegetable Stock (see p. 63) or reduced-sodium canned vegetable broth, divided
⅔ cup fat-free half-and-half, *or* fat-free milk
   Salt and pepper, to taste

Per Serving
Calories: 250
% Calories from fat: 6
Fat (gm): 1.6
Saturated fat (gm): 0.2
Cholesterol (mg): 0
Sodium (mg): 78
Protein (gm): 6.2
Carbohydrate (gm): 51.1
Exchanges
Milk: 0.0
Vegetable: 1.0
Fruit: 0.0
Bread: 3.0
Meat: 0.0
Fat: 0.0

1. Soak corn in cold water to cover 30 minutes.

2. Spray 2 aluminum-foil-lined jelly roll pans with cooking spray. Arrange corn on 1 pan. Arrange remaining vegetables on second pan; spray generously with cooking spray and sprinkle with herbs.

3. Roast corn and other vegetables at 425 degrees until browned and tender, about 40 minutes, removing garlic when soft, after about 20 minutes. Let vegetables stand until cool enough to handle. Remove and discard corn husks. Cut kernels off cobs.

4. Process vegetables and 2 to 3 cups stock in food processor or blender until smooth. Heat vegetable mixture and remaining stock to boiling in large saucepan; reduce heat to medium-low. Stir in half-and-half and cook 3 to 4 minutes, until hot. Season to taste with salt and pepper.

HOT PEPPER VICHYSSOISE

Potato soup will never be boring if served Tex-Mex style. This version, prepared with peppers, packs a punch!

6 main-dish servings (about 1 cup each)

Vegetable cooking spray

1 pound new red potatoes, unpeeled, cut into halves

1 medium leek, cut into ¾-inch pieces (white part only)

1 large poblano chili, cut into ¾-inch pieces

1 medium jalapeño chili, cut into ¾-inch pieces

6 cloves garlic, peeled

1½ teaspoons ground cumin

½ teaspoon chili powder

½ teaspoon dried oregano leaves

½ teaspoon pepper

4 cups Canned Vegetable Stock (see p. 63), *or* canned reduced-sodium vegetable broth, divided

½-¾ cup fat-free half-and-half, *or* fat-free milk

¼ cup minced cilantro

Salt, to taste

6 pieces (⅔ recipe) Roasted Chili Corn Bread (see p. 305)

Per Serving
Calories: 331
% Calories from fat: 7
Fat (gm): 2.5
Saturated fat (gm): 0.5
Cholesterol (mg): 24.7
Sodium (mg): 365
Protein (gm): 10
Carbohydrate (gm): 64.1
Exchanges
Milk: 0.0
Vegetable: 4.0
Fruit: 0.0
Bread: 3.0
Meat: 0.0
Fat: 0.5

1. Spray aluminum-foil-lined jelly roll pan with cooking spray. Arrange vegetables in single layer on pan; spray generously with cooking spray and sprinkle with herbs and pepper.

2. Roast vegetables at 425 degrees until browned and tender, about 40 minutes, removing garlic when tender, after about 20 minutes.

3. Process vegetables and 1 to 2 cups stock in food processor or blender until smooth. Transfer to saucepan; stir in remaining stock, half-and-half, and cilantro; season with salt. Serve warm, or refrigerate until chilled, 4 to 6 hours, and serve cold. Serve with Roasted Chili Corn Bread.

PUREED ROASTED VEGETABLE SOUP

We've served this soup over rice, but it is also delicious served without rice and topped with Garlic Croutons (see p. 677).

6 main-dish servings (about 1½ cups each)

Olive oil cooking spray
1 medium eggplant, peeled
2 pattypan squash
1 medium red bell pepper
1 medium red onion
1 small poblano chili, *or* green bell pepper
3 cloves garlic, peeled
1½ tablespoons herbs de Provence
1 teaspoon pepper
4 cups canned reduced-sodium vegetable broth, divided
1-2 tablespoons lemon juice
1 teaspoon grated lemon rind
Salt, to taste
¾-1¼ cups fat-free plain yogurt
3 cups cooked rice, warm

Per Serving
Calories: 219
% Calories from fat: 4
Fat (gm): 1.1
Saturated fat (gm): 0.2
Cholesterol (mg): 0.5
Sodium (mg): 87
Protein (gm): 6.7
Carbohydrate (gm): 47.4
Exchanges
Milk: 0.0
Vegetable: 3.0
Fruit: 0.0
Bread: 2.0
Meat: 0.0
Fat: 0.0

1. Spray aluminum-foil-lined jelly roll pan with cooking spray. Cut vegetables, except garlic, into 1-inch pieces; arrange vegetables in single layer on pan. Spray vegetables with cooking spray; sprinkle with herbs and pepper.

2. Roast vegetables at 425 degrees until browned and tender, about 40 minutes, removing garlic when soft, after about 20 minutes. Process vegetables and 1 cup broth in food processor or blender until smooth. Heat vegetable mixture, remaining 3 cups broth, lemon juice, and rind in large saucepan to boiling; reduce heat and simmer, uncovered, 5 minutes. Season to taste with salt.

3. Serve soup over rice in bowls; stir 2 to 3 tablespoons yogurt into each bowl.

ROASTED VEGETABLE MINESTRONE

Oven roasting enhances the natural flavors of vegetables, making this soup a favorite in our repertory. Two cups of cooked macaroni or other-shaped pasta can be substituted for 1 can of the beans.

8 main-dish servings (about 1¾ cups each)

Olive oil cooking spray
1   medium eggplant, unpeeled
1   large Idaho potato, unpeeled
2   medium zucchini
2   medium tomatoes
½   small butternut squash, peeled
1   large green bell pepper
1   large red bell pepper
1   teaspoon dried rosemary leaves
¾   teaspoon dried oregano leaves
½   teaspoon dried sage leaves
¼-½   teaspoon dried thyme leaves
1   cup coarsely chopped onion
4   cloves garlic, minced
1   can (15½ ounces) cannellini, *or* Great Northern, beans, rinsed, drained
1   can (15½ ounces) red kidney beans, rinsed, drained
7   cups Canned Vegetable Stock (see p. 63)
2-3   tablespoons white balsamic vinegar
Salt and pepper, to taste

Per Serving
Calories: 224
% Calories from fat: 7
Fat (gm): 2
Saturated fat (gm): 0.2
Cholesterol (mg): 0
Sodium (mg): 269
Protein (gm): 11.7
Carbohydrate (gm): 44.5
Exchanges
Milk: 0.0
Vegetable: 3.0
Fruit: 0.0
Bread: 2.0
Meat: 0.0
Fat: 0.0

1. Line large jelly roll pan with aluminum foil and spray with cooking spray. Cut eggplant, potato, zucchini, tomatoes, squash, and bell peppers into ¾- to 1-inch pieces. Arrange vegetables on jelly roll pan; spray generously with cooking spray and sprinkle with combined herbs. Bake at 425 degrees until vegetables are browned and tender, 30 to 40 minutes.

2. Spray large saucepan with cooking spray; heat over medium heat until hot. Saute onion and garlic until tender, about 5 minutes. Add roasted vegetables, beans, and stock; heat to boiling. Reduce heat and simmer, covered, 10 minutes. Season with vinegar; add salt and pepper, to taste.

ROASTED RATATOUILLE STEW

Roasting vegetables intensifies their natural flavor and sweetness. Serve this full-flavored stew with warm, crusty French bread.

6 main-dish servings (about 2 cups each)

Olive oil cooking spray

8 ounces new potatoes, unpeeled, quartered

4 baby eggplants, unpeeled, cut into 1-inch cubes

3 cups sliced red, *or* green, cabbage

2 medium yellow summer squash, *or* zucchini, sliced

2 cups cauliflower florets

2 cups green beans, cut into halves

2 medium green bell peppers, cut into 1-inch pieces

2 medium onions, sliced

3 cloves garlic, minced

¾-1 teaspoon Italian seasoning

1 cup Mediterranean Stock, *or* Basic Vegetable Stock, (see pp. 60, 58)

1 cup dry red wine, *or* Mediterranean Stock

¼ cup reduced-sodium tomato paste

2 tablespoons balsamic vinegar

1½ tablespoons brown sugar

2 medium tomatoes, cut into wedges

Salt and pepper, to taste

Per Serving
Calories: 197
% Calories from fat: 5
Fat (gm): 1.2
Saturated fat (gm): 0.2
Cholesterol (mg): 0
Sodium (mg): 64
Protein (gm): 5.7
Carbohydrate (gm): 38.4
Exchanges
Milk: 0.0
Vegetable: 5.0
Fruit: 0.0
Bread: 1.0
Meat: 0.0
Fat: 0.0

1. Spray 2 aluminum-foil-lined jelly roll pans with cooking spray. Arrange vegetables in single layer on pans. Generously spray vegetables with cooking spray; sprinkle with Italian seasoning.

2. Roast vegetables at 475 degrees 15 to 20 minutes or until beginning to brown, stirring occasionally.

3. Heat stock, wine, tomato paste, vinegar, and sugar to boiling in small saucepan; pour over vegetables. Add tomatoes to pans.

4. Reduce oven temperature to 350 degrees and bake, covered, 20 to 30 minutes or until vegetables are tender. Season to taste with salt and pepper.

MESQUITE-SMOKED TOFU

 Tofu, lightly smoked, is delicious! It can be smoked on the grill or range-top, following the Notes below. Tempeh can be substituted for the tofu.

4 servings

Vegetable cooking spray
2 packages (10½ ounces each) light firm tofu, sliced lengthwise into halves

Per Serving
Calories: 62
% Calories from fat: 24
Fat (gm): 1.8
Saturated fat (gm): 0
Cholesterol (mg): 0
Sodium (mg): 142
Protein (gm): 10.6
Carbohydrate (gm): 1.8
Exchanges
Milk: 0.0
Vegetable: 0.0
Fruit: 0.0
Bread: 0.0
Meat: 1.5
Fat: 0.0

1. Spray smoker rack generously with cooking spray before placing on grill. Place tofu on rack over medium-hot coals with mesquite chips. Smoke, covered, 20 to 30 minutes, or longer for a more intense smoky flavor.

Notes: Tofu can be smoked on a covered grill. Arrange hot charcoal around edges of grill; place a shallow pan of water in center. Sprinkle hot coals with mesquite chips that have been soaked in water and well drained. Continue as recipe directs.

Tofu can also be smoked on top of the range. Sprinkle 2 to 3 tablespoons mesquite smoking bits (very small mesquite chips, available in canisters at hardware and home improvement stores and some large supermarkets) or mesquite shavings in bottom of large Dutch oven; place wire rack in Dutch oven. Place tofu on rack and cover; heat over high heat 5 minutes. Lift lid just enough to make sure pan is filled with smoke; reduce heat to medium-low and cook, covered, 20 to 30 minutes.

JERK TEMPEH WITH BLACK BEANS AND RICE

Treat yourself to a meal with island flavors! The Caribbean Jerk Seasoning can also be used on eggplant slices and portobello mushrooms.

6 servings

2 packages (8 ounces each) tempeh, cut crosswise into halves
1 tablespoon lime juice
Jerk Seasoning (recipe follows)
Black Beans and Rice (see p. 526)
Fried Plantains (see p. 33)

Per Serving
Calories: 439
% Calories from fat: 16
Fat (gm): 8.3
Saturated fat (gm): 1.3
Cholesterol (mg): 0
Sodium (mg): 250
Protein (gm): 25.6
Carbohydrate (gm): 71.9
Exchanges
Milk: 0.0
Vegetable: 1.0
Fruit: 1.0
Bread: 3.5
Meat: 2.0
Fat: 0.0

1. Brush tempeh pieces with lime juice; sprinkle with Jerk Seasoning, pressing mixture onto tempeh.

2. Grill tempeh over medium-hot coals until browned and hot through, about 5 minutes on each side, or roast at 425 degrees 20 to 30 minutes. Serve with Black Beans and Rice and Fried Plantains.

Jerk Seasoning

(makes about 2 tablespoons)

1½ teaspoons onion powder
1½ teaspoons garlic powder
¾ teaspoon dried thyme leaves
½ teaspoon dried oregano leaves
½ teaspoon ground allspice
½ teaspoon ground ginger
½ teaspoon paprika
¼ teaspoon ground nutmeg
½ teaspoon black pepper
¼-½ teaspoon cayenne pepper

1. Combine all ingredients; store in airtight container until ready to use.

GRILLED TEMPEH WITH POBLANO SOUR CREAM SAUCE

Tempeh is marinated in Fajita Marinade for a flavor of the Southwest.

6 servings

3 packages (8 ounces each) tempeh, cut crosswise into halves
Fajita Marinade (see p. 256)
Vegetable cooking spray
Poblano Sour Cream Sauce (see p. 724)
Cilantro, finely chopped, as garnish

Per Serving
Calories: 260
% Calories from fat: 30
Fat (gm): 9
Saturated fat (gm): 1.5
Cholesterol (mg): 0
Sodium (mg): 26
Protein (gm): 26.8
Carbohydrate (gm): 21.8
Exchanges
Milk: 0.0
Vegetable: 1.0
Fruit: 0.0
Bread: 1.0
Meat: 3.0
Fat: 0.0

1. Place tempeh in shallow glass baking dish; pour Fajita Marinade over. Refrigerate 1 to 2 hours, turning tempeh occasionally; drain.

2. Spray grill rack generously with cooking spray before placing on grill. Spray tempeh on both sides with cooking spray. Place tempeh on rack over medium-hot coals. Grill, covered, until tempeh is browned, 4 to 6 minutes on each side.

3. Arrange tempeh on plates; spoon Poblano Sour Cream Sauce over and garnish with cilantro.

ROASTED TOFU, ONIONS, AND PEPPERS WITH LIME SAUCE

The lime sauce and vegetables are also excellent served over sweet potatoes or yellow winter squash. Tempeh or portobello mushrooms can be substituted for the tofu in this recipe.

4 servings

Vegetable cooking spray
2 packages (10½ ounces each) light firm tofu, sliced lengthwise into 2 halves
2 cups sliced onions

Per Serving
Calories: 179
% Calories from fat: 10
Fat (gm): 2.2
Saturated fat (gm): 0
Cholesterol (mg): 0
Sodium (mg): 149
Protein (gm): 12.8
Carbohydrate (gm): 30.6

1 large bell pepper, sliced
Salt and pepper, to taste
Lime Sauce (recipe follows)
¼ cup finely chopped cilantro

Exchanges
Milk: 0.0
Vegetable: 2.0
Fruit: 0.0
Bread: 1.0
Meat: 1.0
Fat: 0.0

1. Spray aluminum-foil-lined jelly roll pan with cooking spray. Arrange tofu, onions, and bell peppers on pan. Roast at 425 degrees until vegetables are browned and tender, 30 to 40 minutes. Season to taste with salt and pepper.

2. Arrange tofu on plates. Stir vegetables into Lime Sauce; spoon over tofu and sprinkle with cilantro.

Lime Sauce

(makes about 1 cup)

¼ cup sugar
1 tablespoon cornstarch
½ cup lime juice
½ cup water
1 clove garlic, minced
½ teaspoon chili powder, *or* any desired herb

1. Mix sugar and cornstarch in medium saucepan; stir in remaining ingredients and heat to boiling. Boil, stirring constantly, until thickened, about 1 minute.

TANDOORI TEMPEH WITH ORANGE CILANTRO RICE

Tempeh (or tofu) is marinated in a seasoned yogurt mixture for flavor, then grilled or roasted.

4 servings

2 packages (8 ounces each) tempeh, cut crosswise into halves
Tandoori Marinade (recipe follows)

Per Serving
Calories: 363
% Calories from fat: 23
Fat (gm): 9.6
Saturated fat (gm): 1.6
Cholesterol (mg): 0.3
Sodium (mg): 37
Protein (gm): 28
Carbohydrate (gm): 44.1

Vegetable cooking spray

2½ cups (⅔ recipe) Orange Cilantro Rice (see p. 575)

Exchanges
Milk: 0.0
Vegetable: 0.0
Fruit: 0.0
Bread: 3.0
Meat: 3.0
Fat: 0.0

1. Spread all surfaces of tempeh with Tandoori Marinade; place in shallow glass baking dish and refrigerate 3 to 4 hours or overnight.

2. Spray grill rack generously with cooking spray; place tempeh on rack over medium-hot coals. Grill, covered, until tempeh is browned, 4 to 6 minutes on each side. Or, place tempeh in greased, aluminum-foil-lined baking pan and roast at 425 degrees until browned, 20 to 30 minutes. Serve with Orange Cilantro Rice.

Tandoori Marinade

(makes about ½ cup)

⅓ cup fat-free plain yogurt

1 small jalapeño pepper, minced

1 tablespoon finely chopped cilantro, *or* parsley

2 teaspoons minced garlic

1 teaspoon minced gingerroot

1 teaspoon grated lime rind

2 teaspoons paprika

1½ teaspoons ground cumin

1 teaspoon ground coriander

1. Combine all ingredients; refrigerate until ready to use.

ROASTED VEGETABLES WITH MUSHROOM TORTELLINI

A medley of roasted vegetables complement pasta in this colorful dish. Substitute ravioli or a shaped pasta for the tortellini if you want.

4 servings

Vegetable cooking spray
3   medium Italian plum tomatoes
8   ounces small okra, ends trimmed
4   ounces small mushrooms, halved
1   medium zucchini, cut into ¼-inch slices
1   medium yellow summer squash, cut into ¼-inch slices
4   ounces broccoli rabe, rinsed, dried, cut into 3-inch pieces, *or* broccoli, cut into small florets
1½ teaspoons Italian seasoning
    Salt and pepper, to taste
1   package (9 ounces) mushroom, *or* herb, tortellini, cooked, warm
1-2 tablespoons olive oil

Per Serving
Calories: 256
% Calories from fat: 19
Fat (gm): 5.6
Saturated fat (gm): 1.3
Cholesterol (mg): 3.8
Sodium (mg): 337
Protein (gm): 14.6
Carbohydrate (gm): 40.5
Exchanges
Milk: 0.0
Vegetable: 2.0
Fruit: 0.0
Bread: 2.0
Meat: 1.0
Fat: 0.0

1. Line large jelly roll pan with aluminum foil; spray with cooking spray.

2. Cut each tomato into 6 wedges; cut wedges in halves. Arrange tomatoes and remaining vegetables on jelly roll pan; spray generously with cooking spray. Sprinkle vegetables with Italian seasoning; sprinkle lightly with salt and pepper.

3. Roast vegetables at 425 degrees until tender and browned, about 40 minutes, removing broccoli rabe after about 20 minutes. Combine vegetables and tortellini in serving bowl; drizzle with olive oil and toss.

ROASTED EGGPLANT WITH PASTA

Cook the eggplant on a charcoal grill to get a wonderful smoky flavor. The eggplant can be roasted or grilled up to 2 days in advance; refrigerate it in a plastic bag.

6 servings

1 medium eggplant (¾ pound)
1 large tomato, seeded, coarsely chopped
4 green onions and tops, sliced
2 tablespoons balsamic vinegar, *or* red wine vinegar
1 tablespoon olive oil
1-2 teaspoons lemon juice
1 tablespoon finely chopped parsley
1½ cups (6 ounces) fusilli, *or* rotini (spirals or corkscrews), cooked, room temperature

Per Serving
Calories: 140
% Calories from fat: 19
Fat (gm): 3
Saturated fat (gm): 0.5
Cholesterol (mg): 0
Sodium (mg): 7
Protein (gm): 4.5
Carbohydrate (gm): 24
Exchanges
Milk: 0.0
Vegetable: 1.5
Fruit: 0.0
Bread: 1.0
Meat: 0.0
Fat: 0.5

1. Heat oven to 425 degreews. Pierce eggplant 6 to 8 times with fork; place in baking pan. Bake, uncovered, until tender, about 20 minutes. Cool until warm enough to handle easily. Cut eggplant in half; scoop out pulp with large spoon, and cut pulp into ¾-inch pieces.

2. Combine eggplant pulp, tomato, and onions in bowl; stir in vinegar, oil, lemon juice, and parsley. Spoon over pasta and toss.

GRILLED SUMMER VEGETABLES IN PASTA NESTS

For attractive serving, the linguine is shaped into small nests to contain the medley of roasted vegetables.

8 servings

3 tablespoons olive oil, divided
2 tablespoons balsamic vinegar, *or* red wine vinegar
1 teaspoon lemon juice
3 cloves garlic, minced, divided
2 teaspoons crushed caraway seeds

Per Serving
Calories: 197
% Calories from fat: 30
Fat (gm): 6.8
Saturated fat (gm): 0.8
Cholesterol (mg): 0
Sodium (mg): 138
Protein (gm): 6.4
Carbohydrate (gm): 29.1

¼ teaspoon salt

¼ teaspoon pepper

1 medium eggplant, peeled, cut into 1-inch pieces

1 medium zucchini, sliced

1 medium red, *or* green, bell pepper, cut into 1-inch pieces

1 small red onion, cut into 1-inch wedges

Vegetable cooking spray

12 ounces linguine, cooked, warm

1 tablespoon minced parsley

Exchanges
Milk: 0.0
Vegetable: 1.5
Fruit: 0.0
Bread: 1.5
Meat: 0.0
Fat: 1.0

1. Mix 2 tablespoons of oil, vinegar, lemon juice, 2 cloves of garlic, caraway seeds, salt, and pepper; pour over combined vegetables in shallow glass baking dish. Let stand, covered, 30 to 60 minutes.

2. Heat oven to 400 degrees. Spray 2 jelly roll pans with cooking spray; arrange vegetables in single layer on pans. Bake until vegetables are browned and just tender, 30 to 40 minutes.

3. Toss linguine with remaining 1 tablespoon oil, parsley, and remaining garlic. Shape linguine into 8 small nests; spoon vegetables into nests.

FETTUCCINE WITH ROASTED VEGETABLE SAUCE

A unique pasta sauce with a wonderful flavor.

6 servings

Olive oil cooking spray

2 medium zucchini

1 medium eggplant, peeled

1 medium red bell pepper

1 red onion

3 cloves garlic, peeled

1½ teaspoons dried basil leaves

½ teaspoon dried oregano leaves

½ teaspoon dried marjoram leaves

¼ teaspoon crushed red pepper

Per Serving
Calories: 278
% Calories from fat: 9
Fat (gm): 3
Saturated fat (gm): 0.1
Cholesterol (mg): 0
Sodium (mg): 181
Protein (gm): 12.1
Carbohydrate (gm): 50.6
Exchanges
Milk: 0.0
Vegetable: 3.0
Fruit: 0.0
Bread: 2.5
Meat: 0.5
Fat: 0.0

4 cups Canned Vegetable Stock (see
p. 63), *or* reduced-sodium canned
vegetable broth, divided
1-2 tablespoons lemon juice
1 teaspoon grated lemon rind
Salt and pepper, to taste
12 ounces fettuccine, *or* spaghetti, cooked,
warm
6 tablespoons fat-free grated Parmesan
cheese

1. Spray 2 aluminum-foil-lined jelly roll pans with cooking spray. Cut vegetables, except garlic, into ¾ to 1-inch pieces; arrange vegetables in single layer on pans. Spray vegetables generously with cooking spray and sprinkle with herbs and pepper.

2. Roast vegetables at 425 degrees until browned and tender, about 40 minutes, removing garlic when soft, after about 20 minutes.

3. Process vegetables, garlic, and 1 to 2 cups stock in food processor or blender until smooth. Heat vegetable mixture and remaining stock to boiling in large saucepan. Reduce heat and simmer 5 minutes. Stir in lemon juice and rind; season to taste with salt and pepper.

4. Spoon sauce over pasta on serving plates; sprinkle with cheese.

RISOTTO WITH ROASTED TOMATOES

 The creamy texture of risotto comes from the short-grained arborio rice. Arborio rice is available in Italian groceries and large supermarkets.

6 servings

Olive oil cooking spray
3 medium tomatoes, cut into halves
¾ teaspoon dried basil leaves
½ teaspoon dried oregano leaves
¼ teaspoon dried rosemary leaves
1 small onion, chopped
3 cloves garlic, minced

Per Serving
Calories: 133
% Calories from fat: 14
Fat (gm): 2.1
Saturated fat (gm): 0.3
Cholesterol (mg): 0
Sodium (mg): 27
Protein (gm): 3.3
Carbohydrate (gm): 25.7

2   teaspoons olive oil

¾   cup arborio rice

3   cups Basic Vegetable Stock, *or* Canned Vegetable Stock (see pp. 58, 63)

2   tablespoons grated fat-free Parmesan cheese

Salt and pepper, to taste

Exchanges
Milk: 0.0
Vegetable: 1.0
Fruit: 0.0
Bread: 1.5
Meat: 0.0
Fat: 0.0

1.   Spray aluminum-foil-lined jelly roll pan with cooking spray. Arrange tomatoes, cut sides up, on pan; spray generously with cooking spray and sprinkle with combined herbs.

2.   Roast tomatoes until tender, but not too soft, about 20 minutes. Cool tomatoes; seed, if desired, and chop coarsely.

3.   Saute onion and garlic in oil in large saucepan until tender, about 5 minutes. Add rice; cook over medium heat until rice begins to brown, 2 to 3 minutes.

4.   Heat stock to boiling in small saucepan; reduce heat to medium-low to keep stock hot. Add stock to rice mixture, ½ cup at a time, stirring constantly, until stock is absorbed before adding another ½ cup. Continue process until rice is *al dente*, 20 to 25 minutes, adding tomatoes with last ½ cup stock. Stir in cheese; season to taste with salt and pepper.

ROASTED SQUASH, MOROCCAN STYLE

Roasted vegetables and pineapple, combined with couscous, create a perfect filling for oven-roasted acorn squash.

4 servings (about 2 cups each)

Olive oil cooking spray

2   medium acorn squash, cut into halves, seeded

1   medium pineapple, peeled, cored, cut into 1-inch chunks

2   medium onions, sliced

2   cups quartered Brussels sprouts

¼   cup packed light brown sugar

Pinch ground cinnamon

Per Serving
Calories: 450
% Calories from fat: 3
Fat (gm): 1.5
Saturated fat (gm): 0.2
Cholesterol (mg): 0
Sodium (mg): 49
Protein (gm): 11.8
Carbohydrate (gm): 107
Exchanges
Milk: 0.0
Vegetable: 2.5
Fruit: 1.5
Bread: 4.0
Meat: 0.0
Fat: 0.0

Pinch ground nutmeg

½ cup frozen whole-kernel corn, cooked, drained

¼ cup dark raisins

¼ cup finely chopped cilantro leaves

⅔ cup couscous, cooked

Salt and pepper, to taste

1. Spray aluminum-foil-lined jelly roll pan with cooking spray. Place squash halves, pineapple, onions, and Brussels sprouts on pan in single layer; spray generously with cooking spray. Sprinkle squash with brown sugar, cinnamon, and nutmeg. Bake at 400 degrees until vegetables are tender, about 40 minutes. Reserve squash halves.

2. Stir roasted food (except squash halves), corn, raisins, and cilantro into couscous; season to taste with salt and pepper. Spoon couscous mixture into squash halves and serve.

GRILL-ROASTED VEGETABLES WITH POLENTA

 The vegetables can also be oven-roasted at 400 degrees for 30 to 40 minutes. For convenience, the polenta can be made 2 to 3 days in advance.

4 servings (about 1½ cups each)

2 medium eggplant, unpeeled, cut in ½-inch rounds

4 medium tomatoes, cut into wedges

4 medium red onions, cut into wedges

2 medium red bell peppers, cut into 1-inch slices

2 medium yellow summer squash, cut into 1-inch pieces

2 large bulbs garlic, tops trimmed

Vegetable cooking spray

2 tablespoons balsamic, *or* red wine, vinegar

1 tablespoon olive oil, *or* vegetable oil

1 teaspoon lemon juice

½ teaspoon dried rosemary leaves

Per Serving
Calories: 473
% Calories from fat: 14
Fat (gm): 7.8
Saturated fat (gm): 1.2
Cholesterol (mg): 0
Sodium (mg): 513
Protein (gm): 13.5
Carbohydrate (gm): 91.9
Exchanges
Milk: 0.0
Vegetable: 8.0
Fruit: 0.0
Bread: 3.0
Meat: 0.0
Fat: 1.0

½ teaspoon dried sage leaves
½ teaspoon dried thyme leaves
   Herbed Polenta (see p. 580)
4 slices Italian bread, toasted

1. Spray vegetables, including garlic, with cooking spray; place on grill over medium-hot coals. Grill, turning occasionally, until vegetables are browned and tender, about 30 minutes. Combine vegetables, except garlic, in bowl. Mix vinegar, oil, lemon juice, and herbs; drizzle over vegetables and toss.

2. Spray large skillet with cooking spray; heat on grill or range until hot. Cut polenta into 8 wedges; cook in skillet until browned on both sides. Overlap 2 polenta wedges on each serving plate; spoon vegetables over.

3. Separate each garlic bulb into 2 pieces. Squeeze garlic from cloves to spread on bread.

ROASTED VEGETABLES WITH BEANS AND FRUIT

Serve with one of the grilled tofu or tempeh recipes in this chapter.

8 servings (generous 1 cup each)

Olive oil cooking spray
2 medium-sized sweet potatoes, peeled, sliced
2 small parsnips, sliced
2 medium russet potatoes, unpeeled, sliced
3 medium onions, cut into wedges
1 large yellow bell pepper, cut into ¾-inch slices
1 large red bell pepper, cut into ¾-inch slices
1 large fennel bulb, sliced
1 can (15 ounces) Great Northern beans, rinsed, drained
1 can (15 ounces) black beans, rinsed, drained
1½ teaspoons dried marjoram leaves

Per Serving
Calories: 321
% Calories from fat: 12
Fat (gm): 4.6
Saturated fat (gm): 0.6
Cholesterol (mg): 0
Sodium (mg): 192
Protein (gm): 11.9
Carbohydrate (gm): 65.7
Exchanges
Milk: 0.0
Vegetable: 1.0
Fruit: 1.0
Bread: 3.0
Meat: 0.0
Fat: 0.5

½ teaspoon fennel seeds, crushed
¼ teaspoon dried thyme leaves
¾ cup coarsely chopped dried apples
¾ cup coarsely chopped dried peaches, *or*
apricots
3 tablespoons white wine vinegar
2-3 tablespoons olive oil
Salt and pepper, to taste

1. Line 2 large jelly roll pans with aluminum foil and spray with cooking spray. Arrange vegetables, including beans, on pans; spray generously with cooking spray and sprinkle with combined herbs.

2. Roast vegetables at 425 degrees until browned and tender, about 40 minutes, adding dried fruit the last 10 minutes. Combine vegetables and fruit in serving bowl; drizzle with vinegar and oil and toss. Season to taste with salt and pepper.

CASSEROLE OF ROASTED VEGETABLES AND BEANS

A great pack-along dish for tailgate parties or picnics. The casserole is also delicious served at room temperature.

6 servings

Vegetable cooking spray
6 small zucchini
4 ribs celery
2 medium-sized sweet onions
1 medium red, *or* green, bell pepper
½ teaspoon dried oregano leaves
¼ teaspoon ground cinnamon
¾ teaspoon pepper
2 cans (15 ounces each) Great Northern beans, rinsed, drained
1 can (15 ounces) pinto beans, rinsed, drained
2 large tomatoes, coarsely chopped
Salt, to taste

Per Serving
Calories: 329
% Calories from fat: 5
Fat (gm): 1.9
Saturated fat (gm): 0.3
Cholesterol (mg): 0
Sodium (mg): 386
Protein (gm): 21.9
Carbohydrate (gm): 62
Exchanges
Milk: 0.0
Vegetable: 2.0
Fruit: 0.0
Bread: 3.0
Meat: 1.0
Fat: 0.0

¾ cup fresh whole wheat breadcrumbs
½ cup grated fat-free Parmesan cheese
⅓ cup finely chopped cilantro
¼ teaspoon paprika

1. Spray aluminum-foil-lined jelly roll pan with cooking spray. Cut zucchini, celery, onions, and bell pepper into 1-inch pieces and arrange in single layer on pan. Spray vegetables generously with cooking spray and sprinkle with oregano, cinnamon, and pepper.

2. Roast vegetables at 425 degrees until browned and tender, about 35 minutes. Combine roasted vegetables, beans, and tomatoes in greased 2-quart casserole; season to taste with salt.

3. Combine breadcrumbs, cheese, and cilantro; sprinkle over top of casserole. Sprinkle with paprika. Bake at 350 degrees until casserole is browned and hot through, about 20 minutes.

PORTOBELLO MUSHROOMS WITH GRILLED PEPPER RELISH AND POLENTA

Make this recipe with porcini mushrooms if you are fortunate enough to find them in season.

6 servings

Olive oil cooking spray
6 large portobello, *or* porcini, mushrooms (4-5 inches in diameter)
Herbed Polenta (see p. 580)
½ teaspoon dried thyme leaves
¼ teaspoon pepper
Salt, to taste
Grilled Pepper Relish (recipe follows)

Per Serving
Calories: 171
% Calories from fat: 19
Fat (gm): 3.6
Saturated fat (gm): 0.4
Cholesterol (mg): 0
Sodium (mg): 217
Protein (gm): 6.8
Carbohydrate (gm): 26.4
Exchanges
Milk: 0.0
Vegetable: 3.0
Fruit: 0.0
Bread: 1.0
Meat: 0.0
Fat: 0.5

1. Spray mushrooms and polenta wedges with cooking spray; sprinkle mushrooms with thyme and pepper. Grill over medium-hot coals until polenta is lightly browned and mushrooms are tender, about 8 minutes, turning mushrooms occasionally. Sprinkle mushrooms lightly with salt.

2. Place polenta on serving plates, overlapping mushrooms on top. Spoon on Grilled Pepper Relish.

Grilled Pepper Relish

(makes about 2 cups)

  1 medium red bell pepper
  1 medium yellow bell pepper
  2 medium tomatoes
  2 green onions and tops, finely chopped
  2 cloves garlic, minced
  ½ teaspoon ground cumin
  ½ teaspoon sugar
  1 tablespoon balsamic vinegar
  1 tablespoon olive oil
    Salt and pepper, to taste
  2 tablespoons finely chopped fresh cilantro

1. Grill peppers and tomatoes over medium-hot coals until browned and tender, 8 to 10 minutes, turning occasionally. Let vegetables stand until cool. Peel, core, and seed vegetables; chop coarsely.

2. Combine grilled vegetables, green onions, garlic, cumin, sugar, vinegar, and oil in bowl; toss gently. Season to taste with salt and pepper; sprinkle with cilantro.

ROASTED VEGETABLES, MOO-SHU STYLE

For simplicity, we've substituted flour tortillas for the Mandarin Pancakes (see p. 246) traditionally served with moo-shu dishes.

6 servings (2 filled tortillas each)

    Vegetable cooking spray
  1 pound green beans, *or* snow peas
  1 pound white mushrooms, sliced
  4 medium zucchini, cut lengthwise into halves, then sliced
  1 medium onion, thinly sliced
  ¾-1 teaspoon 5-spice powder
    Salt and pepper, to taste

Per Serving
Calories: 363
% Calories from fat: 14
Fat (gm): 5.8
Saturated fat (gm): 0.9
Cholesterol (mg): 0
Sodium (mg): 697
Protein (gm): 12.4
Carbohydrate (gm): 69.3
Exchanges
Milk: 0.0
Vegetable: 4.0
Fruit: 0.0
Bread: 3.0
Meat: 0.0
Fat: 1.0

12 flour tortillas
   Plum Sauce (see p. 734)
2 cups fresh bean sprouts
2 medium carrots, julienne sliced
   Cilantro leaves, as garnish

1. Spray aluminum-foil-lined jelly roll pan with cooking spray. Arrange green beans, mushrooms, zucchini, and onion in single layer on pan. Spray vegetables generously with cooking spray and sprinkle with 5-spice powder.

2. Roast vegetables at 425 degrees until crisp-tender, about 25 minutes. Combine vegetables in bowl; season to taste with salt and pepper.

3. Spread generous tablespoon of Plum Sauce in center of each tortilla. Spoon roasted vegetables onto tortillas; top with bean sprouts, carrots, and cilantro leaves. Roll up, tucking up one end to hold.

SPAGHETTI SQUASH WITH ROASTED TOMATO-HERB SAUCE AND ARTICHOKES

 The squash can also be cooked in the oven; place squash halves, cut sides down, in roasting pan and add 1 inch hot water. Bake, covered, at 400 degrees until flesh is tender, about 45 minutes.

4 servings

2 small spaghetti squash, cut into halves, seeded
   Olive oil cooking spray
½ cup chopped onion
2 cloves garlic, minced
1 package (9 ounces) frozen artichoke hearts, thawed, cut into halves
¼ cup dry white wine, *or* water
   Roasted Tomato-Herb Sauce (recipe follows)
¼ cup grated fat-free Parmesan cheese

Per Serving
Calories: 197
% Calories from fat: 7
Fat (gm): 1.8
Saturated fat (gm): 0.3
Cholesterol (mg): 0
Sodium (mg): 154
Protein (gm): 9.3
Carbohydrate (gm): 40.6
Exchanges
Milk: 0.0
Vegetable: 5.0
Fruit: 0.0
Bread: 1.0
Meat: 0.0
Fat: 0.0

1. Wrap squash loosely in foil; grill over medium-hot coals until flesh is tender, 30 to 40 minutes, turning occasionally.

2. Spray medium saucepan with cooking spray; heat over medium heat until hot. Saute onion and garlic until tender, about 5 minutes. Add artichoke hearts and wine; heat to boiling. Reduce heat and simmer, covered, until artichoke hearts are tender, about 5 minutes. Add tomato sauce and cook over medium heat until hot through.

3. Scrape squash with tines of fork to fluff flesh. Spoon tomato sauce mixture into squash halves and toss; sprinkle with cheese and toss.

 Roasted Tomato-Herb Sauce

(makes about 3 cups)

>   Vegetable cooking spray
>   2½ pounds Italian plum tomatoes, cut into
>   halves
>   1 leek (white part only), cut into ¾-inch
>   pieces
>   1 medium onion, cut into wedges
>   2 medium carrots, cut into ¾-inch pieces
>   3 cloves garlic, peeled
>   ½ teaspoon dried oregano leaves
>   ¼ teaspoon dried marjoram leaves
>   ⅛ teaspoon pepper
>   ½ cup loosely packed basil leaves
>   Salt and pepper, to taste

1. Spray aluminum-foil-lined jelly roll pan with cooking spray; arrange vegetables in single layer on pan. Spray vegetables with cooking spray and sprinkle with oregano, marjoram, and ⅛ teaspoon pepper. Roast at 425 degrees until vegetables are browned and tender, about 40 minutes.

2. Process vegetables and fresh basil in food processor or blender until almost smooth. Season to taste with salt and pepper.

GRILLED VEGETABLE ROLL-UPS

Roll-ups can be grilled and assembled a day in advance; refrigerate, covered. When ready to use, increase baking time to 40 to 45 minutes.

8 servings (2 roll-ups each)

1	large eggplant (1¼ pounds), unpeeled, cut lengthwise into scant ½-inch-thick slices (8 slices)
2	large zucchini, cut lengthwise into scant ½-inch-thick slices (8 slices)
	Olive oil cooking spray
2	teaspoons finely chopped parsley
1	teaspoon dried basil leaves
½	teaspoon dried oregano leaves
½	teaspoon black pepper
½	teaspoon crushed red pepper
2	cups fat-free ricotta cheese
¼	cup (1 ounce) grated fat-free Parmesan cheese
	Salt and pepper, to taste
2	egg whites
	Roasted Tomato-Herb Sauce (see preceding recipe)
¾	cup (3 ounces) shredded fat-free mozzarella cheese

Per Serving
Calories: 149
% Calories from fat: 4
Fat (gm): 0.8
Saturated fat (gm): 0.1
Cholesterol (mg): 0
Sodium (mg): 168
Protein (gm): 16.7
Carbohydrate (gm): 23.7
Exchanges
Milk: 0.0
Vegetable: 3.0
Fruit: 0.0
Bread: 0.0
Meat: 1.5
Fat: 0.0

1. Spray eggplant and zucchini with cooking spray; sprinkle with ½ the combined herbs and black and red pepper. Grill over medium-hot coals until softened, turning once, about 5 minutes.

2. Combine ricotta and Parmesan cheese with remaining herbs and black and red pepper; season to taste with salt and pepper. Mix in egg whites.

3. Spread about 2 tablespoons of cheese mixture on each eggplant and zucchini slice and roll up.

4. Spread about 1 cup tomato sauce in bottom of 13 x 9-inch baking pan. Arrange vegetable rolls, seam sides down, in pan. Spoon remaining tomato sauce over rolls; sprinkle with mozzarella cheese. Bake, uncovered, at 350 degrees 30 minutes.

ROASTED STUFFED PORTOBELLO MUSHROOMS WITH SPINACH-CILANTRO PESTO

 Serve one mushroom as an appetizer or first course. The vegetable stuffing can also be used to fill large white mushroom caps.

4 servings (2 stuffed mushrooms each)

8 large portobello mushrooms (5-6 inches diameter)

Vegetable cooking spray

1 cup finely chopped zucchini

1 cup shredded carrots

3 green onions and tops, thinly sliced

4 tablespoons dry unseasoned bread-crumbs

Spinach-Cilantro Pesto (see p. 730)

Salt and pepper, to taste

½ cup (2 ounces) shredded reduced-fat mozzarella cheese

Per Serving
Calories: 185
% Calories from fat: 20
Fat (gm): 3.9
Saturated fat (gm): 1.8
Cholesterol (mg): 7.6
Sodium (mg): 206
Protein (gm): 16
Carbohydrate (gm): 19.1
Exchanges
Milk: 0.0
Vegetable: 4.0
Fruit: 0.0
Bread: 0.5
Meat: 1.0
Fat: 0.0

1. Remove and chop mushroom stems and chop. Spray large skillet with cooking spray; heat over medium heat until hot. Saute mushroom stems, zucchini, carrots, and green onions until crisp-tender, 8 to 10 minutes. Stir in breadcrumbs and pesto. Season to taste with salt and pepper. Spoon vegetable mixture onto mushrooms.

2. Spray aluminum-foil-lined jelly roll pan with cooking spray; arrange mushrooms on pan. Roast mushrooms at 425 degrees until mushrooms are tender, about 20 minutes, sprinkling with cheese the last 5 minutes of roasting time.

TWO-POTATO VEGGIE PACKETS

Sweet and white potatoes are combined with zucchini and grilled in packets with a great-flavored sauce.

6-8 servings

Vegetable cooking spray

3 medium russet potatoes, unpeeled, cut into 1-inch cubes

1 medium sweet potato, peeled, cut into 1-inch cubes

1 medium zucchini, cut into 1-inch cubes

3 green onions and tops, sliced

1¼ cups fat-free milk, divided

1 tablespoon margarine

2 tablespoons flour

1 teaspoon Dijon-style mustard

1 teaspoon dried parsley leaves

¼ teaspoon celery seeds

¼ teaspoon dried rosemary leaves, crushed

Salt and pepper, to taste

Per Serving
Calories: 179
% Calories from fat: 11
Fat (gm): 2.2
Saturated fat (gm): 0.5
Cholesterol (mg): 0.8
Sodium (mg): 70
Protein (gm): 5.1
Carbohydrate (gm): 35.5
Exchanges
Milk: 0.0
Vegetable: 1.0
Fruit: 0.0
Bread: 2.0
Meat: 0.0
Fat: 0.0

1. Spray a 30 x 18-inch piece of heavy-duty aluminum foil with cooking spray. Arrange potatoes, zucchini, and onions in center of foil.

2. Heat 1 cup milk and margarine to boiling. Mix flour and remaining ¼ cup milk; whisk into boiling milk mixture. Boil, whisking constantly, until thickened, about 1 minute. Remove from heat; stir in mustard and herbs. Season to taste with salt and pepper.

3. Pour sauce over vegetables. Fold foil over vegetables and seal edges to make packet. Place packet on grill over medium-hot coals; grill, turning packet occasionally, until vegetables are tender, about 35 minutes. Carefully open one end of foil packet and transfer vegetable mixture to serving bowl.

GREEK EGGPLANT WITH FETA

Serve warm or at room temperature as an entrée, or present it as a side dish with vegetarian "burgers" or "franks."

4 main-dish servings (about 1½ cups each)

Olive oil cooking spray
- 3 medium eggplant (about 3½ pounds), unpeeled
- 12 ounces red bell peppers, sliced
- 12 ounces yellow bell peppers, sliced
- 1 pound onions, sliced
- 1½ teaspoons dried rosemary leaves
- ¾ teaspoon dried marjoram leaves
- ½ teaspoon dried thyme leaves
- 1 cup (4 ounces) crumbled feta cheese
Salt and pepper, to taste

Per Serving
Calories: 275
% Calories from fat: 22
Fat (gm): 7.6
Saturated fat (gm): 4.4
Cholesterol (mg): 25
Sodium (mg): 332
Protein (gm): 10.7
Carbohydrate (gm): 48.2
Exchanges
Milk: 0.0
Vegetable: 8.0
Fruit: 0.0
Bread: 0.0
Meat: 1.0
Fat: 0.5

1. Line 2 large jelly roll pans with aluminum foil and spray with cooking spray. Cut eggplant into ½-inch slices; cut slices into fourths. Arrange eggplant, bell peppers, and onions on pans. Spray generously with cooking spray and sprinkle with herbs.

2. Roast vegetables at 425 degrees until browned and tender, about 40 minutes. Combine vegetables in serving bowl; sprinkle with cheese and toss. Season to taste with salt and pepper.

MEDITERRANEAN ROASTED EGGPLANT AND TOMATOES

The flavors of dill weed and mint are combined in many Mediterranean dishes. Serve warm or at room temperature, with couscous or Parmesan Polenta (see p. 580).

4 side-dish servings

Olive oil cooking spray
- 1 small eggplant (about 1 pound), unpeeled
- 2 large tomatoes, cut into wedges

Per Serving
Calories: 69
% Calories from fat: 26
Fat (gm): 2.2
Saturated fat (gm): 0.3
Cholesterol (mg): 0
Sodium (mg): 199
Protein (gm): 2
Carbohydrate (gm): 12.3

½ teaspoon dried dill weed
½ teaspoon dried mint leaves
Salt and pepper, to taste
½ tablespoon olive oil

Exchanges
Milk: 0.0
Vegetable: 2.0
Fruit: 0.0
Bread: 0.0
Meat: 0.0
Fat: 0.5

1. Spray aluminum-foil-lined jelly roll pan with cooking spray. Cut eggplant into ½-inch slices; cut slices into fourths. Arrange eggplant and tomatoes on jelly roll pan; spray generously with cooking spray and sprinkle with herbs.

2. Bake vegetables at 425 degrees until browned and very tender, 30 to 40 minutes. Transfer to serving bowl; season to taste with salt and pepper. Drizzle with olive oil.

GRILLED ACORN SQUASH WITH TOFU

Grill roasting adds wonderful flavor to the squash. You can also add aromatic smoke chips, such as apple or cherry, to the coals. The squash can be grilled a day or two in advance, when you are grilling other foods.

8 side-dish servings

4 medium acorn squash
½ cup light firm tofu
1 egg
2 egg whites
3 tablespoons light brown sugar
2 teaspoons margarine, *or* butter
½ teaspoon ground cinnamon
¼ teaspoon ground allspice
⅛ teaspoon ground nutmeg
Salt and pepper, to taste

Per Serving
Calories: 104
% Calories from fat: 15
Fat (gm): 1.9
Saturated fat (gm): 0.4
Cholesterol (mg): 26.6
Sodium (mg): 49
Protein (gm): 3.6
Carbohydrate (gm): 20.4
Exchanges
Milk: 0.0
Vegetable: 0.0
Fruit: 0.0
Bread: 1.5
Meat: 0.0
Fat: 0.0

1. Pierce each squash in several places with sharp knife. Grill over medium-hot coals, turning frequently, until squash is tender, 35 to 40 minutes. Let stand until cool enough to handle.

2. Cut squash into halves; scoop out and discard seeds. Scoop out flesh and mash in large bowl; add tofu, egg, egg whites, brown sugar, margarine, and spices, mixing until smooth. Season to taste with salt and pepper.

3. Spoon mixture into greased 1-quart baking dish. Bake, uncovered, at 350 degrees until mixture is set and toothpick inserted near center comes out clean, about 30 minutes. Let stand 5 minutes before serving.

ROOT VEGGIES AND MASHED POTATOES

 A selection of winter root vegetables, roasted to perfection and served with garlic-spiked mashed potatoes.

4 servings (about 1½ cups each)

Vegetable cooking spray

3 medium beets, peeled, sliced

3 medium turnips, peeled, sliced

3 medium carrots, diagonally cut into 1-inch pieces

1 leek (white parts only), cut into 1-inch pieces

2½ cups halved Brussels sprouts

1 tablespoon caraway seeds

Salt, and pepper, to taste

1½ pounds Idaho potatoes, unpeeled, cubed

4 cloves garlic, peeled

¼ cup fat-free milk, hot

2 tablespoons margarine, cut into pieces

Per Serving
Calories: 451
% Calories from fat: 13
Fat (gm): 6.9
Saturated fat (gm): 1.3
Cholesterol (mg): 0.3
Sodium (mg): 227
Protein (gm): 13.1
Carbohydrate (gm): 90.8
Exchanges
Milk: 0.0
Vegetable: 5.0
Fruit: 0.0
Bread: 4.0
Meat: 0.0
Fat: 1.0

1. Spray aluminum-foil-lined jelly roll pan with cooking spray. Arrange beets, turnips, carrots, leek, and Brussels sprouts on pan in single layer; spray generously with cooking spray. Sprinkle vegetables with caraway seeds; sprinkle lightly with salt and pepper. Bake at 400 degrees until vegetables are tender and lightly browned, about 40 minutes.

2. Cook potatoes and garlic in 2 inches simmering water in covered saucepan until tender, 10 to 15 minutes; drain. Mash potatoes and garlic with masher or electric mixer, adding milk and margarine. Season to taste with salt and pepper.

3. Spoon potatoes onto plates; spoon vegetables over potatoes.

PORTOBELLO MUSHROOMS GRILLED WITH CHILI PASTE

For variety, the Chili Paste is also excellent on tempeh.

6 servings

12 large portobello mushrooms (about 5 inches diameter)
Chili Paste (recipe follows)
Yellow Salsa Rice (see p. 575)
Zucchini from Puebla (see p. 619)

Per Serving
Calories: 221
% Calories from fat: 8
Fat (gm): 2
Saturated fat (gm): 0.5
Cholesterol (mg): 2.4
Sodium (mg): 373
Protein (gm): 6.5
Carbohydrate (gm): 43.1
Exchanges
Milk: 0.0
Vegetable: 3.0
Fruit: 0.0
Bread: 2.0
Meat: 0.0
Fat: 0.0

1. Rub gill sides of mushrooms with Chili Paste. Grill, flat sides down, over medium-hot coals until tender, 8 to 10 minutes. Or roast in oven at 425 degrees until tender, 20 to 30 minutes.

2. Serve with Yellow Salsa Rice and Zucchini from Puebla.

Chili Paste

(makes about ½ cup)

Vegetable cooking spray
2 dried ancho chilies
2 dried pasilla chilies
4 cloves garlic, minced
½ teaspoon salt
2 tablespoons white wine vinegar
Water

1. Spray medium skillet with cooking spray; heat over medium heat until hot. Cook chilies over medium heat until softened, 1 to 2 minutes. Remove and discard stems, seeds, and veins.

2. Process chilies, garlic, salt, and vinegar in food processor or blender, adding a very small amount of water, if necessary, to make a smooth paste.

GRILLED VEGETABLE KABOBS

 If using wooden skewers, soak them for 15 minutes in water before skewering the vegetables.

6 servings

1 package (9 ounces) frozen artichoke hearts, thawed
3 medium zucchini, cut into ½-inch slices
24 cherry tomatoes
3 frozen, Mexican-style all-vegetable "burgers," thawed, cut into quarters
½ cup fat-free French, *or* Italian, salad dressing
½-1 teaspoon ground cumin
3-4 teaspoons lime juice
2 teaspoons grated lime rind
Salt and pepper, to taste
Black Beans and Rice (see p. 526)

Per Serving
Calories: 375
% Calories from fat: 17
Fat (gm): 7.4
Saturated fat (gm): 0.1
Cholesterol (mg): 0
Sodium (mg): 678
Protein (gm): 20
Carbohydrate (gm): 62.2
Exchanges
Milk: 0.0
Vegetable: 3.0
Fruit: 0.0
Bread: 2.5
Meat: 0.5
Fat: 1.0

1. Alternate vegetables and "burgers" on metal skewers. Mix salad dressing, cumin, lime juice and rind in small bowl.

2. Grill kabobs over medium-hot coals until vegetables are tender, 8 to 10 minutes, turning occasionally and basting generously with dressing mixture. Sprinkle lightly with salt and pepper.

3. Spoon Black Beans and Rice onto plates and top with kabobs.

ORIENTAL VEGETABLE SATAY

Vegetables are roasted with Fragrant Basting Sauce and served with a chunky Peanut Sauce.

4 servings

½ medium acorn squash, peeled, seeded, cut into 1-inch pieces

1 pound broccoli florets

½ pound fresh, *or* frozen, thawed, whole okra

2 medium yellow summer squash, cut into 1-inch slices

8 ounces pearl onions, peeled

Fragrant Basting Sauce (see p. 736)

3 cups cooked rice, warm

Peanut Sauce (recipe follows)

Per Serving
Calories: 452
% Calories from fat: 20
Fat (gm): 10.3
Saturated fat (gm): 1.8
Cholesterol (mg): 0
Sodium (mg): 775
Protein (gm): 13.4
Carbohydrate (gm): 78.9
Exchanges
Milk: 0.0
Vegetable: 3.0
Fruit: 0.0
Bread: 4.0
Meat: 0.0
Fat: 2.0

1. Cook acorn squash in 2 inches simmering water in medium saucepan until beginning to soften, about 2 minutes; drain.

2. Arrange vegetables on skewers and place on lightly greased aluminum-foil-lined jelly roll pan. Roast at 425 degrees until lightly browned, about 10 minutes. Baste with half the Basting Sauce, and roast 2 to 3 minutes longer. Turn vegetables and repeat for other side, using remainder of Basting Sauce.

3. Arrange skewers on plates; serve with rice and Peanut Sauce.

Peanut Sauce

(makes about ⅔ cup)

3 tablespoons reduced-sodium soy sauce

3 tablespoons chunky peanut butter

2½ tablespoons sugar

¼ cup thinly sliced green onion, green and white parts

1 tablespoon grated gingerroot

1. Combine all ingredients.

TOMATOES STUFFED WITH PEPPER-ROASTED WILD MUSHROOMS

 A great accompaniment to Cajun Eggplant or Mesquite-Smoked Tofu (see pp. 294, 267).

6 servings

Olive oil cooking spray

16 ounces wild mushrooms (portobello, shiitake, oyster, cremini, etc.)

½ teaspoon coarse-grind pepper

1 cup cooked basmati, *or* brown, rice

¼ cup dry unseasoned breadcrumbs

2 tablespoons fat-free red wine vinaigrette

3 tablespoons finely chopped fresh dill weed, *or* 1½ teaspoons dried dill weed

3 tablespoons finely chopped chives

6 large tomatoes (10-12 ounces each), cored

Salt, to taste

Per Serving
Calories: 136
% Calories from fat: 16
Fat (gm): 2.9
Saturated fat (gm): 0.2
Cholesterol (mg): 0
Sodium (mg): 143
Protein (gm): 6.4
Carbohydrate (gm): 26.6
Exchanges
Milk: 0.0
Vegetable: 4.0
Fruit: 0.0
Bread: 0.5
Meat: 0.0
Fat: 0.0

1. Spray aluminum-foil-lined jelly roll pan with cooking spray. Arrange mushrooms on pan in single layer; spray with cooking spray and sprinkle with pepper.

2. Roast mushrooms at 425 degrees until tender, about 20 minutes; cool slightly. Chop mushrooms; combine with rice, breadcrumbs, vinaigrette, and herbs.

3. Slice tops from tomatoes and scoop out pulp with grapefruit spoon. Chop pulp and stir into mushroom mixture; season to taste with salt. Spoon mushroom mixture into tomatoes. Bake in baking pan at 425 degrees until hot through, 10 to 15 minutes.

GRILLED BEET PUREE

Grilling adds a special flavor to beets, so do try it! Beets can also be roasted at 425 degrees until tender, about 40 minutes.

4 side-dish servings (about ⅓ cup each)

12	ounces beets, scrubbed
¼	cup orange juice
3	tablespoons fat-free sour cream
2	teaspoons grated orange rind
1½	tablespoons minced cilantro
	Salt and pepper, to taste
8	orange segments
	Cilantro sprigs, as garnish

Per Serving
Calories: 47
% Calories from fat: 2
Fat (gm): 0.1
Saturated fat (gm): 0
Cholesterol (mg): 0
Sodium (mg): 43
Protein (gm): 1.8
Carbohydrate (gm): 10.3
Exchanges
Milk: 0.0
Vegetable: 2.0
Fruit: 0.0
Bread: 0.0
Meat: 0.0
Fat: 0.0

1. Grill beets over medium-hot coals until tender, about 30 minutes. Let stand until cool enough to handle. Peel beets.

2. Process beets, orange juice, sour cream, and orange rind in food processor or blender until smooth. Stir in minced cilantro; season to taste with salt and pepper.

3. Spoon beets into serving bowl; garnish with orange segments and cilantro sprigs.

CAJUN EGGPLANT

Packaged Cajun seasoning can be purchased, but we particularly like our homemade blend! The spice blend is also delicious on tempeh and portobello mushrooms.

4-6 side-dish servings

	Vegetable cooking spray
1	large eggplant (1¼-1½ pounds), unpeeled, cut into ½-inch slices
	Cajun Seasoning (recipe follows)

Per Serving
Calories: 47
% Calories from fat: 9
Fat (gm): 0.5
Saturated fat (gm): 0.1
Cholesterol (mg): 0
Sodium (mg): 138
Protein (gm): 1.6
Carbohydrate (gm): 11
Exchanges
Milk: 0.0
Vegetable: 2.0
Fruit: 0.0
Bread: 0.0
Meat: 0.0
Fat: 0.0

1. Lightly spray both sides of eggplant with cooking spray; sprinkle with Cajun Seasoning, pressing mixture onto eggplant.

2. Grill eggplant over medium-hot coals until tender, about 5 minutes per side, or roast in oven at 425 degrees until tender, about 30 minutes.

Cajun Seasoning

(makes about 2 tablespoons)

> 2 teaspoons paprika
> 1 teaspoon onion powder
> 1 teaspoon garlic powder
> ½ teaspoon dried thyme leaves
> ½ teaspoon dried oregano leaves
> ½ teaspoon cayenne pepper
> ½ teaspoon black pepper
> ¼ teaspoon salt

1. Mix all ingredients; store in airtight container until ready to use.

ROASTED PEPERONATA

We've roasted this traditional Italian dish for more intense flavors—faster and easier to cook, too! It's especially good as a topping on vegetarian "franks" or "burgers," or serve it as a side dish with any favorite entrée.

8 side-dish servings (about ⅔ cup each)

> Olive oil cooking spray
> 1 pound green bell peppers, sliced
> 1 pound red bell peppers, sliced
> 1 pound yellow bell peppers, sliced
> 1½ pounds onions, sliced
> 1 teaspoon dried oregano leaves
> ¾ teaspoon dried sage leaves
> ¾ teaspoon dried thyme leaves
> Salt and pepper, to taste

Per Serving
Calories: 83
% Calories from fat: 6
Fat (gm): 0.6
Saturated fat (gm): 0.1
Cholesterol (mg): 0
Sodium (mg): 4.7
Protein (gm): 3
Carbohydrate (gm): 19.3
Exchanges
Milk: 0.0
Vegetable: 3.5
Fruit: 0.0
Bread: 0.0
Meat: 0.0
Fat: 0.0

1. Line jelly roll pan with aluminum foil and spray with cooking spray. Arrange vegetables on pan; spray generously with cooking spray and sprinkle with herbs.

2. Roast vegetables at 425 degrees until browned and very soft, about 45 minutes. Combine in serving bowl; season to taste with salt and pepper.

ROASTED POTATO SALAD

The potatoes are roasted until crusty and brown, lending a unique flavor to this salad.

4 servings (about 1½ cups each)

Olive oil cooking spray
8-10 medium unpeeled Idaho potatoes, cut into eighths (8 cups)
Salt and pepper, to taste
1 medium onion, chopped
1 medium red bell pepper, chopped
1 medium green bell pepper, chopped
½ cup frozen peas, thawed
½ cup thinly sliced celery
Dilled Mayonnaise Dressing (recipe follows)
Lettuce, as garnish
4 rye rolls

Per Serving
Calories: 492
% Calories from fat: 4
Fat (gm): 2
Saturated fat (gm): 0.4
Cholesterol (mg): 0.3
Sodium (mg): 611
Protein (gm): 13.3
Carbohydrate (gm): 107.7
Exchanges
Milk: 0.0
Vegetable: 1.0
Fruit: 0.0
Bread: 6.5
Meat: 0.0
Fat: 0.0

1. Spray aluminum-foil-lined jelly roll pan with cooking spray. Arrange potatoes on pan in single layer; spray generously with cooking spray and sprinkle lightly with salt and pepper. Bake at 400 degrees until potatoes are browned, crusty, and tender, about 30 minutes. Cool to room temperature.

2. Combine potatoes, onion, bell peppers, peas, and celery in large bowl; spoon Dilled Mayonnaise Dressing over and toss. Serve in lettuce-lined bowls with rye rolls.

Dilled Mayonnaise Dressing

(makes about ¾ cup)

¼ cup fat-free mayonnaise, or salad dressing
¼ cup fat-free plain yogurt
2 tablespoons Dijon-style mustard
1 tablespoon lemon juice
2 cloves garlic, minced
½ teaspoon dried dill weed

1. Mix all ingredients; refrigerate until serving time.

VEGETABLE AND WILD RICE SALAD

Other types of rice can be substituted for the wild rice, if desired, or use 1 package (6¼ ounces) long-grain white and wild rice mix, discarding spice packet. Serve this dish warm or at room temperature.

8 side-dish servings (about 1 cup each)

Olive oil cooking spray
2 medium yellow summer squash
1 medium zucchini
1 medium eggplant, peeled
1 medium red bell pepper
3 cloves garlic, peeled
1 tablespoon herbs de Provence
½ cup fat-free honey Dijon salad dressing
¼ cup fat-free plain yogurt
3 tablespoons orange juice
2 teaspoons grated orange rind
3 cups cooked wild rice
Salt and pepper, to taste

Per Serving
Calories: 134
% Calories from fat: 4
Fat (gm): 0.6
Saturated fat (gm): 0.1
Cholesterol (mg): 0.1
Sodium (mg): 178
Protein (gm): 5
Carbohydrate (gm): 28.8
Exchanges
Milk: 0.0
Vegetable: 2.5
Fruit: 0.0
Bread: 1.0
Meat: 0.0
Fat: 0.0

1. Spray aluminum-foil-lined jelly roll pan with cooking spray. Cut vegetables, except garlic, into ¾ to 1-inch pieces. Arrange vegetables in single layer on pan; spray generously with cooking spray and sprinkle with herbs.

2. Roast vegetables at 425 degrees until browned and tender, about 40 minutes, removing garlic when soft, after about 20 minutes. Cool to room temperature.

3. Mash garlic in small bowl; mix in salad dressing, yogurt, orange juice, and rind. Combine vegetables and rice in serving bowl; drizzle dressing over and toss. Season to taste with salt and pepper.

ROASTED MUSHROOM SALAD

The varieties of mushrooms will vary according to season and availability.

6 side-dish servings (about 1 cup each)

Vegetable cooking spray
1½ pounds assorted mushrooms (portobello, cremini, shiitake, etc.)
2 cups cooked orzo, room temperature
1 medium tomato, chopped
3 tablespoons fat-free red wine vinaigrette
3 tablespoons minced fresh dill weed, *or* 1½ teaspoons dried dill weed
3 tablespoons minced fresh chives
Salt and pepper, to taste
Lettuce leaves, as garnish

Per Serving
Calories: 110
% Calories from fat: 18
Fat (gm): 2.5
Saturated fat (gm): 0.1
Cholesterol (mg): 0
Sodium (mg): 118
Protein (gm): 6.4
Carbohydrate (gm): 19.3
Exchanges
Milk: 0.0
Vegetable: 3.0
Fruit: 0.0
Bread: 0.5
Meat: 0.0
Fat: 0.0

1. Spray aluminum-foil-lined jelly roll pan with cooking spray. Arrange mushrooms in single layer on pan; spray generously with cooking spray.

2. Roast mushrooms at 425 degrees until tender, about 20 minutes; cool to room temperature. Slice mushrooms; combine in bowl with orzo, tomato, vinaigrette, and herbs. Season to taste with salt and pepper. Spoon mixture onto lettuce-lined plates.

SWEET ONION SALAD

An unusual salad that is bound to bring compliments to the cook!

6 side-dish servings

Vegetable cooking spray
2 medium Vidalia, *or* Maui, onions (about 12 ounces)
2 medium red onions (about 12 ounces)
1½ teaspoons dried thyme leaves
1 teaspoon dried parsley leaves
¼ teaspoon ground cloves
⅛ teaspoon garlic powder
⅛-¼ teaspoon red cayenne pepper
6 tablespoons fat-free buttermilk salad dressing
4 teaspoons lemon juice
2 teaspoons grated lemon rind
Salt and pepper, to taste
3 cups torn leaf lettuce
3 cups torn curly endive
1½ cups (½ recipe) Croutons (see p. 677)

Per Serving
Calories: 81
% Calories from fat: 7
Fat (gm): 0.7
Saturated fat (gm): 0.1
Cholesterol (mg): 0
Sodium (mg): 145
Protein (gm): 2.8
Carbohydrate (gm): 17.3
Exchanges
Milk: 0.0
Vegetable: 2.0
Fruit: 0.0
Bread: 0.5
Meat: 0.0
Fat: 0.0

1. Spray aluminum-foil-lined jelly roll pan with cooking spray. Cut onions into 2-inch wedges and arrange on pan. Spray onions generously with cooking spray; sprinkle with combined herbs and pepper. Roast at 425 degrees until onions are tender, about 35 minutes.

2. Mix salad dressing, lemon juice, and lemon rind; drizzle over onions in bowl and toss. Season to taste with salt and pepper. Arrange lettuce and endive on plates; top with warm onion mixture and sprinkle with Croutons.

ROASTED ORIENTAL SALAD

You'll enjoy this medley of fresh, wonderful flavors. Hot chili oil is really hot, so use sparingly and taste before adding more.

6 servings

Vegetable cooking spray
1 pound asparagus, ends trimmed
1 pound shiitake mushrooms
½ teaspoon pepper
8 ounces snow peas, strings removed
3 cloves garlic, unpeeled
½ package (7-ounce size) rice noodles
1 medium carrot, shredded
1 small cucumber, seeded, chopped
2 green onions and tops, thinly sliced
2 tablespoons reduced-sodium tamari soy sauce
3 tablespoons rice wine vinegar
1 tablespoon vegetable oil
½ teaspoon hot chili oil
2 teaspoons sugar
1 teaspoon grated gingerroot
⅓ cup finely chopped cilantro
Lettuce leaves, as garnish
6 lime wedges, as garnish

Per Serving
Calories: 183
% Calories from fat: 15
Fat (gm): 3.2
Saturated fat (gm): 0.5
Cholesterol (mg): 0
Sodium (mg): 223
Protein (gm): 5.4
Carbohydrate (gm): 36.5
Exchanges
Milk: 0.0
Vegetable: 4.0
Fruit: 0.0
Bread: 1.0
Meat: 0.0
Fat: 0.5

1. Spray aluminum-foil-lined jelly roll pan with cooking spray. Arrange asparagus and mushrooms on pan; spray generously with cooking spray and sprinkle with pepper.

2. Roast vegetables at 425 degrees for 15 minutes. Add snow peas and garlic to pan; roast until vegetables are tender, about 20 minutes longer. Cool vegetables to room temperature; reserve garlic and coarsely chop roasted vegetables.

3. Place noodles in large bowl; pour cold water over to cover. Let stand until noodles separate and are soft, about 10 minutes. Drain noodles and add to roasted vegetables in large bowl. Add carrot, cucumber, and green onions and toss.

4. Squeeze garlic pulp into small bowl; mix in soy sauce, vinegar, vegetable oil, hot chili oil, sugar, and gingerroot. Drizzle dressing over vegetables; add cilantro and toss. Spoon mixture onto lettuce-lined plates; serve with lime wedges.

GRILLED VEGETABLE BURRITOS

 Roasted vegetables are combined with fat-free half-and-half to create a rich burrito filling.

6 servings

2 medium red bell peppers
2 medium yellow bell peppers
2 medium poblano chilies
Vegetable cooking spray
1 medium onion, sliced
2 cloves garlic, minced
½ cup fat-free half-and-half, *or* fat-free milk
¼ teaspoon dried marjoram leaves
¼ teaspoon dried oregano leaves
¼ teaspoon dried thyme leaves
1 bay leaf
Salt and pepper, to taste
2 cups (⅔ recipe), Refried Beans (see p. 525), warm
6 large flour tortillas (10-inch)
1 cup (½ recipe), Red Tomato Salsa (see p. 9), *or* prepared medium or hot salsa

Per Serving
Calories: 301
% Calories from fat: 10
Fat (gm): 3.5
Saturated fat (gm): 0.5
Cholesterol (mg): 0
Sodium (mg): 195
Protein (gm): 12.6
Carbohydrate (gm): 57.5
Exchanges
Milk: 0.0
Vegetable: 3.0
Fruit: 0.0
Bread: 3.0
Meat: 0.0
Fat: 0.0

1. Grill peppers and poblano chilies over medium-hot coals, turning frequently, until peppers are blistered and blackened, 5 to 8 minutes. Wrap peppers in towel or place in plastic bag; let stand 10 minutes. Peel peppers, discarding skins. Cut peppers into ¼-inch slices.

2. Spray medium skillet with cooking spray; heat over medium heat until hot. Saute onion and garlic until tender, about 5 minutes. Add half-and-half, grilled vegetables, and herbs; heat to boiling. Reduce heat and simmer, uncovered, until mixture is reduced by half; discard bay leaf. Season to taste with salt and pepper.

3. Spoon about ⅓ cup Refried Beans along center of each tortilla; top with about ½ cup vegetable mixture. Fold ends of tortillas in and roll up. Serve with Red Tomato Salsa.

GRILLED VEGETABLE FAJITAS

Cactus "paddles" and poblano peppers are commonly available today in large supermarkets as well as Mexican groceries. If unavailable, substitute another vegetable, such as zucchini, for the cactus and substitute green bell peppers and one jalapeño chili for the poblano peppers.

4 servings (2 fajitas each)

4	medium poblano peppers, cut into 1-inch slices
3	large tomatoes, cut into wedges
2	medium onions, cut into wedges
4	large cactus paddles (*nopales*), cut into 1-inch slices
	Vegetable cooking spray
2	tablespoons olive oil, *or* canola oil
2	tablespoons white distilled vinegar
1	tablespoon lime juice
2	cloves garlic, minced
3-4	dashes cayenne pepper
8	flour, *or* corn, tortillas, warm
¼	cup finely chopped cilantro
8	tablespoons fat-free sour cream
4	avocado slices

Per Serving
Calories: 414
% Calories from fat: 29
Fat (gm): 14.1
Saturated fat (gm): 2.3
Cholesterol (mg): 0
Sodium (mg): 47
Protein (gm): 12.6
Carbohydrate (gm): 64
Exchanges
Milk: 0.0
Vegetable: 3.0
Fruit: 0.0
Bread: 3.5
Meat: 0.0
Fat: 2.0

1. Spray vegetables with cooking spray; place on grill over medium-hot coals. Grill, turning occasionally, until vegetables are browned and tender, about 30 minutes (or bake on greased aluminum-foil-lined jelly roll pan at 400 degrees until brown and tender, 30 to 40 minutes). Combine vegetables in bowl.

2. Mix oil, vinegar, lime juice, garlic, and cayenne pepper; drizzle over vegetables and toss. Spoon about ½ cup of dressed vegetable mixture on each tortilla. Sprinkle with cilantro, top with 1 tablespoon sour cream, and roll up.

3. Place fajitas and avocado slices on serving plates.

GRILLED PORTOBELLO MUSHROOM SANDWICHES

 The sandwiches can also be made with pita bread: make a slit in the tops of 4 pita breads and fill with mushrooms and peppers.

4 servings

1 medium red bell pepper
1 medium yellow bell pepper
   Salt and pepper, to taste
   Olive oil cooking spray
4 large portobello, *or* porcini, mushrooms
   (4-5 inches diameter)
8 slices Italian bread
1 clove garlic, halved
4 tablespoons fat-free mayonnaise
3-4 tablespoons finely chopped basil

Per Serving
Calories: 239
% Calories from fat: 10
Fat (gm): 2.6
Saturated fat (gm): 0.5
Cholesterol (mg): 0
Sodium (mg): 546
Protein (gm): 10.3
Carbohydrate (gm): 43.8
Exchanges
Milk: 0.0
Vegetable: 3.0
Fruit: 0.0
Bread: 2.0
Meat: 0.0
Fat: 0.5

1. Grill bell peppers over medium-hot coals, turning frequently, until peppers are blistered and blackened, 5 to 8 minutes. Wrap peppers in towel or place in plastic bag; let stand 10 minutes. Peel peppers, discarding skins. Cut peppers into ½-inch slices; sprinkle lightly with salt and pepper.

2. Spray both sides of mushrooms with cooking spray; grill, turning occasionally, until tender, about 8 minutes. Season to taste with salt and pepper.

3. Grill bread until toasted, 2 to 3 minutes; rub tops of bread slices with garlic. Mix mayonnaise and basil; spread on 4 bread slices. Top bread with mushrooms, peppers, and remaining bread slices.

VEGGIE POCKET SANDWICHES

 Delicious as a sandwich with sourdough or multigrain bread also!

4 servings

Vegetable cooking spray

1 medium eggplant, unpeeled, cut into 1-inch cubes

1 large sweet potato, unpeeled, cut into ½-inch slices

1 medium green bell pepper, cut into ¾-inch slices

1 large onion, sliced

1 large tomato, cut into 8 wedges

2 tablespoons balsamic, *or* red wine, vinegar

1 tablespoon olive oil, *or* vegetable oil

1 teaspoon lemon juice

2 cloves garlic, minced

1 teaspoon dried oregano leaves

1 teaspoon dried basil leaves

Salt and pepper, to taste

4 pita pockets, cut into halves

Per Serving
Calories: 292
% Calories from fat: 14
Fat (gm): 4.6
Saturated fat (gm): 0.6
Cholesterol (mg): 0
Sodium (mg): 334
Protein (gm): 7.9
Carbohydrate (gm): 56.3
Exchanges
Milk: 0.0
Vegetable: 3.0
Fruit: 0.0
Bread: 2.5
Meat: 0.0
Fat: 1.0

1. Spray aluminum-foil-lined jelly roll pan with cooking spray. Arrange vegetables on pan in single layer and spray generously with cooking spray. Bake at 400 degrees until vegetables are browned and tender, about 30 minutes. Combine vegetables in bowl.

2. Combine vinegar, oil, lemon juice, garlic, oregano, and basil; drizzle over vegetables and toss. Season to taste with salt and pepper. Spoon dressed vegetables into pita pockets.

ROASTED CHILI CORN BREAD

Roasted chilies and corn cut from the cob make this a corn bread to remember!

9 servings (1 piece each)

2 ears corn, in the husks
Vegetable cooking spray
1 small red bell pepper, halved
1 small poblano chili, halved
1 jalapeño chili, halved
3 green onions, white parts only
½ teaspoon ground cumin
½ teaspoon dried oregano leaves
1½ cups all-purpose flour
½ cup plus 1 tablespoon yellow cornmeal
3 tablespoons light brown sugar
2¾ teaspoons baking powder
½-¾ teaspoon salt
1 egg
2 egg whites
1 cup buttermilk
3 tablespoons minced cilantro

Per Serving
Calories: 176
% Calories from fat: 8
Fat (gm): 1.6
Saturated fat (gm): 0.4
Cholesterol (mg): 24.7
Sodium (mg): 283
Protein (gm): 6.3
Carbohydrate (gm): 35
Exchanges
Milk: 0.0
Vegetable: 1.0
Fruit: 0.0
Bread: 2.0
Meat: 0.0
Fat: 0.0

1. Soak corn in water to cover for 30 minutes; drain.

2. Spray aluminum-foil-lined jelly roll pan with cooking spray; arrange vegetables in single layer on pan, with corn to the outside. Spray vegetables, except corn, generously with cooking spray; sprinkle vegetables, except corn, with cumin and oregano.

3. Roast vegetables at 425 degrees until browned and tender, about 40 minutes. Let stand until corn is cool enough to handle. Remove and discard corn husks; cut corn kernels off cobs. Chop remaining vegetables into ¼-inch pieces.

4. Combine flour, ½ cup cornmeal, brown sugar, baking powder, and salt in medium bowl. Whisk egg and egg whites into buttermilk; add to flour mixture, stirring just until combined. Stir in vegetables and cilantro.

5.   Grease 8-inch baking pan and sprinkle with the remaining 1 tablespoon cornmeal; pour batter into pan. Bake at 350 degrees until corn bread is browned and toothpick comes out clean, 35 to 40 minutes. Cool on wire rack; serve warm.

SIX

Pasta

HOMEMADE PASTA

Fresh pasta dough is not difficult to make. A pasta machine is a very simple and expedient way of kneading, rolling, and cutting the dough, producing a high-quality pasta. Rolling and cutting the dough by hand is somewhat more difficult, requiring practice to make thin, delicate pasta. Follow cooking directions in Step 6 carefully. Fresh pasta cooks very quickly—much more quickly than purchased fresh or dried pasta.

4 main-dish servings

1½ cups all-purpose flour
2 large eggs

Per Serving	Exchanges
Calories: 208	Milk: 0.0
% Calories from fat: 13	Vegetable: 0.0
Fat (gm): 3	Fruit: 0.0
Saturated fat (gm): 0.8	Bread: 2.5
Cholesterol (mg): 106.5	Meat: 0.0
Sodium (mg): 32	Fat: 0.5
Protein (gm): 8	
Carbohydrate (gm): 36.1	

1. Mound flour on cutting board, making a well in center. Drop eggs into center of well.

2. Break egg yolks and mix eggs with fork. While mixing eggs, gradually start to incorporate flour into the eggs. As flour is incorporated, it will be necessary to move the mound of flour toward the center, using your hands. Continue mixing until all or almost all flour has been incorporated, forming a soft, but not sticky, ball of dough.

Machine Kneading and Cutting

3. To knead dough using a pasta machine, set machine rollers on widest setting. Cut dough into 2 equal pieces. Lightly flour outside of 1 piece, and pass it through machine. Fold piece of dough into thirds; pass it through machine again, inserting open edges (not the fold) of dough first. Repeat folding and rolling 8 to 12 times or until dough feels smooth and satiny; lightly flour dough only if it begins to feel sticky.

Move machine rollers to next narrower setting. Pass dough (do not fold dough any longer) through rollers, beginning to roll out and stretch dough. Move machine rollers to next narrower

Note: Pasta quantities in recipes throughout are *dry* measurements unless indicated otherwise.

setting; pass dough through rollers. Continue process until pasta is as thin as wished. (Often the narrowest setting on machine makes pasta too thin; 1 or 2 settings from the end is usually best.) Lightly flour dough if it begins to feel even slightly sticky at any time. Repeat above procedures with second piece of dough.

To cut dough using a pasta machine, set cutting rollers for width of pasta desired; pass dough through cutters. Arrange cut pasta in single layer on lightly floured surface.

Hand Kneading and Cutting

3. To knead dough by hand, knead on lightly floured surface until dough is smooth and satiny, about 10 minutes. Cover dough lightly with damp towel and let rest 10 minutes.

Place dough on lightly floured surface. Starting in center of dough, roll with rolling pin from center to edge. Continue rolling, always from center to edge (to keep dough as round as possible) until dough is about $\frac{1}{16}$ inch thick. Lightly flour dough if it begins to feel even slightly sticky at any time.

To cut dough by hand, flour top of dough lightly and roll up. Cut into desired widths with sharp knife. Immediately unroll cut pasta to keep noodles from sticking together and arrange in single layer on lightly floured surface.

Cooking Pasta

4. Pasta can be cooked fresh, or it can be frozen or dried to be cooked later. To freeze pasta, place in heavy plastic freezer bag and freeze. To dry pasta, let stand on floured surface (or hang over rack) until completely dried. (Be sure pasta is completely dried or it will turn moldy in storage.) Store at room temperature in airtight container.

5. To cook fresh, frozen, or dried pasta, heat 4 to 5 quarts lightly salted (optional) water to boiling. Add pasta and begin testing for doneness as soon as water returns to boil. Cooking time will vary from 0 to 2 minutes once water has returned to boil.

Note: Fresh, homemade pasta can be used with any recipe, but it will result in a higher cholesterol count than stated with the recipe, in some cases exceeding the guidelines shown on page vii.

PASTA AND 2-BEAN VEGETABLE SOUP

Make this soup a day or two in advance so flavors can develop; add the tortellini when reheating. Any kind of beans, such as Great Northern, garbanzo, pinto, black, etc.,can be used in the soup.

6 main-dish servings (about 1¼ cups each)

Olive oil cooking spray

½ cup sliced leek (white part only), *or* green onions and tops

3 cloves garlic, minced

2 tablespoons finely chopped cilantro leaves

2 teaspoons dried basil leaves

2 teaspoons dried oregano leaves

2 cans (14½ ounces each) vegetable broth

1 cup water

1 cup quartered Brussels sprouts

1 cup sliced yellow summer squash

1 cup sliced carrots

1 medium tomato, chopped

1 can (15 ounces) black-eyed peas, rinsed, drained

1 can (15 ounces) dark red kidney beans, rinsed, drained

½ package (9-ounce size) fresh reduced-fat cheese tortellini

Salt and pepper, to taste

Per Serving
Calories: 267
% Calories from fat: 14
Fat (gm): 4.6
Saturated fat (gm): 0.8
Cholesterol (mg): 1.3
Sodium (mg): 510
Protein (gm): 14.5
Carbohydrate (gm): 47.6
Exchanges
Milk: 0.0
Vegetable: 2.0
Fruit: 0.0
Bread: 3.0
Meat: 0.0
Fat: 0.5

1. Spray large saucepan with cooking spray; heat over medium heat until hot. Saute leeks and garlic 1 to 2 minutes. Stir in herbs and cook until leek is tender, 3 to 5 minutes.

2. Add broth, water, vegetables, beans, and tortellini; heat to a boil. Reduce heat and simmer, covered, until vegetables are tender and tortellini are *al dente*, about 10 minutes. Season to taste with salt and pepper.

SESAME NOODLE SOUP WITH VEGETABLES

Use oriental sesame oil, which is dark in color and concentrated in flavor; light-colored sesame oil is very delicate in flavor. The fresh Chinese-style noodles are sometimes called soup noodles, chow mein noodles, or spaghetti. Caution: fresh noodles cook very quickly.

4 main-dish servings (about 2 cups each)

½ cup sliced green onions and tops

4 cloves garlic, minced

1 tablespoon sesame oil

2½ cups chopped or thinly sliced napa cabbage

1 cup chopped red bell peppers

1 cup julienned carrots

1 cup sliced shiitake, *or* cremini mushrooms

3 cans (14½ ounces each) reduced-sodium vegetable broth

1 package (12 ounces) fresh Chinese-style noodles

Salt and pepper, to taste

Per Serving
Calories: 281
% Calories from fat: 12
Fat (gm): 3.9
Saturated fat (gm): 0.5
Cholesterol (mg): 0
Sodium (mg): 150
Protein (gm): 4.1
Carbohydrate (gm): 60
Exchanges
Milk: 0.0
Vegetable: 2.0
Fruit: 0.0
Bread: 3.0
Meat: 0.0
Fat: 0.5

1. Saute green onions and garlic in sesame oil in large saucepan until tender, about 5 minutes. Add cabbage, bell peppers, carrots, and mushrooms; saute until vegetables are crisp-tender, about 5 minutes.

2. Add vegetable broth to saucepan; heat to boiling. Stir in noodles; return to boiling. Reduce heat and simmer, uncovered, until noodles are just tender, 1 to 2 minutes. Season to taste with salt and pepper.

ORIENTAL SOUP WITH NOODLES

 The dried chow mein noodles are not the fried ones we have eaten with chop suey for many years. Be sure the correct noodles are used.

4 side-dish servings (about ¾ cup each)

1 ounce oriental dried cloud ears, *or* ½ ounce dried shiitake mushrooms

Hot water

Olive oil cooking spray

½ cup julienned carrots

2 cans (14½ ounces each) reduced-sodium vegetable broth

2 tablespoons dry sherry (optional)

1½ teaspoons reduced-sodium tamari soy sauce

¼-½ teaspoon five-spice powder

2½ ounces snow peas

1 cup sliced mushrooms

¼ cup sliced green onions and tops

½ package (5-ounce size) dried chow mein noodles

Salt and pepper, to taste

Per Serving
Calories: 146
% Calories from fat: 34
Fat (gm): 5.6
Saturated fat (gm): 0.8
Cholesterol (mg): 0
Sodium (mg): 259
Protein (gm): 3.6
Carbohydrate (gm): 21.3
Exchanges
Milk: 0.0
Vegetable: 1.0
Fruit: 0.0
Bread: 1.0
Meat: 0.0
Fat: 1.0

1. Place dried mushrooms in bowl; pour hot water over to cover. Let stand until mushrooms are soft, about 15 minutes; drain. Slice mushrooms, discarding any tough parts.

2. Spray large saucepan with cooking spray; heat over medium heat until hot. Saute dried mushrooms and carrots 3 to 4 minutes. Add vegetable broth, sherry, soy sauce, and five-spice powder. Heat to boiling; reduce heat and simmer, covered, 10 minutes. Stir in snow peas, sliced mushrooms, and green onions; cook until peas are crisp-tender, about 4 minutes.

3. Add noodles to saucepan; cook until noodles are just tender, about 10 minutes. Season to taste with salt and pepper.

GARDEN VEGETABLE AND PASTA SALAD

Steaming is a healthful, fat-free method of cooking vegetables. Steam broccoli and cauliflower florets just until crisp-tender for this delicious, meatless entrée.

4 main-dish servings

1 medium eggplant, unpeeled, cut into ¾-inch pieces
Vegetable cooking spray
2 cups cauliflower florets, steamed, cooled
2 cups broccoli florets, steamed, cooled
10 cherry tomatoes
½ medium green bell pepper, sliced
8 ounces fettuccine, *or* linguine, cooked, room temperature
Basil Vinaigrette (recipe follows)
2 ounces feta cheese, crumbled

Per Serving
Calories: 304
% Calories from fat: 25
Fat (gm): 9
Saturated fat (gm): 2.7
Cholesterol (mg): 12.5
Sodium (mg): 423
Protein (gm): 12.8
Carbohydrate (gm): 47.2
Exchanges
Milk: 0.0
Vegetable: 2.0
Fruit: 0.0
Bread: 2.5
Meat: 0.0
Fat: 1.5

1. Heat oven to 400 degrees. Spray both sides of eggplant with cooking spray; arrange on cookie sheet. Bake until eggplant is tender, about 15 minutes. Cool.

2. Combine eggplant, remaining vegetables, and linguine in large bowl; pour Basil Vinaigrette over and toss. Sprinkle with cheese.

Basil Vinaigrette

(makes about ⅓ cup)

¼ cup balsamic vinegar
1 tablespoon olive oil
2 tablespoons finely chopped fresh basil leaves, *or* 2 teaspoons dried
2 tablespoons finely chopped parsley
¼ teaspoon salt
¼ teaspoon pepper

1. Mix all ingredients; refrigerate until serving time. Stir before using.

BRUSSELS SPROUTS AND GNOCCHI SALAD

Enjoy the first fall harvest of Brussels sprouts in this colorful salad. Pasta shells can be substituted for the gnocchi, if preferred.

8 side-dish servings

2 cups (8 ounces) gnocchi, cooked, room temperature

8 ounces Brussels sprouts, cut into halves, steamed, cooled

1 cup seeded, chopped tomato

1 medium purple, *or* green, bell pepper, sliced

¼ cup thinly sliced red onion

Sun-Dried Tomato and Goat's Cheese Dressing (recipe follows)

2 tablespoons grated Romano cheese

Per Serving
Calories: 172
% Calories from fat: 27
Fat (gm): 5.4
Saturated fat (gm): 0.9
Cholesterol (mg): 3.5
Sodium (mg): 179
Protein (gm): 6.3
Carbohydrate (gm): 26.3
Exchanges
Milk: 0.0
Vegetable: 1.0
Fruit: 0.0
Bread: 1.5
Meat: 0.0
Fat: 1.0

1. Combine gnocchi and vegetables in salad bowl. Pour Sun-Dried Tomato and Goat's Cheese Dressing over salad and toss; sprinkle with grated cheese.

Sun-Dried Tomato and Goat's Cheese Dressing

(makes about ½ cup)

3 sun-dried tomatoes (not in oil)
Hot water

2 tablespoons olive oil

2 tablespoons white wine vinegar

2 tablespoons lemon juice

1 tablespoon goat's cheese, *or* reduced-fat cream cheese, room temperature

2 cloves garlic, minced

½ teaspoon dried marjoram leaves

⅛ teaspoon dried thyme leaves

¼ teaspoon salt

⅛ teaspoon pepper

1. Place tomatoes in small bowl; pour hot water over to cover. Let tomatoes stand until softened, about 15 minutes; drain and finely chop.

2. Mix tomatoes, oil, and remaining ingredients; refrigerate until serving time. Mix again before using.

PASTA AND PORTOBELLO MUSHROOMS VINAIGRETTE

 For extra flavor, grill or smoke the whole portobello mushrooms.

4 main-dish servings

4 large portobello mushrooms, cut into ¾-inch slices

1 tablespoon olive oil

2 medium tomatoes, cut into wedges

1 medium yellow squash, *or* zucchini, diagonally sliced

1 medium green bell pepper, sliced

1 large carrot, diagonally sliced

1 small red onion, sliced

3 cups (8 ounces) rotini (corkscrews), cooked, room temperature

Mixed Herb Vinaigrette (recipe follows)

Lettuce leaves, as garnish

Per Serving
Calories: 422
% Calories from fat: 19
Fat (gm): 9.2
Saturated fat (gm): 1.2
Cholesterol (mg): 0
Sodium (mg): 326
Protein (gm): 12.7
Carbohydrate (gm): 73.9
Exchanges
Milk: 0.0
Vegetable: 2.0
Fruit: 0.0
Bread: 4.0
Meat: 0.0
Fat: 2.0

1. Saute mushrooms in oil in large skillet until tender, about 5 minutes; cool.

2. Combine vegetables and pasta in shallow glass baking dish. Pour Mixed Herb Vinaigrette over and toss.

3. Arrange lettuce on salad plates; spoon salad over.

Mixed Herb Vinaigrette

(makes about ⅔ cup)

- ⅓ cup red wine vinegar
- ¼ cup reduced-sodium vegetable broth, *or* water
- 1 tablespoon olive oil, *or* vegetable oil
- 2 teaspoons sugar
- 2 teaspoons Dijon-style mustard
- 1 teaspoon mustard seeds, crushed
- 3 cloves garlic, minced
- 1 tablespoon finely chopped fresh marjoram leaves, *or* 1 teaspoon dried
- 1 tablespoon finely chopped fresh tarragon leaves, *or* 1 teaspoon dried
- 1 tablespoon finely chopped fresh thyme leaves, *or* ½ teaspoon dried
- ½ teaspoon salt
- ½ teaspoon pepper

1. Mix all ingredients; refrigerate until ready to use. Stir before using.

SMOKED TEMPEH, ARTICHOKE, AND LINGUINE SALAD

Mesquite and hickory chips are most commonly used for smoking foods on the grill. For subtle flavor, try pecan, cherry, or alder wood when smoking the tempeh for this salad.

4 main-dish servings

- 2 packages (8 ounces each) tempeh
- 8 ounces linguine, cooked, room temperature
- 2 cups sliced carrots, steamed until crisp-tender
- 1 package (9 ounces) frozen artichoke hearts, cooked, cut into fourths
- 12 cherry tomatoes, cut into halves

Per Serving
Calories: 491
% Calories from fat: 20
Fat (gm): 11.5
Saturated fat (gm): 1.6
Cholesterol (mg): 0
Sodium (mg): 709
Protein (gm): 36
Carbohydrate (gm): 68
Exchanges
Milk: 0.0
Vegetable: 3.0
Fruit: 0.0
Bread: 3.5
Meat: 3.0
Fat: 0.0

¼ cup sliced green onions and tops
Sour Cream Dressing (recipe follows)

1. Smoke tempeh according to directions in Smoked Tofu recipe (see p. 267); cut into ¾-inch cubes.

2. Combine tempeh, linguine, and vegetables in bowl; spoon Sour Cream Dressing over and toss.

Sour Cream Dressing

(makes about ⅔ cup)

⅓ cup fat-free sour cream
⅓ cup fat-free mayonnaise, or salad dressing
1 tablespoon red wine vinegar
1 clove garlic, minced
½ teaspoon dried rosemary leaves, crushed
½ teaspoon salt
¼ teaspoon pepper

1. Mix all ingredients; refrigerate until serving time. Mix again before using.

SESAME PASTA WITH SUMMER VEGETABLES

These garden vegetables signal the end-of-summer harvest. The vegetables used in this salad can vary according to seasonal availability.

6 side-dish servings

1 small eggplant
1 cup sliced carrots, steamed until crisp-tender
1 cup sliced yellow summer squash, steamed until crisp-tender
1 cup broccoli florets, steamed until crisp-tender
1 medium red bell pepper, sliced
¼ cup sliced green onions and tops
Sesame Dressing (recipe follows)

Per Serving
Calories: 192
% Calories from fat: 30
Fat (gm): 6.6
Saturated fat (gm): 0.7
Cholesterol (mg): 0
Sodium (mg): 428
Protein (gm): 7.2
Carbohydrate (gm): 28.3
Exchanges
Milk: 0.0
Vegetable: 1.5
Fruit: 0.0
Bread: 1.5
Meat: 0.0
Fat: 1.0

    8 ounces thin spaghetti, cooked, room
      temperature
    2 teaspoons toasted sesame seeds

1. Heat oven to 400 degrees. Pierce eggplant 6 to 8 times with fork; place in baking pan. Bake, uncovered, until tender, about 30 minutes. Cool until able to handle easily. Cut eggplant in half; scoop out pulp with a large spoon and cut it into ¾-inch pieces.

2. Combine eggplant and remaining vegetables in bowl; pour Sesame Dressing over and toss. Add pasta and toss; sprinkle with sesame seeds.

Sesame Dressing

(makes about ⅓ cup)

    2 tablespoons reduced-sodium soy sauce
    2 tablespoons sesame oil
    1 teaspoon hot chili oil (optional)
    1 tablespoon balsamic, *or* red wine, vinegar
 1½ tablespoons sugar
    1 clove garlic, minced
    1 tablespoon finely chopped cilantro, *or*
      parsley

1. Mix all ingredients; refrigerate until serving time. Mix again before using.

RICE NOODLE SALAD

If you enjoy the flavor of sesame oil, substitute 1 tablespoon sesame oil for 1 tablespoon of the olive oil in the dressing recipe.

4 servings

    ⅔ package (12-ounce size) rice noodles
      Cold water
    4 quarts boiling water
 1½ cups thinly sliced Chinese cabbage
    2 cups snow peas, steamed

Per Serving
Calories: 246
% Calories from fat: 26
Fat (gm): 7.5
Saturated fat (gm): 1
Cholesterol (mg): 0
Sodium (mg): 197
Protein (gm): 6.6
Carbohydrate (gm): 40.9

¾ cup sliced red bell pepper

¾ cup sliced yellow bell pepper

1 cup sliced mushrooms

1 cup canned, drained lychee fruit, *or* pineapple chunks

½ cup fresh, *or* canned, bean sprouts, rinsed, drained

Citrus Vinaigrette (recipe follows)

Exchanges
Milk: 0.0
Vegetable: 2.0
Fruit: 0.0
Bread: 2.0
Meat: 0.0
Fat: 1.0

1. Place noodles in large bowl; pour cold water over to cover. Let stand until noodles separate and are soft, about 5 minutes. Stir noodles into 4 quarts boiling water. Reduce heat and simmer, uncovered, until tender, about 5 minutes; drain and cool.

2. Combine noodles, Chinese cabbage, snow peas, bell peppers, mushrooms, lychee fruit, and bean sprouts in large bowl. Pour Citrus Vinaigrette over and toss.

Citrus Vinaigrette

(makes about ½ cup)

⅓ cup orange juice

2 tablespoons olive oil

2 cloves garlic, minced

½ teaspoon five-spice powder

¼ teaspoon salt

¼ teaspoon pepper

1. Mix all ingredients; refrigerate until ready to use. Mix again before using.

VEGETABLE LO MEIN

To store leftover gingerroot, place it in a jar, fill with dry sherry, cover, and refrigerate; the gingerroot will last at least 6 months. Gingerroot does not have to be peeled before using.

4 servings

1 package (12 ounces) fresh Chinese-style noodles
4 quarts boiling water
4 Chinese dried black, *or* shiitake, mushrooms
   Hot water
1 tablespoon sesame oil, *or* vegetable oil
1 tablespoon finely chopped fresh gingerroot
3 cloves garlic, minced
2 cups broccoli florets
1 cup sliced carrots
½ cup sliced leek (white part only)
1 cup chopped tomatoes
1 cup sliced kale, *or* bok choy
⅓ cup water
2 tablespoons dry sherry, *or* water
2 teaspoons cornstarch
1 tablespoon black bean paste
2 teaspoons light soy sauce

Per Serving
Calories: 418
% Calories from fat: 9
Fat (gm): 4.2
Saturated fat (gm): 0.6
Cholesterol (mg): 0
Sodium (mg): 275
Protein (gm): 10.6
Carbohydrate (gm): 84.7
Exchanges
Milk: 0.0
Vegetable: 4.0
Fruit: 0.0
Bread: 4.0
Meat: 0.0
Fat: 0.5

1. Cook noodles in 4 quarts boiling water until tender, about 2 minutes; drain and reserve.

2. Place dried mushrooms in bowl; pour hot water over to cover. Let stand until mushrooms are soft, about 15 minutes; drain. Slice mushrooms, discarding tough parts.

3. Heat oil in wok or skillet over medium-high heat until hot. Stir-fry mushrooms, ginger, and garlic 2 minutes. Add remaining vegetables to wok; stir-fry until vegetables are crisp-tender, 5 to 8 minutes. Remove from wok.

4. Combine ⅓ cup water, sherry, and cornstarch; add to wok and heat to boiling. Boil, stirring constantly, until thickened, about 1 minute. Stir in black bean paste and soy sauce. Return vegetable mixture to wok; add noodles. Stir-fry over medium heat until hot through, 2 to 3 minutes.

STIR-FRIED RICE NOODLES WITH VEGETABLES

 Rice noodles are also called cellophane noodles, or "bihon." The dried noodles are soaked in cold water to soften, then drained before using.

4 servings (about 1½ cups each)

1 package (8 ounces) rice noodles
  Cold water
1 tablespoon canola oil
1 cup cut green beans
1 cup cubed yellow summer squash
½ cup thinly sliced celery
½ cup sliced red bell pepper
4 green onions and tops, thinly sliced
1 tablespoon finely chopped fresh gingerroot
2 cups shredded napa cabbage
1 cup canned reduced-sodium vegetable broth
2 tablespoons dry sherry (optional)
2-3 teaspoons light soy sauce
½-1 teaspoon Szechuan chili sauce

Per Serving
Calories: 161
% Calories from fat: 20
Fat (gm): 3.8
Saturated fat (gm): 0.5
Cholesterol (mg): 0
Sodium (mg): 137
Protein (gm): 4.2
Carbohydrate (gm): 29.4
Exchanges
Milk: 0.0
Vegetable: 1.0
Fruit: 0.0
Bread: 1.5
Meat: 0.0
Fat: 0.5

1. Place noodles in large bowl; pour cold water over to cover. Let stand until noodles separate and are soft, about 15 minutes; drain.

2. Heat oil in wok or skillet over medium-high heat until hot. Add green beans, squash, celery, bell pepper, green onions, and gingerroot. Stir-fry until vegetables are tender, 8 to 10 minutes.

3. Add cabbage to wok; stir-fry just until cabbage turns bright in color, about 1 minute. Stir in drained noodles; add vegetable broth, sherry, soy sauce, and chili sauce. Heat to boiling; reduce heat and simmer, uncovered, until noodles have absorbed all liquid, about 5 minutes.

PASTA PEPERONATA

Italian peperonata, a slow-cooked mixture of sweet peppers, onions, and garlic, is also a wonderful filling for pita pockets. For a roasted version of this recipe, see Roasted Peperonata (p. 295).

4 servings

1½	red bell peppers, sliced
1½	green bell peppers, sliced
1½	yellow bell peppers, sliced
3	medium onions, sliced
1	large red onion, sliced
8	cloves garlic, minced
3	tablespoons olive oil, *or* canola oil
3	tablespoons water
1	teaspoon sugar
	Salt and pepper, to taste
8	ounces spaghetti, cooked, warm
¼	cup grated Parmesan cheese (optional)

Per Serving
Calories: 426
% Calories from fat: 25
Fat (gm): 11.8
Saturated fat (gm): 1.6
Cholesterol (mg): 0
Sodium (mg): 8
Protein (gm): 11.1
Carbohydrate (gm): 70.3
Exchanges
Milk: 0.0
Vegetable: 3.0
Fruit: 0.0
Bread: 3.5
Meat: 0.0
Fat: 2.5

1. Saute peppers, onions, and garlic in oil in large skillet 2 to 3 minutes. Add water; cook, covered, over medium to medium-high heat until soft, 2 to 3 minutes.

2. Stir sugar into pepper mixture; cook, uncovered, over medium-low heat until mixture is very soft and browned, about 20 minutes. Season to taste with salt and pepper. Toss with spaghetti; sprinkle with cheese if desired.

PASTA WITH GREENS, RAISINS, AND PINE NUTS

Radicchio, escarole, curly endive, kale, or mustard greens can be substituted for the brightly colored oriental kale in this sweet-and-bitter Italian favorite.

4 servings

⅓	cup dark raisins
½	cup warm water
4	medium onions, sliced

Per Serving
Calories: 436
% Calories from fat: 16
Fat (gm): 7.8
Saturated fat (gm): 1.1
Cholesterol (mg): 0
Sodium (mg): 42
Protein (gm): 13.7
Carbohydrate (gm): 79.6

4 cloves garlic, minced

1 tablespoon olive oil, *or* canola oil

1 teaspoon sugar

12 ounces oriental kale leaves, torn

½ cup reduced-sodium vegetable broth
   Salt and pepper, to taste

8 ounces spaghetti, *or* linguine, cooked, warm

2 tablespoons pine nuts, *or* slivered almonds

Exchanges
Milk: 0.0
Vegetable: 3.0
Fruit: 1.0
Bread: 3.0
Meat: 0.0
Fat: 1.5

1. Soak raisins in warm water 20 minutes; drain and reserve.

2. Saute onions and garlic in oil in large skillet until tender, 3 to 5 minutes. Stir in sugar; cook over low heat until onions are golden, 10 to 15 minutes, stirring occasionally.

3. Stir kale and broth into onion mixture; cook, covered, over low heat until kale is wilted, about 10 minutes. Stir in raisins; season to taste with salt and pepper. Spoon mixture over spaghetti and toss; sprinkle with pine nuts.

"LITTLE EARS" WITH ARTICHOKE HEARTS, MUSHROOMS, AND PEPPERS

Because of their shape, orrechiette are often called "little ears." Other pasta shapes such as cappelletti (little hats), farfalle (bow ties), or rotini (corkscrews) can be substituted.

4 servings

4 ounces shiitake, *or* cremini, mushrooms, sliced

1 red bell pepper, coarsely chopped

1 yellow bell pepper, coarsely chopped

4 cloves garlic, minced

2 teaspoons olive oil, *or* canola oil

½ can (15-ounce size) artichoke hearts, rinsed, drained, cut into fourths

2 tablespoons minced parsley
   Salt and pepper, to taste

3 cups (12 ounces) orrechiette ("little ears"), cooked, warm

Per Serving
Calories: 470
% Calories from fat: 18
Fat (gm): 9.7
Saturated fat (gm): 3.1
Cholesterol (mg): 14.1
Sodium (mg): 233
Protein (gm): 17.1
Carbohydrate (gm): 80.4
Exchanges
Milk: 0.0
Vegetable: 2.0
Fruit: 0.0
Bread: 4.0
Meat: 0.5
Fat: 2.0

¼ cup (1 ounce) crumbled feta cheese

2 tablespoons coarsely chopped walnuts

1. Saute mushrooms, bell peppers, and garlic in oil in large skillet until tender, 3 to 5 minutes. Add artichoke hearts and parsley; cook until hot through, 3 to 4 minutes. Season to taste with salt and pepper.

2. Spoon vegetable mixture over pasta and toss. Spoon onto plates; sprinkle with feta cheese and walnuts.

MAFALDE WITH GARBANZO BEANS, TOMATOES, AND CROUTONS

 This easy-to-make dish has ingredients with many flavor and color contrasts.

4 servings

Vegetable cooking spray

½ cup chopped poblano chili, *or* green bell pepper

⅓ cup chopped onion

1 teaspoon minced garlic

1 can (15½ ounces) garbanzo beans, rinsed, drained

2 cups seeded, chopped Italian plum tomatoes

¼ cup loosely packed chopped, basil leaves

¼ cup fat-free Italian salad dressing

8 ounces mafalde, *or* other flat pasta, cooked, warm

1 ½ cups (½ recipe) Italian-Style, *or* Parmesan, Croutons (see p. 677)

Fat-free Parmesan cheese, grated, as garnish

Per Serving
Calories: 397
% Calories from fat: 9
Fat (gm): 3.9
Saturated fat (gm): 0.6
Cholesterol (mg): 0
Sodium (mg): 717
Protein (gm): 14.8
Carbohydrate (gm): 76.3
Exchanges
Milk: 0.0
Vegetable: 2.0
Fruit: 0.0
Bread: 4.5
Meat: 0.0
Fat: 0.5

1. Spray medium skillet with cooking spray; heat over medium heat until hot. Saute poblano chili, onion, and garlic until tender, 5 to 8 minutes. Add beans and cook, covered, over medium heat until hot through, 3 to 4 minutes. Remove from heat and stir in tomatoes, basil, and salad dressing.

2. Toss pasta and bean mixture in serving bowl; add croutons and toss. Serve with Parmesan cheese.

PASTA FROM PESCIA

 I have fond memories of this hearty dish from the Tuscany region of Italy. Any root vegetable you enjoy can be used in this recipe.

4 servings

3 cups thinly sliced cabbage
1½ cups halved Brussels sprouts
2 medium carrots, diagonally sliced
2 cloves garlic, minced
½ teaspoon dried sage leaves
⅓ cup reduced-sodium vegetable broth
8 small new potatoes, unpeeled, cooked
2 tablespoons grated Parmesan cheese
1 tablespoon minced parsley
Salt and pepper, to taste
8 ounces rigatoni, *or* ziti, cooked, warm

Per Serving
Calories: 486
% Calories from fat: 5
Fat (gm): 2.5
Saturated fat (gm): 0.9
Cholesterol (mg): 2.5
Sodium (mg): 144
Protein (gm): 16.9
Carbohydrate (gm): 102.3
Exchanges
Milk: 0.0
Vegetable: 3.0
Fruit: 0.0
Bread: 6.0
Meat: 0.0
Fat: 0.0

1. Heat cabbage, Brussels sprouts, carrots, garlic, sage, and broth to boiling in large skillet. Reduce heat and simmer, covered, until cabbage is wilted, about 5 minutes. Add potatoes and cook, uncovered, until liquid is gone and cabbage is lightly browned, about 5 minutes.

2. Stir cheese and parsley into vegetables; season to taste with salt and pepper. Spoon mixture over pasta and toss.

PASTA WITH CABBAGE AND POTATOES

 A nourishing entrée, perfect for cool-weather meals.

6 servings

6 cups thinly sliced cabbage

4 cloves garlic, minced

⅓ cup dry white wine, *or* canned vegetable broth

4 medium Idaho potatoes, peeled, cooked, cut into ½-inch cubes

1 teaspoon dried rosemary leaves

1 teaspoon dried sage leaves

½ teaspoon salt

¼ teaspoon pepper

12 ounces pappardelle, *or* other wide pasta, cooked, warm

¼ cup grated Parmesan cheese

1 tablespoon finely chopped parsley

Per Serving
Calories: 349
% Calories from fat: 7
Fat (gm): 2.6
Saturated fat (gm): 1
Cholesterol (mg): 3.3
Sodium (mg): 279
Protein (gm): 11.9
Carbohydrate (gm): 67.9
Exchanges
Milk: 0.0
Vegetable: 2.0
Fruit: 0.0
Bread: 4.0
Meat: 0.0
Fat: 0.0

1. Combine cabbage, garlic, and wine in large skillet; heat to boiling. Cook, covered, over medium-high heat until cabbage is wilted, about 5 minutes; cook, uncovered, 5 minutes more.

2. Stir potatoes, herbs, salt, and pepper into cabbage mixture. Cook over medium to medium-high heat until excess liquid is gone, about 10 minutes.

3. Spoon mixture over pasta and toss; sprinkle with Parmesan cheese and toss. Sprinkle with parsley.

ROTINI AND BEANS NIÇOISE

 Tarragon lends a fresh herb flavor to this pasta and bean combination. Garbanzo or kidney beans can be substituted for any of the beans used.

6 servings

½ cup chopped shallots

2 cups chopped Italian plum tomatoes

1 teaspoon minced garlic

2 teaspoons margarine, *or* butter

Per Serving
Calories: 265
% Calories from fat: 7
Fat (gm): 2.4
Saturated fat (gm): 0.4
Cholesterol (mg): 0
Sodium (mg): 430
Protein (gm): 13.8
Carbohydrate (gm): 53.9

2 tablespoons drained capers

½ teaspoon dried tarragon leaves

2 cups diagonally sliced Italian, *or* regular, green beans, cooked

1 can (13¼ ounces) baby lima beans, rinsed, drained

1 can (15 ounces) cannellini beans, rinsed, drained

4 cups cooked rotini, *or* other-shaped pasta, warm

Salt and pepper, to taste

Fat-free Parmesan cheese, grated, as garnish

Exchanges
Milk: 0.0
Vegetable: 2.0
Fruit: 0.0
Bread: 3.0
Meat: 0.0
Fat: 0.0

1. Saute shallots, tomatoes, and garlic in margarine in large skillet 2 to 3 minutes; cook, covered, over medium heat until tomatoes are wilted, 3 to 5 minutes. Stir in capers and tarragon and cook 1 to 2 minutes longer.

2. Stir all beans into skillet; cook, covered, over medium-low heat until hot through, about 5 minutes. Stir in rotini and season to taste with salt and pepper. Spoon mixture into serving bowl; sprinkle lightly with Parmesan cheese.

RIGATONI WITH ITALIAN "SAUSAGE" AND FENNEL PESTO

 The aromatic flavor of fennel makes this dish very special!

6 servings

Olive oil cooking spray

1 package (12¾ ounces) frozen, Italian-style all-vegetable "burgers", thawed, crumbled

1½ cups thinly sliced fennel bulb, *or* celery

1 cup chopped onion

2 cloves garlic, minced

1 can (8 ounces) reduced-sodium whole tomatoes, drained, chopped

Fennel Pesto (see p. 728)

Per Serving
Calories: 447
% Calories from fat: 26
Fat (gm): 12.8
Saturated fat (gm): 1.7
Cholesterol (mg): 0
Sodium (mg): 372
Protein (gm): 26.1
Carbohydrate (gm): 58
Exchanges
Milk: 0.0
Vegetable: 2.0
Fruit: 0.0
Bread: 3.0
Meat: 2.0
Fat: 1.5

12 ounces rigatoni, *or other tube pasta,* cooked, warm

1. Spray medium skillet with cooking spray; heat over medium heat until hot. Saute "burgers," fennel, onion, and garlic until onion is transparent, 5 to 8 minutes.

2. Stir in tomatoes and Fennel Pesto. Heat to boiling; reduce heat and simmer, covered, until fennel is tender, about 15 minutes. Spoon sauce mixture over pasta and toss.

FETTUCCINE WITH EGGPLANT PERSILLADE

"Persillade" is a French term meaning "with lots of parsley," which this fragrant dish does have.

4 servings

Olive oil cooking spray
1 medium onion, chopped
1 green bell pepper, chopped
1 red bell pepper, chopped
1 small eggplant, unpeeled, cut into ½-inch cubes
2 teaspoons minced roasted garlic
½ cup canned reduced-sodium vegetable broth
Salt and pepper, to taste
½ cup finely chopped parsley
8 ounces whole wheat fettuccine, cooked, warm
2-4 tablespoons grated fat-free Parmesan cheese

Per Serving
Calories: 246
% Calories from fat: 9
Fat (gm): 2.5
Saturated fat (gm): 0.1
Cholesterol (mg): 0
Sodium (mg): 136
Protein (gm): 11.0
Carbohydrate (gm): 48.7
Exchanges
Milk: 0.0
Vegetable: 3.0
Fruit: 0.0
Bread: 2.0
Meat: 0.5
Fat: 0.0

1. Spray large skillet with cooking spray; heat over medium heat until hot. Saute onion, bell peppers, eggplant, and garlic 5 minutes, stirring occasionally. Add broth and heat to boiling; reduce heat and simmer, covered, until eggplant is tender and broth absorbed, about 5 minutes. Season to taste with salt and pepper. Add parsley and toss.

2. Toss vegetable mixture with pasta and spoon onto plates; sprinkle lightly with cheese.

VERY SIMPLE PRIMAVERA

 Very simple to make, and simply good! This primavera can take advantage of any fresh ingredients on hand.

6 servings

Vegetable cooking spray
2 cups thinly sliced onions
4 teaspoons minced garlic
1 teaspoon dried marjoram leaves
½ teaspoon dried basil leaves
1½ cups sliced mushrooms
1 cup thinly sliced green bell peppers
1 cup thinly sliced red bell peppers
8 ounces sugar snap peas, cut into halves
10-12 Italian plum tomatoes, cut into quarters
Salt and pepper, to taste
12 ounces penne, *or* ziti, cooked, warm
¼ cup (1 ounce) grated fat-free Parmesan cheese

Per Serving
Calories: 341
% Calories from fat: 6
Fat (gm): 2.2
Saturated fat (gm): 0.3
Cholesterol (mg): 0
Sodium (mg): 55
Protein (gm): 13.7
Carbohydrate (gm): 69.8
Exchanges
Milk: 0.0
Vegetable: 4.0
Fruit: 0.0
Bread: 3.0
Meat: 0.0
Fat: 0.5

1. Spray large skillet with cooking spray; heat over medium heat until hot. Add onions, garlic, and herbs; saute 2 minutes. Add mushrooms and bell peppers; saute 2 to 3 minutes. Add snap peas and tomatoes; cook, covered, over medium heat until tomatoes are wilted and peas are crisp-tender, 5 to 8 minutes. Season to taste with salt and pepper.

2. Toss vegetables and pasta in bowl; sprinkle with Parmesan cheese and toss.

CREAMY FETTUCCINE PRIMAVERA

The sauce for this dish should be somewhat thin, as it thickens once it is removed from the heat. If made in advance, the sauce will require additional milk when reheating.

4 servings

Garlic-flavored vegetable cooking spray
2 cups sliced mushrooms
2 cups broccoflower, *or* cauliflower, florets
½ cup chopped red bell pepper
½ cup water
1 package (8 ounces) fat-free cream cheese
⅔-1 cup fat-free milk, divided
¼ cup sliced green onions and tops
½ teaspoon Italian seasoning
2 tablespoons grated fat-free Parmesan cheese
Salt and white pepper, to taste
8 ounces fettuccine, *or* linguine, cooked, warm

Per Serving
Calories: 273
% Calories from fat: 8
Fat (gm): 2.5
Saturated fat (gm): 0.1
Cholesterol (mg): 0.7
Sodium (mg): 491
Protein (gm): 20.4
Carbohydrate (gm): 43.2
Exchanges
Milk: 0.5
Vegetable: 2.0
Fruit: 0.0
Bread: 2.0
Meat: 0.5
Fat: 0.0

1. Spray large skillet with cooking spray; heat over medium heat until hot. Saute mushrooms, broccoflower, and bell pepper 3 to 4 minutes. Add water and heat to boiling. Reduce heat and simmer, covered, until broccoflower is tender and water absorbed, about 8 minutes.

2. Heat cream cheese, ⅔ cup milk, green onions, and Italian seasoning in small saucepan over low heat until cream cheese is melted, stirring frequently. Stir in Parmesan cheese and enough remaining milk to make a thin consistency (sauce will thicken when removed from heat). Season to taste with salt and pepper.

3. Pour sauce over fettuccine in serving bowl and toss; add vegetable mixture and toss gently.

CURRIED TORTELLINI WITH BEANS AND SQUASH

Coconut milk adds a subtle Asian flavor to this colorful pasta combination.

6 servings

Olive oil cooking spray
1⅓ cups coarsely chopped onions
⅔ cup red bell pepper
2 teaspoons minced garlic
1 teaspoon curry powder
2 cups diagonally sliced Italian, *or* regular, green beans
2 cups julienned, peeled, seeded butternut, *or* acorn, squash
¼ cup water
1 cup reduced-fat coconut milk
2 packages (9 ounces each) mushroom, *or* herb, tortellini, cooked, warm
Salt and pepper, to taste
3 tablespoons finely chopped cilantro

Per Serving
Calories: 269
% Calories from fat: 25
Fat (gm): 8.3
Saturated fat (gm): 3
Cholesterol (mg): 30
Sodium (mg): 220
Protein (gm): 11.4
Carbohydrate (gm): 44.1
Exchanges
Milk: 0.0
Vegetable: 2.0
Fruit: 0.0
Bread: 2.0
Meat: 0.0
Fat: 1.5

1. Spray large skillet with cooking spray; heat over medium heat until hot. Saute onions, bell pepper, and garlic until tender, 3 to 4 minutes. Stir in curry powder; cook 1 to 2 minutes longer.

2. Add beans, squash, and water to skillet; heat to boiling. Reduce heat and simmer, covered, until vegetables are tender and water gone, 6 to 8 minutes. Stir in coconut milk and cook over medium heat until hot, 2 to 3 minutes. Stir in tortellini. Season to taste with salt and pepper.

3. Spoon pasta mixture into serving bowl; sprinkle with cilantro.

CURRIED PASTA AND VEGETABLES

A delicate curry sauce and angel hair pasta are combined with vegetables and garnished with chopped peanuts and mango chutney.

4 servings

Vegetable cooking spray
½ cup chopped red bell pepper
½ cup chopped yellow bell pepper
1 cup small cauliflower florets
1 cup peas, *or* cut green beans
½ teaspoon crushed red pepper
¼ cup water
Salt and pepper, to taste
2 cups (double recipe) Curry Sauce (see p. 715)
8 ounces angel hair pasta, cooked, warm
2-4 tablespoons chopped dry-roasted peanuts
2 tablespoons finely chopped cilantro
¼ cup chopped mango chutney

Per Serving
Calories: 390
% Calories from fat: 13
Fat (gm): 5.6
Saturated fat (gm): 1.1
Cholesterol (mg): 63.8
Sodium (mg): 84.7
Protein (gm): 13.6
Carbohydrate (gm): 68.7
Exchanges
Milk: 0.0
Vegetable: 2.0
Fruit: 0.5
Bread: 3.5
Meat: 0.0
Fat: 1.0

1. Spray medium skillet with cooking spray; heat over medium heat until hot. Saute bell peppers until tender, 3 to 4 minutes. Add cauliflower, peas, crushed red pepper, and water; heat to boiling. Reduce heat and simmer, covered, until vegetables are tender, 5 to 8 minutes; cook, uncovered, until water has evaporated. Season to taste with salt and pepper.

2. Toss Curry Sauce and pasta in serving bowl; spoon vegetables over and toss. Spoon pasta onto serving plates and sprinkle with peanuts and cilantro; serve a spoonful of chutney on the side of each plate.

LIGHT SUMMER PASTA

The fragrant aroma and flavor of fresh herbs and garlic accent summer ripe tomatoes in this salad.

6 side-dish servings

8 ounces spaghetti, cooked, room temperature

1 pound plum tomatoes, seeded, chopped

¾ cup (3 ounces) cubed (¼ inch) reduced-fat mozzarella cheese

3 tablespoons finely chopped fresh basil leaves, *or* 2 teaspoons dried

2 tablespoons finely chopped parsley
Garlic Vinaigrette (recipe follows)

Per Serving
Calories: 200
% Calories from fat: 30
Fat (gm): 7.6
Saturated fat (gm): 0.6
Cholesterol (mg): 5
Sodium (mg): 234
Protein (gm): 9.8
Carbohydrate (gm): 26.2
Exchanges
Milk: 0.0
Vegetable: 1.0
Fruit: 0.0
Bread: 1.5
Meat: 0.0
Fat: 1.5

1. Combine spaghetti, tomatoes, cheese, and herbs in salad bowl; pour Garlic Vinaigrette over and toss.

Garlic Vinaigrette

(makes about ⅓ cup)

3 tablespoons red wine vinegar
2 tablespoons olive oil
3 cloves garlic, minced
¼ teaspoon salt
⅛ teaspoon pepper

1. Mix all ingredients; refrigerate until serving time. Mix again before using.

MAFALDE WITH SWEET POTATOES AND KALE

Mafalde is a flat pasta with ruffled edges that looks like a miniature version of lasagne noodles. Any flat noodle or spaghetti can be substituted.

4 servings

2 medium-sized sweet potatoes, peeled, cubed (¾ inch)
Olive oil cooking spray
2 medium onions, each cut into 8 wedges, then halved
4 cloves garlic, minced
4 cups sliced kale, *or* Swiss chard
½ cup water
8 ounces mafalde, cooked, warm
2 tablespoons grated fat-free Parmesan cheese

Per Serving
Calories: 338
% Calories from fat: 4
Fat (gm): 1.5
Saturated fat (gm): 0.2
Cholesterol (mg): 0
Sodium (mg): 51
Protein (gm): 11.8
Carbohydrate (gm): 69.5
Exchanges
Milk: 0.0
Vegetable: 2.0
Fruit: 0.0
Bread: 4.0
Meat: 0.0
Fat: 0.0

1. Simmer sweet potatoes in water to cover in medium saucepan until barely tender, 5 to 8 minutes. Drain.

2. Spray large skillet with cooking spray; heat over medium heat until hot. Saute onions and garlic 2 to 3 minutes. Add potatoes, kale, and water; heat to boiling. Reduce heat and simmer, covered, until kale and potatoes are tender and water absorbed, 10 to 12 minutes.

3. Toss vegetable mixture with pasta in serving bowl; sprinkle with cheese before serving.

NOODLES WITH SWEET POTATOES AND SNOW PEAS

Fresh Chinese noodles and oriental flavors make this pasta dish special.

4 servings

Vegetable cooking spray
3 cups peeled, cubed, (½-inch) sweet potatoes
¾ cup diagonally sliced green onions and tops

Per Serving
Calories: 447
% Calories from fat: 3
Fat (gm): 1.7
Saturated fat (gm): 0.3
Cholesterol (mg): 0
Sodium (mg): 108
Protein (gm): 9.1
Carbohydrate (gm): 100.8

3 teaspoons minced garlic

1-2 teaspoons minced gingerroot

3 cups diagonally halved snow peas, strings removed

½ cup chopped red bell pepper

¾ cup canned, reduced-sodium vegetable broth

1-2 teaspoons reduced-sodium tamari soy sauce

1½ teaspoons cornstarch

Salt and pepper, to taste

1-2 teaspoons toasted sesame seeds

1 package (12 ounces) fresh Chinese-style noodles, cooked, warm

Exchanges
Milk: 0.0
Vegetable: 1.0
Fruit: 0.0
Bread: 6.0
Meat: 0.0
Fat: 0.0

1. Spray wok or large skillet with cooking spray; heat over medium heat until hot. Stir-fry potatoes, green onions, garlic, and gingerroot 2 to 3 minutes; cook, covered, over low heat until potatoes are almost tender, 10 to 12 minutes, stirring occasionally.

2. Add snow peas and bell pepper to wok; stir-fry over medium heat until peas are crisp-tender, about 5 minutes. Combine vegetable broth, soy sauce, and cornstarch; add to wok and heat to boiling. Boil, stirring constantly, until thickened, about 1 minute. Season to taste with salt and pepper.

3. Spoon vegetable mixture into serving bowl; sprinkle with sesame seeds. Serve with noodles.

PASTA WITH GREENS AND BEANS

 Mustard greens, Swiss chard, or other bitter greens can be substituted for the kale.

4 servings

1½ cups sliced onions

¾ cup chopped red bell pepper

1 tablespoon minced garlic

1-2 tablespoons olive oil

½-¾ teaspoon crushed red pepper

Per Serving
Calories: 417
% Calories from fat: 12
Fat (gm): 5.9
Saturated fat (gm): 0.7
Cholesterol (mg): 0
Sodium (mg): 282
Protein (gm): 20.6
Carbohydrate (gm): 79.8

1 can (15 ounces) cannellini, *or* Great
   Northern, beans, rinsed, drained
5 cups loosely packed sliced kale
½ cup water
   Salt and pepper, to taste
8 ounces mafalde or other flat pasta,
   cooked, warm
¼ cup grated fat-free Parmesan cheese

Exchanges
Milk: 0.0
Vegetable: 3.0
Fruit: 0.0
Bread: 4.0
Meat: 0.5
Fat: 0.5

1. Saute onions, bell pepper, and garlic in oil in large skillet until tender, 5 to 6 minutes; add crushed red pepper and cook 1 to 2 minutes longer. Add beans, kale, and water to skillet; cook, covered, over medium heat until kale is tender and liquid absorbed, about 10 minutes. Season to taste with salt and pepper.

2. Toss vegetable mixture and pasta; sprinkle with cheese and toss again.

PENNE WITH ASPARAGUS AND PLUM TOMATOES

Perfect for springtime, when asparagus is most abundant. Uncooked tomatoes and crisp-tender asparagus are tossed with warm pasta for the freshest of flavors.

4 servings

   Olive oil cooking spray
¾ cup chopped onion
½ cup chopped yellow bell pepper
1 teaspoon minced garlic
12 ounces fresh asparagus, cut into 1-inch
   pieces
3 tablespoons dry white wine, *or* water
2 cups seeded, chopped Italian plum
   tomatoes
8 ounces penne, cooked, warm
3 tablespoons finely chopped basil
   Salt and pepper, to taste
2-4 tablespoons grated fat-free Parmesan
   cheese

Per Serving
Calories: 295
% Calories from fat: 5
Fat (gm): 1.8
Saturated fat (gm): 0.3
Cholesterol (mg): 0
Sodium (mg): 45
Protein (gm): 12.1
Carbohydrate (gm): 58.0
Exchanges
Milk: 0.0
Vegetable: 2.0
Fruit: 0.0
Bread: 3.0
Meat: 0.5
Fat: 0.0

1. Spray large skillet with cooking spray; heat over medium heat until hot. Saute onion, bell pepper, and garlic until tender, about 5 minutes. Add asparagus and white wine; cook, covered, until asparagus is crisp-tender and wine evaporated, 3 to 5 minutes.

2. Toss asparagus mixture, tomatoes, pasta, and basil in serving bowl; season to taste with salt and pepper and sprinkle with Parmesan cheese.

FETTUCCINE WITH GREENS AND CARAMELIZED ONIONS

 Cajun Eggplant or Mesquite Smoked Tofu (see pp. 294, 267) would be excellent served with this pasta dish.

4 servings

4	medium onions, sliced
1	tablespoon olive oil
1	teaspoon sugar
1	can (14½ ounces) reduced-sodium vegetable broth
1½	cups water
2	cups thinly sliced kale, *or* mustard greens, *or* Swiss chard
2	cups thinly sliced curly endive, *or* spinach
	Salt and pepper, to taste
8	ounces fettuccine, cooked, warm

Per Serving
Calories: 281
% Calories from fat: 18
Fat (gm): 5.8
Saturated fat (gm): 0.5
Cholesterol (mg): 0
Sodium (mg): 151
Protein (gm): 10.3
Carbohydrate (gm): 49.9
Exchanges
Milk: 0.0
Vegetable: 2.0
Fruit: 0.0
Bread: 2.5
Meat: 0.0
Fat: 1.0

1. Cook onions in oil over medium heat in large skillet 5 minutes; reduce heat to low and stir in sugar. Cook until onions are golden in color and very soft, about 20 minutes.

2. Stir broth and water into onions; heat to boiling. Reduce heat and simmer, uncovered, until broth is reduced by ⅓, about 10 minutes. Add greens; simmer, covered, until greens are wilted, 5 to 7 minutes. Simmer, uncovered, until broth is almost absorbed, about 5 minutes. Season to taste with salt and pepper.

3. Spoon onion mixture over pasta and toss.

LINGUINE WITH FENNEL AND SUN-DRIED TOMATO PESTO

Fennel, or anise, lends a fragrant flavor to this light pasta entrée.

6 servings

Olive oil cooking spray
1 cup thinly sliced onion
1 fennel bulb, thinly sliced
¼ cup dry white wine, *or* water
Sun-Dried Tomato Pesto (recipe p. 728)
12 ounces linguine, *or* angel hair pasta, cooked, warm
Salt and pepper, to taste
Fennel tops, as garnish

Per Serving
Calories: 268
% Calories from fat: 29
Fat (gm): 9
Saturated fat (gm): 0.9
Cholesterol (mg): 0
Sodium (mg): 209
Protein (gm): 9.4
Carbohydrate (gm): 38.1
Exchanges
Milk: 0.0
Vegetable: 1.0
Fruit: 0.0
Bread: 2.0
Meat: 0.0
Fat: 2.0

1. Spray large skillet with cooking spray; heat over medium heat until hot. Add onion and fennel and saute 2 to 3 minutes. Cook, covered, over medium-low heat until onion is very soft, 10 to 15 minutes. Stir in wine and simmer, covered, 15 to 20 minutes or until wine is almost gone.

2. Spoon onion mixture and Sun-Dried Tomato Pesto over pasta in serving bowl and toss. Add salt and pepper, to taste; garnish with fennel tops.

ZITI WITH GREMOLATA

The fresh lemon flavor of the Gremolata accents this tomato and pasta dish. Serve with Garlic Bread (see p. 676) and a robust red wine.

8 servings

Olive oil cooking spray
½ cup chopped onion
8 ounces shiitake, *or* cremini, mushrooms, sliced
2 cans (14½ ounces each) diced tomatoes with Italian seasoning, undrained
Salt and pepper, to taste
1 pound ziti, *or* penne, cooked, warm
Gremolata (see p. 731)

Per Serving
Calories: 268
% Calories from fat: 4
Fat (gm): 1.2
Saturated fat (gm): 0.2
Cholesterol (mg): 0
Sodium (mg): 227
Protein (gm): 9.3
Carbohydrate (gm): 53.8
Exchanges
Milk: 0.0
Vegetable: 2.0
Fruit: 0.0
Bread: 3.0
Meat: 0.0
Fat: 0.0

1. Spray large skillet with cooking spray; heat over medium heat until hot. Saute onion and mushrooms until tender, 5 to 8 minutes. Add tomatoes and heat to boiling; reduce heat and simmer, uncovered, until thickened, about 10 minutes. Season to taste with salt and pepper.

2. Toss pasta with tomato mixture and half the Gremolata; pass remaining Gremolata to be added as desired.

PASTA WITH GOAT'S CHEESE AND ONION CONFIT

Try this dish with flavored specialty pastas such as dried mushroom, herb, or black pepper.

4 servings

Olive oil cooking spray
4 cups thinly sliced onions
1 teaspoon minced garlic
½ teaspoon dried sage leaves
½ teaspoon dried rosemary leaves
1 teaspoon sugar
½ cup dry white wine, *or* fat-free milk
2 ounces fat-free cream cheese
2 ounces goat's cheese
Salt and pepper, to taste
8 ounces whole wheat, *or* plain, thin spaghetti, cooked
2-3 tablespoons coarsely chopped walnuts
Sage, *or* rosemary, sprigs, as garnish

Per Serving
Calories: 395
% Calories from fat: 15
Fat (gm): 6.7
Saturated fat (gm): 2.4
Cholesterol (mg): 6.5
Sodium (mg): 144
Protein (gm): 16
Carbohydrate (gm): 66.9
Exchanges
Milk: 0.0
Vegetable: 2.0
Fruit: 0.0
Bread: 4.0
Meat: 0.5
Fat: 0.5

1. Spray large skillet with cooking spray; heat over medium heat until hot. Add onions; cook, covered, over medium-low to low heat until onions are very soft, about 30 minutes.

2. Stir garlic, sage, rosemary, and sugar into onions; cook, uncovered, over medium-low to low heat until onions are caramelized and brown, 15 to 20 minutes. Stir in wine; simmer 2 to 3 minutes longer. Stir in cream cheese and goat's cheese; cook over low heat, stirring, until melted. Season to taste with salt and white pepper.

3. Toss pasta and onion mixture on serving platter. Sprinkle with walnuts and garnish with herb sprigs.

FETTUCCINE WITH ROASTED GARLIC, ONIONS, AND PEPPERS

A dish that is deceptively simple to make, incredibly delicious to eat.

8 side-dish servings

2 bulbs garlic
Olive oil cooking spray
3 medium onions, cut into wedges
2 large red bell peppers, cut into ½-inch slices
2 tablespoons olive oil, *or* vegetable oil
2 tablespoons lemon juice
2 tablespoons finely chopped parsley
½ teaspoon salt
¼ teaspoon pepper
8 ounces fettuccine, cooked, warm

Per Serving
Calories: 151
% Calories from fat: 26
Fat (gm): 4.5
Saturated fat (gm): 0.5
Cholesterol (mg): 0
Sodium (mg): 184
Protein (gm): 5
Carbohydrate (gm): 24.4
Exchanges
Milk: 0.0
Vegetable: 1.5
Fruit: 0.0
Bread: 1.0
Meat: 0.0
Fat: 1.0

1. Heat oven to 400 degrees. Cut a scant ½ inch off tops of garlic bulbs, exposing ends of cloves. Wrap garlic bulbs loosely in aluminum foil. Spray jelly roll pan with cooking spray. Arrange garlic, onions, and bell peppers on pan. Bake vegetables, uncovered, until garlic is very soft and vegetables are tender, 15 to 20 minutes.

2. Cool garlic slightly; squeeze pulp into small bowl. Stir in oil, lemon juice, parsley, salt, and pepper. Spoon garlic mixture over pasta and toss; add onions and peppers and toss. Serve warm.

BUCATINI WITH BRUSSELS SPROUTS AND WALNUTS

Bucatini is a spaghetti-type pasta with a hole in the center. Plain spaghetti can be used.

4 servings

Vegetable cooking spray
2 teaspoons minced garlic
12 ounces Brussels sprouts, cooked crisp-tender, cut into halves

Per Serving
Calories: 367
% Calories from fat: 16
Fat (gm): 6.7
Saturated fat (gm): 0.7
Cholesterol (mg): 0
Sodium (mg): 118
Protein (gm): 14.9
Carbohydrate (gm): 65.4

8 ounces bucatini, *or* spaghetti, cooked, warm

2 cups seeded, chopped Italian plum tomatoes

⅔ cup minced parsley

¼ cup plain breadcrumbs, toasted

¼ cup chopped walnuts

2-4 tablespoons grated fat-free Parmesan cheese

Salt and pepper, to taste

Exchanges
Milk: 0.0
Vegetable: 3.0
Fruit: 0.0
Bread: 3.0
Meat: 0.5
Fat: 1.0

1. Spray skillet with cooking spray; heat over medium heat until hot. Saute garlic 1 to 2 minutes; add Brussels sprouts and cook 2 to 3 minutes longer.

2. Toss pasta with sprouts mixture, tomatoes, parsley, breadcrumbs, walnuts, and Parmesan cheese in serving bowl; season to taste with salt and pepper.

STAR PASTA WITH CARROTS AND GINGER CREAM

 Fresh gingerroot can be very hot in flavor; add more, or less, according to your taste preference. Gingerroot does not have to be peeled before using.

4 servings

1 medium shallot, finely chopped

1 tablespoon minced gingerroot

1 teaspoon margarine, *or* butter

1 cup finely chopped carrots

⅓ cup chopped red bell pepper

½ cup dry white wine

2 tablespoons flour

1 cup fat-free half-and-half, *or* fat-free milk

Salt and pepper, to taste

8 ounces stelline (small star-shaped pasta), *or* orzo, cooked, warm

Cilantro, finely chopped, *or* parsley, as garnish

Per Serving
Calories: 322
% Calories from fat: 6
Fat (gm): 2.1
Saturated fat (gm): 0.3
Cholesterol (mg): 0
Sodium (mg): 84
Protein (gm): 10
Carbohydrate (gm): 58.0
Exchanges
Milk: 0.5
Vegetable: 1.0
Fruit: 0.0
Bread: 3.0
Meat: 0.0
Fat: 1.0

1. Saute shallot and gingerroot in margarine in medium skillet 2 minutes. Stir in carrots, bell pepper, and wine; heat to boiling. Reduce heat and simmer, covered, until vegetables are crisp-tender, 8 to 10 minutes. Cook, uncovered, over medium to medium-high heat until wine has evaporated.

2. Sprinkle flour over vegetables; cook, stirring constantly, 1 to 2 minutes. Stir in half-and-half and heat to boiling. Boil, stirring constantly, until thickened, about 1 minute. Season to taste with salt and pepper. Stir in pasta.

3. Spoon pasta into serving bowl; sprinkle generously with cilantro.

LINGUINE WITH JULIENNED VEGETABLES AND RED PEPPER PESTO

 Any of the pestos (see pp. 727-731) would be excellent in this recipe.

4 servings

Olive oil cooking spray
2 cups julienned zucchini
2 cups peeled, seeded, julienned yellow winter squash, *or* sweet potatoes
½ cup julienned fennel bulb
¼ cup thinly sliced green onions and tops
Salt and pepper, to taste
8 ounces linguine, cooked, warm
Red Pepper Pesto (see p. 729)
2 tablespoons grated fat-free Parmesan cheese

Per Serving
Calories: 335
% Calories from fat: 32
Fat (gm): 12.6
Saturated fat (gm): 1.4
Cholesterol (mg): 0
Sodium (mg): 170
Protein (gm): 13
Carbohydrate (gm): 46.8
Exchanges
Milk: 0.0
Vegetable: 1.0
Fruit: 0.0
Bread: 2.5
Meat: 0.5
Fat: 2.0

1. Spray large skillet with cooking spray; heat over medium heat until hot. Saute zucchini, squash, fennel, and green onions until tender, 8 to 10 minutes. Season to taste with salt and pepper.

2. Toss linguine with Red Pepper Pesto in serving bowl; spoon vegetables over linguine and toss. Sprinkle with Parmesan cheese.

FUSILLI WITH TOMATOES AND CORN

A perfect salad, especially when homegrown tomatoes, corn, and basil are available!

8 side-dish servings

2 cups chopped plum tomatoes
1 cup fresh, *or* frozen, whole-kernel corn, cooked
½ cup sliced green onions and tops
2⅔ cups (6 ounces) fusilli (spirals), *or* corkscrews, cooked, room temperature
Fresh Basil Dressing (recipe follows)

Per Serving
Calories: 135
% Calories from fat: 26
Fat (gm): 4
Saturated fat (gm): 0.6
Cholesterol (mg): 0
Sodium (mg): 141
Protein (gm): 4.1
Carbohydrate (gm): 21.8
Exchanges
Milk: 0.0
Vegetable: 1.0
Fruit: 0.0
Bread: 1.0
Meat: 0.0
Fat: 1.0

1. Combine tomatoes, corn, green onions, and pasta in salad bowl; pour Fresh Basil Dressing over and toss.

Fresh Basil Dressing

(makes about ¼ cup)

⅓ cup red wine vinegar
2 tablespoons olive oil, *or* canola oil
3 tablespoons finely chopped fresh basil leaves, *or* 1½ teaspoons dried
2 cloves garlic, minced
½ teaspoon salt
¼ teaspoon pepper

1. Mix all ingredients; refrigerate until serving time. Stir before using.

"LITTLE EARS" WITH SMOKED TEMPEH AND VEGETABLES

 Smoked Tofu can be used in place of the tempeh, if desired. Smoked tofu can also be purchased in health food and specialty stores.

4 servings

2	packages (8 ounces each) tempeh
3	cups broccoli florets, steamed
1	medium yellow, *or* green, bell pepper, sliced
12	cherry tomatoes, cut into halves
2	cups (8 ounces) "little ears," *or* small pasta shells, cooked
	Mustard Seed Vinaigrette (recipe follows)

Per Serving
Calories: 374
% Calories from fat: 27
Fat (gm): 11.7
Saturated fat (gm): 1.8
Cholesterol (mg): 0
Sodium (mg): 196
Protein (gm): 23.2
Carbohydrate (gm): 47.8
Exchanges
Milk: 0.0
Vegetable: 2.0
Fruit: 0.0
Bread: 2.5
Meat: 2.0
Fat: 1.0

1. Smoke tempeh according to directions in Smoked Tofu recipe (see p. 267); cut tempeh into ¾-inch cubes. Combine tempeh, vegetables, and pasta in serving bowl; pour Mustard Seed Vinaigrette over and toss.

Mustard Seed Vinaigrette

 (makes about ⅓ cup)

2	tablespoons olive oil
2	tablespoons white wine vinegar
2	tablespoons lemon juice
2	medium shallots, finely chopped
2	cloves garlic, finely chopped
¾	teaspoon mustard seeds, crushed
½	teaspoon salt
¼	teaspoon pepper

1. Mix all ingredients; refrigerate until serving time. Stir before using.

FARFALLE WITH ROASTED EGGPLANT AND SQUASH

 In warm summer months, the vegetables can be roasted in advance and the dish served at room temperature.

4 servings

Olive oil cooking spray

4 cups unpeeled, cubed eggplant (1-inch cubes)

4 cups peeled, cubed butternut squash (1-inch cubes)

6 Italian plum tomatoes, each cut lengthwise into 4 wedges

1 large green bell pepper, cut into 1-inch slices

2 teaspoons dried rosemary leaves

1 teaspoon dried tarragon leaves

Salt and pepper, to taste

8 ounces farfalle (bow ties), *or* linguine, cooked, warm

2-3 tablespoon grated fat-free Parmesan cheese

Per Serving
Calories: 376
% Calories from fat: 5
Fat (gm): 2.2
Saturated fat (gm): 0.3
Cholesterol (mg): 0
Sodium (mg): 51.3
Protein (gm): 12.9
Carbohydrate (gm): 81.7
Exchanges
Milk: 0.0
Vegetable: 2.0
Fruit: 0.0
Bread: 4.5
Meat: 0.0
Fat: 0.0

1. Spray aluminum-foil-lined jelly roll pan with cooking spray. Arrange vegetables in single layer on pan; spray generously with cooking spray and sprinkle with herbs. Roast vegetables at 425 degrees until tender and browned, about 40 minutes. Sprinkle very lightly with salt and pepper.

2. Sprinkle pasta with Parmesan cheese in serving bowl and toss; add vegetables and toss.

TAGLIATELLE WITH CHILI-MUSHROOM STROGANOFF SAUCE

Shiitake mushrooms and dried ancho chilies add special flavor accents to this aromatic pasta sauce. The chilies can be quite hot, so adjust amount according to your taste.

6 servings

1	package (1¾ ounces) dried shiitake mushrooms
1-2	dried ancho chilies
3	cups boiling water, divided
2	cups Basic Vegetable Stock (see p. 58), *or* reduced-sodium canned vegetable broth, divided
1	cup chopped onion
8	ounces white mushrooms, halved or quartered
2	teaspoons margarine, *or* butter
¼	cup all-purpose flour
½	teaspoon dried thyme leaves
1	cup fat-free sour cream
1	teaspoon Dijon-style mustard
	Salt and pepper, to taste
12	ounces tagliatelle (flat pasta), *or* fettuccine, cooked, warm
	Parsley, minced, as garnish

Per Serving
Calories: 321
% Calories from fat: 8
Fat (gm): 2.8
Saturated fat (gm): 0.5
Cholesterol (mg): 0
Sodium (mg): 58
Protein (gm): 12.5
Carbohydrate (gm): 62.8
Exchanges
Milk: 0.0
Vegetable: 3.0
Fruit: 0.0
Bread: 3.0
Meat: 0.0
Fat: 0.5

1. Place shiitake mushrooms and chilies in separate bowls; pour 2 cups boiling water over the mushrooms and 1 cup over the chilies. Let stand until vegetables are softened, about 15 minutes.

2. Drain mushrooms, reserving liquid. Remove tough centers from mushrooms and slice. Drain chilies, discarding liquid. Process chilies and 1 cup stock in blender or food processor until smooth.

3. Saute onion and shiitake and white mushrooms in margarine in large skillet until wilted, about 5 minutes. Stir in flour; cook 1 minute longer, stirring frequently. Stir in reserved mushroom liquid, chili mixture, remaining 1 cup stock, and thyme.

Heat to boiling; reduce heat and simmer, covered, until shiitake mushrooms are tender, 10 to 15 minutes. Simmer, uncovered, if necessary, until thickened.

4. Stir in sour cream and mustard; cook until hot through, 2 to 3 minutes. Season to taste with salt and pepper. Toss pasta with sauce in serving bowl; sprinkle generously with parsley.

SOUTHWEST PASTA WITH CILANTRO PESTO

If poblano peppers are not available, substitute green bell peppers and add ½ to 1 teaspoon finely chopped jalapeño pepper to the onions when sauteing. Dried cilantro is not an acceptable substitute for the fresh; if not available, substitute another pesto (see Index).

6 servings

3	medium zucchini, sliced
3	cups peeled, cubed acorn squash
1	medium onion, sliced
3	poblano peppers, sliced
1-1 ½	teaspoons dried oregano leaves
¼-½	teaspoon ground cumin
1	tablespoon olive oil
¾	cup reduced-sodium vegetable broth
2	medium tomatoes, cut into wedges
	Salt and pepper, to taste
12	ounces fettuccine, *or* other flat pasta, cooked, warm
	Cilantro Pesto (see p. 730)

Per Serving
Calories: 408
% Calories from fat: 21
Fat (gm): 10
Saturated fat (gm): 2
Cholesterol (mg): 3.3
Sodium (mg): 196
Protein (gm): 13.8
Carbohydrate (gm): 69.5
Exchanges
Milk: 0.0
Vegetable: 2.0
Fruit: 0.0
Bread: 4.0
Meat: 0.0
Fat: 1.5

1. Saute zucchini and acorn squash, onion, poblano peppers, oregano, and cumin in oil in large skillet 3 minutes; add broth and heat to boiling. Reduce heat and simmer, covered, until acorn squash is crisp-tender, about 5 minutes. Add tomato wedges; cook, covered, until tomatoes soften, 3 to 4 minutes. Season to taste with salt and pepper.

2. Toss fettuccine with Cilantro Pesto; spoon onto serving platter and top with vegetable mixture.

PASTA SANTA FE

Flavors of the Southwest, picante with poblano peppers. If poblano peppers are not available, substitute green bell peppers and add a finely chopped jalapeño chili to the onions when sauteing.

4 servings

1 medium onion, sliced

3 cloves garlic, minced

2 tablespoons canola oil

2 medium zucchini, sliced

2 medium tomatoes, cut into wedges

2 poblano chilies, sliced

1 cup fresh, *or* frozen, thawed, whole-kernel corn

2 tablespoons chili powder

1 teaspoon dried oregano leaves

½ teaspoon ground cumin

2 tablespoons minced cilantro, *or* parsley

½ teaspoon salt

¼ teaspoon pepper

8 ounces *trio maliano* (combination of corkscrews, shells, and rigatoni), cooked, warm

Per Serving
Calories: 350
% Calories from fat: 24
Fat (gm): 9.6
Saturated fat (gm): 1.2
Cholesterol (mg): 0
Sodium (mg): 327
Protein (gm): 11.6
Carbohydrate (gm): 58
Exchanges
Milk: 0.0
Vegetable: 2.0
Fruit: 0.0
Bread: 3.0
Meat: 0.0
Fat: 2.0

1. Saute onion and garlic in oil in large skillet until tender, about 5 minutes. Add remaining vegetables, chili powder, oregano, and cumin. Cook, uncovered, over medium to medium-low heat until vegetables are crisp-tender, 12 to 15 minutes. Stir in cilantro, salt, and pepper.

2. Spoon vegetable mixture over pasta and toss.

PASTA SKILLET CAKES

A great recipe for using leftover pasta! Any flat pasta can be used.

4 servings

1 cup cooked linguine, *or* spaghetti, cut into ½-inch pieces
2 eggs
2 egg whites
½ cup dry plain breadcrumbs
½ cup shredded sweet potato
½ cup shredded zucchini
½ cup finely chopped red bell pepper
¼ cup finely chopped onion
2 tablespoons finely chopped parsley
½ teaspoon dried tarragon, *or* cilantro
1 small jalapeño chili, finely chopped
¼ teaspoon salt
¼ teaspoon white pepper
⅛ teaspoon cayenne pepper
　Vegetable cooking spray
　Lemon Herb Mayonnaise (see p. 733)

Per Serving
Calories: 237
% Calories from fat: 15
Fat (gm): 4.1
Saturated fat (gm): 1
Cholesterol (mg): 106.5
Sodium (mg): 745
Protein (gm): 11
Carbohydrate (gm): 39.7
Exchanges
Milk: 0.0
Vegetable: 2.0
Fruit: 0.0
Bread: 2.0
Meat: 0.0
Fat: 1.0

1. Mix all ingredients, except cooking spray and Lemon Herb Mayonnaise in bowl.

2. Spray 7- or 8-inch skillet with cooking spray; heat over medium heat until hot. Spoon half the mixture into skillet, pressing into an even layer with a pancake turner. Cook over medium heat until browned on the bottom, 3 to 4 minutes. Invert cake onto plate; slide cake back into skillet and cook until browned on the bottom, 3 to 4 minutes. Repeat with remaining mixture.

3. Cut cakes into halves; serve with Lemon Herb Mayonnaise.

MOLDED CAPELLINI CARBONARA

Thin spaghetti or linguine can be substituted for the capellini (angel hair pasta). Fill the center of the mold with a mixture of vegetables, such as the asparagus and tomato mixture in Penne with Asparagus and Plum Tomatoes (see p. 336).

4 servings

Olive oil cooking spray

¼ cup minced shallot

1 teaspoon minced garlic

1 cup seeded, chopped, Italian plum tomatoes

¼ teaspoon crushed red pepper

½ teaspoon dried oregano leaves

2 tablespoons all-vegetable bacon-flavored bits

Salt and pepper, to taste

8 ounces capellini (angel hair pasta), cooked

2 eggs, beaten

2 egg whites, beaten

Per Serving
Calories: 292
% Calories from fat: 14
Fat (gm): 4.5
Saturated fat (gm): 1.1
Cholesterol (mg): 106.5
Sodium (mg): 148
Protein (gm): 13.8
Carbohydrate (gm): 48.5
Exchanges
Milk: 0.0
Vegetable: 1.0
Fruit: 0.0
Bread: 3.0
Meat: 1.0
Fat: 0.0

1. Spray skillet with cooking spray; heat over medium heat until hot. Saute shallot and garlic until tender, 3 to 4 minutes. Add tomatoes, crushed red pepper, and oregano. Cook, covered, over medium heat until tomatoes soften, about 5 minutes. Stir in "bacon" bits; season to taste with salt and pepper.

2. Combine vegetable mixture, pasta, and eggs; spoon into greased 6-cup ring mold. Bake, uncovered, at 350 degrees until set, about 20 minutes. Invert onto serving plate.

POTATO GNOCCHI WITH SAGE CREAM

Fat-free half-and-half is the secret to the rich creaminess of the sauce in this dish.

6 servings

		Per Serving

2 cups fat-free half-and-half, *or* fat-free milk

16-20 medium sage leaves, thinly sliced, *or* ¾ teaspoon dried sage leaves

1 cup chopped onion

2 teaspoons margarine, *or* butter

4 cups small broccoflower florets

½ cup water, divided

2 tablespoons all-purpose flour

½ teaspoon ground nutmeg

1 package (16 ounces) potato gnocchi, cooked, warm

Salt and pepper, to taste

Fat-free Parmesan cheese, grated, as garnish

Per Serving
Calories: 263
% Calories from fat: 2
Fat (gm): 0.6
Saturated fat (gm): 0.2
Cholesterol (mg): 0.9
Sodium (mg): 150
Protein (gm): 13.4
Carbohydrate (gm): 52.4
Exchanges
Milk: 0.0
Vegetable: 2.0
Fruit: 0.0
Bread: 2.5
Meat: 0.0
Fat: 0.0

1. Heat half-and-half and sage leaves (if using dried sage, tie leaves in small cheesecloth bag) to boiling in medium saucepan; reduce heat and simmer 10 minutes. Strain, discarding sage.

2. Saute onion in margarine in large skillet 2 to 3 minutes; add broccoflower and ¼ cup water and heat to boiling. Reduce heat and simmer, covered, until broccoflower is tender and water gone, 5 to 8 minutes.

3. Heat half-and-half mixture to boiling. Mix flour, nutmeg, and remaining ¼ cup water; whisk into half-and-half. Boil, whisking constantly, until thickened, about 1 minute.

4. Pour sauce over vegetables in skillet; mix in gnocchi and season to taste with salt and pepper. Spoon into serving bowl; sprinkle very lightly with Parmesan cheese.

SPINACH GNOCCHI PRIMAVERA

Gnocchi, or dumplings, are often made from potatoes. This spinach version is a delicious variation.

6 servings (3 gnocchi each)

Vegetable cooking spray
½ cup chopped onion
2 cloves garlic, minced
3 packages (10 ounces each) frozen chopped spinach, thawed
⅔ cup all-purpose flour
1 cup reduced-fat ricotta cheese
½ cup grated fat-free Parmesan cheese
1 egg
¼ teaspoon ground nutmeg
½ teaspoon salt (optional)
½ teaspoon pepper
¼ cup all-purpose flour
Primavera Sauce (see p. 714)

Per Serving
Calories: 342
% Calories from fat: 28
Fat (gm): 11.2
Saturated fat (gm): 3.3
Cholesterol (mg): 50.1
Sodium (mg): 482
Protein (gm): 19.8
Carbohydrate (gm): 42.5
Exchanges
Milk: 0.0
Vegetable: 3.0
Fruit: 0.0
Bread: 2.0
Meat: 1.0
Fat: 1.5

1. Spray large skillet with cooking spray; heat over medium heat until hot. Saute onion and garlic until tender, about 5 minutes. Stir in spinach. Cook over medium heat until spinach mixture is quite dry, about 8 minutes, stirring frequently.

2. Stir ⅔ cup flour into spinach. Stir in cheeses, egg, nutmeg, salt, and pepper; cool. Spread ¼ cup flour on a plate. Drop 2 tablespoons spinach mixture into flour; roll into ball. Repeat with remaining spinach mixture, making 18 gnocchi.

3. Heat 3 quarts water to boiling in large saucepan. Add gnocchi to saucepan. Reduce heat and simmer, uncovered, until gnocchi float to surface, about 10 minutes.

4. Toss gnocchi and Primavera Sauce in serving bowl.

SHELLS STUFFED WITH SPINACH AND TOFU

Firm tofu substitutes for ricotta cheese in the deliciously skinny pasta shells. Marinara Sauce or Tomato Sauce with Mushrooms and Sherry (see pp. 700, 703) can be substituted for the Fresh Tomato-Basil Sauce.

4 servings (5 shells each)

Olive oil cooking spray

1½ cups chopped onions

6 cloves garlic, minced

1 package (10 ounces) spinach leaves, torn

¾ cup finely chopped parsley

1½ teaspoons dried basil leaves

½ package (14-ounce size) firm tofu, finely chopped

1½ cups (6 ounces) shredded fat-free mozzarella cheese

2 tablespoons grated fat-free Parmesan cheese

20 jumbo pasta shells (6 ounces), cooked until *al dente*

2 cups (½ recipe) Fresh Tomato-Basil Sauce (see p. 702)

Per Serving
Calories: 395
% Calories from fat: 9
Fat (gm): 4
Saturated fat (gm): 0.3
Cholesterol (mg): 0
Sodium (mg): 579
Protein (gm): 32.1
Carbohydrate (gm): 58.6
Exchanges
Milk: 0.0
Vegetable: 3.0
Fruit: 0.0
Bread: 2.5
Meat: 2.5
Fat: 0.0

1. Spray skillet with cooking spray; heat over medium heat until hot. Saute onions and garlic until transparent, 3 to 5 minutes.

2. Wash spinach; add to skillet with water clinging to leaves. Add parsley and basil and cook, covered, over medium heat until spinach is wilted, 3 to 5 minutes. Remove from heat and cool slightly. Stir in tofu and cheeses.

3. Stuff each shell with about 3 tablespoons tofu-cheese mixture. Arrange shells in baking pan and spoon Fresh Tomato-Basil Sauce over. Bake at 350 degrees, loosely covered, until hot through, 20 to 25 minutes.

VEGETABLE MANICOTTI WITH CREAMED SPINACH SAUCE

Three-Onion Sauce and Tomato Sauce with Mushrooms and Sherry (see pp.712, 703) are also excellent accompaniments for this dish.

4 servings (3 manicotti each)

Olive oil cooking spray
½ cup chopped onion
3 cloves garlic, minced
2 cups loosely packed, chopped spinach leaves
½ cup chopped zucchini
¼ cup chopped yellow summer squash
1 teaspoon dried basil leaves
1 teaspoon dried oregano leaves
¾ cup fat-free ricotta cheese
Salt and pepper, to taste
1 package (8 ounces) manicotti, cooked, room temperature
Creamed Spinach Sauce (see p. 712)

Per Serving
Calories: 476
% Calories from fat: 20
Fat (gm): 10.9
Saturated fat (gm): 3.6
Cholesterol (mg): 13.5
Sodium (mg): 431
Protein (gm): 26.1
Carbohydrate (gm): 72.4
Exchanges
Milk: 1.0
Vegetable: 2.0
Fruit: 0.0
Bread: 3.0
Meat: 1.0
Fat: 1.5

1. Spray large skillet with cooking spray; heat over medium heat until hot. Saute onion and garlic until tender, about 3 minutes. Add remaining vegetables; saute until tender, 5 to 8 minutes. Stir in herbs and cook 2 minutes more. Stir in cheese; season to taste with salt and pepper.

2. Spoon about 3 tablespoons cheese and vegetable mixture into each manicotto; arrange in baking pan. Spoon Creamed Spinach Sauce over manicotti. Bake at 350 degrees, loosely covered with aluminum foil, until manicotti are hot through and sauce is bubbly, 35 to 40 minutes.

MUSHROOM-BROCCOLI MANICOTTI

 Any pasta that is going to be filled and baked should be cooked only until al dente so that the completed dish is not overcooked.

4 servings (3 manicotti each)

Olive oil cooking spray

4 shallots, *or* green onions and tops, chopped

3 cloves garlic, minced

2 cups sliced mushrooms

2 cups finely chopped, cooked broccoli

2 teaspoons dried basil leaves

1 teaspoon dried marjoram leaves

1 cup reduced-fat ricotta cheese

¼ teaspoon salt

¼ teaspoon pepper

1 package (8 ounces) manicotti, cooked, room temperature

Tomato Sauce with Mushrooms and Sherry (see p. 703)

Per Serving
Calories: 394
% Calories from fat: 17
Fat (gm): 7.8
Saturated fat (gm): 0.8
Cholesterol (mg): 7.9
Sodium (mg): 665
Protein (gm): 19.2
Carbohydrate (gm): 63.4
Exchanges
Milk: 0.0
Vegetable: 4.0
Fruit: 0.0
Bread: 3.0
Meat: 0.0
Fat: 1.5

1. Spray large skillet with cooking spray; heat over medium heat until hot. Saute shallots and garlic until tender, 2 to 3 minutes. Add mushrooms; cook, covered, until mushrooms release juices, 3 to 5 minutes. Cook, uncovered, over medium to medium-high heat, until liquid is gone, about 10 minutes. Stir in broccoli, basil, and marjoram; cook 2 to 3 minutes. Stir in cheese, salt, and pepper.

2. Heat oven to 350 degrees. Spoon about 3 tablespoons vegetable-cheese mixture into each manicotto; arrange in baking pan. Spoon Tomato Sauce with Mushrooms and Sherry over manicotti. Bake, loosely covered with aluminum foil, until manicotti are hot through and sauce is bubbly, 30 to 35 minutes.

CHEESE AND VEGETABLE ROTOLI WITH FRESH TOMATO AND HERB SAUCE

 Serve the rotoli whole, or cut each into thirds, arranging the slices cut sides up on the tomato sauce.

4 servings

½ cup chopped onion

½ cup chopped carrot

½ cup chopped mushrooms

2 cloves garlic, minced

1 teaspoon dried basil leaves

1 teaspoon olive oil, *or* canola oil

2 cups small broccoli florets, cooked until crisp-tender

¾ cup fat-free ricotta cheese

½ package (8-ounce size) fat-free cream cheese, softened

¼ cup grated Parmesan cheese

½ cup (2 ounces) shredded reduced-fat mozzarella cheese

½ teaspoon salt (optional)

½ teaspoon pepper

8 lasagne noodles (8 ounces), cooked *al dente*

1½ cups (½ recipe) Fresh Tomato and Herb Sauce (see p. 702)

Parsley sprigs, as garnish

Per Serving
Calories: 335
% Calories from fat: 25
Fat (gm): 9.5
Saturated fat (gm): 3.2
Cholesterol (mg): 12.5
Sodium (mg): 585
Protein (gm): 24.1
Carbohydrate (gm): 41.1
Exchanges
Milk: 0.0
Vegetable: 3.0
Fruit: 0.0
Bread: 2.0
Meat: 1.5
Fat: 1.0

1. Saute onion, carrot, mushrooms, garlic, and basil in oil in large skillet until tender; stir in broccoli.

2. Process sauteed vegetables, all cheeses, salt (if using), and pepper in food processor, using pulse technique, until cheeses are mixed and vegetables are finely chopped.

3. Spread about ⅓ cup vegetable-cheese mixture on 1 lasagne noodle; roll up and place, seam side down, in lightly greased 13 x 9-inch baking pan. Repeat with remaining noodles and vegetable-cheese mixture. Bake at 350 degrees, loosely covered with aluminum foil, until hot, 30 to 40 minutes.

4. Serve rotoli whole or, if desired, cut each rotolo into 3 pieces. Spoon about ⅓ cup Fresh Tomato and Herb Sauce on each plate; arrange rotoli on sauce. Garnish with parsley.

ARTICHOKE RAVIOLI WITH TARRAGON SAUCE

Roasted Red Pepper Sauce or Fresh Tomato and Herb Sauce (see pp. 709, 702) would also be flavorful sauce selections for the ravioli.

4 servings (4 ravioli each)

Olive oil cooking spray

1 package (9 ounces) frozen artichoke hearts, thawed, cooked, finely chopped

¼ cup finely chopped onion

2-3 cloves garlic, minced

⅛-¼ teaspoon ground nutmeg

3 tablespoons dry white wine, *or* water

32 wonton wrappers

Water

Tarragon Sauce (recipe follows)

Per Serving
Calories: 277
% Calories from fat: 4
Fat (gm): 1.3
Saturated fat (gm): 0.2
Cholesterol (mg): 8
Sodium (mg): 579
Protein (gm): 9.4
Carbohydrate (gm): 49.8
Exchanges
Milk: 0.0
Vegetable: 3.0
Fruit: 0.0
Bread: 2.5
Meat: 0.0
Fat: 0.0

1. Spray large skillet with cooking spray; heat over medium heat until hot. Add artichoke hearts, onion, garlic, nutmeg, and wine. Cook over medium heat until liquid is gone, about 5 minutes. Cool.

2. Place about 1 tablespoon artichoke mixture on wonton wrapper; brush edges of wrapper with water. Top with second wonton wrapper and press edges together to seal. Repeat with remaining wonton wrappers and artichoke mixture.

3. Heat about 2 quarts water to boiling in large saucepan; add 4 to 6 ravioli. Reduce heat and simmer, uncovered, until ravioli float to surface and are *al dente*, 3 to 4 minutes. Remove ravioli with slotted spoon; repeat cooking procedure with remaining ravioli. Serve with Tarragon Sauce.

Tarragon Sauce

(makes about 1 cup)

> 2 medium shallots, finely chopped
> 1 tablespoon finely chopped fresh tarragon leaves, *or* ½ teaspoon dried
> ½ cup dry white wine, *or* Canned Vegetable Stock (see p. 63)
> 1 cup Canned Vegetable Stock (see p. 63), divided
> 1 tablespoon flour
> ¼ teaspoon salt
> ⅛ teaspoon ground white pepper

1. Heat shallots, tarragon, and wine to boiling in small saucepan; reduce heat and simmer, uncovered, until mixture is reduced to ¼ cup.

2. Add ½ cup stock; heat to boiling. Mix flour and remaining ½ cup stock; stir into boiling mixture. Boil until thickened (sauce will be thin), stirring constantly. Stir in salt and pepper.

SWEET POTATO RAVIOLI WITH CURRY SAUCE

A light curry-flavored sauce is a delicate accompaniment to this unusual ravioli.

4 servings (4 ravioli each)

> 1 cup cooked, mashed sweet potatoes
> 2 small cloves garlic, minced
> ½-¾ teaspoon ground ginger
> Salt and pepper, to taste
> 32 wonton wrappers
> Water
> Curry Sauce (see p. 715)

Per Serving
Calories: 323
% Calories from fat: 4
Fat (gm): 1.5
Saturated fat (gm): 0.3
Cholesterol (mg): 8
Sodium (mg): 387
Protein (gm): 8.9
Carbohydrate (gm): 65.7
Exchanges
Milk: 0.0
Vegetable: 0.5
Fruit: 0.0
Bread: 4.0
Meat: 0.0
Fat: 0.0

1. Mix sweet potatoes, garlic, and ginger; season to taste with salt and pepper. Spoon about 1 tablespoon potato mixture onto wonton wrapper; brush edges of wrapper with water. Top with second wonton wrapper and press edges together to seal. Repeat with remaining wonton wrappers and potato mixture.

2. Heat about 2 quarts water to boiling in large saucepan; add 4 to 6 ravioli. Reduce heat and simmer, uncovered, until ravioli float to surface and are *al dente*, 3 to 4 minutes. Remove ravioli with slotted spoon; repeat cooking procedure with remaining ravioli. Serve with Curry Sauce.

"SAUSAGE" AND HERBED-CHEESE RAVIOLI WITH WILD MUSHROOM SAUCE

4 servings (4 ravioli each)

Olive oil cooking spray
¼ package (8-ounce size) frozen, thawed, Italian-style all-vegetable "sausage" patties, crumbled
1 small onion, minced
2 cloves garlic, minced
1 cup reduced-fat ricotta cheese
1 teaspoon dried rosemary leaves
32 wonton wrappers
Water
Wild Mushroom Sauce (see p. 717)

Per Serving
Calories: 332
% Calories from fat: 9
Fat (gm): 3.3
Saturated fat (gm): 0.2
Cholesterol (mg): 16
Sodium (mg): 502
Protein (gm): 14.3
Carbohydrate (gm): 56.7
Exchanges
Milk: 0.0
Vegetable: 2.0
Fruit: 0.0
Bread: 3.0
Meat: 1.0
Fat: 0.0

1. Spray small skillet with cooking spray; heat over medium heat until hot. Saute "sausage," onion, and garlic until onion is tender, about 5 minutes. Remove from heat and mix in ricotta cheese and rosemary.

2. Place about 1 tablespoon cheese mixture on wonton wrapper; brush edges of wrapper with water. Top with a second wonton wrapper and press edges together to seal. Repeat with remaining wonton wrappers and cheese mixture.

3. Heat about 2 quarts water to boiling in large saucepan; add 4 to 6 ravioli. Reduce heat and simmer, uncovered, until ravioli float to surface and are *al dente*, 3 to 4 minutes. Repeat cooking procedure with remaining ravioli. Serve with Wild Mushroom Sauce.

EGGPLANT RAVIOLI

The ravioli are easily made with wonton wrappers. Assemble 2 to 3 hours ahead for convenience, and refrigerate in a single layer, covered with plastic wrap.

6 servings (4 ravioli each)

Eggplant Filling (recipe follows)
48 wonton wrappers
Fresh Tomato and Herb Sauce (see p. 702)

Per Serving
Calories: 306
% Calories from fat: 10
Fat (gm): 3.6
Saturated fat (gm): 0.6
Cholesterol (mg): 8
Sodium (mg): 493
Protein (gm): 15.9
Carbohydrate (gm): 54.6
Exchanges
Milk: 0.0
Vegetable: 3.0
Fruit: 0.0
Bread: 2.5
Meat: 1.0
Fat: 0.0

1. Place about 1½ tablespoons eggplant mixture on wonton wrapper; brush edges of wrapper with water. Top with second wonton wrapper and press edges together to seal. Repeat with remaining wonton wrappers and eggplant mixture.

2. Heat about 2 quarts water to boiling in large saucepan; add 4 to 6 ravioli. Reduce heat and simmer, uncovered, until ravioli float to the surface and are *al dente*, 3 to 4 minutes. Remove with slotted spoon; repeat cooking procedure with remaining ravioli. Serve with Fresh Tomato and Herb Sauce.

Eggplant Filling

(makes about 2 cups)

Olive oil cooking spray
½ cup minced onion
½ cup minced green bell pepper
2 teaspoons minced garlic
1 small eggplant (about 12 ounces), peeled, coarsely chopped
1 teaspoon dried oregano leaves
1 teaspoon dried basil leaves
1 teaspoon dried marjoram leaves
½ cup water

1-2 teaspoons light brown sugar

  1 teaspoon balsamic vinegar

  ½ cup (2 ounces) shredded fat-free mozzarella cheese

  ½ cup fat-free ricotta cheese

  ¼ cup (1 ounce) grated fat-free Parmesan cheese

     Salt and pepper, to taste

1. Spray large skillet with cooking spray; heat over medium heat until hot. Saute onion, bell pepper, and garlic until tender, about 5 minutes.

2. Stir eggplant into skillet and saute 1 to 2 minutes. Stir in herbs and water; heat to boiling. Reduce heat and simmer, covered, until vegetables are tender, about 10 minutes. Stir in sugar and vinegar; cook, uncovered, until liquid is almost gone, about 5 minutes.

3. Remove skillet from heat and cool to room temperature; stir in cheeses. Season to taste with salt and pepper.

FETA CHEESE AND SUN-DRIED TOMATO RAVIOLI

Other sauces, such as Roasted Red Pepper Sauce, Many-Cloves Garlic Sauce, or Creamed Spinach Sauce (see pp. 709, 710, 712) would also be excellent with these versatile ravioli.

4 servings (4 ravioli each)

  1 ounce sun-dried tomatoes (not in oil)

  ½ package (8-ounce size) fat-free cream cheese

¼-½ cup (1-2 ounces) crumbled reduced-fat feta cheese

  ½ teaspoon grated lemon rind

  1 teaspoon dried oregano leaves

 32 wonton wrappers

     Mediterranean Tomato-Caper Sauce, warm (see p. 709)

     Fresh oregano, finely chopped, *or* flat-leaf parsley, as garnish

Per Serving
Calories: 327
% Calories from fat: 6
Fat (gm): 2.2
Saturated fat (gm): 0.9
Cholesterol (mg): 10.5
Sodium (mg): 728
Protein (gm): 15.3
Carbohydrate (gm): 61.4
Exchanges
Milk: 0.0
Vegetable: 2.0
Fruit: 0.5
Bread: 3.0
Meat: 0.5
Fat: 0.0

1. Place sun-dried tomatoes in small bowl; pour boiling water over to cover. Let stand until softened, 5 to 10 minutes; drain. Chop tomatoes finely.

2. Mix cheeses, tomatoes, lemon rind, and oregano. Spoon about 1 tablespoon cheese mixture on wonton wrapper; brush edges of wrapper with water. Top with second wonton wrapper and press edges together to seal. Repeat with remaining wonton wrappers and cheese mixture.

3. Heat about 2 quarts water to boiling in large saucepan; add 4 to 6 ravioli. Reduce heat and simmer, uncovered, until ravioli float to the surface and are *al dente*, 3 to 4 minutes. Remove ravioli with slotted spoon; repeat cooking procedure with remaining ravioli. Serve with Mediterranean-Caper Sauce and sprinkle with oregano.

SQUASH AND MUSHROOM LASAGNE

 A white sauce and tomato sauce are combined in this delicate lasagne.

8 servings

Olive oil cooking spray
1 cup sliced onion
1 tablespoon minced garlic
1 pound portobello, *or* cremini, mushrooms, sliced
½ cup dry white wine, *or* canned reduced-sodium vegetable broth
Salt and pepper, to taste
¼ cup finely chopped shallots, *or* green onions and tops
2 teaspoons margarine, *or* butter
¼ cup all-purpose flour
1 teaspoon dried rosemary leaves
½ teaspoon dried thyme leaves
2 cups fat-free milk
2 cups (½ recipe) Marinara Sauce (see p. 700), *or* jarred reduced-sodium spaghetti sauce
½ package (8-ounce size) fat-free cream cheese, cubed
¾ cup (3 ounces) grated fat-free Parmesan cheese, divided

Per Serving
Calories: 256
% Calories from fat: 19
Fat (gm): 5.7
Saturated fat (gm): 0.6
Cholesterol (mg): 1
Sodium (mg): 399
Protein (gm): 13.7
Carbohydrate (gm): 37.7
Exchanges
Milk: 0.0
Vegetable: 2.0
Fruit: 0.0
Bread: 2.0
Meat: 1.0
Fat: 0.0

12 lasagne noodles (10 ounces), cooked
1 pound winter yellow squash (acorn, butternut, Hubbard, etc.), peeled, thinly sliced

1. Spray large skillet with cooking spray; heat over medium heat until hot. Saute onion and garlic 3 to 4 minutes; add mushrooms and saute 5 minutes. Add wine to skillet and heat to boiling. Cook over medium heat until mixture is dry, about 5 minutes, stirring occasionally. Season to taste with salt and pepper.

2. Saute shallots in margarine in medium saucepan until tender, 2 to 3 minutes. Stir in flour and herbs; cook 1 to 2 minutes, stirring constantly. Whisk in milk and heat to boiling; boil, whisking constantly, until thickened, about 1 minute. Mix in Marinara Sauce, cream cheese, and ½ cup Parmesan cheese; cook, stirring frequently, until sauce is hot and cream cheese melted, 5 to 7 minutes. Season to taste with salt and pepper.

3. Stir 1 cup sauce into mushroom mixture. Spread about ½ cup remaining sauce in bottom of 13 x 9-inch baking pan; arrange 4 noodles in pan, overlapping edges. Spoon ½ of mushroom mixture and squash slices over noodles and spread with generous 1 cup sauce. Repeat layers 1 time, ending with layer of noodles and generous 1 cup sauce. Sprinkle with remaining ¼ cup Parmesan cheese.

4. Bake lasagne, loosely covered, until noodles and squash are tender, 50 to 60 minutes. Let stand 10 minutes before serving.

ROASTED RED PEPPER AND SPINACH LASAGNE

For convenience, the recipe uses jarred roasted red peppers, though you can roast your own using the method in Roasted Red Pepper Sauce (see p. 709).

8 servings

Olive oil cooking spray
1 cup chopped onion
2 teaspoons minced roasted garlic
1 teaspoon dried marjoram leaves

Per Serving
Calories: 261
% Calories from fat: 13
Fat (gm): 3.8
Saturated fat (gm): 1.7
Cholesterol (mg): 9.1
Sodium (mg): 386
Protein (gm): 21.4
Carbohydrate (gm): 36.8

½-¾ teaspoon dried oregano leaves

3 cups fat-free milk, divided

¼ cup plus 2 tablespoons all-purpose flour

1 cup (4 ounces) grated fat-free Parmesan cheese, divided

½ package (8-ounce size) fat-free cream cheese, cubed

⅔ cup finely chopped parsley
Salt and pepper, to taste

2 packages (10 ounces each) frozen, thawed, chopped spinach, very well drained

⅔ cup fat-free ricotta cheese

12 lasagne noodles (10 ounces), cooked

1 jar (15 ounces) roasted red peppers, drained, cut into 1-inch slices

1 cup (4 ounces) reduced-fat mozzarella cheese

Exchanges
Milk: 0.5
Vegetable: 2.0
Fruit: 0.0
Bread: 1.5
Meat: 1.0
Fat: 0.0

1. Spray large saucepan with cooking spray; heat over medium heat until hot. Saute onion and garlic until tender, 5 to 8 minutes; stir in marjoram and oregano and cook 1 to 2 minutes longer.

2. Add 2 cups milk to saucepan; heat to boiling. Mix remaining 1 cup milk and flour; whisk into boiling milk mixture. Boil, whisking constantly, until thickened, about 1 minute. Remove from heat; mix in Parmesan and cream cheese, stirring until cream cheese is melted. Stir in parsley; season with salt and pepper.

3. Mix spinach and ricotta cheese; season to taste with salt and pepper.

4. Spread ½ cup sauce in bottom of 13 x 9-inch baking pan. Arrange 4 noodles in pan, overlapping edges. Top with ½ of spinach mixture and ½ of red pepper slices; spread with generous 1 cup sauce. Repeat layers. Place remaining 4 noodles on top of lasagne and spread with remaining 1¼ cups sauce. Sprinkle with mozzarella cheese.

5. Bake lasagne at 350 degrees, loosely covered, until hot through, about 45 minutes. Let stand 10 minutes before serving.

ARTICHOKE LASAGNE

The lasagne can be assembled up to a day in advance and refrigerated, covered. Then bake as directed below, increasing baking time by 15 to 20 minutes.

8 servings

Olive oil cooking spray
1½ cups shiitake mushrooms
1½ cups chopped onions
1 cup chopped red bell pepper
2 teaspoons minced garlic
8 cups loosely packed spinach, torn into bite-sized pieces
2 packages (9 ounces each) frozen, thawed, artichoke hearts, cut into bite-sized pieces
Salt and pepper, to taste
3 cups fat-free milk, divided
¼ cup plus 2 tablespoons flour
1 cup (4 ounces) grated fat-free Parmesan cheese
½ package (8-ounce size) fat-free cream cheese, cubed
⅔ cup finely chopped parsley
½ teaspoon dried thyme leaves
1 teaspoon lemon juice
12 lasagne noodles (10 ounces), cooked
1 cup (4 ounces) shredded reduced-fat mozzarella cheese

Per Serving
Calories: 278
% Calories from fat: 7
Fat (gm): 2.1
Saturated fat (gm): 0.2
Cholesterol (mg): 1.5
Sodium (mg): 438
Protein (gm): 22.5
Carbohydrate (gm): 46.4
Exchanges
Milk: 0.0
Vegetable: 3.0
Fruit: 0.0
Bread: 2.0
Meat: 1.0
Fat: 0.0

1. Spray large skillet with cooking spray; heat over medium heat until hot. Saute mushrooms, onions, bell pepper, and garlic 3 minutes; add spinach and artichoke hearts. Cook, covered, over medium heat until spinach is wilted, about 5 minutes. Cook, uncovered, until mixture is dry. Remove from heat; season to taste with salt and pepper.

2. Heat 2 cups milk to boiling in large saucepan. Mix remaining 1 cup milk and flour; whisk into boiling milk. Boil, whisking constantly, until thickened, about 1 minute. Remove from heat; mix in Parmesan and cream cheese, parsley, thyme, and lemon juice, stirring until cream cheese is melted. Season to taste with salt and pepper.

3. Spread ½ cup sauce mixture in bottom of 13 x 9-inch baking pan; arrange 4 noodles in pan, overlapping edges. Spoon ½ of artichoke mixture over noodles and spread with generous 1 cup sauce. Repeat layers, ending with layer of noodles and generous 1 cup sauce. Sprinkle with mozzarella cheese.

4. Bake lasagne at 350 degrees, loosely covered, until hot through, about 45 minutes. Let stand 10 minutes before cutting.

SEVEN

Loaves, Patties,
AND
Sandwiches

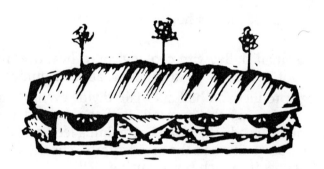

LAYERED VEGETABLE LOAF

4 servings

Vegetable cooking spray

1 medium leek, rinsed, finely chopped

1¾ cups no-cholesterol real egg product

¼ cup fat-free half-and-half, *or* fat-free milk

1 pound broccoli, cooked, finely chopped

¼ teaspoon ground mace

2 cups cubed, cooked carrots

¼ teaspoon dried dill weed

⅔ cup fresh whole wheat breadcrumbs

½ cup (2 ounces) shredded reduced-fat Swiss cheese, divided

½ teaspoon salt (optional)

½ teaspoon ground pepper

2 tablespoons coarsely chopped pine nuts (optional)

1 cup prepared mild, *or* hot, salsa

Per Serving
Calories: 202
% Calories from fat: 15
Fat (gm): 3.4
Saturated fat (gm): 1.7
Cholesterol (mg): 10.1
Sodium (mg): 768
Protein (gm): 19.6
Carbohydrate (gm): 24.4
Exchanges
Milk: 0.0
Vegetable: 3.0
Fruit: 0.0
Bread: 0.5
Meat: 1.5
Fat: 0.0

1. Spray a small skillet with cooking spray; heat over medium heat until hot. Saute leek until softened, about 5 minutes.

2. Mix egg product and half-and-half; divide evenly between 2 medium bowls. Add the broccoli, half the sauteed leek, and mace to one bowl; add the carrots, remaining leek, and dill weed to the other bowl. Stir half the breadcrumbs, cheese, salt, (if using) and pepper into each bowl, mixing well.

3. Line bottom of 9 x 5-inch loaf pan with parchment paper. Spray lightly with cooking spray.

4. Spoon carrot mixture evenly in bottom of pan. Sprinkle with pine nuts, if using. Gently spoon broccoli mixture over carrot layer. Place loaf pan in large roasting pan on oven rack and add 2 inches hot water to roasting pan.

5. Bake, uncovered, at 350 degrees 45 to 55 minutes or until sharp knife inserted near center comes out clean. Cool on wire rack 5 minutes before inverting.

6. Invert loaf onto serving plate; carefully remove parchment. Cut loaf into thick slices and serve with salsa.

BROCCOLI TERRINE WITH LEMON HERB MAYONNAISE

The terrine can also be served with Roasted Red Pepper Sauce or Fresh To-mato-Basil Sauce (see pp. 709, 702)

6-8 servings

1 pound broccoli, cut into 1-inch pieces, cooked until very tender

½ cup fat-free sour cream

¼ cup grated fat-free Parmesan cheese

2-3 teaspoons lemon juice

½ teaspoon dried tarragon leaves

½ teaspoon dried basil leaves

¼ teaspoon dried thyme leaves

Salt and pepper, to taste

3 eggs

2 egg whites

Lemon-Herb Mayonnaise (see p. 733)

Per Serving
Calories: 107
% Calories from fat: 22
Fat (gm): 2.8
Saturated fat (gm): 0.8
Cholesterol (mg): 106.5
Sodium (mg): 369
Protein (gm): 9.5
Carbohydrate (gm): 12.4
Exchanges
Milk: 0.0
Vegetable: 2.0
Fruit: 0.0
Bread: 0.0
Meat: 1.0
Fat: 0.0

1. Process broccoli in food processor until mixture is almost smooth; mix in sour cream, cheese, lemon juice, and herbs. Season to taste with salt and pepper. Mix in eggs and egg whites.

2. Pour mixture into greased loaf pan, 7½ x 3½ inches. Place pan in large roasting pan on middle oven rack; add 2 inches hot water to roasting pan. Bake, covered, at 350 degrees until set, about 1 hour. Remove loaf pan from roasting pan and uncover. Let stand 10 minutes.

3. Loosen sides of loaf with sharp knife and invert onto serving plate, smoothing edges with knife, if necessary. Cool; refrigerate until chilled, 3 to 4 hours.

4. Cut into slices; serve with Lemon Herb Mayonnaise.

SEASONED CAULIFLOWER AND GREEN BEAN LOAF

Vegetables and stuffing crumbs combine in this herb-seasoned loaf.

4-6 servings

Vegetable cooking spray
1 cup sliced green onions and tops
⅔ cup herb-seasoned stuffing cubes
1 pound cauliflower, cooked, finely chopped
8 ounces cut green beans, cooked until crisp-tender
1 ¾ cups no-cholesterol real egg product
¼ cup fat-free milk
1 teaspoon dried tarragon leaves
½ teaspoon caraway seeds, crushed
¾ cup (3 ounces) shredded reduced-fat Cheddar cheese
¼-½ teaspoon salt
¼ teaspoon pepper

Per Serving
Calories: 176
% Calories from fat: 18
Fat (gm): 3.7
Saturated fat (gm): 1.6
Cholesterol (mg): 11.6
Sodium (mg): 683
Protein (gm): 18.2
Carbohydrate (gm): 18.6
Exchanges
Milk: 0.0
Vegetable: 2.0
Fruit: 0.0
Bread: 0.5
Meat: 1.5
Fat: 0.0

1. Spray small skillet with cooking spray; heat over medium heat until hot. Saute green onions until tender, about 8 minutes. Combine stuffing cubes, green onions, and remaining ingredients in bowl.

2. Spoon mixture into greased 9 x 5-inch loaf pan. Place loaf pan in large roasting pan on oven rack and add 2 inches hot water to roasting pan.

3. Bake, uncovered, at 350 degrees until loaf is set and sharp knife inserted near center comes out clean, 50 to 60 minutes. Cool on wire rack 5 minutes; invert onto serving plate.

GREEK-STYLE EGGPLANT LOAF

Eggplant couldn't be more delicious than this! Serve warm, or at room temperature with any roasted vegetables.

4-6 servings

Eggplant Filling (see p. 360)
1 cup cooked brown, *or* basmati rice
⅓ cup unseasoned dry breadcrumbs
¾ cup (3 ounces) crumbled reduced-fat feta cheese
¼ cup chopped sun-dried tomatoes (not in oil)
1 egg
2 egg whites
Mediterranean Tomato-Caper Sauce, *or* Roasted Red Pepper Sauce (see p. 709)

Per Serving
Calories: 362
% Calories from fat: 14
Fat (gm): 5.9
Saturated fat (gm): 2.6
Cholesterol (mg): 60.8
Sodium (mg): 728
Protein (gm): 25.2
Carbohydrate (gm): 55.3
Exchanges
Milk: 0.0
Vegetable: 4.5
Fruit: 0.5
Bread: 1.5
Meat: 2.0
Fat: 0.0

1. Make Eggplant Filling; mix in remaining ingredients, except Mediterranean Tomato-Caper Sauce.

2. Spoon mixture into greased 8½ x 4½-inch loaf pan. Bake at 350 degrees until set, 30 to 35 minutes. Cool on wire rack 10 minutes. Loosen sides of loaf with sharp knife and invert onto serving plate. Serve with Mediterranean Tomato-Caper Sauce.

SPINACH AND BEAN LOAF BAKED IN FILLO

Mediterranean flavors are baked into this colorful and moist loaf.

8 servings

Olive oil cooking spray
2 cups sliced mushrooms
1 small onion, sliced
3 cloves garlic, minced
2 teaspoons dried basil leaves
½ package (8-ounce size) fat-free cream cheese

Per Serving
Calories: 118
% Calories from fat: 19
Fat (gm): 2.9
Saturated fat (gm): 1.1
Cholesterol (mg): 55.8
Sodium (mg): 382
Protein (gm): 13
Carbohydrate (gm): 14.3

1 can (15 ounces) cannellini beans, rinsed, drained
1 package (10 ounces) spinach, sliced
½ cup (2 ounces) shredded fat-free mozzarella cheese
½ cup (2 ounces) reduced-fat feta cheese
Salt and pepper, to taste
2 eggs
1 egg white
6 sheets frozen, thawed, fillo pastry

Exchanges
Milk: 0.0
Vegetable: 1.0
Fruit: 0.0
Bread: 0.5
Meat: 1.0
Fat: 0.0

1. Spray large skillet with cooking spray; heat over medium heat until hot. Add mushrooms, onion, and garlic. Cook, covered, over medium heat until mushrooms are wilted, about 5 minutes. Cook, uncovered, until vegetables are tender. Add basil; cook 1 to 2 minutes longer.

2. Remove skillet from heat; add cream cheese, stirring until melted. Stir in beans, spinach, and cheeses; season to taste with salt and pepper. Stir in eggs and egg white.

3. Spray 9 x 5-inch loaf pan with cooking spray. Arrange 1 sheet of fillo in pan, pressing fillo to sides of pan and allowing edges to extend up slightly above top of pan; spray fillo generously with cooking spray. Arrange second sheet of fillo in pan, turning fillo in opposite direction from first sheet; spray generously with cooking spray. Repeat with remaining 4 sheets fillo.

4. Spoon spinach and bean mixture into fillo-lined pan. Gently fold top edges of fillo in over edge of loaf, forming a decorative edge.

5. Bake loaf at 375 degrees until set in the center, 1¼ to 1½ hours, covering loosely with foil if fillo becomes too brown. Let stand in pan on wire rack 10 minutes. Tilt pan slightly and slide loaf out onto serving plate.

TRI-LAYERED TERRINE WITH ROASTED RED PEPPER SAUCE

Almost too beautiful to eat! The terrine is a perfect appetizer or first course for special occasions. Assemble the terrine 1 to 2 days in advance so that flavors have an opportunity to develop.

6 servings

Soy Bean and Vegetable Spread (see p. 17)
Pine Nut Spinach Pâté (see p. 15)
Wild Mushroom Pâté (see p. 16)
Spinach leaves, carrot curls, fluted mushrooms, and toasted pine nuts, as garnish
Roasted Red Pepper Sauce (see p. 709)

Per Serving
Calories: 252
% Calories from fat: 19
Fat (gm): 5.8
Saturated fat (gm): 0.8
Cholesterol (mg): 0
Sodium (mg): 184
Protein (gm): 17.3
Carbohydrate (gm): 36.8
Exchanges
Milk: 0.0
Vegetable: 4.0
Fruit: 0.0
Bread: 1.0
Meat: 1.0
Fat: 0.5

1. Make Soy Bean and Vegetable Spread, using only ½ cup sour cream. Make Pine Nut Spinach and Wild Mushroom Pâtés.

2. Line an 8½ x 4½ x 3-inch loaf pan or 5-cup mold with plastic wrap. Spoon Soy Bean and Vegetable Spread evenly in bottom of pan; spread Wild Mushroom Pâté over, and Pine Nut Spinach Pâté on top. Refrigerate, covered, at least 1 day or up to 3 days.

3. Invert loaf pan on serving plate; carefully remove plastic wrap. Smooth sides and top of terrine with knife. Garnish plate with spinach leaves, carrot curls, fluted mushrooms, and toasted pine nuts.

4. Cut into slices and serve with Roasted Red Pepper Sauce.

LAYERED EGGPLANT LOAF

Beautiful to serve, delicious to eat, and—best of all—easy to make!

6 servings

1 medium eggplant, unpeeled, sliced lengthwise into generous ¼-inch slices
2 eggs, beaten
1 cup seasoned dry breadcrumbs
Olive oil cooking spray

Per Serving
Calories: 220
% Calories from fat: 12
Fat (gm): 3.1
Saturated fat (gm): 0.8
Cholesterol (mg): 71
Sodium (mg): 701
Protein (gm): 13.1
Carbohydrate (gm): 37.4

Salt and pepper, to taste

1½ cups sliced cremini, *or* white, mushrooms

1 cup sliced yellow summer squash

1 small green bell pepper, sliced

4 cloves garlic, minced

1 can (15 ounces) diced tomatoes,
undrained

2 teaspoons dried basil leaves

¾ cup fat-free ricotta cheese

1 cup cooked, toasted wheat berries,
millet, *or* brown rice

2 tablespoons grated fat-free Parmesan
cheese

Exchanges
Milk: 0.0
Vegetable: 2.0
Fruit: 0.0
Bread: 2.0
Meat: 0.5
Fat: 0.0

1. Dip eggplant slices in egg and coat with breadcrumbs. Spray large skillet with cooking spray; heat over medium heat until hot. Cook eggplant slices until browned on the bottoms, 5 to 7 minutes. Spray tops of eggplant slices generously with cooking spray; turn and cook until browned on other side, 5 to 7 minutes. Sprinkle very lightly with salt and pepper.

2. Spray large skillet with cooking spray; heat over medium heat until hot. Add mushrooms, squash, bell pepper, garlic, tomatoes and liquid, and basil to skillet; heat to boiling. Reduce heat and simmer, uncovered, until vegetables are crisp-tender and juices gone, 8 to 10 minutes, stirring occasionally. Season to taste with salt and pepper.

3. Mix ricotta cheese and wheat berries; pat onto bottom of lightly greased 9-inch springform pan. Place 1 layer of eggplant slices over cheese mixture. Layer vegetable mixture over eggplant. Place remaining eggplant slices in a circle on top, with small ends of slices meeting in the center. Using knife or spatula, tuck or fold large ends of slices down along side of pan. Sprinkle top of eggplant with Parmesan cheese.

4. Bake, uncovered, at 350 degrees until eggplant is tender, 1 to 1¼ hours.

HOLIDAY SWEET POTATO LOAF WITH APPLE-CRANBERRY RELISH

Perfect for Thanksgiving or Christmas. But this loaf is so delicious and easy to make, you'll want to serve it year-round.

6 servings

2½ cups coarsely grated, peeled sweet potatoes
1 small onion, finely chopped
1 large tart cooking apple, finely chopped
½ cup raisins
1 teaspoon dried thyme leaves
½ teaspoon ground cinnamon
¼ teaspoon ground nutmeg
½ cup all-purpose flour
¼ cup orange juice
Salt and pepper, to taste
2 eggs
1 egg white
Apple-Cranberry Relish (recipe follows)

Per Serving
Calories: 421
% Calories from fat: 12
Fat (gm): 5.6
Saturated fat (gm): 1
Cholesterol (mg): 71
Sodium (mg): 63.6
Protein (gm): 7.3
Carbohydrate (gm): 88.9
Exchanges
Milk: 0.0
Vegetable: 0.0
Fruit: 3.0
Bread: 3.0
Meat: 0.0
Fat: 0.5

1. Mix sweet potatoes, onion, apple, raisins, thyme, cinnamon, nutmeg, flour, and orange juice in bowl; season to taste with salt and pepper. Mix in eggs and egg white.

2. Pack mixture in greased 7½ x 3¾-inch loaf pan. Bake, covered, at 350 degrees until loaf is set, about 1 hour. Let stand 10 minutes before serving.

3. Loosen sides of loaf with sharp knife; unmold onto serving plate. Slice loaf and arrange slices on serving platter; serve with Apple-Cranberry Relish.

Apple Cranberry Relish

(makes about 1½ cups)

> 1 cup whole berry cranberry sauce
> ½ medium-tart apple, cored, cut into ½-inch pieces
> ½ orange, cut into segments, coarsely chopped
> ¼ cup chopped pecans, *or* walnuts
> ¼ cup sugar
> 1 tablespoon grated lemon rind

1. Heat all ingredients to simmering in small saucepan. Cook until sugar is dissolved and apple tender, 3 to 5 minutes. Cool; refrigerate until serving time.

ORIENTAL LOAF

Serve this flavorful loaf with stir-fry dishes, or shape the mixture into "burgers" and serve with sauteed onions and bean sprouts.

4 servings

> 1 cup textured vegetable protein
> 1 cup Oriental Stock (see p. 62), *or* canned oriental broth
> ½ cup cooked brown, *or* white, rice
> ⅓ cup sliced green onions and tops
> ¼ cup chopped water chestnuts
> 2 teaspoons minced gingerroot
> 1 clove garlic, minced
> 2 teaspoons chili sesame oil
> 2 teaspoons reduced-sodium tamari soy sauce
> ⅓-½ cup unseasoned dry breadcrumbs
> ¼ cup all-purpose flour
> ½ teaspoon five-spice powder (optional)
> Salt and pepper, to taste
> 1 egg

Per Serving
Calories: 205
% Calories from fat: 19
Fat (gm): 4.5
Saturated fat (gm): 0.9
Cholesterol (mg): 53.3
Sodium (mg): 227
Protein (gm): 18.6
Carbohydrate (gm): 24.9
Exchanges
Milk: 0.0
Vegetable: 0.0
Fruit: 0.0
Bread: 1.5
Meat: 2.0
Fat: 0.0

1. Combine vegetable protein and stock in bowl; let stand until stock is absorbed, 5 to 10 minutes. Mix in remaining ingredients, except salt, pepper, and egg. Season mixture to taste with salt and pepper. Add egg and mix well.

2. Pack mixture into greased 7½ x 3¾-inch loaf pan. Bake, uncovered, at 350 degrees 1 hour. Loosen sides of loaf with sharp knife; unmold onto serving plate.

CHUNKY LOAF WITH VEGETABLES

 This loaf is made with the "chunk-style" textured vegetable protein but "granular" style may be substituted.

4 servings

1 cup chunk-style textured vegetable protein
1 cup Oriental Stock (see p. 62), *or* canned oriental broth
½ cup cooked brown, *or* white rice
½ cup sliced green onions and tops
1 cup chopped Chinese cabbage
½ cup sliced carrots
½ cup sliced celery
2 teaspoons minced gingerroot
2 cloves garlic, minced
1 tablespoon hoisin sauce
2 teaspoons reduced-sodium tamari soy sauce
⅓-½ cup unseasoned dry breadcrumbs
¼ cup all-purpose flour
Salt and pepper, to taste
1 egg

Per Serving
Calories: 218
% Calories from fat: 9
Fat (gm): 2.4
Saturated fat (gm): 0.6
Cholesterol (mg): 54.4
Sodium (mg): 387
Protein (gm): 23.9
Carbohydrate (gm): 28.6
Exchanges
Milk: 0.0
Vegetable: 2.0
Fruit: 0.0
Bread: 1.0
Meat: 2.0
Fat: 0.0

1. Combine vegetable protein and stock in bowl; let stand until stock is absorbed, 5 to 10 minutes. Mix in remaining ingredients, except salt, pepper, and egg. Season to taste with salt and pepper. Add egg and mix well.

2. Pack mixture into greased 7½ x 3¾-inch loaf pan. Bake, uncovered, at 350 degrees 1 hour. Loosen sides of loaf with knife; unmold onto serving plate.

POLKA DOT LOAF

 Morsels of brightly colored vegetables dot this moist loaf.

4-6 servings

Per Serving
Calories: 383
% Calories from fat: 9
Fat (gm): 4.1
Saturated fat (gm): 0.9
Cholesterol (mg): 53.3
Sodium (mg): 292
Protein (gm): 29.3
Carbohydrate (gm): 61.2
Exchanges
Milk: 0.0
Vegetable: 2.0
Fruit: 0.0
Bread: 3.0
Meat: 2.0
Fat: 0.0

- 1 cup textured vegetable protein
- 1 cup Canned Vegetable Stock (see p. 63)
- 1 cup cooked millet
- 1 cup unseasoned dry breadcrumbs
- 1 cup fresh, *or* frozen, thawed, whole-kernel corn
- ½ cup chopped carrots
- ½ cup frozen peas, thawed
- 1 medium red bell pepper, chopped
- ½ cup chopped onion
- 2 cloves garlic, minced
- 1½ teaspoons dried thyme leaves
- ½ teaspoon dried marjoram leaves
- ¼-½ teaspoon crushed red pepper
- Salt and pepper, to taste
- 1 egg

1. Combine vegetable protein and stock in bowl; let stand until stock is absorbed, 5 to 10 minutes. Mix in millet, breadcrumbs, vegetables, and seasonings. Season to taste with salt and pepper. Mix in egg.

2. Pack mixture into greased 7½ x 3¾-inch loaf pan. Bake, uncovered, at 350 degrees 1 hour. Loosen sides of loaf with sharp knife; unmold onto serving plate.

MESQUITE-SMOKED TOFU AND BROWN RICE LOAF

 If you don't want to smoke your own tofu, it can be purchased at health food stores and some supermarkets. This mixture is ideal for shaping into burgers, too.

6-8 servings

Mesquite-flavored vegetable cooking spray
1 cup coarsely chopped broccoli
½ cup chopped onion
2 cloves garlic, minced
1½-2 teaspoons dried rosemary leaves
2 cups loosely packed chopped spinach
3 Italian plum tomatoes, coarsely chopped
2 cups cooked brown rice
5¼ ounces (¼ recipe) Mesquite-Smoked Tofu, finely chopped or crumbled (see p. 267)
¼ cup flour
½ cup canned reduced-sodium vegetable broth
Salt and pepper, to taste
1 egg

Per Serving
Calories: 145
% Calories from fat: 13
Fat (gm): 2.2
Saturated fat (gm): 0.4
Cholesterol (mg): 35.5
Sodium (mg): 69
Protein (gm): 6.8
Carbohydrate (gm): 25.9
Exchanges
Milk: 0.0
Vegetable: 2.0
Fruit: 0.0
Bread: 1.0
Meat: 0.5
Fat: 0.0

1. Spray medium skillet with cooking spray; heat over medium heat until hot. Add broccoli, onion, and garlic to skillet and spray generously with cooking spray. Saute until broccoli is just tender, 8 to 10 minutes. Stir in rosemary; cook 1 to 2 minutes longer. Remove from heat; stir in spinach and tomatoes.

2. Mix vegetable mixture, rice, tofu, flour, and broth; season to taste with salt and pepper. Add egg and mix well. Spray 9 x 5-inch loaf pan with cooking spray; pack loaf mixture in pan.

3. Bake, uncovered, at 350 degrees 1 hour. Loosen sides of loaf with knife; unmold onto serving plate.

TABBOULEH LOAF

Serve the loaf warm, or at room temperature. Wonderful the next day, too, sliced and served in pita breads or whole wheat buns.

6-8 servings

1 cup bulgur
Boiling water
1 cup textured vegetable protein
1 cup Basic Vegetable Stock (see p.58), *or* canned reduced-sodium vegetable broth
1 can (15 ounces) garbanzo beans, rinsed, drained
1 small onion, finely chopped
1 package (9 ounces) frozen artichoke hearts, cooked, finely chopped
1 medium tomato, chopped
⅓ cup raisins
¼ cup sliced black olives
¼ cup all-purpose flour
2 teaspoons dried oregano leaves
1½ teaspoons dried basil leaves
¼ teaspoon dry mustard
Salt and pepper, to taste
2 eggs
2 egg whites
Yogurt-Cucumber Sauce (see p. 733)

Per Serving
Calories: 364
% Calories from fat: 14
Fat (gm): 6
Saturated fat (gm): 1.1
Cholesterol (mg): 71.7
Sodium (mg): 594
Protein (gm): 27.5
Carbohydrate (gm): 56.6
Exchanges
Milk: 0.0
Vegetable: 2.0
Fruit: 0.0
Bread: 3.0
Meat: 2.0
Fat: 0.0

1. Place bulgur in medium bowl; pour boiling water over to cover. Let stand until bulgur is softened, about 20 minutes; drain very well.

2. Place vegetable protein in medium bowl; pour stock over and let stand until stock is absorbed, about 10 minutes.

3. Process beans in food processor or blender until coarsely pureed. Mix garbanzo beans, bulgur, vegetable protein, onion, artichoke hearts, tomato, raisins, black olives, flour, herbs, and dry mustard; season to taste with salt and pepper. Mix in eggs and egg whites.

4. Pack mixture into greased loaf pan, 9 x 5 x 4 inches. Bake, uncovered, at 350 degrees until set, about 1 hour. Loosen sides of loaf with sharp knife; invert onto serving plate. Slice and serve with Yogurt-Cucumber Sauce.

LENTIL LOAF WITH MEDITERRANEAN TOMATO-CAPER SAUCE

 Roasted Red Pepper Sauce or Yogurt-Cucumber Sauce (see pp. 709, 733) are also excellent with this caraway- and fennel-accented loaf.

6 servings

Olive oil cooking spray
¾ cup shredded carrots
½ cup finely chopped onion
½ cup finely chopped celery
3 cloves garlic, minced
1 teaspoon caraway seeds, crushed
1 teaspoon fennel seeds, crushed
1 teaspoon celery seeds, crushed
1 teaspoon ground cumin
1½ cups cooked lentils
1 cup cooked brown rice
1 cup (4 ounces) shredded fat-free mozzarella cheese
½ cup coarsely chopped walnuts
Salt and pepper, to taste
2 eggs
Mediterranean Tomato-Caper Sauce (see p. 709)

Per Serving
Calories: 287
% Calories from fat: 26
Fat (gm): 8.6
Saturated fat (gm): 1
Cholesterol (mg): 71
Sodium (mg): 231
Protein (gm): 19.1
Carbohydrate (gm): 35.8
Exchanges
Milk: 0.0
Vegetable: 2.0
Fruit: 0.0
Bread: 1.5
Meat: 1.5
Fat: 1.0

1. Spray large skillet with cooking spray; heat over medium heat until hot. Saute carrots, onion, celery, garlic, and herbs until vegetables are crisp-tender, about 5 minutes.

2. Mix lentils, rice, vegetable mixture, cheese, and walnuts in bowl; season to taste with salt and pepper. Mix in eggs.

3. Pack mixture into greased loaf pan, 8½ x 4½ x 3 inches. Bake at 350 degrees, uncovered, until set, 45 to 60 minutes. Let stand 10 minutes.

4. Loosen sides of loaf with sharp knife; invert onto serving plate. Slice loaf and serve with Mediterranean Tomato-Caper Sauce.

KASHA LOAF BAKED IN SQUASH HALVES

 You'll enjoy this unique combination of kasha, corn bread stuffing crumbs, and fruit baked in squash halves.

4 servings

Vegetable cooking spray
½ cup sliced celery
½ cup sliced carrots
1 teaspoon finely chopped jalapeño chili
1 cup cooked kasha (roasted buckwheat), *or* cooked brown rice
1 cup corn bread stuffing crumbs
½ cup chopped dried apricots
½ cup dried pitted prunes
1 cup canned reduced-sodium vegetable broth
Salt and pepper, to taste
1 egg
2 egg whites
2 small acorn squash, cut in halves, seeded

Per Serving
Calories: 319
% Calories from fat: 6
Fat (gm): 2.4
Saturated fat (gm): 0.6
Cholesterol (mg): 53.3
Sodium (mg): 196
Protein (gm): 9.6
Carbohydrate (gm): 72.1
Exchanges
Milk: 0.0
Vegetable: 1.0
Fruit: 1.5
Bread: 2.5
Meat: 0.5
Fat: 0.0

1. Spray small skillet with cooking spray; heat over medium heat until hot. Saute celery, carrots, and jalapeño chili until tender, 5 to 8 minutes.

2. In large bowl, combine kasha, stuffing crumbs, sauteed vegetables, and dried fruit. Stir in broth; season to taste with salt and pepper.

3. In medium bowl, beat egg and egg whites; add to loaf mixture and mix well.

4. Spoon mixture into acorn squash halves and place in baking pan. Add 1 inch hot water to pan. Bake, covered, at 350 degrees until squash is fork-tender, about 1 hour.

LOAF-STUFFED POBLANO CHILIES

A loaf mixture with South-of-the-Border flavors, stuffed into one of Mexico's favorite chilies. Poblano chilies can be very hot in flavor; sweet bell peppers may be substituted.

4-6 servings

4-6	large poblano chilies, cut lengthwise into halves, seeded
1	cup textured vegetable protein
½	cup corn bread stuffing crumbs
1¼	cups Canned Vegetable Stock (see p. 63)
1	cup cooked brown, *or* white, rice
¾	cup (3 ounces) shredded reduced-fat mozzarella cheese
¾	cup frozen whole-kernel corn, thawed
¾	cup chopped zucchini
⅓	cup chopped red bell pepper
⅓	cup chopped green bell pepper
1	teaspoon finely chopped jalapeño chili
1-1½	teaspoons dried oregano leaves
½	teaspoon ground cumin
	Salt and pepper, to taste
1	egg
	Cilantro, chopped, as garnish

Per Serving
Calories: 314
% Calories from fat: 16
Fat (gm): 5.7
Saturated fat (gm): 2.9
Cholesterol (mg): 64.6
Sodium (mg): 246
Protein (gm): 30.3
Carbohydrate (gm): 37.6
Exchanges
Milk: 0.0
Vegetable: 2.0
Fruit: 0.0
Bread: 2.0
Meat: 2.0
Fat: 0.0

1. Boil poblano chilies in water to cover until just beginning to soften, about 3 minutes. Drain well.

2. Combine vegetable protein, stuffing crumbs, and stock in bowl; let stand until stock is absorbed, 5 to 10 minutes. Mix in rice, cheese, vegetables, and herbs; season to taste with salt and pepper. Mix in egg.

3. Pack mixture into poblano chili halves and place in baking pan. Bake, loosely covered, at 350 degrees until mixture is hot through and peppers are tender, about 45 minutes. Sprinkle with cilantro.

BEAN AND CORN BREAD LOAF

 Enjoy flavors from the great Southwest in this delicious loaf! And easy to bake in a springform pan.

6 servings

3 cups Canned Vegetable Stock (see p. 63), *or* canned reduced-sodium vegetable broth

1 cup yellow cornmeal
Salt and pepper, to taste
Vegetable cooking spray

1 cup sliced celery

1 large green, *or* red, bell pepper

1 serrano, *or* jalapeño, chili, finely chopped

4 cloves garlic, minced

1 can (15 ounces) red kidney beans, rinsed, drained

1 cup fresh, *or* frozen, whole-kernel corn

2 medium tomatoes, chopped

2 teaspoons dried oregano leaves

1 teaspoon chili powder

1 teaspoon ground cumin

¼ cup finely chopped cilantro

1 cup (4 ounces) shredded reduced-fat Cheddar cheese

Per Serving
Calories: 261
% Calories from fat: 15
Fat (gm): 4.8
Saturated fat (gm): 1.6
Cholesterol (mg): 10.1
Sodium (mg): 464
Protein (gm): 13.6
Carbohydrate (gm): 44.1
Exchanges
Milk: 0.0
Vegetable: 1.0
Fruit: 0.0
Bread: 2.5
Meat: 1.0
Fat: 0.0

1. Heat stock to boiling in large saucepan; gradually stir in cornmeal. Reduce heat and simmer, stirring constantly, until cornmeal has thickened, about 5 minutes. Season to taste with salt and pepper.

2. Spray large skillet with cooking spray; heat over medium heat until hot. Saute celery, bell pepper, chili, and garlic until tender, about 5 minutes.

3. Add beans, corn, tomatoes, and dry herbs to skillet. Cook, covered, over medium heat until tomatoes wilt, about 5 minutes. Cook, uncovered, until mixture is almost dry, 5 to 8 minutes. Remove from heat and cool several minutes; stir in cilantro and season to taste with salt and pepper.

4. Spoon ½ the cornmeal into bottom of greased 9-inch springform pan. Spoon vegetable mixture evenly over cornmeal and sprinkle with cheese. Spoon remaining cornmeal over top of vegetables.

5. Bake, uncovered, at 350 degrees until hot through, 30 to 40 minutes. Remove side of pan and cut into wedges.

BASIC "BURGERS"

Made with prebrowned all vegetable protein crumbles, these versatile "burgers" can be served with melty cheese or a variety of interesting toppings. They can also be modified for other recipes, such as Greek-Style "Burgers" or "Burgers" Provençal (see pp. 390, 389).

6 servings

Per Serving
Calories: 242
% Calories from fat: 17
Fat (gm): 4.5
Saturated fat (gm): 1.2
Cholesterol (mg): 71
Sodium (mg): 508
Protein (gm): 19.8
Carbohydrate (gm): 30.7
Exchanges
Milk: 0.0
Vegetable: 0.0
Fruit: 0.0
Bread: 2.0
Meat: 2.0
Fat: 0.0

1 package (12 ounces) frozen pre-browned vegetable protein crumbles, thawed

2 eggs, lightly beaten

¼ cup dry breadcrumbs

¼ cup finely chopped onion

Vegetable cooking spray

6 whole wheat hamburger buns, toasted

Condiments: mustard, catsup, chopped onion, pickle, etc. (not included in nutritional data)

1. Combine vegetable protein crumbles, eggs, breadcrumbs, and onion; shape mixture into 6 "burgers."

2. Spray large skillet with cooking spray; heat over medium heat until hot. Cook "burgers" until browned, about 5 minutes on each side. Serve in buns with condiments.

Variations:

Herb Seasoned "Burgers"—Add 1 to 2 teaspoons desired herbs such as Italian seasoning, basil, oregano, or sage to the "burger" mixture.

"Cheeseburgers"—Top browned "burgers" with 1 slice reduced-fat Cheddar, Swiss, or Monterey Jack; cover skillet and cook over medium-low heat until cheese is melted, 3 to 4 minutes.

 "Burgers" Deluxe—Add ¼ chopped green or red bell pepper, 2 cloves minced garlic, and 1 to 2 teaspoons dried herbs to the "burger" mixture. Serve cooked "burgers" in toasted buns, topped with lettuce, tomato, and onion slices.

 Smothered "Burgers"—Thinly slice 1 large onion; cook in 1 tablespoon vegetable oil in large skillet over medium to medium-low heat until very soft, 15 to 20 minutes. Season to taste with salt and pepper. Spoon over "burgers."

 Mushroom "Burgers"—Saute 2 to 3 cups sliced mushrooms in 1 tablespoon vegetable oil in large skillet until tender, 5 to 8 minutes; season to taste with salt and pepper. Spoon over "burgers."

VEGETABLE AND TOFU "BURGERS"

 Healthy vegetables, tofu, and crunchy walnuts combine in these honey-sweetened "burgers."

4 servings

2 sun-dried tomato halves (not in oil)
Oriental-flavored cooking spray
⅔ cup finely chopped onion
2 teaspoons minced roasted garlic
2 cups firmly packed chopped spinach
⅔ cup shredded carrots
1 package (10½ ounces) light tofu, well drained, crumbled
2 tablespoons reduced-sodium tamari soy sauce
1 tablespoon honey
7 tablespoons coarsely chopped walnuts
¾ cup dry unseasoned breadcrumbs, divided
Salt and pepper, to taste
4 whole wheat buns, toasted
Spicy brown mustard, *or* mayonnaise (optional)

Per Serving
Calories: 364
% Calories from fat: 30
Fat (gm): 12.5
Saturated fat (gm): 1.4
Cholesterol (mg): 0
Sodium (mg): 778
Protein (gm): 17.9
Carbohydrate (gm): 48.6
Exchanges
Milk: 0.0
Vegetable: 1.0
Fruit: 0.0
Bread: 3.0
Meat: 1.0
Fat: 1.5

1. Pour hot water over tomatoes to cover in small bowl; let stand until softened, about 10 minutes. Drain and chop finely.

2. Spray large skillet with cooking spray; heat over medium heat until hot. Saute onion and garlic 2 to 3 minutes. Add spinach, carrots, tofu, soy sauce, and honey to skillet. Cook, covered, over medium heat until vegetables are tender, about 5 minutes. Cook, uncovered, until mixture is dry, about 5 minutes, stirring occasionally.

3. Process mixture in food processor, using pulse technique, until mixture is finely chopped but not smooth. Stir in walnuts and ½ cup breadcrumbs; season to taste with salt and pepper. Shape mixture into 4 "burgers" and coat with remaining ¼ cup breadcrumbs.

4. Spray large skillet with cooking spray; heat over medium heat until hot. Cook "burgers" until browned on the bottoms, about 5 minutes. Spray tops of "burgers" generously with cooking spray and turn; cook until browned on other side, about 5 minutes. Serve in buns with mustard or mayonnaise.

SMOKED TOFU "BURGERS"

Use our recipe for Smoked Tofu, or purchase tofu already smoked. Make Smoked Tofu a day in advance, if possible, as the smoke flavor increases with refrigerator storage.

4 servings

¼ cup finely chopped red, *or* green, bell pepper

2 tablespoons finely chopped onion

2 cloves garlic, minced

¼ jalapeño chili, minced

1-1½ tablespoons dark sesame oil

4 ounces cremini mushrooms, finely chopped

1-1½ tablespoons reduced-sodium tamari soy sauce

(½ recipe) Smoked Tofu (see p. 267), mashed

¾ cup cooked brown rice

½-⅔ cup unseasoned dry breadcrumbs

Per Serving
Calories: 300
% Calories from fat: 24
Fat (gm): 8.2
Saturated fat (gm): 1.3
Cholesterol (mg): 0
Sodium (mg): 558
Protein (gm): 14.6
Carbohydrate (gm): 43.8
Exchanges
Milk: 0.0
Vegetable: 0.5
Fruit: 0.0
Bread: 2.5
Meat: 1.0
Fat: 1.0

Salt and pepper, to taste
1 egg white
Oriental-flavored cooking spray
4 whole wheat hamburger buns, toasted
1 small onion, sliced

1. Saute bell pepper, chopped onion, garlic, and jalapeño chili in sesame oil in large skillet until tender, about 5 minutes. Add mushrooms and soy sauce; saute, uncovered, until mushrooms are tender, 3 to 4 minutes. Remove from heat.

2. Stir tofu, rice, and breadcrumbs into mixture; season to taste with salt and pepper. Mix in egg white. Shape mixture into 4 "burgers."

3. Spray large skillet with cooking spray; heat over medium heat until hot. Cook "burgers" over medium heat until browned on the bottoms, about 5 minutes. Spray tops of "burgers" with cooking spray and turn; cook until browned on other side, about 5 minutes. Serve in buns with sliced onion.

SQUASH AND TEMPEH PATTIES

Serve these sweet-flavored patties with accompaniments of sour cream and/or applesauce.

4 servings

Olive oil cooking spray
½ cup chopped onion
½ cup chopped red bell pepper
½ jalapeño chili, minced
2 teaspoons minced garlic
1 package (8 ounces) tempeh, crumbled
1½ cups mashed, cooked yellow squash (acorn, butternut, etc.)
2 tablespoons apricot spreadable fruit
1 cup cornbread stuffing crumbs
Salt and pepper, to taste
½ cup applesauce
½ cup fat-free sour cream

Per Serving
Calories: 262
% Calories from fat: 16
Fat (gm): 5
Saturated fat (gm): 0.8
Cholesterol (mg): 0
Sodium (mg): 124
Protein (gm): 16.4
Carbohydrate (gm): 42.4
Exchanges
Milk: 0.0
Vegetable: 1.0
Fruit: 0.0
Bread: 2.5
Meat: 1.0
Fat: 0.0

1. Spray skillet with cooking spray; heat over medium heat until hot. Saute onion, bell pepper, jalapeño chili, and garlic 2 to 3 minutes. Add tempeh to skillet; cook until vegetables are tender, 5 to 8 minutes. Remove from heat; stir in squash and spreadable fruit.

2. Roll stuffing crumbs with rolling pin to make fine crumbs; stir ⅔ cup crumbs into vegetable mixture, reserving remaining crumbs. Season to taste with salt and pepper. Shape mixture into 4 patties; coat with reserved crumbs.

3. Spray large skillet with cooking spray; heat over medium heat until hot. Cook patties over medium heat until browned on the bottoms, about 5 minutes. Spray tops of patties generously with spray and turn; cook until browned on other side, about 5 minutes. Serve patties warm with applesauce and sour cream.

"BURGERS" PROVENÇAL

Open-face "burgers" with flavors from the South of France! This version of ratatouille is very easy and cooks very quickly.

6 servings

  6 Basic "Burgers" (see p. 385)
  ¼ cup finely chopped green bell pepper
  1 teaspoon Italian seasoning
  ½ cup chopped onion
  2 teaspoons minced garlic
  1 tablespoon olive oil
  1 small eggplant, unpeeled, cut into ½-inch cubes
  1 cup chopped red bell peppers
  1 small zucchini, cut into ½-inch cubes
  1 small yellow summer squash, cut into ½-inch cubes
  1 can (14½ ounces) reduced-sodium whole tomatoes, undrained, coarsely chopped
  ½ cup dry red wine, *or* canned reduced-sodium vegetable broth
  1-2 teaspoons sugar

Per Serving
Calories: 306
% Calories from fat: 17
Fat (gm): 5.8
Saturated fat (gm): 1.2
Cholesterol (mg): 71
Sodium (mg): 512
Protein (gm): 20.9
Carbohydrate (gm): 41
Exchanges
Milk: 0.0
Vegetable: 3.0
Fruit: 0.0
Bread: 1.5
Meat: 2.0
Fat: 0.0

1½ teaspoons Italian seasoning
½ teaspoon dried rosemary leaves
¼ teaspoon crushed red pepper
Salt and pepper, to taste
6 slices Italian bread
1 clove garlic, cut in half

1. Make Basic "Burgers," adding bell pepper and Italian seasoning to the mixture.

2. Saute onion and garlic in oil in large skillet 2 to 3 minutes. Add remaining vegetables, wine, sugar, and herbs; heat to boiling. Reduce heat and simmer, covered, until vegetables are tender, 10 to 15 minutes. Simmer, uncovered, until excess juices are gone, 5 to 10 minutes. Season to taste with salt and pepper.

3. Toast bread; rub top side of each slice with cut clove of garlic. Place burgers on bread slices on serving plates; spoon eggplant mixture over.

GREEK-STYLE "BURGERS"

Serve these "burgers" in warm pitas or whole wheat buns, or serve as an entrée, without bread.

6 servings

6 Basic "Burgers" (see p. 385)
¼ cup (1 ounce) crumbled reduced-fat feta cheese
2 teaspoons dried oregano leaves, divided
1 ½ cups chopped onions
2 teaspoons minced garlic
1 tablespoon olive oil
2 cups coarsely chopped tomatoes
2 cups coarsely chopped zucchini
2 teaspoons dried mint leaves
Salt and pepper, to taste
6 pita breads

Per Serving
Calories: 371
% Calories from fat: 16
Fat (gm): 7
Saturated fat (gm): 1.6
Cholesterol (mg): 72.7
Sodium (mg): 723
Protein (gm): 24.7
Carbohydrate (gm): 56
Exchanges
Milk: 0.0
Vegetable: 2.0
Fruit: 0.0
Bread: 3.0
Meat: 2.0
Fat: 0.0

1. Make Basic "Burgers," adding feta cheese and 1 teaspoon oregano leaves to the mixture.

2. Saute onions and garlic in oil 2 to 3 minutes. Add tomatoes, zucchini, mint, and remaining 1 teaspoon oregano. Cook, covered, over medium heat until tomatoes are wilted, about 5 minutes. Cook, uncovered, until vegetables are tender and excess juices absorbed, about 5 minutes. Season to taste with salt and pepper.

3. Arrange cooked "burgers" in pita breads and spoon vegetable mixture inside.

FALAFEL "BURGERS" WITH TAHINI DRESSING

The falafel mixture can also be shaped into "meatballs," if preferred, and baked: coat lightly with unseasoned dry breadcrumbs and place in baking pan. Spray generously with cooking spray; bake at 375 degrees until browned, about 15 minutes.

4 servings

1½ cups cooked garbanzo beans, *or* 1 can (15 ounces) rinsed, drained garbanzo beans, coarsely pureed

¼ cup loosely packed parsley leaves, finely chopped

2 tablespoons chopped green onions and tops

2 cloves garlic, minced

1-2 tablespoons lemon juice

¼ cup all-purpose flour

1¼ teaspoons ground cumin

Salt and pepper, to taste

Olive oil cooking spray

2 pita breads, cut into halves

Tahini Dressing (recipe follows)

¼ cup chopped tomato

¼ cup chopped cucumber

¼ cup thinly sliced green onions and tops

Per Serving
Calories: 291
% Calories from fat: 23
Fat (gm): 7.6
Saturated fat (gm): 0.3
Cholesterol (mg): 0.3
Sodium (mg): 194
Protein (gm): 13.2
Carbohydrate (gm): 45.0
Exchanges
Milk: 0.0
Vegetable: 2.0
Fruit: 0.0
Bread: 2.5
Meat: 0.5
Fat: 1.0

1. Mix garbanzo beans, parsley, chopped green onions, garlic, lemon juice, flour, and cumin in bowl; season to taste with salt and pepper. Shape mixture into 4 "burgers."

2. Spray large skillet with cooking spray; cook over medium heat until hot. Cook "burgers" until browned on the bottoms, 3 to 4 minutes. Spray tops of "burgers" with cooking spray; turn and cook until browned on other side, 3 to 4 minutes.

3. Arrange "burgers" in pita breads; drizzle scant 2 tablespoons Tahini Dressing over each "burger." Spoon combined tomato, cucumber, and sliced green onions into pitas.

Tahini Dressing

⅓ cup fat-free yogurt
2-3 tablespoons tahini (sesame seed paste)
1 small clove garlic, minced
½-1 teaspoon lemon juice

1. Combine all ingredients; refrigerate until ready to use.

TABBOULEH "BURGERS"

The bulgur can be soaked in hot or cold water. The bulgur retains a firmer texture if cold water is used, but the soaking time required is about 2 hours.

6 servings

1 cup bulgur
Boiling water
1 can (15 ounces) garbanzo beans, rinsed, drained
½ cup finely chopped red onion
3 cloves garlic, minced
¼ cup finely chopped parsley
1 teaspoon dried oregano leaves
1 teaspoon dried basil leaves
¼ cup raisins, chopped
½ cup (2 ounces) crumbled reduced-fat feta cheese

Per Serving
Calories: 412
% Calories from fat: 14
Fat (gm): 6.5
Saturated fat (gm): 1.9
Cholesterol (mg): 74.9
Sodium (mg): 798
Protein (gm): 18.6
Carbohydrate (gm): 74.9
Exchanges
Milk: 0.0
Vegetable: 2.0
Fruit: 0.0
Bread: 4.0
Meat: 1.0
Fat: 0.5

Salt and pepper, to taste
2 eggs
Olive oil cooking spray
6 pita breads
⅓ cup chopped tomato
⅓ cup chopped cucumber
¾ cup fat-free yogurt
½ teaspoon dried dill weed

1. Place bulgur in medium bowl; pour boiling water over to cover. Let stand until bulgur is softened, about 20 minutes; drain very well.

2. Process beans in food processor or blender until almost smooth. Mix softened bulgur, beans, onion, garlic, herbs, raisins, and cheese; season to taste with salt and pepper. Mix in eggs. Form mixture into 6 "burgers."

3. Spray large skillet with cooking spray; heat over medium heat until hot. Cook "burgers" over medium heat until browned on the bottoms, about 5 minutes. Spray tops of burgers with cooking spray and turn; cook until browned on other side, about 10 minutes.

4. Serve "burgers" in pita breads. Combine tomato, cucumber, yogurt, and dill weed; spoon into pitas with "burgers."

KASHA-VEGGIE "BURGERS"

 Though the list of ingredients is lengthy, these "burgers" are well worth the effort to make. Prepare double the recipe, and freeze some of the "bur- gers" for future use.

4 servings

Vegetable cooking spray
¾ cup finely chopped zucchini
¾ cup finely chopped mushrooms
¼ cup finely chopped onion
¼ cup finely chopped green bell pepper
2 cloves garlic, minced
½ teaspoon dried basil leaves
½ teaspoon dried dill weed

Per Serving
Calories: 247
% Calories from fat: 12
Fat (gm): 3.6
Saturated fat (gm): 0.8
Cholesterol (mg): 0
Sodium (mg): 398
Protein (gm): 17.3
Carbohydrate (gm): 40.2
Exchanges
Milk: 0.0
Vegetable: 2.0
Fruit: 0.0
Bread: 2.0
Meat: 1.0
Fat: 0.0

¼ teaspoon dried thyme leaves

2 cups loosely packed spinach, finely chopped

1 medium tomato, seeded, chopped

⅔ cup cooked kasha, *or* brown rice

1 cup fresh whole wheat breadcrumbs

½ cup fat-free ricotta cheese

½ cup (2 ounces) shredded fat-free mozzarella cheese

Salt and pepper, to taste

4 whole wheat buns, toasted

1. Spray medium skillet with cooking spray; heat over medium heat until hot. Add zucchini, mushrooms, onion, bell pepper, garlic, and herbs; saute 5 minutes. Add spinach and tomato; cook, covered, over medium heat until tomato wilts. Cook, uncovered, until vegetables are tender, about 5 minutes. Cool.

2. Mix vegetable mixture, kasha, breadcrumbs, and cheeses; season to taste with salt and pepper. Form mixture into 4 "burgers."

3. Spray large skillet with cooking spray; heat over medium heat until hot. Add "burgers" and cook over medium to medium-low heat until browned on the bottoms, 3 to 4 minutes. Spray tops of "burgers" with cooking spray; turn and cook until browned on other side, 3 to 4 minutes. Serve in buns.

LENTIL PITAS WITH FETA CREAM

 Cook the lentils in reduced-sodium canned vegetable broth for extra flavor.

4 servings

1 cup dry lentils, cooked

½ cup finely chopped, seeded tomato

½ cup finely chopped zucchini, *or* yellow summer squash

¼ cup finely chopped green onions and tops

Per Serving
Calories: 311
% Calories from fat: 8
Fat (gm): 3
Saturated fat (gm): 1
Cholesterol (mg): 3
Sodium (mg): 366
Protein (gm): 20
Carbohydrate (gm): 53.9

  3 cloves garlic, minced
  ¼ cup unseasoned dry breadcrumbs
½-¾ teaspoon ground cumin
    Salt and pepper, to taste
  1 egg white
    Olive oil cooking spray
  2 large pita breads, cut into halves
  ½ small cucumber, thinly sliced
    Feta Cream (recipe follows)

Exchanges
Milk: 0.0
Vegetable: 0.5
Fruit: 0.0
Bread: 3.5
Meat: 1.0
Fat: 0.0

1. Process lentils in food processor, or mash with fork, until finely chopped but not smooth (some whole lentils should still be visible). Mix in tomato, zucchini, green onions, garlic, breadcrumbs, and cumin; season to taste with salt and pepper. Mix in egg white; shape mixture into 4 patties.

2. Spray large skillet with cooking spray; heat over medium heat until hot. Cook patties until browned on the bottoms, about 5 minutes. Spray tops of patties with cooking spray and turn; cook over medium heat until browned on other side, about 5 minutes.

3. Place patties in pita breads; top with cucumber slices and spoon Feta Cream over.

Feta Cream

 (makes about ¾ cup)

  ½ cup fat-free yogurt
  ¼ cup (1 ounce) crumbled reduced-fat feta
    cheese
  3 tablespoons finely chopped cilantro
  ½ teaspoon dried dill weed
  ⅛ teaspoon ground white pepper

1. Mix all ingredients; refrigerate until serving time.

GREEK-STYLE GARBANZO "BURGERS" WITH FENNEL GOAT'S CHEESE RELISH

One can (15 ounces) of garbanzo beans, rinsed and drained, can be substituted for the dried beans. The "burgers" can also be served with Feta Cream or Spinach Cilantro Pesto (see pp. 395, 730).

4 servings

3	sun-dried tomatoes (not in oil)
	Olive oil cooking spray
¼	cup finely chopped onion
¼	cup finely chopped red, *or* green, bell pepper
1½	teaspoons minced roasted garlic
¾	teaspoon dried oregano leaves
¾	teaspoon dried thyme leaves
½	teaspoon ground cumin
1½	cups cooked dried garbanzo beans
	Salt, cayenne, and black pepper, to taste
1	egg white
¼-⅓	cup fresh whole wheat breadcrumbs
2	large pita breads, cut into halves, *or* 4 whole wheat hamburger buns
	Fennel Goat's Cheese Relish (recipe follows)

Per Serving
Calories: 302
% Calories from fat: 28
Fat (gm): 9.9
Saturated fat (gm): 2.7
Cholesterol (mg): 7.5
Sodium (mg): 458
Protein (gm): 13.2
Carbohydrate (gm): 43.5
Exchanges
Milk: 0.0
Vegetable: 1.0
Fruit: 0.0
Bread: 2.5
Meat: 0.5
Fat: 1.5

1. Place sun-dried tomatoes in small bowl; pour hot water over to cover. Let stand until tomatoes are softened, about 10 minutes; drain well and chop finely.

2. Spray medium skillet with cooking spray; heat over medium heat until hot. Saute onion, bell pepper, and garlic until tender, about 5 minutes; stir in herbs and cook 1 to 2 minutes longer.

3. Process garbanzo beans in food processor until smooth; mix in vegetable mixture. Season to taste with salt, cayenne, and black pepper. Mix in egg white and enough breadcrumbs for mixture to hold together. Form mixture into 4 "burgers."

4. Spray large skillet with cooking spray; heat over medium heat until hot. Cook "burgers" over medium heat until browned on the bottoms, about 5 minutes. Spray tops of "burgers" generously with cooking spray; turn and cook until browned on other side, about 5 minutes.

5. Arrange "burgers" in pita halves; spoon Fennel Goat's Cheese Relish inside.

Fennel Goat's Cheese Relish

(makes about 1 cup)

⅓ cup thinly sliced fennel bulb
⅓ cup thinly sliced green onions and tops
1-1½ tablespoons olive oil
1-1½ tablespoons balsamic vinegar
¼ cup (1 ounce) crumbled goat's cheese
¼ cup sliced pitted green, *or* ripe, olives
Salt and pepper, to taste

1. Mix fennel, onions, oil, and vinegar; add goat's cheese and olives and toss. Season to taste with salt and pepper. Refrigerate until serving time.

CANNELLINI BEAN PATTIES WITH FRESH TOMATO RELISH

Patties can be lightly coated with cornmeal before cooking for an added bit of "crunch."

4 servings

1 can (15 ounces) cannellini beans, *or* Great Northern beans, rinsed, drained
½ cup finely chopped tomato
¼ cup finely chopped onion
¼ cup finely chopped green bell pepper
1 ½ teaspoons minced garlic
2-4 tablespoons yellow cornmeal
1-1½ teaspoons Italian seasoning
Salt and pepper, to taste
Olive oil cooking spray
4 slices Italian bread, *or* 4 whole wheat hamburger buns

Per Serving
Calories: 231
% Calories from fat: 19
Fat (gm): 5.7
Saturated fat (gm): 0.8
Cholesterol (mg): 0
Sodium (mg): 395
Protein (gm): 11.7
Carbohydrate (gm): 42.9
Exchanges
Milk: 0.0
Vegetable: 2.0
Fruit: 0.0
Bread: 2.0
Meat: 0.0
Fat: 1.0

1 clove garlic, cut in half
Fresh Tomato Relish (recipe follows)

1. Process beans in food processor until almost smooth, or mash coarsely with a fork. Mix in tomato, onion, bell pepper, garlic, cornmeal, and Italian seasoning; season to taste with salt and pepper. Form mixture into 4 patties.

2. Spray large skillet with cooking spray; heat over medium heat until hot. Cook patties over medium heat until browned on the bottoms; spray tops of patties generously with spray and turn. Cook until browned on other side, about 5 minutes.

3. Toast bread; rub tops of bread slices with cut sides of garlic. Arrange patties on bread; spoon Fresh Tomato Relish over.

Fresh Tomato Relish

(makes about 1 cup)

1 cup chopped tomato
1 tablespoon finely chopped lovage, *or* celery, leaves
1 tablespoon finely chopped basil, *or* ½ teaspoon dried basil leaves
1 tablespoon olive oil
1 tablespoon red, *or* white, wine vinegar
Salt and pepper, to taste

1. Mix tomato, herbs, oil, and vinegar; season to taste with salt and pepper. Refrigerate until ready to use.

EGGPLANT PARMESAN SANDWICHES

Thickly sliced eggplant, breaded and sauteed, is served with roasted red peppers on buns with a very simple but flavorful tomato sauce.

4 servings

4 thick slices eggplant (scant ¾ inch thick)
¼ cup no-cholesterol real egg product
⅓ cup seasoned dry breadcrumbs

Per Serving
Calories: 262
% Calories from fat: 8
Fat (gm): 2.2
Saturated fat (gm): 0.5
Cholesterol (mg): 0
Sodium (mg): 765
Protein (gm): 19.4
Carbohydrate (gm): 42.1

2 tablespoons grated fat-free Parmesan cheese

Vegetable cooking spray

4 ounces sliced fat-free mozzarella cheese

2 roasted red peppers, cut into halves

4 French rolls, *or* Hoagie buns, toasted

Pizza Sauce (see p. 700)

Exchanges
Milk: 0.0
Vegetable: 3.0
Fruit: 0.0
Bread: 2.0
Meat: 1.0
Fat: 0.0

1. Dip eggplant slices in egg product and then coat generously with combined breadcrumbs and Parmesan cheese.

2. Spray large skillet with cooking spray; heat over medium heat until hot. Cook eggplant slices over medium heat until browned on the bottoms, about 5 minutes. Spray eggplant slices generously with cooking spray and turn. Cook over medium heat until eggplant slices are tender and browned on other side, about 5 minutes. Top each eggplant slice with 1 ounce cheese; cook, covered, until cheese is melted, 2 to 3 minutes.

3. Place red peppers on bottoms of rolls; top with eggplant, Pizza Sauce, and roll tops.

ITALIAN-STYLE "MEATBALLS"

These meatballs are great in Grinders (see p. 400), or serve with pasta and a wonderful sauce, such as Marinara (see p. 700).

6 servings (4 meatballs each)

1 package (12 ounces) frozen prebrowned vegetable protein crumbles, thawed

2 eggs, lightly beaten

¼ cup Italian-style dry breadcrumbs

2 cloves garlic minced

2 tablespoons grated fat-free Parmesan cheese

2 teaspoons Italian herbs

½ teaspoon fennel seeds, crushed

Per Serving
Calories: 130
% Calories from fat: 13
Fat (gm): 1.9
Saturated fat (gm): 0.5
Cholesterol (mg): 71
Sodium (mg): 376
Protein (gm): 16.3
Carbohydrate (gm): 11.4
Exchanges
Milk: 0.0
Vegetable: 0.0
Fruit: 0.0
Bread: 0.5
Meat: 2.0
Fat: 0.0

1. Combine all ingredients, mashing protein crumbles lightly with fork. Form mixture into 24 balls.

2. Bake in baking pan at 350 degrees until firm, about 10 minutes.

GRINDERS

Serve these fun sandwiches with New England Baked Beans and Roasted Potato Salad (see pp. 519, 296).

6 servings

Fresh Tomato and Herb Sauce (see p. 702)
Salt and pepper, to taste
3   cups sliced green bell peppers
3   cloves garlic, minced
1-2 tablespoons olive oil
Italian-Style "Meatballs" (see p. 399)
6   Italian, *or* Hoagie, rolls, toasted
3   tablespoons grated fat-free Parmesan cheese

Per Serving
Calories: 361
% Calories from fat: 22
Fat (gm): 8.9
Saturated fat (gm): 1.6
Cholesterol (mg): 71
Sodium (mg): 650
Protein (gm): 23.5
Carbohydrate (gm): 49.4
Exchanges
Milk: 0.0
Vegetable: 3.0
Fruit: 0.0
Bread: 2.0
Meat: 2.0
Fat: 0.5

1.   Make Fresh Tomato and Herb Sauce, deleting ½ teaspoon salt; season to taste with salt and pepper.

2.   Saute bell peppers and garlic in oil 5 minutes; reduce heat to medium-low and cook until peppers are very soft, 15 to 20 minutes. Season to taste with salt and pepper.

3.   Arrange "meatballs" on rolls; spoon pepper mixture and Fresh Tomato and Herb Sauce over "meatballs." Sprinkle with cheese.

SOYBEAN-VEGGIE "BURGERS"

These "burgers" pack a hefty nutritional punch and taste as good as they are good for you! Soybeans triple in volume when cooked, so you will need only ⅓ cup of dried soybeans for this recipe.

4 servings

Vegetable cooking spray
½ cup finely chopped onion
½ cup finely chopped carrots
¼ cup finely chopped red bell pepper
4 cloves garlic, minced
1 cup cooked soybeans, coarsely pureed

Per Serving
Calories: 317
% Calories from fat: 20
Fat (gm): 7.3
Saturated fat (gm): 1.3
Cholesterol (mg): 53.3
Sodium (mg): 695
Protein (gm): 16.9
Carbohydrate (gm): 49.6

1 cup cooked basmati, *or* pecan, rice

½ cup seasoned dry breadcrumbs

3 tablespoons finely chopped parsley leaves

Red pepper sauce, to taste

Salt and pepper, to taste

1 egg

4 whole wheat buns, toasted

4 teaspoons spicy brown mustard, *or* horseradish mustard

Lettuce leaves, as garnish

Exchanges
Milk: 0.0
Vegetable: 1.0
Fruit: 0.0
Bread: 3.0
Meat: 1.0
Fat: 0.5

1. Spray medium skillet with cooking spray; heat over medium heat until hot. Add onion, carrots, bell pepper, and garlic and saute until tender, about 8 minutes.

2. Combine soybeans, rice, sauteed vegetables, breadcrumbs, and parsley in bowl; season to taste with red pepper sauce, salt, and pepper. Mix in egg, blending well; form mixture into 4 "burgers."

3. Spray large skillet with cooking spray; heat over medium heat until hot. Add "burgers" and cook over medium to medium-low heat until browned on the bottoms, 3 to 4 minutes. Spray tops of "burgers" with cooking spray; turn "burgers" and cook until browned on other side, 3 to 4 minutes.

4. Spread bottoms of buns with mustard; top with lettuce, "burgers," and bun tops.

SOYBEAN-MUSHROOM "BURGERS"

Dried shiitake mushrooms give an extra-rich flavor to these "burgers." Top "burgers" with additional sauteed mushrooms, if you like.

4 servings

4 dried shiitake mushrooms

Olive oil cooking spray

½ cup finely chopped onion

1 clove garlic, minced

½ cup chopped fresh shiitake, *or* portobello, mushrooms

Per Serving
Calories: 371
% Calories from fat: 22
Fat (gm): 9.3
Saturated fat (gm): 1.9
Cholesterol (mg): 53.3
Sodium (mg): 332
Protein (gm): 18
Carbohydrate (gm): 57.3

½ cup finely chopped red bell pepper

3 tablespoons finely chopped chives, *or* green onion tops

1 cup cooked soybeans, coarsely pureed

1 cup cooked millet, *or* brown pecan rice

½ cup unseasoned dry breadcrumbs

½ teaspoon dried rosemary leaves

Salt and pepper, to taste

1 egg

4 multigrain buns, toasted

Whole-grain mustard, to taste

Exchanges
Milk: 0.0
Vegetable: 1.0
Fruit: 0.0
Bread: 3.5
Meat: 1.0
Fat: 1.0

1. Cover dried mushrooms with boiling water in small bowl; let stand until mushrooms are soft, about 15 minutes. Drain and chop mushrooms, discarding tough stems.

2. Spray medium skillet with cooking spray; heat over medium heat until hot. Saute onion, garlic, fresh and dried mushrooms, bell pepper, and chives until tender, 5 to 8 minutes.

3. Combine soybeans, millet, sauteed vegetables, breadcrumbs, and rosemary; season to taste with salt and pepper. Add egg, mixing well; form mixture into 4 "burgers."

4. Spray large skillet with cooking spray; heat over medium heat until hot. Add "burgers" and cook over medium to medium-low heat until browned on the bottoms, 3 to 4 minutes. Spray tops of "burgers" with cooking spray; turn and cook until browned on other side, 3 to 4 minutes. Serve in buns with mustard.

HERBED VEGGIE "BURGERS"

Serve also as an entrée, accompanied with Baked Tomatoes and Sweet Potato Pone (see pp. 623, 490).

4 servings

Vegetable cooking spray

¾ cup finely chopped broccoflower florets

¾ cup finely chopped mushrooms

¼ cup finely chopped onion

Per Serving
Calories: 313
% Calories from fat: 26
Fat (gm): 9.5
Saturated fat (gm): 1.3
Cholesterol (mg): 1.3
Sodium (mg): 700
Protein (gm): 19.6
Carbohydrate (gm): 40

2 cloves garlic

1½ teaspoons dried basil leaves (divided)

½ teaspoon dried marjoram leaves

¼ teaspoon dried thyme leaves

⅔ cup cooked wild, *or* brown, rice

⅓ cup quick-cooking oats

⅓ cup coarsely chopped toasted walnuts

½ cup 1% fat cottage cheese

½ cup shredded fat-free Cheddar cheese

Salt and pepper, to taste

2 egg whites

⅓ cup fat-free mayonnaise

4 multigrain, *or* whole wheat, buns, toasted

Lettuce leaves, as garnish

Exchanges
Milk: 0.0
Vegetable: 0.0
Fruit: 0.0
Bread: 2.5
Meat: 2.0
Fat: 0.5

1. Spray medium skillet with cooking spray; heat over medium heat until hot. Saute broccoflower, mushrooms, onion, and garlic until tender, 8 to 10 minutes. Add ½ teaspoon basil, marjoram, and thyme and cook 1 to 2 minutes longer. Remove from heat and cool slightly.

2. Stir rice, oats, walnuts, and cheeses into vegetable mixture; season to taste with salt and pepper. Stir in egg whites. Form mixture into 4 "burgers."

3. Spray large skillet with cooking spray; heat over medium heat until hot. Add "burgers" and cook over medium to medium-low heat until browned on the bottoms, 3 to 4 minutes. Spray tops of "burgers" with cooking spray and turn; cook until browned on other side, 3 to 4 minutes.

4. Mix mayonnaise and remaining 1 teaspoon basil. Spread on bottoms of buns and top with lettuce, "burgers," and bun tops.

"CHORIZO"

Our version of chorizo, a well-seasoned Mexican sausage, is made with prebrowned vegetable protein crumbles. The "sausage" patties can be served with eggs or crumbled to serve in quesadillas, nachos, enchiladas, and so on.

6 servings

½-1 teaspoon coriander seeds, crushed
½-1 teaspoon cumin seeds, crushed
1-2 dried ancho chilies
1 package (12 ounces) prebrowned vegetable protein crumbles
2 eggs
2 tablespoons cider vinegar
2 cloves garlic, minced
2 tablespoons paprika
1-1½ teaspoons dried oregano leaves
½ teaspoon salt
Vegetable cooking spray
1 cup (½ recipe) Red Tomato Salsa (see p. 9)
6 tablespoons fat-free sour cream

Per Serving
Calories: 142
% Calories from fat: 13
Fat (gm): 2.2
Saturated fat (gm): 0.6
Cholesterol (mg): 71
Sodium (mg): 476
Protein (gm): 17
Carbohydrate (gm): 14.6
Exchanges
Milk: 0.0
Vegetable: 2.0
Fruit: 0.0
Bread: 0.0
Meat: 2.0
Fat: 0.0

1. Heat seeds in small skillet over medium heat until toasted, stirring frequently. Remove from skillet. Add chili to skillet; cook over medium heat until softened, turning frequently so chili doesn't burn, 1 to 2 minutes. Remove and discard stem, veins, and seeds. Chop chili finely.

2. Combine vegetable protein crumbles, seeds, chili, eggs, vinegar, garlic, paprika, oregano, and salt. Form mixture into 6 patties.

3. Spray large skillet with cooking spray; heat over medium heat until hot. Cook patties over medium to medium-low heat until browned, 3 to 4 minutes on each side. Serve patties with Red Tomato Salsa and sour cream.

MEXI "MEATBALLS"

Accompany these "meatballs" with Black Beans and Rice (see p. 526) and serve with Red Tomato Salsa (see p. 9).

4 servings (4 to 5 meatballs each)

1 cup textured vegetable protein

1 cup Basic Vegetable Stock (see p. 58)

1 egg, lightly beaten

⅓ cup unseasoned dry breadcrumbs

¼ cup all-purpose flour

¼ cup (2 ounces) shredded reduced-fat Monterey Jack cheese

¼ cup finely chopped onion

1 clove garlic, minced

1 teaspoon dried mint leaves

½ teaspoon dried oregano leaves

½ teaspoon ground cumin

½ teaspoon salt

¼ teaspoon cayenne pepper

Per Serving
Calories: 197
% Calories from fat: 21
Fat (gm): 4.7
Saturated fat (gm): 2.1
Cholesterol (mg): 63.4
Sodium (mg): 477
Protein (gm): 22.2
Carbohydrate (gm): 18.9
Exchanges
Milk: 0.0
Vegetable: 0.0
Fruit: 0.0
Bread: 1.0
Meat: 2.0
Fat: 0.0

1. Combine vegetable protein and stock in medium bowl; let stand until stock is absorbed, about 20 minutes. Mix in egg and remaining ingredients. Form mixture into 16 to 20 "meatballs."

2. Bake meatballs in a lightly greased baking pan at 350 degrees until firm and browned, 15 to 20 minutes. Or cook in lightly greased skillet over medium to medium-low heat until browned, about 10 minutes.

Note: Frozen and thawed prebrowned vegetable protein crumbles can be used to make the "meatballs." Substitute 2 cups thawed protein crumbles for the vegetable protein, delete stock, and continue with recipe as above.

PICANTE BLACK BEAN TOSTADAS

The bean patties can also be served in buns, topped with Red or Green Tomato Salsa (see pp. 9, 8).

6 servings

2 cans (15 ounces each) black beans, rinsed, drained
1 cup (4 ounces) shredded reduced-fat Monterey Jack cheese
½ cup chopped onion
½ cup very finely chopped zucchini
4 cloves garlic, minced
1-2 serrano, *or* jalapeño, chilies, minced
1-1½ teaspoons dried oregano leaves
1 teaspoon ground cumin
¼-½ teaspoon crushed red pepper
Salt and pepper, to taste
1 egg white
¼-½ cup unseasoned dry breadcrumbs
Vegetable cooking spray
6 corn, *or* flour, tortillas
1½ cups thinly sliced iceberg lettuce
1½ cups chopped tomatoes
Guacamole (see p. 15)
6 tablespoons fat-free sour cream

Per Serving
Calories: 308
% Calories from fat: 20
Fat (gm): 8
Saturated fat (gm): 2.6
Cholesterol (mg): 13.5
Sodium (mg): 715
Protein (gm): 22.5
Carbohydrate (gm): 48.5
Exchanges
Milk: 0.0
Vegetable: 1.0
Fruit: 0.0
Bread: 2.5
Meat: 1.0
Fat: 1.0

1. Process beans in food processor, or mash with fork, until very finely chopped but not smooth. Mix beans, cheese, onion, zucchini, garlic, serrano chili, herbs, and crushed red pepper; season to taste with salt and pepper. Mix in egg white and enough breadcrumbs to make a firm mixture. Shape mixture into 6 patties.

2. Spray large skillet with cooking spray; heat over medium heat until hot. Cook tortillas until crisp and browned, about 1 minute on each side. Place tortillas on serving plates.

3. Add patties to skillet; cook until browned on bottoms, about 5 minutes; spray tops of patties with cooking spray and turn. Cook until browned on other side, about 5 minutes.

4. Distribute lettuce and tomatoes on tortillas; top with patties. Top patties with dollops of Guacamole and sour cream.

MEATLESS SLOPPY JOES

A sandwich for kids of all ages! Serve with lots of pickles and fresh vegetable relishes.

4 servings

Vegetable cooking spray
½ cup chopped onion
½ cup chopped green, *or* red, bell pepper
1 teaspoon minced garlic
¾ cup sliced mushrooms
½ cup reduced-sodium catsup
⅔ cup water
2 tablespoons light brown sugar
1 tablespoon prepared mustard
1 teaspoon celery seeds
½ teaspoon chili powder
½ cup textured vegetable protein
Salt and pepper, to taste
4 whole wheat hamburger buns, toasted
8 sweet, *or* dill, pickle spears

Per Serving
Calories: 264
% Calories from fat: 11
Fat (gm): 3.5
Saturated fat (gm): 0.7
Cholesterol (mg): 0
Sodium (mg): 428
Protein (gm): 15.1
Carbohydrate (gm): 48.9
Exchanges
Milk: 0.0
Vegetable: 1.0
Fruit: 0.0
Bread: 2.0
Meat: 2.0
Fat: 0.0

1. Spray medium saucepan with cooking spray; heat over medium heat until hot. Saute onion, bell pepper, and garlic until tender, 5 to 8 minutes. Stir in mushrooms, catsup, water, brown sugar, mustard, celery seeds, and chili powder; heat to boiling. Stir in vegetable protein; reduce heat and simmer, covered, 10 minutes. Season to taste with salt and pepper.

2. Spoon sandwich mixture into buns; serve with pickles.

VEGGIE JOES

We recommend using frozen tofu for this recipe, as the texture of frozen, then thawed, tofu is firmer. Tempeh, of course, can be substituted for the tofu.

6 servings

2	packages (10½ ounces each) frozen, light firm tofu, thawed
	Vegetable cooking spray
½	cup chopped green bell pepper
¼	cup sliced green onions and tops
2	cloves garlic, minced
¾	cup sliced carrots
¾	cup small broccoli florets
½	cup whole-kernel corn
3	cans (8 ounces each) reduced-sodium tomato sauce
1½-2	tablespoons cider vinegar
3-4	teaspoons brown spicy mustard
2-3	teaspoons sugar
½	teaspoon celery seeds
	Salt and pepper, to taste
6	sesame seed hamburger buns, toasted
¾	cup (3 ounces) shredded fat-free Cheddar cheese

Per Serving
Calories: 270
% Calories from fat: 13
Fat (gm): 3.9
Saturated fat (gm): 0.6
Cholesterol (mg): 0
Sodium (mg): 513
Protein (gm): 18.7
Carbohydrate (gm): 41.2
Exchanges
Milk: 0.0
Vegetable: 3.0
Fruit: 0.0
Bread: 2.0
Meat: 1.0
Fat: 0.0

1. Press excess liquid from tofu with paper toweling. Crumble tofu, or mash coarsely with a fork.

2. Spray large skillet with cooking spray; heat over medium heat until hot. Saute tofu, bell pepper, onions, and garlic 3 to 4 minutes. Add remaining vegetables and cook, covered, over medium heat until crisp-tender, about 5 minutes.

3. Add tomato sauce, vinegar, mustard, sugar, and celery seeds to skillet; heat to boiling. Reduce heat and simmer, covered, 5 to 10 minutes. Season to taste with salt and pepper.

4. Spoon sandwich mixture into buns; sprinkle with cheese.

MOCK CHICKEN SALAD SANDWICHES

If you prefer a softer texture, cook the tempeh in simmering water 5 to 10 minutes; drain and cool. The salad mixture is also excellent served in scooped-out tomatoes.

4 servings

1	package (8 ounces) tempeh
⅓	cup chopped onion
⅓	cup chopped celery
⅓	cup chopped green bell pepper
2-4	tablespoons sliced green, *or* black, olives
⅓-½	cup fat-free mayonnaise
1-2	teaspoons Dijon mustard
1-2	teaspoons lemon juice
	Salt and pepper, to taste
8	slices whole wheat, *or* light rye, bread, toasted
	Lettuce leaves, as garnish
1	medium tomato, sliced

Per Serving
Calories: 293
% Calories from fat: 22
Fat (gm): 7.7
Saturated fat (gm): 1.4
Cholesterol (mg): 0
Sodium (mg): 690
Protein (gm): 18.1
Carbohydrate (gm): 42.1
Exchanges
Milk: 0.0
Vegetable: 1.0
Fruit: 0.0
Bread: 2.5
Meat: 1.5
Fat: 0.5

1. Crumble tempeh, or mash coarsely with a fork. Combine tempeh, onion, celery, bell pepper, and olives in a bowl. In another bowl, mix mayonnaise, mustard, and lemon juice; stir into tempeh mixture. Season to taste with salt and pepper.

2. Spoon tempeh mixture onto 4 slices of bread; top with lettuce, tomato, and remaining bread slices.

GOAT'S CHEESE HOAGIES

A sandwich full of surprise flavors!

4 servings

	Olive oil cooking spray
4	cups sliced onions
2	cups sliced green bell peppers
2	teaspoons minced garlic
⅓	cup water
¼	cup raisins

Per Serving
Calories: 284
% Calories from fat: 16
Fat (gm): 5.2
Saturated fat (gm): 2.5
Cholesterol (mg): 6.5
Sodium (mg): 382
Protein (gm): 11.5
Carbohydrate (gm): 50.2

1-1½   tablespoons balsamic vinegar
       Salt and pepper, to taste
  ½   package (8-ounce size) fat-free cream
       cheese, softened
  ½   cup (2 ounces) goat's cheese
   4   French rolls, *or* Hoagie buns
  16   spinach leaves

Exchanges
Milk: 0.0
Vegetable: 4.0
Fruit: 0.0
Bread: 2.0
Meat: 0.5
Fat: 0.5

1. Spray large skillet with cooking spray; heat over medium heat until hot. Cook onions, bell peppers, and garlic over medium to medium-low heat, covered, until softened and beginning to brown, 15 to 20 minutes. Add water, raisins, and vinegar; heat to boiling. Reduce heat and simmer, covered, until water has evaporated, 5 to 8 minutes. Season to taste with salt and pepper.

2. Mix cheeses; spread on tops and bottoms of rolls. Arrange spinach leaves on bottoms of rolls; fill with onion mixture and close with tops of rolls.

CRANBERRY CHEESE MELT

 Lots of melty cheese, with cranberry and walnut accents.

4 servings

  ¼   package (8-ounce size) fat-free cream
      cheese, softened
  ¼   cup (1 ounce) shredded smoked
      Gouda, *or* Swiss, cheese
  ¼   cup chopped walnuts
   8 slices whole wheat bread
  ½   medium onion, thinly sliced
  ¼   cup whole-berry cranberry sauce
  ½   cup (2 ounces) shredded fat-free
      Cheddar cheese
      Vegetable cooking spray

Per Serving
Calories: 280
% Calories from fat: 27
Fat (gm): 8.8
Saturated fat (gm): 2.1
Cholesterol (mg): 8.1
Sodium (mg): 548
Protein (gm): 15.9
Carbohydrate (gm): 36.9
Exchanges
Milk: 0.0
Vegetable: 0.0
Fruit: 0.5
Bread: 2.0
Meat: 1.0
Fat: 1.0

1. Mix cream cheese, Gouda cheese, and walnuts; spread on 4 slices bread. Arrange onion slices over cheese; top with cranberry sauce, Cheddar cheese, and remaining bread slices.

2. Spray large skillet with cooking spray; heat over medium heat until hot. Cook sandwiches over medium heat until browned on the bottoms, about 5 minutes. Spray tops of sandwiches with spray and turn; cook until browned on other side, about 5 minutes.

CUCUMBER CHEESE MELT

A marvelous combination of flavors that will keep you coming back for more!

4 servings

¼ package (8-ounce size) fat-free cream cheese, softened

2 tablespoons crumbled blue cheese

8 slices multigrain bread

¼ cup apricot spreadable fruit

16 cucumber slices

4 slices (3 ounces) fat-free Swiss cheese
   Vegetable cooking spray

Per Serving
Calories: 249
% Calories from fat: 11
Fat (gm): 3.1
Saturated fat (gm): 1.1
Cholesterol (mg): 2.6
Sodium (mg): 673
Protein (gm): 13.6
Carbohydrate (gm): 42.9
Exchanges
Milk: 0.0
Vegetable: 2.0
Fruit: 0.0
Bread: 2.0
Meat: 1.0
Fat: 0.0

1. Mix cream cheese and blue cheese; spread on 4 slices of bread. Spread 1 tablespoon spreadable fruit over cheese on each slice; top each with 4 cucumber slices, a slice of Swiss cheese, and remaining bread slices.

2. Spray large skillet with cooking spray; heat over medium heat until hot. Cook sandwiches over medium heat until browned on the bottoms, about 5 minutes. Spray tops of sandwiches with cooking spray and turn; cook until browned on the other side, about 5 minutes.

SUN-DRIED TOMATO PESTO AND CHEESE GRILL

Cilantro Pesto or Mixed Herb Pesto (see pp. 730, 727) can also be used. Thin onion slices can be added to the sandwich or substituted for the tomato slices.

4 servings

8 slices sourdough bread
    Sun-Dried Tomato Pesto (see p. 728)
8 slices (6 ounces) fat-free mozzarella cheese
8 thin slices ripe tomato
    Vegetable cooking spray

Per Serving
Calories: 328
% Calories from fat: 33
Fat (gm): 12
Saturated fat (gm): 1.7
Cholesterol (mg): 0
Sodium (mg): 770
Protein (gm): 21.8
Carbohydrate (gm): 34.1
Exchanges
Milk: 0.0
Vegetable: 1.0
Fruit: 0.0
Bread: 2.0
Meat: 1.5
Fat: 1.5

1. Spread each slice of bread with 1 tablespoon pesto. Top 4 slices with a cheese slice and 2 tomato slices. Top with remaining cheese slices and bread.

2. Spray large skillet with cooking spray; heat over medium heat until hot. Cook sandwiches over medium to medium-low heat until browned on the bottoms, about 5 minutes. Spray tops of sandwiches generously with cooking spray and turn. Cook until browned on the other side, 3 to 5 minutes.

BLUE CHEESE AND PEAR MELT

Blue cheese and pears are perfect flavor companions any way they are served.

4 servings

8 slices honey wheat, *or* light rye, bread
4 slices (3 ounces) fat-free Swiss cheese
¼ cup mango chutney
1 medium pear, cored, cut into ¼-inch slices

Per Serving
Calories: 284
% Calories from fat: 20
Fat (gm): 6.6
Saturated fat (gm): 3.2
Cholesterol (mg): 10.5
Sodium (mg): 780
Protein (gm): 13.6
Carbohydrate (gm): 44.6

½ cup (2 ounces) crumbled blue cheese
Vegetable cooking spray

Exchanges
Milk: 0.0
Vegetable: 0.0
Fruit: 1.0
Bread: 2.0
Meat: 1.0
Fat: 0.5

1. Top 4 slices of bread with Swiss cheese, and spread each with 1 tablespoon chutney; arrange pears on chutney and sprinkle with blue cheese. Top sandwiches with remaining bread slices.

2. Spray large skillet with cooking spray; heat over medium heat until hot. Cook sandwiches until browned on the bottoms, about 5 minutes. Spray tops of sandwiches with cooking spray and turn; cook until browned on the other side, about 5 minutes.

PEANUTTY AND JELLY SANDWICHES

 You won't believe the rich, peanut butter flavor of this creamy, low-fat sandwich spread! Great on raisin bread or crackers, topped with sliced banana or apple.

6 servings

¾ cup canned Great Northern beans, drained

⅓ cup reduced-fat smooth, *or* chunky, peanut butter

2 tablespoons halved raisins

1-2 tablespoons honey

12 slices whole wheat, *or* multigrain, bread

¾ cup grape, *or* other flavor, jelly *or* jam

Per Serving
Calories: 384
% Calories from fat: 18
Fat (gm): 7.9
Saturated fat (gm): 1.7
Cholesterol (mg): 0
Sodium (mg): 389
Protein (gm): 11.9
Carbohydrate (gm): 70.6
Exchanges
Milk: 0.0
Vegetable: 0.0
Fruit: 0.0
Bread: 4.0
Meat: 1.0
Fat: 1.0

1. Process beans in food processor until smooth; mix in peanut butter, raisins, and honey. Spread mixture on 6 slices of bread. Spread remaining slices with jelly and top off sandwiches.

SWISS CHEESE AND SPINACH PINWHEELS

Wonderful sandwiches, because they can be made in advance and refrigerated up to 2 days! Always ready for hungry appetites!

8 servings (2 slices each)

1	large whole wheat lavosh (about 16 inches diameter)
1	package (8 ounces) fat-free cream cheese, softened
1	tablespoon fat-free sour cream
2	tablespoons minced onion
1	teaspoon fennel seeds, crushed
10	slices (7½ ounces) fat-free Swiss cheese
4	cups loosely packed spinach leaves
2	medium tomatoes, thinly sliced
⅓	cup drained, sliced olives

Per Serving
Calories: 177
% Calories from fat: 29
Fat (gm): 5.8
Saturated fat (gm): 0.9
Cholesterol (mg): 0
Sodium (mg): 782
Protein (gm): 13.4
Carbohydrate (gm): 18.4
Exchanges
Milk: 0.0
Vegetable: 1.0
Fruit: 0.0
Bread: 1.0
Meat: 1.0
Fat: 0.5

1. Place lavosh between 2 damp clean kitchen towels; let stand until lavosh is softened enough to roll, 10 to 15 minutes.

2. Mix cream cheese, sour cream, onion, and fennel seeds in small bowl; spread mixture on lavosh. Arrange Swiss cheese, spinach, tomatoes, and olives on cheese. Roll up lavosh tightly; wrap in plastic wrap and refrigerate at least 4 hours, but no longer than 2 days.

3. Trim ends; cut into scant 1-inch slices to serve.

SLICED MUSHROOM PINWHEELS

Easy to make and carry, lavosh sandwiches are great for picnics, as well as home dining.

8 servings (2 slices each)

1	large whole wheat lavosh (about 16 inches diameter)
4	ounces mushrooms
1	package (8 ounces) fat-free cream cheese, softened
1	tablespoon fat-free sour cream

Per Serving
Calories: 122
% Calories from fat: 27
Fat (gm): 3.7
Saturated fat (gm): 0.7
Cholesterol (mg): 0
Sodium (mg): 309
Protein (gm): 6.5
Carbohydrate (gm): 16

1 teaspoon minced garlic

1-2 teaspoons Parisian, *or* Dijon-style, mustard

1 medium onion, thinly sliced

⅓ cup red bell pepper, thinly sliced

3 tablespoons fat-free Italian salad dressing

Exchanges
Milk: 0.0
Vegetable: 1.0
Fruit: 0.0
Bread: 1.0
Meat: 0.0
Fat: 0.5

1. Place lavosh between 2 damp clean kitchen towels; let stand until lavosh is softened enough to roll, 10 to 15 minutes.

2. Remove mushroom stems and chop; slice mushroom caps. Mix cream cheese, chopped mushroom stems, sour cream, garlic, and mustard in small bowl; spread mixture on lavosh. Toss sliced mushrooms, onion, and bell pepper with salad dressing; arrange over cheese mixture. Roll up lavosh tightly; wrap in plastic wrap and refrigerate at least 4 hours, but no longer than 2 days.

3. Trim ends; cut into scant 1-inch slices to serve.

EIGHT

Pizza, Calzones,
AND
Dinner Pies

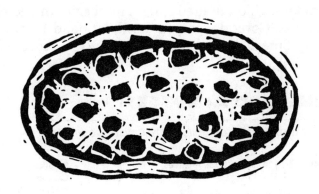

Pizza can be served as an appetizer or a snack, entrée, or even a bread,
so the number of servings in each pizza recipe will vary depending upon
how the pizza is used in a meal. For this reason, the yield for the recipes
has been given in slices, with nutritional information provided per slice.

BASIC PIZZA DOUGH

Quick and easy to make, this dough uses fast-rising yeast and requires no rising.

Makes one 12-inch crust (6 large slices)

1¼ cups all-purpose flour, divided
1 package fast-rising yeast
½ teaspoon sugar
¼ teaspoon salt
½ cup very hot water (120 degrees)

Per Slice
Calories: 99.5
% Calories from fat: 2
Fat (gm): 0.3
Saturated fat (gm): 0
Cholesterol (mg): 0
Sodium (mg): 89
Protein (gm): 3.2
Carbohydrate (gm): 20.7
Exchanges
Milk: 0.0
Vegetable: 0.0
Fruit: 0.0
Bread: 1.5
Meat: 0.0
Fat: 0.0

1. Combine ¾ cup flour, yeast, sugar, and salt in medium bowl; add hot water, stirring until smooth. Mix in enough of remaining ½ cup flour to make a soft dough.

2. Knead dough on floured surface until smooth and elastic, 3 to 5 minutes. Cover dough with bowl; let stand 15 minutes before using. Spread dough on pan according to directions in pizza recipes.

CORNMEAL PIZZA DOUGH

Another fast and easy-to-make, no-rise pizza dough!

Makes one 12-inch crust (6 large slices)

1 cup all-purpose flour, divided
¼ cup yellow cornmeal
1 package fast-rising yeast
½ teaspoon sugar
½ cup very hot water (120 degrees)

Per Slice
Calories: 99
% Calories from fat: 4
Fat (gm): 0.4
Saturated fat (gm): 0.1
Cholesterol (mg): 0
Sodium (mg): 2.3
Protein (gm): 3.1
Carbohydrate (gm): 20.7
Exchanges
Milk: 0.0
Vegetable: 0.0
Fruit: 0.0
Bread: 1.5
Meat: 0.0
Fat: 0.0

1. Combine ½ cup flour, cornmeal, yeast, and sugar in medium bowl; add hot water, stirring until smooth. Mix in enough of remaining ½ cup flour to make a soft dough.

2. Knead dough on floured surface until smooth and elastic, 3 to 5 minutes. Cover dough with bowl; let stand 15 minutes before using. Spread dough on pan according to directions in pizza recipes.

WHOLE WHEAT PIZZA DOUGH

For another flavor variation, substitute rye flour for the whole wheat flour and add ½ teaspoon caraway seeds.

Makes one 12-inch crust (6 large slices)

- ¾ cup all-purpose flour, divided
- 1 package fast-rising yeast
- ¼ teaspoon salt
- ½ cup very hot water (120 degrees)
- 2 teaspoons honey
- ½ cup whole wheat flour

Per Slice
Calories: 101
% Calories from fat: 3
Fat (gm): 0.3
Saturated fat (gm): 0.1
Cholesterol (mg): 0
Sodium (mg): 90
Protein (gm): 3.5
Carbohydrate (gm): 21.6
Exchanges
Milk: 0.0
Vegetable: 0.0
Fruit: 0.0
Bread: 1.5
Meat: 0.0
Fat: 0.0

1. Combine all-purpose flour, yeast, and salt in medium bowl; add hot water and honey, stirring until smooth. Mix in enough whole wheat flour to make a soft dough.

2. Knead dough on floured surface until smooth and elastic, 3 to 5 minutes. Cover dough with bowl; let stand 15 minutes before using. Spread dough on pan according to directions in pizza recipes.

CHEESE PIZZA DOUGH

Two cheeses flavor this crust; fat-free Monterey Jack or Swiss cheese can be substituted for the Cheddar.

Makes one 12-inch crust (6 large slices)

1¼   cups all-purpose flour, divided
1   package fast-rising yeast
½   teaspoon sugar
⅔   cup very hot water (120 degrees)
2   tablespoons grated fat-free Parmesan cheese
¼   cup (1 ounce) shredded fat-free Cheddar cheese

Per Slice
Calories: 112
% Calories from fat: 2
Fat (gm): 0.3
Saturated fat (gm): 0
Cholesterol (mg): 0
Sodium (mg): 49
Protein (gm): 5.4
Carbohydrate (gm): 21.7
Exchanges
Milk: 0.0
Vegetable: 0.0
Fruit: 0.0
Bread: 1.5
Meat: 0.0
Fat: 0.0

1. Combine ¾ cup flour, yeast, and sugar in medium bowl; add hot water, stirring until smooth. Mix in Parmesan cheese and enough remaining ½ cup flour to make smooth dough.

2. Knead dough on floured surface until smooth, kneading in Cheddar cheese. Cover dough with bowl; let stand 15 minutes before using. Spread dough on pan according to directions in pizza recipes.

ZUCCHINI PIZZA CRUST

A baked vegetable crust ready to top with your choice of lightly sauteed vegetables and cheese. See Double Zucchini Pizza (p. 446).

Makes one 12-inch crust (6 large slices)

4   medium zucchini, shredded (about 2 pounds)
   Salt, to taste
⅔   cup finely chopped onion
1   clove garlic, minced
¼   cup whole wheat flour
½   cup (2 ounces) shredded fat-free mozzarella cheese
¼-½   cup (1-2 ounces) grated fat-free Parmesan cheese

Per Slice
Calories: 102
% Calories from fat: 17
Fat (gm): 2
Saturated fat (gm): 0.6
Cholesterol (mg): 71
Sodium (mg): 142
Protein (gm): 10.6
Carbohydrate (gm): 11.7
Exchanges
Milk: 0.0
Vegetable: 0.5
Fruit: 0.0
Bread: 0.5
Meat: 1.0
Fat: 0.0

1 teaspoon Italian seasoning
Pepper, to taste
2 eggs
2 egg whites
Vegetable cooking spray

1. Sprinkle zucchini lightly with salt; let stand in colander 10 minutes. Rinse and drain very well on paper toweling. Mix zucchini, onion, garlic, flour, cheeses, and Italian seasoning; season to taste with pepper. Mix in eggs and egg whites.

2. Spray 12-inch pizza pan with cooking spray; press zucchini mixture evenly on pan. Spray zucchini with cooking spray; bake at 375 degrees until browned, 30 to 40 minutes.

POTATO PIZZA CRUST

Fill this pizza with a medley of lightly sauteed vegetables, top with cheese and bake until melty. Or see Chili Poblano Pizza (p. 442).

6 slices

1 package (1¼ pounds) refrigerated shredded potatoes for hash browns
⅓ cup finely chopped onion
1 egg
1 egg white
¼ teaspoon salt
¼ teaspoon pepper
Vegetable cooking spray

Per Slice
Calories: 93
% Calories from fat: 9
Fat (gm): 0.9
Saturated fat (gm): 0.3
Cholesterol (mg): 35.5
Sodium (mg): 113
Protein (gm): 3.2
Carbohydrate (gm): 18.2
Exchanges
Milk: 0.0
Vegetable: 0.0
Fruit: 0.0
Bread: 1.5
Meat: 0.0
Fat: 0.0

1. Drain potatoes well on paper toweling. Mix potatoes, onion, egg, egg white, salt, and pepper.

2. Spray 12-inch skillet with cooking spray; press potato mixture evenly on bottom and 1 inch up side of skillet. Spray potatoes with cooking spray. Bake at 400 degrees until browned, about 20 minutes.

PIZZA SUPREME

The pizza with everything—"sausage," peppers, mushrooms, onions, cheese, and anything else you think to add!

6 slices

Vegetable cooking spray
Basic Pizza Dough (see p. 418)
Pizza Sauce (see p. 700)
½ package (8-ounce size) frozen Italian-style vegetarian "burgers," thawed, crumbled
½ cup sliced mushrooms
½ cup sliced green bell peppers
½ cup sliced onion
1-2 tablespoons sliced ripe, *or* green, olives
1 teaspoon dried oregano leaves
½ teaspoon fennel seeds (crushed)
¾-1 cup (3-4 ounces) shredded reduced-fat mozzarella cheese

Per Slice
Calories: 241
% Calories from fat: 23
Fat (gm): 6.2
Saturated fat (gm): 1.6
Cholesterol (mg): 7.6
Sodium (mg): 362
Protein (gm): 13.3
Carbohydrate (gm): 32.1
Exchanges
Milk: 0.0
Vegetable: 2.0
Fruit: 0.0
Bread: 1.5
Meat: 1.5
Fat: 0.0

1. Spray 12-inch pizza pan with cooking spray; spread dough on pan, making rim around edge. Spread sauce over dough; sprinkle with crumbled "burgers," mushrooms, bell peppers, onion, and olives. Sprinkle with oregano, fennel seeds, and cheese.

2. Bake pizza at 425 degrees until crust is browned, 15 to 20 minutes.

DELUXE SPINACH-CHEESE PIZZA

Enjoy the combination of 4 cheeses on this flavorful pizza.

6 slices

2 ounces sun-dried tomatoes (not in oil)
Hot water
Olive oil cooking spray
2 cups sliced mushrooms
1 medium onion, sliced

Per Slice
Calories: 224
% Calories from fat: 7
Fat (gm): 1.9
Saturated fat (gm): 1
Cholesterol (mg): 3.5
Sodium (mg): 317
Protein (gm): 17.7
Carbohydrate (gm): 37.5

3 cloves garlic, minced
Basic Pizza Dough (see p. 418)
1 cup fat-free ricotta cheese
½ cup (2 ounces) shredded fat-free mozzarella cheese
¼ cup (1 ounce) grated fat-free Parmesan cheese
1 package (10 ounces) frozen spinach, thawed, well drained
3 tablespoons fat-free sour cream
1 tablespoon lemon juice
¼ teaspoon ground nutmeg
Salt and pepper, to taste
¼ cup (1 ounce) crumbled blue cheese

Exchanges
Milk: 0.0
Vegetable: 1.0
Fruit: 0.0
Bread: 2.0
Meat: 1.0
Fat: 0.0

1. Place tomatoes in bowl and pour hot water over; let stand until softened, about 10 minutes. Drain; slice or coarsely chop.

2. Spray large skillet with cooking spray; heat over medium heat until hot. Cook mushrooms, onion, and garlic over medium heat, covered, until mushrooms are wilted, about 5 minutes. Cook, uncovered, until vegetables are tender and excess liquid is gone, about 5 minutes.

3. Spray 12-inch pizza pan with cooking spray. Spread dough on pan, making rim around edge; bake at 425 degrees 10 minutes.

4. Mix ricotta, mozzarella, and Parmesan cheeses, spinach, sour cream, lemon juice, and nutmeg; season to taste with salt and pepper. Spread cheese mixture evenly on baked crust; top with vegetable mixture and sun-dried tomatoes. Sprinkle pizza with blue cheese.

5. Bake pizza until crust is browned, about 15 minutes.

DEEP-PAN SPINACH PIZZA

We've made this pizza in a springform pan, but use a deep pizza pan if you have one.

6 slices

Vegetable cooking spray
¼ cup finely chopped onion
1 clove garlic, minced
1 package (10 ounces) frozen chopped spinach, thawed, very well drained
Salt and pepper, to taste
Cornmeal Pizza Dough (see p. 418)
¼ cup reduced-sodium tomato sauce
1½ cups fat-free ricotta cheese
2 tablespoons fat-free sour cream
2 tablespoons grated fat-free Parmesan cheese
¾ teaspoon dried oregano leaves
1 medium tomato, sliced
¼ teaspoon Italian seasoning
½ cup (2 ounces) shredded reduced-fat mozzarella cheese

Per Slice
Calories: 195
% Calories from fat: 8
Fat (gm): 1.9
Saturated fat (gm): 1.1
Cholesterol (mg): 5.1
Sodium (mg): 151
Protein (gm): 16.3
Carbohydrate (gm): 30.5
Exchanges
Milk: 0.0
Vegetable: 1.0
Fruit: 0.0
Bread: 1.5
Meat: 1.0
Fat: 0.0

1. Spray medium skillet with cooking spray; heat over medium heat until hot. Saute onion and garlic until tender, 2 to 3 minutes; add spinach and cook until mixture is very dry. Season to taste with salt and pepper.

2. Roll dough on floured surface to circle 13 inches in diameter; ease dough into lightly greased 9-inch springform pan, covering bottom and 2 inches up side of pan. Spread tomato sauce on bottom of dough.

3. Mix ricotta cheese, sour cream, Parmesan cheese, and oregano; spoon onto dough and top with spinach mixture. Fold edge of dough over edge of filling; top center of pizza with tomato slices and sprinkle with Italian seasoning and mozzarella cheese.

4. Bake pizza at 400 degrees until dough is browned, about 20 to 30 minutes. Let stand 5 to 10 minutes before cutting.

BREAKFAST PIZZA

Great for breakfast, brunch, or a light supper. The egg is added last and quickly cooked in the oven.

6 slices

Vegetable cooking spray
Cheese Pizza Dough or Cornmeal Pizza Dough (see pp. 420, 418)
1 cup Pizza Sauce (see p. 700)
½ medium green bell pepper, sliced
½ small onion, sliced
1 cup (4 ounces) shredded fat-free mozzarella cheese
3 tablespoons "bacon"-flavored bits
1 egg

Per Slice
Calories: 197
% Calories from fat: 9
Fat (gm): 1.9
Saturated fat (gm): 0.4
Cholesterol (mg): 35.5
Sodium (mg): 287
Protein (gm): 15.1
Carbohydrate (gm): 29.5
Exchanges
Milk: 0.0
Vegetable: 1.0
Fruit: 0.0
Bread: 1.5
Meat: 1.0
Fat: 0.0

1. Spray 12-inch pizza pan with cooking spray; spread dough on pan, making rim around edge. Spread sauce on dough and sprinkle with bell pepper, onion, cheese, and "bacon" bits.

2. Bake pizza at 425 degrees until crust is browned, 15 to 20 minutes. Remove from oven; break egg into center of pizza. Stir egg with fork and quickly spread over pizza. Return to oven and bake until egg is cooked, 1 to 2 minutes.

RANCH-STYLE PIZZA

Our skinny version of a pizza from a favorite pizzeria.

6 slices

Vegetable cooking spray
Basic Pizza Dough (see p. 418)
¼-½ cup fat-free ranch salad dressing, divided
1 cup (4 ounces) shredded fat-free mozzarella cheese
½ cup (2 ounces) shredded reduced-fat mozzarella cheese

Per Slice
Calories: 171
% Calories from fat: 9
Fat (gm): 1.7
Saturated fat (gm): 1.1
Cholesterol (mg): 5.1
Sodium (mg): 378
Protein (gm): 12.9
Carbohydrate (gm): 25
Exchanges
Milk: 0.0
Vegetable: 0.5
Fruit: 0.0
Bread: 1.5
Meat: 1.0
Fat: 0.0

1 cup thinly sliced spinach
½ cup sliced mushrooms

1. Spray 12-inch pizza pan with cooking spray; spread dough on pan, making rim around edge. Brush dough with ¼ cup salad dressing; sprinkle with cheeses. Toss spinach and mushrooms together; mound in center of pizza.

2. Bake pizza at 425 degrees until crust is browned, 15 to 20 minutes. Drizzle pizza with ¼ cup salad dressing (optional) before serving.

REUBEN PIZZA

Sauerkraut, thousand island salad dressing, and "bacon"-flavored bits create a pizza that challenges the sandwich!

6 slices

Vegetable cooking spray
12 ounces cabbage thinly sliced
½ cup thinly sliced red onion
1½ teaspoons caraway seeds, crushed, divided
2 tablespoons water
½ can (14.2-ounce size) Bavarian-style sweet mild sauerkraut with caraway, rinsed, very well drained
½-1 cup (2-4 ounces) shredded fat-free mozzarella cheese
2-3 teaspoons "bacon"-flavored bits
Whole Wheat Pizza Dough (see p. 419)
½ cup rye flour
¼ cup fat-free thousand island salad dressing

Per Slice
Calories: 185
% Calories from fat: 4
Fat (gm): 0.9
Saturated fat (gm): 0.1
Cholesterol (mg): 0
Sodium (mg): 402
Protein (gm): 8.8
Carbohydrate (gm): 36.9
Exchanges
Milk: 0.0
Vegetable: 1.0
Fruit: 0.0
Bread: 2.0
Meat: 0.5
Fat: 0.0

1. Spray large skillet with cooking spray; heat over medium heat until hot. Add cabbage, onion, and 1 teaspoon caraway seeds; saute 2 to 3 minutes. Add water to skillet; cook, covered, over medium to medium-low heat until cabbage is wilted, 5 to 8 minutes. Stir in sauerkraut; cook, uncovered, over medium-low heat until cabbage mixture is very tender, 15 to 20 minutes. Cool to room temperature; stir in cheese.

2. Make Whole Wheat Pizza Dough, substituting rye flour for the whole wheat flour, and adding the ½ teaspoon caraway seeds.

3. Spray 12-inch pizza pan with cooking spray; spread dough on pan, making rim around edge. Spread salad dressing on dough. Spread cabbage mixture evenly over dough.

4. Bake pizza at 425 degrees until crust is browned, 15 to 20 minutes.

WEST COAST PIZZA

Quick and easy to make because it's made on a purchased focaccia. Serve as a hearty entrée with a crisp green salad.

4 slices

Olive oil cooking spray
1½ cups sliced mushrooms
1 cup small broccoli florets
¾ cup thinly sliced red bell pepper
½ cup sliced carrot
¼ cup thinly sliced green onions
4 cloves garlic, minced
½-¾ cup cooked dried (*or* rinsed, drained, canned) Great Northern beans
Red Tomato Salsa (see p. 9), *or* jarred salsa, divided
1 thin-crust Italian bread shell (focaccia)
½-¾ cup (2-3 ounces) shredded reduced-fat mozzarella cheese
½-¾ cup (2-3 ounces) shredded fat-free mozzarella cheese
½-¾ cup sprouted wheat berries, *or* chick peas

Per Slice
Calories: 351
% Calories from fat: 18
Fat (gm): 7.1
Saturated fat (gm): 2.9
Cholesterol (mg): 13.8
Sodium (mg): 583
Protein (gm): 23.2
Carbohydrate (gm): 50.4
Exchanges
Milk: 0.0
Vegetable: 2.0
Fruit: 0.0
Bread: 2.5
Meat: 2.0
Fat: 0.0

1. Spray large skillet with cooking spray; heat over medium heat until hot. Saute mushrooms, broccoli, bell pepper, carrot, onions, and garlic until tender, 8 to 10 minutes.

2. Mash beans with 3 to 4 tablespoons salsa; spread mixture on bread shell. Spoon about ½ cup salsa over beans; top with sauteed vegetables and cheeses.

3. Bake pizza at 350 degrees until cheese is melted, about 15 minutes. Sprinkle with wheat berries just before serving. Serve with remaining salsa.

CALYPSO PIZZA

 Jalapeño chili accents this island-style fruit and veggie pizza.

6 slices

Vegetable cooking spray
Cheese Pizza Dough (see p. 420)
1 cup rinsed, drained, canned black beans
1 can (8 ounces) pineapple tidbits, drained
¼ cup chopped red bell pepper
1 small jalapeño chili, finely chopped
½ teaspoon minced garlic
½ teaspoon ground cumin
¼ cup hot, *or* mild, salsa
1 teaspoon lime juice
1 cup (4 ounces) shredded reduced-fat Monterey Jack cheese
½ cup (2 ounces) shredded fat-free Cheddar cheese

Per Slice
Calories: 219
% Calories from fat: 16
Fat (gm): 4
Saturated fat (gm): 2.1
Cholesterol (mg): 13.5
Sodium (mg): 373
Protein (gm): 14.1
Carbohydrate (gm): 33.9
Exchanges
Milk: 0.0
Vegetable: 1.0
Fruit: 0.5
Bread: 1.5
Meat: 1.0
Fat: 0.0

1. Spray 12-inch pizza pan with cooking spray; spread dough on pan, making rim around edge. Combine all ingredients, except cheeses, and arrange on crust; sprinkle with cheeses.

2. Bake pizza at 425 degrees until crust is browned, 15 to 20 minutes.

ORIENTAL PIZZA

Stir-fried vegetables create new flavor interest as a pizza topping! Purchased smoked tofu may be substituted for our Mesquite-Smoked Tofu recipe.

6 slices

Oriental-flavored cooking spray
1 cup sliced shiitake, *or* cremini, mushrooms
1 cup thinly sliced bok choy
½ cup small broccoli florets
1 small onion, sliced
½ medium green pepper, sliced
½ cup (2 ounces) snow peas, trimmed
2 teaspoons minced gingerroot
1 clove garlic, minced
1-2 teaspoons reduced-sodium tamari soy sauce
Salt and pepper, to taste
Basic Pizza Dough (see p. 418)
(½ recipe) Mesquite-Smoked Tofu (see p. 267), cut into ½-inch cubes
¾ cup (3 ounces) shredded fat-free mozzarella cheese

Per Slice
Calories: 174
% Calories from fat: 5
Fat (gm): 1
Saturated fat (gm): 0.1
Cholesterol (mg): 0
Sodium (mg): 276
Protein (gm): 13.2
Carbohydrate (gm): 28.6
Exchanges
Milk: 0.0
Vegetable: 1.0
Fruit: 0.0
Bread: 1.5
Meat: 1.0
Fat: 0.0

1. Spray large skillet with cooking spray; heat over medium heat until hot. Stir-fry mushrooms, bok choy, broccoli, onion, green pepper, snow peas, gingerroot, and garlic until tender, 8 to 10 minutes. Season to taste with soy sauce, salt, and pepper; cool to room temperature.

2. Spray 12-inch pizza pan with cooking spray. Spread dough on pan, making rim around edge. Spray dough with cooking spray. Arrange vegetables and tofu on dough; sprinkle with cheese.

3. Bake pizza at 425 degrees until crust is browned, 15 to 20 minutes.

FRENCH-STYLE ONION PIZZA

Called a "Pissaladiere," this onion pizza is more traditionally made on a pastry rather than a pizza crust.

6 slices

Olive oil cooking spray
6 medium onions, thinly sliced (about 6 cups)
2 medium tomatoes, coarsely chopped
¼ cup finely chopped parsley
½ teaspoon dried oregano leaves
¼ teaspoon dried thyme leaves
Salt and pepper, to taste
Basic Pizza Dough (see p. 418)
2-4 tablespoons sliced ripe olives

Per Slice
Calories: 165
% Calories from fat: 9
Fat (gm): 1.6
Saturated fat (gm): 0.2
Cholesterol (mg): 0
Sodium (mg): 191
Protein (gm): 5.1
Carbohydrate (gm): 33.5
Exchanges
Milk: 0.0
Vegetable: 2.0
Fruit: 0.0
Bread: 1.5
Meat: 0.0
Fat: 0.0

1. Spray large skillet with cooking spray; heat over medium heat until hot. Cook onions over medium to medium-low heat until very tender, about 15 minutes. Add tomatoes, parsley, oregano, and thyme; cook over medium heat until mixture is thick, about 15 minutes. Season to taste with salt and pepper; cool to room temperature.

2. Spray 12-inch pizza pan with cooking spray; spread dough on pan, making rim around edge. Spread onion mixture over dough and sprinkle with olives.

3. Bake pizza at 425 degrees until crust is browned, 15 to 20 minutes.

FRESH TOMATO AND BASIL PIZZA

One of the simplest yet most flavorful pizzas you've ever tasted! Use fresh basil if you possibly can.

6 slices

Olive oil cooking spray
Basic Pizza Dough (see p. 418)
Pizza Sauce (see p. 700)
1-2 teaspoons minced plain, *or* roasted, garlic

Per Slice
Calories: 193
% Calories from fat: 9
Fat (gm): 1.8
Saturated fat (gm): 1.1
Cholesterol (mg): 5.1
Sodium (mg): 306
Protein (gm): 14.1
Carbohydrate (gm): 29.4

1 cup (4 ounces) fat-free mozzarella
cheese

½-¾ cup (2-3 ounces) reduced-fat mozzarella cheese

2 medium tomatoes, thinly sliced

12 basil leaves, *or* 1 teaspoon dried basil
leaves

Exchanges
Milk: 0.0
Vegetable: 2.0
Fruit: 0.0
Bread: 1.5
Meat: 1.0
Fat: 0.0

1. Spray 12-inch pizza pan with cooking spray; spread dough
on pan, making rim around edge. Mix Pizza Sauce and garlic;
spread over dough. Sprinkle with cheeses; top with tomato slices
and basil.

2. Bake pizza at 425 degrees until crust is browned, 15 to 20
minutes.

ARTICHOKE AND ROASTED PEPPER PIZZA

 *Roasted green bell peppers add a slightly different flavor; roasted red
peppers can, of course, be substituted.*

6 slices

Olive oil cooking spray

1 medium green bell pepper, cut into ½-
inch slices

Basic Pizza Dough (see p. 418)

½ can (15-ounce size) reduced-sodium
whole tomatoes, drained, coarsely
chopped

½ can (15-ounce size) artichoke hearts,
rinsed, drained, cut into fourths

½ teaspoon Italian seasoning

½ cup (2 ounces) shredded fat-free
mozzarella cheese

¼-½ cup (1-2 ounces) shredded reduced-fat
mozzarella cheese

2 tablespoons grated fat-free Parmesan
cheese

Per Slice
Calories: 169
% Calories from fat: 18
Fat (gm): 3.6
Saturated fat (gm): 0.6
Cholesterol (mg): 2.5
Sodium (mg): 311
Protein (gm): 9
Carbohydrate (gm): 26.8
Exchanges
Milk: 0.0
Vegetable: 1.0
Fruit: 0.0
Bread: 1.5
Meat: 0.5
Fat: 0.0

1. Spray aluminum-foil-lined small baking pan with cooking
spray. Arrange bell pepper in pan; bake at 425 degrees until pepper is tender and browned, 20 to 30 minutes.

2. Spray 12-inch pizza pan with cooking spray; spread dough on pan, making rim around edge. Arrange bell pepper, tomatoes, and artichoke hearts on dough; sprinkle with Italian seasoning and cheeses.

3. Bake pizza until crust is browned, 15 to 20 minutes.

ROASTED RED PEPPER AND CHEESE PIZZA

 For color and flavor variation, try a yellow or green bell pepper.

6 slices

Olive oil cooking spray
1 large red bell pepper, cut into ¾-inch slices
Cornmeal Pizza Dough (see p. 418)
1 cup fat-free ricotta cheese
½ cup (2 ounces) shredded fat-free mozzarella cheese
¼ cup (1 ounce) shredded fat-free Parmesan cheese
3 tablespoons fat-free sour cream
1 tablespoon lemon juice
1 clove garlic, minced
Salt and pepper, to taste
2 green onions, thinly sliced
12-18 fresh basil leaves

Per Slice
Calories: 172
% Calories from fat: 3
Fat (gm): 0.6
Saturated fat (gm): 0.1
Cholesterol (mg): 0
Sodium (mg): 124
Protein (gm): 14.4
Carbohydrate (gm): 29.4
Exchanges
Milk: 0.0
Vegetable: 1.0
Fruit: 0.0
Bread: 1.5
Meat: 1.0
Fat: 0.0

1. Spray aluminum-foil-lined baking pan with cooking spray. Arrange bell pepper slices in pan; spray with cooking spray. Roast at 425 degrees until peppers are soft, but not browned, 20 to 30 minutes.

2. Spray 12-inch pizza pan with cooking spray; spread dough on pan, making rim around edge; bake dough at 425 degrees 15 to 20 minutes.

3. Mix cheeses, sour cream, lemon juice, and garlic; season to taste with salt and pepper. Spread cheese mixture evenly on crust; sprinkle with green onions. Arrange roasted pepper slices and basil leaves attractively on top.

4. Bake at 425 degrees until crust is browned, 15 to 20 minutes.

ROASTED CAPONATA PIZZA

This Mediterranean-inspired pizza combines the flavors of eggplant and a tomato sauce containing raisins, capers, and a blending of herbs and sweet spices.

6 slices

Olive oil cooking spray

2 cups diced, unpeeled eggplant

1 cup coarsely chopped onion

Whole Wheat Pizza Dough (see p. 419)

1 cup (½ recipe) Mediterranean Tomato-Caper Sauce (see p. 709)

½-1 cup (2-4 ounces) shredded fat-free mozzarella cheese

½ cup (2 ounces) crumbled reduced-fat feta cheese

1 tablespoon pine nuts (optional)

Per Slice
Calories: 181
% Calories from fat: 9
Fat (gm): 1.9
Saturated fat (gm): 0.9
Cholesterol (mg): 3.4
Sodium (mg): 312
Protein (gm): 10
Carbohydrate (gm): 32.3
Exchanges
Milk: 0.0
Vegetable: 2.0
Fruit: 0.0
Bread: 1.5
Meat: 0.5
Fat: 0.0

1. Spray aluminum-foil-lined baking pan, 13 x 9 inches, with cooking spray. Arrange eggplant and onion in baking pan; bake at 425 degrees until eggplant is tender and browned, 20 to 30 minutes; cool to room temperature.

2. Spray 12-inch pizza pan with cooking spray; spread dough on pan, making rim around edge. Spread sauce on dough; arrange eggplant mixture on sauce. Sprinkle with cheeses and pine nuts.

3. Bake pizza at 425 degrees until crust is browned, 15 to 20 minutes.

TUSCAN POTATO PIZZA

A hearty pizza with robust flavor.

6 slices

Mesquite-flavored vegetable cooking spray

8 ounces small Russet potatoes, unpeeled, cut into scant ¼-inch slices

Per Slice
Calories: 225
% Calories from fat: 8
Fat (gm): 2.1
Saturated fat (gm): 0.1
Cholesterol (mg): 5
Sodium (mg): 301
Protein (gm): 14.4
Carbohydrate (gm): 38.2

Exchanges
Milk: 0.0
Vegetable: 0.0
Fruit: 0.0
Bread: 2.5
Meat: 1.0
Fat: 0.0

1 medium red onion, thinly sliced
Salt and pepper, to taste
Whole Wheat Pizza Dough (see p. 419)
1-2 teaspoons minced garlic
1-2 teaspoons dried sage leaves
½ teaspoon dried thyme leaves
2 tablespoons sun-dried tomato bits
1 cup (4 ounces) shredded fat-free
mozzarella cheese
½ cup (2 ounces) shredded smoked
mozzarella cheese

1. Spray aluminum-foil-lined jelly roll pan with cooking spray. Arrange potatoes and onions on pan; spray with cooking spray. Bake at 425 degrees until potatoes are almost tender, about 10 minutes. Season to taste with salt and pepper; cool to room temperature.

2. Spray 12-inch pizza pan with cooking spray; spread dough on pan, making rim around edge. Spray dough lightly with cooking spray; spread garlic on crust. Arrange potatoes and onions on crust; sprinkle with herbs, tomato bits, and cheeses.

3. Bake pizza at 425 degrees until browned, 15 to 20 minutes.

PIZZA ON PASTA

A fun pizza, with a crust made of spaghetti!

6 slices

Per Slice
Calories: 305
% Calories from fat: 20
Fat (gm): 6.8
Saturated fat (gm): 2.1
Cholesterol (mg): 9
Sodium (mg): 359
Protein (gm): 18.6
Carbohydrate (gm): 42.7
Exchanges
Milk: 0.0
Vegetable: 2.0
Fruit: 0.0
Bread: 2.0
Meat: 2.0
Fat: 0.0

Olive oil cooking spray
1 package (8 ounces) frozen sausage-style
vegetable protein patties, *or* links,
thawed, crumbled
1 cup sliced mushrooms
1 cup sliced zucchini
½ cup sliced red bell pepper
¼ cup sliced green onions and tops
1½ teaspoons minced garlic
1½ teaspoons Italian seasoning
½ teaspoon dried oregano leaves

Salt and pepper, to taste

8 ounces thin spaghetti, cooked

2 egg whites, lightly beaten

1 medium tomato, sliced

¾-1 cup (3-4 ounces) shredded reduced-fat muenster, *or* mozzarella, cheese

Pizza Sauce (see p. 700), warm

1. Spray large skillet with cooking spray; heat over medium heat until hot. Add "sausage," mushrooms, zucchini, bell pepper, green onions, and garlic; saute until vegetables are tender, about 8 minutes. Stir in Italian seasoning and oregano; cook 1 to 2 minutes longer. Season to taste with salt and pepper. Transfer to large bowl.

2. Spray clean large skillet with cooking spray; heat over medium heat until hot. Mix vegetable mixture, spaghetti, and egg whites. Add to skillet and pat into even layer with pancake turner. Cook, covered, over medium to medium-low heat until browned on the bottom, about 5 minutes. Loosen side and bottom of "pizza" with pancake turner; invert onto large plate. Slide "pizza" back into skillet.

3. Arrange tomato slices over top of "pizza" and sprinkle with cheese; cook, covered, over medium heat until cheese is melted, about 5 minutes. Slide "pizza" onto serving plate; cut into wedges and serve with Pizza Sauce.

ANTIPASTO PIZZA

 A pizza with tempting Mediterranean flavors.

6 slices

Olive oil cooking spray

Cornmeal Pizza Dough (see p. 418)

1 cup (½ recipe) Mediterranean Tomato-Caper Sauce (see p. 709)

½ small zucchini, thinly sliced

½ cup sliced mushrooms

½ cup sliced onion

Per Slice
Calories: 203
% Calories from fat: 13
Fat (gm): 3
Saturated fat (gm): 1
Cholesterol (mg): 3.4
Sodium (mg): 401
Protein (gm): 12
Carbohydrate (gm): 33.2
Exchanges
Milk: 0.0
Vegetable: 2.0
Fruit: 0.0
Bread: 1.5
Meat: 1.0
Fat: 0.0

½ medium red bell pepper, sliced

3 cloves garlic, minced

3-4 pepperoncini, sliced

3-4 frozen (cooked), *or* canned, artichoke
hearts, sliced

2-4 tablespoons sliced ripe olives

¾ cup (3 ounces) shredded fat-free
mozzarella cheese

½ cup (2 ounces) crumbled reduced-fat
feta cheese

1. Spray 12-inch pizza pan with cooking spray; spread dough
on pan, making rim around edge. Spread sauce on dough; top
with vegetables and sprinkle with cheeses.

2. Bake pizza at 425 degrees until crust is browned, 15 to 20
minutes.

LEEK AND FETA PIZZA WITH PESTO SAUCE

 *Use your preference of Mixed Herb, Spinach, or Cilantro Pesto (see pp.
727, 730) on this pizza.*

6 slices

Olive oil cooking spray

4 cups sliced leeks (white parts only)

1 teaspoon dried basil leaves

Salt and pepper, to taste

Basic Pizza Dough (see p. 418)

Sun-Dried Tomato Pesto (see p. 728)

½ cup (2 ounces) shredded fat-free
mozzarella cheese

½ cup (2 ounces) crumbled reduced-fat
feta cheese

2 tablespoons (½ ounce) grated fat-free
Parmesan cheese

Per Slice
Calories: 288
% Calories from fat: 27
Fat (gm): 8.9
Saturated fat (gm): 1.9
Cholesterol (mg): 3.4
Sodium (mg): 428
Protein (gm): 12.1
Carbohydrate (gm): 41.9
Exchanges
Milk: 0.0
Vegetable: 3.0
Fruit: 0.0
Bread: 1.5
Meat: 1.0
Fat: 1.0

1. Spray large skillet with cooking spray; heat over medium
heat until hot. Saute leeks until tender, 8 to 10 minutes. Sprinkle
with basil and cook 1 to 2 minutes longer. Season to taste with
salt and pepper; cool to room temperature.

2. Spray 12-inch pizza pan with cooking spray. Spread dough on pan, making rim around edge. Spread pesto on dough; top with leek mixture and sprinkle with cheeses.

3. Bake pizza at 425 degrees until crust is browned, 15 to 20 minutes.

WILD MUSHROOM PIZZA

 Regular mushrooms can be used for this pizza, but wild mushrooms are more flavorful.

6 slices

Olive oil cooking spray
5 cups sliced wild mushrooms (cremini, portobello, shiitake, etc.)
¼ cup finely chopped shallots, *or* onions
1 teaspoon minced garlic
2 tablespoons water
¼-½ teaspoon dried thyme leaves
Basic Pizza Dough (see p. 418)
¼ cup (½ recipe) Mixed Herb Pesto (see p. 727)
1 cup (4 ounces) shredded fat-free mozzarella cheese, divided

Per Slice
Calories:194
% Calories from fat: 20
Fat (gm): 4.5
Saturated fat (gm): 0.7
Cholesterol (mg): 0.8
Sodium (mg): 336
Protein (gm): 12.5
Carbohydrate (gm): 26.7
Exchanges
Milk: 0.0
Vegetable: 2.0
Fruit: 0.0
Bread: 1.0
Meat: 1.0
Fat: 0.5

1. Spray large skillet with cooking spray; heat over medium heat until hot. Add mushrooms, shallots, garlic, and water to skillet; cook, covered, over medium heat until mushrooms are wilted, about 5 minutes. Cook, uncovered, until mushrooms are tender and liquid is gone, 10 to 12 minutes. Stir in thyme.

2. Spray 12-inch pizza pan with cooking spray. Shape dough into a round; spread on 12-inch pizza pan, making rim around edge. Spread pesto on dough and sprinkle with ½ cup cheese. Spoon mushroom mixture on cheese; sprinkle with remaining ½ cup cheese.

3. Bake pizza at 350 degrees until crust is browned, about 30 minutes.

GAZPACHO PIZZA

Gazpacho, chilled and refreshing, served on a crust!

8 slices

1¼ packages (8-ounce size) fat-free cream cheese, softened

2 tablespoons fat-free mayonnaise

½ teaspoon dry mustard

2 teaspoons finely chopped parsley

2 teaspoons finely chopped chives

1 large whole wheat lavosh, *or* cracker bread, (5¼ ounces)

½ cup chopped avocado

1 cup chopped seeded tomato

1 cup chopped seeded cucumber

½ cup chopped onion

½ cup chopped yellow bell pepper

½ cup chopped green bell pepper

¼ cup fat-free Italian salad dressing

1 teaspoon minced garlic

1 teaspoon minced jalapeño chili

Salt and pepper, to taste

Per Slice
Calories: 153
% Calories from fat: 29
Fat (gm): 5.1
Saturated fat (gm): 0.4
Cholesterol (mg): 0
Sodium (mg): 415
Protein (gm): 7.4
Carbohydrate (gm): 19.9
Exchanges
Milk: 0.0
Vegetable: 1.5
Fruit: 0.0
Bread: 1.0
Meat: 0.0
Fat: 1.0

1. Mix cream cheese, mayonnaise, dry mustard, parsley, and chives. Spread mixture on lavosh.

2. Combine vegetables in large bowl. Combine salad dressing, garlic, and jalapeño chili; pour over vegetables and toss. Season to taste with salt and pepper. Spoon mixture onto lavosh and serve immediately.

TOMATO FILLO PIZZA

Use summer's ripest tomatoes for this delectable pizza.

8 slices

Olive oil cooking spray
8 sheets frozen fillo pastry, thawed
2 cups (8 ounces) shredded fat-free
mozzarella cheese
½ cup thinly sliced onion
1 pound tomatoes, thinly sliced
Salt and pepper, to taste
¼ cup (1 ounce) grated Parmesan cheese
¾ teaspoon dried dill weed
½ teaspoon dried basil leaves

Per Slice
Calories: 79
% Calories from fat: 14
Fat (gm): 1.2
Saturated fat (gm): 0.6
Cholesterol (mg): 2.5
Sodium (mg): 270
Protein (gm): 12
Carbohydrate (gm): 5.4
Exchanges
Milk: 0.0
Vegetable: 0.0
Fruit: 0.0
Bread: 0.5
Meat: 1.0
Fat: 0.0

1. Spray jelly roll pan with cooking spray; place sheet of fillo on pan and spray generously with spray. Repeat with remaining sheets of fillo.

2. Sprinkle mozzarella cheese and onion over fillo; arrange tomato slices on top. Sprinkle lightly with salt and pepper. Sprinkle with Parmesan cheese and herbs.

3. Bake pizza at 375 degrees until fillo is browned and cheese melted, about 15 minutes.

PIZZA, SOUTHWEST-STYLE

A cornmeal crust and mesquite flavor are perfect complements for this pizza.

6 slices

Vegetable cooking spray
1 medium poblano chili, sliced
¾ cup sliced red bell pepper
1 medium onion, thinly sliced
1 small jalapeño chili, finely chopped
2 cloves garlic, minced

Per Slice
Calories: 192
% Calories from fat: 3
Fat (gm): 0.7
Saturated fat (gm): 0.1
Cholesterol (mg): 0
Sodium (mg): 161
Protein (gm): 11.9
Carbohydrate (gm): 35.9

⅔ cup fresh, *or* frozen, thawed, whole-kernel corn

1 teaspoon dried marjoram leaves

Cornmeal Pizza Dough (see p. 418)

Pizza Sauce (see p. 700)

½ teaspoon ground cumin

1 cup (4 ounces) shredded fat-free pizza cheese

Exchanges
Milk: 0.0
Vegetable: 2.0
Fruit: 0.0
Bread: 1.5
Meat: 0.5
Fat: 0.0

1. Spray large skillet with cooking spray; heat over medium heat until hot. Saute poblano chili, bell pepper, onion, jalapeño chili, and garlic until tender, about 8 minutes. Stir in corn and marjoram.

2. Spray 12-inch pizza pan with cooking spray; spread dough on pan, making rim around edge. Spray dough lightly with cooking spray. Mix Pizza Sauce and cumin; spread on dough. Top with vegetable mixture and sprinkle with cheese.

3. Bake pizza at 425 degrees until browned, 15 to 20 minutes.

TACO PIZZA

 Top this baked pizza with your choice of taco ingredients before eating!

6 slices

⅓ package (12-ounce size) prebrowned vegetable protein crumbles

1-2 tablespoons taco seasoning mix

⅔ cup water

Olive oil cooking spray

Cornmeal Pizza Dough (see p. 418)

½ cup (2 ounces) shredded fat-free Cheddar cheese

½ cup (2 ounces) shredded reduced-fat Monterey Jack cheese

½ large green bell pepper, sliced

1 cup chopped lettuce

½ cup chopped tomato

6 tablespoons fat-free sour cream

6 tablespoons reduced-sodium hot, *or* mild, salsa

Per Slice
Calories: 190
% Calories from fat: 10
Fat (gm): 2.2
Saturated fat (gm): 1.1
Cholesterol (mg): 6.8
Sodium (mg): 370
Protein (gm): 14.9
Carbohydrate (gm): 27.8
Exchanges
Milk: 0.0
Vegetable: 0.5
Fruit: 0.0
Bread: 1.5
Meat: 1.5
Fat: 0.0

1. Combine vegetable protein crumbles, taco seasoning mix, and water in medium saucepan; heat to boiling. Reduce heat and simmer, uncovered, until mixture is dry, about 5 minutes. Cool to room temperature.

2. Spray 12-inch pizza pan with cooking spray; spread dough on pan, making rim around edge. Sprinkle dough with vegetable protein crumbles, cheeses, and bell pepper.

3. Bake pizza at 425 degrees until crust is browned, 15 to 20 minutes. Sprinkle with lettuce and tomato and serve immediately with sour cream and salsa.

BLACK BEAN AND JALAPEÑO PIZZA

For quick and easy individual pizzas, assemble ingredients as below, using 4 flour tortillas; bake at 350 degrees until beans are hot and cheese melted, about 10 minutes.

6 slices

Olive oil cooking spray
Cornmeal Pizza Dough, *or* Cheese Pizza Dough (see pp. 418, 420)
1 cup (½ recipe) Red Tomato Salsa (see p. 9), divided
1 cup cooked dried, *or* rinsed, drained, canned, black beans
¼-⅓ cup drained, pickled sliced jalapeño chilies
1 cup (4 ounces) shredded reduced-fat Cheddar cheese

Per Slice
Calories: 191
% Calories from fat: 16
Fat (gm): 3.3
Saturated fat (gm): 1.5
Cholesterol (mg): 10.1
Sodium (mg): 334
Protein (gm): 9.9
Carbohydrate (gm): 30.3
Exchanges
Milk: 0.0
Vegetable: 1.0
Fruit: 0.0
Bread: 2.0
Meat: 0.5
Fat: 0.0

1. Spray 12-inch pizza pan with cooking spray; spread dough on pan, making rim around edge. Spread ¾ cup salsa on dough.

2. Lightly mash black beans with remaining ¼ cup salsa; spoon over pizza. Sprinkle jalapeño chilies and cheese over all.

3. Bake pizza at 425 degrees until crust is browned, 15 to 20 minutes.

CHILI POBLANO PIZZA

Sauteed poblano chilies, called "rajas" in Mexico, top a potato-crusted pizza. Poblano chilies can be quite hot; if so, green bell peppers can be substituted for part of the chilies.

6 slices

Olive oil cooking spray
4 large poblano chilies, sliced
2 cups chopped onions
1 clove garlic, minced
Salt, to taste
Potato Pizza Crust (see p. 421)
½-1 cup (2-4 ounces) shredded reduced-fat Monterey Jack cheese

Per Slice
Calories: 154
% Calories from fat: 16
Fat (gm): 2.8
Saturated fat (gm): 1.3
Cholesterol (mg): 42.3
Sodium (mg): 190
Protein (gm): 7.3
Carbohydrate (gm): 26.1
Exchanges
Milk: 0.0
Vegetable: 1.0
Fruit: 0.0
Bread: 1.5
Meat: 0.5
Fat: 0.0

1. Spray large skillet with cooking spray; heat over medium heat until hot. Add poblano chilies, onions, and garlic, and cook over medium to medium-low heat until chilies are very soft, 20 to 30 minutes. Season to taste with salt.

2. Spread chili mixture in Potato Pizza Crust; sprinkle with cheese. Bake at 400 degrees until cheese is melted, 5 to 10 minutes.

HUEVOS RANCHEROS PIZZA

Pizza crust replaces tortillas in this version of the popular Mexican dish.

6 slices

Vegetable cooking spray
1 large poblano chili, sliced
½ large red bell pepper, sliced
1 small onion, sliced
2 cloves garlic, minced
Salt and pepper, to taste
Cornmeal Pizza Dough, *or* Cheese Pizza Dough (see pp. 418, 420)

Per Slice
Calories: 225
% Calories from fat: 10
Fat (gm): 2.4
Saturated fat (gm): 0.6
Cholesterol (mg): 71
Sodium (mg): 382
Protein (gm): 18.8
Carbohydrate (gm): 32.5
Exchanges
Milk: 0.0
Vegetable: 1.0
Fruit: 0.0
Bread: 1.5
Meat: 1.5
Fat: 0.0

1 cup (½ recipe) Red Tomato Salsa (see p. 9), *or* Pizza Sauce (see p. 700)

"Chorizo" (see p. 404)

1 cup (4 ounces)shredded fat-free Cheddar cheese

1 egg

1. Spray large skillet with cooking spray; heat over medium heat until hot. Saute poblano chili, bell pepper, onion, and garlic, until tender, about 8 minutes. Season to taste with salt and pepper.

2. Spray 12-inch pizza pan with cooking spray; spread dough on pan, making rim around edge. Spread salsa on dough; top with sauteed vegetables, "Chorizo," and cheese.

3. Bake pizza at 425 degrees until crust is browned, 15 to 20 minutes. Remove from oven; break egg into center of pizza. Stir egg with fork and quickly spread over pizza. Return to oven and bake until egg is cooked, 1 to 2 minutes.

PIZZA WITH YELLOW AND GREEN SQUASH

 A pizza with garden-fresh flavors and colors! Substitute fresh herbs, if they are available, using about 2 teaspoons of each.

6 slices

Vegetable cooking spray

1 medium zucchini, cut into scant ¼-inch slices

1 medium yellow summer squash, cut into scant ¼-inch slices

1 medium onion, thinly sliced

2 cloves garlic, minced

Salt and pepper, to taste

Cheese Pizza Dough (see p. 420)

1 medium tomato, thinly sliced

½ teaspoon dried basil leaves

½ teaspoon dried thyme leaves

¼ teaspoon dried oregano leaves

1 cup (4 ounces) shredded reduced-fat mozzarella cheese

Per Slice
Calories: 189
% Calories from fat: 16
Fat (gm): 3.2
Saturated fat (gm): 2.1
Cholesterol (mg): 10.1
Sodium (mg): 188
Protein (gm): 11.8
Carbohydrate (gm): 27.5
Exchanges
Milk: 0.0
Vegetable: 1.0
Fruit: 0.0
Bread: 1.5
Meat: 1.0
Fat: 0.0

1. Spray large skillet with cooking spray; heat over medium heat until hot. Saute both squash, onion, and garlic until crisp-tender, about 3 minutes; season to taste with salt and pepper.

2. Spray 12-inch pizza pan with cooking spray; spread dough on pan, making rim around edge. Spray dough lightly with cooking spray. Arrange tomato slices on dough; top with squash. Sprinkle squash with herbs and cheese.

3. Bake pizza at 425 degrees until browned, 15 to 20 minutes.

SMOKY BROCCOLI AND MUSHROOM PIZZA

Mesquite-flavored cooking spray and smoked mozzarella cheeses give this pizza its wonderful smoky flavor.

6 slices

Vegetable cooking spray
1 cup broccoli florets
1 cup sliced cremini, *or* shiitake mushrooms
1 medium onion, sliced
2 cloves garlic, finely chopped
⅛ teaspoon red pepper flakes
Salt and pepper, to taste
Whole Wheat Pizza Dough (see p. 419)
1 cup fat-free ricotta cheese
3 tablespoons fat-free sour cream
½ teaspoon dried sage
½ cup (2 ounces) shredded smoked mozzarella cheese
½ cup (2 ounces) shredded fat-free mozzarella cheese

Per Slice
Calories: 201
% Calories from fat: 9
Fat (gm): 2.2
Saturated fat (gm): 1.1
Cholesterol (mg): 6.8
Sodium (mg): 265
Protein (gm): 16.5
Carbohydrate (gm): 32
Exchanges
Milk: 0.0
Vegetable: 1.0
Fruit: 0.0
Bread: 1.5
Meat: 1.5
Fat: 0.0

1. Spray large skillet with cooking spray; heat over medium heat until hot. Add broccoli, mushrooms, onion, and garlic and spray generously with cooking spray; saute until crisp-tender, 5 to 8 minutes. Stir in red pepper flakes; season to taste with salt and pepper. Cool to room temperature.

2. Spray 12-inch pizza pan with cooking spray; spread dough on pan, making rim around edge. Spray dough with cooking spray; bake at 425 degrees 10 minutes.

3. Mix ricotta cheese, sour cream, sage, and smoked mozzarella cheese; season to taste with salt and pepper. Spread cheese mixture evenly over dough; top with vegetable mixture. Sprinkle pizza with mozzarella cheese.

4. Bake pizza at 425 degrees until crust is browned, about 15 minutes.

SAGE-SCENTED SWEET POTATO PIZZA

 Something different—try it, you'll like it!

6 slices

Vegetable cooking spray
2 cups sliced sweet potatoes
1 cup sliced onion
1 teaspoon dried sage leaves
Salt and pepper, to taste
Cornmeal Pizza Dough (see p. 418)
2 teaspoons minced roasted garlic
1 cup (4 ounces) shredded reduced-fat Colby-Jack cheese

Per Slice
Calories: 281
% Calories from fat: 13
Fat (gm): 4.2
Saturated fat (gm): 2.2
Cholesterol (mg): 13.5
Sodium (mg): 166
Protein (gm): 11.4
Carbohydrate (gm): 50.3
Exchanges
Milk: 0.0
Vegetable: 1.0
Fruit: 0.0
Bread: 3.0
Meat: 0.5
Fat: 0.5

1. Spray aluminum-foil-lined jelly roll pan with cooking spray. Arrange sweet potatoes and onion on pan; spray with cooking spray and sprinkle with sage. Roast potatoes at 425 degrees until almost tender, 10 to 15 minutes; cool to room temperature. Season to taste with salt and pepper.

2. Spray 12-inch pizza pan with cooking spray. Spread dough on pan, making rim around edge. Sprinkle dough with garlic; arrange potato mixture on dough and sprinkle with cheese.

3. Bake pizza until crust is browned, 15 to 20 minutes.

DOUBLE ZUCCHINI PIZZA

Use yellow summer squash instead of zucchini, if you like.

6 slices

Zucchini Pizza Crust (see p. 420)
Pizza Sauce (see p. 700)
½-¾ cup (2-3 ounces) shredded fat-free mozzarella cheese
1 small zucchini, thinly sliced
½ small onion, sliced
Pepper, to taste
2 tablespoons grated fat-free Parmesan cheese

Per Slice
Calories: 152
% Calories from fat: 12
Fat (gm): 2.1
Saturated fat (gm): 0.6
Cholesterol (mg): 71
Sodium (mg): 236
Protein (gm): 15.9
Carbohydrate (gm): 19.2
Exchanges
Milk: 0.0
Vegetable: 1.5
Fruit: 0.0
Bread: 0.5
Meat: 1.5
Fat: 0.0

1. Spread Zucchini Pizza Crust with Pizza Sauce and sprinkle with mozzarella cheese. Top with zucchini and onion; sprinkle with pepper and Parmesan cheese.

2. Bake pizza at 425 degrees until zucchini is tender and cheese melted, 10 to 15 minutes.

ZUCCHINI AND MUSHROOM PIZZA WITH FILLO CRUST

Serve large pieces as an entrée, smaller pieces for a side dish or appetizer. Any kind of mushrooms can be used, but the wild varieties have the fullest flavor.

8 slices

Olive oil cooking spray
1 cup sliced leeks (white part only), *or* ½ cup each: chopped green onions and onion
4 cups sliced wild mushrooms (cremini, shiitake, portobello, oyster, etc.)
1 teaspoon minced garlic
2 medium zucchini, thinly sliced
½ teaspoon dried thyme leaves
Salt and pepper, to taste

Per Slice
Calories: 69
% Calories from fat: 29
Fat (gm): 2.4
Saturated fat (gm): 1.3
Cholesterol (mg): 5.1
Sodium (mg): 223
Protein (gm): 5.1
Carbohydrate (gm): 8.1
Exchanges
Milk: 0.0
Vegetable: 0.5
Fruit: 0.0
Bread: 0.5
Meat: 0.5
Fat: 0.0

8 sheets frozen, fillo pastry, thawed

1 cup (4 ounces) crumbled reduced-fat feta cheese

¼ cup (1 ounce) grated fat-free Parmesan cheese

1. Spray large skillet with cooking spray; heat over medium heat until hot. Add leeks and cook, covered, over medium heat until wilted, 3 to 4 minutes. Add mushrooms and garlic; cook, covered, 5 minutes. Add zucchini and cook, uncovered, until vegetables are tender, 5 to 8 minutes. Stir in thyme; season to taste with salt and pepper.

2. Spray jelly roll pan with cooking spray; place sheet of fillo on pan and spray generously with spray. Repeat with remaining sheets of fillo. Spoon vegetable mixture evenly over fillo; sprinkle with cheeses.

3. Bake pizza at 375 degrees until fillo is browned and cheese melted, about 15 minutes.

GARDEN PATCH PIZZA

 Pick the best from the season's bounty for this good-for-you pizza!

8 slices

1¼ packages (8-ounce size) fat-free cream cheese, softened

2 tablespoons fat-free sour cream

1 teaspoon Italian seasoning

1 large whole wheat lavosh, *or* cracker bread (5¼ ounces)

1 cup broccoli florets

1 cup chopped, seeded cucumber

2-3 marinated artichoke hearts, drained, sliced

¼ cup sliced carrot

¼ cup thinly sliced green onion

1-2 tablespoons sliced ripe olives

½ cup shredded reduced-fat Havarti cheese

Per Slice
Calories: 149
% Calories from fat: 28
Fat (gm): 4.6
Saturated fat (gm): 0.8
Cholesterol (mg): 5.1
Sodium (mg): 419
Protein (gm): 9.3
Carbohydrate (gm): 17.2
Exchanges
Milk: 0.0
Vegetable: 2.0
Fruit: 0.0
Bread: 0.5
Meat: 0.5
Fat: 0.5

¼ cup French, *or* other flavor, fat-free salad
  dressing

1. Mix cream cheese, sour cream, and Italian seasoning; spread mixture on lavosh. Arrange vegetables and cheese attractively on top.

2. Serve immediately, or refrigerate no longer than 1 hour. Drizzle with salad dressing just before serving.

SPINACH SALAD PIZZA

 This salad on a pizza is made with a large, crisp lavosh cracker. Serve with any salad dressing flavor--sweet-sour, red French, or honey Dijon are good choices.

8 slices

1½ packages (8-ounce size) fat-free cream
  cheese, softened
5-6 tablespoons fat-free sweet-sour salad
  dressing, divided
 1 large whole wheat lavosh, *or* cracker
  bread (5¼ ounces)
 2 cups packed spinach leaves, torn into
  bite-sized pieces
 1 cup sliced mushrooms
 ½ cup thinly sliced red onion
 2 hard-cooked eggs, sliced
 2 tablespoons all-vegetable "bacon"-
  flavored bits

Per Slice
Calories: 162
% Calories from fat: 25
Fat (gm): 4.6
Saturated fat (gm): 0.5
Cholesterol (mg): 53.3
Sodium (mg): 405
Protein (gm): 10.2
Carbohydrate (gm): 19.9
Exchanges
Milk: 0.0
Vegetable: 1.5
Fruit: 0.0
Bread: 1.0
Meat: 0.5
Fat: 0.5

1. Mix cream cheese and 2 tablespoons sweet-sour dressing. Spread mixture on lavosh; top with spinach, mushrooms, onion, hard-cooked eggs, and "bacon" bits.

2. Serve immediately, or refrigerate no longer than 1 hour. Drizzle with remaining sweet-sour dressing just before serving.

APPLE SALAD PIZZA

Use your favorite sweet or tart apple for this pizza and serve as a light lunch or as a side dish with an entrñe.

6 slices

    Vegetable cooking spray
    Basic Pizza Dough (see p. 418)
- 2 cups thinly sliced spinach
- 2 cups chopped, cored red apples
- 2 tablespoons lemon juice
- ¼ cup raisins
- ¼ cup coarsely chopped walnuts, *or* pecans
- ½ teaspoon curry powder (optional)
- ¼ cup (2 ounces) shredded fat-free Cheddar cheese
- ¼ cup (1 ounce) crumbled blue cheese

Per Slice
Calories: 218
% Calories from fat: 19
Fat (gm): 4.9
Saturated fat (gm): 1.2
Cholesterol (mg): 3.5
Sodium (mg): 204
Protein (gm): 7.9
Carbohydrate (gm): 37.7
Exchanges
Milk: 0.0
Vegetable: 1.0
Fruit: 1.0
Bread: 1.5
Meat: 0.0
Fat: 0.5

1. Spray 12-inch pizza pan with cooking spray; spread dough on pan, making rim around edge.

2. Arrange spinach on dough. Sprinkle apples with lemon juice; toss apples with remaining ingredients and arrange on spinach.

3. Bake pizza at 425 degrees until dough is browned, 15 to 20 minutes.

FRUIT ORCHARD PIZZA

Select the season's ripest fruit for this pizza. In the winter season, canned or frozen-and-thawed fruits can be used.

8 slices

- 1½ packages (8-ounce size) fat-free cream cheese, softened
- 2 tablespoons maple syrup, *or* honey
- 1 teaspoon ground cinnamon
- 1 large whole wheat lavosh, *or* cracker bread (5¼ ounces)

Per Slice
Calories: 195
% Calories from fat: 14
Fat (gm): 3.2
Saturated fat (gm): 0
Cholesterol (mg): 0
Sodium (mg): 295
Protein (gm): 8.2
Carbohydrate (gm): 34.2

5-6 cups assorted fresh fruit (strawberries, raspberries, blueberries, sliced peaches, pears, plums, kiwi, etc.)

Raspberry Sauce (see p. 793)

Exchanges
Milk: 0.0
Vegetable: 0.0
Fruit: 1.0
Bread: 1.5
Meat: 0.0
Fat: 0.5

1. Mix cream cheese, maple syrup, and cinnamon. Spread mixture on lavosh; arrange fruit attractively on top.

2. Serve immediately, or refrigerate no longer than 1 hour. Drizzle with Raspberry Sauce just before serving.

PEAR DESSERT PIZZA

 Serve as a dessert, or when in the mood for something a little bit different and wonderful.

6 slices

Basic Pizza Dough (see p. 418)
¼ cup plus 2 tablespoons sugar, divided
Vegetable cooking spray
2 tablespoons honey
2 large ripe pears, cored, sliced
½ teaspoon ground cinnamon
¼ cup (1 ounce) crumbled blue cheese
2 tablespoons raisins
2-4 tablespoons coarsely chopped walnuts

Per Slice
Calories: 244
% Calories from fat: 12
Fat (gm): 3.3
Saturated fat (gm): 1
Cholesterol (mg): 3.5
Sodium (mg): 156
Protein (gm): 5.2
Carbohydrate (gm): 50.2
Exchanges
Milk: 0.0
Vegetable: 0.0
Fruit: 1.5
Bread: 2.0
Meat: 0.0
Fat: 0.5

1. Make Basic Pizza Dough, adding 2 tablespoons sugar to flour.

2. Spray 12-inch pizza pan with cooking spray; spread dough on pan, making rim around edge. Drizzle dough with honey. Arrange pears on dough; spray with cooking spray and sprinkle with remaining ¼ cup sugar and cinnamon. Sprinkle blue cheese, raisins, and walnuts over pears.

3. Bake pizza at 425 degrees until crust is browned, 15 to 20 minutes.

FRUIT FOCACCIA

Dried blueberries would be an excellent addition to this focaccia. Serve as a dessert or a meal accompaniment.

8 servings

½ cup dried cranberries, *or* cherries
½ cup dried fruit bits
1 cup boiling water
1 Focaccia (½ recipe; see p. 673)
2 tablespoons granulated sugar
1 tablespoon melted margarine, *or* butter
⅓ cup packed light brown sugar
Butter-flavored cooking spray

Per Serving
Calories: 253
% Calories from fat: 8
Fat (gm): 2.4
Saturated fat (gm): 0.6
Cholesterol (mg): 1.2
Sodium (mg): 188
Protein (gm): 6.6
Carbohydrate (gm): 52.6
Exchanges
Milk: 0.0
Vegetable: 0.0
Fruit: 0.5
Bread: 3.0
Meat: 0.0
Fat: 0.0

1. Combine dried fruits in bowl; pour boiling water over and let stand until softened, 10 to 15 minutes. Drain.

2. Make Focaccia, adding granulated sugar to the flour mixture. After first rising, spread dough in greased baking pan, 11 x 7 inches. Let rise until double in size, about 30 minutes.

3. Make ¼-inch indentations with fingers to "dimple" dough. Spread margarine over dough; sprinkle with fruit and brown sugar. Spray with cooking spray.

4. Bake focaccia at 425 degrees until browned, 20 to 25 minutes.

LEEK AND ONION FOCACCIA

This delicious pizza is made with focaccia. It can also be made with Basic Pizza Dough (see p. 418), but you will need to double the recipe.

8 servings

1 Focaccia (½ recipe; see p. 673)
½ cup thinly sliced leek (white part only)
½ cup thinly sliced yellow onion
½ cup thinly sliced red onion
½ teaspoon dried sage leaves

Per Serving
Calories: 193
% Calories from fat: 7
Fat (gm): 1.6
Saturated fat (gm): 0.4
Cholesterol (mg): 1.2
Sodium (mg): 171
Protein (gm): 7.1
Carbohydrate (gm): 38.4

1-2   teaspoons olive oil
      Salt and pepper, to taste
1-2   tablespoons grated fat-free Parmesan
      cheese

Exchanges
Milk: 0.0
Vegetable: 1.0
Fruit: 0.0
Bread: 2.5
Meat: 0.0
Fat: 0.0

1.   Make Focaccia; after first rising, spread dough in greased jelly roll pan, 15 x 10 inches. Let stand until dough is doubled in size, about 30 minutes.

2.   Make ¼-inch indentations with fingers to "dimple" the dough. Combine leek, onions, and sage; toss with oil and spread over dough. Sprinkle lightly with salt and pepper; sprinkle lightly with Parmesan cheese.

3.   Bake focaccia at 425 degrees until golden, 20 to 25 minutes.

"SAUSAGE" CALZONES

Hot roll mix makes these calzones fast and easy to prepare. The filling can be prepared a day in advance and refrigerated; heat until warm before assembling calzones.

8 servings

     Olive oil cooking spray
 1   cup sliced carrots
 1   cup cubed zucchini
 1   cup sliced onions
 ½   cup chopped red bell pepper
 ½   cup sliced mushrooms
 4   cloves garlic, minced
 1   package (8 ounces) sausage-style
     vegetable protein links, *or* patties,
     crumbled
 ¾   teaspoon Italian seasoning
 ½-¾ teaspoon fennel seeds, crushed
 1½ cups chopped tomato
 1   cup rinsed, drained, canned cannellini,
     or Great Northern, beans
 ¼   cup sliced ripe olives
     Salt and pepper, to taste

Per Serving
Calories: 398
% Calories from fat: 24
Fat (gm): 11
Saturated fat (gm): 2.6
Cholesterol (mg): 9.2
Sodium (mg): 757
Protein (gm): 20.8
Carbohydrate (gm): 55.8
Exchanges
Milk: 0.0
Vegetable: 2.0
Fruit: 0.0
Bread: 3.0
Meat: 2.0
Fat: 0.5

1 package (16 ounces) hot roll mix
1¼ cups very hot water (120 degrees)
1 tablespoon olive oil
¾ cup (3 ounces) shredded fat-free
   mozzarella cheese
¾ cup (3 ounces) shredded reduced-fat
   mozzarella cheese
2-3 tablespoons fat-free milk

1. Spray large skillet with cooking spray; heat over medium heat until hot. Cook carrots, zucchini, onions, bell pepper, mushrooms, and garlic over medium heat, covered, 5 minutes. Add crumbled vegetable protein links and herbs and cook 1 to 2 minutes longer.

2. Add tomato, beans, and olives to skillet; cook, covered, until vegetables are just tender, 5 to 8 minutes, stirring occasionally. Season to taste with salt and pepper.

3. Make hot roll mix according to package directions for pizza crust, using 1¼ cups very hot water and 1 tablespoon oil. Divide dough into 8 equal pieces. Roll 1 piece dough on floured surface into circle 7 inches in diameter. Spoon about ¾ cup filling on dough and sprinkle with 3 tablespoons combined cheeses. Brush edge of dough with milk and fold in half. Flute edge of dough or press with tines of fork. Place on greased cookie sheet. Repeat with remaining dough, filling, and cheese.

4. Brush tops of calzones with milk. Bake calzones at 375 degrees until browned, about 15 minutes. Let cool on wire rack 5 minutes before serving.

CHEESE AND MUSHROOM CALZONES

Use porcini mushrooms if they are available; portobello or shiitake mushrooms also have a woodsy, rich flavor.

8 servings

Vegetable cooking spray
6 cups sliced porcini, *or* portobello,
   mushrooms

Per Serving
Calories: 312
% Calories from fat: 16
Fat (gm): 5.8
Saturated fat (gm): 1.1
Cholesterol (mg): 4.6
Sodium (mg): 387
Protein (gm): 18
Carbohydrate (gm): 48.4

½ cup chopped broccoli
½ cup chopped onion
2 teaspoons minced roasted garlic
1 teaspoon dried basil leaves
1 cup fat-free ricotta cheese
1 cup (4 ounces) shredded fat-free mozzarella cheese
2 tablespoons grated Parmesan cheese
¼ cup fat-free sour cream
   Salt and pepper, to taste
1 package (16 ounces) hot roll mix
1¼ cups water very hot (120 degrees)
1 tablespoon olive oil
   Fat-free milk, to glaze

Exchanges
Milk: 0.0
Vegetable: 1.0
Fruit: 0.0
Bread: 3.0
Meat: 1.0
Fat: 0.5

1. Spray large skillet with cooking spray; heat over medium heat until hot. Add mushrooms, broccoli, onion, garlic, and basil to skillet; spray generously with cooking spray. Cook, covered, over medium heat until mushrooms have wilted, about 5 minutes. Cook, uncovered, until vegetables are tender, 5 to 8 minutes.

2. Mix sauteed vegetables, cheeses, and sour cream; season to taste with salt and pepper.

3. Make hot roll mix according to package directions for pizza, using 1¼ cups hot water and 1 tablespoon olive oil. Divide dough into 8 equal pieces. Roll 1 piece dough on floured surface into 6- to 7-inch circle; spoon about ⅔ cup mushroom mixture on dough. Brush edge of dough with milk and fold in half. Flute edges of dough or press together with tines of fork. Place on greased cook sheet. Repeat with remaining dough and filling.

4. Brush tops of calzones with milk. Bake calzones at 375 degrees until browned, 15 to 20 minutes. Let cool on wire rack 5 minutes before serving.

SWEET FENNEL CALZONES

Fresh fennel, onion, sour cream, and melty cheese are combined in these golden calzones.

8 servings

Vegetable cooking spray
6 cups thinly sliced fennel bulb
1½ cups chopped onion
⅔ cup chopped red bell pepper
2 cloves garlic, minced
1 cup (4 ounces) shredded fat-free mozzarella cheese
½ cup fat-free sour cream
2 tablespoons finely chopped fennel leaves
Salt and pepper, to taste
1 package (16 ounces) hot roll mix
1¼ cups very hot water (120 degrees)
1 tablespoon olive oil
Fat-free milk, to glaze

Per Serving
Calories: 307
% Calories from fat: 15
Fat (gm): 5.3
Saturated fat (gm): 0.8
Cholesterol (mg): 3.4
Sodium (mg): 378
Protein (gm): 13.8
Carbohydrate (gm): 52
Exchanges
Milk: 0.0
Vegetable: 1.5
Fruit: 0.0
Bread: 3.0
Meat: 0.5
Fat: 0.5

1. Spray large skillet with cooking spray; heat over medium heat until hot. Add fennel, onion, bell pepper, and garlic; cook, covered, over medium to medium-low heat until tender, 15 to 20 minutes, stirring occasionally. Cool until warm; stir in cheese, sour cream, and fennel leaves. Season to taste with salt and pepper.

2. Make hot roll mix according to package directions for pizza, using 1¼ cups hot water and 1 tablespoon olive oil. Divide dough into 8 equal pieces. Roll 1 piece dough on floured surface into 6- to 7-inch circle; spoon about ⅔ cup fennel mixture on dough. Brush edge of dough with milk and fold in half. Flute edges of dough or press together with tines of fork. Place on greased cookie sheet. Repeat with remaining dough and filling.

3. Brush tops of calzones with milk. Bake calzones at 375 degrees until browned, 15 to 20 minutes. Let cool on wire rack 5 minutes before serving.

TORTA RUSTICA

An Italian pizza in a crust-lined deep-dish pie.

8 servings

Olive oil cooking spray

1½ cups chopped onions

1½ teaspoons minced roasted garlic

1 package (8 ounces) frozen, thawed, sausage-style vegetable protein patties, *or* links, crumbled

1 can (16 ounces) reduced-sodium whole tomatoes, undrained, coarsely chopped

3 medium zucchini, sliced

3 cups sliced mushrooms

Salt and pepper, to taste

1 package (16 ounces) hot roll mix

1 cup very hot water (120 degrees)

1 egg

1-1½ cups (4 ounces) shredded reduced-fat mozzarella cheese

Fat-free milk, to glaze

Per Serving
Calories: 368
% Calories from fat: 27
Fat (gm): 11.2
Saturated fat (gm): 2.2
Cholesterol (mg): 34.2
Sodium (mg): 668
Protein (gm): 17
Carbohydrate (gm): 50.4
Exchanges
Milk: 0.0
Vegetable: 2.0
Fruit: 0.0
Bread: 2.0
Meat: 2.0
Fat: 1.0

1. Spray large skillet with cooking spray; heat over medium heat until hot. Saute onions, garlic, and crumbled "sausage" until onions are tender, about 5 minutes. Stir in tomatoes, zucchini, and mushrooms; heat to boiling. Reduce heat and simmer, covered, 5 minutes. Simmer, uncovered, until excess liquid is gone, about 10 minutes. Season to taste with salt and pepper.

2. Make hot roll mix according to package directions, using hot water and egg. Roll ⅔ of dough on floured surface to fit 2-quart casserole or soufflé dish. Ease dough into casserole, allowing dough to extend 1 inch over edge. Spoon half the vegetable mixture into casserole; sprinkle with half the cheese. Top with remaining vegetable mixture and cheese.

3. Roll remaining dough into circle to fit top of casserole. Bring outside edges of dough together and crimp. Cut 1 or 2 slits in top of dough with sharp knife. Brush top of dough with milk.

4. Bake at 400 degrees until crust is browned, about 30 minutes. Let stand 5 to 10 minutes before serving.

ITALIAN "SAUSAGE" PIE

Vegetarian Italian-style "burgers" and vegetables bake into a wonderful pie in no time at all!

6 servings

½ package (16-ounce size) frozen Italian-style vegetable "burgers," crumbled

1 cup chopped tomato

½ cup chopped onion

½ cup sliced zucchini

⅓ cup chopped red bell pepper

1 teaspoon Italian seasoning

¾ cup reduced-fat baking mix

1 cup (4 ounces) shredded fat-free mozzarella cheese

1 tablespoon grated fat-free Parmesan cheese

1 cup fat-free milk

1 egg

2 egg whites, *or* ¼ cup no-cholesterol real egg product

Per Serving
Calories: 205
% Calories from fat: 22
Fat (gm): 5.1
Saturated fat (gm): 0.9
Cholesterol (mg): 36.2
Sodium (mg): 679
Protein (gm): 18.7
Carbohydrate (gm): 21.7
Exchanges
Milk: 0.0
Vegetable: 1.0
Fruit: 0.0
Bread: 1.0
Meat: 2.0
Fat: 0.0

1. Combine "burgers," tomato, onion, zucchini, bell pepper, and Italian seasoning; spoon into lightly greased 9-inch pie pan.

2. Mix baking mix and cheeses in small bowl. Mix milk, egg, and egg whites; stir into dry mixture until blended. Pour batter over vegetable mixture in pie pan. Bake at 400 degrees until set and browned on the top, 35 to 40 minutes. Let stand 5 minutes before cutting.

VEGGIE POT PIE

This skinny version of a family favorite has a top crust only. Use any vegetables you like in this versatile recipe.

4 servings (about 1¼ cups each)

Vegetable cooking spray
½ cup sliced leek (white part only)
½ cup chopped green onions and tops
¾ cup sliced red bell pepper
2 cloves garlic, minced
½ teaspoon dried rosemary leaves
½ teaspoon dried marjoram leaves
¼ teaspoon dried thyme leaves
2 cups Basic Vegetable Stock, *or* Canned Vegetable Stock (see pp. 58, 63)
1 medium sweet potato, peeled, cubed
2 small yellow summer squash, sliced
1 cup cut green beans
½ cup broccoflower, *or* cauliflower florets
1 parsnip, cubed
½ cup whole-kernel corn
3 tablespoons flour
⅓ cup cold water
Salt and pepper, to taste
Pot Pie Pastry (recipe follows)
Fat-free milk, as garnish

Per Serving
Calories: 376
% Calories from fat: 29
Fat (gm): 12.6
Saturated fat (gm): 2.4
Cholesterol (mg): 0
Sodium (mg): 310
Protein (gm): 8.4
Carbohydrate (gm): 60.7
Exchanges
Milk: 0.0
Vegetable: 3.0
Fruit: 0.0
Bread: 2.5
Meat: 0.0
Fat: 2.5

1. Spray large saucepan with cooking spray; heat over medium heat until hot. Saute leek, onions, bell pepper, and garlic until tender, 5 to 8 minutes; stir in herbs and cook 1 to 2 minutes longer. Add stock and remaining vegetables; heat to boiling. Reduce heat and simmer, covered, until vegetables are tender, about 10 minutes.

2. Heat vegetable mixture to boiling. Mix flour and cold water; stir into boiling mixture. Boil, stirring constantly, until thickened. Season to taste with salt and pepper. Pour mixture into 1½-quart soufflé dish or casserole.

3. Roll pastry on floured surface into circle 1 to 1½ inches larger than top of soufflé dish and place on top of dish. Fold edge of pastry under and flute or press with tines of fork. Brush top of pastry lightly with fat-free milk, if using.

4. Bake pie at 425 degrees until pastry is browned, about 20 minutes. Cool on wire rack 5 minutes before serving.

Pot Pie Pastry

    1   cup all-purpose flour
    ¼   teaspoon baking powder
    ¼   teaspoon salt
    4   tablespoons cold margarine, *or* butter, cut
        into pieces
   4-5 tablespoons ice water

1. Combine flour, baking powder, and salt in small bowl; cut in margarine with pastry blender until mixture resembles coarse crumbs. Mix in water, 1 tablespoon at a time, to form dough. Refrigerate, covered, until ready to use.

AUTUMN VEGETABLE PIE

Choose ingredients from your garden or produce market for this savory pie.

4 servings (about 1¼ cups each)

    Olive oil cooking spray
    ½   cup chopped onion
    ½   cup sliced celery
    ½   cup red bell pepper
    2   cloves garlic, minced
    ½   teaspoon dried sage leaves
    ½   teaspoon dried thyme leaves
    2   pinches ground nutmeg
    2   cups Basic Vegetable Stock, *or* Canned
        Vegetable Stock (see pp. 58, 63)
    1   medium sweet potato, peeled, cubed
    1   medium russet potato, unpeeled, cubed

Per Serving
Calories: 396
% Calories from fat: 28
Fat (gm): 12.4
Saturated fat (gm): 2.4
Cholesterol (mg): 0
Sodium (mg): 353
Protein (gm): 9.9
Carbohydrate (gm): 63.8
Exchanges
Milk: 0.0
Vegetable: 3.0
Fruit: 0.0
Bread: 3.0
Meat: 0.0
Fat: 2.5

1 cup cubed, peeled turnip, *or* parsnip
1 cup halved Brussels sprouts
½ cup halved small mushrooms
½ cup lima beans
3 tablespoons flour
⅓ cup cold water
Salt and pepper, to taste
Pot Pie Pastry (see p. 459)
Fat-free milk

1. Spray large saucepan with cooking spray; heat over medium heat until hot. Saute onion, celery, bell pepper, and garlic until tender, about 5 minutes; stir in herbs and cook 1 to 2 minutes longer. Add stock and remaining vegetables; heat to boiling. Reduce heat and simmer, covered, until vegetables are tender, about 10 minutes.

2. Heat vegetable mixture to boiling. Mix flour and cold water; stir into boiling mixture. Boil, stirring constantly, until thickened. Season to taste with salt and pepper. Pour mixture into 1½-quart casserole or soufflé dish.

3. Roll pastry on floured surface into circle 1 to 1½ inches larger than top of soufflé dish and place on top of dish. Fold edge of pastry under and flute or press with tines of fork. Brush top of pastry lightly with fat-free milk, if using.

4. Bake pie at 425 degrees until pastry is browned, about 20 minutes. Cool on wire rack 5 minutes before serving.

SHEPHERD'S VEGGIE POT PIE

Topped with mashed potatoes instead of pastry, this comfort food is sure to please.

4 servings (about 1¼ cups each)

Vegetable cooking spray
1 cup chopped onion
½ cup chopped green bell pepper
½ cup sliced celery
1 clove garlic, minced
½ teaspoon dried savory leaves

Per Serving
Calories: 301
% Calories from fat: 19
Fat (gm): 6.4
Saturated fat (gm): 1.2
Cholesterol (mg): 0.1
Sodium (mg): 150
Protein (gm): 8.3
Carbohydrate (gm): 55.2

¼-½ teaspoon dried thyme leaves

  2 cups Basic Vegetable Stock, *or* Canned Vegetable Stock (see pp. 58, 63)

  1 cup thinly sliced cabbage

  1 cup sliced carrots

  1 medium Idaho potato, unpeeled, cubed

  ¾ cup fresh, *or* frozen, peas

  ¾ cup sliced mushrooms

  3 tablespoons flour

  ⅓ cup cold water

    Salt and pepper, to taste

  2 cups (½ recipe) Real Mashed Potatoes (see p. 610)

  1 tablespoon margarine, *or* butter, melted

    Paprika, as garnish

Exchanges
Milk: 0.0
Vegetable: 2.0
Fruit: 0.0
Bread: 3.0
Meat: 0.0
Fat: 1.0

1. Spray large saucepan with cooking spray; heat over medium heat until hot. Saute onion, bell pepper, celery, and garlic until tender, 5 to 8 minutes; stir in herbs and cook 1 to 2 minutes longer. Stir in stock and remaining vegetables and heat to boiling; reduce heat and simmer, covered, until vegetables are tender, 10 to 15 minutes.

2. Heat vegetable mixture to boiling. Mix flour and cold water; stir into boiling mixture. Boil, stirring constantly, until thickened. Season to taste with salt and pepper. Pour mixture into 1½-quart soufflé dish or casserole.

3. Spoon or pipe potatoes around edge of casserole; drizzle potatoes with margarine and sprinkle with paprika. Bake at 350 degrees until potatoes are lightly browned, 20 to 30 minutes.

USE-IT-UP PIE

So named, because any little tidbits left in the fridge can be used in this tasty pie. Reduced-fat baking mix makes the recipe easy, and keeps it "skinny."

6 servings

Vegetable cooking spray
 1 cup sliced mushrooms
 ½ cup chopped onion
 ½ cup green bell pepper
 ½ cup sliced zucchini
 ½ cup broccoli florets
 1 teaspoon minced garlic
 1 teaspoon dried basil leaves
 1 teaspoon dried oregano leaves
 ¼-½ teaspoon crushed red pepper
 1 cup coarsely chopped tomato
 ½ cup rinsed, drained, canned kidney, *or* black, beans
 ½ cup (2 ounces) shredded reduced-fat Cheddar cheese
Salt and pepper, to taste
 1¼ cups reduced-fat baking mix
 2 tablespoons grated fat-free Parmesan cheese
 2 eggs
 1 cup fat-free milk

Per Serving
Calories: 203
% Calories from fat: 20
Fat (gm): 4.5
Saturated fat (gm): 1.3
Cholesterol (mg): 76.7
Sodium (mg): 675
Protein (gm): 10.7
Carbohydrate (gm): 31
Exchanges
Milk: 0.0
Vegetable: 2.0
Fruit: 0.0
Bread: 1.5
Meat: 0.5
Fat: 0.5

1. Spray large skillet with cooking spray; heat over medium heat until hot. Saute mushrooms, onion, bell pepper, zucchini, broccoli, and garlic until tender, 5 to 8 minutes. Stir in basil, oregano, and red pepper; cook 1 to 2 minutes longer.

2. Remove skillet from heat and stir in tomato, beans, and Cheddar cheese; season to taste with salt and pepper. Spoon mixture into bottom of lightly greased 9-inch pie pan.

3. Mix baking mix, Parmesan cheese, eggs, and milk until smooth; spread mixture evenly over vegetables in pan. Bake at 400 degrees until set and browned on top, 25 to 30 minutes. Let stand 5 minutes before cutting.

MEXICALI PIE

Another easy-to-make pie, perfect for brunch, lunch, or a light supper.

6 servings

½ cup chopped onion

½ can (16-ounce size) dark red kidney beans, rinsed, drained

1 cup frozen whole-kernel corn

1 thinly sliced zucchini, slices cut into halves

¼ cup chopped yellow bell pepper

1 tablespoon drained, canned chopped green chilies

1½ teaspoons chili powder, divided

¼ teaspoon ground cumin

¾ cup reduced-fat baking mix

1 cup (4 ounces) shredded reduced-fat taco cheese

1 cup fat-free milk

1 egg

2 egg whites, *or* ¼ cup no-cholesterol real egg product

Per Serving
Calories: 209
% Calories from fat: 19
Fat (gm): 4.7
Saturated fat (gm): 0.3
Cholesterol (mg): 46.2
Sodium (mg): 531
Protein (gm): 14.6
Carbohydrate (gm): 29.3
Exchanges
Milk: 0.0
Vegetable: 1.0
Fruit: 0.0
Bread: 1.5
Meat: 1.5
Fat: 0.0

1. Combine onion, beans, corn, zucchini, bell pepper, chilies, 1 teaspoon chili powder, and cumin; spoon into lightly greased 9-inch pie pan.

2. Mix baking mix, remaining ½ teaspoon chili powder, and cheese in small bowl. Mix fat-free milk, egg, and egg whites; stir into dry mixture until blended. Pour batter over mixture in pie pan. Bake at 400 degrees until set and browned on the top, 35 to 40 minutes. Let stand 5 minutes before cutting.

ARTICHOKE PIE

All the ingredients of the baked artichoke dip we all love, but made into a wonderful rich and cheesy pie.

8 servings

1 package (8 ounces) fat-free cream cheese, room temperature

1 cup (4 ounces)shredded fat-free mozzarella cheese

¼ cup (1 ounce) grated fat-free Parmesan cheese

2½ teaspoons minced roasted garlic, divided

1 can (14 ounces) artichoke hearts, rinsed, drained, sliced

1 cup fat-free milk

¼ cup fat-free mayonnaise

¼ cup fat-free sour cream, *or* plain yogurt

1 egg

2 egg whites, *or* ¼ cup no-cholesterol real egg product

¾ cup reduced-fat baking mix

Per Serving
Calories: 169
% Calories from fat: 24
Fat (gm): 4.7
Saturated fat (gm): 0.2
Cholesterol (mg): 27.1
Sodium (mg): 755
Protein (gm): 14.2
Carbohydrate (gm): 18.8
Exchanges
Milk: 0.0
Vegetable: 1.0
Fruit: 0.0
Bread: 1.0
Meat: 1.5
Fat: 0.0

1. Mix cheeses and ½ teaspoon roasted garlic; spread in bottom of lightly greased 10-inch pie pan. Mix artichoke hearts and remaining 2 teaspoons roasted garlic; spoon over cheese mixture.

2. Mix milk, mayonnaise, sour cream, egg, and egg whites in small bowl; mix in baking mix until blended. Pour batter over artichoke mixture in pie pan. Bake at 400 degrees until set and browned on the top, 35 to 40 minutes. Let stand 5 minutes before cutting.

RICH TOMATO TART

Rich and full in flavor, this tart has a soft texture, similar to a quiche. Serve as a light entrée, or in smaller portions as a side dish or accompaniment.

6 servings

Olive oil cooking spray
½ cup chopped onion
2 teaspoons minced garlic
1 can (14¼ ounces) reduced-sodium diced tomatoes, drained
½ teaspoon dried marjoram leaves
¼ teaspoon dried thyme leaves
1 tablespoon sugar
1 tablespoon finely chopped parsley
1 tablespoon finely chopped chives
Salt and pepper, to taste
1 egg
4 egg whites, *or* ½ cup no-cholesterol real egg product
½ cup fat-free sour cream
¾ cup cooked brown rice
¾ cup (3 ounces) shredded fat-free mozzarella, *or* Cheddar, cheese
Baked Tart Crust (recipe follows)
1 medium tomato, sliced

Per Serving
Calories: 305
% Calories from fat: 27
Fat (gm): 9.2
Saturated fat (gm): 1.9
Cholesterol (mg): 35.5
Sodium (mg): 290
Protein (gm): 14.9
Carbohydrate (gm): 41.2
Exchanges
Milk: 0.0
Vegetable: 1.0
Fruit: 0.0
Bread: 2.5
Meat: 1.0
Fat: 1.0

1. Spray large skillet with cooking spray; heat over medium heat until hot. Add onion and garlic and cook over medium to medium-low heat until very tender, about 5 minutes.

2. Add canned tomatoes, marjoram, thyme, and sugar to skillet; cook over medium heat until mixture is dry, about 5 minutes. Stir in parsley and chives; season to taste with salt and pepper. Beat egg and egg whites; stir in sour cream until smooth. Mix in rice and cheese; mix in tomato mixture.

3. Spread tomato mixture in Baked Tart Crust. Top with sliced tomato. Bake tart at 350 degrees until filling is set, 25 to 30 minutes. Let stand 5 minutes before cutting.

Baked Tart Crust

1½ cups all-purpose flour
½ teaspoon baking powder
   Pinch salt
 4 tablespoons cold margarine, *or* butter, cut
   into pieces
5-6 tablespoons ice water

1. Combine flour, baking powder, and salt in medium bowl; cut in margarine until mixture resembles coarse crumbs. Add water a tablespoon at a time, mixing lightly with a fork after each addition until dough just holds together. Refrigerate, covered, at least 30 minutes before rolling.

2. Roll dough on lightly floured surface into circle 1 inch larger than 9-inch tart pan. Ease pastry into pan and trim.

3. Line bottom of pastry with aluminum foil and fill with a single layer of pie weights or dried beans. Bake at 400 degrees 15 minutes; remove weights and pierce bottom of crust with tines of fork. Bake until pastry is browned, 10 to 15 minutes longer. Cool on wire rack.

MUSHROOM TART

Be prepared for compliments when serving this attractive tart! White mushrooms can be substituted for the cremini.

6 servings

 2 pounds medium cremini, *or* white,
   mushrooms
 2 tablespoons lemon juice
   Vegetable cooking spray
 2 tablespoons minced shallots
 2 cloves garlic, minced
 1 tablespoon finely chopped parsley
¼ teaspoon dried thyme leaves
1-2 pinches ground nutmeg
   Salt and pepper, to taste
 1 egg
 4 egg whites, *or* ½ cup no-cholesterol real
   egg product

Per Serving
Calories: 282
% Calories from fat: 29
Fat (gm): 9.8
Saturated fat (gm): 1.5
Cholesterol (mg): 35.5
Sodium (mg): 266
Protein (gm): 18.6
Carbohydrate (gm): 34.6
Exchanges
Milk: 0.0
Vegetable: 2.0
Fruit: 0.0
Bread: 1,5
Meat: 2.0
Fat: 0.5

⅔ cup fat-free sour cream

¾ cup cooked brown rice

¾ cup (3 ounces)shredded fat-free mozzarella cheese

Baked Tart Crust (see p. 466)

1. Remove stems from 12 ounces mushrooms; reserve caps. Slice stems and remaining mushrooms; sprinkle with lemon juice.

2. Spray large skillet with cooking spray; heat over medium heat until hot. Add sliced mushrooms, shallots, and garlic; cook, covered, over medium heat until mushrooms wilt and release moisture, about 5 minutes. Cook, uncovered, until mushrooms are tender and liquid evaporated, 5 to 7 minutes. Stir in parsley, thyme, and nutmeg; season to taste with salt and pepper. Beat egg and egg whites; stir in sour cream until smooth. Stir in rice and cheese; stir in mushroom mixture.

3. Make Baked Tart Crust, reducing flour to 1¼ cups and margarine to 3 tablespoons; bake as directed. Spread mushroom mixture evenly in Baked Tart Crust; arrange reserved mushroom caps on top. Spray mushroom caps generously with cooking spray.

4. Bake tart at 350 degrees until filling is set, 25 to 30 minutes. Let stand 5 minutes before cutting.

SPINACH PIE

Three packages (10 ounces each) frozen chopped spinach can be substituted for the fresh. Thaw spinach and drain very well; delete step 1 from recipe.

6 servings

2 pounds fresh spinach, stems removed

Vegetable cooking spray

2 tablespoons minced shallots, *or* onion

1 clove garlic, minced

2-3 pinches ground nutmeg

Salt and pepper, to taste

1 egg

Per Serving
Calories: 340
% Calories from fat: 29
Fat (gm): 11.1
Saturated fat (gm): 2.4
Cholesterol (mg): 106.5
Sodium (mg): 445
Protein (gm): 20.8
Carbohydrate (gm): 41.4

4 egg whites, *or* ½ cup no-cholesterol real
   egg product
½ cup fat-free sour cream
½ cup (2 ounces) grated fat-free Parmesan
   cheese
½ cup (2 ounces) shredded fat-free
   Cheddar, *or* mozzarella, cheese
¾ cup cooked brown rice
   Baked Tart Crust (see p. 466)
2-3 hard-cooked eggs, sliced

Exchanges
Milk: 0.0
Vegetable: 1.0
Fruit: 0.0
Bread: 2.0
Meat: 2.0
Fat: 1.0

1. Wash spinach and place in large saucepan with water that clings to the leaves. Cook, covered, over medium to medium-high heat until spinach is wilted. Drain; press excess liquid from spinach with paper toweling.

2. Spray medium skillet with cooking spray; heat over medium heat until hot. Saute shallots and garlic until tender, 3 to 4 minutes. Add spinach; cook until mixture is very dry, 2 to 3 minutes. Stir in nutmeg; season to taste with salt and pepper. Beat eggs and egg whites; stir in sour cream. Stir in cheeses and rice.

3. Spread spinach mixture evenly in Baked Tart Crust. Bake at 350 degrees until filling is set, 25 to 30 minutes. Arrange hard-cooked eggs on top; let stand 5 minutes before serving.

LEEK PIE

A wonderful pie to make when leeks are in season and moderate in price.

6 servings

2 pounds leeks, trimmed to 14 inches
   Vegetable cooking spray
½ teaspoon dried dill weed
2-3 pinches ground nutmeg
   Salt and pepper, to taste
2 eggs
2 egg whites, *or* ¼ cup no-cholesterol real
   egg product
½ cup fat-free sour cream
   Baked Tart Crust (see p. 465)

Per Serving
Calories: 316
% Calories from fat: 28
Fat (gm): 10
Saturated fat (gm): 2.1
Cholesterol (mg): 71
Sodium (mg): 198
Protein (gm): 10.1
Carbohydrate (gm): 47.7
Exchanges
Milk: 0.0
Vegetable: 4.5
Fruit: 0.0
Bread: 1.5
Meat: 0.5
Fat: 1.5

1. Cook leeks in boiling water to cover in large saucepan until limp, 5 to 7 minutes; drain well on paper toweling. Cut 5 inches of green tops off leeks and reserve. Thinly slice remaining leeks.

2. Spray large skillet with cooking spray; heat over medium heat until hot. Add sliced leeks; cook, covered, over low to medium-low heat until leeks are very soft, about 20 minutes. Stir in dill and nutmeg; season to taste with salt and pepper. Mix eggs, egg whites, and sour cream; stir into leeks.

3. Spread leek mixture in Baked Tart Crust; arrange reserved green tops in spoke pattern on mixture and spray with cooking spray.

4. Bake tart at 350 degrees until filling is set, 30 to 35 minutes. Let stand 5 minutes before cutting.

SWEET ONION TARTE TATIN

You'll hear raves when you serve this beautiful upside-down tart! For best flavor, use one of the sweet onions, such as Vidalia.

6-8 servings

Vegetable cooking spray

1 tablespoon granulated, *or* light brown, sugar

2½ pounds small sweet onions, peeled, cut crosswise into halves

Salt and pepper, to taste

⅓ cup dark, *or* light, raisins

1 teaspoon dried thyme leaves

¼ teaspoon ground allspice

1½ cups Basic Vegetable Stock (see p. 58)

2 teaspoons balsamic vinegar

Baked Tart Crust (see p. 466), unbaked

Per Serving
Calories: 291
% Calories from fat: 25
Fat (gm): 8.3
Saturated fat (gm): 1.6
Cholesterol (mg): 0
Sodium (mg): 126
Protein (gm): 5.9
Carbohydrate (gm): 49.8
Exchanges
Milk: 0.0
Vegetable: 3.0
Fruit: 0.5
Bread: 1.5
Meat: 0.0
Fat: 1.5

1. Spray 12-inch skillet with ovenproof handle with cooking spray; heat over medium heat until hot. Sprinkle bottom of skillet with sugar. Place onion halves, cut sides down, in skillet, fitting in as many as possible. Cut remaining onion halves into pieces, or chop coarsely, and fill in any spaces between onion halves. Sprinkle onions lightly with salt and pepper.

2. Sprinkle raisins, thyme, and allspice over onions. Cook, uncovered, over medium heat until onions begin to brown, 8 to 10 minutes. Add stock and vinegar and heat to boiling. Reduce heat and simmer, covered, until onions are tender, 20 to 25 minutes. Heat to boiling; reduce heat and simmer rapidly, uncovered, until liquid is almost gone.

3. Make Baked Tart Crust, but do not bake. Roll pastry on floured surface into 13-inch circle. Ease pastry into skillet, covering onion mixture; tuck in edges to fit. Bake at 375 degrees until pastry is lightly browned and juices are bubbly, 30 to 35 minutes. Cool in pan on wire rack 10 minutes; place large serving plate over skillet and invert tart onto plate. Serve warm or at room temperature.

CURRIED ONION BAKLAVA

A unique baklava that is not a dessert! This onion baklava can be served in very small pieces as an appetizer, or in larger pieces for an entrée or side dish.

8 side-dish servings

Olive oil cooking spray
2 pounds onions, thinly sliced
3 tablespoons curry powder
¼ cup all-purpose flour
½ cup orange juice, *or* apple juice
¼ cup chopped mango chutney
¼ cup chopped dried apricots
Salt and pepper, to taste
¼ cup ground almonds
½ cup ground ginger snaps
½ teaspoon ground cinnamon
10 sheets frozen fillo, thawed
½ cup water
3 tablespoons sugar
3 tablespoons honey

Per Serving
Calories: 198
% Calories from fat: 15
Fat (gm): 3.4
Saturated fat (gm): 0.4
Cholesterol (mg): 0
Sodium (mg): 57
Protein (gm): 3.6
Carbohydrate (gm): 40.8
Exchanges
Milk: 0.0
Vegetable: 3.0
Fruit: 0.5
Bread: 1.0
Meat: 0.0
Fat: 0.5

1. Spray large skillet with cooking spray; heat over medium heat until hot. Saute onions 5 minutes; stir in curry powder. Cook, covered, over medium-low to low heat until onions are very tender, 15 to 20 minutes. Sprinkle flour over onions; cook, stirring constantly, 1 to 2 minutes.

2. Stir orange juice, chutney, and apricots into onion mixture; heat to boiling. Reduce heat and simmer, uncovered, until apricots are softened and mixture thickened, about 5 minutes. Season to taste with salt and pepper. Cool.

3. Combine almonds, ginger snaps, and cinnamon. Spray bottom of 13 x 9-inch baking pan with cooking spray. Fold 1 sheet of fillo in half crosswise and place in pan; spray with cooking spray and sprinkle with 4 teaspoons almond mixture. Repeat four times, using fillo sheets and almond mixture, and ending with fillo.

4. Spread onion mixture over fillo. Add remaining fillo and almond mixture in layers, as in step 3 above, ending with a layer of fillo. Spray top layer of fillo generously with cooking spray. Score fillo with sharp knife to make serving pieces.

5. Bake baklava at 350 degrees for 45 minutes, covering loosely with foil if becoming too brown. Cut into pieces while hot.

6. Heat water, sugar, and honey to boiling in small saucepan, stirring to dissolve sugar. Pour mixture over hot baklava. Cool 10 to 15 minutes before serving, or cool completely and serve at room temperature.

MOROCCAN-STYLE BEAN AND FILLO PIE

 A fillo pie, filled with a seasoned, mashed garbanzo bean mixture, will please guests as an entrée or side dish.

6 side-dish servings

Vegetable cooking spray
1 cup chopped onion
⅔ cup chopped red bell pepper
2 teaspoons minced garlic
1 teaspoon minced gingerroot
¼ teaspoon crushed red pepper
1½ teaspoons ground cumin
1 teaspoon ground cinnamon
1 tablespoon lemon juice

Per Serving
Calories: 126
% Calories from fat: 26
Fat (gm): 3.8
Saturated fat (gm): 0.4
Cholesterol (mg): 0
Sodium (mg): 295
Protein (gm): 5.2
Carbohydrate (gm): 19.4
Exchanges
Milk: 0.0
Vegetable: 1.0
Fruit: 0.0
Bread: 1.0
Meat: 0.0
Fat: 0.5

1 can (15 ounces) garbanzo beans,
rinsed, drained
Salt and pepper, to taste
10 sheets frozen fillo, thawed
3 tablespoons toasted almonds, chopped
Powdered sugar, to garnish

1. Spray large skillet with cooking spray; heat over medium heat until hot. Saute onion, bell pepper, garlic, gingerroot, and crushed red pepper until onion is tender, 5 to 8 minutes. Stir in cumin, cinnamon, and lemon juice; remove from heat. Add garbanzo beans to skillet, mashing coarsely. Season to taste with salt and pepper.

2. Spray pizza pan or cookie sheet with cooking spray. Fold 1 sheet fillo in half crosswise; place on pan and spray generously with cooking spray. Repeat, using 4 more sheets of fillo. Spoon bean mixture into center of fillo and shape into a flattened round; sprinkle with almonds. Top with remaining fillo, folding and spraying as above. Tuck ends under, forming a pie. Spray generously with cooking spray.

3. Bake pie at 350 degrees until golden, 20 to 25 minutes. Serve warm or at room temperature; sprinkle generously with powdered sugar before serving.

SQUASH AND MUSHROOM GALETTE

Any flavorful wild mushroom, such as shiitake, oyster, or cremini, can be substituted for the portobello mushrooms. This elegant entrée tart can also be cut into smaller wedges and served as a first course.

4-6 servings

1 pound acorn, *or* butternut, squash, cut
into halves, seeds discarded
½ cup thinly sliced leek, white parts only
1 small onion, chopped
1 medium red bell pepper, chopped
2 portobello mushrooms, sliced
8 cloves garlic, minced
1½ teaspoons dried sage leaves

Per Serving
Calories: 339
% Calories from fat: 18
Fat (gm): 7.1
Saturated fat (gm): 1.7
Cholesterol (mg): 58.3
Sodium (mg): 338
Protein (gm): 16.5
Carbohydrate (gm): 54
Exchanges
Milk: 0.0
Vegetable: 1.0
Fruit: 0.0
Bread: 3.0
Meat: 1.0
Fat: 1.0

  1 tablespoon olive oil, *or* canola oil
     Salt and pepper, to taste
     Galette Pastry Dough (recipe follows)
  ½ cup shredded fat-free Cheddar cheese
  2 tablespoons grated Parmesan cheese
  1 egg white, beaten

1.   Place squash, cut sides down, in baking pan. Bake at 375 degrees until very tender, about 1 hour. Scoop squash from shells and mash with fork in large bowl.

2.   Saute leek, onion, bell pepper, mushrooms, garlic, and sage in oil in large skillet until tender, about 5 minutes. Mix into squash; season to taste with salt and pepper.

3.   Roll pastry dough on lightly floured surface to 14-inch circle; transfer to cookie sheet or large pizza pan. Spoon vegetable mixture evenly on dough, leaving 2-inch border around side. Sprinkle with cheeses. Fold edge of dough over edge of vegetable mixture, pleating to fit.

4.   Brush edge of dough with beaten egg white. Bake at 400 degrees until crust is golden, about 25 minutes. Cut into wedges; serve warm.

Galette Pastry Dough

  1 teaspoon active dry yeast
  ⅓ cup warm water (115 degrees)
  1   egg, beaten
  3 tablespoons fat-free sour cream
  1½ cups all-purpose flour
  ¼ teaspoon salt

1.   Stir yeast into warm water in medium bowl; let stand 5 minutes. Add egg and sour cream to yeast mixture, mixing until smooth. Stir in flour and salt, making a soft dough. Knead dough on lightly floured surface until smooth, 12 minutes.

ROASTED PEPERONATA GALETTE

 Cut this attractive galette into smaller pieces for appetizer servings.

4-6 servings

Galette Pastry Dough (see p. 473)
Roasted Peperonata (see p. 295)
½ cup (2 ounces) shredded fat-free mozzarella cheese
1 tablespoon fat-free Parmesan cheese
1 egg white, beaten

Per Serving
Calories: 396
% Calories from fat: 6
Fat (gm): 2.9
Saturated fat (gm): 0.6
Cholesterol (mg): 53.3
Sodium (mg): 292
Protein (gm): 19.8
Carbohydrate (gm): 77
Exchanges
Milk: 0.0
Vegetable: 5.0
Fruit: 0.0
Bread: 3.0
Meat: 1.0
Fat: 0.0

1. Roll pastry dough on floured surface to 14-inch circle; transfer to cookie sheet or large pizza pan. Spoon peperonata mixture evenly onto dough, leaving a 2-inch border around side. Sprinkle with cheeses. Fold edge of dough over edge of vegetable mixture, pleating to fit.

2. Brush edge of dough with beaten egg white. Bake at 400 degrees until crust is golden, about 25 minutes. Cut into wedges; serve warm.

SWEET 'N SPICY VEGETABLE GALETTE

 Sweet vegetables and sweet spices are contrasted with hot jalapeño chili and gingerroot in this picnic-perfect pie.

4-6 servings

Vegetable cooking spray
1 large sweet potato, peeled, cubed
1 medium zucchini, cubed
1 small onion, chopped
½ cup sliced red bell pepper
2-3 teaspoons minced jalapeño chili
2-3 teaspoons minced gingerroot
2 teaspoons minced garlic
½ cup orange juice

Per Serving
Calories: 357
% Calories from fat: 9
Fat (gm): 3.7
Saturated fat (gm): 1.3
Cholesterol (mg): 58.3
Sodium (mg): 312
Protein (gm): 15.8
Carbohydrate (gm): 66.9
Exchanges
Milk: 0.0
Vegetable: 2.0
Fruit: 0.0
Bread: 3.5
Meat: 1.0
Fat: 0.0

     2 tablespoons finely chopped sun-dried
        tomatoes
    ½ teaspoon ground cinnamon
    ½ teaspoon dried thyme leaves
    ¼ teaspoon ground allspice
    ¼ teaspoon ground cloves
     1 cup thinly sliced spinach
        Salt and pepper, to taste
        Galette Pastry Dough (see p. 473)
    ½ cup whole wheat flour
 ¼-½ cup (1-2 ounces) reduced-fat Havarti
        cheese
     1 tablespoon grated fat-free Parmesan
        cheese
     1 egg white, beaten

1. Spray large skillet with cooking spray; heat over medium
heat until hot. Saute potato, zucchini, onion, bell pepper, jalapeño chili, gingerroot, and garlic 5 minutes.

2. Add orange juice, sun-dried tomatoes, and herbs and spices
to skillet; heat to boiling. Reduce heat and simmer, covered, until
vegetables are tender and orange juice absorbed, about 10 minutes. Remove from heat and stir in spinach. Season to taste with
salt and pepper.

3. Make Galette Pastry Dough, substituting ½ cup whole wheat
flour for ½ cup of the all-purpose flour. Roll pastry dough on
floured surface to 14-inch circle; transfer to cookie sheet or large
pizza pan. Spoon vegetable mixture evenly onto dough, leaving
2-inch border around side. Sprinkle with cheeses. Fold edge of
dough over edge of vegetable mixture, pleating to fit.

4. Brush edge of dough with beaten egg white. Bake at 400 degrees until crust is golden, about 25 minutes. Cut into wedges;
serve warm.

NINE

Egg
AND
Cheese Dishes

NOTE: Cholesterol levels are allowably higher in recipes using whole eggs, with the understanding that eggs should be eaten only a few times each week.

EGGS BENEDICT

A popular brunch dish comes back to the table in healthy vegetarian style. Six slices of English Muffin Bread (see p. 666) can be substituted for the English muffins.

6 servings

3 English muffins, halved, toasted
   Spinach leaves, as garnish
6 slices tomato
6 poached eggs
   Mock Hollandaise Sauce (see p. 715)
   Paprika, as garnish
   Parsley leaves, finely chopped, as garnish

Per Serving
Calories: 180
% Calories from fat: 29
Fat (gm): 5.6
Saturated fat (gm): 1.6
Cholesterol (mg): 212.1
Sodium (mg): 461
Protein (gm): 13.7
Carbohydrate (gm): 17.1
Exchanges
Milk: 0.0
Vegetable: 0.0
Fruit: 0.0
Bread: 1.5
Meat: 1.0
Fat: 0.5

1. Top English muffin halves with spinach leaves and tomato slices. Top each with a poached egg.

2. Spoon Mock Hollandaise Sauce over eggs; sprinkle with paprika and parsley.

PIPERADE

Eggs are gently scrambled with a bell pepper and onion mixture in Basque tradition. Serve with squares of warm Focaccia (see p. 673).

4 servings

   Peperonata (see p. 610)
1 large tomato, chopped
4 eggs
4 egg whites, *or* ½ cup no-cholesterol real egg product
2 tablespoons fat-free milk
   Salt and pepper, to taste

Per Serving
Calories: 173
% Calories from fat: 28
Fat (gm): 5.6
Saturated fat (gm): 1.6
Cholesterol (mg): 213.1
Sodium (mg): 129
Protein (gm): 12.9
Carbohydrate (gm): 19.2
Exchanges
Milk: 0.0
Vegetable: 4.0
Fruit: 0.0
Bread: 0.0
Meat: 1.0
Fat: 0.5

1. Make Peperonata, adding chopped tomato during last 10 minutes of cooking time.

2. Beat eggs, egg whites, and fat-free milk. Move Peperonata to side of skillet; add eggs. Cook until eggs are set, stirring occasionally. Gently stir eggs into Peperonata; season to taste with salt and pepper.

HASH AND EGGS

 You'll enjoy the unusual smoky mesquite flavor of this vegetable hash.

4 servings

Vegetable cooking spray
1 cup chopped onions
4 medium Idaho potatoes, unpeeled, cooked, cubed
1 cup frozen peas, thawed
1 cup fresh, *or* frozen, thawed, whole-kernel corn
¼-½ teaspoon dried thyme leaves
Salt and pepper, to taste
4 eggs

Per Serving
Calories: 273
% Calories from fat: 17
Fat (gm): 5.4
Saturated fat (gm): 1.6
Cholesterol (mg): 213
Sodium (mg): 106
Protein (gm): 12.6
Carbohydrate (gm): 45.6
Exchanges
Milk: 0.0
Vegetable: 0.0
Fruit: 0.0
Bread: 3.0
Meat: 1.0
Fat: 0.0

1. Spray large skillet with cooking spray; heat over medium heat until hot. Saute onions 3 to 4 minutes; add potatoes and spray generously with cooking spray. Cook over medium heat until potatoes are browned, stirring frequently. Add peas, corn, and thyme; cook 2 to 3 minutes longer. Season to taste with salt and pepper.

2. Move hash to sides of skillet; add eggs to center of skillet. Cook, covered, over low heat until eggs are cooked, 3 to 4 minutes; season to taste with salt and pepper. Serve from skillet, or transfer to serving platter.

SWEET POTATO HASH WITH POACHED EGGS

A colorful hash dish that's perfect for a hearty breakfast, brunch, or light supper.

4 servings (scant 1 cup each)

Vegetable cooking spray

2 cups cubed (½ inch) peeled sweet potatoes

2 cups cubed (½ inch) unpeeled Idaho potatoes

½ cup chopped onion

½ cup chopped red bell pepper

1 teaspoon dried rosemary leaves

½ teaspoon dried thyme leaves

Salt and pepper, to taste

4 poached, *or* fried, eggs

Per Serving
Calories: 393
% Calories from fat: 13
Fat (gm): 5.8
Saturated fat (gm): 1.7
Cholesterol (mg): 212
Sodium (mg): 171
Protein (gm): 12.3
Carbohydrate (gm): 74.4
Exchanges
Milk: 0.0
Vegetable: 0.5
Fruit: 0.0
Bread: 4.5
Meat: 1.0
Fat: 0.0

1. Spray large skillet with cooking spray; heat over medium heat until hot. Add vegetables and herbs and cook, covered, over medium heat 5 minutes.

2. Spray vegetables lightly with cooking spray and stir. Cook, uncovered, until vegetables are browned and tender, about 10 minutes. Season to taste with salt and pepper.

3. Spoon hash onto plates; top each serving with an egg.

HASH BROWN LOAF WITH EGGS

Served with fried or poached eggs, this loaf is a perfect entrée for brunch or a light supper.

4 servings

¾ cup textured vegetable protein

¾ cup Canned Vegetable Stock (see p. 63)

Vegetable cooking spray

1 cup shredded carrots

1 small onion, finely chopped

¼ cup chopped red bell pepper

2 cloves garlic, minced

Per Serving
Calories: 310
% Calories from fat: 21
Fat (gm): 7.4
Saturated fat (gm): 2
Cholesterol (mg): 211
Sodium (mg): 493
Protein (gm): 36.2
Carbohydrate (gm): 26

¾ cup shredded Idaho potatoes

1½ teaspoons dried thyme leaves

1 teaspoon dried chives

Salt and pepper, to taste

1 cup no-cholesterol real egg product

1 cup (4 ounces) fat-free Cheddar cheese, divided

4 fried, *or* poached, eggs

Exchanges
Milk: 0.0
Vegetable: 2.0
Fruit: 0.0
Bread: 1.0
Meat: 3.0
Fat: 0.0

1. Combine vegetable protein and stock in medium bowl; let stand until stock is absorbed, 5 to 10 minutes.

2. Spray medium skillet with cooking spray; heat over medium heat until hot. Saute carrots, onion, bell pepper, and garlic until tender, about 5 minutes. Stir in potatoes and herbs; season to taste with salt and pepper. Mix in egg product and ¾ cup cheese.

3. Pack mixture into greased 7½ x 3¾-inch loaf pan. Bake, loosely covered, at 350 degrees 45 minutes; uncover and sprinkle with remaining ¼ cup cheese. Bake until loaf is set and cheese melted, about 15 minutes longer. Let stand 10 minutes before serving.

4. Loosen sides of loaf with sharp knife; unmold onto serving plate. Slice loaf and arrange slices on serving plates; serve eggs on top or alongside loaf.

PASTA EGG SALAD

Small bow ties, shells, or elbow macaroni can be substituted for the pasta rings.

4 servings (about 1 cup each)

4 ounces pasta rings, cooked, cooled

5 hard-cooked eggs, coarsely chopped

½ cup sliced snow peas

¼ cup finely chopped onion

¼ cup chopped red bell pepper

Mayonnaise Dressing (recipe follows)

Salt and pepper, to taste

Lettuce leaves, as garnish

1 medium tomato, cut into wedges

Per Serving
Calories: 257
% Calories from fat: 25
Fat (gm): 7.3
Saturated fat (gm): 2.1
Cholesterol (mg): 266.3
Sodium (mg): 516
Protein (gm): 13.2
Carbohydrate (gm): 34.9
Exchanges
Milk: 0.0
Vegetable: 1.0
Fruit: 0.0
Bread: 2.0
Meat: 1.0
Fat: 0.5

1. Combine pasta rings, eggs, snow peas, onion, and bell pepper in large bowl; spoon Mayonnaise Dressing over and toss. Season to taste with salt and pepper.

2. Spoon salad onto lettuce-lined plates; garnish with tomato wedges.

Mayonnaise Dressing

(makes about ⅔ cup)

  ½ cup fat-free mayonnaise
  3 tablespoons white wine vinegar
  1 tablespoon Dijon-style mustard
  ¼ cup finely chopped parsley
  ¼ cup finely chopped chives
  2 tablespoons finely chopped lovage, *or*
    celery, leaves

1. Mix all ingredients; refrigerate until ready to use.

PASTA FRITTATA

A pasta frittata is a delicious way to use leftover linguine, fettuccine, or spaghetti. Vary the vegetables in the topping according to season and availability.

4 servings

  2 medium carrots, sliced
  8 ounces cauliflower florets
  1 cup sliced red bell peppers
  ⅓ cup sliced green onions and tops
  2 cloves garlic, minced
  1 tablespoon olive oil, *or* canola oil
  1 medium zucchini, sliced
  1 medium tomato, chopped
  1 teaspoon dried basil leaves
  ¾ teaspoon dried oregano leaves
  ¾ teaspoon dried marjoram leaves
  4 ounces thin spaghetti, cooked
  4 egg whites

Per Serving
Calories: 249
% Calories from fat: 19
Fat (gm): 5.4
Saturated fat (gm): 1.2
Cholesterol (mg): 2.5
Sodium (mg): 416
Protein (gm): 12
Carbohydrate (gm): 39.5
Exchanges
Milk: 0.0
Vegetable: 3.0
Fruit: 0.0
Bread: 2.0
Meat: 0.0
Fat: 0.5

2 tablespoons grated Parmesan cheese
½ teaspoon salt
¼ teaspoon pepper
Olive oil cooking spray
Parsley, minced, as garnish

1. Saute carrots, cauliflower, bell peppers, onions, and garlic in oil in medium skillet until carrots are crisp-tender, 5 to 7 minutes. Stir in zucchini, tomato, and herbs; saute until vegetables are tender, about 5 minutes more.

2. In bowl, mix spaghetti, egg whites, cheese, salt, and pepper. Spray medium skillet with cooking spray. Add pasta mixture, spreading it evenly. Cook, uncovered, over medium to medium-low heat until browned on bottom, about 5 minutes. Turn and cook until browned on other side, about 5 minutes. Slide frittata onto serving platter; spoon vegetable mixture over and sprinkle with parsley.

VEGETABLE FRITTATA WITH PARMESAN TOAST

 An Italian-style vegetable omelet that is quick and easy to prepare, delicious to eat!

4 servings

Vegetable cooking spray
1 medium poblano chili, sliced
1 medium onion, sliced
2 cups sliced mushrooms
2 cloves garlic, minced
2 tablespoons finely chopped lovage, *or* parsley, leaves
¼ cup vegetable broth
1½ cups no-cholesterol real egg product, *or* 6 eggs
¼ cup fat-free milk
½ cup cooked brown rice
½ cup shredded fat-free Cheddar cheese
¼ teaspoon salt
⅛ teaspoon pepper

Per Serving
Calories: 212
% Calories from fat: 9
Fat (gm): 2.2
Saturated fat (gm): 0.8
Cholesterol (mg): 4.4
Sodium (mg): 590
Protein (gm): 18.4
Carbohydrate (gm): 30
Exchanges
Milk: 0.0
Vegetable: 1.5
Fruit: 0.0
Bread: 1.5
Meat: 1.5
Fat: 0.0

4 slices Italian, *or* French, bread
4 teaspoons grated Parmesan cheese

1. Spray medium ovenproof skillet with cooking spray; heat over medium heat until hot. Saute vegetables 5 minutes; add lovage and broth. Cook, covered, over medium heat until vegetables are tender and liquid is absorbed, about 5 minutes.

2. Beat together egg product and milk; mix in cooked rice, Cheddar cheese, salt, and pepper. Pour mixture over vegetables in skillet. Cook without stirring, uncovered, over medium-low heat until egg is set and lightly browned on bottom, about 10 minutes.

3. Broil frittata 6 inches from heat source until frittata is cooked on top, 3 to 4 minutes; invert frittata onto plate, slide back into skillet, and cook until lightly browned, 3 to 5 minutes.

4. Sprinkle bread with Parmesan cheese; broil 6 inches from heat source until browned, 2 to 3 minutes. Slide frittata onto serving plate; cut into wedges. Serve with Parmesan toast.

"SAUSAGE" AND EGG PIZZA

Tempting for brunch, lunch, or supper.

6 slices

Olive oil cooking spray
2 large poblano chilies, sliced
1 cup chopped onions
1 clove garlic, minced
½ package (8-ounce size) frozen sausage-style vegetable protein links, cut into scant ½-inch slices *or* crumbled
6 eggs
4 egg whites, *or* ½ cup no-cholesterol real egg product
¼ cup fat-free milk
Salt and pepper, to taste
Potato Pizza Crust (see p. 421)
½-1 cup (2-4 ounces) shredded fat-free mozzarella cheese

Per Slice
Calories: 249
% Calories from fat: 28
Fat (gm): 7.7
Saturated fat (gm): 2.1
Cholesterol (mg): 248.7
Sodium (mg): 406
Protein (gm): 19.1
Carbohydrate (gm): 25.6
Exchanges
Milk: 0.0
Vegetable: 1.0
Fruit: 0.0
Bread: 1.5
Meat: 2.0
Fat: 0.0

1. Spray large skillet with cooking spray; heat over medium heat until hot. Add chilies, onions, and garlic; cook over medium to medium-low heat until chilies are very soft, 20 to 30 minutes. Remove from skillet and reserve.

2. Add "sausage" slices to skillet; cook over medium heat 2 to 3 minutes. Beat eggs, egg whites, and milk; pour into skillet. Cook eggs until just set, stirring occasionally. Gently stir reserved chili mixture into eggs; season to taste with salt and pepper. Spoon mixture into Potato Pizza Crust and sprinkle with cheese.

3. Bake pizza at 400 degrees until cheese is melted, about 5 minutes.

VEGETABLE PUFF

Perfect for brunch or lunch, vegetables are baked with an egg custard.

6 servings

Vegetable cooking spray
4 ounces sliced mushrooms
½ cup chopped red bell pepper
½ cup finely chopped shallots
2 cloves garlic, minced
1 pound broccoflower, cooked, coarsely chopped
1 cup finely shredded carrots, cooked
⅔ cup frozen corn, thawed
2 teaspoons lemon juice
¾ teaspoon dried thyme leaves
½ teaspoon salt
½ teaspoon pepper
1 cup fat-free half-and-half, *or* fat-free milk
2 tablespoons flour
1 cup no-cholesterol real egg product
5 large egg whites
½ teaspoon cream of tartar

Per Serving
Calories: 133
% Calories from fat: 3
Fat (gm): 0.5
Saturated fat (gm): 0.1
Cholesterol (mg): 0
Sodium (mg): 359
Protein (gm): 11.8
Carbohydrate (gm): 21.2
Exchanges
Milk: 0.0
Vegetable: 2.0
Fruit: 0.0
Bread: 0.5
Meat: 1.0
Fat: 0.0

1. Spray large skillet with cooking spray; heat over medium heat until hot. Saute mushrooms, bell pepper, shallots, and garlic until tender, about 4 minutes. Stir in broccoflower, carrots, corn, lemon juice, and thyme; saute 5 minutes. Transfer mixture to large bowl and season with salt and pepper.

2. Whisk half-and-half and flour until smooth in small saucepan. Heat to boiling; boil, whisking constantly, until thickened, about 1 minute. Whisk about half the mixture into egg product; whisk egg mixture back into half-and-half. Stir into vegetable mixture.

3. Beat egg whites in large mixer bowl until foamy. Add cream of tartar and continue beating until stiff peaks form; fold into vegetable mixture. Transfer mixture to a lightly greased 1½-quart casserole. Place casserole in a large roasting pan on center rack of oven; add 2 inches hot water to pan.

4. Bake, uncovered, at 375 degrees 35 minutes or until casserole is puffed and lightly browned on top. Serve immediately.

OMELET PUFF WITH VEGETABLE MÉLANGE

 Made with beaten egg whites, this oven-baked omelet soars to new heights. Do not overbeat the whites!

2 servings

5	egg whites
¼	cup water
⅓	cup no-cholesterol real egg product
¼	teaspoon dried tarragon leaves
¼	teaspoon salt
¼	teaspoon pepper
	Vegetable cooking spray
	Vegetable Mélange (recipe follows)
2	slices crusty Italian bread, warm

Per Serving
Calories: 264
% Calories from fat: 7
Fat (gm): 2.1
Saturated fat (gm): 0.4
Cholesterol (mg): 0
Sodium (mg): 662
Protein (gm): 20.5
Carbohydrate (gm): 43.9
Exchanges
Milk: 0.0
Vegetable: 4.0
Fruit: 0.0
Bread: 1.5
Meat: 1.5
Fat: 0.0

1. Beat egg whites in large bowl until foamy; mix in water at high speed, beating until stiff but not dry peaks form.

2. Beat egg product, tarragon, salt, and pepper at high speed in small bowl until thick and lemon colored. Fold egg white mixture into egg product mixture.

3. Spray 10-inch ovenproof skillet with cooking spray; heat over medium heat until hot. Pour egg mixture into skillet; cook over medium to medium-low heat until bottom of omelet is light brown, about 5 minutes.

4. Bake at 325 degrees, uncovered, until omelet is puffed and light brown. Loosen edge of omelet with spatula; slide onto serving platter, carefully folding omelet in half. Spoon Vegetable Mélange over omelet. Serve with Italian bread.

Vegetable Mélange

(makes about 3 cups)

>   Vegetable cooking spray
> 2   medium zucchini, sliced
> 2   medium onions, sliced
> 2   medium tomatoes, cut into wedges
> 4   ounces fresh, *or* frozen, thawed, whole okra
> 1   medium green bell pepper, sliced
> 2   tablespoons canned vegetable broth, *or* water

1. Spray large skillet with cooking spray; heat over medium heat until hot. Saute vegetables until crisp-tender, 3 to 5 minutes. Add broth; cook, covered, over medium-low heat 5 minutes.

SPRING VEGETABLE TERRINE

Spring asparagus and peas are baked in a delicate herb-seasoned egg custard, which is easily unmolded and sliced to serve.

4 servings

>   Vegetable cooking spray
> ⅓   cup thinly sliced green onions and tops
> 1   medium red bell pepper, finely chopped
> 2   cloves garlic, minced
> 1½ pounds fresh asparagus, cut into 1-inch pieces
> 1   package (10 ounces) frozen peas, thawed
> 1   cup fat-free half-and-half, *or* fat-free milk
> 2   tablespoons flour
> 1   tablespoon margarine

Per Serving
Calories: 224
% Calories from fat: 15
Fat (gm): 3.8
Saturated fat (gm): 0.7
Cholesterol (mg): 0
Sodium (mg): 277
Protein (gm): 16.5
Carbohydrate (gm): 32.4
Exchanges
Milk: 0.5
Vegetable: 3.0
Fruit: 0.0
Bread: 1.0
Meat: 0.5
Fat: 0.0

¾ teaspoon dried tarragon leaves

¼ teaspoon ground allspice

½ teaspoon pepper

1 cup no-cholesterol real egg product

1. Spray medium skillet with cooking spray; heat over medium heat until hot. Saute green onions, bell pepper, and garlic until tender, about 5 minutes. Stir in asparagus and peas; set aside.

2. Whisk half-and-half and flour until smooth in small saucepan. Heat to boiling; boil, whisking constantly, until thickened, about 1 minute. Remove from heat and stir in margarine, tarragon, allspice, and pepper. Whisk about half the mixture into egg product; whisk egg product back into saucepan.

3. Line the bottom of 8½ x 4½-inch loaf pan with parchment paper; spray lightly with cooking spray. Combine vegetable and half-and-half mixtures and pour into pan.

4. Bake, uncovered, at 350 degrees 40 minutes or until sharp knife inserted near center comes out clean. Let stand 10 minutes on wire rack before removing from pan. Invert onto serving plate; carefully remove parchment paper and cut into thick slices.

MUSHROOM CUSTARD IN ACORN SQUASH

A delicate-textured custard, robustly flavored with portobello mushrooms, is baked in whole acorn squash.

4 servings

4 small acorn squash (about 1 pound each)

Vegetable cooking spray

8 ounces portobello, *or* cremini, mushrooms, sliced

1 medium onion, chopped

½ teaspoon dried rosemary leaves

½ teaspoon dried thyme leaves

2 eggs

2 egg whites

1½ cups fat-free milk

½ cup reduced-sodium vegetable broth

Per Serving
Calories: 258
% Calories from fat: 17
Fat (gm): 5.4
Saturated fat (gm): 1.4
Cholesterol (mg): 108
Sodium (mg): 258
Protein (gm): 13.1
Carbohydrate (gm): 45.1
Exchanges
Milk: 0.5
Vegetable: 1.0
Fruit: 0.0
Bread: 2.0
Meat: 0.5
Fat: 0.5

¼ teaspoon salt
⅛ teaspoon white pepper

1. Cut small slices from bottoms of squash so they stand upright; cut about 2 inches off stem ends of squash. Scoop out seeds and discard. Stand squash upright in baking pan.

2. Spray medium skillet with vegetable cooking spray; heat over medium heat until hot. Saute mushrooms, onion, rosemary, and thyme until vegetables are tender, about 5 minutes. Cool slightly.

3. Beat eggs and egg whites in medium bowl; beat in milk, broth, salt, and pepper. Stir mushroom mixture into custard; then spoon all into squash cavities. Bake, uncovered, at 350 degrees until custard is set and sharp knife inserted into center comes out clean, about 30 minutes.

MEDITERRANEAN CABBAGE CASSEROLE

 Oregano and mint lend Mediterranean flavors to this casserole.

6 servings

Vegetable Cooking Spray
1 medium cabbage, thinly sliced
2 teaspoons paprika
1 teaspoon sugar
¾ cup dry white wine, *or* Canned Vegetable Stock (see p. 63)
2 tablespoons white wine vinegar
1½ cups no-cholesterol real egg product
1 can (12 ounces) evaporated fat-free milk
½ cup fat-free milk
¾ teaspoon pepper
1 medium green bell pepper, finely chopped
⅓ cup sliced green onions and tops
3 cloves garlic, minced
1 can (14½ ounces) reduced-sodium diced tomatoes, undrained
1 teaspoon dried oregano leaves
½ teaspoon dried mint leaves
Salt and pepper, to taste

Per Serving
Calories: 140
% Calories from fat: 4
Fat (gm): 0.6
Saturated fat (gm): 0.2
Cholesterol (mg): 2.1
Sodium (mg): 205
Protein (gm): 11.9
Carbohydrate (gm): 18.2
Exchanges
Milk: 0.5
Vegetable: 2.0
Fruit: 0.0
Bread: 0.0
Meat: 1.0
Fat: 0.0

1. Spray large skillet with cooking spray; heat over medium heat until hot. Add cabbage, paprika, and sugar; saute 4 to 5 minutes. Add wine and vinegar; heat to boiling. Reduce heat and simmer, covered, until cabbage is wilted, about 10 minutes.

2. Spoon cabbage mixture into greased 11 x 7-inch baking dish. Combine egg product, evaporated milk, fat-free milk, and pepper in bowl; pour over cabbage. Bake, uncovered, at 350 degrees 20 minutes or until sharp knife inserted near center comes out clean.

3. Spray medium saucepan with cooking spray; heat over medium heat until hot. Saute bell pepper, green onions, and garlic until tender, about 5 minutes. Stir in tomatoes, oregano, and mint; simmer, uncovered, 15 minutes or until slightly thickened. Season to taste with salt and pepper.

4. To serve, divide sauce evenly among 6 plates; top each with a square of cabbage casserole.

SWEET POTATO PONE

More of a country-style pudding than a soufflé, this comfort food will become a favorite. Drizzle with warm maple syrup, if you like, and serve with a favorite vegetable and salad of crisp greens.

3 servings

1	small onion, finely chopped
1	tablespoon margarine, *or* butter
3	tablespoons flour
1	cup fat-free milk
½	cup no-cholesterol real egg product, *or* 2 eggs
1	large sweet potato (about 8 ounces), unpeeled, cut into 1-inch cubes, cooked
2	tablespoons packed light brown sugar
¼	teaspoon ground cinnamon
⅛	teaspoon ground nutmeg
⅛	teaspoon ground cloves
¼	teaspoon salt
2-3	dashes white pepper
4	egg whites, beaten to stiff peaks

Per Serving
Calories: 358
% Calories from fat: 16
Fat (gm): 6.2
Saturated fat (gm): 1.4
Cholesterol (mg): 2
Sodium (mg): 606
Protein (gm): 19.6
Carbohydrate (gm): 55.4
Exchanges
Milk: 0.0
Vegetable: 0.5
Fruit: 0.0
Bread: 1.5
Meat: 1.0
Fat: 0.0

1. Saute onion in margarine in saucepan until tender, 3 to 5 minutes. Stir in flour; cook 2 to 3 minutes. Stir in milk; heat to boiling, stirring constantly, until thickened.

2. Beat egg substitute in small bowl until thick and lemon colored, 2 to 3 minutes. Slowly beat about half the milk mixture into egg; then stir egg mixture into milk mixture in saucepan. Cook over low heat, stirring constantly, 1 to 2 minutes. Remove from heat.

3. Coarsely mash sweet potato with fork. Mix sweet potato, brown sugar, spices, salt, and pepper into milk mixture. Mix half the egg whites into milk mixture in saucepan; fold mixture back into remaining egg whites.

4. Spoon mixture into lightly greased 1-quart soufflé dish or casserole. Bake at 375 degrees until puffed and golden (sharp knife inserted halfway between center and edges will come out almost clean), 30 to 35 minutes.

NOODLES FLORENTINE

 Cut into generous squares and serve with a tossed vegetable salad and thick slices of warm multigrain bread.

4 servings

Vegetable cooking spray
1 cup finely chopped red onions
1 medium red bell pepper, chopped
2 cloves garlic, minced
2 teaspoons sugar
½ teaspoon ground nutmeg
Salt and pepper, to taste
1 cup no-cholesterol real egg product
4 packages (10 ounces each) frozen chopped spinach, thawed and drained
2 cups cooked spinach noodles, drained
1 cup fresh whole wheat breadcrumbs
2 slices (2 ounces) reduced-fat Swiss cheese, cut diagonally in half

Per Serving
Calories: 307
% Calories from fat: 14
Fat (gm): 5
Saturated fat (gm): 2
Cholesterol (mg): 36.1
Sodium (mg): 372
Protein (gm): 22.6
Carbohydrate (gm): 47
Exchanges
Milk: 0.0
Vegetable: 3.5
Fruit: 0.0
Bread: 2.0
Meat: 1.5
Fat: 0.0

1.   Spray large saucepan with cooking spray; heat over medium heat until hot. Saute onions, bell pepper, and garlic until softened, about 4 minutes. Stir in sugar and nutmeg; season to taste with salt and pepper.

2.   Transfer onion mixture to large bowl and cool to room temperature; stir in egg product, spinach, noodles, and breadcrumbs.

3.   Spoon mixture into lightly greased 11 x 7½-inch baking dish. Bake, uncovered, at 325 degrees 30 minutes. Top with cheese; bake 10 minutes longer or until sharp knife inserted near center comes out clean. Cool on wire rack 5 minutes before serving.

VEGGIE KUGEL

 This kugel, with lots of veggies, uses no-cholesterol real egg product and evaporated fat-free milk to keep fat and calories in line.

6 servings

¾ cup chopped red bell pepper

¾ cup finely chopped onion

2 tablespoons margarine, *or* butter

8 ounces Brussels sprouts, cut in halves, cooked

8 ounces cubed, peeled sweet potatoes, *or* sliced carrots, cooked

¾ teaspoon dried thyme leaves

½ teaspoon dried marjoram leaves

2 tablespoons flour

1 can (12 ounces) evaporated fat-free milk

1 cup no-cholesterol real egg product

2 packages (10 ounces each) frozen chopped spinach, thawed, well drained

½ teaspoon salt

½ teaspoon pepper

12 ounces no-yolk noodles, cooked

Per Serving
Calories: 385
% Calories from fat: 10
Fat (gm): 4.6
Saturated fat (gm): 0.9
Cholesterol (mg): 1.8
Sodium (mg): 425
Protein (gm): 16.8
Carbohydrate (gm): 71.9
Exchanges
Milk: 0.5
Vegetable: 2.0
Fruit: 0.0
Bread: 3.5
Meat: 0.5
Fat: 0.5

1.   Saute bell pepper and onion in margarine in large saucepan until tender, about 5 minutes; add Brussels sprouts, sweet potatoes, thyme, and marjoram and cook 3 to 4 minutes longer.

2. Mix flour and evaporated milk; add to saucepan and heat to boiling; boil, stirring constantly, until thickened, about 1 minute. Remove from heat and cool to room temperature; stir in egg product, spinach, salt, and pepper. Stir in noodles.

3. Spoon mixture into greased 13 x 9-inch baking dish. Bake at 350 degrees 35 minutes or until sharp knife inserted near center comes out clean. Cool on wire rack 5 minutes; cut into squares.

POTATO KUGEL

This hash brown kugel owes its light texture to beaten egg whites. Served with Mushroom Gravy, it could also be served with a tomato sauce.

6 servings

2 packages (5½ ounces each) hash brown potato mix with onions
3 cups boiling water
6 egg yolks
1½ cups cool water
1 teaspoon baking powder
¼ teaspoon dried thyme leaves
3 tablespoons finely chopped parsley
1 teaspoon salt
½ teaspoon pepper
6 egg whites, beaten to stiff peaks
Vegetable cooking spray
Mushroom Gravy (see p. 716)

Per Serving
Calories: 306
% Calories from fat: 21
Fat (gm): 7.2
Saturated fat (gm): 1.6
Cholesterol (mg): 213
Sodium (mg): 557
Protein (gm): 10.8
Carbohydrate (gm): 49.6
Exchanges
Milk: 0.0
Vegetable: 0.0
Fruit: 0.0
Bread: 3.0
Meat: 1.0
Fat: 1.0

1. Place potato mix in large bowl; pour boiling water over. Let stand 20 to 25 minutes, stirring occasionally.

2. Process egg yolks, 1½ cups water, baking powder, and thyme in food processor or blender until smooth. Mix yolk mixture, parsley, salt, and pepper into potatoes. Fold potato mixture into egg whites.

3. Spray 11 x 7-inch baking dish with cooking spray; place in oven at 300 degrees until hot. Pour kugel mixture into dish; bake until browned and set, about 60 minutes. Serve with Mushroom Gravy.

HUEVOS RANCHEROS

Everyone loves Mexican "country-style eggs" for a hearty breakfast, brunch, or light supper.

6 servings

6 corn tortillas
Vegetable cooking spray
6 eggs
Salt and pepper, to taste
Serrano Tomato Sauce (p. 723)
Refried Beans (p. 525)

Per Serving
Calories: 252
% Calories from fat: 22
Fat (gm): 6.2
Saturated fat (gm): 1.7
Cholesterol (mg): 213
Sodium (mg): 109
Protein (gm): 14.3
Carbohydrate (gm): 35.6
Exchanges
Milk: 0.0
Vegetable: 1.0
Fruit: 0.0
Bread: 2.0
Meat: 1.5
Fat: 0.0

1. Spray tortillas lightly with cooking spray; cook in large skillet until browned, about 1 minute on each side.

2. Spray large skillet with cooking spray; heat over medium heat until hot. Add eggs. Reduce heat to medium-low and cook, covered, until eggs are glazed on top, 3 to 4 minutes. Season to taste with salt and pepper.

3. Arrange tortillas on serving plates; place eggs on tortillas and spoon Serrano Tomato Sauce over. Serve with Refried Beans.

EGGS RANCHEROS WITH BLACK BEANS AND 2 SALSAS

Our adaptation of another Mexican favorite, served with 2 salsas, black beans, and rice.

4 servings

Vegetable cooking spray
1¼ cups no-cholesterol real egg product, *or* 5 eggs
4 corn, *or* flour, tortillas, warm
1 cup (½ recipe) Red Tomato Salsa (see p. 9)
1 cup (½ recipe) Green Tomato Salsa (see p. 8)

Per Serving
Calories: 394
% Calories from fat: 6
Fat (gm): 3
Saturated fat (gm): 0.2
Cholesterol (mg): 0
Sodium (mg): 550
Protein (gm): 21.7
Carbohydrate (gm): 77.3

Seasoned Mashed Black Beans (see p. 524)

3 cups cooked rice, warm

Exchanges
Milk: 0.0
Vegetable: 2.0
Fruit: 0.0
Bread: 4.0
Meat: 1.0
Fat: 0.0

1. Spray medium skillet with cooking spray; heat over medium heat until hot. Beat egg substitute in small bowl until fluffy; add to skillet and cook over medium-low heat until set, 3 to 4 minutes, stirring occasionally.

2. Place tortillas on serving plates; spoon scrambled eggs over. Spoon Salsas alongside; serve with Seasoned Mashed Black Beans and rice.

BREAKFAST BURRITOS

Not to be limited to breakfast, these chunky burritos are perfect for brunch, lunch, or supper.

6 servings (1 burrito each)

Vegetable cooking spray
3 cups cubed, unpeeled Idaho potatoes, cooked
1 cup chopped red, *or* green, bell peppers
1 cup chopped green onions and tops
4 cloves garlic, minced
1½ cups cubed zucchini
¼ cup whole-kernel fresh, *or* frozen, thawed, corn
6 eggs
4 egg whites, *or* ½ cup no-cholesterol real egg product
¼ cup finely chopped cilantro leaves
¾ teaspoon dried oregano leaves
Salt and pepper, to taste
6 flour tortillas (10-inch)
1 cup (4 ounces) shredded reduced-fat mozzarella, *or* Cheddar, cheese
Cilantro, *or* parsley sprigs, as garnish
1-1½ cups mild, *or* hot, salsa

Per Serving
Calories: 398
% Calories from fat: 24
Fat (gm): 10.6
Saturated fat (gm): 4
Cholesterol (mg): 223.1
Sodium (mg): 709
Protein (gm): 21.3
Carbohydrate (gm): 53.7
Exchanges
Milk: 0.0
Vegetable: 1.0
Fruit: 0.0
Bread: 3.0
Meat: 2.0
Fat: 1.0

1. Spray large skillet with cooking spray; heat over medium heat until hot. Add potatoes, bell peppers, green onions, and garlic; cook over medium heat until potatoes are browned and peppers and onions are tender, about 10 minutes. Add zucchini and corn; cook, covered, until zucchini is tender, about 5 minutes.

2. Beat eggs and egg whites; add eggs, chopped cilantro, and oregano to skillet and cook until eggs are set, stirring occasionally. Season to taste with salt and pepper.

3. Spoon mixture onto tortillas; sprinkle each with equal amount of cheese. Fold 2 sides of each tortilla in about 2 inches, then roll up from other side to enclose filling. Garnish with cilantro sprigs; serve with salsa.

MEXICAN SCRAMBLED EGGS WITH "CHORIZO"

 In this recipe, the "Chorizo" is crumbled, rather than being made into patties.

6 servings

Vegetable cooking spray
1 large tomato, chopped
½ cup sliced green onions and tops
2-3 teaspoons finely chopped serrano, *or* jalapeño, chilies
2 small cloves garlic, minced
"Chorizo" (see p. 404), crumbled
6 eggs
6 egg whites, *or* ¾ cup no-cholesterol real egg product
3 tablespoons fat-free milk
Salt and pepper, to taste
Tomatillo Sauce, warm (see p. 724)
6 corn, *or* flour, tortillas

Per Serving
Calories: 327
% Calories from fat: 24
Fat (gm): 8.9
Saturated fat (gm): 2.2
Cholesterol (mg): 284.1
Sodium (mg): 628
Protein (gm): 28.7
Carbohydrate (gm): 34.4
Exchanges
Milk: 0.0
Vegetable: 3.5
Fruit: 0.0
Bread: 1.0
Meat: 3.0
Fat: 0.0

1. Spray large skillet with cooking spray; heat over medium heat until hot. Saute tomato, green onions, chilies, and garlic until tender, about 5 minutes. Add "Chorizo" and cook 3 to 4 minutes.

2. Beat eggs, egg whites, and fat-free milk until foamy; add to skillet. Cook over medium to medium-low heat until eggs are cooked, stirring occasionally; season to taste with salt and pepper. Serve with Tomatillo Sauce and tortillas.

EGGS SCRAMBLED WITH CRISP TORTILLA STRIPS

This is a good recipe to use with day-old or slightly stale tortillas. Complement this hearty egg dish with Refried Beans and "Chorizo" (see pp. 525, 404).

6 servings

- 6 corn tortillas, cut into 2 x ½-inch strips
  Vegetable cooking spray
- 6 eggs
- 6 egg whites, *or* ¾ cup no-cholesterol real egg product
- 3 tablespoons fat-free milk
  Salt and pepper, to taste
- 3 tablespoons crumbled Mexican white cheese, *or* farmer's cheese
- 3 tablespoons finely chopped cilantro
- 1½ cups Poblano Chili Sauce, warm (see p. 722)
  Black Beans and Rice (see p. 526)

Per Serving
Calories: 367
% Calories from fat: 18
Fat (gm): 7.7
Saturated fat (gm): 2.2
Cholesterol (mg): 215.7
Sodium (mg): 480
Protein (gm): 22.9
Carbohydrate (gm): 55.9
Exchanges
Milk: 0.0
Vegetable: 1.0
Fruit: 0.0
Bread: 3.0
Meat: 2.5
Fat: 0.0

1. Spray tortilla strips lightly with cooking spray; cook in skillet over medium to medium-high heat until browned and crisp.

2. Beat eggs, egg whites, and milk until foamy; pour over tortilla strips in skillet. Cook over medium to medium-low heat until eggs are cooked, stirring occasionally. Season to taste with salt and pepper; sprinkle with cheese and cilantro. Serve eggs with Poblano Chili Sauce and Black Beans and Rice.

EGGS SCRAMBLED WITH CACTUS

Cactus paddles, or "nopales," are available canned as well as fresh; the canned cactus do not have to be cooked. Poblano chilies or sweet bell peppers can be substituted, if preferred.

4 servings

1 quart boiling water
8 ounces cactus paddles, sliced
1 teaspoon salt
¼ teaspoon baking soda
Vegetable cooking spray
1 small tomato, chopped
1 cup chopped onions
1 teaspoon finely chopped jalapeño chili
4 eggs
4 egg whites, *or* ½ cup no-cholesterol real egg product
2 tablespoons fat-free milk
Salt and pepper, to taste
4 corn, *or* flour, tortillas, warm

Per Serving
Calories: 179
% Calories from fat: 29
Fat (gm): 5.8
Saturated fat (gm): 1.7
Cholesterol (mg): 213.1
Sodium (mg): 258
Protein (gm): 12.7
Carbohydrate (gm): 18.7
Exchanges
Milk: 0.0
Vegetable: 1.0
Fruit: 0.0
Bread: 1.0
Meat: 2.0
Fat: 0.0

1. Heat water to boiling in medium saucepan; add cactus, 1 teaspoon salt, and baking soda. Reduce heat and simmer, uncovered, until cactus is crisp-tender, about 20 minutes. Rinse well in cold water and drain.

2. Spray large skillet with cooking spray; heat over medium heat until hot. Saute cactus, tomato, onions, and jalapeño chili until onion is tender, 3 to 4 minutes.

3. Beat eggs, egg whites, and fat-free milk until foamy; add to skillet. Cook over medium to medium-low heat until eggs are cooked, stirring occasionally. Season to taste with salt and pepper. Serve with tortillas.

BEAN AND CHEESE CHILES RELLENOS

Authentic chiles rellenos is made with poblano chilies. Green bell (sweet) peppers can be substituted and the rellenos will be delicious, but the flavor of the pepper is not the same. Chiles rellenos is normally coated with a beaten egg-white mixture and deep-fried in oil; our healthful version uses only 1 tablespoon of vegetable oil.

6 servings

6 large poblano chilies
2-3 quarts water
Vegetable cooking spray
½ small jalapeño chili, seeds and veins discarded, minced
4 cloves garlic, minced
1 teaspoon dried oregano leaves
2 packages (8 ounces each) fat-free cream cheese, room temperature
½ cup (2 ounces) Mexican white cheese (*queso blanco*), *or* farmer's cheese, crumbled
1½ cups cooked pinto beans, *or* 1 can (15 ounces) pinto beans, rinsed, drained
1 tablespoon vegetable oil

Per Serving
Calories: 204
% Calories from fat: 25
Fat (gm): 5.5
Saturated fat (gm): 0.4
Cholesterol (mg): 22.3
Sodium (mg): 520
Protein (gm): 17.2
Carbohydrate (gm): 19.4
Exchanges
Milk: 0.0
Vegetable: 1.0
Fruit: 0.0
Bread: 1.0
Meat: 1.5
Fat: 0.5

1. Cut stems from tops of poblano chilies; remove and discard seeds and veins. Heat water to boiling in large saucepan; add peppers. Reduce heat and simmer, uncovered, 2 to 3 minutes, until peppers are slightly softened. Drain well and cool.

2. Spray small skillet with cooking spray; heat over medium heat until hot. Saute jalapeño chili, garlic, and oregano until chili is tender, 2 to 3 minutes.

3. Mix cream cheese, white cheese, beans, and jalapeño chili mixture. Stuff poblano chilies with mixture. Heat oil in medium skillet until hot; saute peppers over medium to medium-high heat until tender and browned on all sides, 6 to 8 minutes. Serve hot.

BLACK BEAN CHEESECAKE WITH SALSA

This unusual entrée can also be served in smaller pieces as an appetizer or first course. It can also be served at room temperature, rather than heating as the recipe directs. Make it a day in advance, as overnight chilling is essential.

8 servings

4	flour tortillas
3	packages (8 ounces each) fat-free cream cheese (not tub type), room temperature
1½	cups no-cholesterol real egg product, *or* 6 eggs
1	can (15 ounces) black beans, rinsed, drained
½	jalapeño chili, finely chopped
2	tablespoons finely chopped onion
2	cloves garlic, minced
2	teaspoons Worcestershire sauce
2	teaspoons dried cumin
½	teaspoon dried oregano leaves
½	teaspoon chili powder
½	teaspoon salt (optional)
½	teaspoon cayenne pepper
	Vegetable cooking spray
1	cup (½ recipe) Red Tomato Salsa (see p. 9) salt withheld

Per Serving
Calories: 205
% Calories from fat: 9
Fat (gm): 1.9
Saturated fat (gm): 0.2
Cholesterol (mg): 0
Sodium (mg): 756
Protein (gm): 22
Carbohydrate (gm): 24.6
Exchanges
Milk: 0.0
Vegetable: 0.0
Fruit: 0.0
Bread: 1.5
Meat: 2.0
Fat: 0.0

1. Lightly grease 9-inch springform pan and line with overlapping tortillas.

2. Beat cream cheese in large bowl until fluffy; beat in egg substitute. Mix in remaining ingredients, except cooking spray and salsa. Transfer mixture to prepared springform pan. Bake at 300 degrees until center is set and sharp knife inserted halfway between center and edge of cheesecake comes out almost clean, 1¾ to 2 hours. Cool to room temperature on wire rack. Refrigerate overnight.

3. Spray large skillet with cooking spray; heat over medium heat until hot. Cook wedges of cheesecake over medium-low heat until browned on both sides. Serve with Red Tomato Salsa.

CHEDDAR CHEESE SOUFFLÉ

 This spectacular soufflé soars above the soufflé dish!

4 servings

Vegetable cooking spray
1-2 tablespoons grated fat-free Parmesan cheese
1 cup fat-free milk
3 tablespoons flour
½ teaspoon dry mustard
½ teaspoon snipped fresh chives
½ teaspoon dried marjoram leaves
¼ teaspoon cayenne pepper
1-2 pinches ground nutmeg
3 egg yolks
¼ cup (1 ounce) shredded fat-free Cheddar cheese
Salt and white pepper, to taste
3 egg whites
¼ teaspoon cream of tartar

Per Serving
Calories: 162
% Calories from fat: 23
Fat (gm): 4.1
Saturated fat (gm): 1.3
Cholesterol (mg): 160.8
Sodium (mg): 340
Protein (gm): 19.3
Carbohydrate (gm): 11.2
Exchanges
Milk: 0.0
Vegetable: 0.0
Fruit: 0.0
Bread: 0.5
Meat: 2.5
Fat: 0.0

1. Spray 1-quart soufflé dish with cooking spray and coat with Parmesan cheese. Attach an aluminum foil collar to dish, extending foil 3 inches above top of dish; spray inside of collar with cooking spray.

2. Mix milk and flour until smooth in small saucepan; mix in mustard, chives, marjoram, cayenne, and nutmeg. Heat to boiling, whisking constantly; boil until thickened, about 1 minute, whisking constantly.

3. To egg yolks in small bowl, whisk in about ½ cup milk mixture. Whisk egg mixture back into saucepan. Add cheese; cook over low heat until melted, whisking constantly. Season to taste with salt and white pepper.

4. In medium bowl, beat egg whites until foamy; add cream of tartar and beat to stiff, but not dry, peaks. Stir about ⅓ of egg whites into cheese mixture; fold cheese mixture into remaining whites in bowl. Spoon into prepared soufflé dish. Bake at 350° until soufflé is puffed, browned, and just set in the center, 35 to 40 minutes. Serve immediately.

CHEESE FONDUE

Flavorful with wine and a hint of garlic, this creamy fondue is made entirely with fat-free cheese!

8 servings (¼ cup fondue each)

1½ cups dry white wine
2-3 large cloves garlic, peeled
  1 package (8 ounces) fat-free cream cheese
  2 cups (8 ounces) shredded fat-free Swiss cheese
  1 tablespoon flour
    Salt, cayenne, and black pepper, to taste
    French, *or* Italian, bread, cubed, for dipping (optional)

Per Serving
Calories: 100
% Calories from fat: 0
Fat (gm): 0
Saturated fat (gm): 0
Cholesterol (mg): 0
Sodium (mg): 547
Protein (gm): 10.8
Carbohydrate (gm): 5
Exchanges
Milk: 0.0
Vegetable: 0.0
Fruit: 0.0
Bread: 0.0
Meat: 1.5
Fat: 0.0

1. Heat wine and garlic cloves to boiling in medium saucepan; reduce heat and boil gently until reduced to ¾ cup. Discard garlic.

2. Add cream cheese and cook over low heat, stirring until melted and smooth. Toss shredded Swiss cheese with flour; add to saucepan and cook, stirring constantly, until melted. Season to taste with salt, cayenne, and black pepper.

3. Serve in fondue pot or bowl with bread cubes for dipping.

Note: Instead of wine, ¾ cup fat-free milk can be substituted. Simmer with garlic 5 minutes, then proceed with recipe as above. If fondue becomes too thick, it can be thinned with white wine, fat-free milk, or water.

WELSH RAREBIT

Perhaps you know this dish as Welsh Rabbit. Whatever the name, the distinctively flavored sauce is rich and delicious. Regular toast can be used instead of pan-grilling the bread in step 3.

6 servings (about ½ cup sauce each)

¼	cup very finely chopped onion
2	tablespoons margarine, *or* butter
¼	cup all-purpose flour
2	cups fat-free milk
½	cup white wine, *or* fat-free milk
2	ounces light pasteurized processed cheese product, cubed
½	cup (2 ounces) reduced-fat sharp Cheddar cheese
¼-½	teaspoon dry mustard
½	teaspoon Worcestershire sauce
	White and cayenne pepper, to taste
6	slices sourdough, *or* multigrain, bread
	Butter-flavored vegetable cooking spray
6	thick slices tomato
	Parsley leaves, finely chopped, as garnish

Per Serving
Calories: 219
% Calories from fat: 31
Fat (gm): 7.6
Saturated fat (gm): 3.4
Cholesterol (mg): 11.5
Sodium (mg): 502
Protein (gm): 9.9
Carbohydrate (gm): 24.1
Exchanges
Milk: 0.0
Vegetable: 0.0
Fruit: 0.0
Bread: 1.5
Meat: 1.0
Fat: 1.0

1. Saute onion in margarine in medium saucepan until tender, 2 to 3 minutes. Stir in flour and cook over medium-low heat, stirring constantly, 1 minute. Whisk in milk and wine; heat to boiling. Boil, whisking constantly, until thickened, about 1 minute.

2. Stir in cheeses, dry mustard, and Worcestershire sauce; cook over low heat until cheeses are melted. Season to taste with white and cayenne pepper.

3. Spray both sides of bread with cooking spray; cook over medium heat in large skillet until browned, 2 to 3 minutes on each side. Broil tomato slices 4 inches from heat source until hot through. Arrange bread on plates; top with tomato slices, and spoon cheese sauce over. Sprinkle with parsley.

CHEESE AND VEGETABLE RAREBIT

 For variation, serve this melty mixture in pita breads, or roll in flour tortillas, tucking up one end to contain the filling.

6 servings

Vegetable cooking spray
⅔ cup small broccoli florets
⅔ cup chopped portobello mushrooms
⅔ cup chopped yellow summer squash
⅓ cup chopped onion
2-3 tablespoons water
½ teaspoon dried marjoram leaves
½ teaspoon dried savory leaves
¼ teaspoon dried thyme leaves
2 tablespoons margarine, *or* butter
¼ cup all-purpose flour
2 cups fat-free milk
½ cup (2 ounces) shredded, *or* cubed, light American cheese
½-1 teaspoon white Worcestershire sauce
Salt and pepper, to taste
6 slices sourdough bread, toasted
2 green onions and tops, sliced

Per Serving
Calories: 185
% Calories from fat: 30
Fat (gm): 6.2
Saturated fat (gm): 2
Cholesterol (mg): 6.4
Sodium (mg): 387
Protein (gm): 8.3
Carbohydrate (gm): 24.1
Exchanges
Milk: 0.0
Vegetable: 1.0
Fruit: 0.0
Bread: 1.5
Meat: 0.0
Fat: 1.0

1. Spray medium skillet with cooking spray; heat over medium heat until hot. Saute broccoli, mushrooms, squash, and chopped onion 3 to 4 minutes; stir in water and herbs. Reduce heat and cook, covered, until vegetables are tender, 5 to 8 minutes.

2. Heat margarine in medium saucepan until melted; stir in flour and cook over medium-low heat, stirring constantly, 1 minute. Whisk in milk and heat to boiling, whisking frequently. Boil, whisking constantly, until thickened, about 1 minute. Remove from heat; add cheese and Worcestershire sauce, whisking until cheese is melted.

3. Stir vegetables into cheese sauce; season to taste with salt and pepper. Spoon vegetable mixture over bread slices on plates; sprinkle with green onions.

QUICHE LORRAINE

Enjoy the rich texture and flavor of this classic quiche, modified to low-fat goodness by using a combination of skim and evaporated fat-free milk. For Spinach Quiche, see the variation following the recipe.

6 servings

Basic Pie Crust (All-Purpose Flour, see p. 757)
Vegetable cooking spray
¼ cup finely chopped onion
¾ cup fat-free milk
½ can (12-ounce size) evaporated fat-free milk
1 egg
2 egg whites
¼ cup fat-free sour cream
¼ teaspoon salt
⅛ teaspoon cayenne pepper
⅛ teaspoon ground nutmeg
1 cup (4 ounces) shredded fat-free Swiss cheese
1 tablespoon flour
2 tablespoons imitation bacon bits

Per Serving
Calories: 264
% Calories from fat: 26
Fat (gm): 7.4
Saturated fat (gm): 1.6
Cholesterol (mg): 37
Sodium (mg): 637
Protein (gm): 14.4
Carbohydrate (gm): 34.3
Exchanges
Milk: 0.5
Vegetable: 0.0
Fruit: 0.0
Bread: 2.0
Meat: 1.0
Fat: 0.5

1. Make Pie Crust, deleting sugar. Roll pastry on floured surface into circle 1 inch larger than inverted 8-inch pie pan. Ease pastry into pan; trim and flute. Line bottom of pastry with aluminum foil and fill with a single layer of pie weights or dried beans. Bake at 425 degrees for 7 minutes; remove pie weights and foil. Bake 3 to 5 minutes longer or until crust is light golden brown. Cool on wire rack.

2. Spray small skillet with cooking spray; place over medium heat until hot. Saute onion until tender, 3 to 5 minutes.

3. Mix skim and evaporated fat-free milk, egg, egg whites, sour cream, salt, cayenne, and nutmeg in medium bowl until smooth. Toss cheese with flour; stir into milk mixture. Stir in imitation bacon bits and onion. Pour into baked pie crust.

4. Bake quiche at 350 degrees until set in the center, and a sharp knife inserted near center comes out clean, about 40 minutes. Cover edge of pie crust with aluminum foil if becoming too brown. Cool quiche on wire rack 5 minutes before cutting.

Variation: **Spinach Quiche**—Replace step 2 as follows: spray medium skillet with vegetable cooking spray; place over medium heat until hot. Saute ¼ cup finely chopped onion until tender, 3 to 5 minutes. Drain ½ package (10-ounce size) frozen, thawed spinach between paper toweling. Add spinach to skillet, cooking over medium to medium-low heat until mixture is quite dry, 3 to 4 minutes. Stir spinach mixture into milk mixture at end of step 3 and proceed as above.

QUICHE IN PEPPER CUPS

For an attractive presentation, use a variety of colored bell peppers.

6 servings

6 red bell peppers, cored, halved lengthwise
Vegetable cooking spray
¾ cup sliced green onions and tops
½ cup chopped green bell pepper
2 cloves garlic, minced
½ teaspoon dried savory leaves
¼ teaspoon dried marjoram leaves
⅛ teaspoon dried thyme leaves
⅔ cup chopped, seeded tomato
2 cups cooked orzo
½ cup (2 ounces) shredded fat-free Swiss cheese
6 eggs, beaten
½ cup fat-free milk
½ teaspoon salt
⅛ teaspoon pepper

Per Serving
Calories: 249
% Calories from fat: 21
Fat (gm): 6.2
Saturated fat (gm): 1.6
Cholesterol (mg): 213.3
Sodium (mg): 380
Protein (gm): 15.4
Carbohydrate (gm): 35.9
Exchanges
Milk: 0.0
Vegetable: 3.0
Fruit: 0.0
Bread: 1.5
Meat: 1.0
Fat: 0.5

1. Cook red bell peppers in boiling water to cover in large saucepan until crisp-tender, 4 to 5 minutes. Drain, cut sides down, on paper toweling.

2. Spray large skillet with cooking spray; heat over medium heat until hot. Saute green onions, chopped bell pepper, and garlic until tender, about 5 minutes. Stir in herbs and cook 1 to 2 minutes longer. Stir in tomato and orzo. Spoon mixture into pepper halves and sprinkle with cheese. Place peppers in sprayed baking pan, 13 x 9 inches.

3. Beat eggs until foamy in medium bowl; beat in milk, salt, and pepper. Pour over mixture in peppers, using about ⅓ cup for each. Bake at 350 degrees until mixture is set and sharp knife inserted near centers of peppers comes out clean, about 45 minutes.

TEN

Bean Dishes

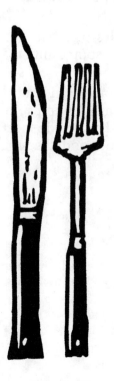

FAVA BEAN BRUSCHETTA

Assembled on Italian bread halves, these bruschetta can be cut into large pieces for a light entrée, or into small pieces for appetizers.

8 servings

1	loaf Italian bread, cut lengthwise into half
	Olive oil cooking spray
2	cloves garlic, cut into halves
	Fava Bean Spread (recipe follows)
2-3	medium tomatoes, thinly sliced
1	medium onion, thinly sliced
1	cup (4 ounces) shredded fat-free mozzarella cheese
1	cup (4 ounces) crumbled reduced-fat feta cheese
¼	cup sliced, pitted black olives
	Parsley, finely chopped, as garnish

Per Serving
Calories: 307
% Calories from fat: 22
Fat (gm): 7.7
Saturated fat (gm): 2.2
Cholesterol (mg): 5.1
Sodium (mg): 761
Protein (gm): 16.9
Carbohydrate (gm): 43.2
Exchanges
Milk: 0.0
Vegetable: 0.0
Fruit: 0.0
Bread: 3.0
Meat: 1.0
Fat: 1.0

1. Spray both cut sides of bread halves with cooking spray; broil 4 inches from heat source until toasted. Rub bread with cut sides of garlic cloves.

2. Spread half of the Fava Bean Spread on each bread half; top with tomato and onion slices and sprinkle with cheeses, olives, and parsley. Place bread on cookie sheet and bake at 450 degrees until bean mixture is hot and cheese melted, 8 to 10 minutes. Cut into serving pieces.

Fava Bean Spread

(makes about 2 cups)

2	cups cooked fresh, *or* dried, fava beans, *or* 1 can (19 ounces) fava beans, rinsed, drained
1	tablespoon olive oil
1	tablespoon lemon juice
¼	cup packed parsley leaves
¼	cup packed basil leaves
	Salt and cayenne pepper, to taste

1. Process all ingredients, except salt and cayenne pepper, in food processor until smooth; season to taste with salt and pepper.

GARLICKY LIMA BEAN SOUP

For those who love garlic! The garlic, of course, can be reduced in amount if you prefer a more subtle dish.

6 side-dish servings (about 1 cup each)

Vegetable cooking spray

2 cups coarsely chopped onions

10 large cloves garlic, peeled, quartered

1 teaspoon crushed red pepper

2 cans (17 ounces each) lima beans, rinsed, drained

3 cups Basic Vegetable Stock (see p. 58), *or* reduced-sodium vegetable broth

1 teaspoon dried thyme leaves

½ cup fat-free half-and-half, *or* fat-free milk

Salt and white pepper, to taste

Cayenne pepper, *or* paprika, as garnish

Parsley, finely chopped, as garnish

Per Serving
Calories: 169
% Calories from fat: 5
Fat (gm): 0.9
Saturated fat (gm): 0.2
Cholesterol (mg): 0
Sodium (mg): 429
Protein (gm): 9.2
Carbohydrate (gm): 31.8
Exchanges
Milk: 0.0
Vegetable: 1.0
Fruit: 0.0
Bread: 2.0
Meat: 0.0
Fat: 0.0

1. Spray large saucepan with cooking spray; heat over medium heat until hot. Cook onions, garlic, and red pepper, covered, over medium to medium-low heat until onions are tender, 8 to 10 minutes. Add beans, stock, and thyme to saucepan; heat to boiling. Reduce heat and simmer, covered, 5 to 10 minutes.

2. Process soup in food processor or blender until smooth; return to saucepan. Stir in half-and-half; cook over medium heat 5 minutes, stirring occasionally. Season to taste with salt and white pepper.

3. Serve soup in bowls; sprinkle lightly with cayenne pepper and parsley.

EASIEST BLACK-EYED PEA AND LENTIL SOUP

This soup will thicken if refrigerated, so stir in additional broth when reheating. The soup freezes well, too.

6 main-dish servings (about 1⅔ cups each)

¾	cup dried black-eyed peas
3	medium carrots, chopped
2	medium ribs celery, sliced
1	medium onion, chopped
1	teaspoon minced garlic
2	tablespoons olive oil
6-8	cups canned reduced-sodium vegetable broth
1	teaspoon dried thyme leaves
½	teaspoon dried marjoram leaves
½	teaspoon dried oregano leaves
1	bay leaf
3	medium tomatoes, chopped
1½	cups dried lentils
	Salt and pepper, to taste

Per Serving
Calories: 356
% Calories from fat: 14
Fat (gm): 5.9
Saturated fat (gm): 0.9
Cholesterol (mg): 0
Sodium (mg): 119
Protein (gm): 20.7
Carbohydrate (gm): 58.3
Exchanges
Milk: 0.0
Vegetable: 2.0
Fruit: 0.0
Bread: 3.0
Meat: 1.0
Fat: 1.0

1. Wash and sort black-eyed peas, discarding any stones. Cover black-eyed peas with 2 inches water in medium saucepan; heat to boiling and boil, covered, 2 minutes. Remove from heat and let stand 1 hour. Drain.

2. Saute carrots, celery, onion, and garlic in oil in large saucepan 5 minutes. Add 6 cups broth, black-eyed peas, and herbs to saucepan; heat to boiling. Reduce heat and simmer, covered, until black-eyed peas are tender, 45 to 60 minutes, adding additional broth if necessary.

3. Stir tomatoes and lentils into soup during last 30 minutes of cooking time. Discard bay leaf; season to taste with salt and pepper.

CURRIED BEAN SOUP

Use any white bean, such as cannellini, navy, soy, lima, or garbanzo in this creamy, rich soup.

6 main-dish servings (about 1¼ cups each)

1 cup chopped onion

1 cup sliced leek (white part only)

3 teaspoons minced garlic

2 tablespoons olive oil

1 tablespoon curry powder

2 cans (15½ ounces each) Great Northern beans, rinsed, drained

3½ cups Basic Vegetable Stock, *or* Canned Vegetable Stock (see pp. 58, 63)

½ cup fat-free half-and-half, *or* fat-free milk

Salt and pepper, to taste

6 tablespoons fat-free sour cream, *or* plain yogurt

3 tablespoons finely chopped cilantro

2 tablespoons finely chopped red bell pepper

Per Serving
Calories: 263
% Calories from fat: 16
Fat (gm): 4.9
Saturated fat (gm): 1
Cholesterol (mg): 0
Sodium (mg): 393
Protein (gm): 13.7
Carbohydrate (gm): 42.5
Exchanges
Milk: 0.0
Vegetable: 1.5
Fruit: 0.0
Bread: 2.5
Meat: 0.5
Fat: 0.5

1. Saute onion, leek, and garlic in oil in large saucepan until tender, 5 to 8 minutes. Stir in curry powder and cook 1 to 2 minutes longer.

2. Add beans and stock to saucepan; heat to boiling. Reduce heat and simmer, covered, 5 minutes. Process bean mixture in food processor or blender until smooth; return to saucepan. Stir in half-and-half; cook over medium heat 2 to 3 minutes. Season to taste with salt and pepper.

3. Serve soup in bowls; top each with a tablespoon of sour cream. Sprinkle with cilantro and bell pepper.

YELLOW AND WHITE BEAN CHILI

Chopped fresh tomato and green onions add perfect color accents to this subtly colored chili. Canned beans can be used in the chili for convenience; use 1 can (15 ounces each) of rinsed, drained Great Northern, garbanzo, and soy beans.

6 servings (about 1¼ cups each)

Per Serving
Calories: 319
% Calories from fat: 22
Fat (gm): 8
Saturated fat (gm): 1.1
Cholesterol (mg): 0
Sodium (mg): 56.9
Protein (gm): 17.2
Carbohydrate (gm): 45.5
Exchanges
Milk: 0.0
Vegetable: 0.0
Fruit: 0.0
Bread: 3.0
Meat: 1.0
Fat: 0.5

- 1 cup chopped onion
- 1 cup thinly sliced leek (white part only)
- 1 cup chopped yellow, *or* white, bell peppers
- 1 jalapeño chili, finely chopped
- 2 teaspoons minced garlic
- 2 teaspoons cumin seeds
- 1-2 tablespoons olive oil
- 1 medium yellow summer squash, cubed
- 2 small red potatoes, peeled, cubed
- 1½ cups cooked, dried Great Northern beans
- 1½ cups cooked, dried garbanzo beans
- 1½ cups cooked, dried soybeans
- 1 can (14½ ounces) reduced-sodium vegetable broth
- ½ cup dry white wine
- 1 teaspoon dried oregano leaves
- ½ teaspoon ground coriander
- ½ teaspoon ground cinnamon
- 1 teaspoon chili powder
- 1 bay leaf
  Salt and pepper, to taste
- 1 small tomato, finely chopped
- 2 green onions and tops, thinly sliced
- 3 tablespoons finely chopped cilantro

1. Saute onion, leek, bell peppers, jalapeño chili, garlic, and cumin seeds in oil in large saucepan until tender, about 8 minutes. Add squash and potatoes; cook 3 to 4 minutes longer.

2. Add all beans, broth, wine, herbs, and spices to saucepan; heat to boiling. Reduce heat and simmer, covered, until vegetables are tender, about 15 minutes. Simmer, uncovered, until thickened, 5 to 10 minutes. Season to taste with salt and pepper. Discard bay leaf.

3. Spoon soup into bowls; sprinkle top of each with tomato, green onions, and cilantro.

TEXAS STEW WITH CHILI-CHEESE DUMPLINGS

With only 30 minutes cooking time, this is a stew you'll prepare often. One green bell pepper and one jalapeño chili can be substituted for the poblano chili.

6 servings (about 1½ cups each)

2 cups chopped onions

1 medium red bell pepper, coarsely chopped

1 medium yellow bell pepper, coarsely chopped

1 large poblano chili, coarsely chopped

3 cloves garlic, minced

2-3 tablespoons chili powder

1½-2 teaspoons ground cumin

1 teaspoon dried oregano leaves

½ teaspoon dried marjoram leaves

2 tablespoons olive oil

2 cans (15 ounces each) reduced-sodium whole tomatoes, undrained, coarsely chopped

1 can (15 ounces) black-eyed peas, rinsed, drained

1 can (15 ounces) red beans, rinsed, drained

1½ cups cubed, peeled butternut, *or* acorn, squash

1 cup fresh, *or* frozen, thawed, okra

Salt and pepper, to taste

Chili-Cheese Dumplings (recipe follows)

Per Serving
Calories: 433
% Calories from fat: 29
Fat (gm): 14.9
Saturated fat (gm): 2.7
Cholesterol (mg): 3.7
Sodium (mg): 713
Protein (gm): 17.4
Carbohydrate (gm): 65.9
Exchanges
Milk: 0.0
Vegetable: 3.0
Fruit: 0.0
Bread: 3.0
Meat: 1.0
Fat: 2.0

1. Saute onions, bell peppers, poblano chili, garlic, and herbs in oil in large saucepan until tender, about 10 minutes. Stir in remaining ingredients, except salt and pepper and Chili-Cheese Dumplings; heat to boiling. Reduce heat and simmer, covered, until okra and squash are tender, 8 to 10 minutes. Season to taste with salt and pepper.

2. Spoon dumpling dough into 6 mounds on top of stew. Cook, uncovered, 5 minutes. Cook, covered, until dumplings are dry, 5 to 10 minutes longer.

Chili-Cheese Dumplings

(makes 6 dumplings)

    ⅔ cup all-purpose flour
    ⅓ cup yellow cornmeal
    1½ teaspoons baking powder
     1 teaspoon chili powder
    ½ teaspoon salt
     2 tablespoons vegetable shortening
    ¼ cup (1 ounce) shredded reduced-fat
       Monterey Jack cheese
     1 tablespoon finely chopped cilantro
    ½ cup fat-free milk

1. Combine flour, cornmeal, baking powder, chili powder, and salt in medium bowl; cut in shortening with pastry blender until mixture resembles coarse crumbs. Mix in cheese and cilantro; stir in milk, forming a soft dough.

WINTER BEAN AND VEGETABLE STEW

Root vegetables and beans combine in this satisfying stew, perfect for cold weather meals. Serve with Multigrain Batter Bread (see p. 668).

6 servings (about 1⅓ cups each)

    1 medium onion, chopped
    1 medium Idaho potato, unpeeled, cut
      into 1-inch cubes
    1 medium sweet potato, peeled, cut into
      1-inch cubes

Per Serving
Calories: 238
% Calories from fat: 20
Fat (gm): 5.7
Saturated fat (gm): 0.7
Cholesterol (mg): 0
Sodium (mg): 399
Protein (gm): 10.8
Carbohydrate (gm): 42.4

1 large carrot, cut into ½-inch pieces
1 medium parsnip, cut into ½-inch
    pieces
½ cup chopped green bell pepper
2 cloves garlic, minced
2 tablespoons olive oil
1 tablespoon flour
1½ cups Basic Vegetable Stock, *or* Canned
    Vegetable Stock (see pp. 58, 63)
1 can (15 ounces) black beans, rinsed,
    drained
1 can (13¼ ounces) baby lima beans,
    rinsed, drained
1 large tomato, cut into wedges
¾ teaspoon dried sage leaves
¼-½ teaspoon dried thyme leaves
    Salt and pepper, to taste
2 green onions and tops, sliced

Exchanges
Milk: 0.0
Vegetable: 2.0
Fruit: 0.0
Bread: 2.0
Meat: 0.0
Fat: 1.0

1. Saute onion, potatoes, carrot, parsnips, bell pepper, and garlic in oil in large saucepan 5 minutes; stir in flour and cook 1 to 2 minutes longer.

2. Add remaining ingredients, except salt and pepper and green onions to saucepan; heat to boiling. Reduce heat and simmer, covered, until vegetables are tender, 15 to 20 minutes. Season to taste with salt and pepper.

3. Serve stew in bowls; sprinkle with green onions.

ADZUKI BEAN PASTITSIO

Any cooked bean you want, or lentils, can be substituted for the adzuki beans in the recipe. Mafalde or fusilli are other pasta choices.

8 servings

    Olive oil cooking spray
⅔ cup chopped onion
½ cup chopped green bell pepper
1 cup cooked adzuki beans
2 cups Mediterranean Tomato-Caper
    Sauce (see p. 709)

Per Serving
Calories: 287
% Calories from fat: 19
Fat (gm): 6.1
Saturated fat (gm): 1.5
Cholesterol (mg): 107.7
Sodium (mg): 195
Protein (gm): 14.8
Carbohydrate (gm): 43.8

  1 teaspoon dried mint leaves
  2 cups elbow macaroni, cooked, divided
  ½ cup grated fat-free Parmesan cheese, divided
2⅓ cups fat-free milk
  2 tablespoons margarine, *or* butter
  4 eggs, lightly beaten
     Nutmeg, ground, as garnish

Exchanges
Milk: 0.0
Vegetable: 3.0
Fruit: 0.0
Bread: 2.0
Meat: 0.5
Fat: 1.0

1. Spray medium saucepan with cooking spray; heat over medium heat until hot. Saute onion and bell pepper until tender, about 5 minutes. Stir in beans, tomato sauce, and mint; cook over medium heat until hot, about 5 minutes.

2. Spoon half the pasta into 13 x 9-inch baking pan. Spoon sauce over evenly; sprinkle with ¼ cup Parmesan cheese. Spoon remaining macaroni over the top.

3. Heat milk and margarine in small saucepan over medium heat until hot, but not boiling. Beat eggs in medium bowl; whisk hot milk into eggs. Pour milk mixture over casserole; sprinkle with remaining cheese and nutmeg.

4. Bake at 350 degrees until topping is set and browned, 50 to 60 minutes. Let stand 5 minutes before cutting.

EGGPLANT AND BEAN CURRY STEW

 The flavorful curry seasoning is created by making a simple paste of onion, garlic, and herbs.

4 servings (about 1 cup each)

  2 medium red potatoes, peeled, cut into ¾-inch cubes
  1 tablespoon olive oil
  1 small eggplant, cut into ¾-inch cubes
  ½ medium onion, chopped
  1 teaspoon minced garlic
  1 teaspoon ground coriander
  ½ teaspoon ground cumin
  ¼ teaspoon crushed red pepper
  ⅛ teaspoon ground turmeric

Per Serving
Calories: 242
% Calories from fat: 21
Fat (gm): 6
Saturated fat (gm): 0.8
Cholesterol (mg): 0
Sodium (mg): 446
Protein (gm): 8.2
Carbohydrate (gm): 41.8
Exchanges
Milk: 0.0
Vegetable: 2.0
Fruit: 0.0
Bread: 2.0
Meat: 0.0
Fat: 1.0

1 tablespoon water
1 can (16 ounces) reduced-sodium whole
  tomatoes, undrained, coarsely chopped
1 can (15 ounces) garbanzo beans,
  rinsed, drained
½ cup water
  Salt and pepper, to taste
¼ cup finely chopped cilantro

1. Saute potatoes in oil in large saucepan until browned; remove and reserve. Add eggplant to saucepan; cook over medium to medium-low heat until lightly browned, stirring frequently. Remove eggplant and reserve.

2. Process onion, garlic, herbs, and 1 tablespoon water in food processor until a smooth paste. Add to saucepan and cook over medium-low heat, 3 to 4 minutes, stirring frequently to prevent burning. Add reserved potatoes and eggplant, tomatoes with liquid, beans, and ½ cup water to saucepan; heat to boiling. Reduce heat and simmer, covered, until eggplant is tender, 20 to 25 minutes. Season to taste with salt and pepper; stir in cilantro.

NEW ENGLAND BAKED BEANS

Long-baked and savory, these beans are the best! All-vegetable "bacon" bits replace the salt pork used in the traditional recipe. If you prefer soaking beans overnight, delete step 1 and proceed with step 2.

4 servings (about 1 cup each)

8 ounces dried navy, *or* Great Northern
  beans, washed and sorted
¾ cup chopped onion
1 clove garlic, minced
3 tablespoons reduced-sodium tomato
  paste
3 tablespoons dark molasses
3 tablespoons packed light brown sugar
2-3 tablespoons all-vegetable bacon-
  flavored bits
½ teaspoon dry mustard
¼ teaspoon dried thyme leaves
½ teaspoon salt

Per Serving
Calories: 299
% Calories from fat: 5
Fat (gm): 1.8
Saturated fat (gm): 0.3
Cholesterol (mg): 0
Sodium (mg): 385
Protein (gm): 14.6
Carbohydrate (gm): 58.9
Exchanges
Milk: 0.0
Vegetable: 0.0
Fruit: 0.0
Bread: 4.0
Meat: 0.0
Fat: 0.0

1. Wash and sort beans, discarding any stones. Cover beans with 2 inches water in large saucepan; heat to boiling and boil, uncovered, 2 minutes. Remove from heat and let stand, covered, 1 hour.

2. Add enough water to beans to cover, if necessary. Heat to boiling; reduce heat and simmer, covered, until beans are tender, about 1¼ hours. Drain beans and reserve liquid.

3. Mix beans and remaining ingredients in 1½-quart casserole; add enough reserved liquid to cover beans. Bake, covered, at 325 degrees, stirring occasionally, 3 hours. Bake, uncovered, until beans are of desired consistency, 45 to 60 minutes.

GINGER-BAKED BEANS

Slow baking adds goodness to this special ginger and sweet-spiced bean dish.

8 servings (about 1 cup each)

1½	cups chopped onions
¼	cup finely chopped gingerroot
4	cloves garlic, minced
2	tablespoons vegetable oil
6	cups cooked dried Great Northern beans, *or* 4 cans (15 ounces each) Great Northern Beans, rinsed, drained
½	cup packed light brown sugar
1	can (6 ounces) reduced-sodium tomato sauce
½	cup light molasses
1	teaspoon dry mustard
1	teaspoon ground ginger
½	teaspoon dried thyme leaves
¼	teaspoon ground cinnamon
¼	teaspoon ground allspice
2	bay leaves
½	cup coarsely ground gingersnap crumbs

Per Serving
Calories: 341
% Calories from fat: 12
Fat (gm): 4.8
Saturated fat (gm): 0.8
Cholesterol (mg): 0
Sodium (mg): 60
Protein (gm): 12.5
Carbohydrate (gm): 64.9
Exchanges
Milk: 0.0
Vegetable: 1.0
Fruit: 0.0
Bread: 4.0
Meat: 0.0
Fat: 0.5

1. Saute onions, gingerroot, and garlic in oil in medium skillet until tender, 5 to 8 minutes. Mix all ingredients, except gingersnap crumbs, in 2-quart casserole.

2. Bake, covered, at 300 degrees 2 hours. Sprinkle top of beans with gingersnap crumbs; bake, uncovered, until beans are thickened to desired consistency, about 30 minutes. Discard bay leaves.

JUST PEACHY BEAN POT

 Peaches and nectar, dried fruit, and mango chutney add special flavor to this bean combo. Mango and mango nectar may be substituted for the peach and peach nectar.

6 servings (about 1⅓ cups each)

1	cup chopped onion
1	clove garlic, minced
1	tablespoon margarine, *or* butter
1-1½	teaspoons curry powder
½-¾	teaspoon ground allspice
¼-½	teaspoon crushed red pepper
1	can (15 ounces) navy beans, rinsed, drained
2	cans (15 ounces each) red kidney beans, rinsed, drained
1½	cups diced peaches
½	cup coarsely chopped mixed dried fruit
½	cup mango chutney
½-¾	cup peach nectar
3	tablespoons cider vinegar

Per Serving
Calories: 332
% Calories from fat: 8
Fat (gm): 3.4
Saturated fat (gm): 0.5
Cholesterol (mg): 0
Sodium (mg): 621
Protein (gm): 17.5
Carbohydrate (gm): 68.8
Exchanges
Milk: 0.0
Vegetable: 0.0
Fruit: 1.5
Bread: 3.0
Meat: 0.5
Fat: 0.0

1. Saute onion and garlic in margarine in small skillet until tender, about 5 minutes. Stir in curry powder, allspice, and crushed red pepper; cook 1 to 2 minutes longer.

2. Mix all ingredients in 2½-quart casserole. Bake, covered, at 350 degrees 30 minutes; bake, uncovered, if thicker consistency is desired, about 15 minutes.

SANTA FE BAKED BEANS

 These baked beans boast flavors of the great Southwest.

4 servings (about 1⅓ cups each)

1 cup chopped onion

½ cup chopped poblano chili, *or* green bell pepper

½-1 serrano, *or* jalapeño, chili, finely chopped

1 tablespoon olive oil

3 cups cooked dried pinto beans, *or* 2 cans (15 ounces each) pinto beans, rinsed, drained

2 cups frozen whole-kernel corn, thawed

6 sun-dried tomatoes (not in oil), cut into fourths

2-3 tablespoons honey

½-1 teaspoon ground cumin

½ teaspoon dried thyme leaves

2 bay leaves

½ cup (2 ounces) crumbled Mexican white, *or* farmer's, cheese

¼ cup finely chopped cilantro

Per Serving
Calories: 400
% Calories from fat: 17
Fat (gm): 8.1
Saturated fat (gm): 2.7
Cholesterol (mg): 12.7
Sodium (mg): 364
Protein (gm): 17.9
Carbohydrate (gm): 69.4
Exchanges
Milk: 0.0
Vegetable: 1.0
Fruit: 0.0
Bread: 4.0
Meat: 0.5
Fat: 1.0

1. Saute onion and chilies in oil in small skillet until tender, about 5 minutes. Combine all ingredients, except cheese and cilantro, in 1½-quart casserole; sprinkle cheese on top.

2. Bake, covered, at 350 degrees until bean mixture is hot, about 30 minutes; discard bay leaves. Sprinkle top of casserole with cilantro before serving.

TUSCAN BEAN BAKE

Easy to combine and bake, these beans are lemon-scented and seasoned with sun-dried tomatoes, garlic, and herbs. Any white beans, such as garbanzo beans, soybeans, or navy beans, can be used.

4 servings (about 1 cup each)

1	cup dried cannellini, *or* Great Northern, beans
1	cup Canned Vegetable Stock (see p. 63), *or* canned reduced-sodium vegetable broth
1	medium onion, chopped
2	teaspoons minced garlic, divided
½	cup chopped red bell pepper
1	teaspoon dried sage leaves
1	teaspoon dried rosemary leaves
2-3	teaspoons grated lemon rind
6	sun-dried tomatoes, sliced
	Salt and pepper, to taste
1	cup fresh whole wheat breadcrumbs
¼	cup minced parsley

Per Serving
Calories: 250
% Calories from fat: 6
Fat (gm): 1.7
Saturated fat (gm): 0.3
Cholesterol (mg): 0
Sodium (mg): 220
Protein (gm): 14.3
Carbohydrate (gm): 45.4
Exchanges
Milk: 0.0
Vegetable: 1.5
Fruit: 0.0
Bread: 2.5
Meat: 0.5
Fat: 0.0

1. Wash and sort beans, discarding any stones. Cover beans with 2 inches water in large saucepan; heat to boiling and boil, uncovered, 2 minutes. Remove from heat and let stand, covered, 1 hour; drain.

2. Combine beans, stock, onion, 1 teaspoon garlic, bell pepper, and herbs in 1½-quart casserole. Bake, covered, at 350 degrees, 30 minutes or until beans are tender. Stir in lemon rind and sun-dried tomatoes; season to taste with salt and pepper.

3. Combine breadcrumbs, parsley, and remaining 1 teaspoon garlic; sprinkle over top of bean mixture and press lightly onto beans to moisten breadcrumbs. Bake, uncovered, until liquid has evaporated, about 20 minutes more.

FRIED LENTILS

Fried lentils ("dal") are a staple of Indian cooking. Normally cooked in a large quantity of clarified, browned butter ("ghee"), we have substituted a small amount of vegetable oil to keep the dish low fat.

8 servings (about ½ cup each)

1½   cups dried red lentils
1   cup chopped onion
1   teaspoon ground turmeric
1   teaspoon crushed cumin seeds
¼   teaspoon crushed red pepper
2   tablespoons vegetable oil
½   cup chopped cilantro, *or* parsley
    Salt, to taste
2   teaspoons grated lemon rind

Per Serving
Calories: 171
% Calories from fat: 20
Fat (gm): 4
Saturated fat (gm): 0.5
Cholesterol (mg): 0
Sodium (mg): 4.4
Protein (gm): 10.5
Carbohydrate (gm): 24.6
Exchanges
Milk: 0.0
Vegetable: 1.0
Fruit: 0.0
Bread: 1.5
Meat: 0.0
Fat: 1.0

1.   Wash and sort lentils, discarding any stones. Cover lentils with 2 inches water and heat to boiling; reduce heat and simmer, covered, until very soft, 30 to 40 minutes. Drain well.

2.   Saute onion, turmeric, cumin seeds, and crushed red pepper in oil in large skillet until onions are tender, 5 to 8 minutes. Reserve ¼ cup onions.

3.   Stir lentils into skillet; cook over low heat, stirring frequently to prevent burning, until mixture is thickened, 10 to 20 minutes. Stir in cilantro; season to taste with salt.

4.   Spoon lentil mixture into serving bowl; sprinkle with reserved ¼ cup onions and lemon rind.

SEASONED MASHED BLACK BEANS

Black beans at their flavorful best—quick and easy too!

6 servings (about ⅔ cup each)

    Vegetable cooking spray
2   medium onions, chopped
4   cloves garlic, minced
1-2   small jalapeño chilies, minced
2   cans (15 ounces each) black beans,
      rinsed, drained

Per Serving
Calories: 158
% Calories from fat: 8
Fat (gm): 1.7
Saturated fat (gm): 0.1
Cholesterol (mg): 0
Sodium (mg): 476
Protein (gm): 12.5
Carbohydrate (gm): 31.2

2 cups Canned Vegetable Stock (see p. 63), *or* canned reduced-sodium vegetable broth
¾-1 teaspoon dried cumin
⅓ cup finely chopped cilantro leaves
Salt and pepper, to taste

Exchanges
Milk: 0.0
Vegetable: 1.0
Fruit: 0.0
Bread: 2.0
Meat: 0.0
Fat: 0.0

1. Spray large skillet with cooking spray; heat over medium heat until hot. Saute onions, garlic, and jalapeño chili until tender, 3 to 4 minutes.

2. Add beans and stock to skillet; cook over medium heat, coarsely mashing beans with fork. Stir in cumin and cilantro. Season to taste with salt and pepper.

REFRIED BEANS

 Two cans (15 ounces each) of pinto beans, rinsed and drained, can be substituted for the dried beans. Then make the recipe, beginning with step 2 and substituting 1 can (14½ ounces) of reduced-sodium vegetable broth for the cooking liquid.

6 servings (about ½ cup each)

1¼ cups dried pinto beans
Water
Vegetable cooking spray
1 medium onion, coarsely chopped
Salt and pepper, to taste

Per Serving
Calories: 106
% Calories from fat: 3
Fat (gm): 0.4
Saturated fat (gm): 0.1
Cholesterol (mg): 0
Sodium (mg): 2
Protein (gm): 6.1
Carbohydrate (gm): 20
Exchanges
Milk: 0.0
Vegetable: 0.0
Fruit: 0.0
Bread: 1.5
Meat: 0.0
Fat: 0.0

1. Wash and sort beans, discarding any stones. Cover beans with 2 inches of water in a large saucepan; heat to boiling and boil, uncovered, 2 minutes. Remove from heat; let stand, covered, 1 hour. Drain beans; cover with 2 inches of water and heat to boiling. Reduce heat and simmer, covered, until beans are tender, 1½ to 2 hours. Drain, reserving 2 cups liquid.

2. Spray large skillet with cooking spray; heat over medium heat until hot. Saute onion until tender, 3 to 5 minutes. Add 1 cup beans and 1 cup reserved liquid to skillet. Cook over high heat, mashing beans until almost smooth with end of meat mallet or potato masher. Add half the remaining beans and liquid; continue cooking and mashing beans. Repeat with remaining beans and liquid. Season to taste with salt and pepper.

BLACK BEANS AND RICE

 If fresh epazote is available, add a sprig or two to the rice while cooking.

6 servings (about ⅔ cup each)

Vegetable cooking spray
¼ cup chopped onion
¼ cup sliced green onions and tops
4 cloves garlic, minced
1 cup long-grain rice
2½ cups Canned Vegetable Stock, *or* Basic Vegetable Stock (see pp. 63, 58)
1 can (15 ounces) black beans, rinsed, drained
2 tablespoons finely chopped cilantro
Salt and pepper, to taste

Per Serving
Calories: 202
% Calories from fat: 5
Fat (gm): 1.2
Saturated fat (gm): 0.1
Cholesterol (mg): 0
Sodium (mg): 247
Protein (gm): 8.5
Carbohydrate (gm): 40.9
Exchanges
Milk: 0.0
Vegetable: 0.0
Fruit: 0.0
Bread: 2.5
Meat: 0.5
Fat: 0.0

1. Spray medium saucepan with cooking spray; heat over medium heat until hot. Saute onion, green onions, and garlic until tender, about 5 minutes. Add rice; cook over medium heat until rice is lightly browned, 2 to 3 minutes, stirring frequently.

2. Add stock to saucepan and heat to boiling; reduce heat and simmer, covered, until rice is tender, 20 to 25 minutes, adding beans during last 5 minutes. Stir in cilantro; season to taste with salt and pepper.

MEXI-BEANS, GREENS, AND RICE

Heartily spiced, the chilies and cayenne pepper in this dish can be decreased if less hotness is desired. Four cans (15 ounces each) pinto beans, rinsed and drained, can be substituted for the dried beans; then delete step 1 in recipe. Serve with Garlic Bread (see p. 676).

8 servings (about 1¼ cups each)

2	cups dried pinto beans
1	medium onion, coarsely chopped
1	medium poblano chili, chopped
1	medium red bell pepper, chopped
4	cloves garlic, minced
1	tablespoon finely chopped gingerroot
2	serrano chilies, finely chopped
2	tablespoons olive oil
2-3	teaspoons chili powder
2	teaspoons dried oregano leaves
1	teaspoon ground cumin
½	teaspoon cayenne pepper
3	cups water
1	can (15 ounces) diced tomatoes, undrained
2	cups coarsely chopped turnip, *or* mustard, greens
	Salt, to taste
5	cups cooked rice, warm
	Cilantro, finely chopped, as garnish

Per Serving
Calories: 361
% Calories from fat: 12
Fat (gm): 4.7
Saturated fat (gm): 0.7
Cholesterol (mg): 0
Sodium (mg): 103
Protein (gm): 14.4
Carbohydrate (gm): 66.7
Exchanges
Milk: 0.0
Vegetable: 2.0
Fruit: 0.0
Bread: 3.5
Meat: 0.5
Fat: 0.5

1. Sort and rinse beans, discarding any stones. Cover beans with 2 inches water in large saucepan; heat to boiling and boil, uncovered, 2 minutes. Remove from heat and let stand, covered, 1 hour; drain.

2. Saute onion, poblano chili, bell pepper, garlic, gingerroot, and serrano chilies in oil in large saucepan until tender, 8 to 10 minutes. Stir in chili powder, herbs, and cayenne pepper; cook 1 to 2 minutes longer.

3. Add 3 cups water and sauteed vegetables to beans; heat to boiling. Reduce heat and simmer, covered, until beans are tender, 1 to 1¼ hours, adding water if necessary. Stir in tomatoes and turnip greens; simmer, uncovered, until mixture is desired thickness, 15 to 30 minutes. Season to taste with salt.

4. Spoon rice into bowls; top with bean mixture and sprinkle generously with cilantro.

BOURBON STREET RED BEANS AND RICE

This New Orleans favorite is best if made with dried beans; however, 2 cans (15 ounces each) rinsed and drained red beans can be substituted for the dried.

4 servings (about 1¼ cups each)

1	cup dried red beans
2-3	cups Canned Vegetable Stock (see p. 63)
1	cup chopped onion
1	cup chopped green bell peppers
1	cup chopped celery
½-1	jalapeño chili, finely chopped
1-1½	teaspoons dried thyme leaves
1	teaspoon dried oregano leaves
½	teaspoon dried sage leaves
¼-½	teaspoon ground cumin
2	bay leaves
¼-½	teaspoon red pepper sauce
⅛-¼	teaspoon cayenne pepper
4-6	drops liquid smoke
	Salt, to taste
4	cups cooked rice, warm

Per Serving
Calories: 431
% Calories from fat: 3
Fat (gm): 1.7
Saturated fat (gm): 0.3
Cholesterol (mg): 0
Sodium (mg): 73
Protein (gm): 16.4
Carbohydrate (gm): 85.2
Exchanges
Milk: 0.0
Vegetable: 2.0
Fruit: 0.0
Bread: 5.0
Meat: 0.5
Fat: 0.0

1. Wash and sort beans, discarding any stones. Cover beans with 2 inches water in large saucepan; heat to boiling and boil 2 minutes. Remove from heat and let stand 1 hour. Drain.

2. Add 2 cups stock to beans and heat to boiling; simmer, covered, 30 minutes. Add vegetables and herbs to saucepan; simmer, covered, until beans are tender, 45 to 60 minutes, adding more stock if necessary (beans should be moist but without excess liquid). Remove bay leaves.

3. Stir red pepper sauce, cayenne pepper, and liquid smoke into beans; season to taste with salt. Serve bean mixture over rice in shallow bowls.

HOPPING JOHN

Be sure to eat your portion of Hopping John before noon on January 1 to guarantee a new year of good luck!

6 servings (about 1 cup each)

Vegetable cooking spray
1¾ cups chopped onions, divided
½ cup chopped celery
3 cloves garlic, minced
1 cup long-grain white rice
3 cups Basic Vegetable Stock (see p. 58), *or* water
1 teaspoon dried oregano leaves
1 bay leaf
2 cans (15 ounces each) black-eyed peas, rinsed, drained
2-3 dashes liquid smoke (optional)
2-3 dashes red pepper sauce
Salt and pepper, to taste

Per Serving
Calories: 306
% Calories from fat: 21
Fat (gm): 7
Saturated fat (gm): 1
Cholesterol (mg): 0
Sodium (mg): 447
Protein (gm): 9.6
Carbohydrate (gm): 50.7
Exchanges
Milk: 0.0
Vegetable: 1.0
Fruit: 0.0
Bread: 3.0
Meat: 0.5
Fat: 1.0

1. Spray large saucepan with cooking spray; heat over medium heat until hot. Saute 1½ cups onions, celery, and garlic until tender, 5 to 8 minutes. Add rice, stock, oregano, and bay leaf; heat to boiling. Reduce heat and simmer, covered, until rice is tender, about 25 minutes.

2. Stir black-eyed peas into rice mixture; season to taste with liquid smoke, red pepper sauce, salt, and pepper. Cook, covered, over medium-low heat 5 minutes. Discard bay leaf.

3. Spoon into serving bowl; sprinkle with remaining ¼ cup onions.

ITALIAN-STYLE BEANS AND VEGETABLES

 This colorful mélange can also be served over pasta, rice, or squares of warm corn bread.

6 servings (about 1¼ cups each)

1½	cups chopped onions
1½	cups chopped portobello mushrooms
4	cloves garlic, minced
2	tablespoons olive oil
2	cups broccoli florets and sliced stems
1	cup sliced yellow summer squash
1	can (15 ounces) garbanzo beans, rinsed, drained
1	can (15 ounces) red kidney beans, rinsed, drained
1	can (14½ ounces) reduced-sodium whole tomatoes, undrained, coarsely chopped
1	teaspoon dried basil leaves
½	teaspoon dried oregano leaves
¼	teaspoon dried thyme leaves
¼-½	teaspoon crushed red pepper
	Salt and pepper, to taste
	Herbed Polenta (see p. 580)

Per Serving
Calories: 304
% Calories from fat: 21
Fat (gm): 7.7
Saturated fat (gm): 1
Cholesterol (mg): 0
Sodium (mg): 641
Protein (gm): 13.3
Carbohydrate (gm): 50.2
Exchanges
Milk: 0.0
Vegetable: 2.0
Fruit: 0.0
Bread: 2.5
Meat: 0.5
Fat: 1.0

1. Saute onions, mushrooms, and garlic in oil in large saucepan until tender, about 10 minutes. Add broccoli and squash; cook, covered, over medium heat 5 minutes.

2. Stir in beans, tomatoes with liquid, herbs, and crushed red pepper; heat to boiling. Reduce heat and simmer, covered, until broccoli is tender, 5 to 8 minutes. Season to taste with salt and pepper.

3. Serve bean mixture over polenta.

STIR-FRIED BEANS AND GREENS

 Oriental foods and flavors combine with beans in this sesame-accented main course.

6 servings (about 1¼ cups each)

8 ounces snow peas, diagonally cut into halves

1 small onion, sliced

1 small red bell pepper, sliced

1 tablespoon finely chopped gingerroot

3-4 cloves garlic, minced

1 serrano, *or* jalapeño, chili, finely chopped

1 tablespoon sesame oil

3 cups thinly sliced bok choy, *or* Chinese cabbage

2 cans (15 ounces each) black-eyed peas, rinsed, drained

1-2 tablespoons reduced-sodium tamari soy sauce

1-2 teaspoons black bean sauce
Pepper, to taste

4 cups Chinese-style egg noodles, *or* rice, cooked, warm

2 teaspoons toasted sesame seeds

Per Serving
Calories: 367
% Calories from fat: 23
Fat (gm): 9.6
Saturated fat (gm): 1.3
Cholesterol (mg): 0
Sodium (mg): 541
Protein (gm): 12.6
Carbohydrate (gm): 58.4
Exchanges
Milk: 0.0
Vegetable: 2.0
Fruit: 0.0
Bread: 3.5
Meat: 0.5
Fat: 1.0

1. Stir-fry snow peas, onion, bell pepper, gingerroot, garlic, and serrano chili in sesame oil in wok or large skillet, 5 to 8 minutes. Stir in bok choy; cook, covered, over medium heat until wilted, 2 to 3 minutes.

2. Stir black-eyed peas into wok; stir-fry until hot, about 5 minutes. Stir in soy sauce and black bean sauce; season to taste with pepper. Serve mixture over noodles or rice; sprinkle with sesame seeds.

BUTTER BEAN AND SPROUTS STIR-FRY

 A mix of beans and fresh vegetables are seasoned with fennel, anise, and gingerroot and accented with a hint of sherry.

6 servings (about 1 cup each)

1 ½ cups halved Brussels sprouts

1 cup sliced onion

½ cup chopped red bell pepper

½ jalapeño chili, minced

1 tablespoon finely chopped gingerroot

¼-½ teaspoon dried fennel seeds

¼-½ teaspoon dried anise seeds

1 tablespoon olive oil

1 can (15 ounces) butter beans, *or* baby lima beans, rinsed and drained

2 cups thinly sliced savoy cabbage, *or* Chinese cabbage

1 large tomato, diced

2 tablespoons dry sherry

2 tablespoons water

1 tablespoon reduced-sodium tamari soy sauce

2 teaspoons cornstarch
Salt and pepper, to taste

1 package (12 ounces) Chinese-style egg noodles

6 tablespoons chopped cashews

Per Serving
Calories: 369
% Calories from fat: 15
Fat (gm): 6.7
Saturated fat (gm): 1.1
Cholesterol (mg): 0
Sodium (mg): 383
Protein (gm): 12.6
Carbohydrate (gm): 69.9
Exchanges
Milk: 0.0
Vegetable: 2.0
Fruit: 0.0
Bread: 3.5
Meat: 0.5
Fat: 1.0

1. Stir-fry Brussels sprouts, onion, bell pepper, jalapeno chili, gingerroot, and fennel and anise seeds in oil in wok or large skillet 5 minutes. Cook, covered, over medium to medium-low heat until Brussels sprouts are crisp-tender, about 10 minutes, stirring occasionally.

2. Stir butter beans, cabbage, and tomato into wok; cook, covered, over medium heat until cabbage is tender, about 5 minutes, stirring occasionally.

3. Mix sherry, water, soy sauce, and cornstarch; stir into vegetable mixture and heat to boiling. Cook, stirring constantly, until thickened, about 1 minute. Season to taste with salt and pepper.

4. Prepare noodles according to package directions. Serve vegetable mixture over noodles; sprinkle with cashews.

ADZUKI BEAN STIR-FRY

Sweet-and-sour in flavor, this colorful stir-fry can be made with any kind of canned or cooked dried bean you like.

4 servings (about 1 cup each)

Vegetable cooking spray
1 small onion, sliced
1 medium red bell pepper, sliced
2 cups halved snow peas
2 teaspoons minced garlic
1 teaspoon minced gingerroot
2 cups cooked dried adzuki beans
1 cup water
⅔ cup orange juice
2 tablespoons reduced-sodium tamari soy sauce
2 tablespoons rice wine vinegar
2 tablespoons honey
½ teaspoon chili paste
4 teaspoons cornstarch
3 cups cooked brown rice, *or* Chinese-style noodles

Per Serving
Calories: 443
% Calories from fat: 4
Fat (gm): 1.9
Saturated fat (gm): 0.3
Cholesterol (mg): 0
Sodium (mg): 349
Protein (gm): 17
Carbohydrate (gm): 91.4
Exchanges
Milk: 0.0
Vegetable: 0.0
Fruit: 0.0
Bread: 6.0
Meat: 0.0
Fat: 0.0

1. Spray wok or large skillet with cooking spray; heat over medium heat until hot. Stir-fry onion, bell pepper, snow peas, garlic, and gingerroot 5 minutes. Add beans and water and heat to boiling; reduce heat and simmer, covered, until vegetables are crisp-tender, 3 to 5 minutes.

2. Heat mixture to boiling. Mix remaining ingredients, except rice; stir into wok. Boil, stirring constantly, until thickened, about 1 minute. Serve over rice or noodles.

CURRIED SOYBEANS AND POTATOES

Make this recipe a day in advance to allow flavors to fully develop. The curry seasoning is a combination of 4 aromatic spices. Any white bean, such as garbanzo, navy, Great Northern, or cannellini, can be substituted for the soybeans.

4 servings (about 1 cup each)

Vegetable cooking spray
1 cup chopped onion
1 medium red bell pepper, chopped
2 teaspoons minced garlic
1 jalapeno chili, finely chopped
2 teaspoons ground turmeric
1 teaspoon ground cumin
½ teaspoon ground coriander
¼ teaspoon ground ginger
4 medium russet potatoes, peeled, cubed
2½ cups cooked dried soybeans, *or* canned soybeans, rinsed, drained
1 medium tart cooking apple, peeled, cored, cubed
1 cup water
2 teaspoons lemon juice
2 tablespoons finely chopped cilantro
Salt and pepper, to taste

Per Serving
Calories: 368
% Calories from fat: 24
Fat (gm): 10.4
Saturated fat (gm): 1.5
Cholesterol (mg): 0
Sodium (mg): 28
Protein (gm): 22
Carbohydrate (gm): 52.7
Exchanges
Milk: 0.0
Vegetable: 2.0
Fruit: 0.0
Bread: 2.5
Meat: 1.5
Fat: 1.0

1. Spray large saucepan with cooking spray; heat over medium heat until hot. Saute onion, bell pepper, garlic, and jalapeño chili until tender, about 5 minutes. Stir in spices; cook over medium-low heat 1 to 2 minutes, stirring constantly so spices do not burn.

2. Add potatoes to saucepan; cook 5 minutes, stirring frequently. Add soybeans, apple, and water; heat to boiling. Reduce heat and simmer, covered, 20 minutes. Simmer, uncovered, until almost dry, 5 to 10 minutes. Stir in lemon juice and cilantro; season to taste with salt and pepper.

BLACK BEAN "MEATBALLS"

Nicely picante and spiced, these "meatballs" will have everyone asking for second servings!

6 servings (5 meatballs each)

2 cans (15 ounces each) black beans, rinsed, drained
1 medium jalapeño chili, chopped
2 teaspoons finely chopped gingerroot
1 cup loosely packed cilantro leaves
¼ cup flaked unsweetened coconut
½ teaspoon curry powder
Salt and pepper, to taste
4 cups cooked kasha, cracked wheat, *or* couscous, warm
2 cups (double recipe) Cucumber Yogurt (see p. 555)

Per Serving
Calories: 284
% Calories from fat: 9
Fat (gm): 3.4
Saturated fat (gm): 1.2
Cholesterol (mg): 0.9
Sodium (mg): 503
Protein (gm): 19.4
Carbohydrate (gm): 55.9
Exchanges
Milk: 0.0
Vegetable: 0.0
Fruit: 0.0
Bread: 3.5
Meat: 1.0
Fat: 0.0

1. Process beans, jalapeño chili, gingerroot, cilantro, coconut, and curry powder in food processor until smooth. Season to taste with salt and pepper. Shape mixture into 30 "meatballs."

2. Bake "meatballs" in baking pan at 350 degrees until hot, 15 to 20 minutes. Serve on kasha; spoon Cucumber Yogurt over.

MEAN BEAN PASTA

Chock full of beans and highly seasoned with herbs, this hearty dish packs a high-protein nutritional punch.

6 servings (about 1 cup each)

2 medium green bell peppers, chopped
¾ cup chopped onion
4 teaspoons minced garlic
2 tablespoons olive oil
4 cups (16 ounces) thinly sliced cabbage
2 medium yellow summer squash
2 teaspoons dried rosemary leaves
1 teaspoon dried sage leaves

Per Serving
Calories: 391
% Calories from fat: 19
Fat (gm): 8.9
Saturated fat (gm): 0.8
Cholesterol (mg): 0
Sodium (mg): 644
Protein (gm): 19.7
Carbohydrate (gm): 67.3
Exchanges
Milk: 0.0
Vegetable: 1.5
Fruit: 0.0
Bread: 4.0
Meat: 0.5
Fat: 1.0

1 teaspoon dried savory leaves

1 can (15 ounces) black beans, rinsed, drained

1 can (15 ounces) garbanzo beans, rinsed, drained
Salt and pepper, to taste

12 ounces whole wheat fettuccine, cooked, warm

¼ cup grated fat-free Parmesan cheese

1. Saute bell peppers, onion, and garlic in oil in large saucepan until tender, about 5 minutes. Add cabbage, squash, and herbs; cook, covered, over medium heat until cabbage is wilted, about 5 minutes. Stir in beans; cook until squash is tender, 5 to 8 minutes, stirring occasionally. Season to taste with salt and pepper.

2. Serve bean mixture over pasta; sprinkle with Parmesan cheese.

BEAN AND PASTA SALAD WITH WHITE BEAN DRESSING

 Pureed beans, fat-free sour cream, and seasonings combine to make a rich, delicious salad dressing—use on green salads too!

6 servings (about 1 cup each)

4 ounces tri-color radiatore, *or* rotini, cooked, cooled

1 can (14¼ ounces) baby lima beans, rinsed, drained

½ can (15-ounce size) Great Northern beans, rinsed, drained

½ package (9-ounce size) artichoke hearts, cooked, cooled, cut into halves

2 cups cut green beans, cooked, cooled

½ cup sliced red bell pepper

¼ cup sliced black olives

½ cup (2 ounces) julienned reduced-fat brick cheese

Per Serving
Calories: 314
% Calories from fat: 19
Fat (gm): 6.7
Saturated fat (gm): 1.4
Cholesterol (mg): 5.1
Sodium (mg): 522
Protein (gm): 16.2
Carbohydrate (gm): 50.1
Exchanges
Milk: 0.0
Vegetable: 2.0
Fruit: 0.0
Bread: 2.5
Meat: 1.0
Fat: 0.5

White Bean Dressing (recipe follows)
Lettuce leaves, as garnish
Parsley, finely chopped, as garnish

1. Combine pasta, vegetables, olives, and cheese in salad bowl; pour White Bean Dressing over and toss. Serve on lettuce-lined plates; garnish with parsley.

White Bean Dressing

(makes about 1½ cups)

- ½ can (15-ounce size) Great Northern beans, rinsed, drained
- ½ cup fat-free sour cream
- 1 tablespoon olive oil
- 2-3 tablespoons red wine vinegar
- 2 cloves garlic
- 1 teaspoon dried oregano leaves
- 1-2 green onions and tops, sliced
- 2 tablespoons finely chopped parsley
  Salt and pepper, to taste

1. Process beans, sour cream, olive oil, vinegar, garlic, and oregano in food processor or blender until smooth. Stir in green onions and parsley; season to taste with salt and pepper. Refrigerate several hours for flavors to blend.

PASTA, WHITE BEAN, AND RED CABBAGE SALAD

A hearty salad with a caraway accent. The salad can be made in advance, but stir in the cabbage just before serving for fresh color.

6 servings (about ⅔ cup each)

- 2¼ cups (6 ounces) rotini (corkscrews), cooked, room temperature
- 1 cup coarsely chopped, *or* sliced, red cabbage
- 1 cup canned, drained and rinsed Great Northern beans
- ½ small onion, chopped
- ½ small red bell pepper, chopped
  Caraway Dressing (recipe follows)

Per Serving
Calories: 185
% Calories from fat: 5
Fat (gm): 1.1
Saturated fat (gm): 0.2
Cholesterol (mg): 0
Sodium (mg): 268
Protein (gm): 8.7
Carbohydrate (gm): 35.9
Exchanges
Milk: 0.0
Vegetable: 1.5
Fruit: 0.0
Bread: 2.0
Meat: 0.0
Fat: 0.0

1. Combine pasta, cabbage, beans, onion, and bell pepper in bowl; stir in Caraway Dressing.

Caraway Dressing

(makes about 1 cup)

- ½ cup fat-free mayonnaise, *or* salad dressing
- ½ cup fat-free sour cream
- 2 teaspoons lemon juice
- 2 cloves garlic, minced
- 1 teaspoon caraway seeds, crushed
- ¼ teaspoon salt (optional)
- ¼ teaspoon pepper

1. Mix all ingredients; refrigerate until serving time. Mix again before using.

BEAN, TOMATO, AND BREAD SALAD

Use summer ripe tomatoes for best flavor. Any kind of beans you like, or have on hand, can be used here.

4 servings (about 1½ cups each)

- 3 cups cubed sourdough bread (½-inch)
  Olive oil cooking spray
- 2 large tomatoes, cubed
- ½ small red onion, thinly sliced
- 1½ cups cooked dried anasazi beans, *or* 1 can (15 ounces) anasazi beans, rinsed, drained
- ¾ cup cooked, dried navy beans, *or* soybeans, *or* ½ can (15-ounce size) navy beans, *or* soybeans, rinsed, drained
- 1 cup chopped roasted red peppers
  Parmesan Vinaigrette (recipe follows)
  Salt and pepper, to taste

Per Serving
Calories: 282
% Calories from fat: 26
Fat (gm): 8.3
Saturated fat (gm): 1.1
Cholesterol (mg): 0
Sodium (mg): 161
Protein (gm): 12.1
Carbohydrate (gm): 42.3
Exchanges
Milk: 0.0
Vegetable: 1.0
Fruit: 0.0
Bread: 2.5
Meat: 0.5
Fat: 1.0

1. Spray bread cubes generously with cooking spray; arrange in single layer on jelly roll pan. Bake at 350 degrees until golden, 10 to 15 minutes, stirring occasionally. Cool.

2. Combine tomatoes, onion, beans, and roasted red peppers in bowl; pour Parmesan Vinaigrette over and toss. Season to taste with salt and pepper. Let stand at room temperature 15 to 30 minutes.

3. Add bread cubes to salad and toss; serve immediately.

Parmesan Vinaigrette

(makes about ½ cup)

2-4 tablespoons olive oil
  4 tablespoons red wine vinegar
  2 tablespoons grated fat-free Parmesan cheese
  2 tablespoons finely chopped fresh basil leaves, *or* 1 teaspoon dried basil leaves
  2 tablespoons finely chopped parsley
  1 tablespoon finely chopped fresh oregano leaves, *or* ½ teaspoon dried oregano leaves
  1 teaspoon minced garlic

1. Mix all ingredients; refrigerate until serving time. Mix again before serving.

VEGETABLE SALAD WITH 2 BEANS

Enjoy the fresh flavors of cilantro and orange and the accent of jalapeño pepper in this bean and vegetable salad.

4 servings (about 1½ cups each)

1 package (10 ounces) frozen baby lima beans, cooked
1 can (15 ounces) garbanzo beans, rinsed, drained
1 large Idaho potato (10-12 ounces), peeled, cubed, cooked
1 medium cucumber, peeled, seeded, chopped
1 medium zucchini, sliced
1 small green bell pepper, chopped
¼ cup chopped cilantro leaves

Per Serving
Calories: 341
% Calories from fat: 24
Fat (gm): 9.4
Saturated fat (gm): 1.3
Cholesterol (mg): 0
Sodium (mg): 463
Protein (gm): 12.6
Carbohydrate (gm): 54.8
Exchanges
Milk: 0.0
Vegetable: 2.0
Fruit: 0.0
Bread: 3.0
Meat: 0.0
Fat: 1.5

Citrus Vinaigrette (recipe follows)
Salt and pepper, to taste
Salad greens, as garnish

1. Combine vegetables and cilantro in salad bowl and toss. Pour dressing over salad and toss; season to taste with salt and pepper.

2. Spoon salad over greens on salad plates.

Citrus Vinaigrette

(makes about ⅔ cup)

- ¼ cup fresh orange juice
- ¼ cup fresh lime juice
- 2 tablespoons olive oil, *or* canola oil
- 1 teaspoon dried cumin
- 1 teaspoon minced jalapeño pepper
- ½ teaspoon paprika
- ¼ teaspoon cayenne

1. Mix all ingredients; refrigerate until ready to serve. Mix again before serving.

ORANGE-MARINATED BEAN SALAD

A medley of beans is enhanced with a fresh accent of orange.

6 servings (about ⅔ cup each)

- 1 can (15 ounces) adzuki beans, rinsed, drained, *or* 1½ cups cooked, dried adzuki beans
- 1 can (15 ounces) red kidney beans, rinsed, drained
- 1 cup thinly sliced cabbage
- ⅓ cup thinly sliced green onions and tops
- 1 small yellow bell pepper, thinly sliced
- ¼ cup thinly sliced celery
- ¼ cup cubed carrot
- Orange Dressing (recipe follows)

Per Serving
Calories: 334
% Calories from fat: 14
Fat (gm): 5.5
Saturated fat (gm): 0.6
Cholesterol (mg): 0
Sodium (mg): 297
Protein (gm): 11
Carbohydrate (gm): 67.1
Exchanges
Milk: 0.0
Vegetable: 2.0
Fruit: 0.0
Bread: 3.0
Meat: 0.5
Fat: 1.0

Salt and white pepper, to taste
3 large red bell peppers, cut into halves
Lettuce leaves, as garnish

1. Combine beans, cabbage, green onions, sliced bell pepper, celery, and carrot; pour Orange Dressing over and toss. Season to taste with salt and white pepper.

2. Spoon salad mixture into bell pepper halves; arrange on lettuce-lined plates.

Orange Dressing

(makes about ½ cup)

⅓ cup orange juice
¼ cup white wine vinegar
2 tablespoons olive oil
2 cloves garlic, minced
1 tablespoon finely chopped parsley
2 teaspoons grated orange rind

1. Mix all ingredients; refrigerate until serving time. Mix again before using.

BLACK BEAN AND SMOKED TOFU SALAD

The smoky flavor of the tofu is a pleasant contrast to the picante chili, fresh-flavored cilantro, and Mustard-Honey Dressing. Purchased smoked tofu can be used.

6 servings (about 1¼ cups each)

2 cans (15 ounces each) black beans, rinsed, drained
Mesquite-Smoked Tofu (see p. 267), cubed
1 large tomato, seeded, chopped
1 medium red bell pepper, chopped
½ cup thinly sliced red onion
¼ cup finely chopped cilantro
¼ cup finely chopped parsley

Per Serving
Calories: 256
% Calories from fat: 28
Fat (gm): 9.6
Saturated fat (gm): 0.9
Cholesterol (mg): 0
Sodium (mg): 587
Protein (gm): 19.8
Carbohydrate (gm): 34.7
Exchanges
Milk: 0.0
Vegetable: 1.0
Fruit: 0.0
Bread: 2.0
Meat: 1.0
Fat: 1.0

1 jalapeño chili, finely chopped
2 teaspoons minced roasted garlic
Mustard-Honey Dressing (recipe follows)
Lettuce leaves, as garnish

1. Combine all ingredients, except Mustard-Honey Dressing and lettuce, in salad bowl; pour dressing over and toss. Serve on lettuce-lined plates.

Mustard-Honey Dressing

(makes about ½ cup)

3-4 tablespoons olive oil
3 tablespoons cider vinegar
1 tablespoon Dijon-style mustard
1-2 tablespoons honey
½ teaspoon dried oregano leaves
1-2 dashes red pepper sauce

1. Mix all ingredients; refrigerate until serving time. Mix again before serving.

BLACK BEAN AND RICE SALAD

Apple adds a fresh flavor accent to this colorful salad; use your favorite variety: sweet or tart.

4 servings (about 2 cups each)

1 cup cooked rice, cooled
1 can (15 ounces) black beans, rinsed, drained
1½ cups sliced bok choy, *or* Chinese cabbage
1½ cups thinly sliced red cabbage
1 cup cubed cucumber, peeled, seeded
2 green onions, green and white parts, sliced
2 tablespoons thinly sliced celery

Per Serving
Calories: 409
% Calories from fat: 24
Fat (gm): 11.9
Saturated fat (gm): 1.5
Cholesterol (mg): 0
Sodium (mg): 376
Protein (gm): 13.6
Carbohydrate (gm): 69.8
Exchanges
Milk: 0.0
Vegetable: 0.0
Fruit: 0.5
Bread: 4.0
Meat: 0.0
Fat: 2.0

1 medium apple, cored, cubed

2 tablespoons dark raisins

¼ cup finely chopped cilantro leaves

3 tablespoons balsamic vinegar

3 tablespoons olive oil, *or* canola oil

1½ teaspoons Dijon-style mustard

Salt and pepper, to taste

1. Combine rice, beans, vegetables, apple, raisins, and cilantro in large bowl; toss to combine.

2. Combine vinegar, oil, and mustard; drizzle over salad and toss. Season to taste with salt and pepper

LENTIL SALAD WITH FETA CHEESE

There are lots of flavor and texture contrasts in this colorful salad. Cook the lentils just until tender so they retain their shape.

6 servings (about 1⅓ cups each)

1½ cups dried brown lentils

3 cups canned reduced-sodium vegetable broth

2 medium tomatoes, coarsely chopped

½ cup thinly sliced celery

½ cup sliced yellow bell pepper

½ cup chopped, seeded cucumber

½ cup chopped onion

½-¾ cup (2-3 ounces) crumbled reduced-fat feta cheese

Balsamic Dressing (recipe follows)

Salt and pepper, to taste

Lettuce leaves, as garnish

Per Serving
Calories: 282
% Calories from fat: 21
Fat (gm): 6.6
Saturated fat (gm): 1.6
Cholesterol (mg): 3.4
Sodium (mg): 184
Protein (gm): 16.4
Carbohydrate (gm): 41.4
Exchanges
Milk: 0.0
Vegetable: 1.0
Fruit: 0.0
Bread: 2.5
Meat: 1.0
Fat: 0.5

1. Wash and sort lentils, discarding any stones. Heat lentils and broth to boiling in large saucepan; reduce heat and simmer, covered, until lentils are just tender, about 25 minutes. Drain any excess liquid; cool to room temperature.

2. Combine lentils, vegetables, and cheese in salad bowl; drizzle Balsamic Dressing over and toss. Season to taste with salt and pepper. Serve on lettuce-lined plates.

Balsamic Dressing

(makes about ⅓ cup)

> 3 tablespoons balsamic, *or* red wine, vinegar
> 2 tablespoons olive oil
> 2 tablespoons lemon juice
> 2 cloves garlic, minced
> ½ teaspoon dried thyme leaves

1. Mix all ingredients; refrigerate until serving time. Mix again before using.

FAVA BEAN SALAD PLATTER

Use the season's most abundant vegetables on this colorful and versatile salad platter. Any cooked vegetables can be served warm or at room temperature.

4 servings

> 4 cups escarole, *or* curly endive, torn
> Fava Bean Spread (see p. 510)
> 8 ounces green beans, cooked
> 2 cups cauliflower florets, cooked
> 4 small tomatoes, cut into wedges
> 1 cup frozen artichoke hearts, cooked
> ¼ cup Greek olives
> 4-8 green onions
> 4 lemon wedges
> 2-4 tablespoons olive oil
> Salt and freshly ground pepper, to taste
> ¼ cup finely chopped fresh basil, *or* oregano, leaves
> ¼ cup finely chopped parsley leaves
> 1¼ pita breads, cut into halves, warm

Per Serving
Calories: 363
% Calories from fat: 30
Fat (gm): 13.3
Saturated fat (gm): 1.9
Cholesterol (mg): 0
Sodium (mg): 411
Protein (gm): 15.5
Carbohydrate (gm): 53.5
Exchanges
Milk: 0.0
Vegetable: 3.0
Fruit: 0.0
Bread: 2.5
Meat: 0.0
Fat: 2.5

1. Arrange escarole on salad plates. Spoon Fava Bean Spread on centers of plates; arrange vegetables and lemon wedges around the spread.

2. Drizzle vegetables with oil; sprinkle with salt and pepper. Sprinkle herbs over vegetables. Serve salads with warm pita breads.

ELEVEN

Grain

Dishes

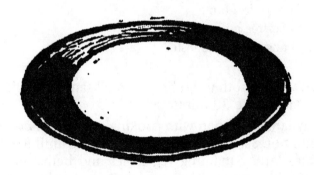

BARLEY-VEGETABLE CHOWDER

 A perfect soup for crisp autumn days; substitute any desired vegetables.

4 main-dish servings (about 1¾ cups each)

2 cans (14½ ounces each) reduced-sodium vegetable broth, divided
⅔ cup barley
Vegetable cooking spray
2 small onions, chopped
1 leek, sliced
2 cloves garlic, minced
1 cup fresh, *or* frozen, lima beans
1 cup fresh, *or* frozen, whole-kernel corn
1 cup finely chopped cabbage
2 medium carrots, sliced
1 teaspoon dried savory leaves
½ teaspoon dried thyme leaves
1 bay leaf
2 tablespoons flour
½ cup fat-free milk
Salt and pepper, to taste

Per Serving
Calories: 312
% Calories from fat: 4
Fat (gm): 1.3
Saturated fat (gm): 0.3
Cholesterol (mg): 0.5
Sodium (mg): 121
Protein (gm): 12.7
Carbohydrate (gm): 66
Exchanges
Milk: 0.0
Vegetable: 2.0
Fruit: 0.0
Bread: 3.5
Meat: 0.0
Fat: 0.0

1. Heat ½ can broth to boiling in small saucepan; stir in barley and let stand 15 to 30 minutes.

2. Spray large saucepan with cooking spray; heat over medium heat until hot. Saute onions, leek, and garlic until tender, about 5 minutes. Add remaining vegetables and herbs; saute 2 to 3 minutes. Add remaining 1½ cans broth and barley mixture; heat to boiling. Reduce heat and simmer, covered, until barley is tender, about 20 minutes.

3. Heat soup to boiling. Mix flour and milk and stir into soup. Boil, stirring constantly, until thickened. Season to taste with salt and pepper. Discard bay leaf.

WHEAT BERRY AND LENTIL STEW WITH DUMPLINGS

Wheat berries have a wonderful, nutty texture. They can be readily purchased at health food stores; barley or another preferred grain can be substituted.

8 servings (about 1⅛ cups each)

1 cup wheat berries
Vegetable cooking spray
2 medium onions, chopped
½ cup chopped celery
4 cloves garlic, minced
1 teaspoon dried savory leaves
3 cups canned reduced-sodium vegetable broth
2 pounds russet potatoes, unpeeled, cubed
2 medium carrots, sliced
1½ cups cooked lentils
Salt and pepper, to taste
Herb Dumplings (recipe follows)

Per Serving
Calories: 414
% Calories from fat: 10
Fat (gm): 4.7
Saturated fat (gm): 0.6
Cholesterol (mg): 0.3
Sodium (mg): 259
Protein (gm): 16.8
Carbohydrate (gm): 78.6
Exchanges
Milk: 0.0
Vegetable: 1.0
Fruit: 0.0
Bread: 5.0
Meat: 0.0
Fat: 0.5

1. Cover wheat berries with 2 to 3 inches water in saucepan; let stand overnight. Heat to boiling; reduce heat and simmer, covered, until wheat berries are tender, 45 to 55 minutes. Drain.

2. Spray large saucepan with cooking spray; heat over medium heat until hot. Saute onions, celery, garlic, and savory until onions are tender, 3 to 5 minutes. Add broth, potatoes, carrots, and lentils and heat to boiling; reduce heat and simmer, covered, until vegetables are just tender, 10 to 15 minutes. Stir in wheat berries. Season to taste with salt and pepper.

3. Spoon dumpling mixture onto top of stew; cook, uncovered, 5 minutes. Cook, covered, until dumplings are dry, 5 to 10 minutes longer.

Herb Dumplings

½ cup all-purpose flour
½ cup yellow cornmeal
1½ teaspoons baking powder
½ teaspoon dried sage leaves
¼ teaspoon dried thyme leaves
½ teaspoon salt
2 tablespoons vegetable shortening
½ cup fat-free milk

1. Combine flour, cornmeal, baking powder, sage, thyme, and salt in medium bowl. Cut in shortening with pastry blender or 2 knives until mixture resembles coarse crumbs. Stir in milk.

BARLEY WITH PEPPERS AND POTATOES

Here's a variation on the delicious Mexican "rajas con papas." If poblano peppers are not available, substitute green bell peppers and 1 to 2 teaspoons of minced jalapeños.

4 servings (about 1½ cups each)

6 large poblano chilies, sliced
2 medium onions, chopped
1 tablespoon olive oil, *or* canola oil
2½ pounds russet potatoes, unpeeled, cooked, cubed
2 cups cooked barley
2 tablespoons finely chopped cilantro leaves
1 teaspoon dried cumin
Salt and cayenne pepper, to taste

Per Serving
Calories: 464
% Calories from fat: 8
Fat (gm): 4.4
Saturated fat (gm): 0.6
Cholesterol (mg): 0
Sodium (mg): 29.3
Protein (gm): 10.2
Carbohydrate (gm): 99.7
Exchanges
Milk: 0.0
Vegetable: 4.0
Fruit: 0.0
Bread: 5.0
Meat: 0.0
Fat: 0.0

1. Saute chilies and onions in oil in large skillet until crisp-tender, about 5 minutes. Add potatoes; saute until browned, 5 to 8 minutes.

2. Add barley to skillet; cook over medium heat until hot through, 3 to 4 minutes. Stir in cilantro and cumin. Season to taste with salt and cayenne pepper.

WHEAT AND BARLEY BOWL

 Grains and greens are cooked together, then combined with tomatoes and toasted nuts.

4 servings (about 1 cup each)

Vegetable cooking spray
¾ cup barley
2½ cups Canned Vegetable Stock (see p. 63), *or* canned reduced-sodium vegetable broth
¼ cup bulgur
½ teaspoon dried thyme leaves
6 ounces thinly sliced turnip greens, kale, *or* spinach
½ cup thinly sliced green onions and tops
¼ cup finely chopped parsley
1 large tomato, coarsely chopped
¼-½ cup coarsely chopped walnuts, toasted
1-2 tablespoons lemon juice
Salt and pepper, to taste

Per Serving
Calories: 257
% Calories from fat: 20
Fat (gm): 6
Saturated fat (gm): 0.6
Cholesterol (mg): 0
Sodium (mg): 66
Protein (gm): 8.6
Carbohydrate (gm): 41.7
Exchanges
Milk: 0.0
Vegetable: 1.0
Fruit: 0.0
Bread: 2.5
Meat: 0.0
Fat: 1.0

1. Spray large saucepan with cooking spray; heat over medium heat until hot. Add barley to saucepan; spray lightly with cooking spray. Cook over medium heat, stirring occasionally, until barley is golden, 5 to 8 minutes.

2. Add stock to saucepan; heat to boiling. Reduce heat and simmer, covered, 40 minutes. Stir in bulgur and thyme; simmer, covered, 15 minutes. Stir in greens, green onions, and parsley; cook, covered, until all liquid is absorbed, about 10 minutes. Stir in tomato, walnuts and lemon juice; cook 5 minutes longer. Season to taste with salt and pepper.

KASHA WITH GREEN VEGGIES

Kasha is buckwheat groats that have been roasted. Traditionally, kasha is mixed with raw egg and cooked in a skillet until dry; this keeps the grains separate while cooking. Buckwheat groats can be substituted in the recipe; delete egg and begin with step 2 in that case.

6 servings

1½ cups kasha

1 egg, beaten

1 large green bell pepper, chopped

½ cup sliced green onions and tops

2 cloves garlic, minced

1 tablespoon olive oil

4 cups Basic Vegetable Stock, *or* Canned Vegetable Stock (see pp. 58, 63)

½ teaspoon dried marjoram leaves

¼ teaspoon dried thyme leaves

8 ounces broccoli rabe, cut into 1-inch pieces, cooked

½ cup frozen, thawed, *or* canned, baby lima beans

¼ cup finely chopped parsley

Salt and pepper, to taste

Per Serving
Calories: 217
% Calories from fat: 18
Fat (gm): 4.7
Saturated fat (gm): 0.9
Cholesterol (mg): 35.5
Sodium (mg): 40
Protein (gm): 8.6
Carbohydrate (gm): 38.8
Exchanges
Milk: 0.0
Vegetable: 1.0
Fruit: 0.0
Bread: 2.0
Meat: 0.0
Fat: 1.0

1. Mix kasha and egg in bowl; transfer to large skillet and cook over medium heat until kasha is dry and grains are separated.

2. Saute bell pepper, green onions, and garlic in oil in large saucepan until tender, about 5 minutes. Add kasha, stock, and herbs to saucepan; heat to boiling. Reduce heat and simmer, covered, until kasha is tender and liquid absorbed, 25 to 30 minutes.

3. Stir broccoli rabe and lima beans into kasha mixture; cook, covered, 3 to 4 minutes. Stir in parsley; season to taste with salt and pepper.

BLACK-EYED PEAS AND GREENS WITH MILLET

A new twist to Hopping John! Your preference in greens might also be kale or mustard greens.

4 servings (about 1½ cups each)

Vegetable cooking spray
1 medium onion, sliced
2 cloves garlic, minced
1 can (14½ ounces) reduced-sodium vegetable broth
3 tablespoons red wine vinegar
6 cups coarsely chopped turnip greens
2 large tomatoes, cut in wedges
1 can (15 ounces) black-eyed peas, rinsed, drained
1 cup millet
2 tablespoons finely chopped cilantro leaves
Salt and pepper, to taste
Red pepper sauce, to taste

Per Serving
Calories: 322
% Calories from fat: 6
Fat (gm): 2.3
Saturated fat (gm): 1.1
Cholesterol (mg): 0
Sodium (mg): 385
Protein (gm): 12.4
Carbohydrate (gm): 63.9
Exchanges
Milk: 0.0
Vegetable: 2.0
Fruit: 0.0
Bread: 3.5
Meat: 0.5
Fat: 0.0

1. Spray large saucepan with cooking spray; heat over medium heat until hot. Saute onion and garlic until tender, about 5 minutes. Add broth and vinegar; heat to boiling. Add greens and tomatoes to saucepan; reduce heat and simmer, covered, until greens are wilted, about 5 minutes.

2. Stir black-eyed peas and millet into saucepan; simmer, covered, until all liquid is absorbed, about 20 minutes. Remove from heat and let stand 5 to 10 minutes. Stir in cilantro; season to taste with salt, pepper, and red pepper sauce.

MEXICAN-STYLE GRAIN AND VEGETABLE CASSEROLE

Rice and millet combine with vegetables and South-of-the-Border flavors. Be sure to toast the millet before cooking to ensure maximum flavor (see directions in next recipe, step 1).

6 servings (about 1¼ cups each)

Vegetable cooking spray
1 large red bell pepper, chopped
1 medium onion, chopped
3 cloves garlic, minced
1 jalapeño chili, finely chopped
2 medium chayote squash, peeled, seeded, cubed
2 cups halved small cremini mushrooms
1 cup fresh, *or* frozen, thawed, whole-kernel corn
¾ teaspoon dried oregano leaves
½ teaspoon ground cumin
½ teaspoon chili powder
Salt and pepper, to taste
2 cups cooked white, *or* brown, rice
2 cups cooked millet
1 cup fat-free sour cream
¾ cup shredded reduced-fat Monterey Jack cheese
2 green onions and tops, sliced

Per Serving
Calories: 293
% Calories from fat: 12
Fat (gm): 4.1
Saturated fat (gm): 1.7
Cholesterol (mg): 10.1
Sodium (mg): 156
Protein (gm): 14
Carbohydrate (gm): 52.6
Exchanges
Milk: 0.0
Vegetable: 2.0
Fruit: 0.0
Bread: 3.0
Meat: 0.5
Fat: 0.0

1. Spray large skillet with cooking spray; heat over medium heat until hot. Saute bell pepper, onion, garlic, and jalapeño chili 5 minutes; add squash, mushrooms, corn, oregano, cumin, and chili powder. Cook, covered, over medium heat until squash and mushrooms are tender, 8 to 10 minutes, stirring occasionally. Season to taste with salt and pepper.

2. Combine rice and millet; season to taste with salt and pepper. Spoon half the mixture into lightly greased 2-quart casserole; top with vegetable mixture and sour cream. Spoon remaining grain mixture on top.

3. Bake casserole, loosely covered, at 300 degrees until hot through, 30 to 40 minutes. Uncover, sprinkle with cheese, and bake until cheese is melted, 5 to 10 minutes longer. Sprinkle with green onions.

MILLET WITH ARTICHOKE HEARTS AND VEGETABLES

 Deeply browned artichoke hearts, seasoned with garlic, add robust flavor to this grain and vegetable combination.

4 servings (about 1½ cups each)

½ cup millet
1¾ cups canned reduced-sodium vegetable broth, divided
2 cans (15 ounces each) artichoke hearts, drained, cut into halves
1 tablespoon margarine, *or* butter
¼ teaspoon garlic powder
2 medium onions, chopped
1 medium green bell pepper, chopped
2 cloves garlic, minced
2 medium tomatoes, chopped
1 medium eggplant, unpeeled, cut into 1-inch pieces
1 medium zucchini, sliced
1 bay leaf
2 tablespoons finely chopped parsley
  Salt and pepper, to taste

Per Serving
Calories: 327
% Calories from fat: 13
Fat (gm): 5.3
Saturated fat (gm): 0.9
Cholesterol (mg): 0
Sodium (mg): 287
Protein (gm): 13.6
Carbohydrate (gm): 65.3
Exchanges
Milk: 0.0
Vegetable: 7.0
Fruit: 0.0
Bread: 1.5
Meat: 0.0
Fat: 1.0

1. Cook millet in large skillet over medium heat until toasted, 2 to 3 minutes. Add 1¼ cups broth and heat to boiling; reduce heat and simmer, covered, until millet is tender and broth is absorbed, about 15 minutes. Remove from heat and let stand, covered, 10 minutes.

2. Saute artichoke hearts in margarine in large skillet until well browned on all sides, 5 to 7 minutes. Remove from skillet and sprinkle with garlic powder.

3. Add onions, bell pepper, and garlic to skillet; saute until tender, 3 to 5 minutes. Add remaining ½ cup broth, remaining vegetables, bay leaf, and parsley; heat to boiling. Reduce heat and simmer, covered, until eggplant is tender, 15 to 20 minutes.

4. Add millet and artichoke hearts to skillet; cook until hot through, 3 to 4 minutes. Discard bay leaf and season to taste with salt and pepper.

CURRIED COUSCOUS

 Couscous, a staple in Mediterranean countries, is one of the fastest, easiest grains to cook. Serve with a selection of condiments so that the dish can be enjoyed with a variety of flavor accents.

4 servings (about 1½ cups each)

Vegetable cooking spray
8 ounces fresh, *or* frozen, thawed, whole okra
1 medium onion, chopped
2 cloves garlic, chopped
2 tablespoons finely chopped parsley
1 cup frozen whole-kernel corn, thawed
1 cup sliced mushrooms
2 medium carrots, sliced
1½ teaspoons curry powder
1 cup Canned Vegetable Stock (see p. 63), *or* canned reduced-sodium vegetable broth
⅔ cup couscous
1 medium tomato, chopped
Salt and pepper, to taste
Cucumber Yogurt (recipe follows)
Onion-Chutney Relish (recipe follows)
¼ cup chopped unsalted peanuts
¼ cup dark raisins

Per Serving
Calories: 304
% Calories from fat: 11
Fat (gm): 3.9
Saturated fat (gm): 0.6
Cholesterol (mg): 0.5
Sodium (mg): 55
Protein (gm): 9.5
Carbohydrate (gm): 60.1
Exchanges
Milk: 0.0
Vegetable: 3.0
Fruit: 1.0
Bread: 2.0
Meat: 0.0
Fat: 0.5

1. Spray large saucepan with cooking spray; heat over medium heat until hot. Saute okra, onion, garlic, and parsley until onion is tender, about 5 minutes. Stir in corn, mushrooms, carrots, and curry powder; cook 2 minutes.

2. Add stock to saucepan and heat to boiling; reduce heat and simmer, covered, until vegetables are tender, 8 to 10 minutes. Stir in couscous and tomato. Remove from heat and let stand, covered, until couscous is tender and broth absorbed, about 5 minutes. Season to taste with salt and pepper.

3. Spoon couscous mixture into serving bowl; serve with Cucumber Yogurt, Onion-Chutney Relish, peanuts, and raisins.

Cucumber Yogurt

(makes about 1 cup)

⅔ cup fat-free plain yogurt
⅔ cup seeded, finely chopped cucumber
1 teaspoon dried dill weed

1. Combine all ingredients; refrigerate until ready to serve.

Onion-Chutney Relish

(makes about 1 cup)

Vegetable cooking spray
4 medium onions, chopped
½ cup chopped mango chutney, purchased
1-1½ teaspoons dried mint leaves

1. Spray large skillet with cooking spray; heat over medium heat until hot. Saute onions 3 to 5 minutes; reduce heat to low and cook until they are very soft and golden, about 15 minutes.

2. Mix onions, chutney, and mint; refrigerate until ready to serve.

FRUITED COUSCOUS WITH SMOKED TOFU

A wonderful combination of flavors and textures. Make Mesquite-Smoked Tofu (see p. 267) a day in advance, as the flavor will heighten. Purchased smoked tofu can also be used.

6 servings (about 1 cup each)

½ cup finely chopped onion
½ cup finely chopped red bell pepper
½ cup finely chopped celery
1½ teaspoons minced garlic

Per Serving
Calories: 303
% Calories from fat: 15
Fat (gm): 5.1
Saturated fat (gm): 1
Cholesterol (mg): 2.5
Sodium (mg): 216
Protein (gm): 15.6
Carbohydrate (gm): 48

1 tablespoon olive oil

1½ teaspoons curry powder

1¼ cups Canned Vegetable Stock (see p. 63), *or* canned reduced-sodium vegetable broth

1 package (10 ounces) couscous Mesquite-Smoked Tofu (see p. 267), cubed

1 can (11 ounces) mandarin orange segments, drained

Salt and pepper, to taste

6 tablespoons (1½ ounces) crumbled reduced-fat feta cheese

Exchanges
Milk: 0.0
Vegetable: 0.5
Fruit: 0.5
Bread: 2.5
Meat: 1.0
Fat: 0.5

1. Saute onion, bell pepper, celery, and garlic in oil in medium saucepan until tender, about 5 minutes. Stir in curry powder; cook 1 to 2 minutes longer, stirring constantly.

2. Add stock to saucepan; heat to boiling. Stir in couscous (discard sauce packet); remove from heat and let stand, covered, 5 minutes. Stir in tofu and orange segments; cook over medium heat until hot, 3 to 4 minutes. Season to taste with salt and pepper.

3. Spoon couscous mixture into serving bowl; sprinkle with cheese.

QUINOA WITH ROASTED EGGPLANT AND SQUASH

Grain recipes are versatile, as almost any grain can be used in them. Couscous, millet, or kasha also would be excellent choices in this recipe.

4 servings (about 1½ cups each)

Vegetable cooking spray

1 small butternut squash, peeled, cubed

1 medium eggplant, unpeeled, cubed

2 medium onions, cut into wedges

2 large bell peppers, cut into thick slices

1 teaspoon dried rosemary leaves

½ teaspoon dried savory leaves

Per Serving
Calories: 282
% Calories from fat: 10
Fat (gm): 3.4
Saturated fat (gm): 0.4
Cholesterol (mg): 0
Sodium (mg): 46
Protein (gm): 8.6
Carbohydrate (gm): 54.8

½ teaspoon dried thyme leaves
2 cups Canned Vegetable Stock (see
   p. 63), *or* water
1 cup quinoa
   Salt and pepper, to taste

Exchanges
Milk: 0.0
Vegetable: 3.0
Fruit: 0.0
Bread: 2.5
Meat: 0.0
Fat: 0.5

1. Spray aluminum-foil-lined jelly roll pan with cooking spray; arrange vegetables in single layer on pan. Spray vegetables generously with cooking spray; sprinkle with herbs. Roast at 425 degrees until vegetables are tender, 35 to 45 minutes.

2. Heat stock to boiling in medium saucepan; add quinoa. Reduce heat and simmer, covered, until quinoa is tender and stock absorbed, about 15 minutes. Combine quinoa and warm vegetables in serving bowl; season to taste with salt and pepper.

QUINOA AND WHEAT BERRY PILAF

The two grains are a contrast in appearance and color. They can be combined with many combinations of vegetables, depending upon season and availability.

4 servings (about 1½ cups each)

½ cup wheat berries
1 cup Canned Vegetable Stock (see p. 63),
   or water
½ cup quinoa
¾ cup chopped green onions and tops
1 medium red bell pepper, chopped
3 cloves garlic, minced
1 tablespoon olive oil
1 cup chopped shiitake, *or* portobello,
   mushrooms
½ cup frozen peas, thawed,
¼ cup finely chopped parsley
   Salt and pepper, to taste

Per Serving
Calories: 248
% Calories from fat: 19
Fat (gm): 5.4
Saturated fat (gm): 0.7
Cholesterol (mg): 0
Sodium (mg): 43
Protein (gm): 8.1
Carbohydrate (gm): 43.8
Exchanges
Milk: 0.0
Vegetable: 1.0
Fruit: 0.0
Bread: 2.5
Meat: 0.0
Fat: 1.0

1. Cover wheat berries with 2 inches water in small saucepan and soak overnight. Heat to boiling; reduce heat and simmer, covered, until tender, 15 to 20 minutes.

2. Heat stock to boiling in small saucepan; add quinoa. Reduce heat and simmer until quinoa is tender and broth absorbed, about 15 minutes.

3. Saute green onions, bell pepper, and garlic in oil in small saucepan until tender, 3 to 4 minutes; add mushrooms and saute until tender, 5 to 8 minutes. Add peas and cook, covered, until hot, 3 to 4 minutes.

4. Combine warm grains, vegetables, and parsley in serving bowl; season to taste with salt and pepper.

ASIAN FRIED RICE

The combination of wild and white rice adds a new dimension to an Asian favorite. Lightly scrambled egg is a traditional addition to many fried rice recipes; it can be omitted, if desired.

4 servings (about 1½ cups each)

Vegetable cooking spray
2 cups sliced broccoli florets and stalks
2 ounces snow peas, cut into halves
2 medium carrots, sliced
¾ cup chopped celery
¾ cup bean sprouts
¾ cup sliced shiitake, *or* white, mushrooms
½ cup chopped red, *or* green, bell pepper
1 clove garlic, minced
1 teaspoon finely chopped gingerroot
½ cup canned reduced-sodium vegetable broth
2 tablespoons reduced-sodium soy sauce
1½ cups cooked white rice
1½ cups cooked wild rice
1 egg, lightly scrambled, crumbled

Per Serving
Calories: 236
% Calories from fat: 8
Fat (gm): 2.1
Saturated fat (gm): 0.5
Cholesterol (mg): 53.3
Sodium (mg): 340
Protein (gm): 10.2
Carbohydrate (gm): 46.9
Exchanges
Milk: 0.0
Vegetable: 2.0
Fruit: 0.0
Bread: 2.5
Meat: 0.0
Fat: 0.0

1. Spray wok or large skillet with cooking spray; heat over medium heat until hot. Stir-fry vegetables and gingerroot until crisp-tender, 5 to 8 minutes.

2. Add broth and soy sauce to wok; stir in rice and scrambled egg and cook 2 to 3 minutes more.

MUSHROOM AND ASPARAGUS PILAF

 The dried Chinese black or shiitake mushrooms impart a hearty, woodsy flavor to this pilaf. The mushrooms are available in large supermarkets or oriental groceries.

6 servings (about 1½ cups each)

3⅓ cups Basic Vegetable Stock (see p. 58), or canned reduced-sodium vegetable broth, divided

2 cups dried Chinese mushrooms
   Vegetable cooking spray

2 large onions, chopped

4 cloves garlic, minced

2 teaspoons dried basil leaves

½ teaspoon dried thyme leaves

½ teaspoon dried savory leaves

1½ pounds asparagus, cut into 1½-inch pieces

¼ cup dry sherry, *or* water

2 packages (6 ounces each) tabbouleh wheat salad mix

¼ teaspoon red pepper sauce
   Salt and pepper, to taste

4 green onions and tops, thinly sliced

¼ cup toasted pecan halves

Per Serving
Calories: 424
% Calories from fat: 23
Fat (gm): 11.7
Saturated fat (gm): 1.2
Cholesterol (mg): 0
Sodium (mg): 597
Protein (gm): 15.2
Carbohydrate (gm): 69.3
Exchanges
Milk: 0.0
Vegetable: 2.0
Fruit: 0.0
Bread: 4.0
Meat: 0.0
Fat: 2.0

1. Heat 2 cups stock to boiling; pour over mushrooms in bowl and let stand until mushrooms are softened, 10 to 15 minutes. Drain, reserving stock. Slice mushrooms, discarding tough stems.

2. Spray large skillet with cooking spray; heat over medium heat until hot. Saute mushrooms, onions, garlic, and herbs until onions are tender, about 5 minutes. Add asparagus; saute 5 minutes more.

3. Add sherry, reserved stock from mushrooms, and remaining 1⅓ cups stock to skillet; heat to boiling. Stir in tabbouleh (discard spice packet). Reduce heat and simmer, covered, until stock is absorbed and tabbouleh is tender, 3 to 5 minutes. Stir in red pepper sauce; season to taste with salt and pepper. Spoon into serving bowl; sprinkle with green onions and pecans.

FRUIT PILAF

An easy pilaf, with dried fruit and nuts, that is simply good.

4 servings (about 1 cup each)

⅔	cup brown rice
⅓	cup wild rice
½	cup sliced green onions and tops
¼	cup thinly sliced celery
1-2	tablespoons margarine, *or* butter
2½	cups Canned Vegetable Stock (see p. 63), *or* canned reduced-sodium vegetable stock
½	teaspoon dried sage, *or* marjoram leaves
¼	teaspoon dried thyme leaves
1	large tart, *or* sweet, apple, peeled, cored, cubed
⅓	cup chopped dried apricots
⅓	cup chopped dried pears
4-6	tablespoons pecan, *or* walnut, halves, toasted
	Salt and pepper, to taste

Per Serving
Calories: 353
% Calories from fat: 23
Fat (gm): 9.2
Saturated fat (gm): 1.2
Cholesterol (mg): 0
Sodium (mg): 80
Protein (gm): 6.4
Carbohydrate (gm): 60.9
Exchanges
Milk: 0.0
Vegetable: 0.0
Fruit: 1.5
Bread: 2.5
Meat: 0.0
Fat: 2.0

1. Saute brown and wild rice, green onions, and celery in margarine in large saucepan until onions are tender, about 5 minutes. Add stock and herbs and heat to boiling; reduce heat and simmer, covered, 45 minutes.

2. Stir apple, apricots, and pears into rice mixture; simmer, covered, until rice is tender and stock absorbed, about 10 minutes. Stir in pecans; season to taste with salt and pepper.

SWEET BULGUR PILAF

A pilaf with sweet accents of yellow squash, raisins, and pie spice.

4 servings (about 1 cup each)

	Vegetable cooking spray
½	cup finely chopped onion
¼	cup thinly sliced green onions and tops
1	large clove garlic, minced

Per Serving
Calories: 263
% Calories from fat: 19
Fat (gm): 6.2
Saturated fat (gm): 1
Cholesterol (mg): 0
Sodium (mg): 44
Protein (gm): 8.7
Carbohydrate (gm): 46.1

1 cup bulgur
2¼ cups Canned Vegetable Stock (see p. 63), *or* canned reduced-sodium vegetable broth
½-¾ teaspoon ground cinnamon
2 cups cubed, peeled butternut, *or* acorn, squash
¼ cup currants, *or* raisins
¼ cup pine nuts, toasted
¼ cup finely chopped parsley
Salt and pepper, to taste

Exchanges
Milk: 0.0
Vegetable: 0.0
Fruit: 0.0
Bread: 3.0
Meat: 0.0
Fat: 1.0

1. Spray large saucepan with cooking spray; heat over medium heat until hot. Saute onion, green onions, garlic, and bulgur until onions are tender, 8 to 10 minutes. Stir in stock and cinnamon and heat to boiling; reduce heat and simmer, covered, 10 minutes.

2. Stir squash and currants into bulgur mixture; simmer, covered, until squash is tender, about 15 minutes. Stir in pine nuts and parsley; season to taste with salt and pepper.

ORIENTAL PILAF

Snow peas, water chestnuts, oriental seasonings, and a combination of brown rice and millet make this pilaf a favorite.

4 servings (about 1¼ cups each)

½ cup brown rice
½ cup millet
½ cup finely chopped onion
¼ cup chopped celery
2-3 teaspoons finely chopped gingerroot
2 cloves garlic, minced
1 tablespoon dark sesame, *or* peanut, oil
2½ cups Oriental Stock (see p. 62), *or* canned oriental broth
1½ cups halved snow peas
½ can (6-ounce size) water chestnuts, rinsed, drained, sliced

Per Serving
Calories: 273
% Calories from fat: 18
Fat (gm): 5.4
Saturated fat (gm): 0.8
Cholesterol (mg): 0
Sodium (mg): 387
Protein (gm): 8.2
Carbohydrate (gm): 47.9
Exchanges
Milk: 0.0
Vegetable: 1.0
Fruit: 0.0
Bread: 3.0
Meat: 0.0
Fat: 0.5

½ cup thinly sliced green onions and tops
2-3 tablespoons reduced-sodium tamari soy
sauce
Salt and pepper, to taste

1.   Saute rice, millet, onion, celery, gingerroot, and garlic in sesame oil in large saucepan until onion is tender, about 10 minutes. Add stock and heat to boiling; reduce heat and simmer,
covered, 15 minutes.

2.   Stir snow peas, water chestnuts, and green onions into grain
mixture; simmer, covered, until grains and snow peas are tender
and stock absorbed, about 10 minutes. Stir in soy sauce; season
to taste with salt and pepper.

ALL-SEASON RISOTTO

*A blending of summer and winter squash provides color and flavor to this
creamy risotto dish. If preferred, the reserved vegetable mixture can be
heated and served to the side rather than mixing it into the risotto.*

6 servings (about 1⅓ cups each)

2 cups peeled, cubed winter yellow squash (acorn, butternut, Hubbard, etc.)
1 medium zucchini, sliced
1½ cups sliced cremini, *or* white, mushrooms
1 medium red bell pepper, chopped
6 plum tomatoes, cut into fourths
2 teaspoons dried oregano leaves
2 tablespoons olive oil, *or* canola oil, divided
1 cup chopped onions
2 cloves garlic, minced
1½ cups arborio rice
2 cans (14½ ounces each) reduced-sodium vegetable broth
2 cups water
¼ cup grated fat-free Parmesan cheese
1 can (15½ ounces) black beans, rinsed, drained

Per Serving
Calories: 391
% Calories from fat: 13
Fat (gm): 6.2
Saturated fat (gm): 0.8
Cholesterol (mg): 0
Sodium (mg): 328
Protein (gm): 14.7
Carbohydrate (gm): 75.9
Exchanges
Milk: 0.0
Vegetable: 2.0
Fruit: 0.0
Bread: 4.0
Meat: 0.0
Fat: 1.0

½ cup frozen peas, thawed
   Salt and pepper, to taste

1. Saute squash, zucchini, mushrooms, bell pepper, tomatoes, and oregano in 1 tablespoon oil in large skillet until tender; remove from heat and reserve.

2. Heat remaining 1 tablespoon oil until hot in large saucepan; add onions and garlic and saute until tender, 3 to 4 minutes. Add rice; cook 2 to 3 minutes, stirring occasionally.

3. Heat broth and water to simmering in medium saucepan; reduce heat to low and keep warm. Add broth to rice mixture, ½ cup at a time, stirring constantly until broth is absorbed before adding next ½ cup. Continue process until rice is *al dente* and mixture is creamy, 20 to 25 minutes.

4. Stir cheese, beans, and peas into rice mixture. Stir in reserved vegetables and heat until hot. Season to taste with salt and pepper. Serve with additional grated cheese if desired.

PORCINI RISOTTO

Use dried shiitake or Chinese black mushrooms if the porcini are not available.

4 servings (about 1 cup each)

¼-½	ounce dried porcini mushrooms
	Hot water
	Olive oil cooking spray
1	small onion, chopped
3	cloves garlic, minced
1	small tomato, seeded, chopped
1	teaspoon dried sage leaves
¼	teaspoon dried thyme leaves
1½	cups arborio rice
1½	quarts Rich Mushroom Stock (see p. 61), *or* canned reduced-sodium vegetable broth
¼	cup grated Parmesan cheese
	Salt and pepper, to taste
2	tablespoons pine nuts, *or* slivered almonds, toasted

Per Serving
Calories: 389
% Calories from fat: 14
Fat (gm): 6.1
Saturated fat (gm): 1.9
Cholesterol (mg): 4.9
Sodium (mg): 135
Protein (gm): 10.2
Carbohydrate (gm): 68
Exchanges
Milk: 0.0
Vegetable: 2.0
Fruit: 0.0
Bread: 4.0
Meat: 0.0
Fat: 1.0

2 tablespoons finely chopped fresh sage,
   or parsley

1. Place mushrooms in bowl; pour hot water over to cover. Let stand until mushrooms are soft, about 15 minutes; drain, reserving liquid. Slice mushrooms, discarding any tough parts.

2. Spray large saucepan with cooking spray; heat over medium heat until hot. Saute mushrooms, onion, and garlic until tender, about 5 minutes. Stir in tomato, sage, and thyme; cook 2 to 3 minutes more. Stir in rice. Cook over medium heat until rice begins to brown, 2 to 3 minutes, stirring frequently.

3. Heat stock and reserved porcini liquid to boiling in medium saucepan; reduce heat to medium-low to keep stock hot. Add stock to rice mixture, ½ cup at a time, stirring constantly until stock is absorbed before adding another ½ cup. Continue process until rice is *al dente* and mixture is creamy, 20 to 25 minutes. Stir in cheese; season to taste with salt and pepper.

4. Serve risotto in bowls; sprinkle with pine nuts and sage.

BROCCOLI AND "SAUSAGE" RISOTTO

 A flavorful risotto, abundantly seasoned with herbs.

6 servings (about 1¼ cups each)

Olive oil cooking spray
1 small onion, chopped
2 cloves garlic, minced
½ teaspoon fennel seeds, crushed
½ teaspoon dried sage leaves
¼ teaspoon dried thyme leaves
¼ teaspoon dried oregano leaves
¼ teaspoon ground allspice
⅛ teaspoon ground mace
1½ cups arborio rice
1½ quarts Canned Vegetable Stock (see
   p. 63), *or* canned reduced-sodium
   vegetable broth
8 ounces frozen "sausage-style" vegetable
   protein patties, thawed, crumbled

Per Serving
Calories: 370
% Calories from fat: 13
Fat (gm): 5.3
Saturated fat (gm): 1.2
Cholesterol (mg): 1.6
Sodium (mg): 344
Protein (gm): 12.6
Carbohydrate (gm): 62.5
Exchanges
Milk: 0.0
Vegetable: 2.0
Fruit: 0.5
Bread: 3.0
Meat: 1.0
Fat: 0.5

2 cups broccoli florets, cooked until crisp-tender

½ cup raisins

2 tablespoons grated Parmesan cheese

Salt and pepper, to taste

Parsley, finely chopped, as garnish

1. Spray large saucepan with cooking spray; heat over medium heat until hot. Add onion and garlic to saucepan; saute until tender, about 5 minutes. Stir in herbs and rice; cook over medium heat until rice begins to brown, 2 to 3 minutes, stirring frequently.

2. Heat stock to boiling in medium saucepan; reduce heat to medium-low to keep stock hot. Add stock to rice mixture, ½ cup at a time, stirring constantly until stock is absorbed before adding another ½ cup. Continue process until rice is *al dente* and mixture is creamy, 20 to 25 minutes, adding "sausage," broccoli, and raisins during last 10 minutes of cooking time. Stir in cheese; season to taste with salt and pepper.

3. Serve risotto in bowls; sprinkle with parsley.

SUMMER SQUASH RISOTTO

A perfect risotto for summer, when squash and tomatoes are fresh from the garden.

4 servings (about 1 cup each)

1 medium zucchini, sliced

1 medium summer yellow squash, sliced

1 tablespoon olive oil

1 medium onion, chopped

3 cloves garlic, minced

8 Italian plum tomatoes, cut into fourths

1½ teaspoons dried oregano leaves

1½ cups arborio rice

1½ quarts Basic Vegetable Stock (see p. 58), *or* canned reduced-sodium vegetable broth

¼ cup grated Romano cheese

Salt and pepper, to taste

2 green onions and tops, sliced

Per Serving
Calories: 423
% Calories from fat: 15
Fat (gm): 7.4
Saturated fat (gm): 2
Cholesterol (mg): 7.2
Sodium (mg): 128
Protein (gm): 11.1
Carbohydrate (gm): 79.5
Exchanges
Milk: 0.0
Vegetable: 3.0
Fruit: 0.0
Bread: 4.0
Meat: 0.0
Fat: 1.5

1. Saute zucchini and yellow squash in oil in large saucepan until crisp-tender, 5 to 7 minutes; remove from saucepan and reserve.

2. Add onion and garlic to saucepan; saute until tender, about 5 minutes. Add tomatoes and oregano; cook until tomatoes are soft, about 3 minutes. Add rice; cook over medium heat until rice begins to brown, 2 to 3 minutes.

3. Heat stock to boiling in small saucepan; reduce heat to medium-low to keep stock hot. Add stock to rice mixture, ½ cup at a time, stirring constantly until stock is absorbed before adding another ½ cup. Continue process until rice is *al dente* and mixture is creamy, 20 to 25 minutes, adding reserved vegetables during last few minutes of cooking time. Stir in cheese; season to taste with salt and pepper.

4. Serve risotto in bowls; sprinkle with green onions.

WINTER VEGETABLE RISOTTO

Arborio rice, a short-grain rice grown in the Arborio region of Italy, can be purchased in Italian groceries and in many supermarkets with ethnic food sections. This rice is especially suited for making risotto, as it cooks to a wonderful creaminess. Other longer-grained rices can be used, but the texture of the risotto will be less creamy.

4 servings (about 1¼ cups each)

Olive oil cooking spray
1 small onion, chopped
3 cloves garlic, minced
1 cup sliced cremini, *or* white, mushrooms
1 teaspoon dried rosemary leaves
1 teaspoon dried thyme leaves
1½ cups arborio rice
6 cups Basic Vegetable Stock (see p. 58),
   or canned reduced-sodium vegetable
   broth
1 cup halved Brussels sprouts, cooked
   until crisp-tender
1 cup cubed, peeled sweet potato, cooked
   until crisp-tender

Per Serving
Calories: 384
% Calories from fat: 8
Fat (gm): 3.3
Saturated fat (gm): 1.4
Cholesterol (mg): 4.9
Sodium (mg): 153
Protein (gm): 11
Carbohydrate (gm): 77.3
Exchanges
Milk: 0.0
Vegetable: 3.0
Fruit: 0.0
Bread: 4.0
Meat: 0.0
Fat: 0.5

¼ cup grated Parmesan cheese
Salt and pepper, to taste
Parsley, minced, as garnish

1. Spray large saucepan with cooking spray; heat over medium heat until hot. Saute onion and garlic until tender, about 5 minutes. Add mushrooms and herbs; cook until mushrooms are tender, 5 to 7 minutes. Stir in rice; cook over medium heat until rice begins to brown, 2 to 3 minutes, stirring frequently.

2. Heat stock just to boiling in medium saucepan; reduce heat to medium-low to keep stock hot. Add stock to rice mixture, ½ cup at a time, stirring constantly until stock is absorbed before adding next ½ cup. Continue process until rice is *al dente* and mixture is creamy, 20 to 25 minutes, adding Brussels sprouts and sweet potato during last 10 minutes of cooking time. Stir in cheese; season to taste with salt and pepper.

3. Serve risotto in bowls; sprinkle with parsley.

RISI BISI

Opinions vary as to whether Risi Bisi is a risotto or a thick soup. If you agree with the latter definition, use an additional ½ to 1 cup of broth to make the mixture a thick-soup consistency.

4 servings (about 1 cup each)

Olive oil cooking spray
1 small onion, chopped
3 cloves garlic, minced
1½ cups arborio rice
2 teaspoons dried basil leaves
1½ quarts canned reduced-sodium vegetable broth
8 ounces frozen tiny peas, thawed
¼ cup grated Parmesan cheese
Salt and pepper, to taste
Parsley, finely chopped, as garnish

Per Serving
Calories: 407
% Calories from fat: 6
Fat (gm): 2.5
Saturated fat (gm): 1.3
Cholesterol (mg): 4.9
Sodium (mg): 291
Protein (gm): 12.2
Carbohydrate (gm): 82.1
Exchanges
Milk: 0.0
Vegetable: 1.0
Fruit: 0.0
Bread: 5.0
Meat: 0.0
Fat: 0.5

1. Spray large saucepan with cooking spray; heat over medium heat until hot. Saute onion and garlic until tender, about 5 minutes. Stir in rice and basil. Cook over medium heat until rice begins to brown, 2 to 3 minutes, stirring frequently.

2. Heat broth to boiling in medium saucepan; reduce heat to medium-low to keep broth hot. Add broth to rice mixture, ½ cup at a time, stirring constantly until broth is absorbed before adding another ½ cup. Continue process until rice is *al dente* and mixture is creamy, 20 to 25 minutes. Stir in peas during last 10 minutes of cooking time. Stir in Parmesan cheese; season to taste with salt and pepper.

3. Serve risotto in bowls; sprinkle with parsley.

RISOTTO-VEGETABLE CAKES

A great way to use leftover risotto!

4 servings

Olive oil cooking spray
1 medium onion, finely chopped
2 cloves garlic, minced
2 teaspoons dried oregano leaves, divided
1 cup arborio rice
4 cups Basic Vegetable Stock (see p. 58), *or* canned reduced-sodium vegetable broth
¼ cup shredded reduced-fat Cheddar, *or* Monterey Jack, cheese
5 tablespoons grated fat-free Parmesan cheese, divided
1 medium zucchini, chopped
2 medium carrots, chopped
1 medium red bell pepper, chopped
½ cup chopped celery
2 egg whites
⅔ cup Italian-seasoned breadcrumbs
8 beefsteak tomatoes, thickly (½ inch) sliced
Salt and pepper, to taste

Per Serving
Calories: 437
% Calories from fat: 9
Fat (gm): 4.3
Saturated fat (gm): 0.9
Cholesterol (mg): 3.8
Sodium (mg): 613
Protein (gm): 17
Carbohydrate (gm): 87.6
Exchanges
Milk: 0.0
Vegetable: 4.0
Fruit: 0.0
Bread: 4.0
Meat: 0.5
Fat: 0.5

1. Spray large saucepan with cooking spray; heat over medium heat until hot. Saute onion, garlic, and 1 teaspoon oregano until tender, about 3 minutes. Add rice; cook 2 to 3 minutes.

2. Heat stock to simmering in medium saucepan; reduce heat to low to keep stock warm. Add stock to rice mixture, ½ cup at a time, stirring constantly until stock is absorbed before adding next ½ cup. Continue process until rice is *al dente* and mixture is creamy, 20 to 25 minutes. Stir in Cheddar cheese and 4 tablespoons Parmesan cheese. Cool to room temperature.

3. Spray large skillet with cooking spray; heat over medium heat until hot. Saute zucchini, carrots, bell pepper, and celery until tender, 5 to 8 minutes. Stir vegetables, egg whites, and breadcrumbs into rice mixture.

4. Form rice mixture into 8 patties, each a scant ¾ inch thick. Broil on lightly greased broiler pan, 6 inches from heat source, until browned, 2 to 4 minutes each side. Top each patty with tomato slice; sprinkle with remaining 1 teaspoon oregano and remaining 1 tablespoon Parmesan cheese. Sprinkle lightly with salt and pepper. Broil until tomato is browned on top, 2 to 3 minutes.

TABBOULEH

 Always a favorite—this tabbouleh version includes finely chopped mint as well as parsley.

4 servings (about 1 cup each)

¾	cup bulgur
1½	cups coarsely chopped seeded tomatoes
¾	cup thinly sliced green onions and tops
¾	cup finely chopped parsley
¼	cup finely chopped mint
⅓-⅔	cup fat-free plain yogurt
¼-⅓	cup lemon juice
1½-2	tablespoons olive oil
	Salt and pepper, to taste

Per Serving
Calories: 176
% Calories from fat: 28
Fat (gm): 5.9
Saturated fat (gm): 0.8
Cholesterol (mg): 0.3
Sodium (mg): 34
Protein (gm): 5.7
Carbohydrate (gm): 28.2
Exchanges
Milk: 0.0
Vegetable: 1.0
Fruit: 0.0
Bread: 1.5
Meat: 0.0
Fat: 1.0

1. Pour boiling water over bulgur to cover; let stand 15 minutes or until bulgur is tender but slightly chewy. Drain well.

2. Mix bulgur, tomatoes, green onions, parsley, and mint; stir in yogurt, lemon juice, and oil. Season to taste with salt and pepper. Refrigerate 1 to 2 hours for flavors to blend.

TABBOULEH AND VEGETABLE SALAD MEDLEY

Two salads—a tabbouleh salad dressed with Lemon-Cinnamon Vinaigrette; and a mixed vegetable salad with chunky Cucumber-Sour Cream Dressing—are lightly combined for a contrast of flavors. If desired, the salads can be arranged side by side on serving plates.

4 servings

1 package (5¼ ounces) tabbouleh wheat salad mix

1 cup cold water

½ cup finely chopped celery

⅓ cup sliced green onions, green and white parts

8 prunes, pitted, chopped

2 tablespoons finely chopped parsley

1 tablespoon finely chopped fresh, *or* 1 teaspoon dried, basil leaves

1 clove garlic, minced

Lemon-Cinnamon Vinaigrette (recipe follows)

Salt and pepper, to taste

2 cups cauliflower florets

¾ cup coarsely chopped red bell pepper

2 medium carrots, diagonally sliced

8 cherry tomatoes, halved

Cucumber-Sour Cream Dressing (recipe follows)

Salad greens, as garnish

¼ cup (1 ounce) crumbled feta cheese

Per Serving
Calories: 382
% Calories from fat: 28
Fat (gm): 12.5
Saturated fat (gm): 2.5
Cholesterol (mg): 6.5
Sodium (mg): 600
Protein (gm): 11.4
Carbohydrate (gm): 61.6
Exchanges
Milk: 0.0
Vegetable: 3.0
Fruit: 1.5
Bread: 1.5
Meat: 0.0
Fat: 2.5

1. Mix tabbouleh and cold water in small bowl (discard spice packet); let stand 30 minutes. Stir celery, green onions, prunes, parsley, basil, and garlic into tabbouleh; add Lemon-Cinnamon Vinaigrette and toss. Season to taste with salt and pepper.

2. Combine cauliflower, bell pepper, carrots, and tomatoes; spoon Cucumber-Sour Cream Dressing over and toss. Season to taste with salt and pepper.

3. Add vegetable salad to tabbouleh salad and toss lightly. Spoon salad into lettuce-lined serving plates; sprinkle with feta cheese.

Lemon-Cinnamon Vinaigrette

(makes about ½ cup)

⅓ cup lemon juice
3 tablespoons olive oil, *or* canola oil
¼ teaspoon dried cinnamon

1. Mix all ingredients; refrigerate until ready to serve. Mix again before serving.

Cucumber-Sour Cream Dressing

(makes about 1 cup)

½ cup fat-free sour cream
¼ cup fat-free plain yogurt
1 teaspoon white wine vinegar
1 teaspoon dried dill weed
½ medium cucumber, peeled, seeded, chopped

1. Combine all ingredients; refrigerate until ready to serve.

VEGETABLE SALAD WITH MILLET

Finely chop the vegetables by hand or in a food processor. Serve this salad in bowls, in beefsteak tomato halves, or use it as a filling for warm pita pockets.

6 servings (about 1⅓ cups each)

1¼ cups millet
3⅓ cups water
½ cup sliced celery
½ medium red bell pepper, sliced
4 green onions and tops, sliced
1 medium carrot, sliced
¼ cup finely chopped parsley
2 tablespoons finely chopped fresh basil, *or* 1 teaspoon dried basil leaves
½ head iceberg lettuce, sliced
½ head green leaf lettuce, sliced
1 medium tomato, coarsely chopped

Per Serving
Calories: 383
% Calories from fat: 23
Fat (gm): 9.6
Saturated fat (gm): 1.4
Cholesterol (mg): 0
Sodium (mg): 238
Protein (gm): 10.3
Carbohydrate (gm): 63.9
Exchanges
Milk: 0.0
Vegetable: 1.0
Fruit: 0.0
Bread: 4.0
Meat: 0.0
Fat: 1.5

Oregano Vinaigrette (recipe follows)
Salt and pepper, to taste
Spinach, *or* lettuce, leaves, as garnish
4 pita pockets

1. Cook millet in large saucepan over medium heat until toasted, 2 to 3 minutes. Add water and heat to boiling; reduce heat and simmer, covered, until millet is tender and liquid absorbed, about 15 minutes. Remove from heat and let stand, covered, 10 minutes. Cool to room temperature.

2. Combine celery, bell pepper, green onions, carrot, parsley, and basil in food processor; process, using pulse technique, until finely chopped. Transfer mixture to large bowl.

3. Add lettuce to food processor; process, using pulse technique, until finely chopped. Transfer mixture to bowl with vegetables.

4. Add tomatoes and millet to vegetable mixture and toss; drizzle with Oregano Vinaigrette and toss. Season to taste with salt and pepper. Spoon salad into spinach-lined salad bowls; serve with pita pockets.

Oregano Vinaigrette

(makes about ⅓ cup)

3 tablespoons olive oil, *or* canola oil
3 tablespoons white wine vinegar
1 teaspoon dried oregano

1. Mix all ingredients; refrigerate until ready to serve.

WHEAT BERRY WALDORF

Wheat berries have a wonderful "toothsome" texture. They can be purchased at health food stores. If wheat berries are unavailable, substitute ⅓ cup bulgur; soak bulgur in 1⅓ cups water until tender.

4 servings (about 1½ cups each)

1¼ cups wheat berries

1½ cups peeled, cored, cubed pineapple

2 medium oranges, cut into segments

1 large unpeeled apple, cored, cubed

1 cup thinly sliced fennel bulb

3 tablespoons coarsely chopped walnuts

2 tablespoons finely chopped parsley leaves

⅓ cup fat-free mayonnaise

2½ teaspoons Dijon-style mustard

1½ tablespoons lemon juice

2 teaspoons sugar

¾ teaspoon crushed fennel seeds
     Lettuce leaves, as garnish

Per Serving
Calories: 319
% Calories from fat: 12
Fat (gm): 4.6
Saturated fat (gm): 0.3
Cholesterol (mg): 0
Sodium (mg): 310
Protein (gm): 7.8
Carbohydrate (gm): 65.8
Exchanges
Milk: 0.0
Vegetable: 0.0
Fruit: 1.5
Bread: 3.0
Meat: 0.0
Fat: 0.5

1. Cover wheat berries with 2 to 3 inches water in saucepan; let stand overnight. Heat to boiling; reduce heat and simmer, covered, until wheat berries are tender, 45 to 55 minutes. Drain and cool.

2. Combine wheat berries, fruit, fennel, walnuts, and parsley in bowl. In separate bowl, combine remaining ingredients, except lettuce; spoon over salad and toss. Serve on lettuce-lined plates.

WHEAT BERRY AND GARDEN TOMATO SALAD

The texture of wheat berries is a perfect complement to crisp cucumbers and sun-ripened tomatoes. Kamut is an excellent grain to substitute for the wheat berries.

4 servings (about 1⅔ cups each)

3	cups cooked wheat berries
4	cups coarsely chopped ripe tomatoes
1½	cups cubed, seeded cucumber
½	cup sliced green onions and tops
¼	cup finely chopped parsley
½	cup (2 ounces) crumbled reduced-fat feta cheese
	Roasted Garlic Vinaigrette (recipe follows)
	Salt and pepper, to taste
	Curly endive, *or* escarole, as garnish

Per Serving
Calories: 281
% Calories from fat: 30
Fat (gm): 10
Saturated fat (gm): 2.4
Cholesterol (mg): 5.1
Sodium (mg): 221
Protein (gm): 9.4
Carbohydrate (gm): 42.7
Exchanges
Milk: 0.0
Vegetable: 2.0
Fruit: 0.0
Bread: 2.0
Meat: 0.0
Fat: 2.0

1. Combine wheat berries, vegetables, and cheese in salad bowl; pour Roasted Garlic Vinaigrette over and toss. Season to taste with salt and pepper. Serve on endive-lined plates.

Roasted Garlic Vinaigrette

2-4	tablespoons olive oil
¼	cup balsamic vinegar
2	teaspoons minced roasted garlic
1	teaspoon dried mint leaves
1	teaspoon dried oregano leaves

1. Mix all ingredients; refrigerate until serving time. Mix again before using.

ORANGE CILANTRO RICE

A perfect accompaniment to grilled or roasted tofu, tempeh, or vegetables. For variation, lemon zest can be substituted for the orange zest.

6 side-dish servings (about ⅔ cup each)

Vegetable cooking spray
½ cup sliced green onions and tops
1 cup long-grain rice
Zest of 1 small orange, grated
2¼ cups water
2 tablespoons finely chopped cilantro
Salt and pepper, to taste

Per Serving
Calories: 118
% Calories from fat: 1
Fat (gm): 0.2
Saturated fat (gm): 0
Cholesterol (mg): 0
Sodium (mg): 2
Protein (gm): 2.3
Carbohydrate (gm): 26
Exchanges
Milk: 0.0
Vegetable: 0.0
Fruit: 0.0
Bread: 1.5
Meat: 0.0
Fat: 0.0

1. Spray medium saucepan with cooking spray; heat over medium heat until hot. Saute onions until tender, 3 to 5 minutes. Add rice and orange zest to saucepan; cook over medium heat until rice is lightly browned, 2 to 3 minutes, stirring frequently.

2. Add water to saucepan and heat to boiling; reduce heat and simmer, covered, until rice is tender, 20 to 25 minutes. Stir in cilantro; season to taste with salt and pepper.

YELLOW SALSA RICE

Ground turmeric contributes subtle flavor and an attractive yellow color to the rice.

6 side-dish servings (about ⅔ cup each)

1 can (14½ ounces) reduced-sodium vegetable broth
½ teaspoon ground turmeric
1 cup long-grain rice
¼ cup prepared medium, *or* hot, salsa
1 medium tomato, chopped
Salt and pepper, to taste
Cilantro, *or* parsley, finely chopped, as garnish

Per Serving
Calories: 130
% Calories from fat: 2
Fat (gm): 0.3
Saturated fat (gm): 0.1
Cholesterol (mg): 0
Sodium (mg): 103
Protein (gm): 2.7
Carbohydrate (gm): 28.4
Exchanges
Milk: 0.0
Vegetable: 1.0
Fruit: 0.0
Bread: 1.5
Meat: 0.0
Fat: 0.0

1. Heat broth and turmeric to boiling in medium saucepan; stir in rice and salsa. Reduce heat and simmer, covered, until rice is tender and liquid absorbed, 20 to 25 minutes; stir in tomato during last 5 minutes of cooking time. Season to taste with salt and pepper.

2. Spoon rice into serving bowl; sprinkle with cilantro.

MEXICAN RED RICE

The tomatoes are pureed in the traditional version of this recipe. We've chosen to chop the tomato for color and flavor.

6 side-dish servings (about ⅔ cup each)

Vegetable cooking spray
1 large tomato, chopped
½ cup chopped onion
1 clove garlic, minced
½ teaspoon dried oregano leaves
¼ teaspoon ground cumin
1 cup long-grain rice
1 can (14½ ounces) reduced-sodium vegetable broth
⅓ cup water
1 carrot, cooked, diced
½ cup frozen peas, thawed
Salt and pepper, to taste

Per Serving
Calories: 149
% Calories from fat: 2
Fat (gm): 0.4
Saturated fat (gm): 0.1
Cholesterol (mg): 0
Sodium (mg): 45
Protein (gm): 3.7
Carbohydrate (gm): 32.5
Exchanges
Milk: 0.0
Vegetable: 0.0
Fruit: 0.0
Bread: 2.0
Meat: 0.0
Fat: 0.0

1. Coat large saucepan with cooking spray; heat over medium heat until hot. Saute tomato, onion, garlic, and herbs until onion is tender, 3 to 5 minutes. Add rice; cook over medium heat until rice is lightly browned, 2 to 3 minutes, stirring frequently.

2. Add broth and water to saucepan; heat to boiling. Reduce heat and simmer, covered, until rice is tender, about 25 minutes, adding carrot and peas during last 5 minutes. Season to taste with salt and pepper.

SPICY RICE

 An aromatic spiced dish of East Indian origins will complement many meals. The turmeric lends a beautiful yellow color to the rice.

8 side-dish servings (about ½ cup each)

1 medium onion, sliced
1 clove garlic, minced
1 tablespoon olive oil
1 cup uncooked basmati, *or* other aromatic, rice
½ cup reduced-fat plain yogurt
1-2 cardamom pods, crushed
¼ teaspoon ground turmeric
¼ teaspoon ground ginger
⅛ teaspoon crushed red pepper
2 cups Canned Vegetable Stock (see p. 63), *or* canned reduced-sodium vegetable broth
Salt and pepper, to taste
1 small tomato, cut into 8 wedges
1 tablespoon finely chopped cilantro

Per Serving
Calories: 166
% Calories from fat: 19
Fat (gm): 3.6
Saturated fat (gm): 0.5
Cholesterol (mg): 1.2
Sodium (mg): 54
Protein (gm): 4.4
Carbohydrate (gm): 27.9
Exchanges
Milk: 0.0
Vegetable: 1.0
Fruit: 0.0
Bread: 1.5
Meat: 0.0
Fat: 0.5

1. Saute onion and garlic in oil in large saucepan until tender, about 8 minutes. Stir in rice; cook over medium heat, stirring frequently, 5 minutes. Stir in yogurt, herbs, and crushed red pepper; cook over medium-high to high heat 5 minutes, stirring frequently.

2. Add stock to saucepan and heat to boiling; reduce heat and simmer, covered, until rice is tender, about 25 minutes. Season to taste with salt and pepper.

3. Spoon rice mixture into serving bowl; arrange tomato wedges on top and sprinkle with cilantro.

TURMERIC RICE

Turmeric contributes color more than flavor to this rice dish. Use instead of plain rice whenever the yellow color is enhancing to a meal.

6 side-dish servings (about ⅔ cup each)

Per Serving
Calories: 120
% Calories from fat: 3
Fat (gm): 0.3
Saturated fat (gm): 0.1
Cholesterol (mg): 0
Sodium (mg): 7
Protein (gm): 2.3
Carbohydrate (gm): 26
Exchanges
Milk: 0.0
Vegetable: 0.0
Fruit: 0.0
Bread: 1.5
Meat: 0.0
Fat: 0.0

- 2¼ cups Basic Vegetable Stock (see p. 58), *or* water
- ¼-½ teaspoon ground turmeric
- ½ teaspoon salt (optional)
- 1 cup long-grain rice
- 2-3 tablespoons finely chopped parsley, *or* cilantro

1. Heat stock, turmeric, and salt, if using, to boiling in small saucepan; stir in rice. Reduce heat and simmer, covered, until rice is tender and stock absorbed, 20 to 25 minutes. Stir in parsley.

WILD RICE SOUFFLÉ

When you're in the mood for something new and different, try this great soufflé!

4 servings

Per Serving
Calories: 210
% Calories from fat: 28
Fat (gm): 6.5
Saturated fat (gm): 2.4
Cholesterol (mg): 168.3
Sodium (mg): 288
Protein (gm): 13
Carbohydrate (gm): 23
Exchanges
Milk: 0.0
Vegetable: 0.0
Fruit: 0.0
Bread: 1.5
Meat: 1.5
Fat: 0.5

- ⅓ cup wild rice
- 1 cup Canned Vegetable Stock (see p. 63), *or* water
- 1 cup fat-free milk
- ¼ cup all-purpose flour
- ½ cup (2 ounces) shredded reduced-fat Cheddar cheese
- ¼ cup finely chopped parsley
- 2 tablespoons finely chopped onion
- ½ teaspoon paprika
- ¼-½ teaspoon dried savory leaves
- ¼-½ teaspoon dried thyme leaves

White pepper

3 egg yolks

3 egg whites, beaten to stiff peaks

1. Rinse rice under cold water and drain. Heat rice and stock to boiling in small saucepan; reduce heat and simmer, covered, until rice is tender and stock absorbed, 45 to 55 minutes.

2. Mix milk and flour in medium saucepan; heat over medium-high heat, whisking constantly, to boiling. Boil, whisking constantly, until thickened. Remove from heat; add cheese and whisk until cheese is melted (sauce will be very thick). Cool slightly; stir in parsley, onion, paprika, and herbs. Season to taste with white pepper.

3. Beat egg yolks in small bowl until thick and lemon colored, about 5 minutes; whisk into cheese mixture. Stir about ¼ of the egg whites into cheese mixture. Fold cheese mixture into remaining egg whites. Fold in rice.

4. Pour mixture into lightly greased 1-quart soufflé dish. Bake at 350 degrees until knife inserted halfway between center and edge comes out clean, 45 to 55 minutes. Serve immediately.

POLENTA

This basic recipe can be varied to your taste by adding sauteed onion and garlic, cheese, herbs, etc. Note the variations below.

6 side-dish servings (about ½ cup each)

3 cups water

¾ cup yellow cornmeal

Salt and pepper, to taste

Per Serving
Calories: 55
% Calories from fat: 9
Fat (gm): 0.5
Saturated fat (gm): 0.1
Cholesterol (mg): 0
Sodium (mg): 5
Protein (gm): 1.2
Carbohydrate (gm): 11.7
Exchanges
Milk: 0.0
Vegetable: 0.0
Fruit: 0.0
Bread: 1.0
Meat: 0.0
Fat: 0.0

1. Heat water to boiling; gradually stir in cornmeal. Cook over medium to medium-low heat, stirring constantly, until polenta thickens enough to hold its shape but is still soft, 5 to 8 minutes.

Variations: **Blue Cheese Polenta**—Stir ½ cup (2 ounces) crumbled blue cheese, *or* other blue veined cheese, into the cooked polenta.

 Goat's Cheese Polenta—Stir ¼ to ½ cup (1 to 2 ounces) crumbled goat's cheese into the cooked polenta.

 Garlic Polenta—Saute ¼ cup finely chopped onion and 4 to 6 cloves minced garlic in 1 tablespoon olive oil; add water, as above, and complete recipe.

HERBED POLENTA

 Gently seasoned with onions, garlic, and basil, the polenta can be served immediately after cooking, or cooled in a pan as the recipe directs.

4-6 side-dish servings (about ⅔ cup each)

Olive oil cooking spray
2 green onions and tops, sliced
1 clove garlic, minced
1 teaspoon dried basil leaves
2½ cups Canned Vegetable Stock, *or* Basic Vegetable Stock (see pp. 63, 58)
¾ cup yellow cornmeal
½ teaspoon salt

Per Serving
Calories: 124
% Calories from fat: 9
Fat (gm): 1.3
Saturated fat (gm): 0.2
Cholesterol (mg): 0
Sodium (mg): 309
Protein (gm): 2.5
Carbohydrate (gm): 22.4
Exchanges
Milk: 0.0
Vegetable: 0.0
Fruit: 0.0
Bread: 1.5
Meat: 0.0
Fat: 0.5

1. Spray large saucepan with cooking spray; heat over medium heat until hot. Saute onions, garlic, and basil until tender, about 5 minutes. Add stock and heat to boiling; gradually stir in cornmeal and salt. Cook over low heat, stirring constantly, until thickened, about 10 minutes.

2. Pour polenta into lightly greased 8-inch cake pan; cool to room temperature. Refrigerate, lightly covered, until polenta is firm, 3 to 4 hours.

3. Spray large skillet with cooking spray; heat over medium heat until hot. Cut polenta into wedges; cook in skillet over medium heat until browned, 3 to 4 minutes on each side.

CORNMEAL AND MILLET MUSH

 A breakfast favorite! Other grains, such as kasha, millet, or wheat berries, can be combined with the cornmeal too.

8 servings (about ½ cup each)

4 cups water
1 cup yellow, *or* white, cornmeal
1 teaspoon salt
2 cups cooked millet
6 tablespoons brown sugar

Per Serving
Calories: 283
% Calories from fat: 8
Fat (gm): 2.7
Saturated fat (gm): 0.4
Cholesterol (mg): 0
Sodium (mg): 278
Protein (gm): 6.7
Carbohydrate (gm): 58.3
Exchanges
Milk: 0.0
Vegetable: 0.0
Fruit: 0.0
Bread: 4.0
Meat: 0.0
Fat: 0.0

1. Heat water to boiling in large saucepan; gradually stir in cornmeal and salt. Reduce heat to medium-low and cook 5 minutes, stirring constantly. Stir in millet and cook until mixture is thick, 3 to 5 minutes longer, stirring constantly.

2. Spoon into bowls; sprinkle with brown sugar.

 Variation: **Fried Mush**—Make cornmeal mixture as above, but pour into greased loaf pan 8½ x 4½ inches. Cool to room temperature; refrigerate until firm, several hours or overnight. Loosen sides of cornmeal mixture with sharp knife; invert onto cutting board. Cut into slices and fry in lightly greased large skillet over medium heat until browned, 3 to 4 minutes on each side. Serve with warm maple syrup.

BEST BREAKFAST CEREAL

Delicious, and nutritious! Although we all appreciate a breakfast that is fast to make, this cereal is even more delicious made with slow-cooking steel-cut oats. Treat yourself!

6 servings (about ⅔ cup each)

3	cups water
1/16	teaspoon salt
1½	cups quick-cooking oats
1½	cups cooked wheat berries
¼	cup chopped toasted pecans, *or* walnuts
½	cup dried fruit bits, *or* raisins
¼-½	cup packed dark brown sugar
1	cup fat-free milk

Per Serving
Calories: 313
% Calories from fat: 13
Fat (gm): 4.9
Saturated fat (gm): 0.6
Cholesterol (mg): 0.7
Sodium (mg): 55
Protein (gm): 9.7
Carbohydrate (gm): 61.4
Exchanges
Milk: 0.0
Vegetable: 0.0
Fruit: 0.5
Bread: 3.5
Meat: 0.0
Fat: 0.5

1. Heat water and salt to boiling in medium saucepan; stir in oats, wheat berries, pecans, and dried fruit bits. Reduce heat and simmer until oatmeal is cooked to desired consistency, about 5 minutes.

2. Stir brown sugar into cereal, or spoon cereal into bowls and sprinkle with sugar. Serve with milk.

TWELVE

Vegetable

Side Dishes

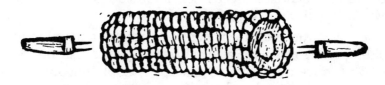

BRAISED WHOLE ARTICHOKES

After the artichokes are tender, continue to cook them slowly until the bottoms are browned and crusty—the resulting flavor is marvelous!

4 servings

4 medium artichokes
    Salt
2-4 teaspoons extra-virgin olive oil

Per Serving
Calories: 80
% Calories from fat: 24
Fat (gm): 2.4
Saturated fat (gm): 0.3
Cholesterol (mg): 0
Sodium (mg): 114
Protein (gm): 4.2
Carbohydrate (gm): 13.4
Exchanges
Milk: 0.0
Vegetable: 2.0
Fruit: 0.0
Bread: 0.0
Meat: 0.0
Fat: 0.5

1. Cut 1 inch from tops of artichokes and trim off stems. Place artichokes in medium saucepan and sprinkle lightly with salt; add 1 inch water. Heat to boiling; reduce heat and simmer, covered, until artichokes are tender, about 30 minutes (bottom leaves will pull out easily).

2. Remove artichokes from pan; discard any remaining water. Holding artichokes with a towel or hot pad, brush bottom of each with olive oil; return to saucepan. Cook, uncovered, over medium to medium-low heat until bottoms of artichokes are deeply browned, 10 to 15 minutes.

ARTICHOKES WITH HOLLANDAISE SAUCE

The Mock Hollandaise Sauce is excellent served over steamed asparagus spears, broccoli, or cauliflower. Also see our delicious recipe for Eggs Benedict (p. 478).

4-6 servings

4-6 whole artichokes, stems trimmed
     Mock Hollandaise Sauce (see p. 715)

Per Serving
Calories: 114
% Calories from fat: 2
Fat (gm): 0.3
Saturated fat (gm): 0.1
Cholesterol (mg): 0.2
Sodium (mg): 396
Protein (gm): 11.9
Carbohydrate (gm): 17.5

Exchanges
Milk: 0.5
Vegetable: 2.0
Fruit: 0.0
Bread: 0.0
Meat: 0.5
Fat: 0.0

1. Slice 1 inch off tops of artichokes and discard. Trim tips of remaining leaves with scissors. Place artichokes in medium saucepan with 2 inches of water; heat to boiling. Reduce heat and simmer, covered, until artichoke leaves pull off easily and bottom is tender when pierced with a fork, about 30 minutes.

2. Place artichokes on serving plates with Mock Hollandaise Sauce on the side for dipping.

ASPARAGUS WITH LEMON-WINE SAUCE

 This rich, delectable sauce is also delicious served with crisp-tender broccoli, cauliflower, green beans, or Brussels sprouts.

4 servings

Vegetable cooking spray

2 tablespoons minced shallots, *or* green onions (white parts)

¼ cup dry white wine, *or* canned reduced-sodium vegetable broth

¾ cup fat-free half-and-half, *or* fat-free milk

2 tablespoons flour

½ teaspoon dried thyme leaves

½ teaspoon dried marjoram leaves

1 tablespoon lemon juice
Salt and white pepper, to taste

1 pound asparagus spears, cooked until crisp-tender, warm

Per Serving
Calories: 85
% Calories from fat: 4
Fat (gm): 0.4
Saturated fat (gm): 0.1
Cholesterol (mg): 0
Sodium (mg): 59
Protein (gm): 4.8
Carbohydrate (gm): 13.4
Exchanges
Milk: 0.0
Vegetable: 2.0
Fruit: 0.0
Bread: 0.5
Meat: 0.0
Fat: 0.0

1. Spray small saucepan with cooking spray; heat over medium heat until hot. Cook shallots over medium to medium-low heat until tender but not browned, 2 to 3 minutes. Add wine and heat to boiling; reduce heat and simmer, uncovered, until wine is evaporated, 3 to 4 minutes.

2. Mix half-and-half, flour, and herbs; stir into saucepan and heat to boiling. Boil, stirring constantly, until sauce is thickened, about 1 minute. Stir in lemon juice; season to taste with salt and pepper.

3. Arrange asparagus in serving dish; spoon sauce over.

ASPARAGUS WITH PEANUT SAUCE

Oriental flavors are the perfect complement to spring's freshest asparagus.

6 servings

2	tablespoons reduced-fat peanut butter
¼	cup sugar
2-3	tablespoons reduced-sodium tamari soy sauce
3-4	teaspoons rice wine (sake), dry sherry, *or* water
1	teaspoon grated gingerroot
1½	pounds asparagus spears, cooked until crisp-tender, chilled

Per Serving
Calories: 95
% Calories from fat: 21
Fat (gm): 2.3
Saturated fat (gm): 0.5
Cholesterol (mg): 0
Sodium (mg): 246
Protein (gm): 4.8
Carbohydrate (gm): 15
Exchanges
Milk: 0.0
Vegetable: 3.0
Fruit: 0.0
Bread: 0.0
Meat: 0.0
Fat: 0.5

1. Mix peanut butter, sugar, soy sauce, rice wine, and gingerroot until smooth.

2. Arrange asparagus on serving platter; spoon peanut sauce over.

GREEK-STYLE GREEN BEANS

Fresh green beans are long simmered with tomatoes, herbs, and garlic in traditional Greek style.

4-6 servings

½	cup chopped onion
4	cloves garlic, minced
1	tablespoon olive oil
¾	teaspoon dried oregano leaves
½	teaspoon dried basil leaves
1	can (28 ounces) reduced-sodium tomatoes, undrained, coarsely chopped

Per Serving
Calories: 123
% Calories from fat: 28
Fat (gm): 4.3
Saturated fat (gm): 0.6
Cholesterol (mg): 0
Sodium (mg): 30
Protein (gm): 4.5
Carbohydrate (gm): 20.5

1 pound green beans
   Salt and pepper, to taste

Exchanges
Milk: 0.0
Vegetable: 4.0
Fruit: 0.0
Bread: 0.0
Meat: 0.0
Fat: 0.5

1. Saute onion and garlic in oil in large skillet until tender, 3 to 4 minutes. Stir in herbs and cook 1 to 2 minutes longer.

2. Add tomatoes with liquid and green beans and heat to boiling; reduce heat and simmer, covered, until beans are very tender, 30 to 40 minutes. Season to taste with salt and pepper.

ORIENTAL GREEN BEANS

Serve these beans as an accompaniment to grilled tofu or portobello mushrooms.

4 servings

    Vegetable cooking spray
¼ cup chopped onion
¼ cup chopped red bell pepper
 2 teaspoons finely chopped gingerroot
 2 cloves garlic, minced
 8 ounces green beans, cut into halves
½ cup sliced water chestnuts
 1 cup cooked dried, *or* canned, adzuki, *or* black, beans
 1 tablespoon rice wine vinegar
1-2 teaspoons reduced-sodium tamari soy sauce
    Salt and pepper, to taste

Per Serving
Calories: 109
% Calories from fat: 2
Fat (gm): 0.2
Saturated fat (gm): 0
Cholesterol (mg): 0
Sodium (mg): 64
Protein (gm): 5.8
Carbohydrate (gm): 22.5
Exchanges
Milk: 0.0
Vegetable: 1.5
Fruit: 0.0
Bread: 1.0
Meat: 0.0
Fat: 0.0

1. Spray wok or large skillet with cooking spray; heat over medium heat until hot. Add onion, bell pepper, gingerroot, and garlic; spray with cooking spray and stir-fry until tender, 3 to 4 minutes.

2. Add green beans and water chestnuts to wok; stir-fry until beans are crisp-tender, 5 to 8 minutes. Stir in adzuki beans, vinegar, and soy sauce; cook 1 to 2 minutes longer. Season to taste with salt and pepper.

GREEN BEAN CASSEROLE

Reduced-fat cream of mushroom soup and fat-free sour cream make this old favorite possible in a new skinny form. We've used fresh green beans, but canned or frozen may be used if you prefer.

6 servings

1 can (10¾ ounces) reduced-fat cream of mushroom soup
½ cup fat-free sour cream
¼ cup fat-free milk
1¼ pounds green beans, cut into 1½-inch pieces, cooked until crisp-tender
½ cup canned French-fried onions

Per Serving
Calories: 81
% Calories from fat: 31
Fat (gm): 2.9
Saturated fat (gm): 0.8
Cholesterol (mg): 1.3
Sodium (mg): 172
Protein (gm): 3
Carbohydrate (gm): 11.6
Exchanges
Milk: 0.0
Vegetable: 2.0
Fruit: 0.0
Bread: 0.0
Meat: 0.0
Fat: 0.5

1. Mix soup, sour cream, and milk in 2-quart casserole; stir in beans.

2. Bake, uncovered, at 350 degrees until mixture is bubbly, about 45 minutes. Sprinkle onions on top during last 5 minutes of baking time.

BEETS DIJON

The easiest way to cook beets is with the skins on; after cooking, the skins slip off easily!

4 servings

Vegetable cooking spray
⅓ cup finely chopped onion
2 cloves garlic, minced
⅓ cup fat-free sour cream
2 tablespoons Dijon-style mustard
2-3 teaspoons lemon juice
Salt and white pepper, to taste
1½ pounds beets, cooked, cubed, *or* sliced, warm
Parsley, minced, as garnish

Per Serving
Calories: 71
% Calories from fat: 7
Fat (gm): 0.6
Saturated fat (gm): 0.1
Cholesterol (mg): 0
Sodium (mg): 185
Protein (gm): 3.5
Carbohydrate (gm): 13.8
Exchanges
Milk: 0.0
Vegetable: 3.0
Fruit: 0.0
Bread: 0.0
Meat: 0.0
Fat: 0.0

1. Spray small saucepan with cooking spray; heat over medium heat until hot. Saute onion and garlic until tender, 3 to 4 minutes. Stir in sour cream, mustard, and lemon juice; heat over low heat until hot. Season to taste with salt and pepper.

2. Spoon sauce over beets; stir gently. Sprinkle with parsley.

HARVARD BEETS

Sweet yet tart, the sauce can also be served over cooked carrots or pearl onions. Vary the amount of vinegar for the tartness you like.

4 servings

3	tablespoons sugar
1½	tablespoons cornstarch
¾	cup water
3-4	tablespoons cider vinegar
2	teaspoons margarine, *or* butter
	Salt and white pepper, to taste
1	pound beets, cooked, sliced, *or* julienned, warm

Per Serving
Calories: 94
% Calories from fat: 18
Fat (gm): 1.9
Saturated fat (gm): 0.4
Cholesterol (mg): 0
Sodium (mg): 70
Protein (gm): 1.1
Carbohydrate (gm): 19.3
Exchanges
Milk: 0.0
Vegetable: 2.0
Fruit: 0.0
Bread: 0.5
Meat: 0.0
Fat: 0.0

1. Mix sugar and cornstarch in small saucepan; whisk in water and vinegar. Heat to boiling, whisking constantly; boil, whisking constantly, until thickened, about 1 minute. Add margarine, whisking until melted. Season to taste with salt and pepper.

2. Pour sauce over beets in serving bowl and toss gently.

HONEY-ROASTED BEETS

The beets are cooked briefly before roasting so they are easier to peel and cut.

6 servings

1½	pounds medium-size beets
	Vegetable cooking spray
2	medium red onions, cut into wedges
4	tablespoons honey, divided
2-3	tablespoons red wine vinegar

Per Serving
Calories: 139
% Calories from fat: 29
Fat (gm): 4.6
Saturated fat (gm): 0.3
Cholesterol (mg): 0
Sodium (mg): 50
Protein (gm): 2.6
Carbohydrate (gm): 23.3

Exchanges
Milk: 0.0
Vegetable: 1.5
Fruit: 1.0
Bread: 0.0
Meat: 0.0
Fat: 1.0

1 tablespoon canola oil
4 cloves garlic, minced
¼ cup currants, *or* raisins
3-4 tablespoons chopped toasted walnuts
   Salt and pepper, to taste
   Parsley, minced, as garnish

1. Simmer beets in water to cover in large saucepan 15 minutes; drain and rinse in cold water. Peel beets; cut into fourths.

2. Line jelly roll pan with aluminum foil; spray with cooking spray. Arrange beets and onions on pan; spray generously with cooking spray and drizzle with 2 tablespoons honey. Roast at 400 degrees until beets are tender, about 40 minutes.

3. Transfer beets and onions to serving bowl. Combine remaining 2 tablespoons honey, vinegar, oil, and garlic; drizzle over beets and toss. Add currants and walnuts and toss; season to taste with salt and pepper. Sprinkle with parsley.

HERB-CRUMBED BROCCOLI

Herb-seasoned breadcrumbs and pecans offer new flavor and texture contrasts in this favorite broccoli dish.

6 servings

Per Serving
Calories: 61
% Calories from fat: 28
Fat (gm): 2.1
Saturated fat (gm): 0.2
Cholesterol (mg): 0
Sodium (mg): 64
Protein (gm): 3.7
Carbohydrate (gm): 8.7
Exchanges
Milk: 0.0
Vegetable: 1.5
Fruit: 0.0
Bread: 0.0
Meat: 0.0
Fat: 0.5

   Vegetable cooking spray
2-4 tablespoons chopped pecans
 ¼ cup dry unseasoned breadcrumbs
 ½ teaspoon dried marjoram leaves
 ¼ teaspoon dried chervil leaves
  2 tablespoons finely chopped parsley
1½ pounds broccoli, cut into florets and stalks sliced, cooked
   Salt and pepper, to taste

1. Spray small skillet with cooking spray; heat over medium heat until hot. Add pecans and spray with cooking spray; cook over medium heat until toasted, 2 to 3 minutes, stirring frequently. Add breadcrumbs, marjoram, and chervil to skillet; cook until crumbs are toasted, 3 to 4 minutes, stirring frequently. Remove from heat and stir in parsley.

2. Season broccoli with salt and pepper to taste; arrange in serving bowl. Spoon crumb mixture over broccoli.

BROCCOLI RABE SAUTEED WITH GARLIC

A simple but flavorful vegetable recipe that can also be made with broccoli or asparagus spears.

4-6 servings

Garlic-flavored vegetable cooking spray
1 pound broccoli rabe, cooked until crisp-tender
4 cloves garlic, minced
Salt and pepper, to taste

Per Serving
Calories: 32
% Calories from fat: 8
Fat (gm): 0.4
Saturated fat (gm): 0.1
Cholesterol (mg): 0
Sodium (mg): 25
Protein (gm): 3.1
Carbohydrate (gm): 5.9
Exchanges
Milk: 0.0
Vegetable: 1.0
Fruit: 0.0
Bread: 0.0
Meat: 0.0
Fat: 0.0

1. Spray large skillet with cooking spray; heat over medium heat until hot. Add broccoli rabe and garlic; spray lightly with cooking spray. Saute over medium to medium-low heat until broccoli is beginning to brown, 4 to 5 minutes. Season to taste with salt and pepper.

SUGAR-GLAZED BRUSSELS SPROUTS AND PEARL ONIONS

If Brussels sprouts are large, cut them into halves for easier eating. The pearl onions can be fresh, frozen, or canned.

4-6 servings

8 ounces small Brussels sprouts
8 ounces small pearl onions
1 tablespoon margarine, *or* butter

Per Serving
Calories: 107
% Calories from fat: 25
Fat (gm): 3.2
Saturated fat (gm): 0.6
Cholesterol (mg): 0
Sodium (mg): 48
Protein (gm): 2.3
Carbohydrate (gm): 19.7

3-4 tablespoons sugar
   Salt and white pepper, to taste

Exchanges
Milk: 0.0
Vegetable: 2.0
Fruit: 0.0
Bread: 0.5
Meat: 0.0
Fat: 0.5

1. Cook Brussels sprouts and onions in 2 inches boiling water in 2 separate covered saucepans until vegetables are crisp-tender, 8 to 10 minutes. Drain well.

2. Heat margarine in medium skillet until melted; stir in sugar. Cook over medium heat until mixture is bubbly; add vegetables and toss to coat. Season to taste with salt and white pepper.

WINE-BRAISED CABBAGE

You'll enjoy the combination of aromatic anise and caraway seeds in this cabbage dish.

4-6 servings

Vegetable cooking spray
¾ cup chopped onion
½ cup chopped green bell pepper
3 cloves garlic, minced
½ teaspoon caraway seeds, crushed
½ teaspoon anise seeds, crushed
1 medium head cabbage, thinly sliced
½ cup dry white wine, *or* canned reduced-sodium vegetable broth
½ cup canned reduced-sodium vegetable broth
2 tablespoons vegetable bacon-flavored bits
   Salt and pepper, to taste

Per Serving
Calories: 118
% Calories from fat: 10
Fat (gm): 1.5
Saturated fat (gm): 0.1
Cholesterol (mg): 0
Sodium (mg): 148
Protein (gm): 6.4
Carbohydrate (gm): 19.3
Exchanges
Milk: 0.0
Vegetable: 3.0
Fruit: 0.0
Bread: 0.5
Meat: 0.0
Fat: 0.0

1. Spray large saucepan with cooking spray; heat over medium heat until hot. Saute onion, green pepper, and garlic 3 to 4 minutes; add caraway and anise seeds and cook 1 minute longer.

2. Add cabbage, wine, and vegetable broth to saucepan; heat to boiling. Reduce heat and simmer, covered, until cabbage is wilted, about 5 minutes. Simmer, uncovered, until cabbage is tender, 10 to 15 minutes. Stir in bacon-flavored bits. Season to taste with salt and pepper.

GINGERED CARROT PUREE

 Cooked until thick, this intensely flavored puree owes its creamy texture to the additions of Idaho potato and half-and-half.

6 servings (about ½ cup each)

2 pounds carrots, sliced

1 medium Idaho potato (8 ounces), peeled, cubed

1-2 tablespoons margarine, *or* butter

¼-½ cup fat-free half-and-half, *or* fat-free milk, heated

¼-½ teaspoon ground ginger

Salt and white pepper, to taste

Ground nutmeg, as garnish

1 tablespoon chopped candied ginger

Per Serving
Calories: 122
% Calories from fat: 16
Fat (gm): 2.2
Saturated fat (gm): 0.4
Cholesterol (mg): 0
Sodium (mg): 132
Protein (gm): 2.4
Carbohydrate (gm): 24.1
Exchanges
Milk: 0.0
Vegetable: 2.5
Fruit: 0.0
Bread: 0.5
Meat: 0.0
Fat: 0.5

1. Cook carrots and potato in 2 inches simmering water until very tender, about 15 minutes; drain.

2. Process carrots and potato in food processor until smooth; transfer mixture to large skillet. Cook mixture over medium to medium-low heat, stirring frequently, until mixture is the consistency of thick mashed potatoes (do not brown), about 15 minutes.

3. Beat margarine and enough half-and-half into carrot mixture to make creamy consistency. Stir in ground ginger; season to taste with salt and white pepper. Spoon into serving bowl; sprinkle with nutmeg and candied ginger.

ORANGE-GLAZED BABY CARROTS

The sweet-spiced orange glaze is also delicious over sweet potatoes or beets.

4 servings

1	package (16 ounces) baby carrots
¾	cup orange juice
½	cup packed light brown sugar
2	tablespoons cornstarch
½	teaspoon ground cinnamon
¼	teaspoon ground allspice
¼	teaspoon ground mace
1	tablespoon margarine, *or* butter
	Salt and white pepper, to taste
1	tablespoon finely chopped parsley

Per Serving
Calories: 191
% Calories from fat: 13
Fat (gm): 3
Saturated fat (gm): 0.6
Cholesterol (mg): 0
Sodium (mg): 145
Protein (gm): 1.8
Carbohydrate (gm): 42.4
Exchanges
Milk: 0.0
Vegetable: 2.0
Fruit: 2.0
Bread: 0.0
Meat: 0.0
Fat: 0.5

1. Cook carrots in 1 inch simmering water in covered medium saucepan until crisp-tender, 10 to 12 minutes; drain.

2. Mix orange juice, brown sugar, cornstarch, and spices in small saucepan; heat to boiling. Boil, stirring constantly, until thickened, about 1 minute. Stir in margarine until melted; season to taste with salt and pepper.

3. Arrange carrots in serving bowl; pour orange sauce over and sprinkle with parsley.

CARROT PUDDING

This recipe makes an excellent side dish although it is served as a dessert in Mexico.

8 servings

2	pounds carrots, cooked, mashed
½	cup sugar
1½	tablespoons margarine, *or* butter, melted
½	cup all-purpose flour
1½	teaspoons baking powder
½	teaspoon ground cinnamon
½	teaspoon salt

Per Serving
Calories: 191
% Calories from fat: 11
Fat (gm): 2.5
Saturated fat (gm): 0.5
Cholesterol (mg): 1.3
Sodium (mg): 339
Protein (gm): 6.3
Carbohydrate (gm): 37.9

½ cup raisins

½ cup (2 ounces) shredded fat-free Cheddar cheese

4 egg whites, beaten to stiff peaks

¼ cup sliced almonds (optional)

Exchanges
Milk: 0.0
Vegetable: 1.5
Fruit: 0.5
Bread: 1.5
Meat: 0.0
Fat: 0.5

1. Mix carrots, sugar, and margarine in medium bowl. Combine flour, baking powder, cinnamon, and salt and add to carrot mixture. Mix in raisins and cheese; fold in beaten egg whites. Spoon mixture into 8-inch-square baking pan; sprinkle with almonds.

2. Bake at 475 degrees 10 minutes; reduce temperature to 350 degrees and bake until browned and set, 50 to 60 minutes. Cut into squares.

CAULIFLOWER WITH CREAMY CHEESE SAUCE

Try making the cheese sauce with other reduced-fat cheeses, such as Havarti, Gruyère, American, or blue, for new flavor variations.

6 servings

1 whole large cauliflower (2 pounds)
Creamy Cheese Sauce (recipe follows)
Paprika, as garnish
Parsley, finely chopped, as garnish

Per Serving
Calories: 102
% Calories from fat: 31
Fat (gm): 3.6
Saturated fat (gm): 1.5
Cholesterol (mg): 5.7
Sodium (mg): 194
Protein (gm): 6.5
Carbohydrate (gm): 11.7
Exchanges
Milk: 0.0
Vegetable: 2.0
Fruit: 0.0
Bread: 0.0
Meat: 0.5
Fat: 0.5

1. Place cauliflower in saucepan with 2 inches of water; heat to boiling. Reduce heat and simmer, covered, until cauliflower is tender, 20 to 25 minutes.

2. Place cauliflower on serving plate; spoon Creamy Cheese Sauce over and sprinkle with paprika and parsley.

Creamy Cheese Sauce

(makes about 1¼ cups)

     2 tablespoons minced onion
     1 tablespoon margarine, *or* butter
     2 tablespoons flour
     1 cup fat-free milk
     ½ cup (2 ounces) cubed reduced-fat pas-
       teurized processed cheese product, *or*
       shredded reduced-fat Cheddar cheese
     ¼ teaspoon dry mustard
   2-3 drops red pepper sauce
       Salt and white pepper, to taste

1. Saute onion in margarine in small saucepan 2 to 3 minutes. Stir in flour; cook over medium-low heat, stirring constantly, 1 minute. Whisk in milk and heat to boiling; boil, whisking constantly, until thickened, about 1 minute.

2. Reduce heat to low. Add cheese, dry mustard, and pepper sauce, whisking until cheese is melted. Season to taste with salt and white pepper.

CAULIFLOWER-FENNEL PUREE

Cooking a pureed vegetable mixture until thick intensifies the flavor of the vegetable.

6 servings (about ½ cup each)

     2 pounds cauliflower, cut into pieces
     1 medium Idaho potato (8 ounces),
       peeled, cubed
1-1½ teaspoons fennel, *or* caraway seeds,
       crushed
   1-2 tablespoons margarine, *or* butter
 ¼-½ cup fat-free half-and-half, *or* fat-free
       milk, heated
       Salt and white pepper, to taste
       Parsley, finely chopped, as garnish

Per Serving
Calories: 90
% Calories from fat: 21
Fat (gm): 2.2
Saturated fat (gm): 0.4
Cholesterol (mg): 0
Sodium (mg): 43
Protein (gm): 3.7
Carbohydrate (gm): 14.8
Exchanges
Milk: 0.0
Vegetable: 1.5
Fruit: 0.0
Bread: 0.5
Meat: 0.0
Fat: 0.5

1. Cook cauliflower and potato in 2 inches simmering water, covered, until very tender, 10 to 12 minutes. Drain.

2. Process vegetables in food processor until smooth; transfer mixture to large skillet and stir in fennel seeds. Cook mixture over medium to medium-low heat, stirring frequently, until mixture is the consistency of very thick mashed potatoes (do not brown), about 15 minutes.

3. Beat margarine and enough half-and-half into mixture to make creamy consistency. Season to taste with salt and white pepper. Spoon into serving bowl; sprinkle with parsley.

CELERY ROOT PUREE

Sometimes the flavor of celery root can be slightly bitter, which a few pinches of sugar will correct.

6 servings (about ½ cup each)

2 pounds peeled celery root, cubed
1 medium Idaho potato, peeled, cubed
¼ cup cubed sweet onion
1-2 tablespoons margarine, *or* butter
¼-½ cup fat-free half-and-half, heated
Nutmeg, ground, to taste
Salt and white pepper, to taste
Parsley, finely chopped, as garnish

Per Serving
Calories: 115
% Calories from fat: 17
Fat (gm): 2.4
Saturated fat (gm): 0.4
Cholesterol (mg): 0
Sodium (mg): 185
Protein (gm): 3.3
Carbohydrate (gm): 22.4
Exchanges
Milk: 0.0
Vegetable: 0.0
Fruit: 0.0
Bread: 1.5
Meat: 0.0
Fat: 0.5

1. Cook celery root, potato, and onion in 2 inches simmering water, covered, until very tender, about 15 minutes; drain.

2. Process vegetables in food processor until smooth; transfer mixture to large skillet. Cook mixture over medium to medium-low heat, stirring frequently, until mixture is the consistency of thick mashed potatoes (do not brown), about 15 minutes.

3. Beat margarine and enough half-and-half into mixture to make creamy consistency. Stir in nutmeg, salt, and white pepper to taste. Spoon into serving bowl; sprinkle with parsley.

SUCCOTASH

Fat-free half-and-half contributes richness without the fat calories in this old-fashioned favorite. Fresh crisp-tender cooked or frozen green beans can be substituted for the baby lima beans.

4 servings (about ¾ cup each)

1 small onion, chopped
1 tablespoon margarine, *or* butter
2 cups frozen baby lima beans
2 cups fresh, *or* frozen, whole kernel corn
½ cup canned reduced-sodium vegetable broth
½ cup fat-free half-and-half
Salt and pepper, to taste

Per Serving
Calories: 146
% Calories from fat: 13
Fat (gm): 2.1
Saturated fat (gm): 0.4
Cholesterol (mg): 0
Sodium (mg): 69
Protein (gm): 6.6
Carbohydrate (gm): 26.7
Exchanges
Milk: 0.0
Vegetable: 0.0
Fruit: 0.0
Bread: 1.5
Meat: 0.0
Fat: 0.5

1. Saute onion in margarine in medium saucepan until tender, 5 to 8 minutes. Stir in lima beans, corn, broth, and half-and-half; heat to boiling. Reduce heat and simmer, covered, until vegetables are tender, about 5 minutes. Season to taste with salt and pepper.

FRIED CORN

Lightly flavored with mesquite, and wonderfully delicious! Use fresh corn, if you can.

4 servings (about ¾ cup each)

Vegetable cooking spray
3 cups fresh corn cut from the cob (3-4 ears), *or* frozen whole-kernel corn, thawed
1 green bell pepper, sliced
1 red bell pepper, sliced
3 cloves garlic, minced
¼ cup water
Salt and pepper, to taste

Per Serving
Calories: 127
% Calories from fat: 2
Fat (gm): 0.3
Saturated fat (gm): 0
Cholesterol (mg): 0
Sodium (mg): 7
Protein (gm): 4.9
Carbohydrate (gm): 31.6
Exchanges
Milk: 0.0
Vegetable: 1.0
Fruit: 0.0
Bread: 1.5
Meat: 0.0
Fat: 0.0

1. Spray large skillet with cooking spray; heat over medium heat until hot. Add corn, bell peppers, and garlic to skillet; spray generously with cooking spray. Cook, covered, over medium-low heat until vegetables are very tender and browned, about 25 minutes, stirring occasionally.

2. Stir water into skillet; cook, covered, over low heat until water is absorbed, about 15 minutes. Season to taste with salt and pepper.

TEX-MEX SWEET CORN

Flavors of the Southwest make corn-on-the-cob better than ever!

6 servings

2-3 tablespoons margarine, *or* butter
½ teaspoon chili powder
½ teaspoon ground cumin
¼ teaspoon dried oregano leaves
¼ teaspoon garlic powder
⅛ teaspoon cayenne pepper
6 ears fresh corn, cooked, warm
Salt, to taste
Cilantro, finely chopped, as garnish

Per Serving
Calories: 153
% Calories from fat: 25
Fat (gm): 4.8
Saturated fat (gm): 0.9
Cholesterol (mg): 0
Sodium (mg): 52
Protein (gm): 4.1
Carbohydrate (gm): 28.5
Exchanges
Milk: 0.0
Vegetable: 0.0
Fruit: 0.0
Bread: 1.5
Meat: 0.0
Fat: 1.0

1. Melt margarine in small saucepan; stir in chili powder, cumin, oregano, garlic powder, and cayenne pepper.

2. Brush margarine mixture on corn; sprinkle lightly with salt and cilantro.

FRESH CORN PUDDING

Best made with fresh corn cut from the cob, but frozen corn will substitute nicely.

4-6 servings

Vegetable cooking spray
2 tablespoons plain, unseasoned bread-crumbs

Per Serving
Calories: 172
% Calories from fat: 22
Fat (gm): 4.3
Saturated fat (gm): 1
Cholesterol (mg): 53.3
Sodium (mg): 466
Protein (gm): 9.2
Carbohydrate (gm): 25.9

2 cups fresh whole-kernel corn, *or* frozen, whole kernel corn, thawed

½ cup fat-free half-and-half, *or* fat-free milk

½ cup fat-free sour cream

1 tablespoon margarine, *or* butter, melted

1 egg

2 egg whites

½ teaspoon baking powder

½ teaspoon dried savory leaves

¼ teaspoon dried thyme leaves

½ teaspoon salt

⅛ teaspoon cayenne pepper

¼ teaspoon black pepper

Exchanges
Milk: 0.0
Vegetable: 0.0
Fruit: 0.0
Bread: 1.5
Meat: 1.0
Fat: 0.0

1. Spray 1-quart soufflé dish lightly with cooking spray; coat with breadcrumbs.

2. Process remaining ingredients in blender or food processor until mixture is coarsely chopped. Pour into soufflé dish. Bake at 350 degrees until puffed and set in the center, 45 to 50 minutes. Serve immediately.

SEASONED EGGPLANT SAUTE

4 servings

Olive oil cooking spray

1 large eggplant (about 1½ pounds), unpeeled, cut into scant ¾-inch cubes

1 cup chopped onions

½ cup chopped red bell pepper

6 cloves garlic, minced

1 teaspoon dried oregano leaves

½ teaspoon dried thyme leaves

¼ teaspoon crushed red pepper

½ cup canned reduced-sodium vegetable broth

Salt and pepper, to taste

2 tablespoons finely chopped parsley

Per Serving
Calories: 83
% Calories from fat: 6
Fat (gm): 0.6
Saturated fat (gm): 0.1
Cholesterol (mg): 0
Sodium (mg): 18
Protein (gm): 2.8
Carbohydrate (gm): 19.3
Exchanges
Milk: 0.0
Vegetable: 3.0
Fruit: 0.0
Bread: 0.0
Meat: 0.0
Fat: 0.0

1. Spray large skillet with cooking spray; heat over medium heat until hot. Saute vegetables until crisp-tender, 8 to 10 minutes; add dried herbs and red pepper and cook 1 to 2 minutes longer.

2. Add vegetable broth to skillet and heat to boiling; reduce heat and simmer, covered, until vegetables are tender and broth absorbed, 15 to 20 minutes. Season to taste with salt and pepper; stir in parsley.

EGGPLANT AND TOMATO CASSEROLE

 Assemble the casserole up to a day in advance, then bake before serving— perfect potluck fare!

8 servings

1 large eggplant (2 pounds), peeled, cut into 1-inch cubes
½ cup seasoned dry breadcrumbs
⅓ cup chopped onion
3 cloves garlic, minced
1½ teaspoons dried oregano leaves, divided
½ teaspoon dried basil leaves
¼ teaspoon dried thyme leaves
   Salt and pepper, to taste
2 eggs
3 medium tomatoes, sliced
¼ cup grated fat-free Parmesan cheese

Per Serving
Calories: 98
% Calories from fat: 16
Fat (gm): 1.9
Saturated fat (gm): 0.5
Cholesterol (mg): 53.3
Sodium (mg): 245
Protein (gm): 5.1
Carbohydrate (gm): 16.9
Exchanges
Milk: 0.0
Vegetable: 2.0
Fruit: 0.0
Bread: 0.5
Meat: 0.0
Fat: 0.5

1. Cook eggplant in 2 inches simmering water in covered medium saucepan until tender, 5 to 8 minutes. Drain well. Mash eggplant with fork; mix in breadcrumbs, onion, garlic, 1 teaspoon oregano, basil, and thyme. Season to taste with salt and pepper. Mix in eggs.

2. Spoon eggplant mixture into baking dish, 11 x 7 inches. Arrange tomatoes in rows over eggplant; sprinkle with cheese and remaining ½ teaspoon oregano.

3. Bake, uncovered, at 350 degrees until casserole is hot and tomatoes tender, about 20 minutes.

FENNEL PUREE

We've included a number of puree recipes, as we love the creamy textures and intense flavors gained from this cooking method.

6 servings (about ½ cup each)

2 pounds fennel bulbs, cubed
1 large Idaho potato (12 ounces), peeled, cubed
¼ cup cubed sweet onion
1-2 tablespoons margarine, *or* butter
¼-½ cup fat-free half-and-half, *or* fat-free milk, heated
Salt and white pepper, to taste
Paprika, as garnish

Per Serving
Calories: 117
% Calories from fat: 16
Fat (gm): 2.3
Saturated fat (gm): 0.4
Cholesterol (mg): 0
Sodium (mg): 113
Protein (gm): 3.2
Carbohydrate (gm): 22.9
Exchanges
Milk: 0.0
Vegetable: 0.0
Fruit: 0.0
Bread: 1.5
Meat: 0.0
Fat: 0.5

1. Cook fennel, potato, and onion in 2 inches simmering water, covered, until very tender, about 15 minutes; drain.

2. Process vegetables in food processor until smooth; transfer mixture to large skillet. Cook mixture over medium to medium-low heat, stirring frequently, until mixture is the consistency of thick mashed potatoes (do not brown), about 15 minutes.

3. Beat margarine and enough half-and-half into fennel mixture to make creamy consistency. Season to taste with salt and white pepper. Spoon into serving bowl; sprinkle with paprika.

LEMON-SPIKED GARLIC GREENS

Kale, collard, turnip, or beet greens make excellent choices for this quick and easy healthful dish.

4 servings

Vegetable cooking spray
¼ cup finely chopped onion
¼ cup finely chopped red bell pepper
4 cloves garlic, minced
1½ pounds greens, washed, stems removed, coarsely chopped
⅓ cup water

Per Serving
Calories: 58
% Calories from fat: 23
Fat (gm): 1.7
Saturated fat (gm): 0.4
Cholesterol (mg): 53.3
Sodium (mg): 43
Protein (gm): 5.9
Carbohydrate (gm): 7

Exchanges
Milk: 0.0
Vegetable: 2.0
Fruit: 0.0
Bread: 0.0
Meat: 0.0
Fat: 0.0

1-2 tablespoons lemon juice
    Salt and pepper, to taste
  1 hard-cooked egg, chopped

1. Spray large saucepan with cooking spray; heat over medium heat until hot. Saute onion, bell pepper, and garlic until tender, 3 to 4 minutes.

2. Add greens and water to saucepan; heat to boiling. Reduce heat and simmer, covered, until greens are wilted and tender, about 5 to 8 minutes, adding more water if necessary. Season to taste with lemon juice, salt, and pepper.

3. Spoon greens into serving bowl; sprinkle with egg.

BRAISED KALE

Packed with vitamins and minerals, kale and other dark leafy greens offer a nutritional bonus. Try other greens such as beet, turnip, or mustard with this recipe too.

4 servings

Per Serving
Calories: 109
% Calories from fat: 27
Fat (gm): 3.5
Saturated fat (gm): 0.5
Cholesterol (mg): 0
Sodium (mg): 232
Protein (gm): 5.7
Carbohydrate (gm): 15.8
Exchanges
Milk: 0.0
Vegetable: 3.0
Fruit: 0.0
Bread: 0.0
Meat: 0.0
Fat: 0.5

  1 medium leek (white part only), *or* 6 green onions and tops, sliced
2-3 teaspoons olive oil
  1 pound kale, rinsed, torn into pieces
  ½ cup water
½-1 teaspoon vegetable bouillon crystals
  ½ cup fat-free sour cream
  1 teaspoon Dijon-style mustard
1-2 tablespoons vegetable bacon-flavored bits
    Salt and pepper, to taste

1. Saute leek in oil in large saucepan until tender, 3 to 4 minutes. Add kale, water, and bouillon crystals; heat to boiling. Reduce heat and simmer, covered, until kale is wilted and tender, about 5 minutes. Drain and discard any excess liquid.

2. Stir sour cream, mustard, and bacon-flavored bits, into kale mixture; cook over low heat 2 to 3 minutes. Season to taste with salt and pepper.

SMASHED POTATOES AND GREENS

 The potatoes are not peeled, giving this dish a rustic character.

4 servings

Vegetable cooking spray
¼ cup finely chopped onion
3 cloves garlic, minced
1½ cups thinly sliced greens (kale, mustard, *or* turnip greens)
¼ cup water
3 medium Idaho potatoes, cubed, cooked
¼ cup fat-free sour cream
2-4 tablespoons fat-free milk
1-2 tablespoons margarine, *or* butter, softened
Salt and pepper, to taste
Paprika, as garnish

Per Serving
Calories: 141
% Calories from fat: 19
Fat (gm): 3.1
Saturated fat (gm): 0.6
Cholesterol (mg): 0.1
Sodium (mg): 60
Protein (gm): 3.8
Carbohydrate (gm): 25.4
Exchanges
Milk: 0.0
Vegetable: 2.0
Fruit: 0.0
Bread: 1.0
Meat: 0.0
Fat: 0.5

1. Spray small skillet with cooking spray; heat over medium heat until hot. Saute onion and garlic until tender, 3 to 4 minutes.

2. Add greens and water to skillet; heat to boiling. Cook, covered, until greens are tender about 5 minutes. Cook, uncovered, until water has evaporated and greens are almost dry.

3. Mash potatoes in bowl; mix in sour cream, milk, and margarine. Stir into greens mixture and cook over low heat until hot through. Season to taste with salt and pepper. Spoon potatoes into serving bowl; sprinkle lightly with paprika.

SAUTEED LEEKS AND PEPPERS

A colorful side dish that will brighten any meal!

6 servings

Olive oil cooking spray

3 medium leeks (white parts only), cut into ½-inch slices

1 small yellow bell pepper, sliced

1 small red bell pepper, sliced

1 small green bell pepper, sliced

½ teaspoon bouquet garni

Salt and pepper, to taste

Per Serving
Calories: 63
% Calories from fat: 5
Fat (gm): 0.4
Saturated fat (gm): 0
Cholesterol (mg): 0
Sodium (mg): 13
Protein (gm): 2
Carbohydrate (gm): 14.6
Exchanges
Milk: 0.0
Vegetable: 2.5
Fruit: 0.0
Bread: 0.0
Meat: 0.0
Fat: 0.0

1. Spray large skillet with cooking spray; heat over medium heat until hot. Add vegetables to skillet; spray with cooking spray. Cook, covered, over medium heat until vegetables are wilted, 5 to 8 minutes.

2. Stir in bouquet garni and cook, uncovered, over medium to medium-low heat until vegetables are tender. Season to taste with salt and pepper.

MUSHROOMS WITH SOUR CREAM

Cooking the mushrooms very slowly until deeply browned intensifies their flavor. Especially delicious served with pierogi, ravioli, or grilled eggplant slices!

4 servings

Vegetable cooking spray

12 ounces shiitake, *or* cremini, mushrooms

¼ cup finely chopped onion

1 teaspoon minced garlic

¼ cup dry white wine, *or* reduced-sodium vegetable broth

¼ teaspoon dried thyme leaves

½ cup fat-free sour cream

Salt and cayenne pepper, to taste

Per Serving
Calories: 80
% Calories from fat: 2
Fat (gm): 0.2
Saturated fat (gm): 0.1
Cholesterol (mg): 0
Sodium (mg): 24
Protein (gm): 3.5
Carbohydrate (gm): 16.5
Exchanges
Milk: 0.0
Vegetable: 2.0
Fruit: 0.0
Bread: 0.5
Meat: 0.0
Fat: 0.0

1. Spray large skillet with cooking spray; heat over medium heat until hot. Slice mushrooms, discarding tough stems. Add mushrooms, onion, and garlic to skillet; spray with cooking spray and saute 3 to 4 minutes.

2. Add wine and thyme to skillet; heat to boiling. Reduce heat and simmer, covered, until mushrooms are very tender, 8 to 10 minutes. Cook, uncovered, on low heat until mushrooms are dry and well browned, 20 to 25 minutes. Stir in sour cream; season to taste with salt and pepper.

GULFPORT OKRA

A Cajun recipe I remember fondly from the Gulfport Diner. Select small okra for best flavor and tenderness.

6 servings

1½ pounds fresh, *or* frozen, thawed, okra
     Vegetable cooking spray
     Garlic powder, to taste
     Salt and pepper, to taste

Per Serving
Calories: 37
% Calories from fat: 4
Fat (gm): 0.2
Saturated fat (gm): 0.1
Cholesterol (mg): 0
Sodium (mg): 6
Protein (gm): 2.1
Carbohydrate (gm): 8.2
Exchanges
Milk: 0.0
Vegetable: 1.5
Fruit: 0.0
Bread: 0.0
Meat: 0.0
Fat: 0.0

1. Trim stems without cutting into tops of okra. Cook okra in boiling water 1 to 2 minutes; drain well.

2. Spray large skillet with cooking spray; heat over medium heat until hot. Add okra and spray with cooking spray; cook over medium heat until well browned, almost black, stirring occasionally. Sprinkle okra generously with garlic powder; season to taste with salt and pepper.

QUARTET OF ONIONS

 Cooked slowly until caramelized, the onion mixture is scented with a combination of mint and sage.

6 servings

Vegetable cooking spray

2 pounds sweet onions, sliced

1 small leek (white part only), thinly sliced

4 ounces shallots, finely chopped

½ cup sliced green onions and tops

½ cup Canned Vegetable Stock (see p. 63), *or* canned reduced-sodium vegetable broth

1-1½ teaspoons dried mint leaves

¼ teaspoon dried sage leaves

Salt and white pepper, to taste

Per Serving
Calories: 90
% Calories from fat: 4
Fat (gm): 0.4
Saturated fat (gm): 0.1
Cholesterol (mg): 0
Sodium (mg): 16
Protein (gm): 2.7
Carbohydrate (gm): 20.1
Exchanges
Milk: 0.0
Vegetable: 4.0
Fruit: 0.0
Bread: 0.0
Meat: 0.0
Fat: 0.0

1. Spray large skillet with cooking spray; heat over medium heat until hot. Saute onions, leek, shallots, and green onions 3 to 4 minutes, stirring frequently. Stir in stock and heat to boiling; reduce heat and simmer, covered, 5 minutes.

2. Stir in herbs and cook, uncovered, over medium-low heat until onion mixture is golden, about 15 minutes. Season to taste with salt and white pepper.

FRUIT-STUFFED VIDALIA ONIONS

 The onions can be poached and filled with fruit up to 1 day in advance; then bake until hot through and tender, 30 to 35 minutes.

4 servings

2 large Vidalia onions, cut crosswise into halves

½ cup water

½ cup dry white wine, *or* water

6 whole peppercorns

4 whole allspice

1 teaspoon mustard seeds

Per Serving
Calories: 142
% Calories from fat: 4
Fat (gm): 0.6
Saturated fat (gm): 0.1
Cholesterol (mg): 0
Sodium (mg): 7
Protein (gm): 1.9
Carbohydrate (gm): 30.5

2 bay leaves

Salt, to taste

Vegetable cooking spray

1 small apple, unpeeled, cored, finely chopped

¼ cup chopped dried fruit

¼ cup golden raisins

2-3 teaspoons sugar

Exchanges
Milk: 0.0
Vegetable: 2.0
Fruit: 1.5
Bread: 0.0
Meat: 0.0
Fat: 0.0

1. Cut small slices off bottoms of onion halves so that onions can stand securely. Remove centers of onions, leaving scant ¾-inch shells; chop onion centers and reserve.

2. Stand onions in medium skillet; add water, wine, peppercorns, allspice, mustard seeds, and bay leaves; heat to boiling. Reduce heat and simmer, covered, until just crisp-tender, about 10 minutes. Remove onions with slotted spoon and transfer to baking pan; sprinkle lightly with salt. Reserve ¼ cup cooking liquid.

3. Spray small skillet with cooking spray; heat over medium heat until hot. Saute reserved onion centers and apple until tender, about 5 minutes. Stir in reserved ¼ cup cooking liquid, dried fruit, raisins, and sugar; cook over medium-low heat until liquid is absorbed. Spoon mixture into onion halves.

4. Bake, covered, at 375 degrees until onions are tender, 20 to 30 minutes.

BRAISED PARSNIPS AND WINTER VEGETABLES

 Idaho or sweet potatoes, winter squash, or Brussels sprouts would be flavorful additions to this colorful vegetable side dish.

6 servings

Olive oil cooking spray

¼ cup minced onion

2 teaspoons minced garlic

2 medium parsnips, peeled, cubed

2 medium carrots, sliced

1 cup julienne-sliced celery root, *or* celery

1 cup shredded red, *or* green, cabbage

Per Serving
Calories: 92
% Calories from fat: 3
Fat (gm): 0.3
Saturated fat (gm): 0.1
Cholesterol (mg): 0
Sodium (mg): 47
Protein (gm): 1.5
Carbohydrate (gm): 19.3

½ cup dry red wine, *or* canned reduced-
    sodium vegetable broth
2 tablespoons light brown sugar
1 teaspoon balsamic, *or* red wine, vinegar
1 teaspoon dried sage leaves
½ teaspoon dried thyme leaves
    Salt and pepper, to taste

Exchanges
Milk: 0.0
Vegetable: 2.0
Fruit: 0.0
Bread: 0.5
Meat: 0.0
Fat: 0.0

1. Spray large skillet with cooking spray; heat over medium heat until hot. Saute onion and garlic 2 to 3 minutes; add parsnips, carrots, celery root, and cabbage and saute until beginning to brown, 4 to 5 minutes.

2. Add remaining ingredients, except salt and pepper, to skillet. Heat to boiling; reduce heat and simmer, covered, until vegetables are tender, 8 to 10 minutes. Season to taste with salt and pepper.

TINY PEAS AND ONIONS

 Mint and dill offer refreshing flavor and are often used together in Mediterranean dishes.

6 servings

1 package (8 ounces) frozen tiny peas
½ package (16-ounce size) frozen small
    whole onions
¼ cup water
2-3 teaspoons margarine, *or* butter
¼-½ teaspoon dried mint leaves
¼-½ teaspoon dried dill weed
    Salt and pepper, to taste

Per Serving
Calories: 63
% Calories from fat: 20
Fat (gm): 1.4
Saturated fat (gm): 0.3
Cholesterol (mg): 0
Sodium (mg): 57
Protein (gm): 2.5
Carbohydrate (gm): 10.4
Exchanges
Milk: 0.0
Vegetable: 0.0
Fruit: 0.0
Bread: 1.0
Meat: 0.0
Fat: 0.0

1. Heat peas, onions, and water to boiling in medium saucepan; reduce heat and simmer until vegetables are tender, 8 to 10 minutes. Drain. Add margarine and herbs to vegetables, stirring until margarine is melted. Season to taste with salt and pepper.

PEPERONATA

Peperonata is Italian-inspired. Sweet bell peppers and onions are slowly cooked until tender and creamy.

8 servings

Olive oil cooking spray
2 cups sliced onions
1 cup sliced green bell pepper
1 cup sliced red bell pepper
6 cloves garlic, minced
¼ cup water
Salt and pepper, to taste

Per Serving
Calories: 36
% Calories from fat: 5
Fat (gm): 0.2
Saturated fat (gm): 0
Cholesterol (mg): 0
Sodium (mg): 2
Protein (gm): 1.3
Carbohydrate (gm): 8.2
Exchanges
Milk: 0.0
Vegetable: 2.0
Fruit: 0.0
Bread: 0.0
Meat: 0.0
Fat: 0.0

1. Spray medium skillet with cooking spray; heat over medium heat until hot. Add onions, bell peppers, and garlic to skillet; cook over medium heat 5 minutes, stirring occasionally.

2. Add water to skillet; cook, covered, over medium-low to low heat until vegetables are very tender and creamy, 20 to 25 minutes, stirring occasionally. Season to taste with salt and pepper.

REAL MASHED POTATOES

Just like grandma used to make! For a country-style variation, leave potatoes unpeeled.

6 servings (about ⅔ cup each)

2 pounds Idaho potatoes, peeled, quartered, cooked until tender
½ cup fat-free sour cream
¼ cup fat-free milk, hot
2 tablespoons margarine, *or* butter
Salt and pepper, to taste

Per Serving
Calories: 165
% Calories from fat: 21
Fat (gm): 3.9
Saturated fat (gm): 0.8
Cholesterol (mg): 0.2
Sodium (mg): 70
Protein (gm): 4.1
Carbohydrate (gm): 29.6
Exchanges
Milk: 0.0
Vegetable: 0.0
Fruit: 0.0
Bread: 2.0
Meat: 0.0
Fat: 0.5

1. Mash potatoes, or beat until smooth, in medium bowl, adding sour cream, milk, and margarine. Season to taste with salt and pepper.

 Variations: **Garlic Mashed Potatoes**—Cook 10 peeled cloves of garlic with the potatoes. Follow recipe above, mashing garlic with potatoes.

 Horseradish Mashed Potatoes—Make Real or Garlic Mashed Potatoes, beating in 2 teaspoons horseradish.

 Potato Pancakes—Make any of the mashed potato recipes above; refrigerate until chilled. Mix in 2 egg whites (or ¼ cup real egg product), 4 chopped green onions and tops, and ¼ cup grated fat-free Parmesan cheese (optional). Form mixture into 8 patties, using about ½ cup mixture for each. Coat patties in flour, dip in beaten egg white, and coat with plain dry breadcrumbs. Cook over medium-high heat in lightly greased large skillet until browned, 3 to 5 minutes on each side.

POTATOES GRATIN

 These potatoes are so rich and creamy you'll never believe they were made without heavy cream!

8 servings (about ½ cup each)

2	tablespoons margarine, *or* butter
3	tablespoons flour
1¾	cups fat-free milk
2	ounces light pasteurized processed cheese product, cubed
½	cup (2 ounces) shredded reduced-fat Cheddar cheese
	Salt and pepper, to taste
2	pounds Idaho potatoes, peeled, cut into scant ¼-inch slices
¼	cup very thinly sliced onion
	Nutmeg, ground, to taste

Per Serving
Calories: 202
% Calories from fat: 23
Fat (gm): 5.1
Saturated fat (gm): 1.7
Cholesterol (mg): 8.5
Sodium (mg): 259
Protein (gm): 7.6
Carbohydrate (gm): 31.7
Exchanges
Milk: 0.0
Vegetable: 0.0
Fruit: 0.0
Bread: 2.0
Meat: 0.5
Fat: 0.5

1. Melt margarine in medium saucepan; stir in flour and cook over medium heat, stirring constantly, 2 minutes. Whisk in milk and heat to boiling; boil, stirring constantly, until thickened. Remove from heat; add cheeses, stirring until melted. Season to taste with salt and pepper.

2. Layer ⅓ of the potatoes and onion in bottom of 2-quart casserole; sprinkle lightly with salt, pepper, and nutmeg. Spoon ⅔ cup sauce over. Repeat layers 2 times, using remaining ingredients.

3. Bake, covered, at 350 degrees for 45 minutes; uncover and bake until potatoes are fork-tender and browned, 20 to 30 minutes more.

 Variations: **Scalloped Potatoes**—Make white sauce as above, increasing margarine to 3 tablespoons, flour to ¼ cup, and milk to 2¼ cups; delete cheeses. Assemble and bake as directed.

TWICE-BAKED POTATOES WITH CHEESE

 These stuffed bakers are always a favorite! The potatoes can be prepared and refrigerated 24 hours in advance; then bake 5 to 10 minutes longer than indicated in recipe.

4 servings

  2 large Idaho potatoes (8 ounces each)
  ¼ cup fat-free sour cream
  ¼ cup fat-free milk
  ¾ cup (3 ounces) shredded reduced-fat sharp, *or* mild, Cheddar cheese, divided
  Salt and pepper, to taste
  Paprika, as garnish

Per Serving
Calories: 177
% Calories from fat: 16
Fat (gm): 3.2
Saturated fat (gm): 1.6
Cholesterol (mg): 11.6
Sodium (mg): 314
Protein (gm): 8.4
Carbohydrate (gm): 29.2
Exchanges
Milk: 0.0
Vegetable: 0.0
Fruit: 0.0
Bread: 2.0
Meat: 0.5
Fat: 0.0

1. Pierce potatoes with a fork and bake at 400 degrees until tender, about 1 hour. Cut into halves; let cool enough to handle.

2. Scoop out inside of potatoes, being careful to leave shells intact. Mash warm potatoes, or beat until smooth, in medium bowl, adding sour cream, milk, and ½ cup of cheese. Season to taste with salt and pepper.

3. Spoon potato mixture into potato shells; sprinkle with remaining ¼ cup cheese and paprika. Bake at 400 degrees until hot through, 15 to 20 minutes.

VEGGIE-STUFFED BAKERS

The potatoes are oven-baked for a crispy skin. The potatoes can be made through step 3 and refrigerated a day in advance; then increase baking time to 30 to 40 minutes.

6 servings

3 large Idaho potatoes (8-10 ounces each)
Vegetable cooking spray
1 cup chopped onion
½ cup fresh, *or* frozen, whole-kernel corn
1 medium red bell pepper, chopped
4 cloves garlic, minced
⅓ cup fat-free sour cream, *or* plain yogurt
¾ cup (3 ounces) shredded fat-free Cheddar cheese, divided
Salt and pepper, to taste
1 cup broccoli florets, cooked until crisp-tender

Per Serving
Calories: 160
% Calories from fat: 2
Fat (gm): 0.3
Saturated fat (gm): 0
Cholesterol (mg): 0
Sodium (mg): 119
Protein (gm): 9
Carbohydrate (gm): 32.4
Exchanges
Milk: 0.0
Vegetable: 1.0
Fruit: 0.0
Bread: 1.5
Meat: 0.5
Fat: 0.0

1. Grease potatoes lightly and bake at 400 degrees until tender, 45 to 60 minutes; let stand until cool enough to handle. Cut potatoes lengthwise into halves; scoop out inside of potatoes, leaving shells intact.

2. Spray medium skillet with cooking spray; heat over medium heat until hot. Saute onion, corn, bell pepper, and garlic until tender, about 5 minutes.

3. Mash potatoes, adding sour cream and half the Cheddar cheese. Mix in sauteed vegetables; season to taste with salt and pepper. Spoon mixture into potato shells; arrange broccoli on top and sprinkle with remaining cheese.

4. Arrange potatoes in baking pan; bake, uncovered, at 350 degrees until hot through, 20 to 30 minutes.

CRISPY FRENCH "FRIES"

Golden brown, delicious, and crisp, these potatoes look and taste like they have been deep-fried: the secret is salting the raw potatoes!

4-6 servings

1 pound Idaho potatoes, unpeeled
2 teaspoons salt
  Vegetable cooking spray
  Salt and pepper, to taste

Per Serving
Calories: 166
% Calories from fat: 1
Fat (gm): 0.2
Saturated fat (gm): 0
Cholesterol (mg): 0
Sodium (mg): 12
Protein (gm): 3.5
Carbohydrate (gm): 38.6
Exchanges
Milk: 0.0
Vegetable: 0.0
Fruit: 0.0
Bread: 2.5
Meat: 0.0
Fat: 0.0

1. Cut potatoes into "fries" 3 to 4 inches long and a scant ½ inch wide. Sprinkle lightly with 2 teaspoons salt and let stand 10 minutes. Rinse potatoes in cold water and dry well on paper toweling.

2. Spray non-stick jelly roll pan with cooking spray. Arrange potatoes in single layer on pan; spray generously with cooking spray, tossing to coat all sides. Sprinkle potatoes lightly with salt and pepper.

3. Bake at 350 degrees until potatoes are golden brown and crisp, 40 to 45 minutes, turning halfway through cooking time.

Note: Potatoes can be held in a 200-degree oven for up to 1 hour.

Variations: **Parmesan "Fries"**—Follow recipe, sprinkling potatoes lightly with grated fat-free Parmesan cheese before baking.

Steak Fries—Cut potatoes into wedges 4 inches long and 1 inch wide. Follow recipe as above, baking until golden brown and crisp, 1 to 1¼ hours.

POTATOES WITH POBLANO CHILIES

In this recipe, roasted poblano chilies are combined with potatoes for a hearty side dish. Serve with a fried egg and salsa for brunch.

4 servings (about ⅔ cup each)

4 medium poblano chilies
   Vegetable cooking spray
1 medium onion, sliced
1 pound Idaho potatoes, unpeeled, cooked, cut into ½-inch cubes
   Salt and pepper, to taste

Per Serving
Calories: 147
% Calories from fat: 2
Fat (gm): 0.3
Saturated fat (gm): 0.1
Cholesterol (mg): 0
Sodium (mg): 11
Protein (gm): 3.7
Carbohydrate (gm): 34
Exchanges
Milk: 0.0
Vegetable: 1.0
Fruit: 0.0
Bread: 1.5
Meat: 0.0
Fat: 0.0

1. Cut chilies into halves; discard stems, seeds, and veins. Place chilies, skin sides up, on broiler pan; broil 6 inches from heat source until skin is blackened and blistered. Place chilies in plastic bag or paper toweling 5 minutes; peel off skin and discard. Cut chilies into strips.

2. Spray large skillet with cooking spray; heat over medium heat until hot. Saute onion 2 to 3 minutes; add chilies and potatoes. Cook over medium heat until onion is tender and potatoes browned, 5 to 8 minutes. Season to taste with salt and pepper.

CANDIED YAMS

Whether called yams or sweet potatoes in your family, the sweet goodness of this dish is the same! If marshmallows are a must, add them 10 minutes before the end of baking time.

8-10 servings

⅓ cup packed light brown sugar
2 tablespoons light corn syrup
1 tablespoon flour
1 tablespoon margarine, *or* butter

Per Serving
Calories: 176
% Calories from fat: 8
Fat (gm): 1.5
Saturated fat (gm): 0.3
Cholesterol (mg): 0
Sodium (mg): 63
Protein (gm): 1.5
Carbohydrate (gm): 39.5

1 can (40 ounces) cut sweet potatoes in syrup, drained, sliced

Exchanges
Milk: 0.0
Vegetable: 0.0
Fruit: 0.0
Bread: 2.5
Meat: 0.0
Fat: 0.0

1. Combine brown sugar, corn syrup, flour, and margarine in small saucepan; heat just to boiling, stirring constantly, and remove from heat.

2. Layer sweet potatoes in 10 x 6-inch baking dish, spooning glaze between each layer and over the top. Bake, uncovered, at 350 degrees until hot, 25 to 30 minutes.

Note: Two pounds fresh sweet potatoes can be substituted for the canned. Peel and slice potatoes. Cook, covered, in medium saucepan in 2 to 3 inches of simmering water until fork-tender, about 10 minutes. Drain well, cool slightly, and proceed with recipe.

ORANGE-LIME SWEET POTATOES

Sweet potatoes are gently sauced with citrus juices; use freshly squeezed juices for best flavor.

4 servings (about ⅔ cup each)

Vegetable cooking spray
1 cup chopped onion
1 teaspoon minced garlic
1 pound sweet potatoes, peeled, cut into 1-inch pieces
1 cup orange juice
¼ cup lime juice
Salt and pepper, to taste

Per Serving
Calories: 143
% Calories from fat: 3
Fat (gm): 0.5
Saturated fat (gm): 0.1
Cholesterol (mg): 0
Sodium (mg): 14
Protein (gm): 2.6
Carbohydrate (gm): 33.5
Exchanges
Milk: 0.0
Vegetable: 0.0
Fruit: 0.5
Bread: 1.5
Meat: 0.0
Fat: 0.0

1. Spray medium skillet with cooking spray; heat over medium heat until hot. Saute onion and garlic 3 to 4 minutes.

2. Add sweet potatoes and juices to skillet; heat to boiling. Reduce heat and simmer, covered, until potatoes are tender, about 10 minutes. Cook, uncovered, until sauce is thickened, 8 to 10 minutes. Season to taste with salt and pepper.

CREAMED SPINACH

For convenience, use packaged salad spinach that has been prewashed.

4 servings

2 packages (10 ounces each) spinach, stems trimmed

¼ cup finely chopped onion

2 teaspoons margarine, *or* butter

2 tablespoons flour

1 cup fat-free milk, *or* fat-free half-and-half

¼ cup fat-free sour cream

Nutmeg, ground, to taste

Salt and pepper, to taste

Per Serving
Calories: 92
% Calories from fat: 20
Fat (gm): 2.2
Saturated fat (gm): 0.5
Cholesterol (mg): 1
Sodium (mg): 145
Protein (gm): 6.6
Carbohydrate (gm): 13.3
Exchanges
Milk: 0.0
Vegetable: 2.5
Fruit: 0.0
Bread: 0.0
Meat: 0.0
Fat: 0.5

1. Rinse spinach and place in large saucepan with water clinging to leaves. Cook, covered, over medium-high heat until spinach is wilted, 3 to 4 minutes. Drain excess liquid.

2. Saute onion in margarine in small saucepan until tender, 3 to 5 minutes. Stir in flour; cook over medium-low heat 1 minute, stirring constantly. Whisk in milk; heat to boiling. Boil, whisking constantly, until thickened, about 1 minute. Remove from heat and stir in sour cream.

3. Pour sauce over spinach and mix lightly; season to taste with nutmeg, salt, and pepper.

Variation: **Spinach au Gratin**—Prepare recipe through step 2. Reserve ¼ cup sauce; mix spinach and remaining sauce and spoon into a small casserole. Spread reserved ¼ cup sauce over spinach; sprinkle with ¼ cup (1 ounce) grated fat-free Parmesan cheese or fat-free Cheddar cheese. Bake, uncovered, at 375 degrees until cheese is melted, 5 to 8 minutes.

APPLE-PECAN ACORN SQUASH

Fruit and maple flavors complement sweet, baked winter squash.

4 servings

1	large acorn squash, cut into quarters, seeded
½	cup coarsely chopped mixed dried fruit
1	small sweet apple, cored, coarsely chopped
¼-½	cup coarsely chopped, toasted pecans
½	teaspoon ground cinnamon
⅛	teaspoon ground nutmeg
⅛	teaspoon ground mace
¼-½	cup maple syrup

Per Serving
Calories: 187
% Calories from fat: 1
Fat (gm): 0.3
Saturated fat (gm): 0.1
Cholesterol (mg): 0
Sodium (mg): 39
Protein (gm): 1.7
Carbohydrate (gm): 47
Exchanges
Milk: 0.0
Vegetable: 0.0
Fruit: 2.0
Bread: 1.0
Meat: 0.0
Fat: 0.0

1. Place squash quarters, cut sides up, in baking pan; add ½ inch hot water. Bake, covered, at 400 degrees until squash is fork-tender, about 30 minutes.

2. Combine dried fruit, apple, pecans, and spices; spoon into squash. Drizzle maple syrup over fruit and squash. Bake, loosely covered, until apples are tender, about 10 minutes longer.

ZUCCHINI FANS PROVENÇAL

Zucchini are thinly sliced, then spread out to form "fans."

4 servings

2	medium sweet onions, thinly sliced, divided
6	cloves garlic, minced, divided
4	small zucchini, cut lengthwise into halves
3	medium tomatoes, thinly sliced
½	cup dry white wine, *or* canned reduced-sodium vegetable broth
	Olive oil cooking spray
	Salt and pepper, to taste
¾	teaspoon dried basil leaves
½	teaspoon dried oregano leaves

Per Serving
Calories: 89
% Calories from fat: 6
Fat (gm): 0.6
Saturated fat (gm): 0.1
Cholesterol (mg): 0
Sodium (mg): 16
Protein (gm): 3.4
Carbohydrate (gm): 15.3
Exchanges
Milk: 0.0
Vegetable: 3.0
Fruit: 0.0
Bread: 0.0
Meat: 0.0
Fat: 0.0

½ teaspoon dried marjoram leaves
¼ teaspoon dried thyme leaves

1. Separate onions into rings; arrange half the onions and garlic in bottom of 11 x 7-inch baking pan.

2. Cut zucchini halves lengthwise into scant ¼-inch slices, cutting to, but not through, small ends. Alternate zucchini and tomato slices in rows over onions, spreading zucchini slices into "fans." Arrange remaining onions and garlic on top.

3. Heat wine to simmering in small saucepan; pour over vegetables. Spray top of vegetables with cooking spray; sprinkle lightly with salt and pepper and combined herbs.

4. Bake, covered, at 350 degrees until zucchini is crisp-tender, about 25 minutes.

ZUCCHINI FROM PUEBLO

If the Mexican white cheese, "queso blanco," is not available, farmer's cheese can be readily substituted. Purchased roasted peppers can be used.

6 servings (about ½ cup each)

Vegetable cooking spray
1 cup chopped onion
2 pounds zucchini, cut diagonally into ¼-inch slices
4 roasted red bell peppers, cut into strips
½ cup Basic Vegetable Stock (see p. 58), *or* canned reduced-sodium vegetable broth
½-1 teaspoon ground cumin
½ cup fat-free milk
Salt and pepper, to taste
2 tablespoons crumbled Mexican white cheese, *or* farmer's cheese

Per Serving
Calories: 62
% Calories from fat: 14
Fat (gm): 1
Saturated fat (gm): 0.1
Cholesterol (mg): 2.6
Sodium (mg): 32
Protein (gm): 2.9
Carbohydrate (gm): 11.8
Exchanges
Milk: 0.0
Vegetable: 2.0
Fruit: 0.0
Bread: 0.0
Meat: 0.0
Fat: 0.0

1. Spray large skillet with cooking spray; heat over medium heat until hot. Saute onion until tender, 5 to 8 minutes. Stir in zucchini, roasted peppers, stock, and cumin. Heat to boiling. Reduce heat and simmer, covered, just until zucchini is crisp-tender, 5 to 8 minutes.

2. Add milk; cook until hot, 1 to 2 minutes. Season to taste with salt and pepper. Spoon zucchini and broth into serving bowl; sprinkle with cheese.

SPAGHETTI SQUASH PARMESAN

The delicate flavor of the squash is complemented with the combination of Italian seasoning and Parmesan cheese.

4 servings

1 spaghetti squash (2½-3 pounds), cut lengthwise into halves, seeded
2 tablespoons sliced green onions and tops
1 teaspoon minced garlic
1-2 tablespoons margarine, *or* butter
¼ cup canned reduced-sodium vegetable broth
1 teaspoon dried Italian seasoning
⅓ cup fat-free Parmesan cheese
Salt and pepper, to taste

Per Serving
Calories: 99
% Calories from fat: 29
Fat (gm): 3.6
Saturated fat (gm): 0.7
Cholesterol (mg): 0
Sodium (mg): 102
Protein (gm): 5.1
Carbohydrate (gm): 14.3
Exchanges
Milk: 0.0
Vegetable: 2.0
Fruit: 0.0
Bread: 0.0
Meat: 0.5
Fat: 0.5

1. Place squash, cut sides down, in baking pan; add ½ inch hot water. Bake, covered, at 400 degrees until squash is fork-tender, 30 to 40 minutes. Remove squash from pan and turn cut sides up. Fluff strands of squash with tines of fork.

2. Saute green onions and garlic in margarine in small saucepan until tender, 3 to 4 minutes. Stir in broth and Italian seasoning; heat to boiling. Spoon half the mixture into each squash half and toss; sprinkle with Parmesan cheese and toss. Season to taste with salt and pepper.

CHAYOTE WITH PUMPKIN SEEDS

The pumpkin seeds ("pepitas") will begin to pop and jump in the skillet, signaling that they are toasted! Chayote squash have the crisp texture of an apple when raw and can be sauteed or steamed until crisp-tender.

4 servings

Vegetable cooking spray
4 teaspoons pumpkin seeds
½ cup finely chopped onion
2 cloves garlic, minced
2 chayote squash, peeled, pitted, cut into ½-inch cubes
Salt and pepper, to taste

Per Serving
Calories: 35
% Calories from fat: 16
Fat (gm): 0.7
Saturated fat (gm): 0.1
Cholesterol (mg): 0
Sodium (mg): 2
Protein (gm): 1.1
Carbohydrate (gm): 7
Exchanges
Milk: 0.0
Vegetable: 1.5
Fruit: 0.0
Bread: 0.0
Meat: 0.0
Fat: 0.0

1. Spray small skillet with vegetable cooking spray; heat over medium heat until hot. Cook pumpkin seeds over medium heat until they are toasted and begin to pop, 3 to 5 minutes. Reserve.

2. Spray large skillet with vegetable cooking spray; heat over medium heat until hot. Saute onion and garlic until tender, 3 to 5 minutes. Add squash and cook over medium heat until squash is crisp-tender, about 20 minutes, stirring occasionally. Season to taste with salt and pepper. Spoon squash into serving bowl; sprinkle with reserved pumpkin seeds.

SAUTEED SUMMER SQUASH WITH SNOW PEAS

The vegetables are best when crisp-tender, so don't overcook! Zucchini or chayote squash may also be used in the recipe.

4 servings

Vegetable cooking spray
2 green onions and tops, sliced
2 cloves garlic, minced
2 medium yellow squash, sliced
2 ounces snow peas, strings trimmed

Per Serving
Calories: 27
% Calories from fat: 10
Fat (gm): 0.3
Saturated fat (gm): 0.1
Cholesterol (mg): 0
Sodium (mg): 2
Protein (gm): 1.4
Carbohydrate (gm): 5.7

2 tablespoons finely chopped lovage, *or* tarragon

Salt and white pepper, to taste

Exchanges
Milk: 0.0
Vegetable: 1.0
Fruit: 0.0
Bread: 0.0
Meat: 0.0
Fat: 0.0

1. Spray a large skillet with cooking spray; heat over medium heat until hot. Saute green onions and garlic 2 to 3 minutes.

2. Add squash, snow peas, and lovage to skillet; spray with cooking spray and cook over medium heat until vegetables are crisp-tender, about 5 minutes. Season to taste with salt and pepper.

TOMATO PUDDING

Dry stuffing cubes can be substituted for the croutons. Two cups coarsely chopped fresh tomatoes can be substituted for the canned tomatoes; simmer until tomatoes wilt and release juices, 5 to 8 minutes.

4 servings

Vegetable cooking spray
½ cup thinly sliced celery
½ cup chopped onion
½ cup chopped green bell pepper
1 can (16 ounces) reduced-sodium whole tomatoes, undrained, coarsely chopped
½ teaspoon celery seeds
½ teaspoon dried marjoram leaves
1 tablespoon light brown sugar
Salt and pepper, to taste
1½ cups (½ recipe) Sourdough Croutons (see p. 677)

Per Serving
Calories: 85
% Calories from fat: 9
Fat (gm): 0.9
Saturated fat (gm): 0.1
Cholesterol (mg): 0
Sodium (mg): 88
Protein (gm): 2.6
Carbohydrate (gm): 17.9
Exchanges
Milk: 0.0
Vegetable: 2.0
Fruit: 0.0
Bread: 0.5
Meat: 0.0
Fat: 0.0

1. Spray medium skillet with cooking spray; heat over medium heat until hot. Saute celery, onion, and bell pepper until tender, about 8 minutes. Stir in tomatoes, celery seed, marjoram, and brown sugar and heat to boiling. Reduce heat and simmer, covered, 2 to 3 minutes. Pour mixture into 1-quart soufflé dish or casserole; season to taste with salt and pepper.

2. Stir croutons into tomato mixture, leaving some of the croutons on the top. Bake at 425 degrees until hot through, about 20 minutes. Serve hot.

HERBED TOMATO HALVES

Select ripe, yet firm tomatoes, and vary the herbs to complement the main dish you're serving them with.

4 servings

4	medium tomatoes, halved
3	tablespoons grated fat-free Parmesan cheese
1	tablespoon dry unseasoned breadcrumbs
½	teaspoon dried basil leaves
½	teaspoon dried marjoram leaves
½	teaspoon dried thyme leaves
⅛-¼	teaspoon garlic powder
2-3	pinches pepper

Per Serving
Calories: 45
% Calories from fat: 9
Fat (gm): 0.5
Saturated fat (gm): 0.1
Cholesterol (mg): 0
Sodium (mg): 60
Protein (gm): 2.8
Carbohydrate (gm): 8.8
Exchanges
Milk: 0.0
Vegetable: 2.0
Fruit: 0.0
Bread: 0.0
Meat: 0.0
Fat: 0.0

1. Place tomatoes in baking pan. Combine remaining ingredients and sprinkle over tomatoes.

2. Bake at 375 degrees until tomatoes are hot and topping is browned, 15 to 20 minutes.

FRIED TOMATOES

Either green or red tomatoes can be used in this recipe—do try both!

4 servings

	Vegetable cooking spray
4	medium green, *or* red, tomatoes, sliced ¼ inch thick
¼	cup all-purpose flour
	Salt and pepper, to taste

Per Serving
Calories: 58
% Calories from fat: 5
Fat (gm): 0.3
Saturated fat (gm): 0
Cholesterol (mg): 0
Sodium (mg): 16
Protein (gm): 2.3
Carbohydrate (gm): 12.2
Exchanges
Milk: 0.0
Vegetable: 1.0
Fruit: 0.0
Bread: 0.5
Meat: 0.0
Fat: 0.0

1. Spray large skillet with cooking spray; heat over medium heat until hot. Coat tomato slices lightly with flour; cook over medium heat until browned, 2 to 3 minutes on each side. Sprinkle lightly with salt and pepper.

Variations: **Sugar-Glazed Fried Tomatoes**—Cook tomatoes as above, but do not coat with flour. After tomatoes are browned, sprinkle lightly with sugar and cook until caramelized, about 1 minute on each side. Do not season with salt and pepper.

Cornmeal-Fried Tomatoes—Cook tomatoes as above, substituting yellow cornmeal for the flour.

GREENS-STUFFED BAKED TOMATOES

We've used turnip greens, but any other flavorful greens, such as kale, mustard greens, or spinach, may be substituted.

6 servings

6 medium tomatoes

10 ounces fresh, *or* frozen, turnip greens, cooked, coarsely chopped

½ teaspoon dried chervil leaves

½ teaspoon dried marjoram leaves

Salt and pepper, to taste

1 tablespoon grated fat-free Parmesan cheese

1 tablespoon dry unseasoned bread-crumbs

Per Serving
Calories: 42
% Calories from fat: 11
Fat (gm): 0.6
Saturated fat (gm): 0.1
Cholesterol (mg): 0
Sodium (mg): 42
Protein (gm): 2.1
Carbohydrate (gm): 9
Exchanges
Milk: 0.0
Vegetable: 2.0
Fruit: 0.0
Bread: 0.0
Meat: 0.0
Fat: 0.0

1. Cut thin slice from tops of tomatoes; scoop pulp from tomatoes, discarding seeds. Chop tomato pulp and mix with turnip greens and herbs; season to taste with salt and pepper.

2. Fill tomatoes with turnip greens mixture and place in baking pan. Sprinkle tops of tomatoes with combined cheese and bread-crumbs. Bake at 350 degrees until tender, about 20 minutes.

THIRTEEN

Salads

AND

Dressings

SPINACH AND MELON SALAD

 An unusual salad, with melon adding color and flavor contrasts.

6 side-dish servings (about 1½ cups each)

8 cups torn spinach
1 cup watermelon balls
1 cup honeydew balls
1 cup cantaloupe balls
⅓ cup thinly sliced cucumber
⅓ cup thinly sliced red onion
   Honey Dressing (recipe follows)

Per Serving
Calories: 81
% Calories from fat: 27
Fat (gm): 2.8
Saturated fat (gm): 0.3
Cholesterol (mg): 0
Sodium (mg): 65
Protein (gm): 2.9
Carbohydrate (gm): 13.7
Exchanges
Milk: 0.0
Vegetable: 1.0
Fruit: 0.5
Bread: 0.0
Meat: 0.0
Fat: 0.5

1. Combine spinach, melon balls, cucumber, and onion in salad bowl; drizzle with Honey Dressing and toss.

Honey Dressing

 (makes ¼ cup)

1-2 tablespoons honey
  1 tablespoon red wine vinegar
  1 tablespoon olive oil
1-2 tablespoons orange juice
1-2 teaspoons lime juice
  ½ teaspoon dried tarragon leaves
2-3 dashes salt
2-3 dashes pepper

1. Mix all ingredients; refrigerate until ready to use. Mix again before using.

WILTED SPINACH SALAD

A delicious favorite that includes vegetable bacon-flavored bits for traditional flavor.

4 side-dish servings

1 package (10 ounces) salad spinach, rinsed, dried

4 green onions and tops, sliced

2 tablespoons vegetable bacon-flavored bits

1 cup fat-free bottled French dressing, *or* sweet-sour salad dressing

2 hard-cooked egg whites, chopped

Salt and pepper, to taste

Per Serving
Calories: 119
% Calories from fat: 9
Fat (gm): 1
Saturated fat (gm): 0.2
Cholesterol (mg): 0
Sodium (mg): 646
Protein (gm): 4.8
Carbohydrate (gm): 19.8
Exchanges
Milk: 0.0
Vegetable: 0.0
Fruit: 0.0
Bread: 1.5
Meat: 0.0
Fat: 0.0

1. Combine spinach, onions, and bacon-flavored bits in salad bowl. Heat French dressing to boiling in small saucepan; immediately pour over salad and toss. Sprinkle egg whites over salad. Season to taste with salt and pepper.

CAESAR SALAD

Traditional anchovies have not been used in our version of Caesar Salad. The egg product used in the dressing is pasteurized, thus safe to eat without cooking.

4 side-dish servings (about 1½ cups each)

4 thick slices French, *or* Italian, bread

1 clove garlic, cut in half

6 cups torn romaine lettuce

2 tablespoons lemon juice

2 tablespoons real egg product

1 tablespoon olive oil

½ teaspoon Worcestershire sauce

2 tablespoons grated fat-free Parmesan cheese

⅛ teaspoon dry mustard

Dash red pepper sauce

Freshly ground pepper, to taste

Per Serving
Calories: 127
% Calories from fat: 30
Fat (gm): 4.4
Saturated fat (gm): 0.6
Cholesterol (mg): 0
Sodium (mg): 200
Protein (gm): 5.3
Carbohydrate (gm): 17.1
Exchanges
Milk: 0.0
Vegetable: 1.0
Fruit: 0.0
Bread: 1.0
Meat: 0.0
Fat: 0.5

1. Rub both sides of bread slices with cut sides of garlic; mince remaining garlic and reserve. Cut bread into ½ to ¾-inch cubes. Bake on jelly roll pan at 425 degrees until croutons are toasted, about 5 minutes.

2. Place lettuce in salad bowl. Beat together lemon juice, reserved garlic, and remaining ingredients, except croutons and pepper. Pour dressing over lettuce and toss; season to taste with pepper. Add croutons and toss again.

12-LAYER SALAD

A new look at an old favorite! This attractive salad may be conveniently assembled, topped with dressing, refrigerated up to a day in advance, and then tossed before serving.

6 main-dish servings (about 2 cups each)

2   cups sliced spinach leaves
2   medium carrots
1½   cups sliced celery
2   cups thinly sliced red cabbage
2   cups small broccoli florets
2   cups chopped iceberg lettuce
1   medium yellow bell pepper, sliced
1   medium tomato, sliced
1½   cups cut green beans, cooked until crisp-tender, cooled
1   cup finely chopped parsley, divided
1   can (15 ounces) dark red kidney beans, rinsed, drained
1   medium red onion, thinly sliced
    Garlic Dressing (recipe follows)
3   hard-boiled eggs, cut into wedges

Per Serving
Calories: 214
% Calories from fat: 14
Fat (gm): 3.7
Saturated fat (gm): 0.9
Cholesterol (mg): 106.5
Sodium (mg): 637
Protein (gm): 14.8
Carbohydrate (gm): 37.8
Exchanges
Milk: 0.0
Vegetable: 3.0
Fruit: 0.0
Bread: 1.0
Meat: 1.0
Fat: 0.0

1. Layer spinach, carrots, celery, cabbage, broccoli, lettuce, pepper, tomato, green beans, ½ cup parsley, kidney beans, and onion in 2½-quart glass salad bowl. Spread dressing over top and sprinkle with remaining ½ cup parsley. Serve immediately or refrigerate up to 24 hours.

2. Before serving, toss salad and place egg wedges on top.

Garlic Dressing

(makes about 1½ cups)

- ¾ cup fat-free mayonnaise, *or* salad dressing
- ¾ cup fat-free sour cream
- 4 cloves garlic, minced
- 1 teaspoon dried basil
- 1 teaspoon dried oregano
- ¾ teaspoon dried tarragon

1. Combine all ingredients; refrigerate until ready to use.

FREEZER COLESLAW

A colorful slaw that is easy to make and convenient to have on hand.

8 side-dish servings (about ¾ cup each)

- 1½ pounds red cabbage, thinly sliced
- 2 carrots, shredded or thinly sliced
- 1 red bell pepper, chopped
- 1 small onion, thinly sliced
- Salt, to taste
- 1 cup water
- ¾ cup cider vinegar
- 1⅔ cups sugar
- 1 teaspoon caraway seeds

Per Serving
Calories: 205
% Calories from fat: 1
Fat (gm): 0.4
Saturated fat (gm): 0
Cholesterol (mg): 0
Sodium (mg): 20
Protein (gm): 1.9
Carbohydrate (gm): 53.1
Exchanges
Milk: 0.0
Vegetable: 2.0
Fruit: 0.0
Bread: 2.0
Meat: 0.0
Fat: 0.0

1. Layer cabbage, carrots, bell pepper, and onion in colander, sprinkling each layer lightly with salt; let stand 1 hour. Rinse well under cold running water; drain.

2. Heat remaining ingredients to boiling in small saucepan; reduce heat and simmer, uncovered, 5 minutes. Cool to room temperature.

3. Mix vegetables and sugar syrup in large bowl. Pack coleslaw in freezer containers or bags and freeze. To serve, thaw in refrigerator or at room temperature.

PASTA COLESLAW

The addition of pasta updates a traditional cabbage slaw.

4 side-dish servings (about 1 cup each)

1½ cups (4 ounces) fusilli (spirals), *or* farfalle (bow ties), cooked, room temperature
1 cup thinly sliced green cabbage
1 medium tomato, chopped
1 medium green bell pepper, chopped
¼ cup sliced celery
Creamy Dressing (recipe follows)

Per Serving
Calories: 139
% Calories from fat: 8
Fat (gm): 1.2
Saturated fat (gm): 0.3
Cholesterol (mg): 0.9
Sodium (mg): 156
Protein (gm): 5.4
Carbohydrate (gm): 27.3
Exchanges
Milk: 0.0
Vegetable: 1.0
Fruit: 0.0
Bread: 1.5
Meat: 0.0
Fat: 0.0

1. Combine pasta, cabbage, tomato, bell pepper, and celery in bowl; stir in Creamy Dressing.

Creamy Dressing

(makes about ½ cup)

¼ cup fat-free mayonnaise, *or* salad dressing
¼ cup low-fat plain yogurt
1 tablespoon lemon juice
2 cloves garlic, minced
½ teaspoon dried tarragon leaves
¼ teaspoon salt (optional)
¼ teaspoon pepper

1. Mix all ingredients. Refrigerate until ready to use.

BROCCOLI SALAD

Serve this hearty salad on a bed of salad greens, spinach, thinly sliced red cabbage, or in scooped-out tomato halves. The blue cheese can be deleted from the dressing, if desired.

6 side-dish servings (about 1¼ cups each)

4½ cups sliced broccoli florets and stalks

1½ cups sliced zucchini

1½ cups chopped green bell peppers

1½ cups sliced mushrooms

12 cherry tomatoes, cut into halves

3 green onions, green and white parts, sliced

2 tablespoons dark raisins

Sour Cream-Mayonnaise Dressing (recipe follows)

Leaf lettuce, as garnish

Per Serving
Calories: 100
% Calories from fat: 13
Fat (gm): 1.7
Saturated fat (gm): 0.8
Cholesterol (mg): 2.7
Sodium (mg): 257
Protein (gm): 5.8
Carbohydrate (gm): 18.8
Exchanges
Milk: 0.0
Vegetable: 4.0
Fruit: 0.0
Bread: 0.0
Meat: 0.0
Fat: 0.0

1. Combine all ingredients in salad bowl; toss with dressing. Serve in lettuce-lined salad bowls.

Sour Cream-Mayonnaise Dressing

(makes about 1¼ cups)

⅓ cup fat-free sour cream

⅓ cup fat-free mayonnaise

3 cloves garlic, minced

3 tablespoons fat-free milk

3 tablespoons crumbled blue cheese

1. Mix all ingredients. Refrigerate until ready to use.

CARROT-RAISIN SALAD

Comfort salad at its best! A small can of drained pineapple tidbits can be added to the salad, if you like.

6 side-dish servings (about ⅓ cup each)

2½ cups shredded carrot (about 3 large)
¾ cup chopped celery
⅓ cup raisins
⅓ cup coarsely chopped walnuts
¾ cup fat-free mayonnaise
½ teaspoon Dijon-style mustard
1-2 teaspoons sugar
⅛ teaspoon salt
Lettuce leaves, as garnish

Per Serving
Calories: 115
% Calories from fat: 30
Fat (gm): 4.1
Saturated fat (gm): 0.3
Cholesterol (mg): 0
Sodium (mg): 460
Protein (gm): 2.6
Carbohydrate (gm): 19.2
Exchanges
Milk: 0.0
Vegetable: 2.0
Fruit: 0.5
Bread: 0.0
Meat: 0.0
Fat: 1.0

1. Combine carrot, celery, raisins, and walnuts in medium bowl. Add remaining ingredients, except lettuce, stirring until blended. Serve on lettuce-lined salad plates.

GERMAN POTATO SALAD

Tart and tangy in flavor, this salad is best served warm from the skillet.

6 side-dish servings (about ⅔ cup each)

Vegetable cooking spray
1 cup chopped onion
1 tablespoon flour
½ cup reduced-sodium canned vegetable broth
1¼ cups cider vinegar
1 tablespoon sugar
½ teaspoon celery seeds
1½ pounds potatoes, peeled, sliced, and cooked, warm
Salt and pepper, to taste
2 tablespoons vegetable bacon-flavored bits

Per Serving
Calories: 125
% Calories from fat: 5
Fat (gm): 0.7
Saturated fat (gm): 0.1
Cholesterol (mg): 0
Sodium (mg): 69.3
Protein (gm): 3
Carbohydrate (gm): 30.7
Exchanges
Milk: 0.0
Vegetable: 0.0
Fruit: 0.0
Bread: 2.0
Meat: 0.0
Fat: 0.0

2 tablespoons finely chopped parsley
leaves

1. Spray medium skillet generously with cooking spray; add onion to skillet and saute until tender and browned, about 5 minutes. Stir in flour; cook 1 minute.

2. Add broth, vinegar, sugar, and celery seeds to onion mixture and heat to boiling; boil, stirring constantly, until thickened, 1 to 2 minutes. Pour mixture over warm potatoes in bowl and toss. Season to taste with salt and pepper; sprinkle with "bacon" bits and parsley. Serve warm.

CREAMY POTATO SALAD

Thanks to fat-free mayonnaise, it's possible to include hard-cooked egg in this salad. For the creamiest salad, toss the potatoes with the dressing while they're still slightly warm.

10 side-dish servings (about ⅔ cup each)

1½ pounds russet potatoes, peeled, cut into
¾-inch cubes

1 cup sliced celery

½ cup thinly sliced green onions and tops

¼ cup chopped green bell pepper

¼ cup chopped red bell pepper

½ cup chopped sweet pickle, *or* pickle
relish

2 hard-cooked eggs, chopped

2-3 tablespoons vegetable bacon-flavored
bits

1 cup fat-free mayonnaise

½ cup fat-free sour cream

2 tablespoons cider vinegar

1 tablespoon prepared mustard

½ teaspoon celery seeds
Salt and pepper, to taste

Per Serving
Calories: 119
% Calories from fat: 11
Fat (gm): 1.5
Saturated fat (gm): 0.4
Cholesterol (mg): 42.6
Sodium (mg): 464
Protein (gm): 3.9
Carbohydrate (gm): 23.4
Exchanges
Milk: 0.0
Vegetable: 0.0
Fruit: 0.0
Bread: 1.5
Meat: 0.0
Fat: 0.0

1. Cook potatoes, covered, in 2 inches simmering water until fork-tender, about 10 minutes. Drain and cool until just warm.

2. Combine potatoes, celery, green onions, green and red bell pepper, sweet pickle, eggs, and bacon flavored bits in large bowl. In small bowl, mix remaining ingredients, except salt and pepper; spoon over vegetable mixture and toss. Season to taste with salt and pepper.

CARIBBEAN POTATO SALAD

Sweet and white potatoes combine with a creamy cumin and lime mayonnaise dressing; olives provide a pungent accent.

8 side-dish servings (about ¾ cup each)

1½   pounds sweet potatoes, peeled, cut into 1 to 1½-inch pieces

1½   pounds russet potatoes, peeled, cut into 1 to 1½-inch pieces

¾   cup fat-free mayonnaise

½   cup fat-free milk

2   teaspoons lime juice

1   teaspoon ground cumin

⅛   teaspoon red cayenne pepper
    Salt, to taste

2   green onions and tops, sliced

¼   cup small pimiento-stuffed olives

Per Serving
Calories: 167
% Calories from fat: 5
Fat (gm): 1
Saturated fat (gm): 0.2
Cholesterol (mg): 0.3
Sodium (mg): 416
Protein (gm): 3.1
Carbohydrate (gm): 37.2
Exchanges
Milk: 0.0
Vegetable: 0.0
Fruit: 0.0
Bread: 2.5
Meat: 0.0
Fat: 0.0

1. Cook potatoes in simmering water in separate large saucepans until tender but not too soft. Drain and cool.

2. Mix mayonnaise, milk, lime juice, cumin, and cayenne pepper; mix gently into combined potatoes in large bowl. Season to taste with salt. Gently stir in green onions and olives. Refrigerate 2 to 3 hours to chill and for flavors to blend.

FRUIT SALAD WITH RASPBERRY YOGURT DRESSING

Use sliced, unpeeled apples and ripe pears in fall and winter months when fresh berries are not available. Serve this healthful salad with Brown Sugar Banana Bread (see p. 680).

4 servings

12 Boston lettuce leaves
1½ cups halved strawberries
1 cup blueberries
1 cup raspberries
1 medium papaya, *or* mango, peeled, sliced, *or* cubed
1 kiwi fruit, peeled, sliced
1 medium orange, peeled, cut into segments
4 slices fresh pineapple, halved
Raspberry Yogurt Dressing (recipe follows)
Poppy seeds, *or* toasted sesame seeds, as garnish

Per Serving
Calories: 257
% Calories from fat: 4
Fat (gm): 1.2
Saturated fat (gm): 0.1
Cholesterol (mg): 0
Sodium (mg): 48
Protein (gm): 5.2
Carbohydrate (gm): 60.1
Exchanges
Milk: 0.0
Vegetable: 0.0
Fruit: 4.0
Bread: 0.0
Meat: 0.0
Fat: 0.0

1. Arrange lettuce on serving plates; arrange fruit on lettuce.

2. Serve Raspberry Yogurt Dressing on the side, or drizzle it over fruit. Sprinkle fruit with poppy seeds.

Raspberry Yogurt Dressing

(makes about 1 cup)

1 cup fat-free raspberry yogurt
2 tablespoons honey
Lime juice, to taste

1. Mix yogurt and honey, adding a few drops of lime juice to taste. Refrigerate until ready to serve.

WALDORF SALAD

Using both red and green apples adds color and flavor interest. If your family enjoys this salad with miniature marshmallows, please add them!

4 side-dish servings (about ¾ cup each)

2	cups unpeeled, cored, cubed red and green apples
1	cup sliced celery
¼	cup raisins
¼	cup coarsely chopped, toasted walnuts, *or* pecans
¼	cup fat-free mayonnaise
¼	cup fat-free sour cream
2-3	teaspoons lemon juice
1-2	tablespoons honey
	Lettuce leaves, as garnish

Per Serving
Calories: 149
% Calories from fat: 26
Fat (gm): 4.7
Saturated fat (gm): 0.3
Cholesterol (mg): 0
Sodium (mg): 227
Protein (gm): 3.5
Carbohydrate (gm): 26.5
Exchanges
Milk: 0.0
Vegetable: 0.5
Fruit: 1.5
Bread: 0.0
Meat: 0.0
Fat: 1.0

1. Combine apples, celery, raisins, and walnuts in medium bowl. Mix remaining ingredients, except lettuce leaves, and stir into apple mixture. Serve on lettuce-lined plates.

SPROUTS AND VEGETABLE SALAD

Use any sprouted beans or grains you like in this salad, mixing flavors and textures.

4 side-dish servings (about 1 cup each)

1	medium tomato, chopped
1	cup broccoli florets
½	cup each: sprouted wheat berries, chick peas, and lentils (see next recipe for sprouting directions)
2	green onions and tops, sliced
	Salt and pepper, to taste
½	cup fat-free blue cheese, *or* other flavor salad dressing
	Lettuce leaves, as garnish
¼	cup (1 ounce) crumbled blue cheese

Per Serving
Calories: 129
% Calories from fat: 16
Fat (gm): 2.5
Saturated fat (gm): 1.4
Cholesterol (mg): 5.2
Sodium (mg): 452
Protein (gm): 5.7
Carbohydrate (gm): 23.5
Exchanges
Milk: 0.0
Vegetable: 1.5
Fruit: 0.0
Bread: 1.0
Meat: 0.0
Fat: 0.5

1. Combine tomato, broccoli, wheat berry sprouts, chick pea sprouts, lentil sprouts, and green onions in salad bowl; sprinkle lightly with salt and pepper. Pour dressing over salad and toss.

2. Spoon salad on lettuce-lined plates; sprinkle with blue cheese.

SPROUTED LENTIL SALAD

All kinds of dried beans and grains can be sprouted. Sprouts are delicious for salads, as garnishes on main dishes and side dishes, or just to eat as snacks. Any favorite sprouted bean or grain can be used in this salad; any fat-free or reduced-fat salad dressing can be substituted for the Tofu Aioli.

4 side-dish servings (about 1 cup each)

Sprouted Lentils (recipe follows)
1 cup torn radicchio leaves
1 cup chopped tomato
½ cup chopped cucumber
½ cup chopped yellow bell pepper
½-⅔ cup (⅓ recipe) Tofu Aioli (see p. 224)
Salt and pepper, to taste

Per Serving
Calories: 86
% Calories from fat: 18
Fat (gm): 1.9
Saturated fat (gm): 0.2
Cholesterol (mg): 0
Sodium (mg): 41
Protein (gm): 6.3
Carbohydrate (gm): 14.3
Exchanges
Milk: 0.0
Vegetable: 3.0
Fruit: 0.0
Bread: 0.0
Meat: 0.0
Fat: 0.5

1. Combine lentils and vegetables in salad bowl; spoon Tofu Aioli over and toss. Season to taste with salt and pepper.

Sprouted Lentils

(makes about 2 cups)

½ cup dried lentils
Water

1. Place lentils in quart jar; add water to cover lentils by 2 to 3 inches and soak overnight. Drain.

2. Return drained lentils to jar and cover with cheesecloth. Let stand at room temperature until lentils have sprouted, about 2 days. Rinse lentils and drain well 3 to 4 times a day until they have sprouted; return to jar and cover with cheesecloth.

3. Refrigerate sprouted lentils until ready to use. Check sprouts daily; if they appear dry, rinse and drain, then return to refrigerator.

Notes: All grains and beans can be sprouted according to the directions above, although they may require shorter or longer times to sprout. The various grains and beans will also yield different amounts.

Wheat berries—½ cup dry wheat berries yield about 1½ cups sprouted wheat berries.

Chick peas—½ cup dry chick peas yield about 1½ cups sprouted chick peas.

MANGO AND BLACK BEAN SALAD

Any tropical fruit, such as pineapple, kiwi, papaya, or star fruit can be used in this refreshing salad.

4 main-dish servings (about 1 cup each)

4	large ripe mangoes, peeled, pitted, cubed
1	cup cubed pineapple
½	medium cucumber, seeded, sliced
¼	cup finely chopped red bell pepper
4	small green onions, thinly sliced
1	can (15 ounces) black beans, rinsed, drained
	Honey-Lime Dressing (recipe follows)
	Romaine lettuce leaves, as garnish
	Mint sprigs, as garnish

Per Serving
Calories: 328
% Calories from fat: 20
Fat (gm): 8.6
Saturated fat (gm): 1.1
Cholesterol (mg): 0
Sodium (mg): 338
Protein (gm): 10.4
Carbohydrate (gm): 65.4
Exchanges
Milk: 0.0
Vegetable: 0.0
Fruit: 2.0
Bread: 2.0
Meat: 0.0
Fat: 1.5

1. Combine mangoes, pineapple, cucumber, bell pepper, green onions, and black beans in bowl; drizzle with Lime Dressing and toss gently.

2. Spoon salad mixture onto lettuce-lined plates. Garnish with mint.

Honey-Lime Dressing

(makes about ⅓ cup)

- 2 tablespoons olive oil
- 1 tablespoon honey
- 3-4 teaspoons lime juice
- 1 teaspoon grated lime rind
- 1 tablespoon tarragon wine vinegar
- 2 tablespoons water
- ½ teaspoon dried mint leaves
- Pinch salt

1. Mix all ingredients; refrigerate until ready to use. Mix again before using.

CACTUS SALAD

The tender cactus paddles, "nopales," are readily available in large supermarkets today—be sure all the thorns have been removed! If not, they can be pulled out easily with tweezers.

6 side-dish servings (about ½ cup each)

- 2 quarts water
- 1½ pounds cactus paddles, cut into ½-inch pieces
- 1 tablespoon salt
- ¼ teaspoon baking soda
- 1½ cups cherry tomato halves
- ½ cup thinly sliced red onion
- Lime Dressing (recipe follows)
- Lettuce leaves, as garnish

Per Serving
Calories: 78
% Calories from fat: 28
Fat (gm): 2.5
Saturated fat (gm): 0.3
Cholesterol (mg): 0
Sodium (mg): 131
Protein (gm): 2.4
Carbohydrate (gm): 12.5
Exchanges
Milk: 0.0
Vegetable: 2.0
Fruit: 0.0
Bread: 0.0
Meat: 0.0
Fat: 0.5

1. Heat water to boiling in large saucepan; add cactus, salt, and baking soda. Reduce heat and simmer, uncovered, until cactus is crisp-tender, about 20 minutes. Rinse well in cold water and drain thoroughly.

2. Combine cactus, tomatoes, and onion in small bowl; pour Lime Dressing over and toss. Serve on lettuce-lined plates.

Lime Dressing

(makes about ¼ cup)

    2 tablespoons lime juice
1–2 tablespoons olive, *or* canola, oil
    1 tablespoon water
    1 teaspoon cider vinegar
    2 teaspoons sugar
    ½ teaspoon dried oregano leaves

1. Combine all ingredients; refrigerate until serving time.

JICAMA SALAD

Jicama adds a marvelous crispness to salads, complementing both fruits and vegetables.

6 side-dish servings (about ⅔ cup each)

    ½ large jicama, peeled (about 12 ounces)
    ½ medium zucchini, sliced
    1 small orange, cut into segments
2–3 thin slices red onion
    Cilantro Lime Dressing (recipe follows)
    Salt and pepper, to taste
    Lettuce leaves, as garnish

Per Serving
Calories: 77
% Calories from fat: 27
Fat (gm): 2.4
Saturated fat (gm): 0.3
Cholesterol (mg): 0
Sodium (mg): 1
Protein (gm): 1.3
Carbohydrate (gm): 13.5
Exchanges
Milk: 0.0
Vegetable: 1.0
Fruit: 0.5
Bread: 0.0
Meat: 0.0
Fat: 0.5

1. Cut jicama into sticks about 1½ x ½ inches. Combine jicama, zucchini, orange, and onion in bowl. Pour Cilantro Lime Dressing over and toss; season to taste with salt and pepper.

2. Arrange lettuce leaves on salad plates; top with salad.

Cilantro Lime Dressing

(makes about ¼ cup)

    2 tablespoons lime juice
    1 tablespoon orange juice
1–2 tablespoons olive, *or* canola, oil
    2 tablespoons finely chopped cilantro
    2 teaspoons sugar

1. Combine all ingredients. Refrigerate until serving time; mix before using.

MACARONI SALAD

Fourth of July signals family picnics, which must include, of course, homemade macaroni salad! Add 1 cup halved or quartered summer-ripe cherry tomatoes for festive color.

6 side-dish servings (about ⅔ cup each)

2 cups cooked elbow macaroni
1 cup frozen baby peas, thawed
½ cup chopped onion
½ cup chopped celery
⅓ cup shredded carrot
¼ cup chopped red bell pepper
¼ cup sliced ripe, *or* pimiento-stuffed, olives
¾ cup fat-free mayonnaise
2 teaspoons prepared mustard
1 teaspoon sugar
Salt and pepper, to taste

Per Serving
Calories: 129
% Calories from fat: 9
Fat (gm): 1.3
Saturated fat (gm): 0.2
Cholesterol (mg): 0
Sodium (mg): 583
Protein (gm): 4
Carbohydrate (gm): 25.6
Exchanges
Milk: 0.0
Vegetable: 0.0
Fruit: 0.0
Bread: 1.5
Meat: 0.0
Fat: 0.0

1. Combine macaroni, peas, onion, celery, carrot, bell pepper, and olives in medium bowl. Add mayonnaise, mustard, and sugar and stir until blended. Season to taste with salt and pepper.

Note: Other pasta, such as rotini, fusilli, ziti, or shells, can be substituted for the macaroni.

MACARONI-BLUE CHEESE SALAD

A not-so-traditional macaroni salad with blue cheese pizazz!

8 side-dish servings

1 cup (4 ounces) elbow macaroni, cooked, room temperature
¾ cup chopped red bell pepper
½ cup chopped cucumber
½ cup shredded carrots

Per Serving
Calories: 82
% Calories from fat: 9
Fat (gm): 0.9
Saturated fat (gm): 0.4
Cholesterol (mg): 1.3
Sodium (mg): 159
Protein (gm): 2.6
Carbohydrate (gm): 16.3

¼ cup thinly sliced green onions and tops
Blue Cheese Dressing (recipe follows)

Exchanges
Milk: 0.0
Vegetable: 2.0
Fruit: 0.0
Bread: 0.5
Meat: 0.0
Fat: 0.0

1. Combine macaroni, bell pepper, cucumber, carrots, and green onions in bowl; stir in Blue Cheese Dressing.

Blue Cheese Dressing

(makes about ½ cup)

½ cup fat-free mayonnaise, *or* salad dressing
2 tablespoons crumbled blue cheese
1 tablespoon red wine vinegar
1 teaspoon celery seeds
½ teaspoon salt (optional)
⅛ teaspoon cayenne pepper
⅛ teaspoon black pepper

1. Mix all ingredients; refrigerate until serving time. Mix again before using.

ORZO WITH SUN-DRIED TOMATOES AND MUSHROOMS

A simple salad, but intensely flavored with sun-dried tomatoes, fresh rosemary, and sherry. If desired, the sherry can be omitted.

4 side-dish servings

2 sun-dried tomatoes
Hot water
Olive oil cooking spray
1½ cups sliced mushrooms
¼ cup thinly sliced green onions and tops
2 cloves garlic, minced
½ cup canned vegetable broth
2 tablespoons dry sherry (optional)
½ cup (4 ounces) orzo, cooked, room temperature

Per Serving
Calories: 135
% Calories from fat: 6
Fat (gm): 0.8
Saturated fat (gm): 0.1
Cholesterol (mg): 0
Sodium (mg): 218
Protein (gm): 5.1
Carbohydrate (gm): 27.2

Exchanges
Milk: 0.0
Vegetable: 0.0
Fruit: 0.0
Bread: 2.0
Meat: 0.0
Fat: 0.0

2 tablespoons finely chopped fresh
rosemary leaves, *or* 1 teaspoon dried

2 tablespoons finely chopped parsley

¼ teaspoon salt

¼ teaspoon pepper

1. Place tomatoes in small bowl; pour hot water over to cover. Let tomatoes stand until softened, about 15 minutes; drain and slice.

2. Spray large skillet with cooking spray; heat over medium heat until hot. Saute mushrooms, green onions, and garlic until mushrooms are tender, 5 to 7 minutes.

3. Add broth and sherry to skillet; heat to boiling. Reduce heat and simmer, uncovered, until liquid is reduced by half, about 5 minutes. Cool to room temperature.

4. Combine orzo and mushroom mixture in bowl; add remaining ingredients and toss.

MIXED VEGETABLES AND ORZO VINAIGRETTE

 The spice turmeric, used in the salad dressing, gives this salad its unusual yellow color. Curry powder can be used instead, imparting the same color but adding a delicate curry flavor.

8 side-dish servings

2 medium zucchini, thinly sliced

8 ounces asparagus, cut into 1½-inch pieces, steamed

1 cup frozen peas, thawed

½ cup sliced carrots, steamed

¾ cup (6 ounces) orzo, cooked
Mustard-Turmeric Vinaigrette (recipe follows)

2 cups torn lettuce leaves

4 cherry tomatoes, cut into halves

Per Serving
Calories: 142
% Calories from fat: 27
Fat (gm): 4.2
Saturated fat (gm): 0.6
Cholesterol (mg): 0
Sodium (mg): 112
Protein (gm): 5.5
Carbohydrate (gm): 20.9
Exchanges
Milk: 0.0
Vegetable: 1.0
Fruit: 0.0
Bread: 1.0
Meat: 0.0
Fat: 1.0

1. Combine zucchini, asparagus, peas, carrots, and orzo in bowl; pour Mustard-Turmeric Vinaigrette over and toss. Spoon onto lettuce-lined salad plates; garnish with tomatoes.

Mustard-Turmeric Vinaigrette

(makes about ½ cup)

¼ cup red wine vinegar
¼ teaspoon ground turmeric
2-3 tablespoons lemon juice
2 tablespoons olive, *or* canola, oil
2 teaspoons Dijon-style mustard
2 cloves garlic, minced
¼ teaspoon salt
¼ teaspoon pepper

1. Heat vinegar and turmeric in small saucepan over medium heat until turmeric is dissolved, stirring constantly, 2 to 3 minutes; cool.

2. Combine vinegar mixture and remaining ingredients; refrigerate until serving time. Mix again before using.

CHILI-DRESSED SALAD WITH RADIATORE

A fun pasta, radiatore look like the tiny radiators for which they are named! Other shaped pastas can be used, if preferred.

4 main-dish servings

Chili Dressing (recipe follows)
3 cups (8 ounces) radiatore, cooked, room temperature
1½ cups broccoflower florets
2 medium tomatoes, cut into wedges
½ cup fresh, *or* frozen, whole-kernel corn, cooked
½ medium avocado, peeled, pitted, cut into ¾-inch pieces
2 tablespoons finely chopped cilantro, *or* parsley
2 cups torn salad greens

Per Serving
Calories: 361
% Calories from fat: 30
Fat (gm): 12.3
Saturated fat (gm): 1.1
Cholesterol (mg): 0
Sodium (mg): 25
Protein (gm): 10.6
Carbohydrate (gm): 54.6
Exchanges
Milk: 0.0
Vegetable: 0.0
Fruit: 0.0
Bread: 4.0
Meat: 0.0
Fat: 2.0

1. Pour dressing over pasta in medium bowl and toss. Add remaining ingredients, toss, and spoon salad over greens on serving plate.

Chili Dressing

(makes about ¼ cup)

> 3 tablespoons lemon juice
> 2 tablespoons olive oil
> ½ teaspoon chili powder
> ¼ teaspoon crushed red pepper

1. Mix all ingredients; refrigerate until serving time. Mix again before using.

FARFALLE SALAD WITH MINTED PESTO

The Minted Pesto provides a refreshing flavor counterpoint to the pasta and vegetables.

6 main-dish servings

> Olive oil cooking spray
> ¼ cup finely chopped shallots, *or* onions
> 3 green onions and tops, sliced
> 2 cloves garlic, minced
> ½ cup dry white wine, *or* Canned Vegetable Stock (see p. 63)
> 2 tablespoons lemon juice
> Minted Pesto (see p. 731)
> 12 ounces farfalle, *or* rotini, cooked, room temperature
> ¾ cup seeded, sliced cucumber
> ½ cup sliced yellow bell pepper
> ½ cup sliced red bell pepper
> 12 cherry tomatoes, halved
> Lettuce leaves, as garnish
> Mint sprigs, as garnish

Per Serving
Calories: 316
% Calories from fat: 17
Fat (gm): 5.9
Saturated fat (gm): 0.7
Cholesterol (mg): 0
Sodium (mg): 24
Protein (gm): 9.9
Carbohydrate (gm): 53.4
Exchanges
Milk: 0.0
Vegetable: 2.0
Fruit: 0.0
Bread: 3.0
Meat: 0.0
Fat: 0.6

1. Spray medium skillet with cooking spray; heat over medium heat until hot. Saute shallots, green onions, and garlic to skillet; saute until tender, 3 to 5 minutes. Add wine and lemon juice; heat to boiling. Reduce heat and simmer, uncovered, until liquid has evaporated, 8 to 10 minutes.

2. Spoon shallot mixture and Minted Pesto over pasta and toss; add cucumber, bell peppers, tomatoes, and toss. Refrigerate to chill lightly, about 1 hour.

3. Spoon salad onto lettuce-lined plates; garnish with mint.

CURRIED PASTA SALAD

Especially delicious with flavored specialty pastas, such as curry, sesame, or tomato.

4 main-dish servings

⅓ cup chopped mango chutney

¼ cup chopped mixed dried fruit

2 tablespoons Dijon-style mustard

1 tablespoon olive oil

1 tablespoon lime juice

8 ounces curry flavor, *or* plain, fettuccine, cooked, cooled

1 cup frozen stir-fry blend vegetables, cooked, cooled to room temperature
Salt, cayenne, and black pepper, to taste

¼ cup sliced green onions and tops

2-4 tablespoons chopped cashews

Per Serving
Calories: 321
% Calories from fat: 22
Fat (gm): 8.1
Saturated fat (gm): 0.9
Cholesterol (mg): 0
Sodium (mg): 207
Protein (gm): 9.3
Carbohydrate (gm): 55.1
Exchanges
Milk: 0.0
Vegetable: 0.0
Fruit: 1.5
Bread: 2.5
Meat: 0.0
Fat: 1.5

1. Combine chutney, dried fruit, mustard, oil, and lime juice; spoon over fettuccine and toss. Add vegetables and toss; season to taste with salt and pepper.

2. Spoon pasta onto serving platter; sprinkle with green onions and cashews.

ANGEL HAIR AND GOAT'S CHEESE SALAD

Goat's cheese adds a creamy texture and piquant accent to this flavorful pasta dish.

6 main-dish servings

Vegetable cooking spray

8 ounces snow peas

8 ounces mushrooms, sliced

3 medium carrots, cut into julienne pieces

4 large plum tomatoes, sliced

2 teaspoons dried oregano leaves

1 teaspoon dried tarragon leaves

½ cup canned reduced-sodium vegetable broth

½ cup fat-free milk

2 teaspoons tomato paste

¼ teaspoon salt

¼ teaspoon pepper

3 ounces goat's cheese, *or* reduced-fat cream cheese

12 ounces capellini (angel hair), *or* thin spaghetti, cooked, warm

Per Serving
Calories: 328
% Calories from fat: 13
Fat (gm): 4.7
Saturated fat (gm): 2.3
Cholesterol (mg): 6.8
Sodium (mg): 197
Protein (gm): 13.9
Carbohydrate (gm): 58.5
Exchanges
Milk: 0.0
Vegetable: 2.0
Fruit: 0.0
Bread: 3.0
Meat: 0.0
Fat: 1.0

1. Spray large skillet with cooking spray; heat over medium heat until hot. Saute vegetables until snow peas are crisp-tender, 6 to 8 minutes. Stir in herbs; cook 1 minute.

2. Stir in broth, milk, and tomato paste; heat to boiling. Reduce heat and simmer, uncovered, until thickened to sauce consistency, about 10 minutes, stirring occasionally. Stir in salt and pepper.

3. In salad bowl, stir goat's cheese into warm pasta until melted; add vegetable mixture and toss.

GARDEN PASTA SALAD WITH CROSTINI

Serve this salad warm, or refrigerate it for several hours and serve cold. Any shaped pasta can be substituted for the shells; breadsticks can be substituted for the crostini.

6 main-dish servings (about 1 cup each)

Olive oil cooking spray
3 cups broccoli florets
2 cups cut asparagus (1-inch pieces)
1 medium yellow bell pepper, cut into 1-inch slices
3 green onions, green and white parts, sliced
¼ cup chopped red onion
½ cup frozen whole-kernel corn, thawed
1 clove garlic, minced
1½ cups small pasta shells, cooked *al dente*, warm
1 can (15 ounces) dark red kidney beans, rinsed, drained
1½ cups halved cherry tomatoes
3 tablespoons finely chopped fresh, *or* 1½ teaspoons dried, basil
1½ tablespoons olive oil, *or* canola oil
1½ tablespoons red wine vinegar
2 tablespoons crumbled feta cheese
4 slices Italian bread for crostini
1 clove garlic, cut in half

Per Serving
Calories: 319
% Calories from fat: 16
Fat (gm): 6.2
Saturated fat (gm): 1.1
Cholesterol (mg): 2.1
Sodium (mg): 297
Protein (gm): 15.5
Carbohydrate (gm): 57.4
Exchanges
Milk: 0.0
Vegetable: 2.0
Fruit: 0.0
Bread: 3.0
Meat: 0.0
Fat: 1.0

1. Spray large skillet with cooking spray; heat over medium heat until hot. Saute broccoli, asparagus, bell pepper, green and red onions, corn, and garlic until crisp-tender, about 5 minutes. Toss with warm pasta, beans, tomatoes, and basil in salad bowl.

2. Combine oil and vinegar; drizzle over salad and toss. Sprinkle with cheese.

3. To make crostini, rub both sides of bread with cut clove of garlic; broil 4 inches from heat source until golden on both sides.

TOSSED GREENS WITH RICE NOODLES AND VEGETABLES

Tender rice noodles and vegetables are bedded on gourmet greens.

4 side-dish servings

½ package (4-ounce size) rice noodles
Cold water
4 cups mesclun, *or* other mixed greens
¼ cup finely chopped mint leaves
¼ cup finely chopped cilantro leaves
Warm Lime Dressing (recipe follows)
1 cup peeled, seeded, chopped cucumber
1 cup chopped tomato
1 cup snow peas, trimmed, cooked until crisp-tender, cooled

Per Serving
Calories: 146
% Calories from fat: 10
Fat (gm): 1.7
Saturated fat (gm): 0.2
Cholesterol (mg): 0
Sodium (mg): 228
Protein (gm): 4.9
Carbohydrate (gm): 29.8
Exchanges
Milk: 0.0
Vegetable: 3.0
Fruit: 0.0
Bread: 1.0
Meat: 0.0
Fat: 0.0

1. Place noodles in large bowl; pour cold water over to cover. Let stand until noodles are separate and soft, about 5 minutes; drain. Stir noodles into 4 quarts boiling water. Reduce heat and simmer, uncovered, until tender, about 5 minutes; drain. Cool.

2. Toss mesclun and herbs with half the Warm Lime Dressing; arrange on large salad plates and top with rice noodles. Toss cucumber, tomato, and snow peas with remaining Warm Lime Dressing and spoon over greens.

Warm Lime Dressing

(makes about ¾ cup)

½ cup water
½ cup lime juice
1 teaspoon cornstarch
2 tablespoons sugar
2 teaspoons minced garlic
2-3 teaspoons reduced-sodium tamari soy sauce
1 teaspoon dark sesame oil
1 teaspoon black bean sauce
½ teaspoon hot chili paste

1. Combine water, lime juice, and cornstarch in small saucepan; stir in remaining ingredients. Heat to boiling; boil, whisking constantly, until thickened, about 1 minute.

ORIENTAL NOODLE SALAD

Use dark oriental sesame oil for the fullest flavor; the light oil is much more subtle in taste.

4 main-dish servings (about 2 cups each)

1	package (3 ounces) ramen noodles
1	cup trimmed snow peas, steamed until crisp-tender
1	cup halved Brussels sprouts, steamed until crisp-tender
1	medium red bell pepper, sliced
1	cup sliced mushrooms
1	cup bean sprouts
2	medium carrots, thinly sliced
½	cup frozen peas, thawed
1	can (11 ounces) mandarin orange segments, drained
¼	cup finely chopped parsley
⅓	cup orange juice
1	tablespoon sesame oil
2	cloves garlic, minced
½	teaspoon five-spice powder
¼	teaspoon salt
¼	teaspoon white pepper
2	teaspoons toasted sesame seeds (optional)

Per Serving
Calories: 252
% Calories from fat: 25
Fat (gm): 7.5
Saturated fat (gm): 0.8
Cholesterol (mg): 13.3
Sodium (mg): 497
Protein (gm): 9.2
Carbohydrate (gm): 41.6
Exchanges
Milk: 0.0
Vegetable: 3.5
Fruit: 0.5
Bread: 1.0
Meat: 0.0
Fat: 1.5

1. Lightly break noodles apart and cook according to package directions, but do not use spice packet; cool.

2. Combine noodles, vegetables, orange segments, and parsley in large salad bowl; toss.

3. In small bowl, combine remaining ingredients, except sesame seeds; pour over salad and toss. Spoon salad onto plates; sprinkle with sesame seeds if desired.

ASIAN-STYLE NOODLE SALAD

 Enjoy the wonderful blending of flavors in this salad. Thin spaghetti or linguine can be substituted for the fresh Asian egg noodles.

4 main-dish servings (about 1¼ cups each)

8 ounces fresh Asian egg noodles, thin spaghetti, *or* linguine, cooked
1 cup fat-free plain yogurt
¼ cup reduced-fat peanut butter
2 tablespoons rice wine vinegar
1 tablespoon reduced-sodium tamari soy sauce
1 teaspoon toasted sesame oil
1 tablespoon sugar
1 tablespoon minced gingerroot
½ teaspoon 5-spice powder
½ teaspoon minced garlic
½ teaspoon cayenne pepper
1 cup shredded carrot
1 medium cucumber, peeled, seeded, cubed
½ cup chopped red bell pepper
¼ cup sliced green onions and tops
¼ cup finely chopped cilantro
Lettuce leaves, garnish

Per Serving
Calories: 388
% Calories from fat: 17
Fat (gm): 7.7
Saturated fat (gm): 1.5
Cholesterol (mg): 1
Sodium (mg): 242
Protein (gm): 14.3
Carbohydrate (gm): 67.3
Exchanges
Milk: 0.0
Vegetable: 3.0
Fruit: 0.0
Bread: 3.5
Meat: 0.0
Fat: 1.5

1. Cook noodles in 4 quarts boiling water until just tender, 1 to 2 minutes (if using spaghetti or linguine, cook according to package directions). Cool to room temperature.

2. Mix yogurt, peanut butter, vinegar, soy sauce, sesame oil, sugar, gingerroot, and seasonings in bowl until smooth. Spoon dressing over noodles and toss; add remaining ingredients, except lettuce, and toss. Spoon salad into lettuce-lined bowls.

FOURTEEN

Breads

POTATO BREAD

Breads made with mashed potatoes are very moist and retain their freshness well. This dough can be conveniently made in advance and refrigerated up to 5 days.

2 loaves (16 servings each)

1 package active dry yeast
1½ cups warm water (110-115 degrees)
2 tablespoons sugar
3 tablespoons margarine, *or* butter, softened
2 eggs
1 cup mashed potatoes, lukewarm
6-6½ cups all-purpose flour
1 cup whole wheat flour
1 teaspoon salt
Fat-free milk, as, garnish

Per Serving
Calories: 121
% Calories from fat: 13
Fat (gm): 1.7
Saturated fat (gm): 0.4
Cholesterol (mg): 13.4
Sodium (mg): 103
Protein (gm): 3.6
Carbohydrate (gm): 22.7
Exchanges
Milk: 0.0
Vegetable: 0.0
Fruit: 0.0
Bread: 1.5
Meat: 0.0
Fat: 0.5

1. Mix yeast and warm water in large bowl; let stand 5 minutes. Mix in sugar, margarine, eggs, and mashed potatoes; mix in 5½ cups all-purpose flour, whole wheat flour, and salt, to make soft dough. Mix in enough remaining 1 cup all-purpose flour to make smooth dough.

2. Knead dough on floured surface until smooth and elastic, about 5 minutes. Place dough in greased bowl; let rise, covered, in warm place until double in size, 1 to 1½ hours. Punch down dough.

3. Divide dough into 2 equal pieces; shape into loaves and place in greased 9 x 5-inch loaf pans. Let stand, loosely covered, until double in size, about 45 minutes.

4. Brush tops of loaves with milk, if using. Bake at 375 degrees until loaves are golden and sound hollow when tapped, about 45 minutes. Remove from pans and cool on wire racks.

PEASANT BREAD

 Five grains and ground nuts are combined in this hearty dense-textured country-style bread. Wonderful toasted, you will want to try this bread with honey.

2 small loaves (8-10 servings each)

2	packages active dry yeast
½	cup warm water (110-115 degrees)
1¼	cups whole wheat flour
½	cup millet
½	cup cracked wheat
½	cup yellow cornmeal
½	cup bulgur wheat
½	cup quick cooking oats
½	cup ground pecans
1	teaspoon salt
1¼	cups lukewarm water
¼	cup honey
2	tablespoons canola oil
1-2	cups unbleached all-purpose flour

Per Serving
Calories: 197
% Calories from fat: 22
Fat (gm): 5
Saturated fat (gm): 0.6
Cholesterol (mg): 0
Sodium (mg): 137
Protein (gm): 5.4
Carbohydrate (gm): 34.2
Exchanges
Milk: 0.0
Vegetable: 0.0
Fruit: 0.0
Bread: 2.0
Meat: 0.0
Fat: 1.0

1. Mix yeast and ½ cup warm water in small bowl; let stand 5 minutes. Mix whole wheat flour, millet, cracked wheat, cornmeal, bulgur, oats, pecans, and salt in large bowl; stir in yeast mixture, 1¼ cups water, honey, and oil. Mix in enough all-purpose flour to make dough easy to handle.

2. Knead dough on floured surface until smooth and elastic, about 5 minutes (dough will be heavy and difficult to maneuver). Place dough in greased bowl; let rise, covered, in warm place until double in size, about 1½ hours. Punch down dough.

3. Divide dough in half; shape into 2 round loaves on greased baking sheet. Let stand, loosely covered, until double in size, about 1½ hours.

4. Bake bread at 350 degrees until loaves are deep golden brown and sound hollow when tapped, about 40 minutes. Transfer to wire racks to cool.

HEARTY VEGETABLE-RYE BREAD

Cauliflower adds a subtle flavor to this aromatic rye loaf.

1 loaf (10-12 servings)

1 package active dry yeast
⅓ cup hot water (110-115 degrees)
1 teaspoon sugar
1 cup pureed cooked cauliflower
1 tablespoon margarine, *or* butter, melted
1 tablespoon light molasses
1 tablespoon spicy brown mustard
2½-3 cups all-purpose flour, divided
1 cup rye flour
½ teaspoon salt
1½ teaspoons caraway seeds, crushed, divided
1½ teaspoons fennel seeds, crushed, divided
1 teaspoon dried dill weed
1 egg white, beaten

Per Serving
Calories: 177
% Calories from fat: 9
Fat (gm): 1.9
Saturated fat (gm): 0.3
Cholesterol (mg): 0
Sodium (mg): 149
Protein (gm): 5.3
Carbohydrate (gm): 34.8
Exchanges
Milk: 0.0
Vegetable: 0.0
Fruit: 0.0
Bread: 2.0
Meat: 0.0
Fat: 0.5

1. Mix yeast, hot water, and sugar in large bowl; let stand 5 minutes. Mix in cauliflower, margarine, molasses, and mustard. Mix in 2 cups all-purpose flour, rye flour, salt, 1 teaspoon caraway seeds, 1 teaspoon fennel seeds, and dill weed. Mix in enough remaining 1 cup all-purpose flour to make smooth dough.

2. Knead dough on floured surface until smooth and elastic, about 5 minutes. Place dough in greased bowl; let stand, covered, in warm place until double in size, about 1 hour. Punch dough down.

3. Shape dough into long or round loaf on greased cookie sheet. Let rise, loosely covered, until double in size, 45 to 60 minutes. Slit top of loaf with sharp knife; brush with egg white, and sprinkle with remaining ½ teaspoon caraway seeds and ½ teaspoon fennel seeds. Bake at 350 degrees until bread is golden and sounds hollow when tapped, 40 to 50 minutes. Cool on wire rack.

ROASTED RED PEPPER BREAD

 Bake this loaf in freeform long or round shape, or in a pan. For convenience, use a jarred fire-roasted red pepper.

1 loaf (16 servings)

2¼-2¾ cups all-purpose flour, divided
   ¾ cup whole wheat flour
   ¼ cup grated fat-free Parmesan cheese
   1 teaspoon Italian seasoning
   ½ teaspoon salt
   1 package fast-rising active dry yeast
 1¼ cups very hot water (125-130 degrees)
   1 tablespoon olive oil
   4 ounces reduced-fat mozzarella cheese, cut into ½-inch cubes
   ½ cup coarsely chopped roasted red pepper
   1 egg white, beaten
   2 teaspoons water
     Italian seasoning, to taste

Per Serving
Calories: 119
% Calories from fat: 16
Fat (gm): 2.2
Saturated fat (gm): 0.9
Cholesterol (mg): 3.8
Sodium (mg): 133
Protein (gm): 5.6
Carbohydrate (gm): 19
Exchanges
Milk: 0.0
Vegetable: 0.0
Fruit: 0.0
Bread: 1.5
Meat: 0.0
Fat: 0.5

1. Combine 2¼ cups all-purpose flour, whole wheat flour, Parmesan cheese, Italian seasoning, salt, and yeast in large bowl; add water and oil, mixing until smooth. Mix in mozzarella cheese and red pepper; mix in enough remaining ½ cup all-purpose flour to make smooth dough.

2. Knead dough on floured surface until smooth and elastic, about 5 minutes. Place dough in greased bowl; let rise, covered, in warm place until double in size, about 30 minutes. Punch dough down.

3. Shape into loaf and place in greased 9 x 5-inch loaf pan, or shape into a round or long loaf on greased cookie sheet. Let stand, covered, until double in size, about 30 minutes.

4. Slit top of loaf with sharp knife. Mix egg white and water; brush over dough and sprinkle with Italian seasoning. Bake at 375 degrees until loaf is golden and sounds hollow when tapped, 35 to 40 minutes. Remove from pan and cool on wire rack.

LIMA BEAN WHEAT BREAD

 Actually, any kind of pureed bean can be used in this moist, dense bread.

3 loaves (10-12 servings each)

2 packages active dry yeast
¼ cup warm water (110-115 degrees)
1 cup cooked dried lima beans, *or* canned lima beans, rinsed, drained
1 cup water
2 cups fat-free milk
4-6 tablespoons margarine, *or* butter, melted
⅓ cup sugar
4½-5½ cups all-purpose flour, divided
1½ cups whole wheat flour
1½ teaspoons salt
Fat-free milk, for glaze

Per Serving
Calories: 125
% Calories from fat: 13
Fat (gm): 1.9
Saturated fat (gm): 0.4
Cholesterol (mg): 0.3
Sodium (mg): 133
Protein (gm): 4
Carbohydrate (gm): 23.2
Exchanges
Milk: 0.0
Vegetable: 0.0
Fruit: 0.0
Bread: 1.5
Meat: 0.0
Fat: 0.5

1. Mix yeast and warm water in small bowl; let stand 5 minutes. Process beans and 1 cup water in food processor or blender until smooth. Mix bean puree, fat-free milk, margarine, and sugar in large bowl. Mix in yeast mixture, 4½ cups all-purpose flour, whole wheat flour, and salt. Mix in enough remaining 1 cup all-purpose flour to make soft dough.

2. Knead dough on floured surface until smooth and elastic, about 5 minutes. Place dough in greased bowl and let rise, covered, in warm place until double in size, about 1 hour. Punch dough down.

3. Divide dough into 3 equal pieces. Shape each piece into oval loaf on greased cookie sheet. Let rise, loosely covered, until double in size, about 45 minutes.

4. Brush loaves with fat-free milk. Bake at 375 degrees until loaves are golden and sound hollow when tapped, about 1 hour. Transfer to wire racks and cool.

SWEET POTATO BRAIDS

Canned pumpkin can be substituted for the sweet potatoes, if desired. For variation, add ½ cup raisins and/or ½ cup coarsely chopped walnuts or pecans to the bread dough.

2 loaves (12 servings each)

2 packages active dry yeast
¼ cup warm fat-free milk (110-115 degrees)
1 cup mashed cooked sweet potatoes
1¾ cups fat-free milk
¼ cup canola oil
1 egg
4 cups all-purpose flour, divided
2 cups whole wheat flour
1 teaspoon salt

Per Serving
Calories: 156
% Calories from fat: 17
Fat (gm): 2.9
Saturated fat (gm): 0.5
Cholesterol (mg): 9.2
Sodium (mg): 105
Protein (gm): 4.9
Carbohydrate (gm): 27.7
Exchanges
Milk: 0.0
Vegetable: 0.0
Fruit: 0.0
Bread: 2.0
Meat: 0.0
Fat: 0.5

1. Mix yeast and warm milk in large bowl; let stand 5 minutes. Stir in sweet potatoes, 1¾ cups fat-free milk, oil, and egg; add 3 cups all-purpose flour, the whole wheat flour, and salt, mixing until smooth. Mix in enough remaining 1 cup all-purpose flour to make smooth dough.

2. Knead dough on floured surface until smooth and elastic, about 5 minutes. Place dough in bowl; let rise, covered, in warm place until double in size, about 1 hour. Punch down dough.

3. Divide dough into 2 equal halves; divide each half into thirds. Roll pieces of dough into strips, 12 inches long. Braid 3 strips; fold ends under and place on greased cookie sheet. Repeat with remaining dough strips. Let rise, loosely covered, until double in size, 30 to 45 minutes.

4. Bake at 375 degrees until breads are golden and sound hollow when tapped, 45 to 55 minutes. Transfer to wire racks and cool.

CRANBERRY-NUT WHEAT LOAF

 Dried cranberries and walnuts make this bread a perfect fall and winter offering.

1 loaf (16 servings)

1 package active dry yeast
¾ cup warm water (110-115 degrees)
3 tablespoons honey
2-3 tablespoons margarine, *or* butter
2 egg whites
1½-2 cups all-purpose flour, divided
1 cup whole wheat flour
1 teaspoon salt
1 cup dried cranberries
⅔ cup coarsely chopped walnuts
Fat-free milk, as garnish

Per Serving
Calories: 153
% Calories from fat: 27
Fat (gm): 4.7
Saturated fat (gm): 0.6
Cholesterol (mg): 0
Sodium (mg): 141
Protein (gm): 4.1
Carbohydrate (gm): 24.6
Exchanges
Milk: 0.0
Vegetable: 0.0
Fruit: 0.5
Bread: 1.0
Meat: 0.0
Fat: 1.0

1. Mix yeast, warm water, and honey in large bowl; let stand 5 minutes. Add margarine, egg whites, 1 cup all-purpose flour, the whole wheat flour, and salt, mixing until smooth. Mix in cranberries, walnuts, and enough remaining 1 cup all-purpose flour to make smooth dough.

2. Knead dough on floured surface until smooth and elastic, about 5 minutes. Place dough in greased bowl; let rise, covered, in warm place until double in size, 1 to 1½ hours. Punch down dough.

3. Shape into loaf and place in greased 9 x 5-inch loaf pan. Let stand, loosely covered, until double in size, about 45 minutes.

4. Brush top of loaf with fat-free milk, if using. Bake at 375 degrees until loaf is golden and sounds hollow when tapped, 35 to 40 minutes. Remove from pan and cool on wire rack.

THREE KINGS' BREAD

 In Mexico, this rich fruit-studded bread is traditionally served to celebrate Twelfth Night on January 6. A tiny china doll is often baked into the dough; the person receiving the piece of bread with the doll must give a party on February 2 to celebrate the Feast of the Candles!

1 loaf (12 servings)

1	package active dry yeast
⅓	cup warm fat-free milk (110-115 degrees)
2¼-2¾	cups all-purpose flour, divided
6	tablespoons margarine, *or* butter, softened
¼	cup plus 2 tablespoons sugar, divided
1	egg
2	egg whites
½	teaspoon salt
¼	cup dark raisins
½	cup candied fruit, divided
¼	cup chopped walnuts (optional)
1-2	tablespoons fat-free milk

Per Serving
Calories: 205
% Calories from fat: 28
Fat (gm): 6.3
Saturated fat (gm): 1.3
Cholesterol (mg): 17.9
Sodium (mg): 174
Protein (gm): 4.2
Carbohydrate (gm): 33.1
Exchanges
Milk: 0.0
Vegetable: 0.0
Fruit: 0.5
Bread: 1.5
Meat: 0.0
Fat: 1.5

1. Mix yeast, warm milk, and ½ cup flour in small bowl; beat well. Let stand, covered, in a warm place for 30 minutes. Beat margarine and ¼ cup sugar in medium bowl until fluffy. Beat in egg, egg whites, and salt. Add yeast mixture, mixing well. Mix in raisins, ¼ cup candied fruit, walnuts (optional), and 1¾ cups flour; mix in remaining ½ cup flour, if necessary, to make soft dough.

2. Knead on floured surface until smooth and elastic, about 5 minutes. Place dough in greased bowl; let stand, covered, in a warm place until dough is double in size, about 1 hour. Punch dough down.

3. Form dough into a round on greased cookie sheet. Make a hole in center of dough, then stretch with fingers into a ring 8 inches in diameter. Let rise, covered, in a warm place until double in size, about 30 minutes. Decorate with remaining ¼ cup of candied fruit.

4. Bake at 375 degrees until bread is golden, 25 to 30 minutes. Brush bread with 1 to 2 tablespoons of milk and sprinkle with remaining 2 tablespoons of sugar. Bake until glazed, 3 to 5 minutes longer. Remove from oven and cool on wire rack.

ORANGE MARMALADE CRESCENTS

Fragrant coffeecakes for special occasions are drizzled with a warm honey and orange topping.

2 loaves (12 servings each)

Potato Bread (see p. 654)
¼ cup sugar
2 tablespoons margarine, *or* butter, softened
¾ cup orange marmalade
½ cup raisins
¼-½ cup sliced almonds, divided
¼ cup light rum, *or* 1-2 teaspoons rum extract
¼ cup honey
2 tablespoons orange juice

Per Serving
Calories: 229
% Calories from fat: 13
Fat (gm): 3.2
Saturated fat (gm): 0.7
Cholesterol (mg): 17.9
Sodium (mg): 151
Protein (gm): 4.9
Carbohydrate (gm): 44.7
Exchanges
Milk: 0.0
Vegetable: 0.0
Fruit: 0.0
Bread: 3.0
Meat: 0.0
Fat: 0.5

1. Make recipe for Potato Bread through step 2, adding ¼ cup sugar to the 2 tablespoons sugar in the recipe.

2. Divide dough into two equal pieces; roll each piece on floured surface into 15 x 6 inch rectangles. Spread each rectangle with 1 tablespoon margarine and place on greased cookie sheets. Make 2-inch cuts at 1-inch intervals along the long sides of dough rectangles.

3. Mix orange marmalade, raisins, half the almonds, and rum; spread half the mixture down center of each rectangle. Crisscross the cut strips over filling; pinch ends of coffeecakes to seal. Curve each coffeecake into crescent shape. Let rise, covered, until impression of finger remains in dough, 1 to 1½ hours.

4. Bake at 375 degrees until coffeecakes are golden, about 20 minutes. Transfer coffeecakes to wire racks.

5. Heat honey and orange juice in small saucepan until hot; brush over coffeecakes and sprinkle with remaining almonds. Serve warm.

APPLE HONEY KUCHEN

 Use your favorite baking apple, tart or sweet, for this brunch bread.

2 kuchens (8-10 servings each)

1	package active dry yeast
¾	cup warm fat-free milk (110-115 degrees)
6	tablespoons granulated sugar, divided
4	tablespoons margarine, *or* butter, divided
1	egg
2-3	cups all-purpose flour
¾	teaspoon salt
1	pound tart, *or* sweet, baking apples, peeled, sliced
½	cup raisins
¼	cup light brown sugar
2	tablespoons grated orange rind
¼	teaspoon ground cinnamon
⅛	teaspoon ground nutmeg
2-4	tablespoons honey
	Fat-free milk, to seal

Per Serving
Calories: 162
% Calories from fat: 19
Fat (gm): 3.4
Saturated fat (gm): 0.7
Cholesterol (mg): 13.5
Sodium (mg): 145
Protein (gm): 2.8
Carbohydrate (gm): 30.9
Exchanges
Milk: 0.0
Vegetable: 0.0
Fruit: 0.0
Bread: 2.0
Meat: 0.0
Fat: 0.5

1. Mix yeast, milk, and 2 tablespoons granulated sugar in large bowl; let stand 5 minutes. Add 2 tablespoons margarine, egg, 2 cups flour, and salt, mixing until smooth. Mix in enough remaining flour to make smooth dough.

2. Knead dough on floured surface until smooth and elastic, about 5 minutes. Place dough in greased bowl; let rise, covered, in warm place until double in size, 1 to 1½ hours. Punch down dough.

3. Heat remaining 2 tablespoons margarine in large skillet until melted; add apples and cook over medium heat until apples are tender, 5 to 8 minutes. Stir in raisins; remove from heat. Mix brown sugar, orange rind, cinnamon, and nutmeg; sprinkle over apple mixture and toss.

4. Divide dough into 2 equal pieces. Roll each piece of dough on floured surface into 12-inch round. Arrange apple mixture on half of each round; drizzle each with 1 to 2 tablespoons honey. Brush edges of dough with milk; fold dough over filling and press edges with tines of fork to seal.

5. Transfer kuchens to greased cookie sheets; sprinkle with remaining 4 tablespoons granulated sugar. Let rise, loosely covered, until impression of finger remains in dough when touched, about 1 hour. Reseal edges of kuchens, if necessary.

6. Bake kuchens at 375 degrees until golden, about 20 minutes. Slide onto wire racks to cool; serve warm.

STICKY BUNS

Impossible to resist, especially when the buns are fresh from the oven! Finger licking is permitted!

24 buns (1 per serving)

3½ cups all-purpose flour, divided

⅓ cup plus 2 tablespoons sugar, divided

1 package active dry yeast

1 tablespoon plus 1 teaspoon ground cinnamon, divided

1 teaspoon salt

1 cup warm fat-free milk (110-115 degrees)

¼ cup fat-free sour cream

1 egg, beaten

Grated rind from 1 orange

Vegetable cooking spray

Sticky Bun Topping (recipe follows)

½ cup pecan pieces

Per Serving
Calories: 200
% Calories from fat: 17
Fat (gm): 3.8
Saturated fat (gm): 0.6
Cholesterol (mg): 9
Sodium (mg): 131
Protein (gm): 3.1
Carbohydrate (gm): 38.9
Exchanges
Milk: 0.0
Vegetable: 0.0
Fruit: 0.0
Bread: 2.5
Meat: 0.0
Fat: 0.5

1. Combine 2 cups flour, ⅓ cup sugar, yeast, 1 tablespoon cinnamon, and salt in large bowl. Stir in milk, sour cream, egg, and orange rind until smooth. Stir in enough remaining 1½ cups flour to make soft dough.

2. Knead dough on floured surface until smooth and elastic, about 5 minutes. Place dough in greased bowl and let stand, covered, in warm place until double in size, 30 to 45 minutes. Punch dough down.

3. Spray three 9-inch-round cake pans with cooking spray; spoon about ½ cup hot Sticky Bun Topping into each and sprinkle with pecan pieces.

4. Combine remaining 2 tablespoons sugar and 1 teaspoon cinnamon in small bowl. Divide dough in half. Roll half the dough on floured surface into rectangle 12 x 7 inches; sprinkle with half the sugar mixture. Roll dough up, beginning with long side; cut into 12 equal slices. Repeat with remaining dough and sugar mixture. Place 8 rolls, cut sides up, in each pan, over the topping.

5. Let rolls rise, covered in warm place, until double in size, about 30 minutes. Bake at 375 degrees until golden, 15 to 20 minutes. Immediately invert rolls onto aluminum foil.

Sticky Bun Topping

    4 tablespoons margarine, *or* butter
  1½ cups packed light brown sugar
    ½ cup light corn syrup
    ¼ cup all-purpose flour

1. Melt margarine in small saucepan; stir in remaining ingredients and cook until bubbly.

Variation: **Cinnamon Rolls**—Do not make Sticky Bun Topping. Make dough as above, mixing in ½ cup raisins. Let dough rise, then roll and shape as above, sprinkling with double the amount of sugar and cinnamon. Place rolls, cut sides up, in sprayed muffin cups. Bake as above, and invert rolls onto wire racks. Mix 2 cups powdered sugar with enough fat-free milk to make a thick glaze; drizzle over slightly warm rolls.

GRANOLA BREAD

A wonderful breakfast bread—serve with plenty of Spiced Rhubarb Jam (see p. 694). For convenience this bread is mixed with an electric mixer and has only 1 rise.

2 loaves (16 servings each)

    2 packages active dry yeast
    ¾ cup warm water (110-115 degrees)
    2 tablespoons light brown sugar
  1¼ cups buttermilk
    3 cups all-purpose flour
 ¾-1½ cups whole wheat flour, divided

Per Serving
Calories: 87
% Calories from fat: 13
Fat (gm): 1.3
Saturated fat (gm): 0.2
Cholesterol (mg): 0.4
Sodium (mg): 111
Protein (gm): 2.6
Carbohydrate (gm): 16.7

　　2 teaspoons baking powder
　　1 teaspoon salt
　2-3 tablespoons margarine, *or* butter,
　　　softened
　1½ cups low-fat granola
　　　Buttermilk, for glaze

Exchanges
Milk: 0.0
Vegetable: 0.0
Fruit: 0.0
Bread: 1.0
Meat: 0.0
Fat: 0.5

1.　Mix yeast, warm water, and brown sugar in large mixer bowl; let stand 5 minutes. Add buttermilk, all-purpose flour, ¾ cup whole wheat flour, baking powder, salt, and margarine, mixing on low speed until smooth. Mix in granola and enough remaining ¾ cup whole wheat flour to make smooth dough (dough will be slightly sticky.)

2.　Knead dough on floured surface until smooth and elastic, about 5 minutes. Divide dough into 2 equal pieces. Roll each piece into a rectangle 18 x 10 inches. Roll up, beginning at short ends; press each end to seal. Place loaves, seam sides down, in greased 9 x 5-inch loaf pans. Let rise, covered, in warm place until double in size, about 1 hour.

3.　Brush tops of loaves with buttermilk. Bake at 375 degrees until loaves are golden and sound hollow when tapped, 40 to 45 minutes. Remove from pans and cool on wire racks.

ENGLISH MUFFIN BREAD

 This quick and easy single-rise bread has a coarse texture similar to English muffins. Delicious warm from the oven, or toasted, with Gingered Honey (see p. 698)

16 servings

Per Serving
Calories: 79
% Calories from fat: 4
Fat (gm): 0.4
Saturated fat (gm): 0.1
Cholesterol (mg): 0.3
Sodium (mg): 163
Protein (gm): 2.9
Carbohydrate (gm): 15.9
Exchanges
Milk: 0.0
Vegetable: 0.0
Fruit: 0.0
Bread: 1.0
Meat: 0.0
Fat: 0.0

　　　　Vegetable cooking spray
　　1-2 teaspoons yellow cornmeal
　2-2½ cups all-purpose flour, divided
　　　½ cup quick-cooking oats
　　　1 package active dry yeast
　　　1 teaspoon salt
　　1¼ cups fat-free milk
　　　1 tablespoon honey
　　　¼ teaspoon baking soda

1. Spray 8 x 4 x 2-inch loaf pan with cooking spray; coat with cornmeal.

2. Combine 1½ cups flour, oats, yeast, and salt in large bowl. Heat milk and honey until warm (110-120 degrees) in small saucepan; stir in baking soda. Add milk mixture to flour mixture, mixing until smooth. Stir in enough of remaining 1 cup flour to make a thick batter. Pour into prepared pan. Let rise, covered, in warm place until double in size, 45 to 60 minutes.

3. Bake at 400 degrees until bread is golden and sounds hollow when tapped, 25 to 30 minutes. Remove from pan immediately and cool on wire rack.

Variation: **Raisin Bread**—Spray loaf pan, but do not coat with cornmeal. Stir 1 teaspoon cinnamon and ½ cup raisins into batter.

BUBBLE LOAF

Also called Bath Buns and Monkey Bread, this pull-apart loaf is easy to make, fun to eat, and perfect for potluck offerings and parties. The recipe can be halved and baked in a 6-cup fluted cake pan.

16 servings

2	packages active dry yeast
1	cup fat-free milk, warm (110-115 degrees)
6	tablespoons margarine, *or* butter, softened
¼	cup sugar
3	eggs
4	cups all-purpose flour
½	teaspoon salt

Per Serving
Calories: 186
% Calories from fat: 27
Fat (gm): 5.5
Saturated fat (gm): 1.2
Cholesterol (mg): 40.2
Sodium (mg): 137
Protein (gm): 5.3
Carbohydrate (gm): 28.3
Exchanges
Milk: 0.0
Vegetable: 0.0
Fruit: 0.0
Bread: 2.0
Meat: 0.0
Fat: 1.0

1. Stir yeast into milk; let stand 2 to 3 minutes. In a large bowl, beat margarine and sugar until fluffy; beat in eggs, 1 at a time. Mix in combined flour and salt alternately with milk mixture, beginning and ending with dry ingredients and beating well after each addition. Let stand, covered, in warm place until dough is double in size, about 1 hour. Punch dough down.

2. Drop dough by large spoonfuls into greased 10-inch tube pan. Let rise, covered, until dough is double in size, about 30 minutes. Bake at 350 degrees until browned, 25 to 30 minutes. Cool in pan on wire rack 10 minutes; remove from pan. Serve warm.

MULTIGRAIN BATTER BREAD

 Batter breads are quick and easy to make, requiring no kneading and only one rise.

2 loaves (16 servings each)

3¼	cups all-purpose flour
1	cup whole wheat flour
¼	cup soy flour, *or* quick-cooking oats
¾	cup quick-cooking oats
¼	cup sugar
½	teaspoon salt
2	packages fast-rising yeast
1	cup cooked brown rice
2¼	cups fat-free milk, hot (125-130 degrees)
2	tablespoons vegetable oil

Per Serving
Calories: 97
% Calories from fat: 13
Fat (gm): 1.4
Saturated fat (gm): 0.2
Cholesterol (mg): 0.3
Sodium (mg): 43
Protein (gm): 3.5
Carbohydrate (gm): 17.9
Exchanges
Milk: 0.0
Vegetable: 0.0
Fruit: 0.0
Bread: 1.0
Meat: 0.0
Fat: 0.5

1. Combine flours, oats, sugar, salt, and yeast in large bowl; stir in rice. Add milk and oil, mixing until smooth. Spoon batter into 2 greased 8½ x 4½-inch bread pans; let stand, loosely covered, until double in size, about 30 minutes.

2. Bake bread at 375 degrees until loaves are browned and sound hollow when tapped, 35 to 40 minutes. Remove from pans and cool on wire racks.

SOFT PRETZELS

 To achieve their typical dense, chewy texture, the pretzels are cooked in boiling water before baking.

12 servings (1 pretzel each)

   1 package active dry yeast
  ½ cup warm water (105-115 degrees)
   1 tablespoon sugar
   1 cup fat-free milk, heated to simmering, cooled
3½-4 cups all-purpose flour, divided
   1 teaspoon salt
   2 quarts water
   1 tablespoon baking soda
   1 egg, beaten
   1 tablespoon cold water
    Toppings: poppy seeds, sesame seeds, coarse salt, herbs, dried onion flakes, etc. (optional)

Per Serving
Calories: 152
% Calories from fat: 5
Fat (gm): 0.8
Saturated fat (gm): 0.2
Cholesterol (mg): 18.1
Sodium (mg): 509
Protein (gm): 5.2
Carbohydrate (gm): 30.2
Exchanges
Milk: 0.0
Vegetable: 0.0
Fruit: 0.0
Bread: 2.0
Meat: 0.0
Fat: 0.0

1. Mix yeast, warm water, and sugar in large bowl; let stand 5 minutes. Add fat-free milk, 2 cups flour, and salt, beating until mixture is smooth. Mix in enough remaining 2 cups flour to make smooth dough.

2. Knead dough on floured surface until smooth and elastic, about 5 minutes. Place dough in greased bowl; let rise, covered, in warm place until double in size, 45 to 60 minutes. Punch dough down.

3. Roll dough on floured surface to rectangle 16 x 12 inches. Cut dough lengthwise into 12 strips, 1 inch wide. Roll one strip dough with palms of hands until rounded and 18 to 20 inches long. Form loop, holding ends of strip and twisting strip 2 times. Bring ends of strip down and fasten at opposite sides of loop to form pretzel shape. Repeat with remaining dough, transferring pretzels to floured surface. Let pretzels stand, lightly covered, 30 minutes (they may not double in size).

4. Heat 2 quarts water to boiling in large saucepan; stir in baking soda. Transfer pretzels, a few at a time, into boiling water; boil until dough feels firm, about 1 minute. Remove pretzels from boiling water with slotted spoon, allowing them to drain well. Place on well-greased aluminum-foil-covered cookie sheets.

5. Mix egg and cold water; brush on tops of pretzels. Sprinkle pretzels with desired toppings. Bake at 400 degrees until pretzels are golden, 18 to 20 minutes. Remove from pans; cool on wire racks.

SQUASH DINNER ROLLS

Use pumpkin, Hubbard, or acorn squash for these rolls; mashed sweet potatoes can be substituted for the squash. If a loaf is preferred, shape and bake the dough in a greased 8½ x 4½-inch loaf pan.

24 servings (1 roll each)

1½-2½	cups all-purpose flour, divided
1	cup whole wheat flour
2	packages fast-rising yeast
1-2	teaspoons salt
½	cup fat-free milk
¼	cup honey
1-2	tablespoons margarine, *or* butter
¾	cup mashed cooked winter squash
1	egg

Per Serving
Calories: 70
% Calories from fat: 11
Fat (gm): 0.9
Saturated fat (gm): 0.2
Cholesterol (mg): 9
Sodium (mg): 100
Protein (gm): 2.2
Carbohydrate (gm): 13.5
Exchanges
Milk: 0.0
Vegetable: 0.0
Fruit: 0.0
Bread: 1.0
Meat: 0.0
Fat: 0.0

1. Combine 1½ cups all-purpose flour, whole wheat flour, yeast, and salt in large mixing bowl. Heat milk, honey, and margarine in small saucepan until very hot (125-130 degrees.) Add milk mixture to flour mixture, mixing until smooth. Mix in squash and egg. Mix in enough remaining 1 cup all-purpose flour to make smooth dough.

2. Knead dough on floured surface until smooth and elastic, about 5 minutes. Place dough in greased bowl; let stand, covered, in warm place until double in size, 30 to 45 minutes. Punch down dough.

3. Divide dough into 24 pieces; shape into round rolls and place in greased muffin tins. Bake at 375 degrees until browned, 20 to 25 minutes.

BOLILLOS

 Bolillos are the crusty, "bobbin-shaped" yeast rolls that are popular throughout Mexico. The dough is similar to French bread dough.

12 servings (1 roll each)

1	package active dry yeast
½	teaspoon sugar
1	cup hot water (110-115 degrees)
2	tablespoons vegetable shortening, room temperature
3½-4	cups all-purpose flour
½	teaspoon salt
2	tablespoons fat-free milk

Per Serving
Calories: 155
% Calories from fat: 15
Fat (gm): 2.5
Saturated fat (gm): 0.6
Cholesterol (mg): 0
Sodium (mg): 91
Protein (gm): 4.1
Carbohydrate (gm): 28.4
Exchanges
Milk: 0.0
Vegetable: 0.0
Fruit: 0.0
Bread: 2.0
Meat: 0.0
Fat: 0.5

1. Mix yeast, sugar, and hot water in medium mixing bowl; add shortening, stirring until melted. Let stand 5 minutes. Mix in 3½ cups of flour and the salt; mix in enough remaining flour to make soft dough.

2. Knead dough on floured surface until smooth and elastic, about 5 minutes. Place dough in greased bowl; let stand, covered, in a warm place until dough is double in size, 1 to 1½ hours. Punch dough down.

3. Divide dough into 12 equal pieces. Roll or pat 1 piece into an oval shape, a scant ½ inch thick. Fold ⅓ of the dough (long edge) toward the center and flatten with palm of hand; fold dough in half in same direction and flatten with palm of hand. Roll dough lightly with hand to make a rounded oval shape. Place, seam side up, on lightly greased cookie sheet. Repeat with remaining dough. Let rolls stand, loosely covered, until double in size, about 1 hour.

4. Brush tops of bolillos lightly with milk. Bake at 375 degrees until lightly browned, about 25 minutes.

PITA BREADS

 Also called Syrian bread or pocket breads, pitas can be eaten plain or split and filled. The breads freeze well, so make lots!

12 servings (1 pita each)

1 package active dry yeast
1⅓ cups hot water (115-125 degrees)
¼ teaspoon sugar
1½ tablespoons olive oil
3-4 cups all-purpose flour, divided
1 teaspoon salt

Per Serving
Calories: 131
% Calories from fat: 14
Fat (gm): 2
Saturated fat (gm): 0.3
Cholesterol (mg): 0
Sodium (mg): 178
Protein (gm): 3.5
Carbohydrate (gm): 24.2
Exchanges
Milk: 0.0
Vegetable: 0.0
Fruit: 0.0
Bread: 2.0
Meat: 0.0
Fat: 0.0

1. Combine yeast, hot water, and sugar in large bowl; let stand 5 minutes. Add oil, 3 cups flour, and salt, mixing until smooth. Mix in enough remaining 1 cup flour to make smooth dough.

2. Knead dough on floured surface until smooth and elastic, about 5 minutes. Place dough in greased bowl; let stand, covered, in warm place until double in size, about 1 hour. Punch dough down.

3. Shape dough into 12 balls; let stand, loosely covered, 30 minutes (dough will not double in size). Roll balls of dough on floured surface into rounds 5 to 6 inches in diameter. Place rounds 2 to 3 inches apart on cookie sheets; let stand, 30 minutes.

4. Bake breads, 1 pan at a time, at 500 degrees until pitas are puffed and brown, 3 to 5 minutes. Cool on wire racks.

WHOLE WHEAT LAVOSH

A flat cracker bread that is perfect to serve with dips and spreads, or as an accompaniment to soups and salads.

6 servings

½ cup fat-free milk, heated (115 degrees)
1 package active dry yeast
2⅓ cups whole wheat flour
1 cup all-purpose flour, divided
½ teaspoon salt
1 egg white
1 tablespoon water

Per Serving
Calories: 186
% Calories from fat: 4
Fat (gm): 0.8
Saturated fat (gm): 0.2
Cholesterol (mg): 0.3
Sodium (mg): 150
Protein (gm): 7.7
Carbohydrate (gm): 38.5
Exchanges
Milk: 0.0
Vegetable: 0.0
Fruit: 0.0
Bread: 2.5
Meat: 0.0
Fat: 0.0

1. Mix milk and yeast in large bowl; let stand 5 minutes. Mix in whole wheat flour, ½ cup all-purpose flour, and salt; mix in enough remaining ½ cup all-purpose flour to make a smooth dough. Let stand, covered, 15 to 20 minutes.

2. Divide dough into 8 equal pieces. Roll each piece on lightly floured surface into a 3-inch round; place on greased cookie sheet. Beat egg white and water; brush over top of dough.

3. Bake lavosh at 425 degrees until crisp and browned, 5 to 8 minutes, turning lavosh over halfway through baking time. (Lavosh will become crisper upon cooling, so do not overbake.) Cool on wire rack.

FOCACCIA

This delicious Italian bread is very versatile and can be used in many ways—see Leek and Onion Focaccia and Fruit Focaccia (p. 451). Focaccia can be frozen, so bake extra to have on hand.

2 focaccia (10 servings each)

5½ cups bread flour, divided
1 package (¼ ounce) fast-rising yeast
1 teaspoon sugar
1 teaspoon salt

Per Serving
Calories: 139
% Calories from fat: 5
Fat (gm): 0.8
Saturated fat (gm): 0.2
Cholesterol (mg): 1
Sodium (mg): 131
Protein (gm): 5.2
Carbohydrate (gm): 28.2

1¾ cups very hot water (125-130 degrees)
Olive oil cooking spray
¼ cup (1 ounce) grated Parmesan cheese

Exchanges
Milk: 0.0
Vegetable: 0.0
Fruit: 0.0
Bread: 2.0
Meat: 0.0
Fat: 0.0

1. Combine 4 cups flour, yeast, sugar, and salt in large mixing bowl. Add water, mixing until smooth. Mix in enough remaining 1½ cups flour to make soft dough.

2. Knead dough on floured surface until dough is smooth and elastic, about 5 minutes. Place dough in greased bowl; turn greased side up and let rise, covered, in warm place until double in size, about 1 hour. Punch dough down.

3. Divide dough into halves. Roll 1 piece dough on floured surface to fit jelly roll pan, 15 x 10 inches. Grease pan lightly; ease dough into pan. Repeat with remaining dough. Let dough rise until double in size, 45 to 60 minutes.

4. Make ¼-inch-deep indentations with fingers to "dimple" the dough; spray lightly with cooking spray and sprinkle with Parmesan cheese.

5. Bake focaccia at 425 degrees until browned, about 30 minutes. Cool in pans on wire racks. Serve warm or at room temperature.

SPINACH-MUSHROOM FLATBREAD

 This attractive bread is made in a freeform shape and topped with spinach and Parmesan cheese. The bread can be made in advance and reheated at 300 degrees, loosely wrapped in aluminum foil, 15 to 20 minutes.

1 loaf (12-16 servings)

3-3½ cups all-purpose flour, divided
1½ cups whole wheat flour
2 tablespoons sugar
1½ teaspoons dried rosemary leaves, crushed
½ teaspoon dried thyme leaves
½ teaspoon salt
1 package fast-rising yeast
2 cups very hot water (125-130 degrees)
Olive oil cooking spray

Per Serving
Calories: 190
% Calories from fat: 5
Fat (gm): 1
Saturated fat (gm): 0.4
Cholesterol (mg): 1.3
Sodium (mg): 123
Protein (gm): 7
Carbohydrate (gm): 38.8
Exchanges
Milk: 0.0
Vegetable: 0.0
Fruit: 0.0
Bread: 2.5
Meat: 0.0
Fat: 0.0

¼ cup sliced onion

3 cloves garlic, minced

2 cups torn spinach leaves

1 cup sliced cremini, *or* white, mushrooms

¼ cup (2 ounces) shredded reduced-fat
mozzarella cheese

2-3 tablespoons grated fat-free Parmesan
cheese

1. Combine 2½ cups all-purpose flour, the whole wheat flour, sugar, herbs, salt, and yeast in large mixing bowl; add water, mixing until smooth. Mix in enough remaining 1 cup all-purpose flour to make soft dough.

2. Knead dough on floured surface until smooth and elastic, about 5 minutes. Place dough in greased bowl; let rise, loosely covered, in warm place until double in size, 30 to 45 minutes. Punch dough down.

3. Pat dough on floured surface into a round. Pull the edges of the dough into a freeform shape, about 10 x 14 inches. Transfer dough to greased cookie sheet and let stand 20 minutes (dough will rise, but will not double in size).

4. Spray medium skillet with cooking spray; heat over medium heat until hot. Saute onion and garlic until tender, 3 to 4 minutes. Add spinach and mushrooms; cook, covered, over medium to medium-low heat until spinach is wilted, about 5 minutes. Cook, uncovered, until mushrooms are tender, about 5 minutes. Remove from heat and reserve.

5. Bake bread at 350 degrees until golden, about 20 minutes. Arrange spinach mixture over top of bread; sprinkle with cheeses. Continue baking until spinach mixture is hot and cheese melted, 5 to 10 minutes. Remove from cookie sheet and cool on wire rack.

GARLIC BREAD

Select a good quality French or Italian loaf for this aromatic bread, or use a sourdough bread for an interesting flavor variation.

4 servings

4 thick slices French, *or* Italian, bread
   Olive oil cooking spray
2 cloves garlic, cut into halves

Per Serving
Calories: 71
% Calories from fat: 10
Fat (gm): 0.8
Saturated fat (gm): 0.2
Cholesterol (mg): 0
Sodium (mg): 152
Protein (gm): 2.3
Carbohydrate (gm): 13.5
Exchanges
Milk: 0.0
Vegetable: 0.0
Fruit: 0.0
Bread: 1.0
Meat: 0.0
Fat: 0.0

1. Spray both sides of bread generously with cooking spray. Broil on cookie sheet 4 inches from heat source until browned, about 1 minute on each side.

2. Rub both sides of hot toast with cut sides of garlic.

Variation: **Parmesan Garlic Bread**—Combine 2 teaspoons grated Parmesan cheese and 1 teaspoon minced garlic. Spray bread with cooking spray as above and spread top of each slice with cheese mixture. Broil as above, or wrap loosely in aluminum foil and bake at 350 degrees until warm, about 5 minutes.

CROUTONS

 Croutons can brighten a soup, add crunch to a salad, and provide a flavor accent for many dishes. Store croutons up to 2 weeks, or freeze. Bake at 300 degrees 5 to 7 minutes if they need freshening.

12 servings (¼ cup each)

3 cups cubed firm, *or* day-old, French, *or* Italian, bread (½-¾ inch cubes)
Vegetable cooking spray

Per Serving
Calories: 20
% Calories from fat: 13
Fat (gm): 0.3
Saturated fat (gm): 0.1
Cholesterol (mg): 0
Sodium (mg): 39
Protein (gm): 0.6
Carbohydrate (gm): 3.7
Exchanges
Milk: 0.0
Vegetable: 0.0
Fruit: 0.0
Bread: 0.0
Meat: 0.0
Fat: 0.0

1. Spray bread cubes with cooking spray; arrange in single layer on jelly roll pan. Bake at 375 degrees until browned, 8 to 10 minutes, stirring occasionally. Cool; store in airtight container.

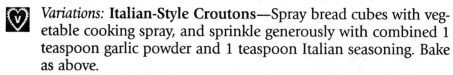

Variations: **Italian-Style Croutons**—Spray bread cubes with vegetable cooking spray, and sprinkle generously with combined 1 teaspoon garlic powder and 1 teaspoon Italian seasoning. Bake as above.

Sourdough Croutons—Spray sourdough bread cubes with vegetable cooking spray, and sprinkle with 2 teaspoons bouquet garni. Bake as above.

Parmesan Croutons—Spray bread cubes with vegetable cooking spray, and sprinkle with 1 to 2 tablespoons grated fat-free Parmesan cheese. Bake as above.

Rye Caraway Croutons—Spray rye bread cubes with vegetable cooking spray, and sprinkle with 2 teaspoons crushed caraway seed. Bake as above.

Sesame Croutons—Spray bread cubes with vegetable cooking spray, and sprinkle with 2 to 3 teaspoons sesame seeds. Bake as above.

Herb Croutons—Spray multigrain or whole wheat bread cubes with vegetable cooking spray, and sprinkle with 2 teaspoons dried herbs or herb combinations, such as basil, tarragon, oregano, savory, rosemary, etc. Bake as above.

GREEN CHILI CORN BREAD

Corn bread, Southwest-style! If using mild canned chilies, consider adding a teaspoon or so of minced jalapeño chili for a piquant accent. Serve this flavorful corn bread warm.

9 servings

Vegetable cooking spray
¼ cup chopped red bell pepper
2 cloves garlic, minced
½ teaspoon cumin seeds, crushed
1¼ cups yellow cornmeal
¾ cup all-purpose flour
2 teaspoons baking powder
½ teaspoon baking soda
1 teaspoon sugar
½ teaspoon salt
1¼ cups buttermilk
½ cup canned cream-style corn
1 can (4 ounces) chopped hot, *or* mild, green chilies, well drained
1 egg
2 egg whites
3½ tablespoons margarine, *or* butter, melted

Per Serving
Calories: 184
% Calories from fat: 29
Fat (gm): 6.1
Saturated fat (gm): 1.3
Cholesterol (mg): 24.9
Sodium (mg): 563
Protein (gm): 5.6
Carbohydrate (gm): 27.6
Exchanges
Milk: 0.0
Vegetable: 0.0
Fruit: 0.0
Bread: 2.0
Meat: 0.0
Fat: 1.0

1. Spray small skillet with cooking spray; heat over medium heat until hot. Saute bell pepper, garlic, and cumin seeds until pepper is tender, 2 to 3 minutes.

2. Combine cornmeal, flour, baking powder, baking soda, sugar, and salt in large bowl. Add buttermilk, bell pepper mixture, and remaining ingredients; mix until smooth. Spread batter in greased 8-inch-square baking pan.

3. Bake at 425 degrees until corn bread is golden, about 30 minutes. Cool in pan on wire rack.

THREE-GRAIN MOLASSES BREAD

 Molasses and brown sugar give this hearty quick bread a special flavor.

1 loaf (16 servings)

1 cup all-purpose flour
1 cup whole wheat flour
1 cup yellow cornmeal
1 teaspoon baking soda
½ teaspoon salt
1¼ cups water
½ cup light molasses
½ cup packed light brown sugar
3 tablespoons vegetable oil

Per Serving
Calories: 155
% Calories from fat: 17
Fat (gm): 3
Saturated fat (gm): 0.4
Cholesterol (mg): 0
Sodium (mg): 153
Protein (gm): 2.5
Carbohydrate (gm): 30.5
Exchanges
Milk: 0.0
Vegetable: 0.0
Fruit: 0.0
Bread: 2.0
Meat: 0.0
Fat: 0.5

1. Mix all ingredients in large bowl. Pour batter into greased 9 x 5-inch loaf pan.

2. Bake bread at 350 degrees until wooden pick comes out clean, about 1 hour. Remove bread from pan and cool on wire rack.

FRUITED BRAN BREAD

 Use any combination of dried fruit you want in this quick and healthy, no-rise batter bread.

1 loaf (16 servings)

1¼ cups all-purpose flour
½ cup whole wheat flour
2 teaspoons baking powder
½ teaspoon baking soda
½ teaspoon salt
1½ cups whole bran cereal
1⅓ cups buttermilk
¾ cup packed light brown sugar
3 tablespoons margarine, *or* butter, softened
1 egg
1 cup coarsely chopped mixed dried fruit
¼-½ cup chopped walnuts

Per Serving
Calories: 169
% Calories from fat: 20
Fat (gm): 4.2
Saturated fat (gm): 0.8
Cholesterol (mg): 14.1
Sodium (mg): 261
Protein (gm): 4.1
Carbohydrate (gm): 33.1
Exchanges
Milk: 0.0
Vegetable: 0.0
Fruit: 0.0
Bread: 2.0
Meat: 0.0
Fat: 0.5

1. Combine all-purpose flour, whole wheat flour, baking powder, baking soda, salt, and bran cereal in medium bowl. Add buttermilk, brown sugar, margarine, and egg to bowl; stir just until dry ingredients are moistened. Gently fold in dried fruit and walnuts.

2. Spread batter in greased and floured 9 x 5-inch loaf pan. Bake at 350 degrees until wooden pick inserted in center comes out clean, about 1 hour. Remove from pan; cool completely on wire rack before slicing.

BROWN SUGAR BANANA BREAD

Brown sugar gives this banana bread a caramel flavor; the applesauce adds moistness. It's the best!

16 servings

4	tablespoons margarine, *or* butter, softened
¼	cup applesauce
2	eggs
2	tablespoons fat-free milk, *or* water
¾	cup packed light brown sugar
1	cup mashed banana (2-3 medium bananas)
1¾	cups all-purpose flour
2	teaspoons baking powder
½	teaspoon baking soda
¼	teaspoon salt
¼	cup coarsely chopped walnuts, *or* pecans

Per Serving
Calories: 151
% Calories from fat: 28
Fat (gm): 4.8
Saturated fat (gm): 0.9
Cholesterol (mg): 26.7
Sodium (mg): 160
Protein (gm): 2.9
Carbohydrate (gm): 24.9
Exchanges
Milk: 0.0
Vegetable: 0.0
Fruit: 0.5
Bread: 1.0
Meat: 0.0
Fat: 1.0

1. Beat margarine, applesauce, eggs, milk, and brown sugar in large mixer bowl until smooth. Add banana and blend at low speed; beat at high speed 1 to 2 minutes.

2. Combine flour, baking powder, baking soda, and salt; mix into batter. Mix in walnuts. Pour batter into greased loaf pan, 8 x 4 x 2 inches.

3. Bake at 350 degrees until bread is golden and toothpick inserted in center comes out clean, 55 to 60 minutes. Cool in pan on wire rack 10 minutes; remove from pan and cool to room temperature.

MINT AND CITRUS TEA BREAD

Fine textured and lightly scented with mint, orange, and lemon, this bread is a delicious addition to any meal.

1 loaf (16 servings)

½ cup fat-free milk

2 tablespoons finely chopped fresh mint, *or* 2 teaspoons dried mint leaves

2 tablespoons grated orange rind

1 tablespoon grated lemon rind

¼ cup orange juice

5 tablespoons margarine, *or* butter, softened

¾ cup sugar

2 eggs

1½ cups all-purpose flour

½ cup whole wheat flour

1½ teaspoons baking powder

½ teaspoon salt

½ cup powdered sugar

Fat-free milk, for glaze

Nutmeg, ground, as garnish

Per Serving
Calories: 153
% Calories from fat: 25
Fat (gm): 4.4
Saturated fat (gm): 0.9
Cholesterol (mg): 26.8
Sodium (mg): 151
Protein (gm): 2.9
Carbohydrate (gm): 26
Exchanges
Milk: 0.0
Vegetable: 0.0
Fruit: 0.0
Bread: 1.5
Meat: 0.0
Fat: 1.0

1. Heat milk, mint, orange rind, and lemon rind in small saucepan to simmering; strain and cool. Add orange juice.

2. Beat margarine and sugar until smooth in medium bowl; beat in eggs. Mix in combined all-purpose and whole wheat flour, baking powder, and salt alternately with milk mixture, beginning and ending with dry ingredients.

3. Pour batter into greased 8½ x 4½-inch loaf pan. Bake at 325 degrees until bread is golden and toothpick inserted in center comes out clean, about 45 minutes. Remove from pan and cool on wire rack.

4. Mix powdered sugar with enough fat-free milk to make medium glaze consistency; drizzle glaze over bread and sprinkle lightly with nutmeg.

SOUR CREAM COFFEECAKE WITH APPLE-DATE FILLING

An irresistible offering, this moist cake is filled with apples, dates, sugar, and spices. Serve warm, if desired.

24 servings

½ cup margarine, *or* butter, softened
¼ cup unsweetened applesauce
1 cup granulated sugar
⅓ cup packed light brown sugar
3 eggs
1½ teaspoons vanilla
3 cups all-purpose flour
1½ teaspoons baking powder
1½ teaspoons baking soda
1 teaspoon ground cinnamon
½ teaspoon salt
1½ cups fat-free sour cream
Apple-Date Filling (recipe follows)
Cream Cheese Glaze (recipe follows)

Per Serving
Calories: 198
% Calories from fat: 21
Fat (gm): 4.6
Saturated fat (gm): 1
Cholesterol (mg): 26.6
Sodium (mg): 235
Protein (gm): 3.8
Carbohydrate (gm): 36.1
Exchanges
Milk: 0.0
Vegetable: 0.0
Fruit: 0.0
Bread: 2.0
Meat: 0.0
Fat: 1.0

1. Beat margarine, applesauce, and sugars in large bowl until smooth. Beat in eggs, 1 at a time; beat in vanilla. Combine flour, baking powder, baking soda, cinnamon, and salt and mix in alternately with sour cream, beginning and ending with dry ingredients.

2. Spoon ⅓ of batter into greased and floured 12-cup fluted cake pan; spoon ½ of Apple-Date Filling over batter. Repeat layers, ending with batter.

3. Bake at 325 degrees until toothpick inserted in center of cake comes out clean, about 1 hour. Cool in pan on wire rack 10 minutes; remove from pan and cool to room temperature.

4. Place coffeecake on serving plate; spoon Cream Cheese Glaze over.

Apple-Date Filling

(makes about 1 cup)

½ cup dried apples, coarsely chopped
¼ cup chopped dates
⅔ cup water
⅓ cup packed light brown sugar
1 tablespoon flour
¼ teaspoon ground nutmeg
⅛ teaspoon salt

1. Combine all ingredients in small saucepan and heat to boiling; reduce heat and simmer, uncovered, until apples are tender and mixture is thick, 5 to 8 minutes. Cool.

Cream Cheese Glaze

(makes ½ cup)

2 ounces fat-free cream cheese, room
temperature
1 cup powdered sugar

1. Beat cream cheese and powdered sugar until smooth; refrigerate until ready to use.

CRANBERRY COFFEECAKE

Quick and easy to make, this sweet-tart coffeecake can be ready to bake in less than 10 minutes.

12 servings

1½ cups fresh, *or* frozen, thawed,
cranberries
1 cup sugar, divided
1 teaspoon grated orange rind
1½ cups all-purpose flour
2 teaspoons baking powder
½ teaspoon salt
1 egg
¼ cup orange juice
¼ cup fat-free milk
3 tablespoons margarine, *or* butter, softened
¼-½ cup chopped pecans

Per Serving
Calories: 180
% Calories from fat: 25
Fat (gm): 5
Saturated fat (gm): 0.8
Cholesterol (mg): 17.8
Sodium (mg): 185
Protein (gm): 2.6
Carbohydrate (gm): 31.8
Exchanges
Milk: 0.0
Vegetable: 0.0
Fruit: 0.0
Bread: 2.0
Meat: 0.0
Fat: 1.0

1. Arrange cranberries in greased 8-inch-square baking pan; sprinkle with ½ cup sugar and the orange rind. Mix remaining ingredients until just moistened in medium bowl; drop by spoonfuls onto cranberries, spreading batter evenly to sides of pan.

2. Bake coffeecake at 400 degrees until wooden pick inserted in center comes out clean, 25 to 30 minutes. Immediately invert coffeecake onto serving plate. Serve warm.

VINEGAR BISCUITS

Every grandmother no doubt had her version of this old-fashioned biscuit recipe.

12 biscuits (1 per serving)

¾	cup fat-free milk
¼	cup cider vinegar
2	cups all-purpose flour
1½	teaspoons baking soda
1	teaspoon cream of tartar
½	teaspoon salt
3	tablespoons vegetable shortening, melted

Per Serving
Calories: 109
% Calories from fat: 27
Fat (gm): 3.2
Saturated fat (gm): 0.8
Cholesterol (mg): 0.3
Sodium (mg): 255
Protein (gm): 2.7
Carbohydrate (gm): 17.1
Exchanges
Milk: 0.0
Vegetable: 0.0
Fruit: 0.0
Bread: 1.0
Meat: 0.0
Fat: 0.5

1. Mix milk and vinegar in glass measure. Combine flour, baking soda, cream of tartar, and salt in medium bowl; add milk mixture and shortening, mixing until blended.

2. Knead dough on generously floured surface 1 to 2 minutes. Pat dough into ½ inch thickness; cut into 12 biscuits with 3-inch-round cutter. Bake on greased cookie sheet at 425 degrees until golden, 10 to 12 minutes.

QUICK SELF-RISING BISCUITS

Two cups all-purpose flour can be substituted for the self-rising flour; then add 3 teaspoons baking powder and ½ teaspoon salt.

18 servings (1 biscuit each)

2 cups self-rising flour
1 tablespoon vegetable shortening
¾-1 cup fat-free milk
1 tablespoon margarine, *or* butter, melted

Per Serving
Calories: 65
% Calories from fat: 21
Fat (gm): 1.4
Saturated fat (gm): 0.3
Cholesterol (mg): 0.2
Sodium (mg): 189
Protein (gm): 1.7
Carbohydrate (gm): 10.8
Exchanges
Milk: 0.0
Vegetable: 0.0
Fruit: 0.0
Bread: 1.0
Meat: 0.0
Fat: 0.0

1. Measure flour into medium bowl; cut in margarine until mixture resembles coarse crumbs. Stir enough milk into flour mixture to make a soft dough. Roll dough on floured surface to ½ inch thickness; cut into 18 biscuits with 2-inch cutter.

2. Place biscuits in greased 13 x 9-inch baking pan; brush with melted margarine. Bake at 425 degrees until golden, about 15 minutes.

Variations: **Chive Biscuits**—Mix 3 tablespoons snipped fresh or dried chives into biscuit dough.

Parmesan Biscuits—Brush biscuits with melted margarine as above; sprinkle with 2 tablespoons grated fat-free Parmesan cheese.

SWEET POTATO BISCUITS

Sweet potatoes offer moistness and a delicate sweetness to these biscuits. For a nonsweet biscuit, white potatoes can be substituted.

18 servings (1 biscuit each)

¾	cup mashed, cooked sweet potatoes
3-4	tablespoons margarine, *or* butter, melted
⅔	cup fat-free milk
1¾-2	cups all-purpose flour, divided
4	teaspoons baking powder
1	tablespoon brown sugar
½	teaspoon salt
	Fat-free milk, for glaze
	Nutmeg, ground, as garnish

Per Serving
Calories: 82
% Calories from fat: 23
Fat (gm): 2.1
Saturated fat (gm): 0.4
Cholesterol (mg): 0.1
Sodium (mg): 161
Protein (gm): 1.8
Carbohydrate (gm): 14
Exchanges
Milk: 0.0
Vegetable: 0.0
Fruit: 0.0
Bread: 1.0
Meat: 0.0
Fat: 0.5

1. Mix sweet potatoes and margarine in medium bowl; stir in ⅔ cup milk. Mix in 1¾ cups flour, baking powder, brown sugar, and salt. Mix in remaining ¼ cup flour if dough is too sticky to handle easily.

2. Knead dough on floured surface 5 to 6 times. Roll on floured surface to ½ inch thickness; cut into 18 biscuits with 2-inch biscuit cutter and place close together on greased baking sheet. Brush biscuits lightly with milk and sprinkle lightly with nutmeg.

3. Bake biscuits at 425 degrees until golden, 12 to 15 minutes.

"LITTLE PANTS" BISCUITS

These Mexican-inspired sugar and cinnamon-topped breads are sort of a cross between a biscuit and a cookie. They are usually made into "pants" shapes but can be cut into rounds or squares if you prefer.

18 servings (1 biscuit each)

4	tablespoons vegetable shortening
½	cup sugar, divided
2	cups all-purpose flour
2	teaspoons baking powder
½	teaspoon salt

Per Serving
Calories: 101
% Calories from fat: 27
Fat (gm): 3
Saturated fat (gm): 0.8
Cholesterol (mg): 0.1
Sodium (mg): 100
Protein (gm): 1.7
Carbohydrate (gm): 16.7

½ cup plus 2 tablespoons fat-free milk, divided

½ teaspoon ground cinnamon

Exchanges
Milk: 0.0
Vegetable: 0.0
Fruit: 0.0
Bread: 1.0
Meat: 0.0
Fat: 0.5

1. Beat shortening and 6 tablespoons sugar in medium bowl until smooth. Beat in combined flour, baking powder, and salt alternately with ½ cup milk to form soft dough.

2. Roll dough on floured surface into a rectangle, a scant ½ inch thick. Cut dough into 18 trapezoid shapes, 2½ inches long on the bottom, 1½ inches on the top, and 3 inches on the sides. Cut out a small wedge of dough from the bottom, center of each piece to form "pants legs."

3. Lightly brush biscuits with remaining 2 tablespoons of milk. Mix the remaining 2 tablespoons of sugar with the cinnamon; sprinkle over biscuits.

4. Bake at 350 degrees on lightly greased cookie sheet until browned, 15 to 20 minutes. Serve warm.

WILD RICE MUFFINS

 Wild rice adds crunchy texture and a nutritional boost to these muffins.

12 servings (1 muffin each)

½ cup uncooked wild rice
2 cups water
1 teaspoon salt, divided
1 cup fat-free milk
4 tablespoons margarine, *or* butter, melted
1 egg, beaten
2 egg whites
1 cup all-purpose flour
½ cup whole wheat flour
3 tablespoons baking powder
1 tablespoon sugar

Per Serving
Calories: 136
% Calories from fat: 30
Fat (gm): 4.5
Saturated fat (gm): 0.9
Cholesterol (mg): 18.1
Sodium (mg): 494
Protein (gm): 4.6
Carbohydrate (gm): 19.4
Exchanges
Milk: 0.0
Vegetable: 0.0
Fruit: 0.0
Bread: 1.5
Meat: 0.0
Fat: 0.5

1. Heat rice, water, and ½ teaspoon salt to boiling in small saucepan; reduce heat and simmer, covered, until rice is tender, 45 to 50 minutes. Drain, if necessary, and cool.

2. Mix milk, margarine, egg, egg whites, and rice in large bowl. Add combined all-purpose and whole wheat flour, baking powder, sugar, and remaining ½ teaspoon salt, mixing just until dry ingredients are moistened.

3. Spoon batter into 12 greased muffin cups. Bake at 400 degrees until muffins are browned, 20 to 25 minutes. Remove from pans and cool on wire racks.

CARDAMOM-PEAR MUFFINS

Any dried fruit you like can be substituted for the pears, and nutmeg can be substituted for the cardamom.

12 servings (1 muffin each)

1 cup fat-free milk
4 tablespoons margarine, *or* butter, melted
1 egg
2 cups all-purpose flour
⅓ cup plus 2 tablespoons sugar, divided
3 teaspoons baking powder
½ teaspoon salt
1 cup chopped dried pears
1 teaspoon grated orange, *or* lemon, rind
½ teaspoon ground cardamom, *or* nutmeg

Per Serving
Calories: 193
% Calories from fat: 21
Fat (gm): 4.5
Saturated fat (gm): 1
Cholesterol (mg): 18.1
Sodium (mg): 232
Protein (gm): 3.7
Carbohydrate (gm): 35.4
Exchanges
Milk: 0.0
Vegetable: 0.0
Fruit: 0.0
Bread: 2.0
Meat: 0.0
Fat: 1.0

1. Mix milk, margarine, and egg in medium bowl. Add combined flour, ⅓ cup sugar, baking powder, and salt, mixing just until dry ingredients are moistened. Gently mix in pears and orange rind.

2. Spoon batter into 12 greased muffin cups; sprinkle with remaining 2 tablespoons sugar and cardamom. Bake at 400 degrees until muffins are browned and toothpicks inserted in centers of muffins come out clean, 20 to 25 minutes. Remove from pans and cool on wire racks.

HIGH-ENERGY MUFFINS

 These muffins pack a nutritional punch, thanks to the addition of pureed beans.

24 servings (1 muffin each)

3 cups cooked, dried red kidney beans, *or* 2 cans (15 ounces each) red kidney beans, rinsed, drained

⅓ cup fat-free milk

4 tablespoons margarine, *or* butter, softened

¾ cup packed light brown sugar

3 eggs

1 teaspoon vanilla

1 cup all-purpose flour

½ cup whole wheat flour

1 teaspoon baking soda

½ teaspoon salt

1 teaspoon ground cinnamon

½ teaspoon ground allspice

¼ teaspoon ground nutmeg

¼ teaspoon ground mace

¾ cup raisins

　Cinnamon Streusel (recipe follows)

　Vanilla Glaze (recipe follows)

Per Serving
Calories: 174
% Calories from fat: 19
Fat (gm): 3.7
Saturated fat (gm): 0.8
Cholesterol (mg): 26.7
Sodium (mg): 146
Protein (gm): 4.1
Carbohydrate (gm): 31.9
Exchanges
Milk: 0.0
Vegetable: 0.0
Fruit: 0.0
Bread: 2.0
Meat: 0.0
Fat: 0.5

1. Process beans and milk in food processor until mixture is smooth. Beat margarine, brown sugar, eggs, and vanilla until smooth in medium bowl; beat in bean mixture. Add combined all-purpose and whole wheat flour, baking soda, salt, and spices, mixing just until blended. Mix in raisins.

2. Spoon mixture into 24 greased muffin cups and sprinkle with Cinnamon Streusel. Bake at 375 degrees until toothpicks inserted in centers come out clean, 20 to 25 minutes. Cool muffins in pans 5 minutes; remove and cool on wire racks.

3. Drizzle muffins with Vanilla Glaze.

Cinnamon Streusel

(makes about ¾ cup)

- ½ cup packed light brown sugar
- 2 tablespoons quick-cooking oats
- 2 tablespoons flour
- ¼ teaspoon ground cinnamon
- 2 tablespoons cold margarine, *or* butter, cut into pieces

1. Combine brown sugar, oats, flour, and cinnamon in small bowl; cut in margarine until mixture resembles coarse crumbs.

Vanilla Glaze

(makes about ⅓ cup)

- 1 cup powdered sugar
- 1 teaspoon vanilla
- 2-3 tablespoons fat-free milk

1. Mix powdered sugar and vanilla with enough milk to make medium glaze consistency.

BLUEBERRY PANCAKES WITH BLUEBERRY MAPLE SYRUP

For special occasions or just for fun, drizzle pancake batter into heart or other shapes in the skillet!

4 main-dish servings

- ¾ cup fat-free milk
- 1 egg
- 1 tablespoon margarine, *or* butter, melted
- ¾ cup all-purpose flour
- ¼ cup whole wheat flour
- 1-2 tablespoons sugar
- 2 teaspoons baking powder
- ½ teaspoon salt
- ⅛ teaspoon ground nutmeg
- ¾ cup fresh, *or* frozen, thawed, blueberries
  Blueberry Maple Syrup (recipe follows), *or* light pancake syrup, heated

Per Serving
Calories: 308
% Calories from fat: 14
Fat (gm): 4.7
Saturated fat (gm): 1.1
Cholesterol (mg): 54
Sodium (mg): 511
Protein (gm): 6.9
Carbohydrate (gm): 60.9
Exchanges
Milk: 0.0
Vegetable: 0.0
Fruit: 2.0
Bread: 2.0
Meat: 0.0
Fat: 1.0

1. Mix milk, egg, and margarine in medium bowl; add remaining ingredients, except blueberries and syrup, and beat until almost smooth. Gently mix in blueberries.

2. Pour batter into lightly greased large skillet, using about ¼ cup batter for each pancake. Cook over medium heat until bubbles form in pancakes and they are browned on the bottoms, 3 to 5 minutes. Turn pancakes; cook until browned on other side, 3 to 5 minutes.

3. Serve pancakes with Blueberry Maple Syrup.

Blueberry Maple Syrup

(makes 4 servings, about ¼ cup each)

    ½-¾ cup maple syrup
      ½ cup fresh, *or* frozen, blueberries
      1 teaspoon grated orange rind
      1 teaspoon grated lemon rind

1. Heat all ingredients in small saucepan over medium-high heat until hot through, 3 to 5 minutes.

BUTTERMILK BUCKWHEAT PANCAKES

Whole wheat flour can be substituted for the buckwheat flour if you want.

4 main-dish servings

      1 cup buttermilk
      1 egg
    1-2 tablespoons vegetable oil
      ½ cup all-purpose flour
      ½ cup buckwheat flour
      1 tablespoon sugar
      1 teaspoon baking powder
      ½ teaspoon baking soda
      ½ teaspoon salt
      1 teaspoon grated orange rind
    ½-1 cup maple syrup, light pancake syrup,
         or Blueberry Maple Syrup (see previous
         recipe), heated

Per Serving
Calories: 291
% Calories from fat: 18
Fat (gm): 5.8
Saturated fat (gm): 1.3
Cholesterol (mg): 55.5
Sodium (mg): 593
Protein (gm): 7.1
Carbohydrate (gm): 54
Exchanges
Milk: 0.0
Vegetable: 0.0
Fruit: 1.5
Bread: 2.0
Meat: 0.0
Fat: 1.0

1. Mix buttermilk, egg, and oil in medium bowl; add remaining ingredients, except maple syrup, and beat until almost smooth.

2. Pour batter into lightly greased large skillet, using about ¼ cup batter for each pancake. Cook over medium heat until bubbles form in pancakes and they are browned on the bottoms, 3 to 5 minutes. Turn pancakes; cook until browned on other side, 3 to 5 minutes.

3. Serve pancakes with warm syrup.

CREPES

Cooked crepes can be kept warm in a 200-degree oven while cooking remaining crepes. Crepes can also be made in advance and frozen; layer crepes in plastic wrap and wrap in aluminum foil. To heat, place unwrapped crepes on cookie sheet; bake at 325 degrees until hot, 5 to 8 minutes.

4 servings (2 each)

½ cup all-purpose flour
½ cup fat-free milk
1 egg
2 egg whites
1 tablespoon margarine, melted, *or* canola oil
¼ teaspoon salt
Vegetable cooking spray

Per Serving
Calories: 120
% Calories from fat: 33
 (will decrease when filled)
Fat (gm): 4.3
Saturated fat (gm): 1
Cholesterol (mg): 53.8
Sodium (mg): 226
Protein (gm): 6
Carbohydrate (gm): 13.8
Exchanges
Milk: 0.0
Vegetable: 0.0
Fruit: 0.0
Bread: 1.0
Meat: 0.0
Fat: 1.0

1. Combine all ingredients, except cooking spray, in small bowl; beat until smooth (batter will be thin).

2. Spray 8-inch crepe pan or small skillet with cooking spray; heat over medium heat until hot. Pour scant ¼ cup batter into pan, tilting pan to coat bottom evenly with batter.

3. Cook over medium heat until browned on the bottom, 2 to 3 minutes. Turn crepe and cook until browned on other side, 2 to 3 minutes.

Variation: **Dessert Crepes**—Add 1 to 2 tablespoons sugar to crepe batter; cook as above.

STUFFED FRENCH TOAST

A rich breakfast entrée with a sweet surprise inside! Serve with warm maple syrup or a drizzle of honey.

4 main-dish servings

¾ cup no-cholesterol real egg product

⅓ cup fat-free half-and-half, *or* fat-free milk

1 teaspoon ground cinnamon

¼ teaspoon ground nutmeg

4 thick (1-inch) slices sourdough, *or* Italian, bread

4 tablespoons fat-free cream cheese

4 teaspoons strawberry, *or* other flavor, spreadable fruit preserves

1-2 tablespoons margarine, *or* butter

1 cup maple syrup, *or* light pancake syrup, warm

Per Serving
Calories: 353
% Calories from fat: 9
Fat (gm): 3.7
Saturated fat (gm): 0.8
Cholesterol (mg): 0
Sodium (mg): 376
Protein (gm): 8.8
Carbohydrate (gm): 71.2
Exchanges
Milk: 0.0
Vegetable: 0.0
Fruit: 3.0
Bread: 2.0
Meat: 0.0
Fat: 0.5

1. Combine egg product, half-and-half, and spices in shallow bowl.

2. Cut a pocket into the side of each bread slice; fill with cream cheese and spreadable fruit. Soak bread in egg mixture, turning to soak both sides.

3. Cook bread in margarine in large skillet on low to medium-low heat until browned, about 5 minutes on each side. Serve with warm syrup.

SPICED PEAR BUTTER

Use ripe pears that are still firm for this gently spiced spread.

Makes 1½ pints (48 servings of 1 tablespoon)

2½ pounds firm, ripe pears, peeled, cored, chopped

½ cup water

1 tablespoon lemon juice

¾ teaspoon ground ginger

½ teaspoon ground cinnamon

Per Serving
Calories: 47
% Calories from fat: 2
Fat (gm): 0.1
Saturated fat (gm): 0
Cholesterol (mg): 0
Sodium (mg): 0
Protein (gm): 0.1
Carbohydrate (gm): 12

⅛ teaspoon ground nutmeg

2-2¼ cups sugar

Exchanges
Milk: 0.0
Vegetable: 0.0
Fruit: 0.75
Bread: 0.0
Meat: 0.0
Fat: 0.0

1. Heat pears and water to boiling in large saucepan; reduce heat and simmer, covered, until pears are very tender, about 10 minutes. Process pears and liquid in food processor or blender until smooth.

2. Return pear puree to saucepan; stir in remaining ingredients. Heat mixture to boiling; reduce heat and simmer, uncovered, stirring frequently, until mixture thickens to desired consistency, 10 to 20 minutes.

3. Pour pear butter into 3 sterilized half-pint jars and seal; cool. Store in refrigerator up to 2 weeks.

SPICED RHUBARB JAM

Cook this jam to desired consistency, as it is not made with pectin.

Makes 2 pints (64 servings of 1 tablespoon)

1½ pounds rhubarb, cut into 1 to 2-inch pieces (about 6 cups)

2 cups sugar

1 cup water

2 pieces gingerroot (each 1 inch), cut lengthwise in halves

1 cinnamon stick

¼ teaspoon ground cardamom

Per Serving
Calories: 27
% Calories from fat: 1
Fat (gm): 0
Saturated fat (gm): 0
Cholesterol (mg): 0
Sodium (mg): 1
Protein (gm): 0.1
Carbohydrate (gm): 6.8
Exchanges
Milk: 0.0
Vegetable: 0.0
Fruit: 0.5
Bread: 0.0
Meat: 0.0
Fat: 0.0

1. Combine rhubarb, sugar, and water in large saucepan; heat to boiling. Reduce heat and simmer, covered, until rhubarb is tender, about 10 minutes. Strain rhubarb, reserving juice.

2. Return juice to saucepan; add gingerroot, cinnamon, and cardamom and heat to boiling. Simmer rapidly, stirring occasionally, until very thick, 10 to 15 minutes. Discard cinnamon stick and gingerroot.

3. Stir rhubarb into juice mixture; simmer longer, if necessary to achieve desired thickness, stirring constantly to prevent sticking and burning.

4. Pour jam into sterilized jars and seal; cool. Store in refrigerator.

ORANGE-ROSEMARY JELLY

 A subtle herb-flavored jelly that's especially wonderful with biscuits.

Makes 2 pints (64 servings of 1 tablespoon)

1 cup boiling water
2 tablespoons rosemary leaves, crushed
1 can (6 ounces) frozen orange juice concentrate
1 package (1¾ ounces) powdered fruit pectin
¼ cup lemon juice
1 tablespoon distilled white vinegar
Pinch salt
1 drop red food color (optional)
3⅓ cups sugar

Per Serving
Calories: 47
% Calories from fat: 0
Fat (gm): 0
Saturated fat (gm): 0
Cholesterol (mg): 0
Sodium (mg): 2
Protein (gm): 0.1
Carbohydrate (gm): 12.2
Exchanges
Milk: 0.0
Vegetable: 0.0
Fruit: 0.75
Bread: 0.0
Meat: 0.0
Fat: 0.0

1. Pour boiling water over rosemary in small bowl; let stand until cool. Strain; discard rosemary. Combine rosemary water and orange juice concentrate in 2-cup measure; add water to measure 2 cups.

2. Combine orange juice mixture and remaining ingredients, except sugar, in large saucepan; heat to boiling. Stir in sugar and return to boiling, stirring constantly. Boil hard 1 minute, stirring constantly.

3. Pour jelly into sterilized jars and seal; cool. Store in refrigerator.

TARRAGON WINE JELLY

 A delicious jelly that will make any occasion jolly!

Makes 3 pints (96 servings of 1 tablespoon)

4	cups dry white wine
2	tablespoons dried tarragon leaves
6	cups sugar
1	package (6 ounces) liquid pectin

Per Serving
Calories: 58
% Calories from fat: 0
Fat (gm): 0
Saturated fat (gm): 0
Cholesterol (mg): 0
Sodium (mg): 10
Protein (gm): 0
Carbohydrate (gm): 14.1
Exchanges
Milk: 0.0
Vegetable: 0.0
Fruit: 1.0
Bread: 0.0
Meat: 0.0
Fat: 0.0

1. Heat wine and tarragon to boiling in medium saucepan; reduce heat and simmer, covered, 10 minutes. Strain. Return wine to saucepan; add sugar and heat to boiling, stirring occasionally. Stir in pectin and heat to boiling; boil hard 1 minute, stirring constantly.

2. Pour jelly into sterilized jars and seal; cool. Store in refrigerator.

ROSE GERANIUM JELLY

 Simply delicious, and one of my favorites for gift giving. Serve with a plain cracker, biscuits, or bread.

Makes 2 pints (64 servings of 1 tablespoon)

1	cup boiling water
½	cup packed torn rose geranium leaves
1	can (6 ounces) frozen apple juice concentrate
1	package (1¾ ounces) powdered fruit pectin
2-3	tablespoons lemon juice
1	tablespoon distilled white vinegar
	Pinch salt
3½	cups sugar

Per Serving
Calories: 49
% Calories from fat: 0
Fat (gm): 0
Saturated fat (gm): 0
Cholesterol (mg): 0
Sodium (mg): 2
Protein (gm): 0
Carbohydrate (gm): 12.8
Exchanges
Milk: 0.0
Vegetable: 0.0
Fruit: 0.75
Bread: 0.0
Meat: 0.0
Fat: 0.0

1. Pour boiling water over rose geranium leaves in small bowl; let stand until cool. Strain; discard rose geranium leaves. Combine rose geranium water and apple juice concentrate in 2-cup measure; add water to measure 2 cups.

2. Combine apple juice mixture and remaining ingredients, except sugar, in large saucepan; heat to boiling. Stir in sugar and return to boiling, stirring constantly. Boil hard 1 minute, stirring constantly.

3. Pour jelly into sterilized jars and seal; cool. Store in refrigerator.

Variation: **Apple-Mint Jelly**—Substitute ½ cup loosely packed mint leaves, or 3 tablespoons dried mint leaves, for the rose geranium leaves. Make recipe as above.

EASY GINGER JELLY

Serve on crackers, homemade bread, or biscuits. The flavor of this jelly is subtle—use more gingerroot if a stronger flavor is desired.

Makes 2 half-pints (32 servings of 1 tablespoon)

2 jars (8 ounces each) apple jelly

4-6 quarter-size slices gingerroot (⅛ inch thick), coarsely chopped

Per Serving
Calories: 39
% Calories from fat: 0
Fat (gm): 0
Saturated fat (gm): 0
Cholesterol (mg): 0
Sodium (mg): 2
Protein (gm): 0
Carbohydrate (gm): 10.1
Exchanges
Milk: 0.0
Vegetable: 0.0
Fruit: 0.5
Bread: 0.0
Meat: 0.0
Fat: 0.0

1. Heat jelly and ginger to boiling over medium heat in small saucepan. Remove from heat and let stand until cool.

2. Spoon jelly and ginger into sterilized jars and seal. Refrigerate at least 3 days before serving. Store in refrigerator.

GINGERED HONEY

For best flavor make this aromatic honey 2 weeks in advance of serving. Serve on toast, crackers, biscuits, or pancakes, or spoon over ice cream or fruit!

Makes 1 pint (32 servings of 1 tablespoon)

4 ounces gingerroot, peeled, sliced paper-thin

1⅓ cups honey, clover *or* other flavor, warm

Per Serving
Calories: 46
% Calories from fat: 0
Fat (gm): 0
Saturated fat (gm): 0
Cholesterol (mg): 0
Sodium (mg): 1
Protein (gm): 0
Carbohydrate (gm): 11.9
Exchanges
Milk: 0.0
Vegetable: 0.0
Fruit: 0.75
Bread: 0.0
Meat: 0.0
Fat: 0.0

1. Loosely fill sterilized pint jar with gingerroot; fill to top with warm honey, covering ginger completely. Cool to room temperature; seal and refrigerate at least 2 weeks before using. Store in refrigerator.

FIFTEEN

Sauces

AND

Condiments

PIZZA SAUCE

A simple sauce that can also be used on "burgers," loaves, or other entrées.

4 servings (¼ cup each)

Olive oil cooking spray
1 small onion, chopped
¼ cup chopped green bell pepper
2 cloves garlic, minced
1 can (8 ounces) reduced-sodium tomato sauce
½ teaspoon dried basil leaves
¼ teaspoon dried oregano leaves
Salt and pepper, to taste

Per Serving
Calories: 37
% Calories from fat: 2
Fat (gm): 0.1
Saturated fat (gm): 0
Cholesterol (mg): 0
Sodium (mg): 18
Protein (gm): 1.5
Carbohydrate (gm): 7.8
Exchanges
Milk: 0.0
Vegetable: 1.5
Fruit: 0.0
Bread: 0.0
Meat: 0.0
Fat: 0.0

1. Spray medium saucepan with cooking spray; heat over medium heat until hot. Saute onion, bell pepper, and garlic until tender, about 5 minutes.

2. Stir in tomato sauce and herbs; heat to boiling. Reduce heat and simmer, uncovered, until sauce thickens, about 5 minutes. Season to taste with salt and pepper.

MARINARA SAUCE

A classic Italian tomato sauce, seasoned very simply. Serve over any desired pasta.

8 servings (about ½ cup each)

2 medium onions, chopped
6-8 cloves garlic, minced
1-2 tablespoons olive oil
2 cans (16 ounces each) plum tomatoes, drained, chopped
½ cup dry white wine, *or* tomato juice
¼ cup tomato paste
2-3 tablespoons lemon juice
½ teaspoon salt
¼ teaspoon pepper

Per Serving
Calories: 62
% Calories from fat: 28
 (10% with 2 ozs. pasta)
Fat (gm): 2.1
Saturated fat (gm): 0.3
Cholesterol (mg): 0
Sodium (mg): 384
Protein (gm): 1.9
Carbohydrate (gm): 10.1
Exchanges
Milk: 0.0
Vegetable: 2.0
Fruit: 0.0
Bread: 0.0
Meat: 0.0
Fat: 0.5

1. Saute onions and garlic in oil in large saucepan until tender, about 5 minutes. Stir in tomatoes, wine, and tomato paste; heat to boiling. Reduce heat and simmer, uncovered, until mixture is medium sauce consistency, about 20 minutes. Stir in lemon juice, salt, and pepper.

TOMATO AND "MEAT" SAUCE

A perfect sauce for pasta, lasagne, and tomato sauce-based casseroles.

8 servings (about ½ cup each)

Olive oil cooking spray
1 medium onion, chopped
3 cloves garlic, minced
2 cans (14½ ounces each) reduced-sodium diced tomatoes
½ package (12-ounce size) frozen pre-browned vegetable protein crumbles, *or* 1 cup textured vegetable protein
⅓ cup finely chopped parsley
¼ cup water
¾ teaspoon Italian herbs
¾ teaspoon dried basil leaves
½ teaspoon dried oregano leaves
⅛ teaspoon ground nutmeg
Salt and pepper, to taste

Per Serving
Calories: 61
% Calories from fat: 5
Fat (gm): 0.3
Saturated fat (gm): 0.1
Cholesterol (mg): 0
Sodium (mg): 110
Protein (gm): 6.2
Carbohydrate (gm): 9.2
Exchanges
Milk: 0.0
Vegetable: 2.0
Fruit: 0.0
Bread: 0.0
Meat: 0.5
Fat: 0.0

1. Spray large saucepan with cooking spray; heat over medium heat until hot. Saute onion and garlic until tender, 3 to 5 minutes.

2. Add remaining ingredients, except salt and pepper; heat to boiling. Reduce heat and simmer, uncovered, until thickened, about 20 minutes, stirring occasionally. Season to taste with salt and pepper.

FRESH TOMATO-BASIL SAUCE

This fresh tomato sauce has an intense basil flavor. For interesting variations, other fresh herbs such as rosemary, tarragon, or sage can be substituted for the basil. Serve over a more delicate pasta, such as angel hair or thin spaghetti.

8 servings (about ½ cup each)

5 cups chopped tomatoes
1 small onion, chopped
5 cloves garlic, minced
½ cup dry red, *or* white, wine
2 tablespoons tomato paste
1 tablespoon sugar
2 tablespoons finely chopped fresh thyme leaves, *or* 1½ teaspoons dried
2 bay leaves
3-4 tablespoons finely chopped fresh basil leaves, *or* 1½ teaspoons dried
½ teaspoon salt
⅛ teaspoon crushed red pepper
¼ teaspoon ground black pepper

Per Serving
Calories: 58
% Calories from fat: 8
   (2% with 2 ozs. pasta)
Fat (gm): 0.6
Saturated fat (gm): 0.1
Cholesterol (mg): 0
Sodium (mg): 122
Protein (gm): 1.7
Carbohydrate (gm): 10.9
Exchanges
Milk: 0.0
Vegetable: 2.0
Fruit: 0.0
Bread: 0.0
Meat: 0.0
Fat: 0.0

1. Combine all ingredients, except basil, salt, and peppers, in medium saucepan; heat to boiling. Reduce heat and simmer, covered, 5 minutes. Simmer, uncovered, until sauce is reduced to medium consistency, about 20 minutes.

2. Stir in basil, salt, and both peppers; simmer 5 to 10 minutes longer. Discard bay leaves.

FRESH TOMATO AND HERB SAUCE

Prepare and enjoy this sauce when garden-ripened tomatoes are at their peak flavor. Use fresh herbs if at all possible. Serve over any desired pasta.

6 servings (about ½ cup each)

¼ cup finely chopped onion
3 cloves garlic, minced
1 tablespoon olive oil
5 cups peeled, seeded, chopped tomatoes

Per Serving
Calories: 66
% Calories from fat: 36
   (10% with 2 ozs. pasta)
Fat (gm): 2.9
Saturated fat (gm): 0.4
Cholesterol (mg): 0
Sodium (mg): 106
Protein (gm): 1.8
Carbohydrate (gm): 10.1

2 tablespoons finely chopped fresh basil leaves, *or* 1½ teaspoons dried

1 tablespoon finely chopped fresh thyme leaves, *or* ½ teaspoon dried

1 tablespoon finely chopped fresh oregano leaves, *or* 1 teaspoon dried

2 bay leaves

½ teaspoon salt

½ teaspoon pepper

Exchanges
Milk: 0.0
Vegetable: 2.0
Fruit: 0.0
Bread: 0.0
Meat: 0.0
Fat: 0.5

1. Saute onion and garlic in oil in large saucepan until tender, about 5 minutes. Add tomatoes and herbs to saucepan. Cook, covered, over medium-high heat until tomatoes release liquid and begin to wilt, about 5 minutes. Reduce heat and simmer, uncovered, until mixture is very thick, about 20 minutes. Discard bay leaves; stir in salt and pepper.

2. If a smooth sauce is desired, process in food processor or blender until smooth.

TOMATO SAUCE WITH MUSHROOMS AND SHERRY

Flavors of mushrooms, sherry, rosemary, and oregano meld in a delicious tomato sauce. Serve over spinach fettuccine, thin spaghetti, or linguine.

4 servings (about ½ cup each)

1 small onion, finely chopped

2 cloves garlic, minced

1 tablespoon olive oil

4 cups sliced mushrooms

3 tablespoons dry sherry, *or* water

1 can (28 ounces) crushed tomatoes, undrained

2 tablespoons finely chopped parsley

½ teaspoon dried rosemary leaves, crushed

½ teaspoon dried oregano leaves

1 teaspoon sugar

¼ teaspoon salt

¼ teaspoon pepper

Per Serving
Calories: 118
% Calories from fat: 29
  (11% with 2 ozs. pasta)
Fat (gm): 4.2
Saturated fat (gm): 0.6
Cholesterol (mg): 0
Sodium (mg): 462
Protein (gm): 3.8
Carbohydrate (gm): 16.3
Exchanges
Milk: 0.0
Vegetable: 3.0
Fruit: 0.0
Bread: 0.0
Meat: 0.0
Fat: 1.0

1. Saute onions and garlic in oil in medium saucepan 2 to 3 minutes. Add mushrooms and sherry; cook, covered, over medium-high heat until mushrooms are wilted and release liquid. Reduce heat and cook, uncovered, stirring occasionally, until mushrooms are soft and have darkened.

2. Stir in tomatoes, herbs, and sugar; heat to boiling. Reduce heat and simmer, covered, 10 to 15 minutes. Stir in salt and pepper.

BOLOGNESE-STYLE "MEAT" SAUCE

 Traditionally, Bolognese sauce is made with chopped beef or Italian sausage. All-vegetable protein crumbles are used for the vegetarian version of this sauce. Serve with spaghetti or use a shaped pasta such as farfalle (bow ties) or ruote (wheels).

4 servings (about ½ cup each)

Vegetable cooking spray
1 small onion, finely chopped
¼ cup thinly sliced carrot
¼ cup thinly sliced celery
3 cloves garlic, minced
½ teaspoon dried oregano leaves
½ teaspoon dried tarragon leaves
½ teaspoon dried thyme leaves
⅛ teaspoon ground nutmeg
1 can (8 ounces) reduced-sodium tomato sauce
1 can (8 ounces) reduced-sodium whole tomatoes, drained, chopped
¼ cup dry white wine, *or* tomato juice
⅔ package (12-ounce size) frozen pre-browned vegetable protein crumbles, thawed
Salt and pepper, to taste

Per Serving
Calories: 145
% Calories from fat: 2
 (3% with 2 ozs. pasta)
Fat (gm): 0.3
Saturated fat (gm): 0.1
Cholesterol (mg): 0
Sodium (mg): 286
Protein (gm): 15.2
Carbohydrate (gm): 18.3
Exchanges
Milk: 0.0
Vegetable: 2.0
Fruit: 0.0
Bread: 0.0
Meat: 2.0
Fat: 0.0

1. Spray medium saucepan with cooking spray; heat over medium heat until hot. Saute onion, carrot, celery, and garlic until crisp-tender, about 5 minutes; stir in herbs and cook 1 to 2 minutes longer.

2. Add tomato sauce, tomatoes, wine, and protein crumbles to saucepan; heat to boiling. Reduce heat and simmer, uncovered, until thick sauce consistency, about 15 minutes. Season to taste with salt and pepper.

TOMATO AND "MEATBALL" SAUCE

 You'll savor the full-bodied herb flavors in this updated version of a traditional pasta sauce. Serve with spaghetti or one of the more unusually shaped pastas such as cappelletti (little hats) or gnocchi.

6 servings (about 1⅓ cups each)

1	cup chopped onion	
3	cloves garlic, minced	
1	tablespoon olive oil	
1	can (16 ounces) reduced-sodium whole tomatoes, drained, chopped	
1	can (8 ounces) reduced-sodium tomato sauce	
1	tablespoon tomato paste	
1	teaspoon dried basil leaves	
½	teaspoon dried tarragon leaves	
½	teaspoon dried oregano leaves	
⅛	teaspoon crushed red pepper	
½	teaspoon salt	
¼	teaspoon black pepper	
	Italian-Style "Meatballs" (see p. 399)	
½	cup no-cholesterol real egg product	

Per Serving
Calories: 183
% Calories from fat: 14
Fat (gm): 2.8
Saturated fat (gm): 0.3
Cholesterol (mg): 0
Sodium (mg): 613
Protein (gm): 18.5
Carbohydrate (gm): 21.4
Exchanges
Milk: 0.0
Vegetable: 3.0
Fruit: 0.0
Bread: 0.0
Meat: 2.0
Fat: 0.0

1. Saute onion and garlic in oil in large saucepan 2 to 3 minutes. Stir in tomatoes, tomato sauce, tomato paste, herbs, and red pepper; heat to boiling. Reduce heat and simmer, uncovered, 10 minutes; stir in salt and pepper.

2. Make "Meatballs", substituting ½ cup no-cholesterol egg product for the whole eggs. Add "Meatballs" to tomato mixture. Simmer, uncovered, until medium sauce consistency, 10 to 15 minutes.

PEASANT BEAN SAUCE WITH TOMATOES AND SAGE

Hearty and chunky with 2 types of beans, this sauce is excellent served over one of the tube-shaped pastas such as ziti, mostaccioli, or rigatoni.

8 servings (about ½ cup each)

1 can (15½ ounces) red kidney beans, drained
1 can (15 ounces) cannellini, *or* Great Northern beans, drained
½ cup chopped onion
½ cup chopped celery
2 cloves garlic, minced
1 can (16 ounces) plum tomatoes, drained, chopped
2 cups Canned Vegetable Stock (see p. 63), *or* canned reduced-sodium vegetable broth
1 teaspoon dried sage leaves
¼ teaspoon salt
⅛ teaspoon pepper

Per Serving
Calories: 121
% Calories from fat: 4
 (3% with 2 ozs. pasta)
Fat (gm): 1.2
Saturated fat (gm): 0.5
Cholesterol (mg): 0
Sodium (mg): 300
Protein (gm): 9.2
Carbohydrate (gm): 25.1
Exchanges
Milk: 0.0
Vegetable: 1.0
Fruit: 0.0
Bread: 1.0
Meat: 0.5
Fat: 0.0

1. Heat beans, onion, celery, and garlic to boiling in large saucepan. Reduce heat and simmer, covered, 5 minutes.

2. Stir in tomatoes, stock, and sage; heat to boiling. Reduce heat and simmer, uncovered, until mixture is desired sauce consistency, about 20 minutes. Stir in salt and pepper.

CREOLE SAUCE

Creole flavors accent this substantial sauce. If you enjoy okra, it would be an excellent addition. Serve over spaghetti or tube-shaped pasta.

8 servings (about ½ cup each)

1½ cups sliced green bell peppers
¾ cup sliced carrots
½ cup sliced onion
½ cup sliced celery
3 cloves garlic, minced

Per Serving
Calories: 77
% Calories from fat: 40
 (14% with 2 ozs. pasta)
Fat (gm): 3.6
Saturated fat (gm): 0.5
Cholesterol (mg): 0
Sodium (mg): 173
Protein (gm): 1.7
Carbohydrate (gm): 10.6

2 tablespoons olive oil

1 medium tomato, chopped

1 teaspoon dried basil leaves

1 teaspoon dried oregano leaves

1 teaspoon paprika

½ teaspoon dried thyme leaves

½ teaspoon gumbo file powder (optional)

1 bay leaf

¼ teaspoon cayenne pepper

½ teaspoon salt

1 can (14½ ounces) reduced-sodium vegetable broth

1 can (8 ounces) reduced-sodium tomato sauce

Exchanges
Milk: 0.0
Vegetable: 2.0
Fruit: 0.0
Bread: 0.0
Meat: 0.0
Fat: 0.5

1. Saute bell peppers, carrots, onion, celery, and garlic in oil until peppers are tender, 8 to 10 minutes. Stir in tomato, combined herbs, gumbo file powder, bay leaf, cayenne pepper, and salt. Cook over medium heat 2 to 3 minutes, stirring frequently.

2. Add broth and tomato sauce; heat to boiling. Reduce heat and simmer, uncovered, until vegetables are tender and sauce is thickened to desired consistency, about 20 minutes. Discard bay leaf.

PEPERONATA-TOMATO SAUCE

Italian peperonata, a slow-cooked mixture of bell peppers and onions, is combined with tomato sauce for a perfect pasta topping.

4 servings (about ½ cup each)

1 medium red bell pepper, sliced

1 medium green bell pepper, sliced

1 medium yellow bell pepper, sliced

1 medium onion, sliced

3 cloves garlic, minced

2 tablespoons olive oil

2 tablespoons water

2 cans (8 ounces each) reduced-sodium tomato sauce

½ teaspoon salt

¼ teaspoon pepper

Per Serving
Calories: 135
% Calories from fat: 45
  (18% with 2 ozs. pasta)
Fat (gm): 6.9
Saturated fat (gm): 0.9
Cholesterol (mg): 0
Sodium (mg): 302
Protein (gm): 3
Carbohydrate (gm): 16
Exchanges
Milk: 0.0
Vegetable: 3.0
Fruit: 0.0
Bread: 0.0
Meat: 0.0
Fat: 1.5

1. Saute bell peppers, onion, and garlic in oil in medium saucepan 2 to 3 minutes. Add water; cook, covered, over medium to medium-high heat until peppers are wilted. Cook, uncovered, over medium-low heat until peppers mixture and onions are very soft and browned, about 20 minutes.

2. Stir tomato sauce into peppers mixture; heat to boiling. Reduce heat and simmer, uncovered, until mixture is thick sauce consistency, 10 to 15 minutes. Stir in salt and pepper.

EGGPLANT SAUCE

12 servings (about ½ cup each)

1	pound eggplant, unpeeled, cut into 1½-inch pieces	
1	cup chopped onion	
½	cup chopped green bell pepper	
6	cloves garlic, minced	
2	tablespoons olive oil	
3	cups chopped tomatoes	
¾	teaspoon dried tarragon leaves	
¾	teaspoon dried thyme leaves	
1	can (28 ounces) crushed tomatoes, undrained	
½	cup dry red wine	
2	tablespoons drained capers	
2	teaspoons sugar	
½	teaspoon salt	
¼	teaspoon pepper	

Per Serving
Calories: 83
% Calories from fat: 26
Fat (gm): 2.6
Saturated fat (gm): 0.4
Cholesterol (mg): 0
Sodium (mg): 317
Protein (gm): 2.2
Carbohydrate (gm): 12.5
Exchanges
Milk: 0.0
Vegetable: 2.5
Fruit: 0.0
Bread: 0.0
Meat: 0.0
Fat: 0.5

1. Saute eggplant, onion, bell pepper, and garlic in oil in large saucepan 5 minutes. Add chopped tomatoes and herbs, and saute until onion is crisp-tender, 5 to 7 minutes.

2. Stir canned tomatoes, wine, capers, and sugar into vegetable mixture; heat to boiling. Reduce heat and simmer, covered, until eggplant is tender, about 20 minutes. Simmer, uncovered, until desired sauce consistency, about 10 minutes more. Stir in salt and pepper.

MEDITERRANEAN TOMATO-CAPER SAUCE

Flavors of the Mediterranean combine in this fragrant tomato sauce. The sauce is not cooked but should be made in advance for flavors to meld. The sauce can be used hot, also; just heat before using.

4 servings (about ½ cup each)

2	cans (8 ounces each) reduced-sodium tomato sauce	
2	teaspoons minced garlic	
1	teaspoon dried oregano leaves	
1	teaspoon ground cumin	
1	teaspoon ground coriander	
1	teaspoon paprika	
	Pinch ground cardamom	
	Pinch ground cinnamon	
	Pinch ground cloves	
2	teaspoons lime juice	
¼	cup raisins	
2-3	teaspoons drained capers	
	Salt and pepper, to taste	

Per Serving
Calories: 83
% Calories from fat: 3
Fat (gm): 0.3
Saturated fat (gm): 0
Cholesterol (mg): 0
Sodium (mg): 88
Protein (gm): 2.7
Carbohydrate (gm): 18.3
Exchanges
Milk: 0.0
Vegetable: 2.0
Fruit: 0.5
Bread: 0.0
Meat: 0.0
Fat: 0.0

1. Combine all ingredients; refrigerate at least 2 hours for flavors to blend.

ROASTED RED PEPPER SAUCE

Fast and easy to make, this is a sauce you'll want to prepare often.

8 servings (3 tablespoons each)

4	large red bell peppers, cut into halves	
1	teaspoon sugar	

Per Serving
Calories: 41
% Calories from fat: 7
Fat (gm): 0.4
Saturated fat (gm): 0
Cholesterol (mg): 0
Sodium (mg): 0
Protein (gm): 1.6
Carbohydrate (gm): 9.4
Exchanges
Milk: 0.0
Vegetable: 1.5
Fruit: 0.0
Bread: 0.0
Meat: 0.0
Fat: 0.0

1. Place peppers, skin sides up, on broiler pan. Broil 4 to 6 inches from heat source until skins are blistered and blackened. Place peppers in plastic bag for 5 minutes; remove and peel off skins.

2. Process peppers and sugar in food processor or blender until smooth. Refrigerate until ready to use.

Note: 1 jar (12 ounces) roasted red peppers, drained, can be substituted for the peppers in the recipe.

MANY-CLOVES GARLIC SAUCE

Cooked slowly until caramelized, the garlic becomes very sweet in flavor.

4 servings (about ½ cup each)

25 cloves garlic, peeled

2 teaspoons olive oil

1¾ cups Basic Vegetable Stock, divided (see p. 58)

¼ cup dry white wine, *or* Basic Vegetable Stock

2 tablespoons flour

2 tablespoons finely chopped parsley

⅛ teaspoon salt

2 dashes white pepper

Per Serving
Calories: 78
% Calories from fat: 29
Fat (gm): 2.6
Saturated fat (gm): 0.4
Cholesterol (mg): 0
Sodium (mg): 76
Protein (gm): 0.5
Carbohydrate (gm): 2.5
Exchanges
Milk: 0.0
Vegetable: 2.0
Fruit: 0.0
Bread: 0.0
Meat: 0.0
Fat: 1.0

1. Cook garlic in oil in medium skillet, covered, over medium to medium-low heat until tender, about 10 minutes. Cook, uncovered, over medium-low to low heat until garlic cloves are golden brown, about 10 minutes. Mash cloves slightly with a fork.

2. Add 1½ cups stock and wine to skillet and heat to boiling. Mix flour and remaining ¼ cup stock and stir into boiling mixture. Boil, stirring constantly, until thickened, about 1 minute. Stir in parsley, salt, and pepper.

ALFREDO SAUCE

Serve this famous Parmesan-flavored sauce over traditional fettuccine noodles.

4 servings (about ½ cup each)

3 tablespoons margarine, *or* butter
¼ cup all-purpose flour
2½ cups fat-free milk
¼ cup grated Parmesan cheese
⅛ teaspoon ground nutmeg
½ teaspoon salt
¼ teaspoon pepper

Per Serving
Calories: 187
% Calories from fat: 52
  (24% with 2 ozs. pasta)
Fat (gm): 10.7
Saturated fat (gm): 3.1
Cholesterol (mg): 7.4
Sodium (mg): 561
Protein (gm): 8.7
Carbohydrate (gm): 13.9
Exchanges
Milk: 0.5
Vegetable: 0.0
Fruit: 0.0
Bread: 0.5
Meat: 0.5
Fat: 2.0

1. Melt margarine in medium saucepan; stir in flour. Cook over medium heat 1 minute, stirring constantly. Stir in milk; heat to boiling. Boil, stirring constantly, until thickened, 1 to 2 minutes.

2. Reduce heat to low and stir in cheese, nutmeg, salt, and pepper; cook 1 to 2 minutes.

GORGONZOLA SAUCE

Although higher in fat content than some of the other blue cheeses, Gorgonzola lends richness of flavor to this creamy sauce.

6 servings (about ⅓ cup each)

3 tablespoons margarine, *or* butter
¼ cup all-purpose flour
2 cups fat-free milk
¼ cup dry white wine, *or* fat-free milk
3 ounces Gorgonzola cheese, crumbled
¼ teaspoon pepper

Per Serving
Calories: 156
% Calories from fat: 59
  (24% with 2 ozs. pasta)
Fat (gm): 10.2
Saturated fat (gm): 1.2
Cholesterol (mg): 14
Sodium (mg): 271
Protein (gm): 6.4
Carbohydrate (gm): 8.1
Exchanges
Milk: 0.0
Vegetable: 0.0
Fruit: 0.0
Bread: 0.5
Meat: 0.5
Fat: 2.0

1. Melt margarine in medium saucepan; stir in flour. Cook over medium heat 1 minute, stirring constantly. Stir in milk and wine; heat to boiling. Boil, stirring constantly, until thickened, 1 to 2 minutes.

2. Reduce heat to low, and stir in cheese and pepper; cook 1 to 2 minutes.

THREE-ONION SAUCE

 This onion mixture is cooked very slowly until the onions are caramelized.

4 servings (about ½ cup each)

1½	cups cleaned, sliced leeks
1½	cups chopped red onions
6	shallots, sliced
3	tablespoons olive oil
¼	cup all-purpose flour
1	can (14½ ounces) reduced-sodium vegetable broth
¼	teaspoon dried thyme leaves
½	teaspoon salt
¼	teaspoon pepper

Per Serving
Calories: 196
% Calories from fat: 47
 (25% with 2 ozs. pasta)
Fat (gm): 10.5
Saturated fat (gm): 1.4
Cholesterol (mg): 0
Sodium (mg): 317
Protein (gm): 3
Carbohydrate (gm): 23.9
Exchanges
Milk: 0.0
Vegetable: 1.0
Fruit: 0.0
Bread: 1.0
Meat: 0.0
Fat: 2.0

1. Saute leeks, onions, and shallots in oil in medium saucepan 2 to 3 minutes. Reduce heat to medium-low and cook slowly until mixture is golden brown, 20 to 25 minutes. Stir in flour; cook over medium heat 1 to 2 minutes more.

2. Stir broth, thyme, salt, and pepper into leek mixture; heat to boiling. Boil, stirring constantly, until thickened, 1 to 2 minutes.

CREAMED SPINACH SAUCE

 This sauce clings nicely, so serve over a substantial pasta such as farfalle (bow ties), radiatore, or a filled tortellini.

6 servings (about ½ cup each)

2	cloves garlic, minced
2	tablespoons margarine, *or* butter
¼	cup all-purpose flour
3	cups 2% milk

Per Serving
Calories: 141
% Calories from fat: 40
 (17% with 2 ozs. pasta)
Fat (gm): 6.6
Saturated fat (gm): 2.8
Cholesterol (mg): 9
Sodium (mg): 284
Protein (gm): 8
Carbohydrate (gm): 14.4

1½ pounds fresh spinach, cleaned, chopped

2 teaspoons dried basil leaves

⅛-¼ teaspoon ground nutmeg

4-6 dashes red pepper sauce

¼-½ teaspoon salt

Exchanges
Milk: 0.5
Vegetable: 2.0
Fruit: 0.0
Bread: 0.0
Meat: 0.0
Fat: 1.0

1. Saute garlic in margarine in large saucepan 1 to 2 minutes. Stir in flour and cook over medium heat 1 to 2 minutes more. Stir in milk; heat to boiling. Boil, stirring constantly, until thickened, 1 to 2 minutes.

2. Stir spinach and remaining ingredients into sauce. Cook, uncovered, over medium heat until spinach is cooked, 5 to 7 minutes.

ARTICHOKE SAUCE

 Minced jalapeño peppers add a hint of piquancy to this sauce. Serve over fusilli (spirals), rotini (corkscrews), or other-shaped pastas.

4 servings (about ½ cup each)

1 cup sliced onion

2 cloves garlic, minced

1 tablespoon olive oil

1 can (14 ounces) artichoke hearts, drained, rinsed, and sliced

¼ teaspoon minced, seeded jalapeño peppers

2 tablespoons flour

1 cup canned reduced-sodium vegetable broth

¼ cup grated Parmesan cheese

2 tablespoons finely chopped parsley

¼ teaspoon salt

¼ teaspoon pepper

Per Serving
Calories: 149
% Calories from fat: 32
   (16% with 2 ozs. pasta)
Fat (gm): 5.7
Saturated fat (gm): 1.7
Cholesterol (mg): 4.9
Sodium (mg): 372
Protein (gm): 7.3
Carbohydrate (gm): 20.4
Exchanges
Milk: 0.0
Vegetable: 4.0
Fruit: 0.0
Bread: 0.0
Meat: 0.0
Fat: 1.0

1. Saute onion and garlic in oil in medium saucepan until tender, about 5 minutes. Stir in artichoke hearts and jalapeño peppers; cook over medium heat 10 minutes. Stir in flour; cook 1 to 2 minutes more.

2. Stir broth into artichoke mixture; heat to boiling. Boil, stirring constantly, until thickened, 1 to 2 minutes.

3. Reduce heat to low, and stir in Parmesan cheese, parsley, salt, and pepper; cook 1 to 2 minutes.

PRIMAVERA SAUCE

Select vegetables from the season's bounty for this rich, flavorful sauce. Serve over fettuccine, linguine, or spaghetti.

6 servings (about 1 cup each)

3	tablespoons margarine, *or* butter
¼	cup all-purpose flour
2	cups 2% milk
¼	cup dry white wine, *or* canned reduced-sodium vegetable broth
2	cups broccoli florets, steamed until crisp-tender
2	cups cauliflower florets, steamed until crisp-tender
1	cup diagonally sliced carrots, steamed until crisp-tender
1	medium red bell pepper, sliced
¼	cup grated Parmesan cheese
¼-½	teaspoon ground nutmeg
¼	teaspoon salt
¼	teaspoon pepper

Per Serving
Calories: 174
% Calories from fat: 44
  (26% with 2 ozs. pasta)
Fat (gm): 8.9
Saturated fat (gm): 2.9
Cholesterol (mg): 9.3
Sodium (mg): 298
Protein (gm): 7.4
Carbohydrate (gm): 16.4
Exchanges
Milk: 0.5
Vegetable: 2.0
Fruit: 0.0
Bread: 0.0
Meat: 0.0
Fat: 2.0

1. Melt margarine in medium saucepan; stir in flour. Cook over medium heat 1 minute, stirring constantly. Stir in milk and wine; heat to boiling. Boil, stirring constantly, until thickened, 1 to 2 minutes.

2. Stir in vegetables; cook over medium heat until hot through, 2 to 3 minutes. Reduce heat to low and stir in cheese, nutmeg, salt, and pepper; cook 1 to 2 minutes more.

CURRY SAUCE

Delicious tossed with pasta, or served over cooked cauliflower or broccoli.

4 servings (about ½ cup each)

Vegetable cooking spray
¼ cup finely chopped onion
4 cloves garlic, minced
2 tablespoons flour
2 teaspoons curry powder
¼ teaspoon cayenne pepper
2 cups Basic Vegetable Stock, *or* Canned Vegetable Stock (see pp. 58, 63)
1 tablespoon cornstarch
¼ cup dry white wine, *or* Basic Vegetable Stock
Salt and pepper, to taste

Per Serving
Calories: 50
% Calories from fat: 8
Fat (gm): 0.4
Saturated fat (gm): 0
Cholesterol (mg): 0
Sodium (mg): 8
Protein (gm): 1.1
Carbohydrate (gm): 8.3
Exchanges
Milk: 0.0
Vegetable: 0.5
Fruit: 0.0
Bread: 0.5
Meat: 0.0
Fat: 0.0

1. Spray medium saucepan with cooking spray; heat over medium heat until hot. Saute onion and garlic 2 to 3 minutes; stir in flour, curry powder, and pepper. Cook 1 minute longer, stirring constantly.

2. Stir stock into saucepan; heat to boiling. Mix cornstarch and wine; stir into boiling mixture. Boil until sauce is thickened, about 1 minute, stirring constantly. Season to taste with salt and pepper.

MOCK HOLLANDAISE SAUCE

This creamy-textured Hollandaise Sauce is almost too good to be true. Enjoy it with Eggs Benedict and Artichokes with Hollandaise Sauce (see pp. 478, 584).

6 servings (about ¼ cup each)

6 ounces fat-free cream cheese
⅓ cup fat-free sour cream
3-4 tablespoons fat-free milk
1-2 teaspoons lemon juice

Per Serving
Calories: 36
% Calories from fat: 1
Fat (gm): 0
Saturated fat (gm): 0
Cholesterol (mg): 0.1
Sodium (mg): 188
Protein (gm): 5.1
Carbohydrate (gm): 2.8

½-1 teaspoon Dijon-style mustard
⅛ teaspoon ground turmeric

Exchanges
Milk: 0.0
Vegetable: 0.0
Fruit: 0.0
Bread: 0.0
Meat: 0.5
Fat: 0.0

1. Heat all ingredients in small saucepan over medium-low to low heat until melted and smooth, stirring constantly. Serve immediately.

MUSHROOM GRAVY

Serve over "burgers," potato pancakes, or grilled eggplant slices, or serve over bowls of warm polenta.

6 servings (about ¼ cup each)

Vegetable cooking spray
1 cup sliced cremini, *or* white mushrooms
⅓ cup finely chopped onion
1 clove garlic, minced
1 cup Canned Vegetable Stock (see p. 63)
2 tablespoons flour
Salt and pepper, to taste

Per Serving
Calories: 27
% Calories from fat: 7
Fat (gm): 0.2
Saturated fat (gm): 0
Cholesterol (mg): 0
Sodium (mg): 10
Protein (gm): 0.8
Carbohydrate (gm): 4.6
Exchanges
Milk: 0.0
Vegetable: 1.0
Fruit: 0.0
Bread: 0.0
Meat: 0.0
Fat: 0.0

1. Spray medium saucepan with cooking spray; heat over medium heat until hot. Saute mushrooms, onion, and garlic until tender, about 5 minutes.

2. Mix stock and flour; add to saucepan and heat to boiling. Boil, stirring constantly, until thickened, about 1 minute. Season to taste with salt and pepper.

WILD MUSHROOM SAUCE

 Rich in flavor, this versatile sauce will complement many dishes. Serve over grilled tempeh or eggplant, or over "burgers."

8 servings (about ⅓ cup each)

Olive oil cooking spray
¼ cup finely chopped shallots
2 cloves garlic, minced
2 cups chopped or sliced wild mushrooms (portobello, shiitake, cremini, etc.)
⅓ cup dry sherry, *or* Basic Vegetable Stock (see p. 58)
2-3 tablespoons lemon juice
¼-½ teaspoon dried thyme leaves
2 cups Basic Vegetable Stock (see p. 58)
2 tablespoons cornstarch
Salt and pepper, to taste

Per Serving
Calories: 34
% Calories from fat: 5
Fat (gm): 0.2
Saturated fat (gm): 0
Cholesterol (mg): 0
Sodium (mg): 5
Protein (gm): 0.7
Carbohydrate (gm): 5.3
Exchanges
Milk: 0.0
Vegetable: 1.0
Fruit: 0.0
Bread: 0.0
Meat: 0.0
Fat: 0.0

1. Spray medium saucepan with cooking spray; heat over medium heat until hot. Saute shallots and garlic until tender, 3 to 4 minutes. Stir in mushrooms; cook, covered, over medium-low heat until mushrooms are wilted, about 5 minutes. Stir in sherry, lemon juice, and thyme; heat to boiling. Reduce heat and simmer, uncovered, until mushrooms are tender and excess liquid is gone, about 5 minutes.

2. Mix stock and cornstarch; stir into saucepan and heat to boiling. Boil, stirring constantly, until thickened, about 1 minute. Season to taste with salt and pepper.

PAPRIKASH SAUCE

Suit your preference of hot or sweet paprika in this recipe. Reduced-fat sour cream adds a wonderful creamy texture and richness to the sauce. Serve over any kind of pasta.

6 servings (about ½ cup each)

Per Serving
Calories: 97
% Calories from fat: 17
   (8% with 2 ozs. pasta)
Fat (gm): 1.9
Saturated fat (gm): 0.1
Cholesterol (mg): 7.6
Sodium (mg): 230
Protein (gm): 2.9
Carbohydrate (gm): 14.2
Exchanges
Milk: 0.0
Vegetable: 0.0
Fruit: 0.0
Bread: 1.0
Meat: 0.0
Fat: 0.5

1 medium red bell pepper, sliced
1 medium green bell pepper, sliced
1 large onion, sliced
1 tablespoon margarine, *or* butter
2 tablespoons flour
1 tablespoon sweet Hungarian paprika
½ teaspoon salt
¼ teaspoon pepper
1 can (8 ounces) reduced-sodium tomato sauce
½ cup canned reduced-sodium vegetable broth
½ cup dry white wine, *or* canned reduced-sodium vegetable broth
½ cup reduced-fat sour cream

1. Cook bell peppers and onion in margarine in large skillet over medium heat until peppers are very soft, 10 to 15 minutes. Stir in flour, paprika, salt, and pepper; cook 3 to 5 minutes, stirring occasionally.

2. Stir in tomato sauce, broth, and wine; heat to boiling. Reduce heat and simmer, uncovered, until sauce is thickened, 5 to 7 minutes. Stir in sour cream.

CINCINNATI CHILI SAUCE

5-Way Cincinnati Chili gained fame in the chili parlors of Cincinnati. The "meat" sauce is seasoned with sweet spices and generally has a hint of dark chocolate. The chili is served alone, 1 way; 2 ways, over spaghetti; 3 ways, with added beans; 4 ways, with chopped onions; 5 ways, with shredded cheese!

8 servings (about ½ cup each)

Olive oil cooking spray
- ½ cup chopped onion
- 4 cloves garlic, minced
- 1 can (28 ounces) reduced-sodium crushed tomatoes, undrained
- 1 can (8 ounces) reduced-sodium tomato sauce
- ½ cup water
- ½ package (12-ounce size) frozen pre-browned vegetable protein crumbles, thawed
- 2 tablespoons chili powder
- 2 teaspoons dried oregano leaves
- 1 teaspoon ground cinnamon
- 1 teaspoon ground allspice
- ½ teaspoon paprika
- 1 tablespoon cocoa
- ½ teaspoon salt
- ½ teaspoon pepper

Per Serving
Calories: 79
% Calories from fat: 8
  (5% with 2 ozs. pasta)
Fat (gm): 0.7
Saturated fat (gm): 0.1
Cholesterol (mg): 0
Sodium (mg): 269
Protein (gm): 7
Carbohydrate (gm): 12.9
Exchanges
Milk: 0.0
Vegetable: 1.0
Fruit: 0.0
Bread: 0.0
Meat: 1.0
Fat: 0.0

1. Spray large saucepan with cooking spray; heat over medium heat until hot. Saute onion and garlic until tender, about 5 minutes.

2. Stir remaining ingredients into saucepan; heat to boiling. Reduce heat and simmer, covered, 15 minutes; simmer, uncovered, until sauce is thickened, about 15 minutes more.

CHILI TOMATO SAUCE

 A very simple but versatile sauce that can be used with tacos, enchiladas, and other favorite Mexican dishes.

8 servings (about ¼ cup each)

1	can (16 ounces) reduced-sodium tomato sauce
¼	cup water
2–2½	tablespoons chili powder
2	cloves garlic, minced
	Salt and pepper, to taste

Per Serving
Calories: 30
% Calories from fat: 10
Fat (gm): 0.3
Saturated fat (gm): 0
Cholesterol (mg): 0
Sodium (mg): 36
Protein (gm): 1.3
Carbohydrate (gm): 5.9
Exchanges
Milk: 0.0
Vegetable: 0.8
Fruit: 0.0
Bread: 0.0
Meat: 0.0
Fat: 0.0

1. Combine tomato sauce, water, chili powder, and garlic in small saucepan; heat to boiling. Reduce heat and simmer, uncovered, 2 to 3 minutes. Season to taste with salt and pepper.

ENCHILADA SAUCE

 Many Mexican sauces are a simple combination of pureed ingredients that are then cooked or fried until thickened to desired consistency.

8 servings (about ¼ cup each)

1	ancho chili, stem, seeds, and veins discarded
	Boiling water
2	medium tomatoes, chopped
1	red bell pepper, chopped
1	small onion, chopped
2	cloves garlic, minced
½	teaspoon dried marjoram leaves
⅛	teaspoon ground allspice
	Vegetable cooking spray
1	bay leaf
	Salt, to taste

Per Serving
Calories: 15
% Calories from fat: 8
Fat (gm): 0.2
Saturated fat (gm): 0
Cholesterol (mg): 0
Sodium (mg): 3.6
Protein (gm): 0.6
Carbohydrate (gm): 3.4
Exchanges
Milk: 0.0
Vegetable: 0.0
Fruit: 0.0
Bread: 0.0
Meat: 0.0
Fat: 0.0

1. Cover ancho chili with boiling water in small bowl; let stand until softened, 10 to 15 minutes. Drain.

2. Process ancho chili, tomatoes, bell pepper, onion, garlic, marjoram, and allspice in food processor or blender until almost smooth.

3. Spray small skillet with cooking spray; heat over medium heat until hot. Fry sauce and bay leaf over medium heat until thickened to a medium consistency; discard bay leaf and season to taste with salt. Serve hot.

MOLE SAUCE

Mole is the most popular and traditional of all the Mexican sauces (see Enchiladas Mole, p. 251). Piquant with chilies and fragrant with sweet spices, the sauce is also flavored with unsweetened chocolate. Even this simplified version of the delicious mole is somewhat time consuming to make, so double the recipe and freeze half!

8 servings (about ⅓ cup each)

Vegetable cooking spray
3 mulato chilies
4 ancho chilies
4 pasilla chilies
Boiling water
1 tablespoon sesame seeds
4 whole peppercorns
2 whole cloves
⅛ teaspoon coriander seeds
Cinnamon stick, ½-inch piece
2 tablespoons raisins
2 tablespoons whole, *or* slivered, almonds
2 tablespoons pumpkin seeds
¼ cup chopped onion
2 cloves garlic, finely chopped
1 small corn tortilla
1 small tomato, chopped
1-1½ cups canned reduced-sodium vegetable broth
1-2 tablespoons unsweetened cocoa
Salt, to taste

Per Serving
Calories: 68
% Calories from fat: 25
Fat (gm): 1.9
Saturated fat (gm): 0.2
Cholesterol (mg): 0
Sodium (mg): 101
Protein (gm): 1.5
Carbohydrate (gm): 11.2
Exchanges
Milk: 0.0
Vegetable: 2.0
Fruit: 0.0
Bread: 0.0
Meat: 0.0
Fat: 0.5

1. Spray medium skillet with cooking spray; heat over medium heat until hot. Cook all chilies over medium heat until softened; remove and discard stems, seeds, and veins (if chilies are already soft, the cooking step can be omitted). Pour boiling water over chilies to cover in bowl; let stand 10 to 15 minutes. Drain, reserving ¾ cup liquid.

2. Spray small skillet with cooking spray; heat over medium heat until hot. Add sesame seeds and spices and cook over medium heat until seeds are toasted, 1 to 2 minutes, stirring constantly; remove from skillet. Add raisins, almonds, and pumpkin seeds to skillet and cook over medium heat until toasted, 1 to 2 minutes, stirring constantly; remove from skillet. Add onion and garlic to skillet; saute until tender, 2 to 3 minutes, and remove from skillet.

3. Spray tortilla lightly with cooking spray; cook in skillet over medium heat until browned, about 1 minute on each side. Cool tortilla; cut into 1-inch pieces.

4. Process chilies, onion mixture, and tomato in blender until smooth. Add sesame seed-spice mixture, raisin mixture, reserved chili liquid, and tortilla; process, adding enough vegetable broth to make smooth, thick mixture.

5. Spray large skillet with cooking spray; heat over medium heat until hot. Add sauce; stir in cocoa and remaining vegetable broth. Heat to boiling; reduce heat and simmer, uncovered, 5 minutes, stirring frequently. Season to taste with salt.

POBLANO CHILI SAUCE

 Fast and easy to make, this sauce will vary in hotness depending upon the individual poblano chili and the amount of chili powder used.

8 servings (about ¼ cup each)

Vegetable cooking spray
2 medium tomatoes, chopped
½ medium poblano chili, seeds and veins discarded, chopped
1 small onion, chopped
2 cloves garlic, minced
1-2 tablespoons chili powder
Salt and pepper, to taste

Per Serving
Calories: 16
% Calories from fat: 14
Fat (gm): 0.3
Saturated fat (gm): 0
Cholesterol (mg): 0
Sodium (mg): 13
Protein (gm): 0.6
Carbohydrate (gm): 3.4
Exchanges
Milk: 0.0
Vegetable: 0.5
Fruit: 0.0
Bread: 0.0
Meat: 0.0
Fat: 0.0

1. Spray large skillet with cooking spray; heat over medium heat until hot. Cook tomatoes, poblano chili, onion, garlic, and chili powder until poblano chili and onion are very tender, 8 to 10 minutes.

2. Process mixture in food processor or blender until smooth; season to taste with salt and pepper.

SERRANO TOMATO SAUCE

 Use garden ripe tomatoes for best flavor; any hot chili can be substituted for the serrano chili.

6 servings (about ⅓ cup each)

2 large tomatoes, cut into wedges
Vegetable cooking spray
1 small onion, finely chopped
1 serrano chili, seeds and veins discarded, minced
1 clove garlic, minced
Salt, to taste

Per Serving
Calories: 18
% Calories from fat: 8
Fat (gm): 0.2
Saturated fat (gm): 0
Cholesterol (mg): 0
Sodium (mg): 4
Protein (gm): 0.6
Carbohydrate (gm): 4
Exchanges
Milk: 0.0
Vegetable: 1.0
Fruit: 0.0
Bread: 0.0
Meat: 0.0
Fat: 0.0

1. Process tomatoes in food processor or blender until almost smooth.

2. Spray medium skillet with cooking spray; heat over medium heat until hot. Saute onion, serrano chili, and garlic until tender, 3 to 4 minutes. Add tomatoes and heat to boiling; cook over medium to medium-high heat until mixture thickens to a medium sauce consistency, 5 to 8 minutes. Season to taste with salt; serve warm.

TOMATILLO SAUCE

Made with Mexican green tomatoes ("tomatillos"), this sauce is very fast and easy to make. It can be served over flautas, enchiladas, and tacos.

8 servings (about ¼ cup each)

1½ pounds tomatillos
½ medium onion, chopped
1 clove garlic, minced
½ small serrano chili, minced
3 tablespoons finely chopped cilantro
Vegetable cooking spray
2-3 teaspoons sugar
Salt and white pepper, to taste

Per Serving
Calories: 38
% Calories from fat: 19
Fat (gm): 1.0
Saturated fat (gm): 0
Cholesterol (mg): 0
Sodium (mg): 2
Protein (gm): 1.2
Carbohydrate (gm): 7.6
Exchanges
Milk: 0.0
Vegetable: 2.0
Fruit: 0.0
Bread: 0.0
Meat: 0.0
Fat: 0.0

1. Remove and discard husks from tomatillos. Simmer, covered, in 1 inch of water in large saucepan until tender, 5 to 8 minutes. Cool; drain.

2. Process tomatillos, onion, garlic, serrano chili, and cilantro in food processor or blender, using pulse technique, until almost smooth. Spray large skillet with cooking spray; heat over medium heat until hot. Add sauce and "fry" over medium heat until slightly thickened, about 5 minutes. Season to taste with sugar, salt, and pepper.

POBLANO SOUR CREAM SAUCE

This versatile sauce is also excellent served with vegetable fajitas or enchiladas or over Vegetable Crepes (see p. 222).

4 servings (about ⅓ cup each)

Vegetable cooking spray
1 large poblano chili, thinly sliced
1 small onion, chopped
2 cloves garlic, minced
1 cup fat-free sour cream
¼-½ teaspoon ground cumin
Salt and pepper, to taste

Per Serving
Calories: 49
% Calories from fat: 2
Fat (gm): 0.1
Saturated fat (gm): 0
Cholesterol (mg): 0
Sodium (mg): 39
Protein (gm): 4.3
Carbohydrate (gm): 9.1
Exchanges
Milk: 0.0
Vegetable: 2.0
Fruit: 0.0
Bread: 0.0
Meat: 0.0
Fat: 0.0

1. Spray small saucepan with cooking spray; heat over medium heat until hot. Saute poblano chili, onion, and garlic until very tender, about 10 minutes. Stir in sour cream and cumin; cook over low heat until hot, 2 to 3 minutes. Season to taste with salt and pepper.

JALAPEÑO CON QUESO SAUCE

A versatile sauce to enhance enchiladas and other tortilla dishes. This goes especially well with Potatoes with Poblano Chilies (see p. 615).

8 servings (about ¼ cup each)

Vegetable cooking spray
1 teaspoon finely chopped jalapeño chili
1 teaspoon ground cumin
½ teaspoon dried oregano leaves
8 ounces reduced-fat pasteurized processed cheese product, cubed
⅓-½ cup fat-free milk
1¼ cups (5 ounces) shredded fat-free Cheddar cheese

Per Serving
Calories: 92
% Calories from fat: 30
Fat (gm): 3.2
Saturated fat (gm): 2
Cholesterol (mg): 13.4
Sodium (mg): 562
Protein (gm): 12.2
Carbohydrate (gm): 4.4
Exchanges
Milk: 0.0
Vegetable: 0.0
Fruit: 0.0
Bread: 0.0
Meat: 2.0
Fat: 0.0

1. Spray medium saucepan with cooking spray; heat over medium heat until hot. Saute jalapeño chili until tender, about 2 minutes; stir in cumin and oregano.

2. Add processed cheese product; cook over low heat, stirring frequently, until melted. Stir in ⅓ cup milk and Cheddar cheese. Stir in additional milk if needed for desired consistency, cooking until hot through, 1 to 2 minutes.

GARBANZO SALSA

A colorful salsa with fresh flavors that will complement "burgers," loaves, and many other entrées.

8 servings (about ⅓ cup each)

1 can (15 ½ ounces) garbanzo beans, rinsed, drained
¾ cup chopped, seeded cucumber
¾ cup quartered cherry tomatoes
3 green onions and tops, thinly sliced

Per Serving
Calories: 76
% Calories from fat: 29
Fat (gm): 2.5
Saturated fat (gm): 0.3
Cholesterol (mg): 0
Sodium (mg): 221
Protein (gm): 2.9
Carbohydrate (gm): 11

¼ cup chopped yellow bell pepper
2 tablespoons finely chopped mint
2 tablespoons finely chopped cilantro
2-3 cloves minced garlic
2-2½ teaspoons olive oil
Lemon juice, to taste

Exchanges
Milk: 0.0
Vegetable: 1.0
Fruit: 0.0
Bread: 0.5
Meat: 0.0
Fat: 0.5

1. Combine beans, cucumber, tomatoes, onions, bell pepper, herbs, and garlic in bowl. Drizzle with oil and toss; season to taste with lemon juice.

TROPICAL SALSA

A fruit and vegetable salsa with cool refreshing flavor!

6 servings (about ¼ cup each)

½ cup cubed papaya, *or* mango
½ cup cubed pineapple
½ cup chopped tomato
¼ cup chopped, seeded cucumber
¼ cup canned black beans, rinsed, drained
½ teaspoon minced jalapeño chili
2 tablespoons finely chopped cilantro
¼ cup orange juice
1 tablespoon lime juice
2-3 teaspoons sugar

Per Serving
Calories: 32
% Calories from fat: 6
Fat (gm): 0.2
Saturated fat (gm): 0
Cholesterol (mg): 0
Sodium (mg): 30.4
Protein (gm): 1
Carbohydrate (gm): 7.6
Exchanges
Milk: 0.0
Vegetable: 0.0
Fruit: 0.5
Bread: 0.0
Meat: 0.0
Fat: 0.0

1. Combine papaya, pineapple, tomato, cucumber, black beans, jalapeño chili, and cilantro in small bowl. Combine orange and lime juice and sugar in separate bowl; add to other ingredients and toss. Refrigerate until serving time.

MIXED HERB PESTO

Packaged fresh herbs are readily available in most supermarkets. Each ½-ounce package yields about ¼ cup of packed herb leaves. Serve pesto sauces at room temperature, mixing with hot pasta.

4 servings (about 2 tablespoons each)

½ cup packed fresh basil leaves, *or* 2 tablespoons dried	**Per Serving** Calories: 134 % Calories from fat: 77 (31% with 2 ozs. pasta) Fat (gm): 12
½ cup packed fresh parsley leaves	Saturated fat (gm): 1.9 Cholesterol (mg): 2.4
¼ cup packed fresh oregano leaves, *or* 2 tablespoons dried	Sodium (mg): 330 Protein (gm): 4 Carbohydrate (gm): 4.9
3 cloves garlic	**Exchanges** Milk: 0.0
2 tablespoons grated Parmesan cheese	Vegetable: 1.0
1 ounce walnuts (about 14 medium)	Fruit: 0.0 Bread: 0.0
2 tablespoons olive oil	Meat: 0.0
2 teaspoons lemon juice	Fat: 2.5
½ teaspoon salt	
¼ teaspoon pepper	

1. Combine herbs, garlic, Parmesan cheese, and walnuts in food processor or blender. Process, adding oil and lemon juice gradually, until mixture is very finely chopped. Stir in salt and pepper. Serve at room temperature.

SPINACH PESTO

Serve with any favorite pasta, or as a topping for sliced tomato or vegetable salads.

4 servings (about 2 tablespoons each)

1 cup loosely packed fresh spinach	**Per Serving** Calories: 68 % Calories from fat: 86 (16% with 2 ozs. pasta)
3 tablespoons finely chopped fresh basil leaves, *or* 1 tablespoon dried	Fat (gm): 6.8 Saturated fat (gm): 0.9 Cholesterol (mg): 0
1-2 cloves garlic	Sodium (mg): 22
1 tablespoon grated fat-free Parmesan cheese	Protein (gm): 1 Carbohydrate (gm): 1.4 **Exchanges**
2 tablespoons olive oil	Milk: 0.0 Vegetable: 0.0
1-2 teaspoons lemon juice	Fruit: 0.0
Salt and pepper, to taste	Bread: 0.0 Meat: 0.0 Fat: 1.5

1. Process all ingredients, except lemon juice, salt, and pepper, in food processor or blender until smooth. Season with lemon juice.

2. Let stand 2 to 3 hours for flavors to blend, or refrigerate until serving time. Season to taste with salt and pepper. Serve at room temperature.

SUN-DRIED TOMATO PESTO

Use yellow or red sun-dried tomatoes in this flavorful pesto.

4 servings (2 tablespoons each)

½ cup sun-dried tomatoes (not in oil)
½ cup boiling water
½ cup packed basil leaves
2 cloves garlic
3 tablespoons olive oil
2 tablespoons grated fat-free Parmesan cheese
Salt and pepper, to taste

Per Serving
Calories: 118
% Calories from fat: 75
  (28% with 2 ozs. pasta)
Fat (gm): 10.4
Saturated fat (gm): 1.4
Cholesterol (mg): 0
Sodium (mg): 164
Protein (gm): 2.2
Carbohydrate (gm): 5.5
Exchanges
Milk: 0.0
Vegetable: 0.0
Fruit: 0.0
Bread: 0.5
Meat: 0.0
Fat: 2.0

1. Soak tomatoes in boiling water in bowl until softened, about 10 minutes. Drain, reserving liquid.

2. Process tomatoes, basil, garlic, oil, and cheese in food processor or blender, adding enough reserved liquid to make a smooth, spoonable paste. Season to taste with salt and pepper. Serve at room temperature.

FENNEL PESTO

Perfect with pasta, or to serve with sliced tomatoes. Or stir into fat-free sour cream for a marvelous veggie dip.

6 servings (scant ¼ cup each)

1 tablespoon fennel seeds
Hot water
1 cup chopped fennel bulb, *or* celery
½ cup loosely packed parsley
2 cloves garlic

Per Serving
Calories: 71
% Calories from fat: 61
  (17% with 2 ozs. pasta)
Fat (gm): 5
Saturated fat (gm): 0.6
Cholesterol (mg): 0
Sodium (mg): 42
Protein (gm): 2.6
Carbohydrate (gm): 4.6

14 walnut halves (about 1 ounce)
3 tablespoons water
1 tablespoon olive oil
¼ cup grated fat-free Parmesan cheese
Salt and pepper, to taste

Exchanges
Milk: 0.0
Vegetable: 1.0
Fruit: 0.0
Bread: 0.0
Meat: 0.0
Fat: 1.0

1. Place fennel seeds in small bowl; pour hot water over to cover. Let stand 10 minutes; drain.

2. Process fennel, fennel seeds, parsley, and garlic in food processor or blender until finely chopped. Add walnuts, 3 tablespoons water, and oil; process until walnuts are finely chopped. Stir in Parmesan cheese; season to taste with salt and pepper. Serve at room temperature.

RED PEPPER PESTO

Make this pesto with jarred roasted peppers, or make your own, following step 1 in the recipe for Roasted Red Pepper Sauce (see p. 709).

4 servings (about 2 tablespoons each)

1 cup roasted red peppers
1 cup packed fresh basil
2 cloves garlic
¼ cup grated fat-free Parmesan cheese
1 teaspoon sugar
1 teaspoon balsamic vinegar
3 tablespoons olive oil
Salt and pepper, to taste

Per Serving
Calories: 124
% Calories from fat: 71
  (30% with 2 ozs. pasta)
Fat (gm): 10.3
Saturated fat (gm): 1.4
Cholesterol (mg): 0
Sodium (mg): 46
Protein (gm): 2.7
Carbohydrate (gm): 6.8
Exchanges
Milk: 0.0
Vegetable: 1.0
Fruit: 0.0
Bread: 0.0
Meat: 0.0
Fat: 2.0

1. Process all ingredients, except salt and pepper, in food processor or blender until smooth. Season to taste with salt and pepper. Serve at room temperature.

CILANTRO PESTO

A pesto with a very fresh flavor. As with any pesto, serve at room temperature, adding it to hot pasta. The flavor of dried cilantro is not acceptable in this recipe; if the fresh herb is not available, substitute fresh tarragon or oregano.

6 servings (about 2 tablespoons each)

1½ cups packed cilantro leaves
½ cup packed parsley
1 clove garlic
¼ cup grated Parmesan cheese
3 tablespoons pine nuts, *or* walnuts
1 tablespoon olive oil
1 tablespoon lemon juice
¼ teaspoon salt
¼ teaspoon pepper

Per Serving
Calories: 70
% Calories from fat: 73
 (20% with 2 ozs. pasta)
Fat (gm): 6.1
Saturated fat (gm): 1.1
Cholesterol (mg): 3.3
Sodium (mg): 173
Protein (gm): 3.5
Carbohydrate (gm): 1.7
Exchanges
Milk: 0.0
Vegetable: 0.5
Fruit: 0.0
Bread: 0.0
Meat: 0.0
Fat: 1.5

1. Combine herbs, garlic, Parmesan cheese, and pine nuts in food processor or blender. Process, adding oil and lemon juice gradually, until mixture is very finely chopped. Stir in salt and pepper. Serve at room temperature.

SPINACH-CILANTRO PESTO

Any favorite herb can be substituted for the cilantro.

4 servings (about 2 tablespoons each)

1 cup loosely packed spinach leaves
¼ cup finely chopped cilantro
3 cloves garlic
¼ teaspoon ground cumin
1 tablespoon grated fat-free Parmesan cheese
1-2 teaspoons olive oil
1-2 teaspoons lime juice
1-2 tablespoons water
Salt and pepper, to taste

Per Serving
Calories: 22
% Calories from fat: 47
 (9% with 2 ozs. pasta)
Fat (gm): 1.2
Saturated fat (gm): 0.2
Cholesterol (mg): 0
Sodium (mg): 24
Protein (gm): 1.2
Carbohydrate (gm): 1.9
Exchanges
Milk: 0.0
Vegetable: 0.0
Fruit: 0.0
Bread: 0.0
Meat: 0.0
Fat: 0.5

1. Process all ingredients, except water, salt, and pepper, in food processor or blender until smooth; add water if necessary for consistency. Season to taste with salt and pepper. Serve at room temperature.

MINTED PESTO

Try this pesto using different mints, such as peppermint, spearmint, lemon mint, etc. The refreshing flavor is a complement to vegetables and salads, as well as pasta dishes.

8 servings (about 2 tablespoons each)

1 cup packed mint leaves
½ cup fresh parsley
2 cloves garlic, minced
2 tablespoons grated fat-free Parmesan cheese
2 tablespoons walnut pieces
2-3 tablespoons olive oil
2-3 tablespoons Basic Vegetable Stock (see p. 58), *or* water
Salt and pepper, to taste

Per Serving
Calories: 51
% Calories from fat: 78
(19% with 2 ozs. pasta)
Fat (gm): 4.6
Saturated fat (gm): 0.5
Cholesterol (mg): 0
Sodium (mg): 15
Protein (gm): 1.2
Carbohydrate (gm): 1.7
Exchanges
Milk: 0.0
Vegetable: 0.0
Fruit: 0.0
Bread: 0.0
Meat: 0.0
Fat: 1.0

1. Process all ingredients, except stock, salt, pepper, in food processor or blender until smooth. Stir in enough stock to make a spoonable mixture; season to taste with salt and pepper. Serve at room temperature.

GREMOLATA

Gremolata is a pungent mixture of finely chopped parsley, lemon rind, and garlic that can be added to soups or pasta as a flavor accent.

4 servings (about 2 tablespoons each)

1 cup packed parsley
1-2 teaspoons grated lemon rind
4 large cloves garlic

Per Serving
Calories: 10
% Calories from fat: 10
Fat (gm): 0.1
Saturated fat (gm): 0
Cholesterol (mg): 0
Sodium (mg): 9
Protein (gm): 0.6
Carbohydrate (gm): 2

Exchanges
Milk: 0.0
Vegetable: 0.0
Fruit: 0.0
Bread: 0.0
Meat: 0.0
Fat: 0.0

1. Process parsley, lemon rind, and garlic in food processor until finely minced, using pulse technique. Refrigerate until serving time. Stir into sauces and soups as desired.

GINGERED TOMATO RELISH

12 servings (about 2 tablespoons each)

1½ cups chopped tomatoes
½ cup finely chopped zucchini
¼ cup finely chopped carrot
¼ cup finely chopped onion
1 tablespoon grated gingerroot
Salt and pepper, to taste

Per Serving
Calories: 9
% Calories from fat: 10
Fat (gm): 0.1
Saturated fat (gm): 0
Cholesterol (mg): 0
Sodium (mg): 4
Protein (gm): 0.4
Carbohydrate (gm): 2
Exchanges
Milk: 0.0
Vegetable: 0.0
Fruit: 0.0
Bread: 0.0
Meat: 0.0
Fat: 0.0

1. Combine all ingredients, except salt and pepper, in medium skillet. Cook, covered, over medium heat until tomatoes are soft and mixture is bubbly. Simmer, uncovered, until excess liquid is gone, about 10 minutes. Season to taste with salt and pepper. Serve warm.

CRANBERRY COULIS

This mildly tart sauce is used as a flavor accent in White Bean and Sweet Potato Soup with Cranberry Coulis (see p. 110). It is also excellent served over fruit, cake, or ice cream.

6 servings (about 3 tablespoons each)

1½ cups fresh, *or* frozen, cranberries
1 cup orange juice

Per Serving
Calories: 59
% Calories from fat: 2
Fat (gm): 0.1
Saturated fat (gm): 0
Cholesterol (mg): 0
Sodium (mg): 1
Protein (gm): 0.4
Carbohydrate (gm): 14.8

2-3 tablespoons sugar

1-2 tablespoons honey

Exchanges
Milk: 0.0
Vegetable: 0.0
Fruit: 1.0
Bread: 0.0
Meat: 0.0
Fat: 0.0

1. Heat cranberries and orange juice to boiling in small saucepan; reduce heat and simmer, covered, until cranberries are tender, 5 to 8 minutes. Add sugar and honey and process mixture in food processor or blender until almost smooth.

LEMON-HERB MAYONNAISE

Delicious served with Pasta Skillet Cakes (p. 349), with vegetable salads, or as a dip with vegetable relishes.

6 servings (about 2 tablespoons each)

½ cup fat-free mayonnaise

¼ cup fat-free sour cream

1-2 teaspoons lemon juice

1 teaspoon grated lemon rind

½ teaspoon dried tarragon leaves

⅛ teaspoon dried thyme leaves

Per Serving
Calories: 23
% Calories from fat: 1
Fat (gm): 0
Saturated fat (gm): 0
Cholesterol (mg): 0
Sodium (mg): 260
Protein (gm): 0.7
Carbohydrate (gm): 5.2
Exchanges
Milk: 0.0
Vegetable: 0.0
Fruit: 0.0
Bread: 0.5
Meat: 0.0
Fat: 0.0

1. Mix all ingredients; refrigerate until serving time.

YOGURT-CUCUMBER SAUCE

For flavor variation, substitute ¾ teaspoon each dried oregano and mint leaves for the dill weed. Serve with African Fava Patties (see p. 47) or over sliced tomatoes and cucumbers.

6 servings (¼ cup each)

1 cup fat-free yogurt

¼ cup fat-free sour cream

⅓ cup finely chopped, seeded, peeled cucumber

Per Serving
Calories: 30
% Calories from fat: 3
Fat (gm): 0.1
Saturated fat (gm): 0
Cholesterol (mg): 0.7
Sodium (mg): 36
Protein (gm): 3
Carbohydrate (gm): 4.5

2 cloves garlic, minced
2-3 teaspoons dried dill weed
Salt and white pepper, to taste

Exchanges
Milk: 0.0
Vegetable: 1.0
Fruit: 0.0
Bread: 0.0
Meat: 0.0
Fat: 0.0

1. Combine yogurt, sour cream, cucumber, garlic, and dill weed in bowl; season to taste with salt and pepper. Refrigerate, covered, until serving time.

MUSTARD SAUCE

Serve this spicy sauce with Baked Spinach Balls or Mixed Vegetable Egg Rolls (see pp. 43, 46).

8 servings (about 2 tablespoons each)

¾ cup fat-free sour cream
3-4 teaspoons Dijon-style mustard
1½-2 tablespoons honey
1 tablespoon chopped chives

Per Serving
Calories: 27
% Calories from fat: 4
Fat (gm): 0.1
Saturated fat (gm): 0
Cholesterol (mg): 0
Sodium (mg): 39
Protein (gm): 1.5
Carbohydrate (gm): 5.4
Exchanges
Milk: 0.0
Vegetable: 1.0
Fruit: 0.0
Bread: 0.0
Meat: 0.0
Fat: 0.0

1. Mix all ingredients; refrigerate until ready to serve.

PLUM SAUCE

A fragrant and flavorful sauce to serve with oriental appetizers, or with kabobs of baked or broiled cubed tofu.

8 servings (about 2 tablespoons each)

¾ cup oriental plum sauce
2-3 tablespoons tamari, *or* reduced-sodium, soy sauce
2 tablespoons rice wine vinegar, *or* cider vinegar

Per Serving
Calories: 37
% Calories from fat: 1
Fat (gm): 0
Saturated fat (gm): 0
Cholesterol (mg): 0
Sodium (mg): 258
Protein (gm): 0.6
Carbohydrate (gm): 9

1 tablespoon grated gingerroot
1-2 teaspoons brown sugar
1 green onion and top, thinly sliced
2 cloves garlic, minced

Exchanges
Milk: 0.0
Vegetable: 0.0
Fruit: 0.0
Bread: 0.5
Meat: 0.0
Fat: 0.0

1. Mix all ingredients; refrigerate until ready to serve.

TAMARI DIPPING SAUCE

 An excellent sauce for egg rolls, wontons, potstickers, or whenever an oriental flavor accent is desired.

12 servings (1 tablespoon each)

½ cup reduced-sodium tamari, *or* soy,
sauce
2 tablespoons rice wine vinegar
4 teaspoons lemon juice
2 teaspoons honey

Per Serving
Calories: 15
% Calories from fat: 0
Fat (gm): 0
Saturated fat (gm): 0
Cholesterol (mg): 0
Sodium (mg): 405
Protein (gm): 1.2
Carbohydrate (gm): 2.1
Exchanges
Milk: 0.0
Vegetable: 0.0
Fruit: 0.0
Bread: 0.0
Meat: 0.0
Fat: 0.0

1. Mix all ingredients; refrigerate until ready to use.

TAMARI MARINADE

A simple but flavorful marinade that is especially nice for tofu or tempeh. Use as a dipping sauce, too.

4 servings (1 tablespoon each)

2 tablespoons reduced-sodium tamari soy sauce
2 tablespoons cider vinegar
1½ teaspoons minced garlic
½-1 teaspoon chili powder

Per Serving
Calories: 11
% Calories from fat: 5
Fat (gm): 0.1
Saturated fat (gm): 0
Cholesterol (mg): 0
Sodium (mg): 307
Protein (gm): 1
Carbohydrate (gm): 1.7
Exchanges
Milk: 0.0
Vegetable: 0.0
Fruit: 0.0
Bread: 0.0
Meat: 0.0
Fat: 0.0

1. Mix all ingredients; refrigerate until ready to use.

FRAGRANT BASTING SAUCE

Delicious with broiled or grilled tofu, tempeh, and vegetable kabobs.

6 servings (about 2 tablespoons each)

2 tablespoons reduced-sodium soy sauce
¼ cup rice wine, *or* dry sherry
¼ cup packed light brown sugar
1 tablespoon finely chopped green onion and top
1 teaspoon grated lemon rind
2 teaspoons sesame oil
1 teaspoon black bean sauce
1-2 dashes hot chili sesame oil

Per Serving
Calories: 55
% Calories from fat: 24
Fat (gm): 1.5
Saturated fat (gm): 0.2
Cholesterol (mg): 0
Sodium (mg): 197
Protein (gm): 0.6
Carbohydrate (gm): 10.3
Exchanges
Milk: 0.0
Vegetable: 0.0
Fruit: 0.0
Bread: 0.5
Meat: 0.0
Fat: 0.5

1. Combine all ingredients; refrigerate until ready to use.

SIXTEEN

Desserts

MOM'S RHUBARB STREUSEL CAKE

With Mom's approval, we've added a streusel, rich and crispy, and a light orange glaze to this wonderfully moist cake.

12 servings

½ cup margarine, *or* butter, softened
1⅓ cups sugar
1 egg, beaten
1 teaspoon vanilla
2 cups all-purpose flour
1 teaspoon baking soda
1 teaspoon ground cinnamon
½ teaspoon ground nutmeg
½ teaspoon salt
1 cup buttermilk
2 cups sliced fresh, *or* frozen, thawed, rhubarb (scant 1-inch pieces)
⅓ cup raisins
2 teaspoons grated orange rind
Crisp Streusel (recipe follows)
Orange Glaze (recipe follow)

Per Serving
Calories: 342
% Calories from fat: 27
Fat (gm): 10.4
Saturated fat (gm): 2.2
Cholesterol (mg): 18.5
Sodium (mg): 336
Protein (gm): 4.1
Carbohydrate (gm): 59.3
Exchanges
Milk: 0.0
Vegetable: 0.0
Fruit: 1.0
Bread: 3.0
Meat: 0.0
Fat: 1.5

1. In medium bowl, beat margarine and sugar until smooth; beat in egg and vanilla. Mix in combined flour, baking soda, cinnamon, nutmeg, and salt alternately with buttermilk, beginning and ending with dry ingredients. Mix in rhubarb, raisins, and orange rind.

2. Pour batter into greased and floured 13 x 9-inch baking pan. Sprinkle Crisp Streusel over cake. Bake at 350 degrees until toothpick inserted in center comes out clean, 35 to 40 minutes.

3. Cool in pan on wire rack 15 minutes; drizzle with Orange Glaze.

Crisp Streusel

- ½ cup packed light brown sugar
- 2 tablespoons quick-cooking oats
- 2 tablespoons flour
- 2 tablespoons cold margarine, *or* butter, cut into pieces

1. Combine brown sugar, oats, and flour in small bowl; cut in margarine with pastry blender to form crumbly mixture.

Orange Glaze

- ½ cup powdered sugar
- 1 teaspoon grated orange rind
- 2-4 teaspoons orange juice

1. Mix powdered sugar and orange rind with enough orange juice to make glaze consistency.

GLAZED ORANGE CHIFFON CAKE

Sometimes called Sunshine Cake, this cake has a perfect, tender texture and a delicate orange flavor.

12 servings

- 2¼ cups cake flour
- 1⅔ cups granulated sugar
- 1 tablespoon baking powder
- ¼ teaspoon salt
- ¾ cup orange juice, *or* water
- ⅓ cup canola oil
- 5 egg yolks
- 1 teaspoon vanilla
- 2 teaspoons grated orange rind
- 7 egg whites
- ½ teaspoon cream of tartar
- 2 cups powdered sugar
- 2-3 tablespoons orange juice
  Nutmeg, ground, as garnish

Per Serving
Calories: 358
% Calories from fat: 21
Fat (gm): 8.4
Saturated fat (gm): 1.5
Cholesterol (mg): 88.8
Sodium (mg): 163
Protein (gm): 5
Carbohydrate (gm): 66.3
Exchanges
Milk: 0.0
Vegetable: 0.0
Fruit: 0.0
Bread: 4.0
Meat: 0.0
Fat: 1.5

1. Combine flour, granulated sugar, baking powder, and salt in large mixing bowl. Mix orange juice, oil, egg yolks, vanilla, and orange rind in bowl; add to flour mixture and beat at medium speed until smooth.

2. With clean beaters and in separate large bowl, beat egg whites until foamy. Add cream of tartar and beat to very stiff but not dry peaks. Stir about ¼ of egg whites into cake batter; fold batter back into remaining egg whites. Pour batter into ungreased 10-inch tube pan.

3. Bake at 325 degrees until cake is golden and springs back when touched (cracks in top of cake will appear dry), 55 to 60 minutes. Invert cake pan on a funnel or bottle until cake is completely cool. Loosen side of cake and invert onto serving plate.

4. Mix powdered sugar with enough orange juice to make glaze consistency. Spoon glaze over top of cool cake; sprinkle with nutmeg.

CHOCOLATE BUTTERMILK CAKE WITH MOCHA FROSTING

 A chocolate dream come true, this cake is 3 layers high and generously covered with creamy mocha frosting!

16 servings

6 tablespoons vegetable shortening
1 cup granulated sugar
½ cup packed light brown sugar
2 eggs
2 egg whites
1 teaspoon vanilla
2 cups cake flour
½ cup unsweetened cocoa
2 teaspoons baking powder
½ teaspoon baking soda
½ teaspoon salt
1 cup buttermilk
Mocha Frosting (recipe follow)

Per Serving
Calories: 351
% Calories from fat: 17
Fat (gm): 6.9
Saturated fat (gm): 1.8
Cholesterol (mg): 27.3
Sodium (mg): 195
Protein (gm): 4.1
Carbohydrate (gm): 71.5
Exchanges
Milk: 0.0
Vegetable: 0.0
Fruit: 0.0
Bread: 4.5
Meat: 0.0
Fat: 1.0

1. Grease and flour three 8-inch-round cake pans. Line bottoms of pans with waxed paper.

2. Beat shortening, sugars, eggs, egg whites, and vanilla in large bowl until smooth. Mix in combined flour, cocoa, baking powder, baking soda, and salt alternately with buttermilk, beginning and ending with dry ingredients.

3. Pour equal amounts of batter into prepared pans. Bake at 350 degrees until toothpicks inserted in centers of cakes come out clean, 25 to 30 minutes. Cool in pans on wire racks 10 minutes; invert onto wire racks. Peel off waxed paper and cool cake layers completely.

4. Place 1 cake layer on serving plate; frost with about ½ cup frosting. Repeat with second cake layer and frosting. Top with third cake layer; frost top and side of cake.

Mocha Frosting

(makes about 2½ cups)

  5 cups powdered sugar
  ½ cup unsweetened cocoa
  2-3 teaspoons instant coffee crystals
  1-2 tablespoons margarine, *or* butter, softened
  1 teaspoon vanilla
  4-5 tablespoons fat-free milk

1. Combine powdered sugar, cocoa, coffee crystals, and margarine in large bowl; beat in vanilla and enough milk to make spreadable consistency.

FLOURLESS CHOCOLATE CAKE

It's hard to believe that a cake so sinfully rich and wonderful can actually be low in fat! Although regular cocoa can be used, the Dutch process cocoa lends a special flavor.

8 servings

  ½ cup Dutch process cocoa
  ¾ cup packed light brown sugar
  3 tablespoons flour
  2 teaspoons instant espresso coffee crystals

Per Serving
Calories: 335
% Calories from fat: 22
Fat (gm): 8.9
Saturated fat (gm): 3.6
Cholesterol (mg): 27.1
Sodium (mg): 107
Protein (gm): 6.3
Carbohydrate (gm): 66.1

⅛ teaspoon salt
Pinch pepper
¾ cup fat-free milk
1 teaspoon vanilla
2 ounces unsweetened, *or* bittersweet, chocolate, chopped
2 ounces semisweet chocolate, chopped
1 egg
3 egg whites
⅛ teaspoon cream of tartar
⅓ cup granulated sugar
"Rich" Chocolate Frosting (recipe follows)

Exchanges
Milk: 0.0
Vegetable: 0.0
Fruit: 0.0
Bread: 4.0
Meat: 0.0
Fat: 1.0

1. Combine cocoa, brown sugar, flour, coffee crystals, salt, and pepper in medium saucepan; gradually stir in milk and vanilla to make smooth mixture. Heat over medium heat, stirring frequently, until mixture is hot and sugar dissolved (do not boil).

2. Remove saucepan from heat; add chocolate, stirring until melted. Whisk about ½ cup chocolate mixture into 1 egg; whisk egg mixture back into saucepan. Cool to room temperature.

3. Beat egg whites until foamy in medium bowl; add cream of tartar and beat to soft peaks. Continue beating, adding sugar gradually, until stiff but not dry peaks form. Stir about ¼ of the egg whites into cooled chocolate mixture; fold chocolate mixture back into egg whites.

4. Lightly grease bottom and side of 9-inch cake pan; line bottom of pan with parchment paper. Pour batter into pan. Place pan in large roasting pan on center oven rack; add 1 inch hot water to pan.

5. Bake cake at 350 degrees until just firm when lightly touched, 25 to 30 minutes (do not test with toothpick as cake will still be soft in the center). Cool completely on wire rack; refrigerate, covered, 8 hours or overnight.

6. Loosen side of cake from pan with sharp knife. Remove from pan and place on serving plate. Frost with "Rich" Chocolate Frosting.

"Rich" Chocolate Frosting

(makes about ¾ cup)

> 1-2 tablespoons margarine, *or* butter, softened
> 1½ cups powdered sugar
> ¼ cup Dutch process cocoa
> ½ teaspoon vanilla
> 3-4 tablespoons fat-free milk

1. Mix margarine, powdered sugar, cocoa, and vanilla with enough milk to make spreadable consistency.

COFFEE-FROSTED COCOA CAKE

A perfect cake to carry for shared dinners and picnics.

16 servings

> 1½ cups sugar
> ½ cup margarine, *or* butter, softened
> 2 eggs
> 1 teaspoon vanilla
> 2 cups all-purpose flour
> ¾ cup unsweetened cocoa
> 2 teaspoons baking soda
> 1 teaspoon salt
> 1 cup fat-free milk
>   Coffee Frosting (recipe follows)

Per Serving
Calories: 240
% Calories from fat: 27
Fat (gm): 7.6
Saturated fat (gm): 1.6
Cholesterol (mg): 26.9
Sodium (mg): 385
Protein (gm): 3.9
Carbohydrate (gm): 41.6
Exchanges
Milk: 0.0
Vegetable: 0.0
Fruit: 0.0
Bread: 2.5
Meat: 0.0
Fat: 1.5

1. Combine sugar and margarine in large bowl; beat until light and fluffy. Add eggs one at a time, beating well after each addition. Stir in vanilla.

2. Combine flour, cocoa, baking soda, and salt in medium bowl. Mix dry ingredients into egg mixture alternately with milk, blending well. Spread batter in greased and floured 13 x 9-inch cake pan.

3. Bake cake at 350 degrees 25 to 35 minutes or until toothpick inserted in center comes out clean and cake begins to pull away from sides of pan. Cool completely on wire rack. Frost with Coffee Frosting.

Coffee Frosting

(makes about ½ cup)

- 1 tablespoon instant coffee granules
- 1 tablespoon hot water
- 1 tablespoon margarine, *or* butter, softened
- 1 cup powdered sugar
- 2-3 tablespoons fat-free milk

1. Dissolve coffee in hot water in medium bowl. Beat in margarine, powdered sugar, and enough milk for spreading consistency.

CHOCOLATE-CHERRY PUDDING CAKE

Served warm, this fudgy favorite will bring smiles to kids of all ages.

14 servings

- 1¾ cups all-purpose flour
- 1¼ cups granulated sugar
- ⅓ cup unsweetened cocoa
- 3 tablespoons baking powder
- ¾ cup fat-free milk
- ½ cup unsweetened applesauce
- 1 cup fresh, *or* frozen, thawed, sweet cherries, pitted
- ¼ cup chopped pecans
- 1¼ cups packed dark brown sugar
- 3 cups hot water
- ¼ cup unsweetened cocoa

Per Serving
Calories: 242
% Calories from fat: 7
Fat (gm): 1.9
Saturated fat (gm): 0.2
Cholesterol (mg): 0
Sodium (mg): 264
Protein (gm): 3
Carbohydrate (gm): 55.1
Exchanges
Milk: 0.0
Vegetable: 0.0
Fruit: 1.5
Bread: 2.0
Meat: 0.0
Fat: 0.0

1. Combine flour, granulated sugar, ⅓ cup cocoa, and baking powder in large bowl; stir in milk and applesauce just until dry ingredients are moistened. Fold in cherries and pecans. Spoon batter into greased and floured 13 x 9-inch baking pan.

2. Combine brown sugar, hot water, and ¼ cup cocoa in medium bowl, stirring until smooth. Pour brown sugar mixture over batter.

3. Bake at 350 degrees 35 to 40 minutes or until set (cake will have a pudding-like texture). Serve warm or at room temperature.

CARROT CAKE WITH CREAM CHEESE FROSTING

Moist and sweetly spiced, you'll make this cake over and over again.

16 servings

3 cups shredded carrots
½ cup raisins for baking
1 cup packed light brown sugar
⅓ cup vegetable oil
3 eggs
2 cups all-purpose flour
1 teaspoon baking powder
1 teaspoon baking soda
1 teaspoon ground cinnamon
¼ teaspoon ground allspice
¼ teaspoon ground nutmeg
¼ teaspoon salt
Cream Cheese Frosting (recipe follows)

Per Serving
Calories: 346
% Calories from fat: 24
Fat (gm): 9.7
Saturated fat (gm): 2.7
Cholesterol (mg): 44.9
Sodium (mg): 255
Protein (gm): 4.7
Carbohydrate (gm): 62.2
Exchanges
Milk: 0.0
Vegetable: 1.0
Fruit: 0.0
Bread: 5.0
Meat: 0.0
Fat: 2.0

1. Mix carrots, raisins, brown sugar, oil, and eggs in large bowl. Mix in combined remaining ingredients, except Cream Cheese Frosting.

2. Pour batter equally into 2 greased and floured 8-inch-round cake pans. Bake at 350 degrees until toothpicks inserted in cakes come out clean, 25 to 30 minutes. Cool in pans on wire rack 10 minutes; remove from pans and cool.

3. Place 1 cake layer on serving plate and frost. Top with remaining cake layer; frost top and side of cake.

Cream Cheese Frosting

(makes about 3 cups)

1 package (8 ounces) reduced-fat cream cheese, softened
2 tablespoons margarine, *or* butter, softened
4-5 cups powdered sugar
1 teaspoon vanilla

1. Beat cream cheese and margarine in medium bowl until smooth; beat in powdered sugar and vanilla.

SPICE CAKE WITH PENUCHE FROSTING

The flavor combination of sweet cake spices and creamy caramel fudge (penuche) frosting is too good to be true!

10 servings

4	tablespoons margarine, *or* butter, softened
¾	cup sugar
1	egg
½	teaspoon vanilla
1⅓	cups all-purpose flour
2	teaspoons baking powder
¾	teaspoon ground cinnamon
¼	teaspoon ground nutmeg
¼	teaspoon ground ginger
¼	teaspoon salt
⅔	cup fat-free milk
	Penuche Frosting (recipe follows)

Per Serving
Calories: 342
% Calories from fat: 23
Fat (gm): 8.7
Saturated fat (gm): 1.8
Cholesterol (mg): 21.6
Sodium (mg): 233
Protein (gm): 3.1
Carbohydrate (gm): 63.6
Exchanges
Milk: 0.0
Vegetable: 0.0
Fruit: 0.0
Bread: 4.0
Meat: 0.0
Fat: 1.5

1. Beat margarine, sugar, egg, and vanilla in large bowl until smooth. Mix in combined flour, baking powder, spices, and salt alternately with milk, beginning and ending with dry ingredients. Pour into greased and floured 8- or 9-inch-round cake pan.

2. Bake at 350 degrees until cake is browned and springs back when touched, about 40 minutes. Cool in pan on wire rack 10 minutes; remove from pan and cool to room temperature.

3. Place cake on serving plate; spread top and side with Penuche Frosting.

Penuche Frosting

(makes about 2½ cups)

3	tablespoons margarine, *or* butter
½	cup packed light brown sugar
2-2½	cups powdered sugar
½	teaspoon vanilla
2-4	tablespoons fat-free milk

1. Melt margarine in medium saucepan; stir in brown sugar and cook over medium heat until bubbly. Stir in powdered sugar, vanilla, and enough milk to make spreading consistency.

Note: Use the frosting immediately as it tends to thicken quickly. If frosting becomes too thick, thin with a few drops of hot water.

PINEAPPLE UPSIDE-DOWN CAKE

Invert the cake immediately after baking so all the warm caramel topping releases from the pan.

8-10 servings

3	tablespoons light corn syrup
5	tablespoons margarine, *or* butter, softened, divided
⅔	cup packed light brown sugar
2-3	tablespoons chopped pecans
1	can (8 ounces) sliced pineapple in its own juice, drained, slices cut in halves
4	maraschino cherries, cut in halves
⅔	cup granulated sugar
1	egg
½	teaspoon pineapple extract, *or* vanilla
1⅓	cups all-purpose flour
2	teaspoons baking powder
¼	teaspoon salt
⅔	cup fat-free milk
	Light whipped topping, as garnish

Per Serving
Calories: 347
% Calories from fat: 23
Fat (gm): 9.1
Saturated fat (gm): 1.7
Cholesterol (mg): 27
Sodium (mg): 264
Protein (gm): 4
Carbohydrate (gm): 63.8
Exchanges
Milk: 0.0
Vegetable: 0.0
Fruit: 0.5
Bread: 3.5
Meat: 0.0
Fat: 1.5

1. Heat corn syrup and 1 tablespoon margarine until melted in small skillet. Stir in brown sugar and pecans and cook over medium heat until mixture is bubbly, 2 to 3 minutes. Pour topping mixture into ungreased 9-inch-round cake pan; arrange pineapple slices and cherries on top.

2. Beat remaining 4 tablespoons margarine, granulated sugar, egg, and pineapple extract in medium bowl until smooth. Mix in combined flour, baking powder, and salt alternately with milk, beginning and ending with dry ingredients. Pour batter over topping in pan.

3. Bake at 350 degrees until cake springs back when touched, about 40 minutes. Loosen side of cake with sharp knife and invert onto serving plate. Serve warm with whipped topping.

BOSTON CREAM CAKE

A family favorite, with chocolatey glaze and a luxurious cream filling. Although sometimes called a "pie," it is, indeed, a cake.

12 servings

8 tablespoons margarine, *or* butter, softened
1¼ cups sugar
2 eggs
1 teaspoon vanilla
2⅔ cups all-purpose flour
3 teaspoons baking powder
½ teaspoon salt
1⅔ cups fat-free milk
Vanilla Cream Filling (recipe follows)
Chocolate Glaze (recipe follows)

Per Serving
Calories: 353
% Calories from fat: 23
Fat (gm): 9.3
Saturated fat (gm): 2
Cholesterol (mg): 54.2
Sodium (mg): 305
Protein (gm): 6.6
Carbohydrate (gm): 61.3
Exchanges
Milk: 0.0
Vegetable: 0.0
Fruit: 0.0
Bread: 4.0
Meat: 0.0
Fat: 1.5

1. Beat margarine, sugar, eggs, and vanilla until smooth in medium bowl. Mix in combined flour, baking powder, and salt alternately with milk, beginning and ending with dry ingredients. Pour batter equally into 2 greased and floured 8- or 9-inch-round cake pans.

2. Bake at 350 degrees until cakes spring back when touched, about 40 minutes. Cool in pans on wire rack 10 minutes; remove from pans and cool to room temperature.

3. Place 1 cake layer on serving plate; spread with Vanilla Cream Filling. Top with second cake layer and spoon Chocolate Glaze over.

Vanilla Cream Filling

(makes about ¼ cup)

¼ cup sugar
2 tablespoons cornstarch
1 cup fat-free milk
1 egg, beaten
½ teaspoon vanilla

1. Mix sugar and cornstarch in small saucepan; stir in milk. Heat over medium-high heat, stirring constantly, until mixture comes to a boil; boil, stirring constantly, until thickened.

2. Whisk about ½ of milk mixture into beaten egg in small bowl; whisk egg mixture back into saucepan. Cook over very low heat, whisking constantly, 30 to 60 seconds. Remove from heat; stir in vanilla and cool.

Chocolate Glaze

1 cup powdered sugar
2 tablespoons unsweetened cocoa
½ teaspoon vanilla
1-2 tablespoons fat-free milk

1. Combine powdered sugar and cocoa in small bowl; stir in vanilla and enough milk to make glaze consistency.

PUMPKIN-GINGER CAKE WITH WARM RUM SAUCE

Moist with pumpkin and savory with spices, a perfect choice for fall and winter holidays.

8 servings

½ cup canned pumpkin
½ cup packed light brown sugar
¼ cup margarine, *or* butter, softened
¼ cup light molasses
1 egg
1½ cups all-purpose flour
½ teaspoon baking powder
½ teaspoon baking soda
½ teaspoon ground allspice
½ teaspoon ground cloves
½ teaspoon ground ginger
Warm Rum Sauce (recipe follows)

Per Serving
Calories: 304
% Calories from fat: 28
Fat (gm): 9.5
Saturated fat (gm): 2
Cholesterol (mg): 27.3
Sodium (mg): 235
Protein (gm): 4.8
Carbohydrate (gm): 48.6
Exchanges
Milk: 0.0
Vegetable: 0.0
Fruit: 0.0
Bread: 3.0
Meat: 0.0
Fat: 2.0

1. Combine pumpkin, brown sugar, margarine, molasses, and egg in large mixer bowl; beat at medium speed until light and fluffy.

2. Combine flour, baking powder, baking soda, allspice, cloves, and ginger in medium bowl; add to pumpkin mixture. Blend at low speed until moistened. Pour batter into greased and floured 8-inch-square baking pan.

3. Bake cake at 350 degrees until toothpick inserted in center comes out clean, 30 to 40 minutes. Cool in pan on wire rack 10 minutes; remove from pan. Cool completely on wire rack. Serve with Warm Rum Sauce.

Warm Rum Sauce

(makes 1½ cups)

- ¼ cup sugar
- 1 tablespoon cornstarch
- 1¼ cups fat-free milk
- 2 tablespoons rum, *or* ½ teaspoon rum extract
- 2 tablespoons margarine, *or* butter
- ½ teaspoon vanilla
- ⅛ teaspoon ground nutmeg

1. Mix sugar and cornstarch in small saucepan; stir in milk and rum. Cook over medium heat until mixture boils and thickens, stirring constantly.

2. Remove from heat; stir in margarine, vanilla, and nutmeg. Serve warm.

BANANA-CINNAMON CAKE

Bananas add flavor and moistness to this picnic-perfect cake.

10 servings

- 1½ cups all-purpose flour
- ½ cup packed light brown sugar
- 2 teaspoons baking powder
- 1 teaspoon baking soda
- 1 teaspoon ground cinnamon
- ¼ teaspoon salt
- 1 package (6 ounces) reduced-fat custard-style banana yogurt
- 1 cup ripe banana, mashed (1 medium banana)
- 2 tablespoons margarine, *or* butter, softened
- 2 egg whites

Per Serving
Calories: 235
% Calories from fat: 19
Fat (gm): 5
Saturated fat (gm): 0.9
Cholesterol (mg): 0.1
Sodium (mg): 326
Protein (gm): 3.7
Carbohydrate (gm): 44.4
Exchanges
Milk: 0.0
Vegetable: 0.0
Fruit: 0.5
Bread: 2.5
Meat: 0.0
Fat: 0.5

1 teaspoon vanilla
Powdered Sugar Frosting (recipe
follows)

1. Combine flour, sugar, baking powder, baking soda, cinnamon, and salt in large bowl. Mix yogurt, banana, margarine, egg whites, and vanilla; stir into flour mixture and mix well. Pour batter into greased and floured 9-inch baking pan.

2. Bake at 375 degrees 25 to 30 minutes or until cake springs back when lightly touched in center. Cool in pan on wire rack 10 minutes; invert onto wire rack and cool completely. Spread with Powdered Sugar Frosting.

Powdered Sugar Frosting

(makes about ½ cup)

1 cup powdered sugar
2 tablespoons margarine, *or* butter, melted
2 tablespoons fat-free milk

1. Combine powdered sugar, margarine, and milk in small bowl; beat until smooth. Spread frosting over cooled cake.

LEMON POUND CAKE

Savor the rich flavor of this cake. It may also be served with Tart Lemon Sauce (p. 808), if desired.

12 servings

¾ cup sugar
⅓ cup margarine, *or* butter, softened
1 cup reduced-fat sour cream
3 egg whites
2 teaspoons lemon juice
1 tablespoon grated lemon rind
2½ cups cake flour
1 teaspoon baking soda
¼ teaspoon salt
Lemon Syrup (recipe follows)
Powdered sugar, as garnish

Per Serving
Calories: 230
% Calories from fat: 26
Fat (gm): 6.5
Saturated fat (gm): 1
Cholesterol (mg): 6.3
Sodium (mg): 235
Protein (gm): 3.5
Carbohydrate (gm): 38.8
Exchanges
Milk: 0.0
Vegetable: 0.0
Fruit: 0.0
Bread: 2.5
Meat: 0.0
Fat: 1.0

1. Beat sugar and margarine in large bowl until light and fluffy. Beat in sour cream, egg whites, lemon juice, and lemon rind until smooth. Mix in combined flour, baking soda, and salt, beating until smooth, about 1 minute. Spoon batter into greased and floured 6-cup fluted cake pan.

2. Bake cake 40 to 50 minutes or until toothpick inserted in center comes out clean. Cool in pan on wire rack 20 minutes; invert onto wire rack.

3. With a skewer or tines of fork, pierce cake top at 1-inch intervals. Spoon warm Lemon Syrup over cake; sprinkle with powdered sugar.

Lemon Syrup

(makes about ⅔ cup)

> ⅔ cup powdered sugar
> ¼ cup lemon juice
> 3 tablespoons water

1. Combine sugar, lemon juice, and water in small saucepan. Heat to boiling, stirring constantly until sugar is dissolved. Cool slightly.

ORANGE POPPY SEED CAKE

This citrus-fresh cake is a perfect addition to any brunch menu.

12 servings

> ½ cup sugar
> 6 tablespoons margarine, *or* butter, softened
> 2 egg whites
> 1 egg
> ¾ cup reduced-fat sour cream
> 2 tablespoons frozen orange juice concentrate, thawed
> 2 cups cake flour
> 2 tablespoons poppy seeds
> 1 teaspoon baking powder
> ½ teaspoon baking soda
> ¼ teaspoon salt
> Citrus Glaze (recipe follows)

Per Serving
Calories: 227
% Calories from fat: 31
Fat (gm): 7.8
Saturated fat (gm): 1.3
Cholesterol (mg): 22.5
Sodium (mg): 215
Protein (gm): 3.5
Carbohydrate (gm): 35.5
Exchanges
Milk: 0.0
Vegetable: 0.0
Fruit: 0.0
Bread: 2.5
Meat: 0.0
Fat: 1.0

1. In large bowl, beat sugar and margarine until smooth and fluffy. Beat in egg whites, egg, sour cream, and orange juice until smooth.

2. Combine cake flour, poppy seeds, baking powder, baking soda, and salt in medium bowl; add to sour cream mixture. Beat on medium-high speed until smooth, about 1 to 2 minutes. Pour batter into greased and floured 6-cup fluted cake pan.

3. Bake cake at 350 degrees 40 to 55 minutes or until toothpick inserted in center comes out clean. Cool in pan on wire rack 25 to 30 minutes; invert onto wire rack and cool. Spoon Citrus Glaze over cake.

Citrus Glaze

   1 cup powdered sugar
3-4 tablespoons orange juice

1. Combine sugar and enough orange juice to make glaze consistency.

RASPBERRY-ORANGE SWIRL CAKE

A swirl of raspberry puree enhances flavor and appearance in this delectable cake.

14 servings

  2 cups fresh, *or* frozen, thawed raspberries
  1 package (18½ ounces) reduced-fat yellow cake mix
  1 cup water
  2 tablespoons frozen orange juice concentrate, thawed
  3 egg whites
  ½ teaspoon orange extract
  2 teaspoons grated orange rind
  2 cups powdered sugar
  ½ teaspoon orange extract
3-4 tablespoons fat-free milk

Per Serving
Calories: 229
% Calories from fat: 11
Fat (gm): 2.7
Saturated fat (gm): 0.9
Cholesterol (mg): 0
Sodium (mg): 266
Protein (gm): 1.9
Carbohydrate (gm): 49.6
Exchanges
Milk: 0.0
Vegetable: 0.0
Fruit: 1.0
Bread: 2.0
Meat: 0.0
Fat: 0.5

1. Process raspberries in food processor or blender until smooth; strain and discard seeds.

2. Combine cake mix, water, orange juice, egg whites, and ½ teaspoon orange extract in mixer bowl. Beat on medium-high speed until smooth, about 2 minutes; stir in orange rind.

3. Pour half the batter into greased and floured 12-cup fluted cake pan; spoon on raspberry puree and top with remaining batter. With a knife, cut through batter a few times to marbleize.

4. Bake cake at 350 degrees 40 to 45 minutes or until toothpick inserted in center comes out clean. Cool in pan on wire rack 20 minutes; remove from pan. Cool completely on wire rack.

5. Combine powdered sugar and ½ teaspoon orange extract in small bowl; stir in enough milk to make glaze consistency. Spoon over cake.

PINEAPPLE-LEMON TRIFLE

Select your prettiest glass bowl for serving this attractive dessert. A fruit puree replaces the more traditional preserves, enhancing the use of fresh fruits in this recipe.

12 servings

1 package (18¼ ounces) reduced-fat
   white cake mix
1½ cups water
3 egg whites
1½ cups pineapple chunks in juice, drained
   Lemon Custard (recipe follows)
1 pint strawberries, sliced
2 medium bananas, sliced
¾ cup frozen light whipped topping,
   thawed

Per Serving
Calories: 191
% Calories from fat: 16
Fat (gm): 3.6
Saturated fat (gm): 0.8
Cholesterol (mg): 36
Sodium (mg): 192
Protein (gm): 3.3
Carbohydrate (gm): 38.6
Exchanges
Milk: 0.0
Vegetable: 0.0
Fruit: 1.0
Bread: 1.5
Meat: 0.0
Fat: 0.0

1. Prepare cake mix according to package directions, using 1½ cups water and 3 egg whites. Pour batter into lightly greased and floured 13 x 9-inch baking pan.

2. Bake cake at 350 degrees 28 to 30 minutes or until top springs back when touched. Cool on wire rack. Cut half the cake into 1-inch cubes. (Reserve or freeze remaining cake for another use.)

3. Process pineapple chunks in blender or food processor until smooth. Layer ⅓ of cake cubes in bottom of 2-quart glass serving bowl. Spoon ⅓ of Lemon Custard and ⅓ of pineapple puree over cake cubes; top with ⅓ of strawberries and bananas. Repeat layers twice. Refrigerate until chilled, about 1 hour. Garnish with whipped topping.

Lemon Custard

(makes about 2 cups)

- ¼ cup sugar
- 2 tablespoons cornstarch
- 2 tablespoons flour
- 1 cup fat-free milk
- ½ cup lemon juice
- 2 eggs, slightly beaten
- ¼ teaspoon ground nutmeg

1. Mix sugar, cornstarch, and flour in medium saucepan; stir in milk and lemon juice. Cook over medium heat until mixture boils and thickens; boil 1 minute, stirring constantly.

2. Stir about ½ cup milk mixture into eggs; stir egg mixture back into saucepan. Cook over low heat, stirring constantly, until thickened. Remove from heat and cool; stir in nutmeg. Refrigerate until chilled, 1 to 2 hours.

CASSATA SICILIANA

Filled with ricotta cheese, candied fruit, and chocolate chips, cassata is an Italian dessert traditionally served during the Christmas holidays.

10 servings

- 1 package (6.95 ounces) angel food loaf cake mix
- ½ cup water
- 1 cup low-fat ricotta cheese
- ¼ cup sugar
- 2 tablespoons, finely chopped mixed candied fruit
- 1 ounce semisweet chocolate, finely chopped

Per Serving
Calories: 183
% Calories from fat: 12
Fat (gm): 2.5
Saturated fat (gm): 0.2
Cholesterol (mg): 0.5
Sodium (mg): 270
Protein (gm): 4.4
Carbohydrate (gm): 34.2
Exchanges
Milk: 0.0
Vegetable: 0.0
Fruit: 0.0
Bread: 2.5
Meat: 0.0
Fat: 0.0

1 teaspoon grated lemon rind
¼ cup dark rum
Chocolate Sauce (recipe follows)

1.   Combine cake mix and water in large bowl. Mix at low speed until moistened. Beat 2 minutes at high speed. Pour into ungreased 9 x 5-inch loaf pan. Bake at 375 degrees 25 to 30 minutes or until cracks on top appear dry. Cool completely in pan tipped on side on wire rack. Remove cake from pan. With a serrated knife, slice cake horizontally into three equal layers.

2.   Combine ricotta cheese, sugar, candied fruit, chocolate, and lemon rind in small bowl. Place 1 cake layer, crust side down, in a 9 x 5-inch loaf pan lined with plastic wrap. Brush cake with 1 tablespoon rum; spread with half of the ricotta mixture. Top with second cake layer, brush with 1 tablespoon rum, and spread with remaining ricotta mixture. Top with remaining cake layer, and brush with remaining rum. Cover with plastic wrap, pressing firmly to compact layers.

3.   Refrigerate cake, weighted with a 16-ounce can, overnight. Remove cake from pan; slice and arrange on serving plate. Drizzle with Chocolate Sauce.

Chocolate Sauce

 (makes about 1 cup)

¼ cup unsweetened cocoa
2 tablespoons sugar
1 tablespoon cornstarch
⅓ cup dark corn syrup
¼ cup 2% milk
1 teaspoon margarine, *or* butter
2 teaspoons vanilla

1.   Combine cocoa, sugar, and cornstarch in small saucepan. Stir in corn syrup and milk until smooth. Cook over medium heat until mixture boils and thickens, stirring constantly. Remove from heat; stir in margarine and vanilla. Cool.

BASIC PIE CRUST (All-Purpose Flour)

 This pastry contains a minimum of margarine yet is not difficult to handle or roll. Use cold margarine and ice water, as the recipe directs.

8 servings (one 8- or 9-inch pie crust)

1¼ cups all-purpose flour

2 tablespoons sugar

¼ teaspoon salt

3 tablespoons cold margarine, *or* butter

4-5 tablespoons ice water

Per Serving
Calories: 121
% Calories from fat: 33
   (will decrease in pie servings)
Fat (gm): 4.4
Saturated fat (gm): 0.9
Cholesterol (mg): 0
Sodium (mg): 117
Protein (gm): 2.1
Carbohydrate (gm): 18.1
Exchanges
Milk: 0.0
Vegetable: 0.0
Fruit: 0.0
Bread: 1.0
Meat: 0.0
Fat: 1.0

1. Combine flour, sugar, and salt in medium bowl. With pastry blender or 2 knives, cut in margarine until mixture resembles coarse crumbs. Sprinkle with water, 1 tablespoon at a time, mixing lightly with a fork after each addition until pastry just holds together.

2. On lightly floured surface, roll dough into a circle 2 inches larger in diameter than pie pan. Wrap pastry around rolling pin and unroll into 8- or 9-inch pie or tart pan, easing it into bottom and side of pan. Trim edges, fold under, and flute. Bake as pie recipe directs.

Note: When a pie crust is baked before it is filled, the recipe will indicate baking with weights so that bottom of crust remains flat. Line bottom of pastry with aluminum foil and fill with a single layer of pie weights or dried beans. Remove weights and foil 5 minutes before end of baking time indicated in recipe. If not using weights or dried beans, piercing the bottom of the pastry with the tines of a fork will help crust remain flat.

BASIC PIE CRUST (Cake Flour)

This pastry also contains a minimum of margarine but uses cake flour, which is lower in calories than all-purpose flour.

8 servings (one 8- or 9-inch pie crust)

1¼ cups cake flour
1 tablespoon sugar
¼ teaspoon salt
3 tablespoons cold margarine, *or* butter
3-4 tablespoons ice water

Per Serving
Calories: 106
% Calories from fat: 38
  (will decrease in pie servings)
Fat (gm): 4.4
Saturated fat (gm): 0.9
Cholesterol (mg): 0
Sodium (mg): 117
Protein (gm): 1.4
Carbohydrate (gm): 14.9
Exchanges
Milk: 0.0
Vegetable: 0.0
Fruit: 0.0
Bread: 1.0
Meat: 0.0
Fat: 1.0

1. Combine cake flour, sugar, and salt in medium bowl. With pastry blender or 2 knives, cut in margarine until mixture resembles coarse crumbs. Sprinkle with water, 1 tablespoon at a time, mixing lightly with a fork after each addition until pastry just holds together.

2. On lightly floured surface, roll dough into a circle 2 inches larger in diameter than pie pan. Wrap pastry around rolling pin and unroll into 8- or 9-inch pie or tart pan, easing it into bottom and side of pan. Trim edges, fold under, and flute. Bake as pie recipe directs.

Note: When a pie crust is baked before it is filled, the recipe will indicate baking with weights so that bottom of crust remains flat. Line bottom of pastry with aluminum foil and fill with a single layer of pie weights or dried beans. Remove weights and foil 5 minutes before end of baking time indicated in recipe. If not using weights or dried beans, piercing the bottom of the pastry with the tines of a fork will help crust remain flat.

MERINGUE PIE CRUST

Light, airy, delicious, and versatile. Fill this crust with scoops of low-fat frozen yogurt or ice cream, and top with a light drizzle of Warm Rum Sauce or Bittersweet Chocolate Sauce (see pp. 750, 794).

8 servings (one 8- or 9-inch pie crust)

4 egg whites
½ teaspoon cream of tartar
1 cup sugar

Per Serving
Calories: 98
% Calories from fat: 0
Fat (gm): 0
Saturated fat (gm): 0
Cholesterol (mg): 0
Sodium (mg): 28
Protein (gm): 1.8
Carbohydrate (gm): 24.2
Exchanges
Milk: 0.0
Vegetable: 0.0
Fruit: 1.0
Bread: 0.0
Meat: 0.5
Fat: 0.0

1. Beat egg whites and cream of tartar in medium bowl to soft peaks. Gradually beat in sugar, beating to stiff peaks. Spoon mixture into ungreased 8- or 9-inch glass pie pan, spreading on bottom and up side to form a large bowl shape.

2. Bake at 350 degrees 40 minutes or until crust is firm to touch and very lightly browned. Cool on wire rack.

GRAHAM CRACKER CRUMB CRUST

Mix this crust right in the pie pan—quick and easy!

8 servings (one 8- or 9-inch pie crust)

1¼ cups graham cracker crumbs
2 tablespoons sugar
3 tablespoons margarine, *or* butter, melted

Per Serving
Calories: 131
% Calories from fat: 44
(will decrease in pie servings)
Fat (gm): 6.4
Saturated fat (gm): 0.8
Cholesterol (mg): 0
Sodium (mg): 148
Protein (gm): 1.3
Carbohydrate (gm): 17.2
Exchanges
Milk: 0.0
Vegetable: 0.0
Fruit: 0.0
Bread: 1.0
Meat: 0.0
Fat: 1.0

1. Combine graham crumbs, sugar, and margarine in 8- or 9-inch pie pan; pat mixture evenly on bottom and side of pan.

2. Bake at 350 degrees 8 to 10 minutes or until edge or crust is lightly browned. Cool on wire rack.

VANILLA CRUMB CRUST

A perfect recipe when a delicately flavored crust is desired.

8 servings (from 8- or 9-inch pie crust)

1 cup vanilla wafer cookie crumbs
2 tablespoons margarine, *or* butter, melted

Per Serving
Calories: 83
% Calories from fat: 51
    (will decrease in pie servings)
Fat (gm): 4.7
Saturated fat (gm): 0.9
Cholesterol (mg): 7.8
Sodium (mg): 64
Protein (gm): 0.6
Carbohydrate (gm): 9.4
Exchanges
Milk: 0.0
Vegetable: 0.0
Fruit: 0.0
Bread: 0.5
Meat: 0.0
Fat: 1.0

1. Combine vanilla crumbs and margarine in 8- or 9-inch pie pan; pat mixture evenly on bottom and side of pan.

2. Bake 8 to 10 minutes or until edge of crust is lightly browned. Cool on wire rack.

GINGERSNAP CRUMB CRUST

Gingersnaps provide a zesty flavor accent in this crust.

8 servings (from 8- or 9-inch pie crust)

½ cup graham cracker crumbs
½ cup gingersnap cookie crumbs
2 tablespoons margarine, *or* butter

Per Serving
Calories: 84
% Calories from fat: 46
    (will decrease in pie servings)
Fat (gm): 4.3
Saturated fat (gm): 0.7
Cholesterol (mg): 0
Sodium (mg): 113
Protein (gm): 0.9
Carbohydrate (gm): 10.5
Exchanges
Milk: 0.0
Vegetable: 0.0
Fruit: 0.0
Bread: 0.5
Meat: 0.0
Fat: 1.0

1. Combine graham crumbs, gingersnap crumbs, and margarine in 8- or 9-inch pie pan; pat mixture evenly on bottom and side of pan.

2. Bake at 350 degrees 8 to 10 minutes or until edge of crust is lightly browned. Cool on wire rack.

GRANDMA'S LEMON MERINGUE PIE

 A perfect flavor combination of sweet and tart, topped with a mile-high meringue! Be sure to spread the meringue while filling is hot, and seal to the edge of the crust to prevent weeping.

10 servings

    Baked Reduced-Fat Pie Crust (recipe follows)
2 cups sugar, divided
½ cup cornstarch
1½ cups water
½ cup lemon juice
1 egg
2 tablespoons margarine, or butter
4 egg whites
¼ teaspoon cream of tartar

Per Serving
Calories: 316
% Calories from fat: 18
Fat (gm): 6.5
Saturated fat (gm): 1.5
Cholesterol (mg): 21.3
Sodium (mg): 110
Protein (gm): 3.7
Carbohydrate (gm): 61.6
Exchanges
Milk: 0.0
Vegetable: 0.0
Fruit: 0.0
Bread: 4.0
Meat: 0.0
Fat: 0.5

1. Make pastry, using 9-inch pie pan. Line bottom of pastry with aluminum foil and fill with layer of pie weights or dry beans. Bake at 400 degrees for 10 minutes; remove foil and pie weights. Continue baking until crust is golden, 5 to 8 minutes. Cool on wire rack.

2. Combine 1½ cups sugar and cornstarch in medium saucepan; stir in water and lemon juice. Heat to boiling; boil, whisking constantly, until thickened, about 1 minute.

3. Beat egg in small bowl; whisk about 1 cup of lemon mixture into egg mixture. Whisk egg mixture back into saucepan; cook over very low heat, whisking constantly, 30 to 60 seconds. Remove from heat; add margarine, stirring until melted. Pour filling into pie crust.

4. Using clean beaters and large bowl, beat egg whites until foamy; add cream of tartar and beat to soft peaks. Beat to stiff peaks, adding remaining ½ cup sugar gradually. Spread meringue over hot filling, sealing well to edge of pie crust. Bake at 400 degrees until meringue is browned, about 5 minutes. Cool to room temperature before cutting. Refrigerate leftover pie.

Baked Reduced-Fat Pie Crust

(for one 8- or 9-inch pie)

- 1¼ cups all-purpose flour
- 2 tablespoons sugar
- ¼ teaspoon salt
- 3-4 tablespoons vegetable shortening, *or* butter
- 4-5 tablespoons ice water

1.   Combine flour, sugar, and salt in medium bowl. Cut in shortening with pastry blender until mixture resembles coarse crumbs. Sprinkle with ice water, 1 tablespoon at a time, mixing with fork just until dough holds together.

2.   Roll pastry on floured surface to circle 2 inches larger than inverted pie pan. Ease pastry into pan; trim and flute edge. Bake as recipe directs.

DOUBLE-CRUST APPLE PIE

Nothing is more American than real homemade apple pie. Enjoy it warm with a generous scoop of fat-free frozen yogurt or a slice of reduced-fat Cheddar cheese.

10 servings

- Double Crust Pastry (recipe follows)
- 8 cups peeled, cored, sliced tart baking apples
- 1 cup sugar
- 4-5 tablespoons all-purpose flour
- ¾ teaspoon ground cinnamon
- ¼ teaspoon ground nutmeg
- ⅛ teaspoon ground cloves
- ⅛ teaspoon salt
- 2 tablespoons margarine, *or* butter, cut into pieces (optional)

Per Serving
Calories: 297
% Calories from fat: 19
Fat (gm): 6.3
Saturated fat (gm): 1.2
Cholesterol (mg): 0
Sodium (mg): 200
Protein (gm): 3.1
Carbohydrate (gm): 58.9
Exchanges
Milk: 0.0
Vegetable: 0.0
Fruit: 1.0
Bread: 3.5
Meat: 0.0
Fat: 1.5

1. Roll ⅔ of pastry on floured surface to form circle 2 inches larger than inverted 9-inch pie pan; ease pastry into pan.

2. Toss apples with combined sugar, flour, spices, and salt in large bowl; arrange apples in pastry shell and dot with margarine, if using.

3. Roll remaining pastry to fit top of pie and place over apples. Trim edges of pastry to within ½ inch of pan; fold top pastry over bottom pastry and flute. Cut vents in top crust.

4. Bake pie at 425 degrees until apples are fork-tender and pastry browned, 40 to 50 minutes. Cover pastry with aluminum foil if it is becoming too brown. Cool 10 to 15 minutes before cutting.

Double-Crust Pastry

(makes double crust for 8- or 9-inch pie)

- 2 cups all-purpose flour
- 3 tablespoons sugar
- ½ teaspoon salt
- 5 tablespoons cold margarine, *or* butter, cut into pieces
- 6-7 tablespoons ice water

1. Combine flour, sugar, and salt in medium bowl; cut in margarine with pastry blender until mixture resembles coarse crumbs. Add water, a tablespoon at a time, mixing with fork, until dough forms. Refrigerate until ready to use.

TARTE TATIN

Caramelized sugar contributes special flavor to this French-style upside-down apple tart.

8 servings

- 1 cup cake flour
- 2 tablespoons sugar
- 3 tablespoons cold margarine, *or* butter
- 2-3 tablespoons ice water
- 5 cups Granny Smith apples (about 2½ lbs.), peeled, cored, and cut into scant ½-inch slices

Per Serving
Calories: 279
% Calories from fat: 24
Fat (gm): 7.6
Saturated fat (gm): 1.5
Cholesterol (mg): 0
Sodium (mg): 83.1
Protein (gm): 1.4
Carbohydrate (gm): 53.8

½ cup sugar

¼ teaspoon ground nutmeg

1 tablespoon lemon juice

¼ cup sugar

2 tablespoons margarine, *or* butter

Exchanges
Milk: 0.0
Vegetable: 0.0
Fruit: 1.5
Bread: 2.0
Meat: 0.0
Fat: 1.0

1. Combine cake flour and sugar in medium bowl. With pastry blender or 2 knives, cut in margarine until mixture resembles coarse crumbs. Sprinkle in water, 1 tablespoon at a time, mixing lightly with a fork after each addition until pastry just holds together. Cover dough and refrigerate 15 minutes. On lightly floured surface, roll pastry into 11-inch circle; cover loosely with plastic wrap and set aside.

2. Toss apples with combined ½ cup sugar and nutmeg; sprinkle with lemon juice. Set aside. Place ¼ cup sugar in 10-inch skillet with oven-proof handle. Cook over medium heat until sugar melts and is golden brown, about 5 minutes, stirring occasionally (watch carefully—the sugar can burn easily). Add apple mixture and margarine; cook 5 minutes or until apples are just tender, stirring occasionally. Remove from heat.

3. Arrange apples in skillet so they are slightly mounded in the center. Place pastry on top of apples; tuck in edges. Cut slits in pastry to allow steam to escape. Bake at 425 degrees 20 to 25 minutes or until lightly browned. Invert onto serving platter. Serve warm or at room temperature.

OLD-FASHIONED BUTTERMILK PIE

 Carry on Grandma's best tradition with this pie!

8 servings

Gingersnap Crumb Crust (see p. 760)

¾ cup sugar

1 tablespoon margarine, *or* butter, softened

1 egg

2 egg whites

3 tablespoons flour

¼ teaspoon salt

1 cup buttermilk

Nutmeg, ground, as garnish

Per Serving
Calories: 205
% Calories from fat: 29
Fat (gm): 6.7
Saturated fat (gm): 1.3
Cholesterol (mg): 27.8
Sodium (mg): 251
Protein (gm): 3.9
Carbohydrate (gm): 33.1
Exchanges
Milk: 0.0
Vegetable: 0.0
Fruit: 0.0
Bread: 2.0
Meat: 0.0
Fat: 1.5

1. Make pie crust, using 8-inch pie pan; do not bake.

2. Mix sugar and margarine in medium bowl until blended; beat in egg and egg whites. Stir in flour, salt, and buttermilk until well blended.

3. Pour filling into prepared crust; bake at 350 degrees 40 minutes or until sharp knife inserted near center comes out clean. Sprinkle with nutmeg and serve warm or chilled.

SPICED SWEET POTATO PIE

 A change from traditional pumpkin, this pie will brighten any winter holiday table.

10 servings

Basic Pie Crust (All-Purpose Flour, see p. 757)

1½ cups sweet potatoes, peeled, cooked, and mashed

¾ cup packed light brown sugar

1 egg

2 egg whites

1½ cup fat-free milk

1 teaspoon ground cinnamon

1 teaspoon ground ginger

½ teaspoon ground mace

¼ teaspoon salt

Frozen light whipped topping, thawed (optional)

Per Serving
Calories: 218
% Calories from fat: 11
Fat (gm): 2.5
Saturated fat (gm): 0.6
Cholesterol (mg): 22
Sodium (mg): 140
Protein (gm): 5
Carbohydrate (gm): 44.1
Exchanges
Milk: 0.0
Vegetable: 0.0
Fruit: 0.0
Bread: 2.5
Meat: 0.0
Fat: 0.5

1. Prepare pie crust, using 8-inch pie pan. Pierce bottom of pastry with fork; bake at 425 degrees without weights 10 minutes or until very light brown. Cool on wire rack.

2. Beat sweet potatoes, brown sugar, egg, and egg whites in medium bowl until smooth. Mix in milk, cinnamon, ginger, mace, and salt. Pour into pie crust.

3. Bake at 350 degrees about 45 minutes or until sharp knife inserted near center comes out clean. Serve warm or at room temperature; garnish with whipped topping.

BANANA-STRAWBERRY CREAM PIE

 Strawberries add a new twist to this old favorite. Refrigerate until the cream filling is set and well chilled before slicing.

8 servings

Graham Cracker Crumb Crust (see p. 759)

¼ cup graham cracker crumbs
1 tablespoon margarine, *or* butter
⅓ cup sugar
¼ cup cornstarch
2 tablespoons flour
⅓ teaspoon salt
2½ cups fat-free milk
3 egg yolks
1 teaspoon vanilla
¼ teaspoon ground cinnamon
⅓ teaspoon ground nutmeg
1 cup sliced strawberries
2 medium bananas

Per Serving
Calories: 250
% Calories from fat: 30
Fat (gm): 8.5
Saturated fat (gm): 1.7
Cholesterol (mg): 81.1
Sodium (mg): 226
Protein (gm): 5.4
Carbohydrate (gm): 38.9
Exchanges
Milk: 0.0
Vegetable: 0.0
Fruit: 0.5
Bread: 2.0
Meat: 0.0
Fat: 1.5

1. Make pie crust, adding ¼ cup graham crumbs and 1 tablespoon margarine to recipe and using 9-inch pie pan.

2. Mix sugar, cornstarch, flour, and salt in medium saucepan; stir in milk. Cook over medium heat until mixture boils and thickens; boil 1 minute, stirring constantly.

3. Stir about ½ cup of mixture into egg yolks; stir egg mixture back into saucepan. Cook over low heat, stirring constantly until thickened. Remove from heat; stir in vanilla, cinnamon, and nutmeg. Cool to room temperature, stirring frequently. Refrigerate until chilled, 1 to 2 hours.

4. Set aside 4 to 6 strawberry slices. Slice 1 to 1½ bananas and arrange in crust with remaining strawberries. Spoon custard into crust; refrigerate until set, 4 to 6 hours. Slice remaining banana and garnish pie with banana and strawberry slices.

TOASTED COCONUT CREAM TART

Tucked in a tart pan for a new look, you'll enjoy this updated version of an old favorite.

8 servings

    Basic Pie Crust (Cake Flour, see p. 758)
⅓ cup sugar
2 tablespoons cornstarch
1½ cups 2% milk
1 egg, slightly beaten
¼ cup flaked, toasted, unsweetened coconut

Per Serving
Calories: 170
% Calories from fat: 26
Fat (gm): 4.9
Saturated fat (gm): 1.1
Cholesterol (mg): 30
Sodium (mg): 85
Protein (gm): 3.8
Carbohydrate (gm): 28
Exchanges
Milk: 0.0
Vegetable: 0.0
Fruit: 0.0
Bread: 2.0
Meat: 0.0
Fat: 1.0

1. Prepare pie crust, using 9-inch tart pan. Line pastry with weights, and bake at 375 degrees 10 to 15 minutes or until lightly browned. Cool on wire rack.

2. Mix sugar and cornstarch in small saucepan; stir in milk. Cook over medium heat until mixture boils and thickens; boil 1 minute, stirring constantly.

3. Stir about ½ cup of mixture into egg; stir egg mixture back into saucepan. Cook over low heat, stirring constantly, until thickened. Stir in 3 tablespoons of coconut.

4. Pour custard into cooled pie crust, spreading evenly. Sprinkle with remaining 1 tablespoon coconut. Cool to room temperature. Refrigerate until set, 2 to 4 hours.

CHOCOLATE RUM PIE

Dutch or European process cocoa gives a special rich chocolate flavor to the filling in this delicious pie.

8 servings

    Vanilla Crumb Crust (see p. 760)
*1 envelope unflavored gelatin
½ cup 2% milk
½ cup sugar
2 tablespoons dark rum

Per Serving
Calories: 170
% Calories from fat: 30
Fat (gm): 5.7
Saturated fat (gm): 0.9
Cholesterol (mg): 10
Sodium (mg): 83
Protein (gm): 2.8
Carbohydrate (gm): 25.6

½ cup Dutch process cocoa

1 teaspoon rum extract

1 envelope (1.3 ounces) whipped topping (such as Dream Whip)

½ cup 2% milk

Exchanges
Milk: 0.0
Vegetable: 0.0
Fruit: 0.0
Bread: 2.0
Meat: 0.0
Fat: 0.5

1. Make pie crust, using 8-inch pie pan.

2. Sprinkle gelatin over ½ cup milk in small saucepan; let stand 2 to 3 minutes. Stir in sugar and rum. Cook over low heat, stirring constantly, until gelatin and sugar are dissolved. Remove from heat; stir in cocoa and rum extract.

3. Refrigerate until gelatin mixture is partially set (consistency of unbeaten egg whites). Blend whipped topping and ½ cup milk in deep bowl; beat at high speed until topping forms soft peaks, about 4 minutes. Fold topping into gelatin mixture. Spoon mixture into cooled crust; refrigerate until set, 2 to 4 hours.

Note: This recipe is not appropriate for strict vegetarians.

KEY LIME PIE

Use key lime juice in this pie, if available, for the best flavor.

8 servings

Basic Pie Crust (Cake Flour, see p. 758)

¾ cup sugar

*1 envelope unflavored gelatin

1¼ cups fat-free milk

6 ounces reduced-fat cream cheese, softened

⅓-½ cup fresh lime juice

Lime slices, as garnish

Fresh mint, as garnish

Per Serving
Calories: 222
% Calories from fat: 29
Fat (gm): 7.3
Saturated fat (gm): 3.5
Cholesterol (mg): 17
Sodium (mg): 155
Protein (gm): 5.3
Carbohydrate (gm): 35
Exchanges
Milk: 0.5
Vegetable: 0.0
Fruit: 0.0
Bread: 2.0
Meat: 0.0
Fat: 1.0

1. Prepare pie crust, using 8-inch pie pan. Line pastry with weights (see Note, p. 758), and bake at 425 degrees until golden brown, 15 to 20 minutes. Cool on wire rack.

2. Mix sugar and gelatin in small saucepan; stir in milk. Cook over low heat until sugar and gelatin are dissolved, stirring constantly; remove from heat.

3. Beat cream cheese in small bowl until fluffy; beat in lime juice until smooth. Gradually add milk mixture, mixing until smooth. Pour mixture into cooled pie crust. Refrigerate until set, about 2 to 4 hours. Garnish with lime slices and mint.

*Note: This recipe is not appropriate for strict vegetarians.

KIWI TART

Add other sliced spring or summer fruit to this tart if you wish.

8 servings

Basic Pie Crust (Cake Flour, see p. 758)
¼ cup sugar
2 tablespoons cornstarch
1¼ cups 2% milk
1 tablespoon lemon juice
1 egg, slightly beaten
5 medium kiwi fruit, peeled and sliced

Per Serving
Calories: 168
% Calories from fat: 20
Fat (gm): 3.8
Saturated fat (gm): 1
Cholesterol (mg): 29
Sodium (mg): 78
Protein (gm): 3.7
Carbohydrate (gm): 30.4
Exchanges
Milk: 0.0
Vegetable: 0.0
Fruit: 1.0
Bread: 1.0
Meat: 0.0
Fat: 1.0

1. Prepare pie crust, using 9-inch tart pan. Line pastry with weights (see Note, p. 758), and bake at 425 degrees 10 to 15 minutes or until lightly browned. Cool on wire rack.

2. Mix sugar and cornstarch in small saucepan; stir in milk and lemon juice. Cook over medium heat until mixture boils and thickens; boil 1 minute, stirring constantly. Stir about ½ cup milk mixture into egg; stir egg mixture back into saucepan. Cook over low heat, stirring constantly, until thickened, about 1 minute.

3. Spoon hot custard into cooled pie crust, spreading evenly; cool to room temperature. Lightly cover custard with plastic wrap; refrigerate 2 to 4 hours or until set. Just before serving, arrange kiwi slices in overlapping circles on custard.

LEMON CLOUD PIE

Other flavors of this wonderful dessert are easy. Just substitute another low-fat fruit yogurt for the lemon: strawberry, raspberry, or cherry are possible choices.

8 servings

Meringue Pie Crust (see p. 759)
1½ cups frozen light whipped non-dairy topping, thawed
1½ cups low-fat custard-style lemon yogurt
2 tablespoons grated lemon rind
Lemon slices, as garnish

Per Serving
Calories: 170
% Calories from fat: 17
Fat (gm): 3.5
Saturated fat (gm): 0.3
Cholesterol (mg): 2
Sodium (mg): 62
Protein (gm): 3.6
Carbohydrate (gm): 35.5
Exchanges
Milk: 0.5
Vegetable: 0.0
Fruit: 2.0
Bread: 0.0
Meat: 0.0
Fat: 0.5

1. Bake pie crust, using 9-inch pie pan.

2. Combine whipped topping, yogurt, and lemon rind in small bowl. Spoon into center of meringue shell. Garnish with lemon slices. Serve immediately or refrigerate until ready to eat.

RASPBERRY-GLAZED BLUEBERRY TART

Imagine this tart, abundant with just-picked, perfectly ripe berries! Top helpings with a small scoop of low-fat frozen vanilla or lemon yogurt.

8 servings

Basic Pie Crust (All-Purpose Flour, see p. 757)
1 tablespoon sugar
4 cups fresh blueberries
¾ cup raspberry spreadable fruit
1 tablespoon raspberry-flavor liqueur (optional)
2 teaspoons cornstarch
¼ teaspoon ground cinnamon
¼ teaspoon ground nutmeg

Per Serving
Calories: 169
% Calories from fat: 13
Fat (gm): 2.6
Saturated fat (gm): 0.4
Cholesterol (mg): 0
Sodium (mg): 70
Protein (gm): 2
Carbohydrate (gm): 13
Exchanges
Milk: 0.0
Vegetable: 0.0
Fruit: 1.0
Bread: 1.0
Meat: 0.0
Fat: 0.5

1. Prepare pie crust, adding 1 tablespoon sugar to recipe and using 9-inch tart pan. Line pastry with weights (see Note, p. 757), and bake at 425 degrees until golden brown, 10 to 12 minutes. Cool on wire rack.

2. Arrange blueberries in cooled crust. Combine spreadable fruit, liqueur, cornstarch, cinnamon, and nutmeg in small saucepan. Heat to boiling, stirring constantly. Remove from heat and spoon over blueberries. Refrigerate until glaze is slightly firm, about 30 minutes.

PEAR TART WITH CRÈME ANGLAISE

Select pears that are just ripe, but not soft, for this elegant and delicate tart.

8 servings

Basic Pie Crust (Cake Flour, see p. 758)
2 pounds pears (4 large), peeled, cored, and sliced ¼ inch thick
¼ cup all-purpose flour
3 tablespoons sugar
½ teaspoon ground cinnamon
¼ teaspoon ground nutmeg
Crème Anglaise (recipe follows)

Per Serving
Calories: 210
% Calories from fat: 14
Fat (gm): 3.5
Saturated fat (gm): 0.6
Cholesterol (mg): 25
Sodium (mg): 66
Protein (gm): 3.6
Carbohydrate (gm): 42
Exchanges
Milk: 0.0
Vegetable: 0.0
Fruit: 1.0
Bread: 2.0
Meat: 0.0
Fat: 0.5

1. Prepare pie crust, using 9-inch tart pan. Line pastry with weights (see Note, p. 758), and bake at 425 degrees 10 to 12 minutes or until lightly browned. Cool on wire rack.

2. Toss pears with combined flour, sugar, cinnamon, and nutmeg. Arrange pears in overlapping circles in crust. Bake at 375 degrees 20 to 25 minutes or until pears are tender. Serve warm with Crème Anglaise.

Crème Anglaise

(makes about 1 cup)

1 tablespoon cornstarch
2 teaspoons sugar
1 cup fat-free milk
1 egg yolk
⅛-¼ teaspoon ground nutmeg

1. Mix cornstarch and sugar in small saucepan; stir in milk. Cook over medium heat until mixture boils and thickens, stirring constantly.

2. Stir about ½ cup milk mixture into egg yolk; stir egg yolk mixture back into saucepan.

3. Cook over low heat, stirring constantly, until thickened (mixture will coat back of spoon). Remove from heat; stir in nutmeg. Serve warm or refrigerate.

RUSTIC COUNTRY FRUIT TART

Perfect for a lazy-day summer picnic, this tumble of garden fruits is lightly glazed and encased in a free-form pastry.

8 servings

Basic Pie Crust (All-Purpose Flour, see p. 757)
¼ cup all-purpose flour
2 tablespoons cold margarine, *or* butter
1 pint raspberries
1 pint strawberries, sliced
1 cup seedless grapes
3 medium apricots, pitted, cut into halves
3 medium peaches, *or* nectarines, peeled, pitted, cut into halves
¼ cup all-purpose flour
⅓ cup sugar
½ teaspoon ground cinnamon
¼ cup apricot spreadable fruit
2 tablespoons water

Per Serving
Calories: 295
% Calories from fat: 23
Fat (gm): 7.8
Saturated fat (gm): 1.5
Cholesterol (mg): 0
Sodium (mg): 152
Protein (gm): 4
Carbohydrate (gm): 54.4
Exchanges
Milk: 0.0
Vegetable: 0.0
Fruit: 1.0
Bread: 2.5
Meat: 0.0
Fat: 1.0

1. Prepare pie crust, adding ¼ cup flour and 2 tablespoons margarine to recipe. Roll pastry on lightly floured surface into a 12-inch circle (edges do not need to be even). Transfer pastry to a 12-inch pizza pan.

2. Toss fruits with combined ¼ cup flour, sugar, and cinnamon. Arrange fruits in center of pastry, leaving a 2- to 3-inch border around outer edge. Gently gather and fold outer edge of pastry over fruits (fruits will not be completely enclosed, as tart should have a rustic look).

3. Bake tart at 425 degrees 20 to 25 minutes, or until crust is lightly browned and fruit is tender. Heat spreadable fruit and water in small saucepan until warm; brush over fruit. Cut into wedges and serve warm.

SPRING BERRY CHEESECAKE

16 servings

½	cup vanilla wafer cookie crumbs
2	tablespoons margarine, *or* butter, melted
1	cup low-fat cottage cheese
1	package (8 ounces) fat-free cream cheese, softened
1	cup fat-free sour cream
⅓	plus ¼ cup sugar, divided
3	eggs
½	cup fat-free milk
2	tablespoons lemon juice
3	tablespoons finely grated lemon rind
3	tablespoons all-purpose flour
1	teaspoon vanilla
⅛	teaspoon salt
1	quart strawberries, *or* blueberries, sliced

Per Serving
Calories: 122
% Calories from fat: 23
Fat (gm): 3.1
Saturated fat (gm): 0.8
Cholesterol (mg): 42.6
Sodium (mg): 209
Protein (gm): 6.7
Carbohydrate (gm): 16.6
Exchanges
Milk: 0.0
Vegetable: 0.0
Fruit: 0.5
Bread: 0.5
Meat: 0.5
Fat: 0.5

1. Combine vanilla wafer crumbs and margarine and press in bottom of 9-inch springform pan.

2. Process cottage cheese in food processor or blender until smooth. Transfer cottage cheese to large bowl. Add cream cheese, sour cream, and ⅓ cup sugar and beat until light and fluffy. Add eggs one at a time, beating well after each addition. Stir in milk, lemon juice, lemon rind, flour, vanilla, and salt; blend well.

3. Pour mixture into prepared crust and bake at 325 degrees 50 minutes or until center is set. Cool on wire rack. Refrigerate 8 hours or overnight.

4. Combine berries and ¼ cup sugar in medium bowl; cover and refrigerate. Spoon strawberries over cheesecake slices.

NEW YORK-STYLE CHEESECAKE

There is only one word for this cheesecake—spectacular!

12 servings

Graham Cracker Crumb Crust (see p. 759)

3 packages (8 ounces each) fat-free cream cheese, softened

¾ cup sugar

2 eggs

2 tablespoons cornstarch

1 teaspoon vanilla

1 cup reduced-fat sour cream

Per Serving
Calories: 209
% Calories from fat: 28
Fat (gm): 6.2
Saturated fat (gm): 3.2
Cholesterol (mg): 45
Sodium (mg): 452
Protein (gm): 10.4
Carbohydrate (gm): 258
Exchanges
Milk: 0.0
Vegetable: 0.0
Fruit: 0.0
Bread: 1.5
Meat: 1.0
Fat: 1.0

1. Make crumb crust, patting mixture on bottom and ½ inch up side of 9-inch springform pan.

2. Beat cream cheese and sugar in large bowl until light and fluffy; beat in eggs, cornstarch, and vanilla. Add sour cream, mixing until well blended. Pour mixture into prepared crust.

3. Bake at 325 degrees until cheesecake is set but still slightly soft in the center, 45 to 50 minutes. Turn oven off; let cheesecake cool in oven with door ajar for 3 hours. Refrigerate 8 hours or overnight.

LEMON MERINGUE CHEESECAKE

Never has a cheesecake filling been quite as smooth and delicate as this. The filling is slightly soft, so chill very well before cutting.

12 servings

Basic Pie Crust (All-Purpose Flour, see p. 757)

3 packages (8 ounces each) fat-free cream cheese, softened

4 egg yolks

⅔ cup lemon juice

2 tablespoons flour

1 cup sugar

⅓ cup cornstarch

⅔ cup water

2 teaspoons grated lemon rind

4 egg whites

¼ teaspoon cream of tartar

⅓ cup powdered sugar

Per Serving
Calories: 224
% Calories from fat: 13
Fat (gm): 3.3
Saturated fat (gm): 0.8
Cholesterol (mg): 81
Sodium (mg): 441
Protein (gm): 11.6
Carbohydrate (gm): 35.4
Exchanges
Milk: 0.0
Vegetable: 0.0
Fruit: 0.0
Bread: 2.5
Meat: 1.0
Fat: 0.0

1. Prepare pie crust, using 9-inch pie pan. Line pastry with weights (see Note, p. 757), and bake at 425 degrees until golden, 12 to 15 minutes. Cool on wire rack.

2. Beat cream cheese and egg yolks in medium bowl until smooth; beat in lemon juice and flour.

3. Mix sugar and cornstarch in medium saucepan; stir in water and lemon rind. Cook over medium heat, stirring constantly, until mixture thickens and boils; boil 1 minute, stirring constantly. Remove from heat. Gradually stir in cheese mixture, mixing until completely blended. Pour hot mixture into prepared crust.

4. Beat egg whites and cream of tartar in large bowl until foamy. Gradually beat in powdered sugar, beating to stiff but not dry peaks. Spread meringue over top of pie, sealing it to edge of crust. Bake at 425 degrees until meringue is golden, about 10 minutes. Cool to room temperature on wire rack; refrigerate at least 4 hours before serving.

CHOCOLATE FILLO CHEESECAKE

12 servings

Vegetable cooking spray

2 tablespoons dry unseasoned bread-crumbs

6 sheets frozen fillo pastry, thawed

3 packages (8 ounces each) fat-free cream cheese, softened

1 cup reduced-fat sour cream

⅔ cup sugar

⅓ cup Dutch process cocoa

2 eggs

3 tablespoons flour

½ teaspoon ground cinnamon

Per Serving
Calories: 159
% Calories from fat: 8
Fat (gm): 1.4
Saturated fat (gm): 0.3
Cholesterol (mg): 45
Sodium (mg): 358
Protein (gm): 12.3
Carbohydrate (gm): 22.4
Exchanges
Milk: 0.0
Vegetable: 0.0
Fruit: 0.0
Bread: 1.0
Meat: 1.5
Fat: 0.0

1. Lightly spray 9-inch springform pan with cooking spray; sprinkle with breadcrumbs.

2. Working quickly, spray each fillo sheet lightly with cooking spray. Layer fillo in bottom of pan, turning each slightly so that corners are staggered. Bake at 375 degrees 6 to 8 minutes or until lightly browned. Cool on wire rack.

3. Reduce oven temperature to 350 degrees. Beat cream cheese until fluffy in large bowl; mix in sour cream, sugar, and cocoa. Beat in eggs; mix in flour and cinnamon. Pour mixture into fillo crust; gently fold edges of fillo inward so that edges of fillo do not extend outside of pan.

4. Bake 50 minutes or until center of cheesecake is almost set. Cover edges of fillo crust with aluminum foil during last 15 or 20 minutes of baking time if beginning to get too brown. Cool on wire rack 10 minutes. Carefully remove side of pan; cool to room temperature. Cover loosely and refrigerate 8 hours or overnight.

CHOCOLATE CHIP COOKIES

5 dozen cookies (1 per serving)

8 tablespoons margarine, *or* butter, softened

1 cup packed light brown sugar

½ cup granulated sugar

1 egg

1 teaspoon vanilla

2½ cups all-purpose flour

½ teaspoon baking soda

½ teaspoon salt

⅓ cup fat-free milk

½ package (12-ounce size) reduced-fat semisweet chocolate morsels

Per Serving
Calories: 66
% Calories from fat: 27
Fat (gm): 2
Saturated fat (gm): 0.7
Cholesterol (mg): 3.6
Sodium (mg): 70
Protein (gm): 0.8
Carbohydrate (gm): 11.2
Exchanges
Milk: 0.0
Vegetable: 0.0
Fruit: 0.0
Bread: 0.5
Meat: 0.0
Fat: 0.5

1. Beat margarine and sugars in medium bowl until fluffy; beat in egg and vanilla. Mix in combined flour, baking soda, and salt alternately with milk, beginning and ending with dry ingredients. Mix in chocolate morsels.

2. Drop cookies by tablespoonfuls onto greased cookie sheets. Bake at 375 degrees until browned, about 10 minutes. Cool on wire racks.

RAISIN OATMEAL COOKIES

Moist and chewy, just the way they should be!

2½ dozen cookies (1 per serving)

6 tablespoons margarine, *or* butter, softened

¼ cup fat-free sour cream

1 egg

1 teaspoon vanilla

1 cup packed light brown sugar

1½ cups quick-cooking oats

1 cup all-purpose flour

½ teaspoon baking soda

¼ teaspoon baking powder

1 teaspoon ground cinnamon

½ cup raisins for baking

Per Serving
Calories: 90
% Calories from fat: 27
Fat (gm): 2.7
Saturated fat (gm): 0.5
Cholesterol (mg): 7.1
Sodium (mg): 57
Protein (gm): 1.5
Carbohydrate (gm): 15.3
Exchanges
Milk: 0.0
Vegetable: 0.0
Fruit: 0.0
Bread: 1.0
Meat: 0.0
Fat: 0.5

1. Mix margarine, sour cream, egg, and vanilla in large bowl; beat in brown sugar. Mix in combined oats, flour, baking soda, baking powder, and cinnamon. Mix in raisins.

2. Drop dough onto greased cookie sheets, using 2 tablespoons for each cookie. Bake at 350 degrees until browned, 12 to 15 minutes. Cool on wire racks.

FROSTED SUGAR COOKIES

 Rich, crisp, and generously frosted, these cookies will flatter any holiday or special occasion.

6 dozen cookies (1 per serving)

10	tablespoons margarine, *or* butter, softened
2	tablespoons fat-free sour cream
1	egg
1	teaspoon lemon extract
1	cup powdered sugar
2	cups all-purpose flour
1	teaspoon baking powder
¼	teaspoon salt
	Sugar Frosting (recipe follows)
	Cinnamon, ground as garnish

Per Serving
Calories: 48
% Calories from fat: 31
Fat (gm): 1.7
Saturated fat (gm): 0.3
Cholesterol (mg): 3
Sodium (mg): 45
Protein (gm): 0.5
Carbohydrate (gm): 7.7
Exchanges
Milk: 0.0
Vegetable: 0.0
Fruit: 0.0
Bread: 0.5
Meat: 0.0
Fat: 0.5

1. Beat margarine, sour cream, egg, and lemon extract in medium bowl until smooth; mix in sugar. Mix in combined flour, baking powder, and salt. Refrigerate dough 4 to 6 hours.

2. Roll dough on floured surface to ¼ inch thickness. Cut out cookies with 2-inch cookie cutters. Bake at 375 degrees on greased cookie sheets until lightly browned, 8 to 10 minutes. Cool on wire racks.

3. Frost cookies with Sugar Frosting; sprinkle very lightly with cinnamon.

Sugar Frosting

 (makes about ¾ cup)

2	cups powdered sugar
½	teaspoon lemon extract, *or* vanilla
2-3	tablespoons fat-free milk

1. In small bowl, mix powdered sugar, lemon extract, and enough milk to make spreadable consistency.

GLAZED CHOCOLATE SHORTBREAD SQUARES

Rich, chocolatey, and crisp!

5 dozen squares (1 per serving)

1½ cups all-purpose flour
¼ cup unsweetened cocoa
¾ cup sugar
¼ teaspoon salt
8 tablespoons margarine, *or* butter, softened
2 egg whites
2 teaspoons vanilla
   Sugar Glaze (recipe follows)

Per Serving
Calories: 44
% Calories from fat: 31
Fat (gm): 1.6
Saturated fat (gm): 0.3
Cholesterol (mg): 0
Sodium (mg): 29
Protein (gm): 0.5
Carbohydrate (gm): 7.2
Exchanges
Milk: 0.0
Vegetable: 0.0
Fruit: 0.0
Bread: 0.5
Meat: 0.0
Fat: 0.5

1. Combine flour, cocoa, sugar, and salt in medium-size bowl; cut in margarine with pastry blender or 2 knives until mixture resembles coarse crumbs. Mix in egg whites and vanilla, stirring just enough to form a soft dough.

2. Place dough in bottom of greased jelly roll pan, 15 x 10 inches. Pat and spread dough, using fingers and small spatula, until bottom of pan is evenly covered. Pierce dough with tines of fork.

3. Bake at 350 degrees until firm to touch, 20 to 25 minutes. Cool slightly on wire rack. Spoon glaze over shortbread and cut into squares while warm.

Sugar Glaze

(makes about 1 cup)

1 cup powdered sugar
2-3 tablespoons fat-free milk

1. In a small bowl, mix powdered sugar with enough milk to make glaze consistency.

CARDAMOM CRISPS

For flavor variations, ground cinnamon or allspice can be substituted for the cardamom. These cookies require some care in spreading in the pan but are well worth the effort!

5 dozen cookies (1 per serving)

1¾	cups all-purpose flour
¾	cup sugar
1½	teaspoons ground cardamom
¼	teaspoon salt
8	tablespoons margarine, *or* butter, softened
2	egg whites
1	teaspoon vanilla
1	egg white, beaten
	Vanilla Glaze (recipe follows)

Per Serving
Calories: 46
% Calories from fat: 30
Fat (gm): 1.5
Saturated fat (gm): 0.3
Cholesterol (mg): 0
Sodium (mg): 29
Protein (gm): 0.6
Carbohydrate (gm): 7.4
Exchanges
Milk: 0.0
Vegetable: 0.0
Fruit: 0.0
Bread: 0.5
Meat: 0.0
Fat: 0.5

1. Combine flour, sugar, cardamom, and salt in medium-size bowl; cut in margarine with pastry blender or 2 knives until mixture resembles coarse crumbs. Mix in 2 egg whites and vanilla, stirring just enough to form a soft dough.

2. Place dough in bottom of greased jelly roll pan, 15 x 10 inches. Pat and spread dough, using fingers and small spatula or knife, until bottom of pan is evenly covered. Brush dough with 1 beaten egg white.

3. Bake at 350 degrees until edges of cookies are lightly browned, 20 to 25 minutes. Cool in pan several minutes. Drizzle glaze over warm cookies and cut into squares.

Vanilla Glaze

(makes about ½ cup)

1 cup powdered sugar
1 teaspoon vanilla
1-2 tablespoons fat-free milk

1. Mix powdered sugar with vanilla and enough milk to make glaze consistency.

COCOA-GLAZED COOKIE CRISPS

Bake cookie crisps only until beginning to brown, and cut while warm for best results.

5 dozen cookies (1 per serving)

1¾ cups all-purpose flour
¾ cup packed light brown sugar
¼ teaspoon salt
8 tablespoons margarine, *or* butter, softened
2 egg whites
1 teaspoon vanilla
1 egg white, beaten
Cocoa Glaze (recipe follows)

Per Serving
Calories: 46
% Calories from fat: 30
Fat (gm): 1.6
Saturated fat (gm): 0.3
Cholesterol (mg): 0
Sodium (mg): 31
Protein (gm): 0.6
Carbohydrate (gm): 7.6
Exchanges
Milk: 0.0
Vegetable: 0.0
Fruit: 0.0
Bread: 0.5
Meat: 0.0
Fat: 0.5

1. Combine flour, brown sugar, and salt in medium-size bowl; cut in margarine with pastry blender or 2 knives until mixture resembles coarse crumbs. Mix in 2 egg whites and vanilla, stirring just enough to form a soft dough.

2. Place dough in bottom of greased jelly roll pan, 15 x 10 inches. Pat and spread dough, using fingers and small spatula or knife, until bottom of pan is evenly covered. Brush dough with 1 beaten egg white.

3. Bake dough at 350 degrees until edges of cookies are lightly browned, 20 to 25 minutes. Cool in pan several minutes. Drizzle glaze over warm cookies and cut into squares.

Cocoa Glaze

(makes about ½ cup)

1 cup powdered sugar
2 tablespoons unsweetened cocoa
1-2 tablespoons fat-free milk

1. Mix powdered sugar and cocoa in small bowl. Mix in enough milk to make glaze consistency.

FROSTED COCOA BROWNIES

Very chocolatey and slightly chewy, you'll never guess these brownies are low in fat.

25 brownies (1 per serving)

1 cup all-purpose flour
1 cup sugar
¼ cup unsweetened cocoa
5 tablespoons margarine, *or* butter, melted
¼ cup fat-free milk
1 egg
2 egg whites
¼ cup honey
1 teaspoon vanilla
Cocoa Frosting (recipe follows)

Per Serving
Calories: 111
% Calories from fat: 24
Fat (gm): 3.1
Saturated fat (gm): 0.6
Cholesterol (mg): 8.6
Sodium (mg): 42
Protein (gm): 1.5
Carbohydrate (gm): 20.4
Exchanges
Milk: 0.0
Vegetable: 0.0
Fruit: 1.5
Bread: 0.0
Meat: 0.0
Fat: 0.5

1. Combine flour, sugar, and cocoa in medium bowl; add margarine, milk, egg, egg whites, honey, and vanilla, mixing until smooth. Pour batter into greased and floured 8-inch-square baking pan.

2. Bake at 350 degrees until brownies spring back when touched, about 30 minutes. Cool in pan on wire rack; spread with Cocoa Frosting.

Cocoa Frosting

(makes about ½ cup)

1 cup powdered sugar
2-3 tablespoons unsweetened cocoa
1 tablespoon margarine, *or* butter, softened
2-3 tablespoons fat-free milk

1. In small bowl, beat powdered sugar, cocoa, margarine, and enough milk to make spreading consistency.

SUGARED LEMON SQUARES

Just like the favorites you remember, but much "skinnier"!

25 squares (1 per serving)

¾ cup all-purpose flour

4 tablespoons margarine, *or* butter, softened

2 tablespoons reduced-fat sour cream

2 tablespoons granulated sugar

1 cup granulated sugar

1 egg

2 egg whites

1 tablespoon grated lemon rind

3 tablespoons lemon juice

½ teaspoon baking powder

¼ teaspoon salt

Powdered sugar, as garnish

Per Serving
Calories: 71
% Calories from fat: 27
Fat (gm): 2.1
Saturated fat (gm): 0.4
Cholesterol (mg): 8.9
Sodium (mg): 57
Protein (gm): 1
Carbohydrate (gm): 12.2
Exchanges
Milk: 0.0
Vegetable: 0.0
Fruit: 0.0
Bread: 1.0
Meat: 0.0
Fat: 0.5

1. Mix flour, margarine, sour cream, and 2 tablespoons granulated sugar in small bowl to form soft dough. Pat dough into bottom and ¼ inch up sides of 8 x 8-inch baking pan. Bake until lightly browned, about 20 minutes. Cool on wire rack.

2. Mix 1 cup granulated sugar and remaining ingredients, except powdered sugar, in small bowl; pour over baked pastry. Bake at 350 degrees until no indentation remains when touched in the center, 20 to 25 minutes. Cool on wire rack; cut into squares. Sprinkle lightly with powdered sugar.

FIG AND PEAR BARS

Chewy, dense, and oh, so good! A fruit bar at its best.

30 bars (1 per serving)

¾ cup chopped dried figs

¾ cup chopped dried pears

½ cup water

2 tablespoons packed light brown sugar

5 tablespoons margarine, *or* butter, softened

2 tablespoons granulated sugar

3 egg whites

Per Serving
Calories: 77
% Calories from fat: 23
Fat (gm): 2.1
Saturated fat (gm): 0.4
Cholesterol (mg): 0.1
Sodium (mg): 68
Protein (gm): 1.4
Carbohydrate (gm): 13.8

              1 teaspoon vanilla
          1 ¾ cups all-purpose flour
            ½ teaspoon baking soda
            ¼ teaspoon salt
              2 tablespoons 2% milk

Exchanges
Milk: 0.0
Vegetable: 0.0
Fruit: 0.5
Bread: 0.5
Meat: 0.0
Fat: 0.5

1.   In small saucepan, heat figs, pears, water, and brown sugar to boiling. Reduce heat and simmer, uncovered, until fruit is softened and mixture is thick, about 20 minutes. Process mixture in food processor or blender until smooth. Cool.

2.   Beat margarine and granulated sugar in medium-size bowl until fluffy; beat in egg whites and vanilla. Mix in combined flour, baking soda, and salt. Shape dough into 4 logs, each about 5 x 2 x ½ inches. Wrap each in plastic wrap and refrigerate about 1 hour.

3.   Roll 1 log on floured surface into 12 x 5-inch flat rectangle. Using ¼ of the fruit mixture, spread a 1-inch strip down center of dough. Fold sides of dough over the filling, pressing edges to seal. Cut log in half and place, seam side down, on greased cookie sheet. Repeat with remaining dough logs and filling. Brush tops of logs with milk.

4.   Bake until lightly browned, about 12 minutes. Cool on wire racks; cut into 1½-inch bars.

CHOCOLATE FUDGE MERINGUES

 Better bake several batches as these won't last long!

24 cookies (1 per serving)

              3 egg whites
            ½ teaspoon cream of tartar
            ¼ teaspoon salt
              2 cups powdered sugar
            ½ cup unsweetened cocoa
              1 ounce semisweet chocolate, finely
                chopped

Per Serving
Calories: 43
% Calories from fat: 11
Fat (gm): 0.5
Saturated fat (gm): 0
Cholesterol (mg): 0
Sodium (mg): 29
Protein (gm): 0.8
Carbohydrate (gm): 9.1
Exchanges
Milk: 0.0
Vegetable: 0.0
Fruit: 0.0
Bread: 0.5
Meat: 0.0
Fat: 0.0

1. In medium-size bowl, beat egg whites until foamy. Add cream of tartar and salt; beat to soft peaks. Beat in sugar gradually, beating until mixture forms stiff, shiny peaks. Fold in cocoa; fold in chopped chocolate.

2. Drop mixture by tablespoons onto parchment or aluminum-foil-lined cookie sheets. Bake at 300 degrees until cookies feel crisp when touched, 20 to 25 minutes. Cool in pans on wire racks.

ORANGE-ALMOND MERINGUES

 Party perfect!

24 cookies (1 per serving)

   3 egg whites
½ teaspoon orange extract
½ teaspoon cream of tartar
¼ teaspoon salt
¾ cup sugar
½ cup chopped toasted almonds

Per Serving
Calories: 34
% Calories from fat: 21
Fat (gm): 0.8
Saturated fat (gm): 0.1
Cholesterol (mg): 0
Sodium (mg): 29
Protein (gm): 0.8
Carbohydrate (gm): 6.4
Exchanges
Milk: 0.0
Vegetable: 0.0
Fruit: 0.0
Bread: 0.5
Meat: 0.0
Fat: 0.0

1. In medium-size bowl, beat egg whites until foamy. Add orange extract, cream of tartar, and salt; beat to soft peaks. Beat in sugar gradually, beating until mixture forms stiff, shiny peaks. Fold in almonds.

2. Drop mixture by tablespoons onto parchment or aluminum-foil-lined cookie sheets. Bake at 300 degrees until cookies begin to brown and feel crisp when touched, 20 to 25 minutes. Cool in pans on wire racks.

PEPPERMINT CLOUDS

Although wonderful cookies any time, peppermint always reminds me of Christmas holidays.

24 cookies (1 per serving)

3 egg whites
½ teaspoon cream of tartar
¼ teaspoon salt
¾ cup sugar
⅓ cup (2 ounces) crushed peppermint
candies

Per Serving
Calories: 34
% Calories from fat: 0
Fat (gm): 0
Saturated fat (gm): 0
Cholesterol (mg): 0
Sodium (mg): 30
Protein (gm): 0.4
Carbohydrate (gm): 8.4
Exchanges
Milk: 0.0
Vegetable: 0.0
Fruit: 0.0
Bread: 0.5
Meat: 0.0
Fat: 0.0

1. In medium-size bowl, beat egg whites until foamy. Add cream of tartar and salt; beat to soft peaks. Beat in sugar gradually, beating until mixture forms stiff, shiny peaks. Reserve 2 tablespoons crushed candy; fold remaining candy into egg white mixture.

2. Drop mixture by tablespoons onto parchment or aluminum-foil-lined cookie sheets. Sprinkle tops of cookies with reserved candy. Bake at 300 degrees until cookies begin to brown and feel crisp when touched, 20 to 25 minutes. Cool in pans on wire racks.

HAZELNUT MACAROONS

Use any favorite nuts in these moist and crunchy macaroons.

30 cookies (1 per serving)

4 egg whites
⅛ teaspoon cream of tartar
¼ teaspoon salt
1 cup sugar
1 cup canned sweetened coconut
¼ cup finely chopped hazelnuts, *or* pecans

Per Serving
Calories: 44
% Calories from fat: 28
Fat (gm): 1.4
Saturated fat (gm): 0.8
Cholesterol (mg): 0
Sodium (mg): 25.6
Protein (gm): 0.7
Carbohydrate (gm): 7.6
Exchanges
Milk: 0.0
Vegetable: 0.0
Fruit: 0.0
Bread: 0.5
Meat: 0.0
Fat: 0.5

1. In medium-size bowl, beat egg whites until foamy. Add cream of tartar and salt; beat to soft peaks. Beat in sugar gradually, beating until mixture forms stiff, shiny peaks. Fold in coconut; fold in hazelnuts.

2. Drop mixture by tablespoons onto parchment or aluminum-foil-lined cookie sheets. Bake at 300 degrees until cookies begin to brown and feel crisp when touched, 20 to 25 minutes. Cool in pans on wire racks.

ANISE-ALMOND BISCOTTI

Crisp—because they're baked twice—biscotti are perfect for dunking into coffee, tea, or Vin Santo, the Italian way!

60 bars (1 per serving)

Per Serving
Calories: 41
% Calories from fat: 26
Fat (gm): 1.2
Saturated fat (gm): 0.2
Cholesterol (mg): 7.1
Sodium (mg): 40
Protein (gm): 1
Carbohydrate (gm): 6.7
Exchanges
Milk: 0.0
Vegetable: 0.0
Fruit: 0.0
Bread: 0.5
Meat: 0.0
Fat: 0.0

4 tablespoons margarine, *or* butter, softened

¾ cup sugar

2 eggs

2 egg whites

2½ cups all-purpose flour

2 teaspoons crushed anise seeds

1½ teaspoons baking powder

½ teaspoon baking soda

¼ teaspoon salt

⅓ cup (1 ounce) whole blanched almonds

1. In medium-size bowl, beat margarine, sugar, eggs, and egg whites until smooth. Mix in combined flour, anise seeds, baking powder, baking soda, and salt. Mix in almonds.

2. Shape dough on greased cookie sheets into 4 slightly flattened rolls, 1½ inches in diameter. Bake at 350 degrees until lightly browned, about 20 minutes. Let stand on wire rack until cool enough to handle; cut bars into ½-inch slices. Arrange slices, cut sides down, on ungreased cookie sheets.

3. Bake biscotti at 350 degrees until toasted on the bottom, 7 to 10 minutes; turn and bake until biscotti are golden on other side and feel almost dry, 7 to 10 minutes. Cool on wire racks.

APRICOT-SESAME BISCOTTI

Biscotti become crisper as they cool, so bake only until almost dry.

60 bars (1 per serving)

2½ cups all-purpose flour
1 teaspoon baking powder
½ teaspoon baking soda
¾ cup packed light brown sugar
2 tablespoons grated orange rind
2 tablespoons sesame seeds, toasted
2 eggs
2 egg whites
½ cup finely chopped dried apricots

Per Serving
Calories: 37
% Calories from fat: 9
Fat (gm): 0.4
Saturated fat (gm): 0.1
Cholesterol (mg): 7.1
Sodium (mg): 21
Protein (gm): 1
Carbohydrate (gm): 7.4
Exchanges
Milk: 0.0
Vegetable: 0.0
Fruit: 0.0
Bread: 0.5
Meat: 0.0
Fat: 0.0

1. Combine flour, baking powder, baking soda, brown sugar, orange rind, and sesame seeds in large bowl. Mix eggs and egg whites; stir into flour mixture until smooth. Mix in dried apricots.

2. Shape dough on greased cookie sheets into 4 slightly flattened rolls, 1½ inches in diameter. Bake at 350 degrees until lightly browned, about 20 minutes. Let stand on wire rack until cool enough to handle; cut bars into ½-inch slices.

3. Arrange slices, cut sides down, on ungreased cookie sheets. Bake biscotti until toasted on the bottom, 7 to 10 minutes; turn and bake until biscotti are golden on other side and feel almost dry, 7 to 10 minutes. Cool on wire racks.

SPICED ORANGE COMPOTE

A perfect dessert for winter, when many fresh fruits are not yet available. Serve with cookies. Cardamom Crisps (see p. 780) would bring smiles.

8 servings

5 oranges, peeled, sliced
⅓ cup orange juice
3 tablespoons packed light brown sugar
2-3 tablespoons orange-flavored liqueur

Per Serving
Calories: 72
% Calories from fat: 1
Fat (gm): 0.1
Saturated fat (gm): 0
Cholesterol (mg): 0
Sodium (mg): 2
Protein (gm): 0.8
Carbohydrate (gm): 16.8

4 whole allspice
1 cinnamon stick
Mint sprigs, as garnish

Exchanges
Milk: 0.0
Vegetable: 0.0
Fruit: 1.0
Bread: 0.0
Meat: 0.0
Fat: 0.0

1. Place oranges in shallow glass bowl. Mix orange juice, brown sugar, orange liqueur, allspice, and cinnamon in small saucepan. Heat just to boiling; pour over orange slices. Refrigerate, covered, 8 hours or overnight for flavors to blend. Garnish with mint.

HONEY-LIME MELON WEDGES

A recipe that is so simple, but so very good.

4 servings

1 small cantaloupe, *or* other melon in season
3-4 tablespoons honey
4 lime wedges
Nutmeg, ground, as garnish

Per Serving
Calories: 112
% Calories from fat: 3
Fat (gm): 0.5
Saturated fat (gm): 0
Cholesterol (mg): 0
Sodium (mg): 15
Protein (gm): 1.5
Carbohydrate (gm): 28.1
Exchanges
Milk: 0.0
Vegetable: 0.0
Fruit: 2.0
Bread: 0.0
Meat: 0.0
Fat: 0.0

1. Cut melon into wedges. Drizzle honey over melon. Squeeze juice from lime wedges over each slice and sprinkle with nutmeg.

HONEY-BROILED PINEAPPLE SLICES

This dessert beckons a selection of cookie accompaniments. Choose among Chewy Chocolate Brownies, Fig and Pear Bars, or Hazelnut Macaroons (see pp. 782, 783, 786).

4 servings (2 pineapple slices each)

1 medium pineapple (1½ pounds), peeled, cored, and cut into eight ½-inch slices

Per Serving
Calories: 143
% Calories from fat: 4
Fat (gm): 0.7
Saturated fat (gm): 0
Cholesterol (mg): 0
Sodium (mg): 3
Protein (gm): 0.8
Carbohydrate (gm): 36.5

3 tablespoons honey	**Exchanges**
2 tablespoons frozen orange juice concentrate, thawed	Milk: 0.0
	Vegetable: 0.0
	Fruit: 2.5
2 tablespoons minced fresh cilantro, *or* mint	Bread: 0.0
	Meat: 0.0
	Fat: 0.0

1. Preheat broiler to medium-high. Arrange pineapple rings on broiler pan. Combine honey and orange concentrate in small bowl; brush onto pineapple.

2. Broil pineapple slices 6 inches from heat source 3 minutes; turn and baste with honey mixture. Broil 2 to 3 minutes more or until golden. Sprinkle with cilantro.

FRESH BERRY RHUBARB

Frozen rhubarb can also be used so you can enjoy this light dessert all year.

6 servings (½ cup each)

½ cup sugar	**Per Serving**
½ cup water	Calories: 103
	% Calories from fat: 3
	Fat (gm): 0.3
4 cups sliced rhubarb (about 16 ounces)	Saturated fat (gm): 0.1
	Cholesterol (mg): 0
¼ teaspoon ground cinnamon	Sodium (mg): 5.3
1 cup sliced strawberries	Protein (gm): 1
	Carbohydrate (gm): 25.6
1 cup blueberries	**Exchanges**
	Milk: 0.0
	Vegetable: 0.0
	Fruit: 1.5
	Bread: 0.0
	Meat: 0.0
	Fat: 0.0

1. Combine sugar and water in medium-size saucepan. Heat to boiling; reduce heat and add rhubarb. Simmer, uncovered, 10 minutes or until rhubarb is tender, stirring occasionally.

2. Remove rhubarb from heat and stir in cinnamon; cool completely. Stir in strawberries and blueberries.

WINE-POACHED PLUMS

White port wine is unique in this recipe, but red port can be used if you prefer.

4 servings

    2 cups white port wine
⅓-½ cup sugar
    1 cinnamon stick
    1 whole nutmeg
   12 medium plums

Per Serving
Calories: 247
% Calories from fat: **4**
Fat (gm): 1.2
Saturated fat (gm): 0.1
Cholesterol (mg): 0
Sodium (mg): 5
Protein (gm): 1.8
Carbohydrate (gm): 57.6
Exchanges
Milk: 0.0
Vegetable: 0.0
Fruit: 4.0
Bread: 0.0
Meat: 0.0
Fat: 0.0

1. Combine wine, sugar, cinnamon, and nutmeg in medium-size saucepan. Heat to boiling, add plums, and reduce heat to low. Gently simmer plums, covered, 10 to 15 minutes or until tender. Remove plums to serving dish.

2. Bring poaching liquid to a boil over high heat. Boil gently 12 to 15 minutes or until slightly thickened. Serve over plums.

CARAMEL APPLE SLICES

Serve these fragrant apple slices over low-fat frozen vanilla yogurt for a sumptuous sundae, or serve over pancakes, waffles, or crepes.

4 servings

  2 large apples (sweet or tart)
½ cup apple cider
¼ cup packed light brown sugar
     Cinnamon, ground, as garnish
     Nutmeg, ground, as garnish

Per Serving
Calories: 104
% Calories from fat: 2
Fat (gm): 0.3
Saturated fat (gm): 0
Cholesterol (mg): 0
Sodium (mg): 5
Protein (gm): 0.1
Carbohydrate (gm): 24.1
Exchanges
Milk: 0.0
Vegetable: 0.0
Fruit: 1.5
Bread: 0.0
Meat: 0.0
Fat: 0.0

1. Cut apples into fourths and core. Cut apples further into scant ¼-inch slices and place in medium-size skillet. Pour apple cider over; sprinkle with brown sugar. Heat to boiling; reduce heat and simmer, uncovered, until apples are crisp-tender, 3 to 4 minutes. Remove apples to serving dish with slotted spoon.

2. Heat cider mixture to boiling; boil until mixture is reduced to a syrup consistency. Pour syrup over apples, and sprinkle very lightly with cinnamon and nutmeg.

Note: Apples can be sliced in advance. Rinse them in 1 cup water mixed with 2 tablespoons lemon juice to prevent apples from turning brown.

MIXED FRUIT KABOBS WITH RASPBERRY SAUCE

Bittersweet Chocolate Sauce (p. 794) would also be an excellent sauce choice for the kabobs.

8 servings (2 kabobs each)

2 bananas
2 kiwi fruit, peeled
2 peaches, pitted
2 pears, cored
   Vegetable cooking spray
¼ cup apple, *or* orange, juice
   Raspberry Sauce (recipe follows)

Per Serving
Calories: 110
% Calories from fat: 5
Fat (gm): 0.6
Saturated fat (gm): 0
Cholesterol (mg): 0
Sodium (mg): 1
Protein (gm): 1.1
Carbohydrate (gm): 27.8
Exchanges
Milk: 0.0
Vegetable: 0.0
Fruit: 2.0
Bread: 0.0
Meat: 0.0
Fat: 0.0

1. Cut each piece of fruit into 8 equal pieces. Alternately thread fruit onto sixteen 6-inch wooden or metal skewers.

2. Coat a grill or broiling pan with non-stick cooking spray. Grill or broil, 6 inches from medium-hot heat source, 5 to 8 minutes or until bananas are golden, rotating kabobs occasionally. Baste with apple juice. Serve with Raspberry Sauce.

Raspberry Sauce

(makes about 1 cup)

   1 pint fresh, *or* frozen, thawed, raspberries
  ¼ cup sugar
   1 teaspoon lemon juice

1. In a blender or food processor, combine raspberries, sugar, and lemon juice. Puree until smooth. Strain the puree; discard seeds.

PEARS BELLE HÉLÈNE

Tuck a Cocoa-Glazed Cookie Crisp (see p. 781) beside each serving to complete this elegant offering.

4 servings

  4 cups water
  ¼ cup sugar
  4 small pears, peeled with stem intact
  1 cup frozen low-fat vanilla yogurt
    Bittersweet Chocolate Sauce (recipe follows)

Per Serving
Calories: 183
% Calories from fat: 5
Fat (gm): 1.1
Saturated fat (gm): 0
Cholesterol (mg): 0
Sodium (mg): 0
Protein (gm): 2.3
Carbohydrate (gm): 43.9
Exchanges
Milk: 0.0
Vegetable: 0.0
Fruit: 2.0
Bread: 1.0
Meat: 0.0
Fat: 0.0

1. Combine water and sugar in small saucepan; heat to boiling. Add pears; reduce heat to low and gently simmer, covered, 10 to 15 minutes or until pears are tender.

2. Cool pears in syrup; refrigerate until chilled, 1 to 2 hours. Drain.

3. To serve, flatten a scoop of yogurt in each of 4 dessert dishes. Place a pear on top and drizzle with Bittersweet Chocolate Sauce.

Bittersweet Chocolate Sauce

(makes about 1½ cups)

- ¾   cup unsweetened cocoa
- ½   cup sugar
- ¾   cup fat-free milk
- 2   tablespoons margarine, *or* butter
- 1   teaspoon vanilla
- ¼-½   teaspoon ground cinnamon

1.   Mix cocoa and sugar in small saucepan; stir in milk and add margarine. Heat over medium heat until boiling, stirring constantly. Reduce heat and simmer until sauce is smooth and slightly thickened, 3 to 4 minutes.

2.   Stir in vanilla and cinnamon. Serve warm or at room temperature.

STRAWBERRY-KIWI SHORTCAKE

This moist, nutritious whole wheat shortcake is made to order for a duo of fresh fruit.

8 servings

- 1   cup all-purpose flour
- 1   cup whole wheat flour
- ⅓   cup sugar
- 1½   teaspoons baking powder
- ½   teaspoon baking soda
- ¼   teaspoon salt
- ⅔   cup buttermilk
- 4   tablespoons margarine, *or* butter, melted
- 1   egg
- 2   egg whites
- 1½   teaspoons vanilla
- 3   cups sliced strawberries
- 1   cup peeled, sliced kiwi fruit

Per Serving
Calories: 227
% Calories from fat: 29
Fat (gm): 7.3
Saturated fat (gm): 1.5
Cholesterol (mg): 27.4
Sodium (mg): 319
Protein (gm): 6.5
Carbohydrate (gm): 39.1
Exchanges
Milk: 0.0
Vegetable: 0.0
Fruit: 1.0
Bread: 2.0
Meat: 0.0
Fat: 1.0

1.   Combine flours, sugar, baking powder, baking soda, and salt in medium-size bowl. Mix buttermilk, margarine, egg, egg whites, and vanilla in small bowl until smooth; stir into flour mixture, mixing only until dry ingredients are moistened.

2. With floured hands, lightly pat dough into lightly greased 8-inch (round or square) baking pan. Bake at 400 degrees 12 to 15 minutes or until toothpick inserted near center comes out clean. Cool on wire rack 10 minutes.

3. Slice cake into wedges or squares and top with strawberries and kiwi fruit.

FRAN'S RHUBARB CRUNCH

Recipes from neighbors are the best. With a crunchy sweet crust on top and bottom, you'll lick your bowl clean and ask for more! The recipe can be halved and baked in a 9-inch-square baking pan, if desired. Thank you, Fran!

16 servings

1 cup all-purpose flour
1 cup whole wheat flour
1½ cups packed light brown sugar
1 cup quick-cooking oats
½ cup bran, *or* quick-cooking oats
2 teaspoons ground cinnamon
10 tablespoons margarine, *or* butter, melted
2 pounds fresh, *or* frozen, thawed, rhubarb, cut into 1-inch pieces (8 cups)
2 cups granulated sugar
¼ cup cornstarch
2 cups water
2 teaspoons vanilla

Per Serving
Calories: 341
% Calories from fat: 10
Fat (gm): 7.9
Saturated fat (gm): 1.5
Cholesterol (mg): 0
Sodium (mg): 94
Protein (gm): 3.8
Carbohydrate (gm): 66.9
Exchanges
Milk: 0.0
Vegetable: 0.0
Fruit: 1.0
Bread: 3.0
Meat: 0.0
Fat: 1.5

1. Combine flours, brown sugar, oats, bran, and cinnamon in large bowl; stir in margarine to make a crumbly mixture. Press half the mixture evenly on bottom of 13 x 9-inch baking pan. Arrange rhubarb evenly over crust.

2. Combine granulated sugar and cornstarch in medium saucepan; add water and heat to boiling. Boil, stirring constantly, until thickened, about 1 minute. Stir in vanilla. Pour mixture over rhubarb.

3. Sprinkle remaining crumb mixture over rhubarb. Bake, at 350 degrees, uncovered, until bubbly around the edges, 55 to 60 minutes.

APPLE-CRANBERRY CRISP

 Apples and cranberries are happy companions in this streusel-topped fruit crisp.

6 servings

2½ pounds cooking apples, peeled, cored, and sliced
1 cup fresh, *or* frozen, thawed cranberries
½ cup packed light brown sugar
2 tablespoons flour
1 teaspoon finely chopped crystallized ginger
Streusel Topping (recipe follows)

Per Serving
Calories: 283
% Calories from fat: 12
Fat (gm): 3.9
Saturated fat (gm): 0.7
Cholesterol (mg): 0
Sodium (mg): 43
Protein (gm): 1.9
Carbohydrate (gm): 64
Exchanges
Milk: 0.0
Vegetable: 0.0
Fruit: 2.0
Bread: 2.0
Meat: 0.0
Fat: 0.5

1. Combine apples, cranberries, brown sugar, flour, and ginger in a 1-quart glass casserole. Sprinkle Streusel Topping over fruit.

2. Bake, uncovered, at 350 degrees 30 to 40 minutes or until apples are tender. Serve warm.

Streusel Topping

⅓ cup quick-cooking oats
3 tablespoons flour
3 tablespoons packed light brown sugar
1½ tablespoons cold margarine, *or* butter

1. Combine oats, flour, and brown sugar in small bowl; cut in margarine with pastry cutter or 2 knives until mixture resembles coarse crumbs.

CHERRY-BERRY GRUNT

 A wonderful campfire dessert brought indoors and given a cherry accent.

8 servings

¾ cup all-purpose flour
2 tablespoons sugar
1 teaspoon baking powder
¼ teaspoon salt

Per Serving
Calories: 151
% Calories from fat: 26
Fat (gm): 4.5
Saturated fat (gm): 0.9
Cholesterol (mg): 0.1
Sodium (mg): 163
Protein (gm): 2
Carbohydrate (gm): 26.9

3 tablespoons margarine, *or* butter
3 tablespoons fat-free milk
1½ cups dark sweet cherries, pitted
1½ cups blueberries
3 tablespoons sugar
1 tablespoon lemon juice
1 tablespoon grated lemon rind
¼ teaspoon ground cinnamon

Exchanges
Milk: 0.0
Vegetable: 0.0
Fruit: 0.5
Bread: 1.0
Meat: 0.0
Fat: 1.0

1. Combine flour, 2 tablespoons sugar, baking powder, and salt in medium-size bowl. Cut in margarine with pastry blender or 2 knives until mixture resembles coarse crumbs. Mix in milk, stirring just enough to form a soft dough; set aside.

2. Combine cherries, blueberries, 3 tablespoons sugar, lemon juice, lemon rind, and cinnamon in Dutch oven or large saucepan. Heat to boiling; reduce heat and simmer, uncovered, 5 minutes.

3. Drop dough by rounded tablespoonfuls onto berry mixture. Cook, uncovered, 10 minutes; cover and cook an additional 10 minutes. Serve warm.

BAKED FRUIT COMPOTE WITH MERINGUE PUFFS

 Spoonfuls of meringue add a creative touch to warm, baked fruits.

4 servings

2 cups peeled, pitted, sliced peaches
1 pint raspberries
¼ cup sugar
3 egg whites
3 tablespoons sugar
½ teaspoon vanilla
¼ teaspoon ground nutmeg
2 tablespoons sliced toasted almonds

Per Serving
Calories: 181
% Calories from fat: 11
Fat (gm): 2.3
Saturated fat (gm): 0.2
Cholesterol (mg): 0
Sodium (mg): 42
Protein (gm): 4.5
Carbohydrate (gm): 38.7
Exchanges
Milk: 0.0
Vegetable: 0.0
Fruit: 2.0
Bread: 0.0
Meat: 1.0
Fat: 0.0

1. Combine peaches, raspberries, and ¼ cup sugar in medium-size bowl. Divide evenly among 4 custard cups and place in baking pan or on cookie sheet. Bake at 375 degrees 10 to 15 minutes or until heated through.

2. Beat egg whites in small bowl until soft peaks form. Gradually add 3 tablespoons sugar, beating until stiff peaks form. Add vanilla and nutmeg; beat 1 minute. Spoon meringue over warm peach mixture. Bake until lightly browned, about 10 minutes. Sprinkle with almonds and serve immediately.

BANANAS FOSTER

A taste of New Orleans!

4 servings

¼ cup packed light brown sugar
1½ teaspoons cornstarch
½ cup water
1 tablespoon rum
1 teaspoon vanilla
2 medium bananas, peeled and sliced
¼ cup toasted pecan halves
1⅓ cups frozen low-fat vanilla yogurt

Per Serving
Calories: 236
% Calories from fat: 20
Fat (gm): 5.5
Saturated fat (gm): 0.5
Cholesterol (mg): 0
Sodium (mg): 5
Protein (gm): 3.4
Carbohydrate (gm): 43
Exchanges
Milk: 0.0
Vegetable: 0.0
Fruit: 2.0
Bread: 1.0
Meat: 0.0
Fat: 1.0

1. Mix brown sugar and cornstarch in small saucepan; stir in water. Cook over medium heat until thickened, stirring constantly. Reduce heat to low; stir in rum and vanilla.

2. Gently stir in bananas and simmer 1 to 2 minutes or until bananas are warm; stir in pecans. Serve warm over frozen yogurt.

PRALINE SUNDAES

Fresh peach slices would make a flavorful addition to the sundaes, or select one of the cookies from this chapter.

4 servings

¼ cup packed light brown sugar
1½ teaspoons cornstarch
½ cup water
1 tablespoon bourbon, *or* brandy
1 teaspoon margarine, *or* butter
½ teaspoon vanilla

Per Serving
Calories: 256
% Calories from fat: 20
Fat (gm): 5.7
Saturated fat (gm): 1.9
Cholesterol (mg): 45
Sodium (mg): 72
Protein (gm): 8.3
Carbohydrate (gm): 41.1

2 tablespoons chopped pecans
1 pint frozen low-fat vanilla yogurt

Exchanges
Milk: 0.0
Vegetable: 0.0
Fruit: 0.0
Bread: 3.0
Meat: 0.0
Fat: 1.0

1. Mix sugar and cornstarch in small saucepan; stir in water. Heat to boiling over medium heat, stirring constantly until thickened, about 1 minute.

2. Stir in bourbon; cook 10 to 15 seconds. Remove from heat; stir in margarine, vanilla, and pecans. Serve warm over frozen yogurt.

ORANGE-PINEAPPLE SHERBET

 Use an ice cream maker to produce the smoothest texture in sherbets and ices. To keep orange segments whole, add them just before freezing is completed.

8 servings (about ½ cup each)

½ cup sugar
⅓ cup water
1 can (15¼ ounces) unsweetened crushed pineapple, undrained
1¼ cups buttermilk
¼ cup orange juice
1 can (11 ounces) mandarin orange segments, drained

Per Serving
Calories: 67
% Calories from fat: 5
Fat (gm): 0.4
Saturated fat (gm): 0.2
Cholesterol (mg): 1
Sodium (mg): 42
Protein (gm): 1.6
Carbohydrate (gm): 15.4
Exchanges
Milk: 0.0
Vegetable: 0.0
Fruit: 1.0
Bread: 0.0
Meat: 0.0
Fat: 0.0

1. Heat sugar and water to boiling in medium saucepan, stirring until sugar is dissolved. Cool to room temperature.

2. Process pineapple, buttermilk, sugar syrup mixture, and orange juice in food processor or blender until smooth. Freeze in ice cream maker according to manufacturer's directions, adding oranges just before sherbet is frozen. Or pour into 8-inch-square baking dish and freeze until slushy, about 2 hours; spoon into bowl and beat until fluffy, then stir in oranges, return to pan, and freeze until firm, 6 hours or overnight.

GINGER-CITRUS SORBET

Slightly tart, slightly zesty, very refreshing!

6 servings

3½ cups water
1½ cups sugar
¼ cup peeled, minced gingerroot
2 teaspoons grated orange rind
⅓ cup orange juice
2 tablespoons lemon juice

Per Serving
Calories: 190
% Calories from fat: 0
Fat (gm): 0.1
Saturated fat (gm): 0
Cholesterol (mg): 0
Sodium (mg): 1
Protein (gm): 0.2
Carbohydrate (gm): 50.6
Exchanges
Milk: 0.0
Vegetable: 0.0
Fruit: 3.0
Bread: 0.0
Meat: 0.0
Fat: 0.0

1. Combine water, sugar, gingerroot, and orange rind in medium saucepan. Heat to boiling over medium-high heat, stirring until sugar is dissolved; reduce heat and simmer 7 to 10 minutes. Cool to room temperature; stir in orange juice and lemon juice.

2. Freeze mixture in ice cream maker according to manufacturer's directions. Or pour into 8-inch-square baking dish and freeze until slushy, 2 to 4 hours; spoon into bowl and beat until fluffy, then return to pan and freeze until firm, 6 hours.

LEMON ICE

Serve this sweet-and-tart ice as a dessert or as a refreshing palate cleanser between dinner courses.

8 servings

2 cups water
1 cup sugar
1 cup fresh lemon juice
½ cup grated lemon rind

Per Serving
Calories: 101
% Calories from fat: 0
Fat (gm): 0
Saturated fat (gm): 0
Cholesterol (mg): 0
Sodium (mg): 1.3
Protein (gm): 0.2
Carbohydrate (gm): 27.6
Exchanges
Milk: 0.0
Vegetable: 0.0
Fruit: 0.0
Bread: 1.5
Meat: 0.0
Fat: 0.0

1. Combine water and sugar in medium saucepan. Heat to boiling over medium-high heat, stirring until sugar is dissolved. Reduce heat and simmer, uncovered, 5 minutes. Remove from heat; cool to room temperature. Stir in lemon juice and lemon rind.

2. Freeze mixture in ice cream maker according to manufacturer's directions. Or pour into 8-inch-square baking dish and freeze until slushy, about 2 hours; spoon into bowl and beat until fluffy, then return to pan and freeze until firm, 6 hours or overnight.

PINEAPPLE-CHAMPAGNE ICE

Champagne-inspired for a touch of elegance.

8 servings

2½ cups unsweetened pineapple juice
½ cup dry champagne, *or* sparkling wine
⅓ teaspoon ground nutmeg
8 slices (½ inch thick) fresh pineapple
Mint sprigs, as garnish

Per Serving
Calories: 99
% Calories from fat: **4**
Fat (gm): 0.5
Saturated fat (gm): 0.1
Cholesterol (mg): 0
Sodium (mg): 2
Protein (gm): 0.6
Carbohydrate (gm): 22.4
Exchanges
Milk: 0.0
Vegetable: 0.0
Fruit: 1.5
Bread: 0.0
Meat: 0.0
Fat: 0.0

1. Mix pineapple juice, champagne, and nutmeg. Freeze mixture in ice cream maker according to manufacturer's directions. Or pour mixture into 9-inch-square baking dish and freeze until slushy, about 2 hours; spoon into bowl and beat until fluffy, then return to pan and freeze until firm, 6 hours or overnight.

2. To serve, place pineapple slices on dessert plates. Top each with a scoop of Pineapple-Champagne Ice. Garnish with mint.

MIXED FRUIT TORTONI

Traditionally made with heavy cream and candied fruits, our version of this Italian favorite uses fresh seasonal fruits and low-fat topping.

12 servings

1½ cups fresh, *or* frozen, thawed, raspberries

  3 envelopes (1.3 ounces each) low-fat whipped topping mix

1½ cups 2% milk

  ½ cup pitted, halved sweet cherries, divided

  ⅓ cup peeled, pitted, cubed apricots

  ⅓ cup peeled, cored, cubed pineapple,

  4 tablespoons sugar

  ¼ cup chopped pistachio nuts, *or* slivered almonds, divided

Per Serving
Calories: 126
% Calories from fat: 28
Fat (gm): 3.5
Saturated fat (gm): 0.7
Cholesterol (mg): 2
Sodium (mg): 32
Protein (gm): 2.1
Carbohydrate (gm): 18.2
Exchanges
Milk: 0.0
Vegetable: 0.0
Fruit: 1.5
Bread: 0.0
Meat: 0.0
Fat: 0.5

1. Process raspberries in food processor or blender until smooth; strain and discard seeds.

2. Blend whipped topping and milk in large bowl; beat at high speed until topping forms soft peaks, about 4 minutes. Fold raspberry puree into whipped topping.

3. Reserve 12 cherry halves. Combine remaining cherries, apricots, and pineapple in small bowl; sprinkle with sugar and stir. Fold fruit and 2 tablespoons nuts into whipped topping mixture.

4. Spoon mixture equally into 12 cupcake liners; garnish tops of each with reserved cherry halves and remaining nuts. Place cupcake liners in muffin or baking pan; freeze until firm, 6 hours or overnight.

Note: If desired, ½ teaspoon sherry extract can be folded into the whipped topping mixture.

ORANGE BAKED ALASKA

Create any desired flavor of frozen yogurt by substituting another liqueur for the orange. Try cherry, raspberry, or a non-fruit flavor such as almond, hazelnut, or coffee.

8 servings

Gingersnap Crumb Crust (see p. 760)
½ cup graham cracker crumbs
1 tablespoon margarine, *or* butter
4 cups frozen low-fat vanilla yogurt, slightly softened
2 tablespoons orange-flavored liqueur, *or* orange juice concentrate
½ teaspoon ground nutmeg
3 egg whites
⅛ teaspoon cream of tartar
¼ cup sugar

Per Serving
Calories: 332
% Calories from fat: 25
Fat (gm): 9.2
Saturated fat (gm): 2.5
Cholesterol (mg): 45
Sodium (mg): 245
Protein (gm): 10.7
Carbohydrate (gm): 50
Exchanges
Milk: 0.0
Vegetable: 0.0
Fruit: 0.0
Bread: 3.5
Meat: 0.0
Fat: 2.0

1. Make crumb crust, adding ½ cup graham cracker crumbs and 1 tablespoon margarine to recipe and using 8-inch pie pan.

2. Mix frozen yogurt, liqueur, and nutmeg; spoon into cooled pie crust. Cover with plastic wrap and freeze until firm, 8 hours or overnight.

3. In medium-size bowl, beat egg whites with cream of tartar to soft peaks. Gradually add sugar, beating to stiff peaks. Spread meringue over frozen pie, carefully sealing to edge of crust. Bake at 500 degrees 3 to 5 minutes or until meringue is golden. Serve immediately.

CHOCOLATE BAKED ALASKA

For an added chocolate accent, drizzle each serving with 1 to 2 tablespoons of Bittersweet Chocolate Sauce (see p. 794).

8 servings

Vanilla Crumb Crust (see p.760)
¼ cup vanilla wafer cookie crumbs
1 tablespoon margarine, *or* butter
4 cups frozen low-fat chocolate yogurt, slightly softened

Per Serving
Calories: 301
% Calories from fat: 27
Fat (gm): 9.1
Saturated fat (gm): 2.7
Cholesterol (mg): 39.8
Sodium (mg): 169
Protein (gm): 10.2
Carbohydrate (gm): 44.2

  3   egg whites
  ⅛   teaspoon cream of tartar
  ¼   cup sugar

Exchanges
Milk: 0.0
Vegetable: 0.0
Fruit: 0.0
Bread: 3.0
Meat: 0.0
Fat: 2.0

1.   Make crumb crust, adding ¼ cup cookie crumbs and 1 table-spoon margarine to recipe and using 8-inch pie pan.

2.   Spoon frozen yogurt into cooled pie crust; cover with plastic wrap and freeze until firm, 8 hours or overnight.

3.   In medium-size bowl, beat egg whites with cream of tartar to soft peaks. Gradually add sugar, beating to stiff peaks. Spread meringue over frozen pie, carefully sealing to edge of crust. Bake at 500 degrees 3 to 5 minutes or until meringue is golden. Serve immediately.

FROZEN PEPPERMINT CAKE ROLLS

This beautiful dessert is deceptively easy to prepare, using cake mix. The cake rolls can be frozen, securely wrapped in aluminum foil, up to 1 month.

20 servings

  4   eggs
  1   package (18¾ ounces) yellow cake mix
  ½   cup water
      Powdered sugar, as garnish
  ¾   cup crushed peppermint candies
  1½ quarts frozen low-fat vanilla yogurt, slightly softened
      Bittersweet Chocolate Sauce (see p. 794)

Per Serving
Calories: 249
% Calories from fat: 16
Fat (gm): 4.4
Saturated fat (gm): 1
Cholesterol (mg): 42.4
Sodium (mg): 212
Protein (gm): 5.1
Carbohydrate (gm): 47
Exchanges
Milk: 0.0
Vegetable: 0.0
Fruit: 0.0
Bread: 3.0
Meat: 0.0
Fat: 1.0

1.   Lightly grease 2 jelly roll pans, 15 x 10 inches, and line with parchment or baking paper; grease parchment and sprinkle with flour.

2.   Beat eggs in medium-size bowl at high speed until thick and lemon-colored, about 5 minutes. Mix in cake mix and water on low speed. Pour batter into prepared pans; bake 15 minutes or until cakes spring back when touched. Immediately invert cakes onto clean kitchen towels sprinkled with powdered sugar. Remove foil and roll cake up in towels, starting at short ends. Cool on wire racks 15 minutes (no longer, or cakes will be too cool to fill and roll easily).

3. Fold peppermint candies into frozen yogurt. Unroll cakes; spread with frozen yogurt mixture. Roll cakes up and wrap in plastic wrap; freeze until firm, 8 hours or overnight.

4. Arrange cakes on serving platters; sprinkle with powdered sugar. Cut into slices; drizzle with Bittersweet Chocolate Sauce.

ICE CREAM JELLY ROLL CAKE

A versatile cake that can be filled with your flavor choice of fat-free ice cream, frozen yogurt, or light whipped topping and sliced fruit.

8 servings

- 3 egg yolks
- ½ teaspoon vanilla
- ¾ cup sugar, divided
- 3 egg whites
- ¾ cup cake flour
- 1 teaspoon baking powder
- ¼ teaspoon salt
- 1-1½ quarts strawberry, *or* other flavor, fat-free ice cream, slightly softened
  Powdered sugar, as garnish
  Whole strawberries, as garnish

Per Serving
Calories: 229
% Calories from fat: 8
Fat (gm): 2
Saturated fat (gm): 0.6
Cholesterol (mg): 79.9
Sodium (mg): 197
Protein (gm): 7.2
Carbohydrate (gm): 47.2
Exchanges
Milk: 0.0
Vegetable: 0.0
Fruit: 0.0
Bread: 2.5
Meat: 0.0
Fat: 0.0

1. Grease jelly roll pan, 15½ x 10½ x 1 inches. Line bottom of pan with parchment or baking paper; grease and flour paper.

2. Beat egg yolks and vanilla in medium bowl until thick and lemon colored, 3 to 5 minutes. Gradually beat in ¼ cup sugar, beating 2 minutes longer.

3. Using clean beaters and large bowl, beat egg whites to soft peaks; gradually beat in remaining ½ cup granulated sugar, beating to stiff, glossy peaks. Fold egg yolks into whites; sprinkle combined flour, baking powder, and salt over mixture and fold in. Spread batter evenly in prepared pan, using metal spatula.

4. Bake at 375 degrees until cake is golden and springs back when touched, 10 to 12 minutes. Immediately invert cake onto large kitchen towel sprinkled with powdered sugar; peel off paper and discard. Roll cake up in towel, beginning at short end. Cool on wire rack 30 to 60 minutes.

5. Unroll cake; spread with ice cream. Reroll cake and freeze until ice cream is firm, 6 to 8 hours.

6. Trim ends from cake and place cake on serving plate. Sprinkle cake generously with powdered sugar and garnish with strawberries.

 Variations: **Chocolate Ice Cream Jelly Roll Cake**—Make cake as above, adding ¼ cup unsweetened cocoa to the flour mixture. Fill cake with chocolate chip or chocolate fudge fat-free ice cream.

 Easy Cake Mix Jelly Roll Cakes—Prepare 2 jelly roll pans as above. Replace steps 2 and 3 as follows: beat 4 eggs in large bowl until thick and lemon colored; mix in ½ cup water. Mix in 1 package (18¼ ounces) yellow or chocolate light cake mix. Spread batter in pans and bake at 325 degrees until cakes spring back when touched, 8 to 10 minutes. Complete as above. Makes 2 cakes.

"RICH" CHOCOLATE PUDDING

 Unbelievably rich in flavor, smooth in texture. Use Dutch or European process cocoa for fullest flavor. Offer Hazelnut Macaroons (see p. 786) as an accompaniment to this dessert.

4 servings

½ cup sugar
⅓ cup unsweetened cocoa
3 tablespoons cornstarch
⅛ teaspoon salt
2 cups 2% milk
1 egg yolk, slightly beaten
2 teaspoons vanilla

Per Serving
Calories: 216
% Calories from fat: 17
Fat (gm): 4.3
Saturated fat (gm): 2
Cholesterol (mg): 62.3
Sodium (mg): 135
Protein (gm): 6.2
Carbohydrate (gm): 41.2
Exchanges
Milk: 0.5
Vegetable: 0.0
Fruit: 0.0
Bread: 2.0
Meat: 0.0
Fat: 0.5

1. Mix sugar, cocoa, cornstarch, and salt in medium saucepan; stir in milk. Cook over medium heat until mixture boils and thickens, stirring constantly; boil 1 minute, stirring constantly.

2. Stir about ½ cup milk mixture into egg yolk. Stir egg yolk mixture back into saucepan. Cook over low heat, stirring constantly, 30 to 60 seconds. Stir in vanilla.

3. Spoon into dessert bowls. Refrigerate, covered with plastic wrap, until chilled, 1 to 2 hours.

BAKED CEREAL PUDDING

 Eat warm from the oven, or refrigerate for a chilled dessert. Either way, this comfort food is just delicious.

6 servings (½ cup each)

2	eggs
2	egg whites
¼	cup sugar
¼	cup packed brown sugar
¾	cup natural wheat and barley cereal (Grape-Nuts)
2	cups fat-free milk
2	tablespoons margarine, *or* butter, melted
1	teaspoon vanilla
⅛	teaspoon salt

Per Serving
Calories: 214
% Calories from fat: 24
Fat (gm): 5.8
Saturated fat (gm): 1.4
Cholesterol (mg): 72.3
Sodium (mg): 262
Protein (gm): 7.9
Carbohydrate (gm): 33.2
Exchanges
Milk: 0.0
Vegetable: 0.0
Fruit: 0.0
Bread: 2.0
Meat: 0.5
Fat: 1.0

1. Beat eggs, egg whites, and sugars in medium bowl; mix in remaining ingredients.

2. Pour mixture into 1-quart soufflé dish or casserole. Place dish in roasting pan on oven rack; pour 2 inches hot water into pan. Bake, uncovered, at 375 degrees until pudding is set, about 50 minutes, stirring well halfway through baking time.

3. Remove soufflé dish from pan; cool on wire rack. Serve warm, or refrigerate and serve chilled.

OLD-FASHIONED BAKED RICE PUDDING

Serve warm with Tart Lemon Sauce or Raspberry Sauce (see pp. 808, 793).

6 servings

½ cup uncooked rice
3 cups fat-free milk
⅓ cup sugar
¼ cup golden raisins
½ teaspoon ground cinnamon
2 dashes ground nutmeg

Per Serving
Calories: 158
% Calories from fat: 2
Fat (gm): 0.3
Saturated fat (gm): 0.2
Cholesterol (mg): 2
Sodium (mg): 65
Protein (gm): 5.4
Carbohydrate (gm): 34
Exchanges
Milk: 0.5
Vegetable: 0.0
Fruit: 0.5
Bread: 1.0
Meat: 0.0
Fat: 0.0

1. Combine rice, milk, sugar, raisins, cinnamon, and nutmeg in 2-quart casserole.

2. Bake, uncovered, at 350 degrees until rice is tender and milk is absorbed, about 2½ hours, stirring occasionally. Serve warm or chilled.

BLUEBERRY BREAD PUDDING WITH TART LEMON SAUCE

Serve this pudding with Raspberry Sauce (p. 793) for a double-berry treat!

8 servings

3 tablespoons margarine, *or* butter, softened
6 slices whole wheat bread
1 egg
2 egg whites
½ cup sugar
¼ teaspoon salt
2 cups fat-free milk
1 teaspoon vanilla
1 cup fresh, *or* frozen, blueberries
Tart Lemon Sauce (recipe follows)

Per Serving
Calories: 302
% Calories from fat: 29
Fat (gm): 10
Saturated fat (gm): 2.2
Cholesterol (mg): 80.9
Sodium (mg): 332
Protein (gm): 7.7
Carbohydrate (gm): 47.7
Exchanges
Milk: 0.0
Vegetable: 0.0
Fruit: 0.0
Bread: 3.0
Meat: 0.0
Fat: 2.0

1. Spread margarine on one side of each slice of bread; cut into 2-inch squares and place in greased 9-inch dish or 1-quart casserole.

2. Combine egg, egg whites, sugar, and salt in medium bowl. Heat milk in small saucepan until just boiling; stir milk into egg mixture. Stir in vanilla and blueberries; pour over bread cubes.

3. Place baking dish in a 10 x 15-inch roasting pan; pour 1 inch hot water into pan. Bake, uncovered, at 350 degrees 35 to 40 minutes or until knife inserted near center comes out clean. Serve warm or room temperature with Tart Lemon Sauce

Tart Lemon Sauce

(makes 1½ cups)

  2 tablespoons margarine, *or* butter
⅔-1 cup sugar
  1 cup lemon juice
  2 eggs, slightly beaten

1. Melt margarine over low heat in small saucepan; stir in sugar and lemon juice. Cook over medium heat until sugar is dissolved.

2. Whisk about ½ cup of hot lemon mixture into eggs. Whisk egg mixture back into mixture in saucepan; cook over low heat until thickened, 2 to 3 minutes, whisking constantly. Serve warm or room temperature.

Variation: **Raisin Bread Pudding**—Substitute ⅓ cup raisins for the blueberries. Sprinkle raisins over bread squares in step 1; complete recipe as above.

WARM INDIAN PUDDING

Molasses and sweet spices signal the welcome flavors of the fall season.

6 servings

  ¼ cup yellow cornmeal
2¾ cups fat-free milk, divided
  ¾ cup light molasses
  ⅓ cup packed light brown sugar
  ¼ teaspoon salt
  3 tablespoons margarine, *or* butter

Per Serving
Calories: 277
% Calories from fat: 19
Fat (gm): 6.1
Saturated fat (gm): 1.3
Cholesterol (mg): 2
Sodium (mg): 143
Protein (gm): 5.3
Carbohydrate (gm): 35

¼   cup dark raisins
½   teaspoon ground cinnamon
¼   teaspoon ground nutmeg
⅛   teaspoon ground cloves
⅛   teaspoon ground ginger
¼   cup fat-free milk

Exchanges
Milk: 0.5
Vegetable: 0.0
Fruit: 0.5
Bread: 2.5
Meat: 0.0
Fat: 0.5

1. Combine cornmeal and 1 cup milk in a small bowl; set aside.

2. Heat remaining 1¾ cups milk in a medium saucepan until steaming. Stir in cornmeal mixture and cook until thickened, 15 minutes, stirring occasionally. Stir in molasses, sugar, and salt. Cook 2 to 3 minutes to dissolve sugar. Remove from heat; stir in margarine, raisins, cinnamon, nutmeg, cloves, and ginger.

3. Spoon mixture into greased 1½-quart casserole. Pour ¼ cup milk over mixture; bake, uncovered, 1¼ hours or until knife inserted near center comes out clean. Serve warm.

BROWN SUGAR APPLE PUDDING

Topped and baked with a batter and brown sugar syrup, this is the best apple pudding you will ever eat!

10 servings

Vegetable cooking spray
  6   cups peeled, cored, sliced (¼ inch) apples
  ½   cup packed light brown sugar
  ¼   cup margarine, *or* butter, softened
1½   teaspoons ground cinnamon
  1   egg
  ½   teaspoon vanilla
  ¾   cup all-purpose flour
  2   teaspoons baking powder
  ¼   teaspoon salt
  ½   cup fat-free milk
Brown Sugar Syrup (recipe follows)

Per Serving
Calories: 220
% Calories from fat: 23
Fat (gm): 5.8
Saturated fat (gm): 1.2
Cholesterol (mg): 21.5
Sodium (mg): 198
Protein (gm): 2.4
Carbohydrate (gm): 41.1
Exchanges
Milk: 0.0
Vegetable: 0.0
Fruit: 0.5
Bread: 2.0
Meat: 0.0
Fat: 1.0

1. Lightly spray 1½-quart casserole with cooking spray; arrange apple slices in casserole and set aside.

2. Combine brown sugar, margarine, and cinnamon in medium bowl; stir in egg and vanilla. Mix in combined flour, baking powder, and salt alternately with milk, stirring only until blended. Spread batter over apple slices.

3. Pour Brown Sugar Syrup over batter. Bake, uncovered, at 375 degrees 50 to 55 minutes or until apples are tender. Serve warm or at room temperature.

Brown Sugar Syrup

½ cup packed light brown sugar
2 tablespoons flour
1 teaspoon margarine, *or* butter
1 cup water
½ teaspoon vanilla

1. Combine brown sugar, flour, and margarine in small saucepan. Stir in water and heat to boiling, stirring constantly. Boil 2 to 3 minutes, stirring constantly. Remove from heat and stir in vanilla.

LEMON VELVET PUDDING

Top this velvet-textured custard with fresh peaches, strawberries, or other seasonal fruit. Serve a plate of Apricot-Sesame Biscotti (see p.788) on the side.

4 servings

½ cup sugar
3 tablespoons cornstarch
⅛ teaspoon salt
2 cups 2% milk
1 egg yolk, slightly beaten
2 tablespoons lemon juice
1 teaspoon lemon extract

Per Serving
Calories: 200
% Calories from fat: 16
Fat (gm): 3.6
Saturated fat (gm): 1.9
Cholesterol (mg): 62.3
Sodium (mg): 130
Protein (gm): 4.8
Carbohydrate (gm): 37.4
Exchanges
Milk: 0.5
Vegetable: 0.0
Fruit: 0.0
Bread: 2.0
Meat: 0.0
Fat: 0.5

1. Mix sugar, cornstarch, and salt in medium saucepan; stir in milk. Cook over medium heat until mixture boils and thickens, stirring constantly; boil 1 minute stirring constantly.

2. Whisk about ½ cup milk mixture into egg yolk. Whisk egg yolk mixture back into saucepan; whisk in lemon juice and extract. Cook over low heat, stirring constantly, 30 to 60 seconds.

3. Spoon pudding into dessert dishes. Refrigerate, covered with plastic wrap, until chilled, 1 to 2 hours.

FRESH APRICOT CUSTARD

A delicate custard with fresh apricots gently folded throughout. Serve with cookies: Cardamom Crisps (see p. 780) would be nice.

6 servings

½ cup sugar
3 tablespoons cornstarch
2 cups fat-free milk
½ cup apricot nectar
2 egg yolks, slightly beaten
2 tablespoons margarine, *or* butter
1½ cups peeled, coarsely chopped fresh apricots (7 medium apricots)

Per Serving
Calories: 193
% Calories from fat: 26
Fat (gm): 5.8
Saturated fat (gm): 1.4
Cholesterol (mg): 72.3
Sodium (mg): 90
Protein (gm): 4.4
Carbohydrate (gm): 32
Exchanges
Milk: 0.0
Vegetable: 0.0
Fruit: 0.5
Bread: 1.5
Meat: 0.0
Fat: 1.0

1. Mix sugar and cornstarch in medium saucepan; stir in milk and apricot nectar. Cook over medium heat until mixture boils and thickens, stirring constantly; boil 1 minute, stirring constantly.

2. Whisk about ½ cup milk mixture into egg yolks; whisk egg yolk mixture back into saucepan. Cook over low heat, stirring constantly, 30 to 60 seconds. Remove from heat; stir in margarine. Refrigerate, covered with plastic wrap, until chilled, 1 to 2 hours.

3. Stir custard until fluffy; stir in apricots. Spoon into dessert dishes.

CARAMEL FLAN

Unbelievably delicate and fine in texture, this flan is one you'll serve over and over again.

8 servings

¼ cup sugar
4 cups fat-free milk
⅓ cup sugar
3 eggs
4 egg whites, *or* ½ cup no-cholesterol real egg product
2 teaspoons vanilla

Per Serving
Calories: 140
% Calories from fat: 14
Fat (gm): 2.1
Saturated fat (gm): 0.7
Cholesterol (mg): 81.9
Sodium (mg): 114
Protein (gm): 8.3
Carbohydrate (gm): 21.3
Exchanges
Milk: 0.5
Vegetable: 0.0
Fruit: 0.0
Bread: 1.0
Meat: 0.0
Fat: 0.5

1. Heat ¼ cup sugar in small skillet over medium-high heat until sugar melts and turns golden, stirring occasionally (watch carefully as the sugar can burn easily!). Quickly pour syrup into bottom of 2-quart soufflé or casserole and tilt bottom to spread caramel. Set aside to cool.

2. Heat milk and ⅓ cup sugar until steaming and just beginning to bubble at edges. Beat eggs and egg whites in medium bowl; stir in hot milk mixture and vanilla. Pour mixture through strainer into soufflé dish.

3. Place soufflé dish in roasting pan on middle oven rack. Cover dish with lid or aluminum foil. Pour 2 inches hot water into roasting pan. Bake at 350 degrees 1 hour or until sharp knife inserted halfway between center and edge of custard comes out clean. Remove soufflé dish from roasting pan and cool to room temperature on wire rack. Refrigerate 8 hours or overnight.

4. To unmold, loosen edge of custard with sharp knife. Place rimmed serving dish over soufflé dish and invert.

ORANGE FLAN

 This flan is scented with orange for a subtle flavor accent.

8 servings

¼ cup sugar

3¾ cups fat-free milk

¼ cup frozen orange juice concentrate

⅓ cup sugar

3 eggs

6 egg whites, *or* ¾ cup no-cholesterol real egg product

⅛-¼ teaspoon orange extract

Per Serving
Calories: 152
% Calories from fat: 12
Fat (gm): 2.1
Saturated fat (gm): 0.7
Cholesterol (mg): 81.8
Sodium (mg): 124
Protein (gm): 9.1
Carbohydrate (gm): 24
Exchanges
Milk: 0.5
Vegetable: 0.0
Fruit: 0.0
Bread: 1.0
Meat: 0.0
Fat: 0.5

1. Heat ¼ cup sugar in small skillet over medium-high heat until sugar melts and turns golden, stirring occasionally (watch carefully as the sugar can burn easily!). Quickly pour syrup into bottom of 2-quart soufflé or casserole and tilt bottom to spread caramel. Set aside to cool.

2. Heat milk, orange juice concentrate, and ⅓ cup sugar in medium saucepan until steaming and just beginning to bubble at edges. Beat eggs and egg whites in medium-size bowl; stir in hot milk mixture and orange extract. Pour mixture through strainer into soufflé dish.

3. Place soufflé dish in roasting pan on middle oven rack. Cover dish with lid or aluminum foil. Pour 2 inches hot water into roasting pan. Bake at 350 degrees 1 hour or until sharp knife inserted halfway between center and edge of custard comes out clean. Remove soufflé dish from roasting pan and cool to room temperature on wire rack. Refrigerate 8 hours or overnight.

4. To unmold, loosen edge of custard with sharp knife. Place rimmed serving dish over soufflé dish and invert.

HERBED CUSTARD BRULÉE

Scented with herbs, the delicate custard is topped with a sprinkling of caramelized sugar.

6 servings

3 cups fat-free milk

2 tablespoons minced fresh, *or* ½ teaspoon dried, basil leaves

2 tablespoons minced fresh, *or* ½ teaspoon dried, cilantro leaves

2 tablespoons minced fresh, *or* ½ teaspoon dried, tarragon leaves

2 eggs

6 egg whites, *or* ¾ cup no-cholesterol real egg product

½ cup granulated sugar

3 tablespoons packed light brown sugar

Per Serving
Calories: 176
% Calories from fat: 10
Fat (gm): 1.9
Saturated fat (gm): 0.7
Cholesterol (mg): 73
Sodium (mg): 142
Protein (gm): 9.9
Carbohydrate (gm): 30
Exchanges
Milk: 0.5
Vegetable: 0.0
Fruit: 0.0
Bread: 1.5
Meat: 0.0
Fat: 0.5

1. Combine milk, basil, cilantro, and tarragon in medium-size saucepan. Heat to boiling; remove from heat, cover, and let stand 10 minutes. Strain; discard herbs.

2. Beat eggs, egg whites, and granulated sugar in medium bowl 5 minutes or until pale yellow. Gradually add milk mixture to eggs, beating constantly. Pour mixture into 8 custard cups or oven-proof ramekins.

3. Place cups in 10 x 15-inch roasting pan on center oven rack; pour 2 inches hot water into pan. Bake at 350 degrees 20 minutes or until knife inserted halfway between center and edge of custard comes out clean. Remove cups from roasting pan and cool to room temperature on wire rack. Refrigerate until completely chilled, 2 to 4 hours.

4. Preheat oven to 150 degrees. Sprinkle brown sugar evenly in small baking dish and bake 10 minutes or until moisture is evaporated (do not melt sugar).

5. Turn oven to broil. Sprinkle brown sugar evenly over chilled custards. Place on cookie sheet and broil, 4 inches from heat source, until sugar is melted and caramelized, 2 to 3 minutes. Serve immediately.

CHILLED RASPBERRY SOUFFLÉ

Serve this delicate soufflé with Raspberry Sauce (see p. 793).

6 servings (about ½ cup each)

⅓ cup sugar

½ cup water

3 teaspoons lemon juice

*1 package (¼ ounce) unflavored gelatin

2 cups fresh, *or* frozen, thawed, raspberries

2 envelopes (1.3 ounces each) low-fat whipped topping mix

1 cup 2% milk

Fresh raspberries, as garnish

Mint sprigs, as garnish

Per Serving
Calories: 69
% Calories from fat: 14
Fat (gm): 1
Saturated fat (gm): 0.5
Cholesterol (mg): 3
Sodium (mg): 30
Protein (gm): 2.7
Carbohydrate (gm): 10.9
Exchanges
Milk: 0.0
Vegetable: 0.0
Fruit: 1.5
Bread: 0.0
Meat: 0.0
Fat: 1.0

1. Combine sugar, water, and lemon juice in medium saucepan; sprinkle in gelatin. Let stand 2 to 3 minutes. Heat to simmering over medium heat, stirring constantly until sugar and gelatin are dissolved. Cool; refrigerate until mixture is consistency of unbeaten egg whites.

2. Process 2 cups raspberries in food processor or blender until smooth; strain and discard seeds.

3. Blend whipped topping mix and milk in medium bowl; beat at high speed until topping forms soft peaks, about 4 minutes. Stir raspberry puree into gelatin mixture; fold in whipped topping.

4. Spoon soufflé mixture into serving dish or individual stemmed dessert dishes. Chill 2 to 4 hours or until set. Garnish with fresh raspberries and mint.

Note: This recipe is not appropriate for strict vegetarians.

PEACH-ALLSPICE SOUFFLÉS

6 servings

Vegetable cooking spray
1½ cups chopped fresh peaches, *or* frozen, thawed, *or* canned, drained peaches
2 teaspoons lemon juice
1 teaspoon vanilla
1 teaspoon sugar
⅛ teaspoon ground allspice
2 egg yolks
4 egg whites
⅛ teaspoon cream of tartar
¼ cup sugar
Powdered sugar, as garnish

Per Serving
Calories: 85
% Calories from fat: 18
Fat (gm): 1.7
Saturated fat (gm): 0.5
Cholesterol (mg): 71
Sodium (mg): 39
Protein (gm): 3.6
Carbohydrate (gm): 14.1
Exchanges
Milk: 0.0
Vegetable: 0.0
Fruit: 1.0
Bread: 0.0
Meat: 0.5
Fat: 0.0

1. Spray six 1-cup soufflé dishes or custard cups with cooking spray; place dishes on baking sheet and set aside.

2. Process peaches, lemon juice, vanilla, 1 teaspoon sugar, and allspice in food processor or blender until smooth. Add egg yolks, one at a time, processing until smooth.

3. Beat egg whites and cream of tartar in large bowl until soft peaks form. Gradually beat in ¼ cup sugar, beating to stiff peaks. Fold in peach mixture. Spoon into prepared dishes.

4. Bake at 450 degrees 7 minutes; reduce heat to 425 degrees and bake 7 minutes more or until soufflés are lightly browned and sharp knife inserted near centers comes out clean. Sprinkle with powdered sugar, and serve immediately.

Note: Soufflé can be baked in a 1-quart soufflé dish. Bake at 450 degrees for 10 minutes; reduce heat to 425 degrees and bake 10 minutes more or until sharp knife inserted near center comes out clean.

SEVENTEEN

Veg Express

Recipes in Veg Express guarantee that you'll have dinner on the table in a streamlined 20 to 30 minutes.

Accomplishing this feat does require some organization on the part of the cook, however, and it's necessary to take advantage of the high-quality convenience and ready-to-use ingredients indicated in the recipes. Read the recipe through and assemble equipment and ingredients before you start; then cook your way to a delicious reward!

As convenience foods may be higher in fat and/or sodium, some of the recipes in Veg Express exceed the nutritional criteria (see pg. vii) established for percentage of calories from fat and/or sodium in this book.

VERY QUICK BEAN AND VEGETABLE STEW

Pureed beans provide a perfect thickening for the stew, and canned vegetables make it extra quick.

6 servings (about 1¼ cups each)
Prep/Cook Time: 20 minutes

8	ounces egg noodles
	Vegetable cooking spray
3	carrots, sliced
¾	cup chopped onion
2	teaspoons minced garlic
1	can (15 ounces) navy beans, rinsed, drained
2	cups vegetable broth, divided
2	cans (16 ounces each) Italian-style zucchini with mushrooms in tomato sauce
1	can (15 ounces) black beans, rinsed, drained
1	cup frozen peas
1½	teaspoons dried Italian seasoning
	Salt and pepper, to taste

Per Serving
Calories: 365
% Calories from fat: 7
Fat (gm): 3
Saturated fat (gm): 0.5
Cholesterol (mg): 32.6
Sodium (mg): 1479
Protein (gm): 18.1
Carbohydrate (gm): 69.7
Exchanges
Milk: 0.0
Vegetable: 2.0
Fruit: 0.0
Bread: 4.0
Meat: 0.0
Fat: 0.5

1. Cook noodles according to package directions.

2. Spray large saucepan with cooking spray; heat over medium heat until hot. Saute carrots, onion, and garlic 5 minutes.

3. Puree navy beans with half the broth in blender. Add to sauteed vegetables in saucepan. Add remaining broth, zucchini, black beans, peas, and Italian seasoning. Heat to boiling. Reduce heat and simmer, uncovered, until vegetables are tender, about 10 minutes. Season to taste with salt and pepper.

4. Spoon stew over noodles in shallow bowls.

FETTUCCINE WITH FRESH FENNEL AND BRUSSELS SPROUTS

Brussels sprouts cook more quickly when halved.

4 servings
Prep/Cook Time: 15–20 minutes

8	ounces spinach fettuccine
	Olive oil cooking spray
1	fennel bulb, thinly sliced
1	medium onion, thinly sliced
8	ounces small Brussels sprouts, halved
1/4	cup water, *or* vegetable broth
1	tablespoon lemon juice
	Salt and pepper, to taste
2	ounces shredded, *or* shaved, Parmesan cheese
4	tablespoons toasted pine nuts, *or* slivered almonds

Per Serving
Calories: 337
% Calories from fat: 32
Fat (gm): 12.3
Saturated fat (gm): 4.2
Cholesterol (mg): 78.1
Sodium (mg): 360
Protein (gm): 18.2
Carbohydrate (gm): 41.1
Exchanges
Milk: 0.0
Vegetable: 0.0
Fruit: 0.0
Bread: 2.5
Meat: 2.0
Fat: 1.0

1. Cook fettuccine according to package directions.

2. Spray large skillet with cooking spray; heat over medium heat until hot. Saute fennel and onion 3 to 4 minutes. Add Brussels sprouts and water and heat to boiling; reduce heat and simmer, covered, until sprouts are crisp-tender, 5 to 8 minutes. Stir in lemon juice; season to taste with salt and pepper.

3. Spoon fennel and sprouts mixture over pasta on serving platter; sprinkle with Parmesan cheese and pine nuts.

WINE-GLAZED RAVIOLI AND ASPARAGUS

A reduction of vegetable broth, white wine, and orange juice creates an elegant and fragrant sauce for flavorful pasta.

4 servings
Prep/Cook Time: 20 minutes

1	package (9 ounces) fresh mushroom ravioli
2	cups canned reduced-sodium vegetable broth
1	cup dry white wine

Per Serving
Calories: 290
% Calories from fat: 32
Fat (gm): 10.6
Saturated fat (gm): 3.6
Cholesterol (mg): 26.8
Sodium (mg): 254
Protein (gm): 8.2
Carbohydrate (gm): 33

1 cup orange juice
1/4 teaspoon crushed red pepper
1 pound asparagus, cut into 1-inch pieces
2 tablespoons margarine, *or* butter
   Salt and pepper, to taste

Exchanges
Milk: 0.0
Vegetable: 1.0
Fruit: 0.0
Bread: 2.0
Meat: 0.0
Fat: 1.5

1. Cook ravioli according to package directions.

2. Heat vegetable broth, white wine, orange juice, and crushed red pepper to boiling in large skillet; boil, uncovered, 10 minutes or until liquid is reduced to about 1/2 cup.

3. Add asparagus to skillet; cook, covered, over medium heat until crisp-tender, 3 to 4 minutes. Add ravioli and margarine; season to taste with salt and pepper.

20-MINUTE RAVIOLI

Use any favorite flavor of refrigerated fresh ravioli with this quick and nutritious bean sauce.

4 servings
Prep/Cook Time: 20 minutes

1 package (9 ounces) fresh sun-dried tomato ravioli
3/4 cup chopped onion
2 teaspoons minced garlic
1 tablespoon olive oil
3/4 cup canned kidney beans, rinsed, drained
1 large tomato, cubed
1/2 teaspoon dried thyme leaves
   Salt and pepper, to taste

Per Serving
Calories: 234
% Calories from fat: 35
Fat (gm): 9.4
Saturated fat (gm): 3.8
Cholesterol (mg): 32.8
Sodium (mg): 320
Protein (gm): 9.5
Carbohydrate (gm): 29.1
Exchanges
Milk: 0.0
Vegetable: 0.0
Fruit: 0.0
Bread: 2.0
Meat: 1.0
Fat: 1.0

1. Cook ravioli according to package directions.

2. Saute onion and garlic in oil in large skillet until tender, about 5 minutes. Stir in beans, tomato, and thyme; cook 2 to 3 minutes. Stir in ravioli and cook 2 to 3 minutes longer. Season to taste with salt and pepper.

GREAT GARLIC PASTA

Slow cooking gives a sweet, mellow flavor to the garlic. Prepared peeled garlic can be found in jars in the produce section of most supermarkets.

4 servings
Prep/Cook Time: 15-20 minutes

8	ounces (2 cups) orrechiette, *or* cappelletti
1	cup tiny peas
1/3	cup slivered (1/4 -inch pieces), *or* thinly sliced, garlic
2–3	teaspoons olive oil
2	tablespoons minced fresh parsley
1	tablespoon minced fresh rosemary, *or* 1 teaspoon crushed dried rosemary leaves
1/4–1/3	cup freshly grated Parmesan cheese
	Salt and pepper, to taste

Per Serving
Calories: 302
% Calories from fat: 15
Fat (gm): 5
Saturated fat (gm): 1.4
Cholesterol (mg): 3.9
Sodium (mg): 132
Protein (gm): 12.1
Carbohydrate (gm): 52.2
Exchanges
Milk: 0.0
Vegetable: 2.0
Fruit: 0.0
Bread: 3.0
Meat: 0.0
Fat: 1.0

1.   Cook pasta according to package directions, adding peas 1 minute before end of cooking time; drain.

2.   Cook garlic over very low heat in oil in small skillet until very tender but not browned, about 10 minutes. Add herbs; toss with pasta and cheese in serving bowl. Season to taste with salt and pepper.

ASPARAGUS AND WHITE BEANS, ITALIAN-STYLE

Imagine yourself in a medieval town in Tuscany while enjoying this spring asparagus and bean saute.

4 servings
Prep/Cook Time: 15-20 minutes

8	ounces linguine, *or* thin spaghetti
1	pound asparagus, cut into 2-inch pieces
2	teaspoons minced garlic
2-3	teaspoons olive oil
2	cups chopped Italian plum tomatoes
1	can (15 ounces) cannellini, *or* Great Northern, beans, rinsed, drained
1	teaspoon dried rosemary leaves, *or* Italian seasoning

Per Serving
Calories: 339
% Calories from fat: 16
Fat (gm): 6.1
Saturated fat (gm): 1.4
Cholesterol (mg): 3.9
Sodium (mg): 458
Protein (gm): 15.8
Carbohydrate (gm): 58.7
Exchanges
Milk: 0.0
Vegetable: 2.0
Fruit: 0.0
Bread: 3.0
Meat: 0.5
Fat: 1.0

1 cup canned reduced-sodium vegetable
broth
Salt and pepper, to taste
$1/4-1/2$ cup (1 to 2 ounces) shredded Parmesan
cheese

1. Cook pasta according to package directions.

2. Saute asparagus and garlic in oil in large skillet until crisp-tender, 3 to 4 minutes. Stir in remaining ingredients, except salt, pepper, and cheese; heat to boiling. Reduce heat and simmer rapidly until mixture has thickened, 3 to 5 minutes. Season to taste with salt and pepper.

3. Serve vegetable mixture over pasta; sprinkle with cheese.

THAI FRIED RICE

Although packaged coconut ginger rice is delicious, any kind of leftover rice can be used, making this speedy dish even faster to prepare!

2 servings
Prep/Cook Time: 15-20 minutes

Per Serving
Calories: 337
% Calories from fat: 20
Fat (gm): 7.6
Saturated fat (gm): 0.9
Cholesterol (mg): 212
Sodium (mg): 483
Protein (gm): 19.6
Carbohydrate (gm): 47.4
Exchanges
Milk: 0.0
Vegetable: 3.0
Fruit: 0.0
Bread: 2.0
Meat: 1.0
Fat: 1.5

1 package (6.4 ounces) Thai coconut
ginger rice, *or* $1^1/2$ cups cooked rice
1 package (16 ounces) frozen vegetable
stir-fry blend with sugar snap peas
6 green onions and tops, sliced, divided
$1/2-1$ teaspoon hot chili sesame oil
2 eggs, lightly beaten
2-3 tablespoons Thai peanut sauce (see Tip)
1-2 tablespoons reduced-sodium tamari
sauce

1. Cook rice according to package directions.

2. Stir-fry frozen vegetables and 4 green onions in sesame oil in large skillet until tender, 3 to 4 minutes. Move vegetables to side of skillet.

3. Add eggs to skillet; cook over medium heat until set, stirring occasionally, about 2 minutes. Break up eggs with spatula and mix with vegetables; stir in rice and peanut and tamari sauces.

4. Spoon rice mixture into serving dish and garnish with remaining 2 green onions.

Tip: Mix 1 to 2 tablespoons reduced-fat peanut butter, 2 to 3 teaspoons reduced-sodium tamari soy sauce, and $^1/_2$ to 1 teaspoon minced gingerroot as a substitute for the Thai peanut sauce.

THAI STIR-FRY

 With a few convenience foods in your pantry, everyday vegetables can be transformed into an exotic meal.

4 servings
Prep/Cook Time: 20 minutes

Per Serving	
Calories: 238	
% Calories from fat: 20	
Fat (gm): 5.4	
Saturated fat (gm): 1	
Cholesterol (mg): 0	
Sodium (mg): 1433	
Protein (gm): 10.2	
Carbohydrate (gm): 38.3	

Exchanges
Milk: 0.0
Vegetable: 2.0
Fruit: 0.0
Bread: 2.0
Meat: 0.0
Fat: 1.0

1	package (6.4 ounces) Thai coconut ginger rice (see Tips)
	Vegetable cooking spray
8	green onions and tops, sliced
8	ounces broccoli florets
8	ounces carrots, thinly sliced
$^1/_2$–1	cup Thai peanut sauce
$^1/_2$	cup canned reduced-sodium vegetable broth
2	teaspoons cornstarch
$^1/_4$	cup finely chopped cilantro
$^1/_4$	cup dry-roasted peanuts (optional)

1. Prepare rice according to package directions.

2. Spray large skillet with cooking spray; heat over medium heat until hot. Saute onions, broccoli, and carrots until crisp-tender, 4 to 5 minutes. Stir in peanut sauce; stir in combined vegetable broth and cornstarch; heat to boiling. Boil, stirring, until thickened, about 1 minute.

3. Serve vegetable mixture over rice; sprinkle with cilantro and peanuts.

Tips: An aromatic rice, such as basmati or jasmine, can be substituted for the Thai rice; cook with light coconut milk, if desired, or sprinkle with flaked coconut when serving.

SESAME ASPARAGUS STIR-FRY

Check the Asian section of your supermarket for the interesting selection of sauces available for noodles and rice.

4 servings (about 1 cup each)
Prep/Cook Time: 18-20 minutes

1 package (18 ounces) Chinese egg noodles
Vegetable cooking spray
8 ounces asparagus, cut into 1-inch pieces
1/4 teaspoon dried pepper flakes
1 can (15 ounces) black beans, rinsed, drained
1 jar (14 ounces) Mandarin sesame sauce for noodles and rice
1 small tomato, coarsely chopped

Per Serving
Calories: 387
% Calories from fat: 14
Fat (gm): 6.2
Saturated fat (gm): 0.8
Cholesterol (mg): 0
Sodium (mg): 1187
Protein (gm): 9.3
Carbohydrate (gm): 74.6
Exchanges
Milk: 0.0
Vegetable 0.0
Fruit: 0.0
Bread: 5.0
Meat: 0.0
Fat: 0.5

1. Cook noodles according to package directions.

2. Spray wok or medium skillet with cooking spray; heat over medium heat until hot. Stir-fry asparagus over medium-high heat 3 to 4 minutes or until browned. Add red pepper flakes; cook 1 minute longer.

3. Stir beans and Mandarin sesame sauce into skillet and cook 2 to 3 minutes; stir in tomato. Serve over noodles.

FALAFEL "BURGERS"

The falafel mixture can also be shaped into 1-inch balls and cooked as the recipe directs; serve with Yogurt Cucumber Sauce as appetizers, or in pitas for sandwiches.

4 servings
Prep/Cook Time: 20 minutes

1 package (6 ounces) falafel mix
1/2 cup shredded carrots
1/4 cup sunflower kernels
2 tablespoons thinly sliced green onions and tops
Vegetable cooking spray
Yogurt Cucumber Sauce (recipe follows)

Per Serving
Calories: 258
% Calories from fat: 32
Fat (gm): 8.4
Saturated fat (gm): 1
Cholesterol (mg): 3.5
Sodium (mg): 582
Protein (gm): 11.4
Carbohydrate (gm): 28.1
Exchanges
Milk: 0.0
Vegetable: 0.0
Fruit: 0.0
Bread: 2.0
Meat: 1.0
Fat: 1.5

1. Prepare falafel mix with water according to package directions; mix in carrots, sunflower kernels, and green onions. Shape mixture into 8 "burgers" about ¹/₂ inch thick.

2. Spray large skillet with cooking spray; heat over medium heat until hot. Place "burgers" in skillet and spray tops with cooking spray. Cook patties until browned, 4 to 5 minutes on each side.

3. Make Yogurt Cucumber Sauce while "burgers" are cooking; serve with "burgers."

Yogurt Cucumber Sauce

(makes about 1¹/₃ cups)

> 1 cup reduced-fat plain yogurt
> 1 cup shredded, *or* chopped, cucumber
> ¹/₂ teaspoon dried dill weed
> ¹/₂ teaspoon dried mint leaves
> Salt and white pepper, to taste

Mix yogurt, cucumber, and herbs. Season to taste with salt and pepper.

EGGPLANT POLENTA STACK

Purchase packaged flavored polenta in the produce section; choose any favorite for this dish.

4 servings
Prep/Bake Time: 30 minutes

> 8 slices (³/₄-inch) eggplant (about 1 pound)
> 2 egg whites, lightly beaten, *or* ¹/₄ cup no-cholesterol real egg product
> ¹/₂ cup Italian-seasoned dry bread crumbs
> ¹/₄ cup grated Parmesan cheese
> Olive oil cooking spray
> 8 slices (¹/₂-inch) tomato
> Salt and pepper, to taste
> 1 package (16 ounces) prepared Italian-herb polenta, cut into 8 slices
> 2–4 ounces reduced-fat feta, *or* goat, cheese, crumbled

Per Serving
Calories: 222
% Calories from fat: 18
Fat (gm): 4.5
Saturated fat (gm): 2.4
Cholesterol (mg): 9
Sodium (mg): 624
Protein (gm): 10.9
Carbohydrate (gm): 35.1
Exchanges
Milk: 0.0
Vegetable: 0.0
Fruit: 0.0
Bread: 2.0
Meat: 1.0
Fat: 0.0

1. Dip eggplant slices in egg whites and coat with combined breadcrumbs and Parmesan cheese. Spray large skillet with cooking spray and heat over medium heat until hot. Cook eggplant until browned on the bottom, about 8 minutes; spray tops of slices with cooking spray and turn. Cook until eggplant is tender and browned on the bottom, about 8 minutes longer.

2. Arrange eggplant slices in baking pan; top each with a slice of tomato; sprinkle lightly with salt and pepper. Top tomato slices with polenta and sprinkle with feta cheese.

3. Bake at 500 degrees until polenta is warm and cheese softened, about 5 minutes.

TWO-CHEESE RISOTTO

This flavorful risotto is quickly prepared with a simplified method that requires little stirring. Serve with a salad and green vegetable for a simple but elegant meal.

4 servings (about 1 cup each)
Prep/Cook Time: 30 minutes

Vegetable cooking spray
1/2 cup finely chopped onion
1 cup arborio rice
2 1/2 cups vegetable broth
1/2 cup dry white wine
1 cup (4 ounces) shredded Parmesan cheese
1/4–1/2 cup (1 to 2 ounces) crumbled blue cheese
2–3 tablespoons chopped chives, *or* Italian parsley
Salt and pepper, to taste

Per Serving
Calories: 345
% Calories from fat: 22
Fat (gm): 8.3
Saturated fat (gm): 5.2
Cholesterol (mg): 21.1
Sodium (mg): 525
Protein (gm): 13.9
Carbohydrate (gm): 47.3
Exchanges
Milk: 0.0
Vegetable: 0.0
Fruit: 0.0
Bread: 3.0
Meat: 1.0
Fat: 1.5

1. Spray large saucepan with cooking spray; heat over medium heat until hot. Add onion and saute 1 to 2 minutes. Add rice, vegetable broth, and wine and heat to boiling. Reduce heat and simmer, covered, until rice is *al dente* and liquid absorbed, 20 to 25 minutes, stirring occasionally.

2. Stir in cheeses and chives. Season to taste with salt and pepper.

SWEET POTATO CHIPOTLE CHILI

Chipotle chilies are dried, smoked jalapeño chilies. When canned, they are in adobo sauce, which is made with ground chilies and spices. The chilies add a distinctive smoky flavor to this robust dish; taste before adding a second chili, as they can be fiercely hot!

4 servings (1¹/₂ cups each)
Prep/Cook Time: 30 minutes

Per Serving
Calories: 399
% Calories from fat: 12
Fat (gm): 5.4
Saturated fat (gm): 0.6
Cholesterol (mg): 0
Sodium (mg): 932
Protein (gm): 18.7
Carbohydrate (gm): 72.1
Exchanges
Milk: 0.0
Vegetable: 2.0
Fruit: 0.0
Bread: 4.0
Meat: 0.0
Fat: 1.0

2	cups frozen stir-fry pepper blend
1	teaspoon minced garlic
1–2	teaspoons minced gingerroot
1	teaspoon cumin seeds
1–2	tablespoons peanut, *or* canola, oil
3	cups cubed, peeled sweet potatoes (¹/₂-inch)
1	can (14¹/₂ ounces) chili-style chunky tomatoes, undrained
2	cans (15 ounces each) black beans, rinsed, drained
1–2	chipotle chilies in adobo sauce, chopped
1	cup water, *or* vegetable broth
	Salt, to taste

1. Saute pepper blend, garlic, gingerroot, and cumin seeds in oil in large saucepan until tender, about 5 minutes.

2. Add remaining ingredients, except salt, to saucepan; heat to boiling. Reduce heat and simmer, covered, until sweet potatoes are tender, about 15 minutes. Season to taste with salt.

ARTICHOKE TORTELLINI BAKE

Refrigerated fresh tortellini and ravioli are convenient to have on hand for speedy meal preparation—use any favorite kind in this dish.

4 servings
Prep/Bake Time: 30 minutes

1	package (9 ounces) mozzarella-garlic tortellini
	Vegetable cooking spray
2	cups (4 ounces) sliced mushrooms
1	small onion, sliced
1	teaspoon minced garlic
2	tablespoons flour
1	cup fat-free milk
	Salt and cayenne pepper, to taste
1	can (14 ounces) artichoke hearts, drained
1/2–1	cup (2–4 ounces) shredded reduced-fat Italian 6-cheese blend, divided
1–2	tablespoons seasoned dry bread crumbs

Per Serving
Calories: 267
% Calories from fat: 21
Fat (gm): 6.4
Saturated fat (gm): 3.4
Cholesterol (mg): 29.1
Sodium (mg): 523
Protein (gm): 16.9
Carbohydrate (gm): 37.4
Exchanges
Milk: 0.0
Vegetable: 1.0
Fruit: 0.0
Bread: 2.0
Meat: 1.0
Fat: 0.5

1. Cook tortellini according to package directions.

2. Spray large saucepan with cooking spray; heat over medium heat until hot. Saute mushrooms, onion, and garlic until tender, about 5 minutes. Stir in flour; cook 1 to 2 minutes. Add milk and heat to boiling; boil, stirring constantly, until thickened, 1 to 2 minutes. Season to taste with salt and cayenne pepper.

3. Stir in artichokes, tortellini, and all but 2 tablespoons of the cheese. Pour into greased 1 1/2-quart casserole; sprinkle with bread crumbs and remaining 2 tablespoons cheese.

4. Bake at 375 degrees until bubbly and browned on the top, about 15 minutes.

DUTCH PANCAKE WITH SPICED FRUIT MÉLANGE

A spectacular brunch or lunch entrée that will win raves!

4 servings
Prep/Bake Time: 30 minutes

Dutch Pancake (recipe follows)
Vegetable cooking spray
3 medium tart cooking apples, unpeeled, cored, sliced
1 cup mixed dried fruit
¼ cup dried cranberries, *or* cherries
¼ cup sugar
½ cup orange juice
1 teaspoon ground cinnamon
Maple syrup, warm

Per Serving
Calories: 465
% Calories from fat: 17
Fat (gm): 9.1
Saturated fat (gm): 2.1
Cholesterol (mg): 106.8
Sodium (mg): 321
Protein (gm): 11.7
Carbohydrate (gm): 88.4
Exchanges
Milk: 0.0
Vegetable: 0.0
Fruit: 3.0
Bread: 3.0
Meat: 0.0
Fat: 1.5

1. Make Dutch Pancake.

2. Spray large skillet with cooking spray; heat over medium heat until hot. Add apples to skillet and cook 2 to 3 minutes. Add remaining ingredients, except maple syrup, and cook, covered, over medium heat until apples are just tender, 8 to 10 minutes. Heat to boiling and cook, uncovered, until liquid is syrupy, 2 to 3 minutes.

3. Spoon fruit mixture into hot Dutch Pancake; cut into wedges and serve with maple syrup.

Dutch Pancake

2 eggs
½ cup no-cholesterol real egg product, *or* 4 egg whites
¾ cup non-fat milk
¾ cup all-purpose flour
1 tablespoon sugar
¼ teaspoon salt
2 tablespoons margarine, *or* butter

1. Whisk all ingredients, except margarine, in large bowl until almost smooth (batter will be slightly lumpy).

2. Heat margarine in large skillet with ovenproof handle until melted and bubbly; pour in batter. Bake, uncovered, at 425 degrees until pancake is puffed and browned, 20 to 25 minutes (do not open door during first 15 minutes). Serve warm.

EGGS AND MUSHROOMS À LA KING

A brunch or light supper favorite that's fast and easy to make. For a special touch, add 1 to 2 tablespoons of dry sherry to the sauce.

4 servings
Prep/Cook Time: 30 minutes

2 cups sliced cremini mushrooms
½ cup chopped onion
1-2 tablespoons margarine, *or* butter
¼ cup all-purpose flour
½ teaspoon dried thyme leaves
3 cups fat-free milk
4 hard-cooked eggs, chopped
Salt and pepper, to taste
4 English muffins, split, toasted, *or* waffles
2-4 tablespoons imitation bacon bits

Per Serving
Calories: 355
% Calories from fat: 26
Fat (gm): 10.2
Saturated fat (gm): 2.6
Cholesterol (mg): 216.2
Sodium (mg): 520
Protein (gm): 20.5
Carbohydrate (gm): 44.5
Exchanges
Milk: 1.0
Vegetable: 0.0
Fruit: 0.0
Bread: 2.0
Meat: 1.0
Fat: 1.5

1. Saute mushrooms and onion in margarine until onion is tender and mushrooms are beginning to brown, 8 to 10 minutes. Sprinkle with flour and thyme; cook 1 to 2 minutes longer. Stir in milk and heat to boiling; boil, stirring, until thickened, about 1 minute.

2. Reduce heat and stir in eggs; season to taste with salt and pepper. Serve over English muffins; sprinkle with bacon bits.

PORTOBELLO MONTE CRISTO GRILL

A fabulous sandwich, dipped in egg batter and grilled to golden goodness.

4 servings
Prep/Cook Time: 20 minutes

4 large portobello mushrooms, stems removed
2 tablespoons olive oil
1 teaspoon Italian seasoning
Salt and pepper, to taste
8 slices sourdough bread, divided
1 roasted red pepper, cut into 1-inch strips
3-4 ounces fat-free feta cheese, sliced
1 egg
1/4 cup fat-free milk

Per Serving
Calories: 252
% Calories from fat: 34
Fat (gm): 9.6
Saturated fat (gm): 1.6
Cholesterol (mg): 63.4
Sodium (mg): 674
Protein (gm): 11.7
Carbohydrate (gm): 30.2
Exchanges
Milk: 0.0
Vegetable: 0.0
Fruit: 0.0
Bread: 2.0
Meat: 1.0
Fat: 1.0

1. Saute mushrooms in oil in large skillet just until tender, 5 to 8 minutes, turning once. Sprinkle mushrooms with Italian seasoning and salt and pepper to taste.

2. Place mushrooms on 4 slices of bread; top with roasted red pepper, feta cheese, and remaining bread slices. Beat egg and milk together in pie plate. Dip sandwiches in egg mixture, and then grill in greased skillet over medium heat until browned on both sides.

CURRIED SWEET POTATO COUSCOUS

Versatile couscous blends easily with a variety of vegetable flavors.

4 servings
Prep/Cook Time: 20 minutes

1/4 cup sliced onion
2 cloves garlic, minced
1-2 tablespoons olive oil
2 medium sweet potatoes, cooked, diced
1-1 1/2 teaspoons curry powder
1/4 cup raisins
1 cup reduced-sodium vegetable broth
2/3 cup couscous

Per Serving
Calories: 317
% Calories from fat: 25
Fat (gm): 9
Saturated fat (gm): 1
Cholesterol (mg): 0
Sodium (mg): 136
Protein (gm): 7.5
Carbohydrate (gm): 53.3
Exchanges
Milk: 0.0
Vegetable: 0.0
Fruit: 0.0
Bread: 3.0
Meat: 0.0
Fat: 2.0

1 cup thinly sliced kale
Salt and pepper, to taste
4 tablespoons chopped walnuts

1. Saute onion and garlic in olive oil in large saucepan until tender, 2 to 3 minutes. Stir in sweet potatoes; cook over medium heat until potatoes are lightly browned, about 5 minutes. Stir in curry powder, raisins, and broth; heat to boiling. Add couscous and kale, stirring with a fork.

2. Remove from heat and let stand, covered, until couscous is tender and broth is absorbed, about 5 minutes. Season to taste with salt and pepper. Sprinkle each serving with walnuts.

BARLEY AND VEGETABLE MÉLANGE

Topped with an egg, this hearty dish is perfect for any meal.

4 servings
Prep/Cook Time: 30 minutes

Per Serving
Calories: 265
% Calories from fat: 27
Fat (gm): 8.4
Saturated fat (gm): 2.1
Cholesterol (mg): 211.1
Sodium (mg): 517
Protein (gm): 12.6
Carbohydrate (gm): 37.4
Exchanges
Milk: 0.0
Vegetable: 1.0
Fruit: 0.0
Bread: 2.0
Meat: 1.0
Fat: 1.0

3 cups reduced-sodium vegetable broth, *or* water
1 cup quick-cooking barley
Vegetable cooking spray
1/3 cup sliced green onions and tops
1 cup sliced mushrooms
2 cloves garlic, minced
1 large zucchini, diced
2 cup halved cherry tomatoes
Salt and pepper, to taste
4 fried, *or* poached, eggs

1. Heat vegetable broth to boiling in medium saucepan; stir in barley. Reduce heat and simmer, covered, until barley is tender, 10 to 12 minutes. Remove from heat and let stand 5 minutes.

2. Spray large skillet with cooking spray; heat over medium heat until hot. Add onions, mushrooms, and garlic and saute until tender, about 5 minutes. Add zucchini and tomatoes; saute until zucchini is lightly browned, 5 to 8 minutes.

3. Add barley to skillet, stirring to combine; season to taste with salt and pepper. Top each serving with an egg.

ITALIAN "MEATBALLS" WITH POLENTA

Keep soy "meatballs" in your freezer for cooking convenience. They cook quickly and can be used for many great dishes.

4 servings
Prep/Cook Time: 20 minutes

Per Serving
Calories: 273
% Calories from fat: 21
Fat (gm): 6.5
Saturated fat (gm): 2
Cholesterol (mg): 3.9
Sodium (mg): 1412
Protein (gm): 18
Carbohydrate (gm): 37.7
Exchanges
Milk: 0.0
Vegetable: 1.0
Fruit: 0.0
Bread: 2.0
Meat: 2.0
Fat: 0.0

1	package (12 ounces) frozen soy "meatballs"
1	can (28 ounces) Italian-seasoned diced tomatoes, undrained
1	tablespoon minced roasted garlic
	Polenta (see p. 579)
1/4-1/2	cup shredded Parmesan cheese

1. Heat frozen "meatballs," tomatoes and liquid, and garlic to boiling in large skillet; reduce heat and simmer until "meatballs" are hot through, 8 to 10 minutes. Simmer, uncovered, until tomato mixture is thickened to a medium consistency, about 10 minutes.

2. While "meatballs" are cooking, make Polenta. Serve "meatballs" and tomatoes over Polenta. Sprinkle each serving with 1 to 2 tablespoons cheese.

GREAT GREEK SALAD

Tofu adds a healthy twist to this classic salad. Fresh herbs lend a flavor accent.

4 servings
Prep/Cook Time: 20 minutes

Per Serving
Calories: 102
% Calories from fat: 23
Fat (gm): 2.7
Saturated fat (gm): 0.6
Cholesterol (mg): 53.1
Sodium (mg): 774
Protein (gm): 9.3
Carbohydrate (gm): 10.6
Exchanges
Milk: 0.0
Vegetable: 2.0
Fruit: 0.0
Bread: 0.0
Meat: 1.0
Fat: 0.0

1	package (10 ounces) light extra-firm tofu, cut into 1/2-inch cubes
1	cup sliced, seeded cucumber
1/3	cup thinly sliced red onion
1/4	cup sliced sun-dried tomatoes (not oil packed), softened
1/2	cup fat-free Italian, *or* vinaigrette, dressing
2-3	tablespoons chopped fresh, *or* 1 tablespoon dried, oregano, *or* basil leaves

¼ cup chopped parsley
4 cups sliced romaine lettuce
¼ cup crumbled fat-free feta cheese
8 pitted Kalamata olives, halved
1 hard-cooked egg, sliced

1. Combine tofu, cucumber, onion, tomatoes, dressing, and herbs in large bowl; toss well. Add lettuce and toss. Spoon onto salad plates; top with remaining ingredients.

CURRIED TOFU AND VEGETABLES

Serve this quick curry with basmati rice or crusty bread.

4 servings
Prep/Cook Time: 30 minutes

¼ cup chopped onion
2-3 teaspoons finely chopped gingerroot
1 tablespoon canola oil
1 tablespoon curry powder
1 teaspoon ground cumin
1 small eggplant, cut into ½-inch cubes
2 cups cubed, peeled winter squash, *or* sweet potato (½-inch cubes)
1½ cups cut (1-inch) green beans
1 cup canned reduced-sodium vegetable broth
1 package (10 ounces) light firm tofu, cubed
   Salt and pepper, to taste
¼ cup shredded unsweetened coconut

Per Serving
Calories: 159
% Calories from fat: 30
Fat (gm): 5.8
Saturated fat (gm): 1.4
Cholesterol (mg): 0
Sodium (mg): 185
Protein (gm): 8.3
Carbohydrate (gm): 21.9
Exchanges
Milk: 0.0
Vegetable: 1.0
Fruit: 0.0
Bread: 1.0
Meat: 1.0
Fat: 0.0

1. Saute onion and ginger in oil in large saucepan 2 minutes; add curry powder and cumin and saute 2 to 3 minutes longer.

2. Add eggplant and squash; saute until lightly browned, about 5 minutes. Stir in green beans and broth. Heat to boiling; reduce heat and simmer, covered, until vegetables are tender, about 15 minutes. Stir in tofu; heat until hot through. Season to taste with salt and pepper. Spoon into serving bowl and sprinkle with coconut.

WHITE BEAN MASHERS WITH SAUTEED VEGETABLES

 A quick and delicious dinner. Substitute cannellini or lima beans for the Great Northern, if you prefer.

6 servings
Prep/Cook Time: 30 minutes

Per Serving
Calories: 145
% Calories from fat: 20
Fat (gm): 3.3
Saturated fat (gm): 0.9
Cholesterol (mg): 2.1
Sodium (mg): 218
Protein (gm): 8.1
Carbohydrate (gm): 24.9
Exchanges
Milk: 0.0
Vegetable: 2.0
Fruit: 0.0
Bread: 1.0
Meat: 0.0
Fat: 0.5

1½ pounds Idaho potatoes (4 medium), peeled, cubed
4 large cloves garlic, peeled
1 can (15 ounces) Great Northern beans, rinsed, drained
8 ounces sliced portobello mushrooms
1 cup small broccoli florets
2 green onions, sliced
1 tablespoon margarine, *or* butter
Salt and pepper, to taste
3-4 tablespoons fat-free milk
3-4 tablespoons shredded Parmesan cheese

1. Place potatoes and garlic in medium saucepan with water to cover; heat to boiling. Reduce heat and simmer, covered, 10 minutes. Add beans and simmer until potatoes are tender, about 10 minutes. Drain.

2. While potatoes are cooking, saute mushrooms, broccoli, and green onions in margarine in large skillet until tender and browned, about 8 minutes. Season to taste with salt and pepper.

3. Mash potato mixture with electric mixer or potato masher, adding milk, cheese, and salt and pepper to taste. Spoon onto serving platter. Spoon sauteed vegetables over.

SPICY GRITS WITH BLACKEYE SALSA

Try these spicy grits with habanero or serrrano chilies if you want to increase the heat! Be sure to make the Blackeye Salsa first so flavors can blend while you make the grits.

4 servings
Prep/Cook Time: 25 minutes

2	cups water
1-2	tablespoons chopped jalapeño chili
¹/₂	teaspoon ground cumin
¹/₂	teaspoon salt
²/₃	cup quick-cooking grits
1	cup (4 ounces) shredded reduced-fat Monterey Jack cheese
¹/₂	can (15-ounce size) black-eyed peas, rinsed, drained, coarsely chopped
	Blackeye Salsa (recipe follows)

Per Serving
Calories: 258
% Calories from fat: 22
Fat (gm): 5.6
Saturated fat (gm): 4.1
Cholesterol (mg): 20
Sodium (mg): 1007
Protein (gm): 14.8
Carbohydrate (gm): 36.8
Exchanges
Milk: 0.0
Vegetable: 1.0
Fruit: 0.0
Bread: 2.0
Meat: 1.0
Fat: 1.0

1. Combine water, jalapeño chili, cumin, and salt in medium saucepan; heat to boiling. Gradually stir in grits; reduce heat and simmer, stirring occasionally until thickened, about 5 minutes. Add cheese and black-eyed peas, stirring until cheese is melted. Spoon onto plates; top with Blackeye Salsa.

Blackeye Salsa

(makes about 1³/₄ cups)

¹/₂	can (15-ounce size) black-eyed peas, rinsed, drained, coarsely chopped
1	cup chopped tomatoes
¹/₄	cup chopped green onions and tops
1-2	teaspoons minced jalapeño chili
1	tablespoon lime juice
¹/₂	teaspoon ground cumin
¹/₂	teaspoon salt

1. Combine all ingredients in small bowl.

EL PASO SUCCOTASH

Delicious served over rice or with warm corn bread.

4 servings
Prep/Cook Time: 20 minutes

Per Serving	

Calories: 280
% Calories from fat: 12
Fat (gm): 3.9
Saturated fat (gm): 0.8
Cholesterol (mg): 1.2
Sodium (mg): 484
Protein (gm): 15.2
Carbohydrate (gm): 48.8

Exchanges
Milk: 0.0
Vegetable: 0.0
Fruit: 0.0
Bread: 3.0
Meat: 1.0
Fat: 0.0

- 1/2 cup chopped onion
- 1/2 cup chopped poblano chili, *or* green bell pepper
- 1 teaspoon minced jalapeño chili
- 1 teaspoon minced garlic
- 2 teaspoons chili powder
- 1 teaspoon ground cumin
- 1 tablespoon margarine, *or* butter
- 1 tablespoon flour
- 1 cup fat-free milk
- 1 can (15 ounces) lima beans, rinsed, drained
- 1 can (15 ounces) black-eyed peas, *or* red beans, rinsed, drained
- 1 cup frozen whole-kernel corn
  Salt and pepper, to taste
- 1 medium tomato, chopped
- 2 tablespoons chopped cilantro
- 2-3 teaspoons lime juice

1. Saute onion, chilies, garlic, chili powder, and cumin in margarine in large saucepan until tender, about 5 minutes. Stir in flour and cook 1 minute. Stir in milk; heat to boiling, stirring until thickened, about 1 minute.

2. Stir in beans and corn; heat to simmering. Season to taste with salt and pepper. Stir in remaining ingredients.

INDEX

A

Achiote Oil, 259
Acorn Squash
   Apple-Pecan, 618
   "Sausage" Stuffed, 217
   Tofu, Grilled, 288
Adzuki Bean Pastitsio, 517
Adzuki Bean Stir-Fry, 533
African Fava Patties with Yogurt-Cucumber
      Sauce, 47
Aioli, Tofu, 224
Alfredo Sauce, 711
Alsatian Peasant Soup, 129
Ancho Chili Stew, Mexican, 157
Angel Hair and Goat's Cheese Salad, 647
Anise-Almond Biscotti, 787
Antipasto Pizza, 435
Appetizers
   Baklava, Curried Onion, 470
   Bread, Artichoke-Stuffed, 39
   Bruschetta, Fava Bean, 510
   Bruschetta, Mushroom, 41
   Calzones, 51
   Cheese and Spinach Squares, 42
   Chili Bonzos, 3
   Croustades, Curried Onion, 38
   Dips and Spreads
      Artichoke Dip, Baked, 7
      Artichoke Pâté, 22
      Bean Dip, Mexican, 10
      Cheese Spread, Chutney, 26
      Chili con Queso, 12
      Curry Dip, 8
      Eggrolls, Mixed Vegetable, 46
      Eggplant Caviar, 20
      Eggplant Marmalade, 25
      Fava Bean Spread, 510
      Garlic and Herb Cannellini Dip,
         Roasted 18
      Garlic and Three-Cheese Spread,
         Roasted, 37
      Guacamole, 2
      Hummus, Black Bean, 20
      Hummus, Spicy Orange, 19
      Hummus, Sun-Dried Tomato, 18
      "Liver," Faux Chopped, 24
      Mushroom Spread, Garden, 23
      Onion Dip, Toasted, 6
      Pâté, Pine Nut Spinach, 15
      Pâté, Wild Mushroom, 16
      Pinto Bean and Avocado Dip, 11
      Queso Fundido, 13
      Salsa, Green Tomato, 8
      Salsa, Red Tomato, 9
      Sombrero Dip, 14
      Soy Bean and Vegetable Spread, 17
   Empanadas, Fruit, 34
   Fava Patties with Yogurt-Cucumber
      Sauce, African, 47
   Focaccia, Onion and Blue Cheese, 51
   Fruit Nuggets, 5
   Gorp, By Golly, 2
   Hot Stuff!, 48
   Jicama with Lime and Cilantro, 33
   Mushrooms Stuffed with Orzo, 37
   Nachos, 32
   Pinwheels, Curried, 40
   Pita Chips, 53
   Plantains, Fried Ripe, 33
   Pot Stickers, Five-Spice, 44
   Quesadillas, 30
      Black Bean, 29
      Goat's Cheese with Tropical Fruit
         Salsa, 28
   Quiches, Spinach and Cheese, Mini-, 42
   Shells with Spinach Pesto, Ricotta
      Stuffed, 35
   Spinach Balls, Baked, 43
   Strudels, Apple-Cabbage, 50
   Tofu Satay, Indonesian-Style, 48
   Tortellini Kabobs with Many-Cloves
      Garlic Sauce, 49
   Tortilla Chips, Baked, 55
   Tortilla Wedges, 31
   Vegetables, Stuffed, 36
   Veggie Crisps, 4
Apple
   -Cabbage Strudels, 50
   -Cranberry Crisp, 796
   Cranberry Relish, 376
   -Date Filling, 683
   Honey Kuchen, 663
   -Mint Jelly, 697
   Pie, Double Crust, 762
   Pudding, Brown Sugar, 810
   Salad Pizza, 449
Apricot Custard, Fresh, 812
Apricot-Sesame Biscotti, 788
Artichoke(s)
   Braised Whole, 584
   Dip, Baked, 7
   with Hollandaise Sauce, 584
   Lasagne, 365
   and Mushroom Soup, Cream of, 83
   Pâté, 22
   Pie, 464

Ravioli with Tarragon Sauce, 347
and Roasted Pepper Pizza, 431
Sauce, 713
Spaghetti Squash with Roasted Tomato-Herb Sauce and, 282
-Stuffed Appetizer Bread, 39
Tortellini Bake, 829
Asian Fried Rice, 558
Asian-Style Noodle Salad, 651
Asparagus
  with Lemon-Wine Sauce, 585
  with Peanut Sauce, 586
  Stir-Fry, Sesame, 825
  and White Beans, Italian-Style, 822
  Wine-Glazed Ravioli and, 820
Avocado Dip, Pinto Bean and, 11
Avocado Sour Cream, 71

B

Baked Alaska, Chocolate, 803
Baked Beans (*see* Beans and Legumes)
Bakers, Veggie Stuffed, 613
Baklava, Curried Onion, 470
Balsamic Dressing, 544
Banana(s)
  Bread, Brown Sugar, 680
  Cinnamon Cake, 750
  Foster, 798
  -Strawberry Cream Pie, 766
Barbecued Tempeh and Peppers, 215
Barley
  Bowl, Wheat and, 549
  with Peppers and Potatoes, 548
  -Vegetable Chowder, 546
Basil Dressing, Fresh, 343
Basil Soup, Fresh, 83
Batter Bread, Multigrain, 668
Beans and Legumes (*also see* Salads, Sandwiches and Patties, Soups, and Stews)
  Adzuki, Stir-Fry, 533
  Asparagus and White, Italian-Style, 822
  Baked
    Ginger, 520
    New England, 519
    Pot, Just Peachy, 521
    Santa Fe, 522
    Tuscan, Bake, 523
  Black, and Jalapeño Pizza, 441
  Black-Eyed Peas and Greens with Millet, 551
  Black-Eyed Pea and Lentil Soup, Easiest, 512
  Bruschetta, Fava, 510
  Butter, and Sprouts Stir-Fry, 532
  Cannellini Dip, Roasted Garlic and Herb, 18
  and Cheese Chiles Rellenos, 499
  Cheesecake with Salsa, Black, 500
  Chili
    Bonzos, 3
    Sweet Potato, Chipotle, 828
    Yellow and White, 514

and Cornbread Loaf, 384
Curry Stew, Eggplant and, 518
Fava Patties with Yogurt-Cucumber Sauce, African, 67
and Fillo, Moroccan Style, 471
and Fruit, Roasted Vegetables with, 278
Gazpacho, 73
Fava Spread, 510
and Greens, Stir-Fried, 531
Gumbo, Black, and Okra, 150
Hopping John, 529
Hummus
  Black, 20
  Spicy Orange, 19
  Sun-Dried Tomato, 18
Lentils
  Fried, 524
  Ravioli with Gingered Tomato Relish, 235
  Salad with Feta Cheese, 543
  "Liver," Faux Chopped, 24
Loaf Baked in Fillo, Spinach and, 371
Mashed, Seasoned Black, 524
Mashers with Sauteed Vegetables, White, 836
"Meatballs," Black, 535
Mexi-Beans, Greens, and Rice, 527
Pasta, Mean, 535
and Pasta Salad with White Bean Dressing, 536
Pasta, White, and Red Cabbage Salad, 537
Pastitsio, Adzuki, 517
Pinto, and Avocado Dip, 11
Pot, Just Peachy, 521
Quesadilla, Black, 29
Red, and Rice, Bourbon Street, 528
Refried, 525
and Rice, Black, 526
Rotini and Beans Niçoise, 326
Salads
  Lentil, with Feta Cheese, 543
  and Pasta Salad with White Bean Dressing, 536
  and Rice, Black, 542
  and Smoked Tofu, Black 541
  White, Pasta and Red Cabbage, 537
Sauce with Tomatoes and Sage, Peasant, 706
Soups
  Black-Eyed Pea and Lentil, Easiest, 512
  Chili, Black and White, 153
  Chili, Yellow and White, 514
  Classic, Black, 127
  Curried, 513
  Gazpacho, 73
  Lima, Garlicky, 511
  Navy, 132
  with Sun-Dried Tomatoes and Cilantro Cream, Black, 134
  and Vegetable Soup, Four-, 130
Soybean and Vegetable Spread, 17
Soybeans and Potatoes, Curried, 534

Stews
  Eggplant and, Curry, 518
  with Fusilli, Spiced, 167
  and Squash Stew, 148
  Texas, with Chili-Cheese Dumplings,
    515
  Winter, and Vegetable, 516
  Vegetable, Thickened, 142
  and Vegetable, Hot 'n Spicy, 153
  and Vegetable, Very Quick, 819
  and Vegetable, Winter, 516
  and Vegetables, Italian-Style, 530
  Succotash, El Paso, 838
  Tomato and Bread Salad, 538
  with Tomatoes and Sage, Peasant, 706
  Tortellini with Beans and Squash,
    Curried, 331
  Tostados, Picante Black, 406
Beet(s)
  Borscht, 84
  Dijon, 588
  Harvard, 589
  Honey-Roasted, 589
  Puree, Grilled, 294
  Soup, Dilled, 66
Berry
  Cheesecake, Spring, 773
  Rhubarb, Fresh, 790
  Soup, Very, 64
Biscotti (*see* Cookies)
Biscuits (*see* Breads)
Black-Eyed Pea and Lentil Soup, Easiest,
  512
Black-Eyed Peas and Greens with Millet,
  551
Blue Cheese
  Dressing, 642
  and Pear Melt, 412
  Polenta, 580
Blueberry
  Bread Pudding with Tart Lemon Sauce,
    808
  Maple Syrup, 691
  Pancakes with Blueberry Maple Syrup,
    690
Bolillos, 671
Bolognese-Style "Meat" Sauce, 704
Boston Cream Cake, 748
Bread(s)
  Artichoke-Stuffed Appetizer, 39
  Banana, Brown Sugar, 680
  Biscuits
    Chive, 685
    "Little Pants," 686
    Parmesan, 685
    Quick Self-Rising, 685
    Sweet Potato, 686
    Vinegar, 684
  Bolillos, 671
  Braids, Sweet Potato, 659
  Bran, Fruited, 679
  Bruschetta, 54
  Buns, Sticky, 664
  Coffeecake, Cranberry, 683

Coffeecake with Apple-Date Filling,
    Sour Cream, 682
  Cornbread, Green Chili, 678
  Cornbread, Roasted Chili, 305
  Cranberry-Nut Wheat Loaf, 660
  Crepes, 692
  Crepes, Dessert, 692
  Crescents, Orange Marmalade, 662
  Croustades, 55
  Croutons, 677
    Herb, 677
    Italian-Style, 677
    Parmesan, 677
    Rye-Caraway, 677
    Sesame, 677
    Sourdough, 677
  Dumplings, Chili Cheese, 516
  Dumplings, Herb, 146, 548
  English Muffin, 666
  Flatbread, Spinach-Mushroom, 674
  Focaccia, 673
    Fruit, 451
    Leek and Onion, 451
    Onion and Blue Cheese, 51
  French Toast, Stuffed, 693
  Garlic, 676
  Granola, 665
  Kuchen, Apple Honey, 663
  Lavosh, Easy Herb, 53
  Lavosh, Whole Wheat, 673
  Lima Bean Wheat, 658
  Loaf, Bubble, 667
  Mint and Citrus Tea, 681
  Muffins
    Cardamom-Pear, 688
    High Energy, 689
    Wild Rice, 687
  Multigrain Batter, 668
  Pancakes
    Buttermilk Buckwheat, 691
    with Blueberry Maple Syrup,
      Blueberry, 690
    Dutch, with Spiced Fruit Mélange,
      830
    Mandarin, 246
  Parmesan Garlic, 676
  Pastry Dough, Galette, 473
  Peasant, 655
  Pita, 672
  Pizza Dough
    Basic, 418
    Cheese, 420
    Cornmeal, 418
    Whole Wheat, 419
  Pretzels, Soft, 669
  Pudding(s) (*see* Desserts)
  Raisin, 667
  Roasted Red Pepper 657
  Rolls, Cinnamon, 665
  Rolls, Squash Dinner, 670
  -Rye, Hearty Vegetable, 656
  Tamale Dough, 258
  Three-Grain Molasses, 679
  Three Kings, 661

Broccoli
Rabe Sauteed with Garlic, 591
and Cheese Rotoli with Many-Cloves
Garlic Sauce, 188
Herb-Crumbed, 590
and Mushroom Pizza, Smoky, 444
and Pasta Soup, Herbed, 86
and "Sausage" Risotto, 564
Soup, Cream of, 85
Terrine with Lemon Herb Mayonnaise,
369
Salad with Sour Cream-Mayonnaise
Dressing, 631
Bruschetta, 54
Fava Bean, 510
Mushroom, 41
Brussels Sprouts
Bucatini with, and walnuts, 340
Fettuccine with, and Fresh Fennel, 820
and Gnocchi Salad, 314
and Pearl Onions, Sugar-Glazed, 591
"Burgers" (*see* Sandwiches)
Burritos, Breakfast, 495
Burritos with Poblano Chili Sauce,
Vegetarian, 250
Butter Bean and Sprouts Stir-Fry, 532
Buttermilk Pie, Old Fashioned, 764

C
Cabbage
with Chili Tomato Sauce, Stuffed, 229
-Fennel Strudel, 226
and Potato Hash, 230
with Quinoa, Sweet Spiced, 205
Ragout with Real Mashed Potatoes, 147
and Sauerkraut Casserole, 204
Soup, Roasted, 87
Wine-Braised, 592
Cactus Salad, 639
Caesar Salad, 627
Cajun Eggplant, 294
Cajun Seasoning, 295
Cake(s)
Banana Cinnamon, 750
Boston Cream, 748
Carrot, with Cream Cheese Frosting,
745
Cassata Siciliana, 755
Chiffon, Glazed Orange, 739
Cheesecakes
Chocolate Fillo, 776
Lemon Meringue, 775
New York-Style, 774
Spring Berry, 773
Chocolate
Buttermilk, with Mocha Frosting, 740
Cherry Pudding, 744
Coffee-Frosted Cocoa, 743
Flourless, 741
Ice Cream Jelly Roll, 806
Jelly Roll, Easy Cake Mix, 806
Jelly Roll, Ice Cream, 805
Orange Poppy Seed, 752
Pineapple Upside Down, 747
Pound Cake, Lemon, 751

Pumpkin-Ginger, with Warm Rum
Sauce, 749
Raspberry-Orange Swirl, 753
Rhubarb Streusel, Mom's, 738
Rolls, Frozen Peppermint, 804
Shortcake, Strawberry-Kiwi, 794
Spice, with Penuche Frosting, 746
Calzones, 51
Cheese and Mushroom, 453
"Sausage," 452
Cannellini
and Cabbage Soup, 135
Casserole, 191
Patties with Fresh Tomato Relish, 397
Capellini Carbonara, Molded, 350
Caponata Pizza, Roasted, 433
Caramel Apple Slices, 791
Caramel Flan, 813
Caraway Dressing, 538
Cardamom Crisps, 780
Cardamom-Pear Muffins, 688
Caribbean
Ginger Bean Stew, 162
Potato Salad, 634
Sweet and Sour Stew, 160
Carrot(s)
Cake with Cream Cheese Frosting, 745
Orange-Glazed Baby, 594
Pudding, 594
Puree, Gingered, 593
-Raisin Salad, 632
Soup, Dilled, 88
Cassata Siciliana, 756
Casseroles
Acorn Squash with Tofu, Grilled, 288
Artichoke Tortellini Bake, 829
Baked Beans (*see* Beans)
Cabbage, Mediterranean, 489
Cabbage and Sauerkraut, 204
Cannelloni, 191
Capellini Carbonara, Molded, 350
Chiliquiles, 182
Eggplant
Baked in Eggplant, 202
Lasagne, 187
Parmesan, and Spaghetti, 190
Provençal, 194
Ragout, Baked, 201
Soufflé, 196
and Tomato, 601
and Tomato Sauce Parmesan, 192
and Zucchini, 197
Enchilada Stack, 181
Fusilli and Cheese Primavera, 184
Goulash, 203
Grain and Vegetable, Mexican-Style, 552
Grain and Veggie, Mixed, 176
Green Bean, 588
Kugel, Potato, 493
Lasagne
Artichoke, 365
Eggplant, 187
with Eggplant Sauce, Veggie, 185
"Mexican-Style," 179
Roasted Red Pepper and Spinach, 363

"Sausage," 186
Squash and Mushroom, 362
Macaroni and Cheese Primavera, 174
Manicotti with Creamed Spinach Sauce,
    Vegetable, 354
Manicotti, Mushroom-Broccoli, 355
"Meatball," Mexican 180
"Meatball" and Dilled Potato, Swedish,
    206
Mexican-Style Grain and Vegetable, 552
Moussaka, Vegetable-Barley, 193
Noodles Florentine, 491
Pasta Bake, Spinach, 177
Pastitsio, 200
Pastitsio, Adjuki Bean, 517
Potatoes, Gratin, 611
Potatoes, Scalloped, 612
Pudding
    Carrot, 594
    Corn, Fresh, 599
    Tomato, 622
Ratatouille, 195
of Roasted Vegetables and Beans, 279
Rotoli
    Broccoli and Cheese, with Many-
        Cloves Garlic Sauce, 188
    with Fresh Tomato Herb Sauce,
        Cheese and Vegetable, 356
    with Marinara Sauce, Spinach-
        Mushroom, 189
Shells Stuffed with Spinach and Tofu,
    353
Spaghetti and Eggplant Parmesan, 190
Spinach au Gratin, 617
Swedish "Meatball" and Dilled Potato,
    206
Sweet Potato Pone, 490
Terrine, Spring Vegetable, 487
Tetrazzini, Vegetarian, 183
Torta Rustica, 456
Vegetable and Mixed Rice, 178
Vegetable Puff, 485
Vegetables and Beans, Roasted, 279
Veggie Kugel, 492
Wild Rice, Cheese, and Vegetable,175
Yams, Candied, 615
Zucchini Fans Provençal, 618
Zucchini and Mushrooms Parmesan,
    199
Cauliflower
    with Creamy Cheese Sauce, 595
    -Fennel Puree, 596
    and Green Bean Loaf, Seasoned, 370
    Soup with Cheese, Cream of, 89
Celery Root Puree, 597
Cereal, Best Breakfast, 582
Cereal Pudding, Baked, 807
Chayote with Pumpkin Seeds, 621
Chayote Squash Soup with Cilantro
    Cream, 77
Cheese
    -cake with Salsa, Black Bean, 500
    Cheddar, Soufflé, 501
    Chiles Rellenos, Bean and, 499
    Chili con Queso, 12

Crepes, Spinach, 221
Fondue, 502
Fusilli and, Primavera, 184
Lasagne
    Artichoke, 365
    Eggplant, 187
    with Eggplant Sauce, Veggie, 185
    "Mexican-Style," 179
    Roasted Red Pepper and Spinach,
        363
    "Sausage," 186
    Squash and Mushroom, 362
Macaroni and, Primavera, 174
Melt
    Blue Cheese and Pear, 412
    Cranberry, 410
    Cucumber, 411
and Mushroom Calzones, 453
Nachos, 32
Pizza Dough, 420
Quesadillas, 30
    Black Bean, 29
    Goat's, with Tropical Fruit Salsa, 28
Queso Fundido, 13
Quiche
    Lorraine, 505
    Mini-, Spinach and, 42
    in Pepper Cups, 506
    Spinach, 506
Ricotta Stuffed Shells with Spinach
    Pesto, 35
Risotto, Two-, 827
Sandwiches
    Hoagies, Goat's Cheese, 409
    Melt
        Blue Cheese and Pear, 412
        Cranberry Cheese, 410
        Cucumber Cheese, 411
    Pinwheels, Swiss Cheese and
        Spinach, 414
Sauce(s)
    Alfredo, 711
    Creamy, 596
    Gorgonzola, 711
    Jalapeño con Queso, 725
    and Vegetable Rarebit, 504
    Welsh Rarebit, 503
Soufflé, Cheddar, 501
and Spinach Squares, 42
Spread, Chutney, 26
Spread, Roasted Garlic and Three, 37
-Stuffed Pasta Shells with Simple Tomato
    Sauce, 237
and Vegetable Rarebit, 504
and Vegetable Rotoli, with Fresh Tomato
    Herb, 356
Welsh Rarebit, 503
Wontons, Cranberry-, 45
Cheesecakes (*see under* Cakes)
Cherry Soup, Sweet, 64
Cherry-Berry Grunt, 796
Chicken Salad Sandwiches, Mock, 409
Chickpea and Pasta Soup, 137
Chiles Rellenos, Bean and Cheese,
    499

Chili
  Black and White Bean, 153
  Bonzos, 3
  sin Carne, 126
  -Cheese Dumplings, 516
  Dressing, 645
  Mac, 127
  Paste, 290
  Poblano Pizza, 442
  con Queso, 12
  Stew, 154
  Sweet Potato Chipotle, 828
  -Tomato Sauce, 179
Chiliquiles, 182
Chimichangas, 256
Chive Biscuits, 685
Chocolate
  Baked Alaska, 803
  Buttermilk Cake with Mocha Frosting, 740
  Cake, Flourless, 741
  -Cherry Pudding Cake, 744
  Chip Cookies, 777
  Fillo Cheesecake, 776
  Frosting, "Rich," 743
  Fudge Meringues, 784
  Glaze, 749
  Ice Cream Jelly Roll Cake, 806
  Pudding, "Rich," 806
  Rum Pie, 767
  Sauce, 756
  Sauce, Bittersweet, 794
  Shortbread Squares, Glazed, 779
Chop Suey, 241
Chopped "Liver," Faux 24
"Chorizo," 404
Chowder
  Barley-Vegetable, 546
  Hearty Corn and Potato, 92
  Potato, 106
  Roasted Corn and Potato, 262
Chutney Cheese Spread, 26
Cilantro
  Lime Dressing, 640
  Pesto, 730
  sour Cream, 77
Cincinnati Chili Sauce, 719
Cinnamon Streusel, 690
Cinnamon Rolls, 665
Citrus Glaze, 753
Citrus Vinaigrette, 540
Cocoa
  Brownies, Frosted, 782
  Frosting,782
  Glaze, 781
  -Glazed Cookie Crisps, 781
Coconut Cream Tart, Toasted, 767
Coffee Frosting, 744
Coffee-Frosted Cocoa Cake, 743
Coffeecake(s) (*see under* Breads)
Coleslaw, Freezer, 629
Coleslaw, Pasta, 630
Condiments
  Avocado Sour Cream, 72
  Cajun Seasoning, 295

Chili Paste, 290
Feta Cream, 395
Honey, Gingered, 698
Jam, Rhubarb, Spiced, 694
Jelly(ies)
  Apple-Mint, 697
  Ginger, Easy, 697
  Orange-Rosemary, 695
  Rose Geranium, 696
  Tarragon Wine, 696
Jerk Seasoning, 268
Maple Syrup, Blueberry, 691
Pear Butter, Spiced, 693
Relish(es)
  Apple-Cranberry, 376
  Fennel Goat's Cheese, 397
  Gremolata, 731
  Onion-Chutney, 555
  Pepper, Grilled, 281
  Tomato, Fresh, 398
Sour Sauce, 119
Cookies
  Biscotti
    Anise-Almond, 787
    Apricot-Sesame 788
  Brownies, Frosted Cocoa, 782
  Cardamom Crisps, 780
  Chocolate Chip, 777
  Crisps, Cocoa-Glazed, 781
  Fig and Pear Bars, 783
  Lemon Squares, Sugared, 783
  Macaroons, Hazelnut, 786
  Meringues
    Chocolate Fudge, 784
    Orange-Almond, 785
    Peppermint Clouds, 786
  Raisin-Oatmeal, 777
  Shortbread Squares, Glazed Chocolate, 779
  Sugar, Frosted, 778
Corn
  Fried, 598
  Mélange, Spiced, 212
  and Potato Chowder, Hearty, 92
  and Potato Chowder, Roasted, 262
  Pudding, Fresh, 599
  Soup, Creamed, 93
  Soup with Epazote, 94
  Tex-Mex Sweet, 599
Corn Bread Loaf, Bean and, 384
Corn Bread, Roasted Chili, 305
Cornmeal and Millet Mush, 581
Cornmeal Pizza Dough, 418
Couscous, Curried, 554
Couscous with Smoked Tofu, Fruited, 555
Cranberry
  Cheese Melt, 410
  Coffeecake, 683
  Coulis, 732
  -Cheese Wontons, 45
  -Nut Wheat Loaf, 660
Cream
  of Artichoke and Mushroom Soup, 83
  of Broccoli Soup, 85
  of Cauliflower Soup with Cheese, 89

Cheese Frosting, 745
Cheese Glaze, 683
of Mushroom Soup, 97
of Tomato Soup, 112
Creamed Corn Soup, 9
Creamed Vegetable Soup, Lightly, 11
Crème Anglaise, 772
Creole Sauce, 706
Creole Skillet Stew, Easy, 151
Crepes
Dessert, 692
Spinach Cheese, 221
Vegetable, 222
Croustades, 55
Croustades, Curried Onion, 38
Croutons
Herb, 677
Italian-Style, 677
Parmesan, 677
Rye-Caraway, 677
Sesame, 677
Sourdough, 677
Crust(s) (*see* Pie Crusts)
Cucumber
Cheese Melt, 422
and Sorrel Soup, 68
Soup, Herbed, 67
-Sour Cream Dressing, 571
Yogurt, 555
Curried
Bean Soup, 513
Coconut Soup, Vietnamese, 119
Couscous, 554
Onion Baklava, 470
Onion Croustades, 38
Pasta Salad, 646
Pasta and Vegetables, 332
Pinwheels, 40
Soybeans and Potatoes, 534
Stew, Mediterranean, 171
Sweet Potato Couscous, 832
Tofu and Vegetables, 835
Tortellini with Beans and Squash, 331
Vegetable and Coconut Stew,
Vietnamese, 165
Curry
Dip, 8
Sauce, 715
Vegetable, 233
Custard Brulée, Herbed, 815
Custard Topping, 194

D

Desserts (*also see* Cakes, Cookies, Fillings
and Toppings, Frostings and
Glazes, Pies, Puddings and
Custards, Sauces)
Apple Slices, Caramel, 791
Bananas Foster,798
Crisp, Apple-Cranberry, 796
Fruit Compote with Meringue Puffs,
Baked 797
Frozen,
Baked Alaska, Chocolate, 803
Baked Alaska, Orange, 803

Ice, Lemon, 800
Ice Pineapple-Champagne, 801
Sherbet, Orange-Pineapple, 799
Sorbet, Ginger-Citrus, 800
Sundaes, Praline, 798
Tortoni, Mixed Fruit, 802
Grunt, Cherry-Berry 796
Kabobs with Raspberry Sauce, Mixed
Fruit, 792
Melon Wedges, Honey-Lime, 789
Orange Compote, Spiced 788
Pears Belle Hélène, 793
Pineapple Slices, Honey-Broiled, 789
Plums, Wine-Poached, 791
Raspberry Soufflé, Chilled, 816
Rhubarb Crunch, Fran's, 795
Rhubarb, Fresh Berry, 790
Soufflé, Chilled Raspberry, 816
Soufflés, Peach-Allspice, 817
Dim Sum Platter with Stir-Fried Vegetables,
241
Dips and Spreads (*see under* Appetizers)
Dressing(s) (*see* Salad Dressings)
Dumplings, Chili-Cheese, 516
Dumplings, Herb, 146, 548

E

Egg(s)
Benedict, 478
Burritos, Breakfast, 495
Custard in Acorn Squash, Mushroom,
488
Frittata with Parmesan Toast, Vegetable,
483
Frittata, Pasta, 482
Hash
and, 479
Brown Loaf with, 480
with Poached, Sweet Potato, 480
Huevos Rancheros, 494
Kugel, Potato, 493
Kugel, Veggie, 492
and Mushrooms à la King, 831
Noodles Florentine, 491
Omelet Puff with Vegetable Mélange,
486
Piperade, 478
Pizza, Sausage and, 484
Quiche
Lorraine, 505
in Pepper Cups, 506
Spinach, 506
Spinach and Cheese, Mini-, 42
Rancheros with Black Beans and 2
Salsas, 494
Salad, Pasta, 481
Scrambled
with Cactus, 498
with "Chorizo," Mexican, 496
with Crisp Tortilla Strips, 497
Soufflé, Wild Rice, 578
Sweet Potato Pone, 490
Terrine, Spring Vegetable, 487
Vegetable Mélange 487
Vegetable Puff, 485

Egg Rolls, Mixed Vegetable, 46
Eggplant
    Baked in Eggplant, 202
    and Bean Curry Stew, 518
    Cajun, 294
    Casserole Soufflé, 196
    Caviar, 20
    in Eggplant Shells, Creamed, 220
    Filling, 360
    Lasagne, 187
    Loaf, Layered, 373
    Marmalade, 25
    Parmesan Sandwiches, 398
    with Pasta, Roasted, 273
    Polenta Stack, 826
    Provençal, 194
    Ragout, Baked, 201
    Ravioli, 360
    Sauce, 708
    Saute, Seasoned, 600
    Soup with Roasted Red Pepper Sauce,
        69
    and Tomato Casserole, 601
    and Tomato Sauce Parmesan, 192
    and Vegetable Saute, 211
    and Zucchini Casserole, 197
Empanada Pastry, 35
Empanadas, Fruit, 34
Enchilada
    Mole, 251
    Sauce, 720
    Stack, 181
    Vegetable, 252
English Muffin Bread, 666
Entrées (*also see* Casseroles, Cheese, Eggs,
        Beans and Legumes, Grains,
        Grilled and Roasted Dishes,
        Loaves, Pasta, Salads, Sandwiches
        and Patties, Soups, and Stews)
    Burritos with Poblano Chili Sauce,
        Vegetarian, 250
    Cabbage with Chili Tomato Sauce,
        Stuffed, 229
    Chimichangas, 256
    Chop Suey, 241
    Corn Mélange, Spiced, 212
    Crepes, Spinach Cheese, 221
    Crepes, Vegetable, 222
    Curry, Vegetable, 233
    Dim Sum Platter with Stir-Fried
        Vegetables, 241
    Enchiladas, Vegetable, 252
    Enchiladas Mole, 251
    5-Spice, 239
    Flautas with Tomatillo Sauce, 253
    Grapevine Leaves, Stuffed, 232
    Hash, Cabbage and Potato, 230
    Leek Cakes, Serbian, 227
    Loaf, Teem Seem, 243
    Niçoise Platter, 223
    Pasta Shells with Simple Tomato Sauce,
        Cheese- Stuffed, 237
    Portobello Mushrooms, Stuffed, 213
    Ravioli with Gingered Tomato Relish,
        Lentil, 235

"Sausage" Stuffed Acorn Squash, 217
Spaghetti Squash and Spaghetti, 210
Spaghetti Squash Stuffed with Vegetable
        Saute, 219
Stir-Fry(ied)
    Green on Green, with Tofu, 236
    Spring Vegetable, 238
    Szechuan Vegetable, 240
    Tempeh "Steak" with Red and
        Green, 247
Strudel
    Cabbage-Fennel, 226
    Leek and Mushroom, 225
    with Wild Mushroom Sauce,
        Vegetable, 224
Sweet Potato Cakes, 212
Tacos Picadillo, 248
Tacos with "Chorizo" and Potatoes,
        249
Tamales, Three-Chili, 257
Tamales with Beans, Veggie, 258
Tempeh
    Fajitas, 250
    Moo-Shu, 244
    Orange-Scented Vegetables with, 214
    and Peppers, Barbecued, 215
    Saute, and Garden Vegetable, 216
    "Steak" with Red and Green Stir-Fry,
        247
Tofu Ranchero, 259
Tomato Halves, Red and Yellow,
        Stuffed, 218
Tortellini and Vegetable Kabobs,
        Marinated, 234
Tostadas, Vegetable, 254
Vegetables Paprikash, 231

F
Fajitas
    Grilled Vegetable, 302
    Marinade, 256
    Tempeh, 255
Falafel "Burgers," 825
Farfalle with Roasted Eggplant and
        Squash, 345
Farfalle Salad with Minted Pesto, 645
Fava
    Bean Bruschetta, 510
    Bean Salad Platter, 544
    Bean Spread, 510
Fennel
    Calzones, Sweet, 455
    Fettuccine with Fresh, and Brussels
        Sprouts, 820
    Pesto, 728
    Puree, 602
    and Sun-Dried Tomato Pesto, Linguine
        with, 338
Feta Cream, 395
Feta Cheese and Sun-Dried Tomato
        Ravioli, 361
Fettuccine
    with Eggplant, Persillade, 328
    with Greens and Caramelized Onions,
        337

Primavera, Creamy 330
with Roasted Garlic, Onions, and
Peppers, 340
with Roasted Vegetable Sauce, 274
Fillings and Toppings
Apple-Date Filling, 683
Cinnamon Streusel, 690
Custard, 194
Eggplant, 360
Sticky Bun Topping, 665
Streusel, Crisp, 739
Streusel Topping, 796
Syrup, Lemon, 752
Five-Spice Stir-Fry, 239
Flan (*see under* Puddings and Custards)
Flautas with Tomatillo Sauce, 253
Focaccia, 673
Fruit, 451
Leek and Onion, 451
Onion and Blue Cheese, 51
Fondue, Cheese, 502
French
"Fries," Crispy, 614
"Fries," Parmesan, 614
"Fries," Steak, 614
-Style Onion Pizza, 430
Toast, Stuffed, 693
Fried Mush, 581
Fried Tomatoes, Sugar-Glazed, 624
Frittata with Parmesan Toast, Vegetable,
483
Frittata, Pasta, 482
Frostings and Glazes
Chocolate,"Rich," 743
Citrus, 753
Cocoa, 781
Coffee, 744
Cream Cheese, 683, 745
Mocha, 741
Orange, 739
Penuche, 746
Powdered Sugar, 751
Sugar, 778, 779
Vanilla, 690, 780
Fruit
Compote with Meringue Puffs, Baked,
797
Kabobs with Raspberry Sauce, Mixed, 792
Mélange, Dutch Pancake with Spiced,
830
Nuggets, 5
Tart, Rustic Country, 772
Tortoni, Mixed, 802
Fruited Bran Bread, 679
Fusilli with Fresh Tomatoes and Corn, 343
Fusilli and Cheese Primavera, 184

G

Galette Pastry Dough, 473
Garbanzo Bean Soup, 136
Garbanzo Salsa, 725
Garden Mushroom Spread, 23
Garlic
Bread, 676
Dressing, 629

Greens, Lemon-Spiked, 603
and Herb Cannellini Dip, Roasted, 18
Mashed Potatoes, 611
Pasta, Great, 822
Polenta, 580
Sauce, Many Cloves, 710
Soup with Toast, 95
and Three-Cheese Spread, Roasted, 27
Vinaigrette, 333
Gazpacho, 71
Bean, 73
Pizza, 438
White, 72
German Potato Salad, 632
Ginger(ed)
Baked Beans, 520
-Citrus Sorbet, 800
Honey, 698
Jelly, Easy, 697
Tomato Relish, 732
Gingersnap Crumb Crust, 760
Glaze(s) (*see under* Frostings and Glazes)
Gnocchi
Potato, with Sage Cream, 351
Salad, Brussels Sprouts and, 314
Spinach, Primavera, 352
Goat's Cheese
Dressing, 314
Hoagies, 409
Polenta, 580
Quesadillas with Tropical Fruit Salsa, 28
Relish, Fennel, 397
Gorgonzola Sauce, 711
Gorp, By Golly, 2
Goulash Casserole, 203
Graham Cracker Crumb Crust, 759
Grains
Barley
with Peppers and Potatoes, 548
- Vegetable Chowder, 546
and Vegetable Mélange, 833
Black-Eyed Peas and Greens with
Millet, 551
Cereal, Best Breakfast, 582
Couscous
Curried, 554
Curried Sweet Potato, 832
with Smoked Tofu, Fruited, 555
Fried Rice, Asian, 558
Grits with Blackeye Salsa, Spicy, 837
Kasha with Green Veggies, 550
Kasha Loaf Baked in Squash Halves,
382
Millet with Artichoke Hearts and
Vegetables, 553
Millet, Vegetable Salad with, 571
Mush, Cornmeal and Millet, 581
Mush, Fried, 581
Polenta, 579
Blue Cheese, 580
Eggplant, Stack, 826
Garlic, 580
Grill Roasted Vegetables with, 277
Goat's Cheese, 580
Grill-Roasted Vegetables with, 277

Herbed, 580
Portobello Mushrooms with Grilled
 Pepper Relish and, 280
Quinoa with Roasted Eggplant and
 Squash, 556
Rice
 Fried, Thai, 823
 Mexican Red, 576
 Orange Cilantro, 575
 Pilaf
  Fruit, 560
  Oriental, 561
  Mushroom and Asparagus, 559
  Quinoa and Wheat Berry, 557
  Sweet Bulgur, 560
 Risi Bisi, 567
 Risotto
  All-Season, 562
  Broccoli and "Sausage," 564
  Porcini, 563
  Soufflé, Wild Rice, 578
  Summer Squash, 565
  Two-Cheese, 827
  Vegetable Cakes, 568
  Winter Vegetable, 566
  Spicy, 577
 Thai-Fried, 823
 Turmeric, 578
 Yellow Salsa, 575
Tabbouleh, 569
Tabbouleh and Vegetable Salad Medley,
 570
and Vegetable Casserole, Mexican-
 Style, 552
and Veggie Casserole, Mixed, 176
Wheat and Barley Bowl, 549
Wheat Berry
 and Garden Tomato Salad, 574
 and Lentil Stew with Dumplings, 547
 Waldorf, 573
Granola Bread, 665
Grapevine Leaves, Stuffed, 232
Gravy, Mushroom, 716
Greek
 Eggplant with Feta, 287
 Lemon-Rice Soup, 120
 Lentil Stew, 172
 Salad, Great, 834
 -Style "Burgers," 390
 -Style Eggplant Loaf, 371
 -Style Garbanzo "Burgers" with Fennel
  Goat's Cheese Relish, 396
 -Style Green Beans, 586
Green
 Bean Casserole, 588
 Beans Oriental, 587
 Chili Corn bread, 678
 on Green Stir-Fry with Tofu, 236
 Tomato Salsa, 8
Greens
 Lemon-Spiked Garlic, 603
 with Rice Noodles and Vegetables,
  Tossed, 649
 and Smashed Potatoes, 604

-Stuffed Baked Tomatoes, 624
Gremolata, 731
Grilled Foods (*see* Roasted and Grilled)
Grinders, 400
Guacamole, 15
Gumbo, Black Bean and Okra, 150

H
Harvard Beets, 589
Hash
 Brown Loaf with Eggs, 480
 Cabbage and Potato, 230
 and Eggs, 479
 with Poached Eggs, Sweet Potato, 480
Hazelnut Macaroons, 786
Herb(ed)
 Croutons, 677
 Lavosh, Easy, 53
 Pesto, Mixed, 727
 Polenta, 580
Hollandaise Sauce, Mock, 715
Honey
 -Broiled Pineapple Slices, 789
 Dressing, 626
 Gingered, 698
 -Lime Dressing, 639
 -Lime Melon Wedges, 789
Hopping John, 529
Hot Stuff!, 48
Hot Sour Soup, 118
Huevos Rancheros, 494
Huevos Rancheros Pizza, 442
Hummus (*see under* Appetizers)

I
Ice (*see* Desserts, Frozen)
Ice Cream (*see* Desserts, Frozen)
Indian Lentil Soup, 139
Indian Pudding, Warm, 809
Indonesian-Style Tofu Satay, 48
Ingredients information, ix-xii
Italian
 "Meatballs" with Polenta, 834
 "Sausage" Pie, 457
 -Style Beans and Vegetables, 530
 -Style Croutons, 677
 -Style "Meatballs," 399

J
Jalapeño con Queso Sauce, 725
Jelly(ies) (*see under* Condiments)
Jerk Seasoning, 268
Jerk Tempeh with Black Beans and Rice,
 268
Jicama with Lime and Cilantro, 33
Jicama Salad, 640

K
Kabobs, Grilled Vegetable, 291
Kale, Braised, 603
Kasha
 with Green Veggies, 550
 Loaf Baked in Squash Halves, 382
 -Veggie "Burgers," 393

Key Lime Pie, 768
Kiwi Tart, 769
Kugel, Potato, 493
Kugel, Veggie, 492

L

Lasagne (*see under* Pasta)
Lavosh, Whole Wheat, 673
Leeks
  Cakes, Serbian, 227
  and Feta Pizza with Pesto Sauce, 436
  and Mushroom Strudel, 225
  and Onion Focaccia, 451
  and Peppers, Sauteed, 605
  Pie, 468
Lemon
  -Cinnamon Vinaigrette, 571
  Cloud Pie, 770
  Custard, 755
  Herb Mayonnaise, 733
  Ice, 800
  Meringue Cheesecake, 775
  Meringue Pie, Grandma's, 761
  Pound Cake, 751
  Sauce, Tart, 809
  Squares, Sugared, 783
  Syrup, 752
  Velvet Pudding, 811
Lentils
  Fried, 524
  Loaf with Mediterranean Tomato-Caper
    Sauce, 381
  Pitas with Feta Cream, 394
  Ravioli with Gingered Tomato Relish,
    235
  Salad with Feta Cheese, 543
  Salad, Sprouted, 637
  Soup, Country, 138
  Soup, Indian, 139
  Sprouted, 637
  Stew with Dumplings, Wheat Berry and,
    547
  Stew, Green, 172
Lima Bean Soup, Garlicky, 511
Lima Bean Wheat Bread, 658
Lime
  Dressing, 640
  Dressing, Warm, 649
  Sauce, 270
Linguine
  with Fennel and Sun-Dried Tomato
    Pesto, 338
  with Julienned Vegetables and Red
    Pepper Pesto, 342
  Soup, Sun-Dried Tomato and, 109
"Little Ears" with Artichoke Hearts,
    Mushrooms, and Peppers, 323
"Little Ears" with Smoked Tempeh and
    Vegetables, 344
"Little Pants" Biscuits, 686
Lo Mein, Vegetable, 320
Loaves
  Bean and Cornbread, 384
  Cauliflower and Green Bean, Seasoned,
    370

"Chorizo," 404
Eggplant, Greek-Style, 371
Eggplant, Layered, 373
Kasha, Baked in Squash Halves, 382
Hash Brown, with Eggs, 480
Lentil, with Mediterranean Tomato-
    Caper Sauce, 381
Oriental, 376
Polka Dot, 378
Spinach and Bean, Baked in Fillo, 371
-Stuffed Poblano Chilies, 383
Sweet Potato, with Apple Cranberry
    Relish, Holiday, 375
Tabbouleh, 380
Teem Seem, 243
Terrine
  Broccoli, with Lemon Herb
    Mayonnaise, 369
  Spring Vegetable, 487
  Tri-Layered, with Roasted Red Pepper
    Sauce, 373
Tofu and Brown Rice, Mesquite Smoked,
    379
Vegetable, Layered, 368
with Vegetables, Chunky, 377

M

Macaroni
  -Blue Cheese Salad, 641
  and Cheese, 174
  and Cheese Primavera, 174
  Salad, 641
Macaroons, Hazelnut, 786
Mafalde with Sweet Potatoes and Kale, 334
Mafalde with Garbanzo Beans, Fresh
    Tomatoes, and Croutons, 324
Mandarin Pancakes, 246
Mango and Black Bean Salad, 638
Manicotti, Mushroom-Broccoli, 355
Manicotti with Creamed Spinach Sauce,
    Vegetable, 354
Marinade(s) (*see under* Sauces)
Marinara Sauce, 700
Mashed Potatoes, Root Veggies and, 289
Mayonnaise Dressing, 482
Mayonnaise Dressing, Dilled, 297
"Meatballs"
  Black Bean, 535
  Italian, with Polenta, 834
  Italian-Style, 399
  Mexi, 405
  Swedish, 207
  in Tomato Chili Sauce, 158
  and Vegetable Soup, 125
Mediterranean
  Cabbage Casserole, 489
  Curried Stew, 171
  Roasted Eggplant and Tomatoes, 288
  Stock, 60
  -Style Vegetable Soup, 121
  Tomato-Caper Sauce, 709
Melon Soup, Fragrant, 65
Melon Wedges, Honey-Lime, 789
Meringue(s) (*see under* Cookies)
Meringue Pie Crust, 759

Mexi "Meatball" Soup, 115
Mexi-Beans, Greens, and Rice, 527
Mexicali Pie, 463
Mexican
  Ancho Chili Stew, 157
  Bean Dip, 10
  "Meatball" Casserole, 180
  Red Rice, 576
  Scrambled Eggs with "Chorizo," 496
  -Style Grain and Vegetable Casserole,
    552
  -Style Lasagne, 179
  -Style Vegetable Stew, 158
Millet, Vegetable Salad with, 571
Millet with Artichoke Hearts and
    Vegetables, 553
Minestrone
  Light, 122
  Roasted Vegetable, 265
  Summer, 123
Mint and Citrus Tea Bread, 681
Minted Pesto, 731
Mocha Frosting, 741
Molasses Bread, Three-Grain, 679
Mole Sauce, 721
Mole, Enchiladas, 251
Moo-Shu Tempeh, 244
Moroccan-Style Bean and Fillo Pie, 471
Moussaka, Vegetable-Barley, 193
Muffins (*see under* Breads)
Mush, Cornmeal and Millet, 581
Mush, Fried, 581
Mushroom(s)
  à la King, Eggs and, 831
  and Asparagus Pilaf, 559
  and Barley Soup, Savory, 99
  -Broccoli Manicotti, 355
  Bruschetta, 41
  Custard in Acorn Squash, 488
  Gravy, 716
  Grilled with Chili Paste, Portobello,
    290
  with Grilled Pepper Relish and Polenta,
    Portobello, 280
  Pâté, Wild, 16
  Pinwheels, Sliced, 414
  Pizza, Wild, 437
  Portobello Monte Cristo Grill, 832
  Salad, Roasted, 298
  Sauce, Wild, 717
  Soup, Black, 96
  Soup, Cream of, 97
  Soup, Tortellini and, 98
  with Sour Cream, 605
  Stock, Rich, 61
  Stuffed with Orzo, 37
  Tart, 466
  Tortellini, Roasted Vegetables with,
    272
Mustard
  -Honey Dressing, 542
  Sauce, 734
  -Seed Vinaigrette, 344
  -Turmeric Vinaigrette, 644

N
Nachos, 32
Navy Bean Soup, 132
New England Baked Beans, 519
New York-Style Cheesecake, 774
Niçoise Platter, 223
Noodle(s)
  Florentine, 491
  Soup, Tempeh, 100
  with Sweet Potatoes and Snow Peas,
    334
Nutritional data, vi-viii

O
Okra, Gulfport, 606
Omelet Puff with Vegetable Mélange, 486
Onion(s)
  and Blue Cheese Focaccia, 51
  Chutney Relish, 555
  Dip, Toasted, 6
  Fruit-Stuffed Vidalia, 607
  and Leek Soup with Pasta, 103
  Quartet of, 607
  Salad, Sweet, 299
  Sauce, Three-, 712
  Soup, French, 102
  Soup with Mushrooms, Three-, 103
  Soup, Vidalia, 101
  Tarte Tatin, Sweet, 469
  Tiny Peas and, 609
Orange
  -Almond Meringues, 785
  Baked Alaska, 803
  Chiffon Cake, Glazed, 739
  Cilantro Rice, 575
  Compote, Spiced, 788
  Dressing, 541
  Flan, 814
  Glaze, 739
  Hummus, Spicy, 19
  Marinated Bean Salad, 540
  Marmalade Crescents, 662
  -Pineapple Sherbet, 799
  Poppy Seed Cake, 752
  -Rosemary Jelly, 695
Oregano Vinaigrette, 572
Oriental
  Green Beans, 587
  Loaf, 376
  Noodle Salad, 650
  Pilaf, 561
  Pizza, 429
  Salad, Roasted, 300
  Soup with Noodles, 312
  Stock, 62
  Vegetable Satay, 292
  Watercress Soup, 116
Orzo, Mushrooms Stuffed with, 37
Orzo with Sun-dried Tomatoes and
    Mushrooms, 642

P
Pancakes, Potato, 611
Pancakes (*see under* Breads)

Paprikash Sauce, 718
Paprikash, Vegetables, 231
Parmesan
　Biscuits,685
　Croutons, 677
　Garlic Bread, 676
　Vinaigrette,539
Parsnips and Winter Vegetables, Braised, 608
Pasta (*also see* Casseroles, Salads)
　Bucatini with Brussels Sprouts and Walnuts, 340
　with Cabbage and Potatoes, 326
　Capellini Carbonara, Molded, 350
　with Cilantro Pesto, Southwest, 347
　Farfalle with Roasted Eggplant and Squash, 345
　Fettuccine
　　with Eggplant Persillade, 328
　　with Fresh fennel and Brussels Sprouts, 820
　　with Greens and Caramelized Onions, 337
　　Primavera, Creamy, 330
　　with Roasted Garlic, Onions, and Peppers, 340
　　with Roasted Vegetable Sauce, 274
　Frittata, 482
　Fusilli with Fresh Tomatoes and Corn, 343
　Fusilli and Cheese Primavera, 184
　Garlic, Great, 822
　with Goat's Cheese and Onion Confit, 339
　with Greens and Beans, 335
　with Greens, Raisins, and Pine Nuts, 322
　Homemade, 308
　Lasagne
　　Artichoke, 365
　　Eggplant, 187
　　with Eggplant Sauce, Veggie, 185
　　"Mexican-Style," 179
　　Roasted Red Pepper and Spinach, 363
　　"Sausage," 186
　　Squash and Mushroom, 362
　Light Summer, 333
　Linguine with Julienned Vegetables and Red Pepper Pesto, 342
　Linguine with Fennel and Sun-Dried Tomato Pesto, 338
　"Little Ears" with Artichoke Hearts, Mushrooms, and Peppers, 323
　"Little Ears" with Smoked Tempeh and Vegetables, 344
　Lo Mein, Vegetable, 320
　Mafalde with Garbanzo Beans, Fresh Tomatoes, and Croutons, 324
　Mafalde with Sweet Potatoes and Kale, 334
　Manicotti, Mushroom-Broccoli, 355
　Manicotti with Creamed Spinach Sauce, Vegetable, 354
　Mean Bean, 535
　Noodles, Florentine, 491
　Noodles with Sweet Potatoes and Snow Peas, 334
　Nests, Grilled Summer Vegetables in, 273
　Orzo, Mushrooms Stuffed with, 37
　Pastitsio, 200
　Pastitsio, Adzuki Bean, 517
　Penne with Fresh Asparagus and Plum Tomatoes, 336
　Peperonata, 322
　from Pescia, 325
　Pizza on, 434
　Potato Gnocchi with Sage Cream, 351
　Primavera, Very Simple, 329
　Ravioli
　　20 -minute, 821
　　Artichoke, with Tarragon Sauce, 357
　　and Asparagus, Wine-Glazed, 820
　　with Curry Sauce, Sweet Potato, 358
　　Eggplant, 360
　　Feta Cheese and Sun-Dried Tomato, 361
　　Lentil, with Gingered Tomato Relish, 235
　　with Tarragon Sauce, Artichoke, 347
　　with Wild Mushroom Sauce, 359
　Rice Noodles with Vegetables, Stir-Fried, 321
　Rigatoni with Italian "Sausage" and Fennel Pesto, 327
　Roasted Eggplant with, 273
　Rotini and Beans Niçoise, 326
　Rotoli
　　with Fresh Tomato Herb Sauce, Cheese and Vegetable, 356
　　with Many-Cloves Garlic Sauce, Broccoli and Cheese 188
　　with Marinara Sauce, Spinach-Mushroom, 189
　Santa Fe, 348
　Shells with Simple Tomato Sauce, Cheese-Stuffed, 237
　Shells with Spinach Pesto, Ricotta Stuffed, 35
　Shells Stuffed with Spinach and Tofu, 353
　Skillet Cakes, 349
　Soup
　　with Noodles, Oriental 312
　　and 2-Bean Vegetable, 310
　　Two-Bean and, 124
　　with Vegetables, Sesame Noodle, 311
　Spaghetti and Eggplant Parmesan, 190
　Spaghetti, Spaghetti Squash and, 210
　Spinach Gnocchi Primavera, 352
　Star, with Carrots and Ginger Cream, 341
　Tagliatelle with Chili-Mushroom Stroganoff Sauce, 346
　Tetrazzini, Vegetarian, 183
　Tortellini
　　Artichoke, bake, 829
　　with Beans and Squash, Curried 331

Kabobs with Many-Cloves Garlic Sauce, 49
Roasted Vegetables with Mushroom, 272
and Vegetable Kabobs, Marinated, 234
and Vegetables, Curried, 332
Vegetables in, Nests, Grilled Summer, 273
White Bean and Red Cabbage Salad, 537
Wontons, Cranberry-Cheese, 45
Ziti with Gremolata, 338
Pâté, Pine Nut Spinach, 15
Pâté, Wild Mushroom, 16
Patties (*see* Sandwiches)
Pea Soup, Chilled, 74
Peach-Allspice Soufflés, 817
Peanut Sauce, 292
Peanut Butter Soup, Creamy, 104
Peanutty and Jelly Sandwiches, 413
Pear(s)
Belle Héléne, 793
Butter, Spiced, 693
Dessert Pizza, 450
Melt, Blue Cheese and, 412
Tart with Crème Anglaise, 771
Peas and Onions, Tiny, 609
Peas and Beans, Southern Stewed, 149
Penne with Fresh Asparagus and Plum Tomatoes, 336
Penuche Frosting, 746
Peperonata,610
Galette, Roasted, 474
-Roasted, 295
-Tomato Sauce, 707
Pepper Relish, Grilled, 281
Peppermint Clouds, 786
Peppermint Cake Rolls, Frozen, 804
Pesto (*see* Sauces)
Pies (*also see* Pie Crusts)
Dessert
Apple, Double-Crust, 762
Buttermilk, Old-Fashioned, 764
Chocolate Rum, 767
Cream, Banana-Strawberry, 766
Key Lime, 768
Lemon Cloud, 770
Lemon Meringue, Mom's, 761
Sweet Potato, Spiced, 765
Savory
Artichoke, 464
Baklava, Curried Onion, 470
Bean and Fillo, Moroccan-Style, 471
Calzones
Cheese and Mushroom, 453
"Sausage," 452
Sweet Fennel, 455
Galette
Roasted Peperonata, 474
Squash and Mushroom, 472
Vegetable, Sweet 'n Spicy, 474
Italian "Sausage," 457
Leek, 468

Mexicali, 463
Pot Pie, Shepherd's Veggie, 460
Spinach, 467
Tart, Mushroom, 466
Tarte Tatin, Sweet Onion, 469
Tomato, "Rich," 465
Use-It-Up, 462
Vegetable, Autumn, 459
Veggie Pot, 458
Tart
Blueberry, Raspberry-Glazed, 770
Coconut Cream, Toasted, 767
Fruit, Rustic Country, 772
Kiwi, 768
Pear, with Crème Anglaise, 771
Tarte Tatin, 763
Pie Crusts
Basic (All-Purpose Flour), 757
Basic (Cake Flour), 758
Crumb
Gingersnap, 760
Graham Cracker, 759
Vanilla, 760
Galette Dough, 451
Meringue, 759
Pastry
Double Crust, 763
Empanada, 35
Pot Pie, 459
Reduced-Fat, Baked, 762
Pilaf (*see under* Grains)
Pine Nut Spinach Pâté, 15
Pineapple
-Champagne Ice, 801
-Lemon Trifle, 754
Slices, Honey-Broiled, 789
Upside-Down Cake, 747
Pinto Bean and Avocado Dip, 11
Piperade, 478
Pita Breads, 682
Pita Chips, 53
Pizza
Antipasto, 435
Apple Salad, 449
Artichoke and Roasted Pepper, 431
Black Bean and Jalapeño, 441
Breakfast, 425
Broccoli and Mushroom, Smoky, 444
Calypso, 428
Caponata, Roasted, 433
Chili Poblano, 442
Dough (*see* Pizza Crusts)
Fruit Orchard, 449
Garden Patch, 447
Gazpacho, 438
Huevos Rancheros, 442
Leek and Feta, with Pesto Sauce, 436
Onion, French-Style, 430
Oriental, 429
on Pasta, 434
Pear Dessert, 450
Potato, Tuscan, 433
Ranch-Style, 425
Red Pepper and Cheese, Roasted, 432
Reuben, 426

Salad, Spinach, 448
Sauce, 700
"Sausage" and Egg, 484
Southwest-Style, 439
Spinach, Deep-Pan, 424
Spinach-Cheese, Deluxe, 422
Supreme, 422
Sweet Potato, Sage-Scented, 445
Taco, 440
Tomato and Basil, Fresh, 430
Tomato Fillo, 439
West Coast, 427
Wild Mushroom, 437
with Yellow and Green Squash, 443
Zucchini, Double, 446
Zucchini and Mushroom, Fillo Crust, 446
Pizza Crusts and Dough
Basic, 418
Cheese, 420
Cornmeal, 418
Potato, 421
Whole Wheat, 419
Zucchini, 420
Plantains, Fried Ripe, 33
Plum Sauce, 734
Plums, Wine-Poached, 791
Poblano
Chili Sauce, 722
Chili Soup, 70
Chilies, Loaf-Stuffed, 383
Sour Cream Sauce, 724
Polenta (*see under* Grains)
Porcini Risotto, 563
Portobello Mushroom(s)
Grilled with Chili Paste, 290
with Grilled Pepper Relish and Polenta, 280
Sandwiches, Grilled, 303
with Spinach-Cilantro Pesto, Roasted Stuffed, 285
Roasted Stuffed, 213
Pot Pie
Pastry, 459
Shepherd's Veggie, 460
Veggie, 458
Potato(es)
Bread, 654
with Cheese, Twice-Baked, 612
Chowder, 106
Garlic Mashed 611
Gnocchi with Sage Cream, 351
Gratin, 611
Greens and Smashed, 604
Horseradish Mashed, 611
Kugel, 493
Pancakes, 611
Pizza Crust, 421
Pizza, Tuscan, 433
with Poblano Chilies, 615
Real Mashed, 610
Salad, Creamy, 633
Salad, Roasted, 296
Scalloped, 612
Veggie Packets, Two-, 286

Potstickers, Five-Spice, 44
Pound Cake, Lemon, 751
Powdered Sugar Frosting, 751
Pozole, 114
Praline Sundaes, 798
Pretzels, Soft, 669
Primavera
Fusilli and Cheese, 184
Macaroni and Cheese, 174
Very Simple, 329
Pumpkin Soup, Cinnamon-Spiced, 107
Pumpkin-Ginger Cake with Warm Rum Sauce, 749
Puddings and Custards
Apple, Brown Sugar, 810
Apricot, Fresh, 812
Bread, Blueberry with Tart Lemon Sauce, 808
Bread, Raisin, 809
Brulée, Herbed, 815
Cereal, Baked, 807
Chocolate, "Rich," 806
Crème Anglaise, 772
Cream Filling, Vanilla, 748
Flan, Caramel, 813
Flan, Orange, 814
Indian, Warm, 809
Lemon, 755
Lemon Velvet, 811
Rice, Old-Fashioned Baked, 808
Trifle, Pineapple-Lemon, 754
Puree
Cauliflower-Fennel, 596
Celery Root, 597
Fennel, 602
Gingered Carrot, 593

Q
Quesadillas (*see under* Appetizers)
Queso Fundido, 13
Quiche(s) (*see under* Eggs)
Quinoa and Wheat Berry Pilaf, 557
Quinoa with Roasted Eggplant and Squash, 556

R
Ragout, Cabbage with Real Mashed Potatoes, 147
Raisin
Bread, 667
Bread Pudding, 809
Oatmeal Cookies, 777
Raspberry
-Glazed Blueberry Tart, 770
-Orange Swirl Cake, 753
Sauce, 793
Soufflé, Chilled, 816
Ratatouille, 195
Ratatouille Stew, Roasted, 266
Ravioli (*see under* Pasta)
Red Beans and Rice, Bourbon Street, 528
Red Pepper
and Cheese Pizza, Roasted, 432
Pesto, 729
Sauce, Roasted, 709

Soup, Sweet, 75
and Spinach Lasagne, Roasted, 363
Reduced-Fat Pie Crust, Baked, 762
Refried Beans, 525
Relish(es) (*see under* Condiments)
Rellenos, Bean and Cheese Chili, 499
Reuben Pizza, 426
Rhubarb
Crunch, Fran's, 795
Fresh Berry, 790
Jam, Spiced, 694
Streusel Cake, Mom's, 738
Rice (*see under* Grains)
Ricotta Stuffed Shells with Spinach Pesto, 35
Rigatoni with Italian "Sausage" and Fennel Pesto, 327
Risi Bisi, 567
Risotto (*see under* Grains)
Roasted and Grilled Dishes
Artichokes, 282
Beet Puree, 294
Beets, Honey Roasted, 589
Casserole of, Vegetables and Beans, 279
Eggplant
Cajun, 294
with Feta, Greek, 287
with Pasta, 273
and Tomatoes, Mediterranean, 288
Fajitas, Vegetable, 302
Farfalle with Roasted Eggplant and Squash, 345
Fettuccine with Roasted Garlic, Onions, and Peppers, 340
Fettuccine with Roasted Vegetable Sauce, 274
Kabobs, Vegetable, 291
Peperonata, 295
Polenta, 280
Portobello Mushrooms
with Chili Paste, 290
with, Pepper Relish and Polenta, 280
with Spinach-Cilantro Pesto, 285
Potato Veggie Packets, Two, 286
Ratatouille Stew, 266
Red Pepper Bread, 657
Risotto with, Tomatoes, 275
Roll-Ups, Vegetable, 284
Root Veggies and Mashed Potatoes, 289
Salad(s)
Mushroom, 298
Oriental, 300
Potato, 296
Sweet Onion, 299
Vegetable and Wild Rice, 297
Sandwiches, Veggie Pocket, 304
Sandwiches, Portobello Mushroom, 303
Satay, Oriental Vegetable, 292
Soups
Chowder, Corn and Potato, 262
Minestrone, Vegetable, 265
Vegetable, Pureed, 262
Vichyssoise, Hot Pepper, 263
Spaghetti Squash with Roasted Tomato-Herb Sauce and Artichokes, 282

Squash, Moroccan Style, 276
Tempeh (*see* Tempeh)
Tofu (*see* Tofu)
Tomatoes Stuffed with Pepper-Roasted Wild Mushrooms, 293
Vegetable(s)
with Beans and Fruit, 278
Burritos, 301
Moo-Shu Style, 281
with Mushroom Tortellini, 272
in Pasta Nests, Summer, 273
with Polenta, 277
Rolls (*see under* Breads)
Roll-Ups, Grilled Vegetable, 284
Rose Geranium Jelly, 696
Rotini and Beans Niçoise, 326
Rotoli (*see under* Pasta)
Rum Sauce, Warm, 750
Rye Caraway Croutons, 677

S
Salad(s) (*also see* Beans and Legumes)
12-Layer, 628
Bean
Black, Mango and, 638
Black, and Rice, 542
Black, and Smoked Tofu, 541
Fava Platter, 544
Orange Marinated, 540
and Pasta with White Bean Dressing, 536
Tomato, and Bread, 538
Vegetable, with 2, 539
Broccoli, with Sour Cream-Mayonnaise Dressing, 631
Cactus, 639
Caesar, 627
Carrot-Raisin, 632
Coleslaw, Freezer 629
Fruit, with Raspberry Yogurt Dressing, 635
Greek, Great, 834
Jicama, 640
Lentil, with Feta Cheese, 543
Lentils, Sprouted, 637
Mushroom, Roasted, 298
Oriental, Roasted, 300
Pasta
Angel Hair and Goat's Cheese, 647
Bean and, with White Bean Dressing, 536
Coleslaw, 630
Curried, 646
Egg Salad, 481
Farfelle, with Minted Pesto, 645
Garden, with Crostini, 648
Gnocchi, Brussels Sprouts and, 314
Greens with Rice Noodles and Vegetables, Tossed, 649
Macaroni, 641
Macaroni-Blue Cheese, 641
Noodle, Asian-Style, 651
Noodles, Oriental, 650
Orzo with Sun-Dried Tomatoes and Mushrooms, 642

and Portobello Mushrooms
Vinaigrette, 315
with Radiatore, Chili Dressed, 644
Rice Noodle, 318
Smoked Tempeh, Artichoke, and
Linguine, 316
with Summer Vegetables, Sesame, 317
White Bean, and Red Cabbage, 537
Vegetable and, Garden, 313
Potato(es)
Caribbean, 634
Creamy, 633
German 632
Roasted, 296
Spinach and Melon, 626
Spinach, Wilted, 627
Sprouts and Vegetable, 636
Vegetable and Wild Rice, 297
Vegetables and Orzo Vinaigrette, Mixed,
643
Waldorf, 636
Waldorf, Wheat Berry, 573
Salad Dressings
Balsamic, 544
Blue Cheese, 642
Caraway, 538
Chili, 645
Cilantro Lime, 640
Creamy, 630
Cucumber-Sour Cream, 571
Garlic, 629
Honey, 626
Honey-Lime, 639
Lime, 640
Lime, Warm, 649
Mayonnaise, Dilled, 297
Mustard-Honey, 542
Orange, 541
Raspberry Yogurt Dressing, 635
Sesame, 318
Sour Cream, 317
Sour Cream-Mayonnaise, 631
Sun-Dried Tomato and Goat's Cheese,
314
Tahini, 392
Vinaigrette
Basil, 313
Basil, Fresh, 343
Citrus, 319, 540
Garlic, 333
Lemon-Cinnamon, 571
Lime, Warm, 649
Mixed Herb, 316
Mustard Seed, 344
Oregano, 572
Parmesan, 539
Roasted Garlic, 574
White Bean, 537
Salsa (*see under* Appetizers and Sauces)
Sandwiches and Patties
"Burgers"
Basic, 385
Provençal, 389
Falafel, 825
Falafel, with Tahini Dressing, 391

Greek-Style, 390
Greek-Style Garbanzo, with Fennel
Goat's Cheese Relish, 396
Herbed Veggie, 402
Kasha Veggie, 393
Smoked Tofu, 387
Soybean Mushroom, 401
Soybean Veggie, 400
Tabbouleh, 392
Vegetable and Tofu, 386
"Chicken" Salad, Mock, 409
Eggplant Parmesan, 398
Grill, Portobello Monte Cristo, 832
Grill, Sun-Dried Tomato Pesto and
Cheese, 412
Grinders, 400
Hoagies, Goat's Cheese, 409
Melt
Blue Cheese and Pear, 412
Cranberry Cheese, 410
Cucumber Cheese, 411
Peanutty and Jelly, 413
with Fresh Tomato Relish, Cannellini
Bean, 397
Pinwheels, Sliced Mushroom, 414
Pinwheels, Swiss Cheese and Spinach,
414
Pitas with Fennel Cream, Lentil, 394
"Sloppy Joes," Meatless, 407
Squash and Tempeh, 388
Tostadas, Picante Black Bean, 406
Veggie Joes, 408
Veggie Pocket, 304
Satay, Indonesian-Style Tofu, 48
Satay, Oriental Vegetable, 292
Sauces (*also see* Condiments and Jellies)
Aioli, Tofu, 224
Alfredo, 711
Artichoke, 713
Basting, Fragrant, 736
Bean, with Tomatoes and Sage, Peasant,
706
Blackeye Salsa, 837
Cheese, Creamy, 596
Chili, Cincinnati, 719
Chili Tomato, 720
Creole, 706
Cucumber Yogurt, 555
Curry, 715
Dessert
Chocolate, 756
Chocolate, Bittersweet, 794
Coulis, Cranberry, 732
Crème Anglaise, 772
Lemon, Tart, 809
Raspberry, 793
Rum, Warm, 750
Eggplant, 708
Enchilada, 720
Fragrant Basting, 736
Garbanzo Salsa, 725
Garlic, Many Cloves, 710
Gorgonzola, 711
Gravy, Mushroom, 716
Hollandaise, Mock, 715

Jalapeño con Queso, 725
Lime, 270
Marinades
    Fajita, 256
    Tamari, 736
    Tandoori, 271
Marinara, 700
Mayonnaise, Lemon Herb, 733
Mole, 721
Mushroom, Wild, 717
Mustard, 734
Paprikash, 718
Peanut, 292
Peperonata-Tomato, 707
Pesto
    Cilantro, 730
    Fennel, 728
    Herb, Mixed, 727
    Minted, 731
    Red Pepper, 729
    Spinach, 727
    Spinach-Cilantro, 730
    Sun-Dried Tomato, 728
Plum, 734
Poblano Chili, 722
Poblano Sour Cream, 724
Primavera, 714
Red Pepper, Roasted 709
Sour Cream, Minted, 197
Spinach, Creamed, 712
Tamari Dipping, 735
Tamari Marinade, 735
Tarragon, 358
Three-Onion, 712
Tomatillo, 724
Tomato
    -Basil, Fresh, 702
    -Caper, Mediterranean 709
    -Chili, 179
    and Herb, Fresh, 702
    Herb, Roasted, 283
    and "Meat," 701
    "Meat," Bolognese-Style, 704
    and "Meatball," 705
    with Mushrooms and Sherry, 703
    Pizza, 700
    Relish, Gingered, 732
    Salsa, Green, 8
    Salsa, Red, 9
    Serrano, 723
    Simple, 237
Tropical Salsa, 726
Yogurt Cucumber, 733, 826
Sauerkraut Casserole, Cabbage and, 204
"Sausage"
    Calzones, 452
    and Egg Pizza, 484
    and Herbed-Cheese Ravioli with Wild
        Mushroom Sauce, 359
    Lasagne, 18
    Stuffed Acorn Squash, 217
Serbian Leek Cakes, 227
Sesame
    Croutons, 677
    Dressing, 318

Noodle Soup with Vegetables, 311
Pasta with Summer Vegetables, 317
Shells Stuffed with Spinach and Tofu, 353
Sherbet, Orange-Pineapple, 799
Side Dishes
    Acorn Squash, Apple Pecan, 618
    Artichokes with Hollandaise Sauce, 584
    Artichokes, Braised Whole, 584
    Asparagus with Lemon-Wine Sauce, 585
    Asparagus with Peanut Sauce, 586
    Beans, Refried, 525
    Beet(s)
        Dijon, 589
        Harvard, 589
        Honey Roasted, 589
        Puree, Grilled, 294
    Black Beans, Seasoned, Mashed, 524
    Broccoli, Herb-Crumbed, 590
    Broccoli Rabe Sauteed with Garlic, 591
    Brussels Sprouts and Pearl Onions,
            Sugar-Glazed, 591
    Cabbage, Wine-Braised, 592
    Carrot Pudding, 594
    Carrot Puree, Gingered, 593
    Carrots, Orange-Glazed Baby, 594
    Cauliflower with Creamy Cheese Sauce,
        595
    Cauliflower-Fennel Puree, 596
    Celery Root Puree, 597
    Chayote with Pumpkin Seeds, 621
    Corn
        Fried, 598
        Pudding, Fresh, 599
        Tex-Mex, Sweet, 599
    Eggplant Saute, Seasoned, 600
    Eggplant and Tomato Casserole, 601
    Fennel Puree, 602
    Green Bean(s)
        Casserole, 588
        Greek-Style, 586
        Oriental, 587
    Greens, Lemon-Spiked Garlic, 603
    Kale, Braised, 603
    Leeks and Peppers, Sauteed, 605
    Lentils, Fried, 524
    Mushrooms with Sour Cream, 605
    Okra, Gulfport, 606
    Onions, Vidalia, Fruit-Stuffed, 607
    Onions, Quartet of, 607
    Parsnips and Winter Vegetables, Braised,
        608
    Peas and Onions, Tiny, 609
    Peperonata, 610
    Peperonata, Roasted, 295
    Potato(es)
        and Greens, Smashed, 604
        Bakers,Veggie-Stuffed, 613
        with Cheese, Twice-Baked, 612
        "Fries," Crispy French, 614
        "Fries," Parmesan, 614
        "Fries," Steak, 614
        Garlic Mashed, 611
        Gratin, 611
        Mashed, Horseradish, 611
        Mashed, Real, 610

Pancakes, 611
with Poblano Chilies, 615
Scalloped, 612
Sweet, Orange Lime, 616
Yams, Candied, 615
Spaghetti Squash Parmesan, 620
Spinach, Creamed,617
Spinach au Gratin, 617
Squash with Snow Peas, Sauteed
Summer, 621
Squash, Moroccan Style, Roasted, 276
Succotash, 598
Tomato(es)
Cornmeal Fried, 624
Fried, 623
Fried, Sugar Glazed, 624
Greens-Stuffed Baked, 624
Halves, Herbed, 623
Pudding, 622
Zucchini from Pueblo, 619
Zucchini Fans Provençal, 618
Sherbets (*see under* Desserts)
Sorbets (*see under* Desserts)
Sloppy Joes, Meatless, 407
Soft Pretzels, 669
Soufflés (*also see under* Desserts)
Cheddar Cheese, 501
Eggplant Casserole, 196
Soup(s) (*see also* Beans and Legumes,
Pasta, and Roasted and Grilled
Dishes)
Alsatian Peasant, 129
Artichoke and Mushroom, Cream of, 107
Basil, Fresh, 83
Bean
Black-Eyed Pea and Lentil, Easiest,
512
Black, and Okra Gumbo, 150
Chickpea and Pasta, 137
Chili, Black and White, 153
Classic Black, 127
Curried, 513
Garbanzo, 136
Garlicky Lima, 511
Gazpacho, 73
Navy, 132
Pasta and Two-, Vegetable, 310
with Sun-Dried Tomatoes and
Cilantro Cream, Black, 134
and Sweet Potato, with Cranberry
Coulis, White, 110
and Vegetable, Four-, 130
-Thickened, 133
Tuscan, 131
Beet, Dilled, 66
Berry, Very, 64
Borscht, Beet, 84
Broccoli, Cream of, 85
Broccoli and Pasta, Herbed, 86
Cabbage, Russian, 87
Cabbage, Cannellini and, 135
Carrot, Dilled, 88
Cauliflower, with Cheese, Cream of, 89
Chayote Squash, with Cilantro Sour
Cream, 77

Cherry, Sweet, 64
Chili
sin Carne, 126
Mac, 127
Sweet Potato Chipotle, 828
Yellow and White Bean, 514
Chowder
Barley Vegetable, 546
Corn and Potato, Hearty, 92
Potato, 106
Roasted Corn and Potato, 262
Coconut, Vietnamese Curried, 119
Corn, with Epazote, 94
Corn, Creamed, 93
Cucumber, Herbed, 67
Cucumber and Sorrel, 68
Eggplant, with Roasted Red Pepper
Sauce, 69
Garden Harvest, 91
Garlic, with Toast, 95
Gazpacho, 71
Bean, 73
White, 72
Hot Sour, 118
Lemon-Rice, Greek, 120
Lentil, Country, 138
Lentil, Indian, 139
"Meatball," Mexi, 115
"Meatball" and Vegetable, 125
Melon, Fragrant, 65
Minestrone
Light, 122
Roasted Vegetable, 265
Summer, 123
Mushroom
and Barley, Savory, 99
Black, 96
Cream of, 97
Rich, Stock, 61
Noodle, Tempeh, 100
Onion
French, 102
and Leek, with Pasta, 103
with Mushrooms, Three-, 103
Vidalia, 101
Pea, Chilled, 74
Oriental, with Noodles, 312
Peanut Butter, Creamy, 104
Poblano Chili, 70
Pozole, 114
Pumpkin, Cinnamon-Spiced, 107
Red Pepper, Sweet, 75
Sesame Noodle with Vegetables, 311
Snow Pea, 76
Spinach with Onion Flowers, 108
Spinach and Tortellini, 106
Split Pea, 140
Squash
Orange-Scented, 79
Summer, 78
Winter, 80
Stock
Mediterranean, 60
Oriental, 62
Vegetable, Basic, 58

Vegetable, Canned, 63
Vegetable, Roasted, 59
Tomatillo, with Cilantro, 81
Tomato
    Cream of, 112
    and Leek, Ripe, 82
    and Linguine, Sun-Dried, 109
    Two, 112
Tortellini and Mushroom, 98
Tortellini, with Kale, 96
Tortilla, 113
Vegetable
    Lightly Creamed, 111
    Lime-Scented, 90
    Mediterranean-Style, 121
    with Orzo, 128
    Roasted, Pureed, 264
Vichyssoise, 105
Vichyssoise, Hot Pepper, 263
Watercress, Oriental, 116
Wonton, 117
Sour Cream
    Avocado, 71
    Cilantro, 77
    Coffeecake with Apple-Date Filling, 682
    Dressing, 317
    Minted, 197
    -Mayonnaise Dressing, 631
Sourdough Croutons, 677
Southern Vegetable Stew, 152
Southern Stewed Peas and Beans, 149
Southwest Pasta with Cilantro Pesto, 347
Soybean
    Mushroom "Burgers," 401
    and Vegetable Spread, 17
    -Veggie "Burgers," 400
Spaghetti, and Eggplant Parmesan, 190
Spaghetti Squash
    Parmesan, 620
    with Roasted Tomato-Herb Sauce and
        Artichokes, 282
    and Spaghetti, 210
    Stuffed with Vegetable Saute, 219
Spicy Rice, 577
Spinach
    Balls, Baked, 43
    Cheese Crepes, 221
    and Cheese Mini-Quiches, 42
    -Cheese Pizza, Deluxe, 422
    -Cilantro Pesto, 730
    Creamed, 617
    Gnocchi Primavera, 352
    au Gratin, 617
    and Melon Salad, 626
    -Mushroom Flatbread, 674
    -Mushroom Rotoli with Marinara Sauce,
        189
    Pasta Bake, 177
    Pesto, 727
    Pie, 467
    Pizza, Deep-Pan, 424
    Quiche, 506
    Salad Pizza, 448
    Salad, Wilted, 627
    Sauce, Creamed, 712

Soup with Onion Flowers, 108
    Squares, and Cheese, 42
    and Tortellini Soup, 106
Split Pea Soup, 140
Sprouts and Vegetable Salad, 636
Squash
    Dinner Rolls, 670
    Moroccan Style, Roasted, 276
    and Mushroom Galette, 472
    and Mushroom Lasagne, 362
    with Snow Peas, Sauteed Summer, 621
    Soup
        Orange-Scented, 79
        Summer, 78
        Winter, 80
    Stew, Orange and Ginger, 159
Stew(s) (*also see* Beans and Legumes)
    Ancho Chili, Mexican, 157
    Bean
        Caribbean Ginger, 162
        with Polenta, Three-, 166
        and Squash, 148
        Vegetable, Hot and Spicy, 153
        Vegetable, Thickened, 142
        and Vegetable, Very Quick, 819
        and Vegetable, Winter, 516
    Cabbage Ragout with Real Mashed
        Potatoes, 147
    Cannelloni, 191
    Caribbean Sweet and Sour, 160
    Chili, 154
    Chili, Black and White Bean, 153
    with Couscous, Garden, 170
    Curried, Mediterranean, 171
    with Dumplings, Veggie, 145
    with Fusilli, Spiced Bean, 167
    Gumbo, Black Bean and Okra, 150
    Hasty, 143
    Lentil, Greek, 172
    "Meatballs" in Tomato Chili Sauce,
        158
    Orange and Ginger, 159
    Peas and Beans, Southern Stewed, 149
    Ratatouille, Roasted, 266
    Skillet, Easy Creole, 151
    Squash, Orange and Ginger, 159
    Squash and Potato, Sweet-Sour, 163
    Vegetable, Mexican-Style, 158
    Vegetable, Southern, 152
Sticky Bun Topping, 665
Sticky Buns, 664
Stir-Fry(ied)
    Adzuki Bean, 533
    Beans and Greens, 531
    Butter Bean and Sprouts, 532
    Dim-Sum Platter with, Vegetables, 241
    Five-Spice, 239
    Green on Green, with Tofu, 236
    Rice Noodles with Vegetables, 321
    Sesame Asparagus, 825
    Spring Vegetable, 238
    Szechuan Vegetable, 240
    Tempeh "Steak" with Red and Green
        247
    Thai, 824

Stocks (*see under* Soups)
Strawberry-Kiwi Shortcake, 794
Streusel, 690
   Crisp, 739
   Topping, 796
Stroganoff, Creamy Vegetable and
     "Burger," 144
Strudel
   Apple-Cabbage, 50
   Cabbage-Fennel, 226
   Vegetable, with Wild Mushroom Sauce,
     224
Succotash, 598
Succotash, El Paso, 838
Sugar Cookies, Frosted, 778
Summer Squash Risotto, 565
Sun-Dried Tomato
   and Goat's Cheese Dressing, 314
   Hummus, 18
   and Linguine Soup, 109
   Pesto, 728
   Pesto and Cheese Grill, 412
Swedish "Meatball" and Dilled Potato
     Casserole, 206
Swedish "Meatballs," 207
Sweet Onion Tarte Tatin, 469
Sweet Potato(es)
   Biscuits, 686
   Braids, 658
   Cakes, 212
   Chili, Chipotle, 828
   Couscous, Curried, 832
   Hash with Poached Eggs, 480
   Loaf with Apple Cranberry Relish,
     Holiday, 375
   Orange-Lime, 616
   Pie, Spiced, 765
   Pizza, Sage-Scented, 445
   Pone, 490
   Ravioli with Curry Sauce, 358
Sweet-Sour Squash and Potato Stew, 163
Swiss Cheese and Spinach Pinwheels, 414
Symbols for vegetarian types, viii
Syrup, Lemon, 752
Syrup, Blueberry Maple, 691
Szechuan Vegetable Stir-Fry, 240

T

Tabbouleh, 569
   "Burgers," 392
   Loaf, 380
   and Vegetable Salad Medley, 570
Taco(s)
   with "Chorizo" and Potatoes, 249
   Picadillo, 248
   Pizza, 440
Tagliatelle with Chili-Mushroom
     Stroganoff Sauce, 346
Tahini Dressing, 392
Tamale(s)
   with Beans, Veggie, 258
   Dough, 258
   Three-Chili, 257
Tamari Dipping Sauce, 735
Tamari Marinade, 736

Tandoori Tempeh with Orange Cilantro
     Rice, 270
Tandoori Marinade, 271
Tarragon Wine Jelly, 696
Tart Crust, Baked, 466
Tarte Tatin, 763
Tempeh
   Barbecued, and Peppers, 215
   Chop Suey, 241
   Enchiladas Mole, 251
   Fajitas, 255
   Grilled, with Poblano Sour Cream
     Sauce, 269
   Jerk, with Black Beans and Rice, 268
   "Little Ears" with Smoked, and
     Vegetables, 344
   Moo-Shu, 244
   Patties, Squash and, 388
   Sandwiches, Mock "Chicken" Salad,
     409
   Saute, Garden Vegetable and, 216
   Smoked, Artichoke, and Linguine Salad,
     316
   Soup, Noodle, 100
   "Steak" with Red and Green Stir-Fry, 247
   Szechuan Vegetable Stir-Fry, 240
   Tandoori, with Orange Cilantro Rice,
     270
   Vegetables with, Orange-Scented, 214
Terrine
   Broccoli, with Lemon Herb Mayonnaise,
     369
   Spring Vegetable, 487
   Tri-Layered, with Roasted Red Pepper
     Sauce, 373
Tetrazzini, Vegetarian, 183
Tex-Mex Vegetable Stew, 156
Texas Stew with Chili-Cheese Dumplings,
     515
Thai Fried Rice, 823
Thai Stir-Fry, 824
Three Kings Bread, 661
Tofu
   Acorn Squash with, 288
   Aioli, 224
   "Burgers," Smoked, 387
   "Burgers," Vegetable and, 386
   Couscous with Smoked, Fruited, 555
   Curried, and Vegetables, 835
   Hot Sour Soup, 118
   Mesquite-Smoked, 267
   Mesquite-Smoked, and Brown Rice Loaf,
     379
   Ranchero, 259
   Roasted, Onions and Peppers with Lime
     Sauce, 269
   Salad, Black Bean and Smoked, 541
   Salad, Great Greek, 834
   Satay, Indonesian-Style, 48
   Shells Stuffed with Spinach, 353
   Soup, Hot Sour, 118
   Soup, Mediterranean-Style Vegetable,
     121
   Stew, Caribbean Sweet and Sour, 160
   Stew, and Vegetable, 164

Stir-Fry with, Green on Green, 236
Vegetables Marengo, 169
Veggie Joes, 408
Tomatillo Soup with Cilantro, 81
Tomatillo Sauce, 724
Tomato(es)
    and Basil Pizza, Fresh, 430
    Cornmeal Fried, 624
    Fillo Pizza, 439
    Fried, 623
    Fried, Sugar-Glazed, 624
    Greens-Stuffed Baked, 624
    Halves, Herbed, 623
    Halves, Red and Yellow, Stuffed, 218
    Pudding, 622
    Relish, Fresh, 398
    Relish, Gingered, 732
    Sauce(s) (*see under* Sauces)
    Soup(s) (*see under* Soup)
    Stuffed with Pepper-Roasted Wild
        Mushrooms, 293
    Tart, Rich, 465
Torta Rustica, 456
Tortellini
    Kabobs with Many-Cloves Garlic Sauce,
        49
    Soup
        with Kale, 96
        and Mushroom, 98
        Spinach and, 106
    and Vegetable Kabobs, Marinated, 234
Tortilla
    Chips, Baked, 55
    Soup, 113
    Strips, Baked, 81
    Wedges, 31
Tortoni, Mixed Fruit, 802
Tostadas, Vegetable, 254
Trifle, Pineapple-Lemon, 754
Turmeric Rice, 578
Tuscan
    Bean Soup, 131
    Bean Stew, 523
    Potato Pizza, 433
Two-Bean and Pasta Soup, 124

V
Vanilla Cream Filling, 748
    Crumb Crust, 760
    Glaze, 690, 780
Vegetable(s)
    -Barley Moussaka, 193
    and "Burger" Stroganoff, Creamy,
        144
    Burritos, Grilled, 301
    Galette, Sweet 'n Spicy, 474
    Marengo, 169
    Mélange, 487
    and Mixed Rice Casserole, 178
    Moo-Shu Style, Roasted, 281
    and Orzo Vinaigrette, Mixed, 643
    Pie, Autumn, 459

Puff, 485
-Rye Bread, Hearty, 656
Salad(s) (*see under* Salads)
Soup(s) (*see under* Soups)
Stew(s) (*see under* Stews)
Stock (*see under* Soups)
Stuffed, 36
Tajine, 173
Vegetarian Tetrazzini, 183
Vegetarian types, viii
Veggie
    Burgers, Herbed, 402
    Crisps, 4
    Joes, 408
    Kugel, 492
    Lasagne with Eggplant Sauce, 185
    Mélange with Bulgur, 146
    Stew with Dumplings, 145
Vichyssoise, Hot Pepper, 263
Vichyssoise, 105
Vietnamese Curried Vegetable and
        Coconut Stew, 165
Vietnamese Curried Coconut Soup, 119
Vinaigrette (*see under* Salad Dressings)
Vinegar Biscuits, 684

W
Waldorf, Wheat Berry, 573
Waldorf Salad, 636
Welsh Rarebit, 503
Wheat and Barley Bowl, 549
Wheat Berry
    and Garden Tomato Salad, 574
    and Lentil Stew with Dumplings,
        547
    Waldorf, 573
White Bean and Sweet Potato Soup with
        Cranberry Coulis, 110
White Bean Dressing, 537
Wild Rice
    Cheese, and Vegetable Casserole, 175
    Muffins, 687
    Salad, Vegetable and, 297
    Soufflé, 578
Wonton Soup, 117
Wontons, Cranberry-Cheese, 45

Y, Z
Yams, Candied, 615
Yellow and White Bean Chili, 514
Yogurt, Cucumber, 555
Yogurt Cucumber Sauce, 733
Ziti with Gremolata, 338
Zucchini
    Fans Provençal, 618
    and Garlic Spread, Roasted, 21
    and Mushrooms Parmesan, 199
    and Mushroom Pizza with Fillo Crust,
        446
    Pizza Crust, 420
    Pizza, Double, 446
    from Pueblo, 619